Government and Politics of the
United States

COMPARATIVE GOVERNMENT AND POLITICS SERIES

Published

Maura Adshead and Jonathan Tonge
Politics in Ireland: Convergence and Divergence in a Two-Polity Ireland

Rudy Andeweg and Galen A. Irwin
Governance and Politics of the Netherlands (3rd edition)

Tim Bale
European Politics: A Comparative Introduction (3rd edition)

Nigel Bowles and Robert K. McMahon
Government and Politics of the United States (3rd edition)

Paul Brooker
Non-Democratic Regimes (3rd edition)

Kris Deschouwer
The Politics of Belgium: Governing a Divided Society (2nd edition)

Robert Elgie
Political Leadership in Liberal Democracies

Rod Hague and Martin Harrop
* Comparative Government and Politics: An Introduction (9th edition)

Paul M. Heywood
The Government and Politics of Spain

Xiaoming Huang
Politics in Pacific Asia: An Introduction

B. Guy Peters
Comparative Politics: Theories and Methods
[Rights: World excluding North America]

Tony Saich
Governance and Politics of China (3rd edition)

Eric Shiraev
Russian Government and Politics (2nd edition)

Anne Stevens
Government and Politics of France (3rd edition)

Ramesh Thakur
The Government and Politics of India

Forthcoming

Tim Haughton
Government and Politics of Central and Eastern Europe

* Published in North America as **Political Science: A Comparative Introduction (7th edition)**

Comparative Government and Politics
Series Standing Order ISBN 978–0–333–71693–9 hardback
Series Standing Order ISBN 978–0–333–69335–3 paperback
(outside North America only)

You can receive future titles in this series as they are published by placing a standing order. Please contact your bookseller or, in the case of difficulty, write to us at the address below with your name and address, the title of the series and one of the ISBNs quoted above.

Customer Services Department, Macmillan Distribution Ltd, Houndmills, Basingstoke, Hampshire, RG21 6XS, UK

Government and Politics of the United States

Third Edition

Nigel Bowles

and

Robert K. McMahon

palgrave
macmillan

First edition 1993
Second edition 1998
Third edition 2014

Published by
PALGRAVE MACMILLAN

Palgrave Macmillan in the UK is an imprint of Macmillan Publishers Limited, registered in England, company number 785998, of Houndmills, Basingstoke, Hampshire RG21 6XS.

Palgrave Macmillan in the US is a division of St Martin's Press LLC, 175 Fifth Avenue, New York, NY 10010.

Palgrave Macmillan is the global academic imprint of the above companies and has companies and representatives throughout the world.

Palgrave® and Macmillan® are registered trademarks in the United States, the United Kingdom, Europe and other countries

ISBN 978-0-333-94862-0   hardback
ISBN 978-0-333-94861-3   paperback

This book is printed on paper suitable for recycling and made from fully managed and sustained forest sources. Logging, pulping and manufacturing processes are expected to conform to the environmental regulations of the country of origin.

A catalogue record for this book is available from the British Library.

A catalog record for this book is available from the Library of Congress.

Typeset by Cambrian Typesetters, Camberley, Surrey

Printed in China

Dedicated to the memory of

Gavin F. Cameron
1969–2007

Reader in Macroeconomics, University of Oxford
Friend and Scholar

Contents

List of Illustrative Material

Tables

Figures

Exhibits

Map

List of Abbreviations

AAA   Agricultural Adjustment Act
AARP   American Association of Retired Persons
ABA   American Bar Association
ABM   Anti-Ballistic Missile
ACA   Affordable Care Act
ACDA   Arms Control and Disarmament Agency
ACLU   American Civil Liberties Union
AFDC   Aid to Families with Dependent Children
AFL–CIO   American Federation of Labor and Congress of Industrial
          Organizations
AHIPAC   American Hellenic Institute Public Affairs Committee
AID   Agency for International Development
AMA   American Medical Association
APSA   Parties Committee of the American Political Science
          Association
ARRA   American Recovery and Reinvestment Bill
ATRA   American Taxpayer Relief Act
BCRA   Bipartisan Campaign Finance Reform Act
BICA   Budget and Impoundment Control Act
BOB   Bureau of the Budget
CBO   Congressional Budget Office
CEA   Council of Economic Advisors
CEQ   Council on Environmental Quality
CINC   Commanders-in-Chief
CPG   Conditional Party Government
CPSC   Consumer Product Safety Commission
CREEP   Committee to Re-elect the President
DEA   Drug Enforcement Administration
DHS   Department of Homeland Security
DNC   Democratic National Committee
DNI   Director of National Intelligence
DPC   Domestic Policy Council
ECV   electoral college vote
EEOC   Equal Employment Opportunities Commission
EOA   Economic Opportunity Act
EOP   Executive Office of the President
EPA   Environmental Protection Agency
EPC   Economic Policy Council

ESEA	Elementary and Secondary Education Act
FAA	Federal Aviation Administration
FAS	Foreign Agricultural Service
FBI	Federal Bureau of Investigation
FCC	Federal Communications Commission
FDA	Food and Drug Administration
FDIC	Federal Deposit Insurance Corporation
FEC	Federal Election Commission
FECA	Federal Election Campaign Act
FNSEA	Fédération Nationale des Syndicats d'Expoitants d'Agricoles (National Federation of Agricultural Holders' Unions)
FOMC	Federal Open Market Committee
FSO	Foreign Service Officer
GAO	Government Accountability Office
GDP	gross domestic product
GNP	gross national product
GOP	Grand Old Party
GPRA	Government Performance and Results Act
GRS	General Revenue Sharing
GS	General Schedule
HAVA	Help America Vote Act
HUD	Housing and Urban Development
ICC	Interstate Commerce Commission
IMF	International Monetary Fund
INS	Immigration and Naturalization Service
IRS	Internal Revenue Service
JCS	Joint Chiefs of Staff
LIBOR	London Interbank Overnight Lending Rate
MBA	Master's in Business Administration
NAACP	National Association for the Advancement of Colored Persons
NAM	National Association of Manufacturers
NCLB	No Child Left Behind Act
NDAA	National Defense Authorization Act
NDCP	Office of National Drug Control Policy
NEA	National Educational Association
NEC	National Economic Council
NGA	National Governors' Association
NOW	National Organization for Women
NPR	National Performance Review
NRA	National Rifle Association
NSA	National Security Adviser
NSC	National Security Council
NSS	National Security Staff

NYA	National Youth Administration
OA	Office of Administration
OASDI	Old Age, Survivors, and Disability Insurance system
OBRA	Omnibus Budget Reconciliation Act
OEO	Office of Economic Opportunity
OMB	Office of Management and Budget
OPM	Office of Personal Management
OHSA	Occupational Health and Safety Administration
OSTP	Office of Science and Technology
PAC	political action committee
PACE	Professional Administrative Career Examination
PBO	performance-based organization
PWA	Public Works Administration
RNC	Republican National Committee
SALT I	Strategic Arms Limitation Treaty
SEC	Securities and Exchange Commission
SES	Senior Executive Service
TANF	Temporary Aid to Needy Families
TARP	Troubled Assets Relief Programme
TVA	Tennessee Valley Authority
UAW	United Automotive Workers
UCA	unanimous consent agreement
USAF	United States Air Force
USCC	United States Catholic Conference United States Chamber of Commerce
USIAUS	Information Agency
USNCB	US National Central Bureau
USTR	Office of the United States Trade Representative
VP	Vice-President
WHO	White House Office
WTO	World Trade Organization

Preface to the Third Edition and Acknowledgements

Three years ago Nigel Bowles generously allowed me to begin work on an updated version of his book. His editor at Palgrave, Steven Kennedy, suggested it would be no more than a 'light revision'. I offer my gratitude to Nigel for his constant support both as friend and mentor, and for his patience in reading many versions of every chapter in this book. I remain hugely grateful to Steven for his invaluable editorial advice, encouragement and support (despite his idea of a 'light revision' differing vastly from mine). I would also like to thank the patient and very helpful anonymous review employed by the publishers for all of his or her excellent advice on earlier drafts of the chapters.

The biggest debt owed is to my wife Claire for her constant love and encouragement, especially during the many evenings when she had to put our four children to bed because 'Daddy is working'. Without her help, and the welcome distractions from Molly, Oran, Noah and Jonah, this book would never have been finished. We make a very good team in which I seem to sit down quite a bit more than she does, and where she keeps all of us moving forwards.

In Oxford, Desmond King has been a mentor since 1994 when I sat in his M.Phil seminars, and a friend since 2003 when Molly McMahon and Samuel King were born. Other friends have supported me in numerous ways and they include: David Myatt and Charlotte Vinnicombe, Christopher Wallace, Stephen Fisher and Heather Hamill, Richard and Maria Nichol, and Trevor McCrisken.

At Radley College (where acronyms rule) I have been supported by Andrew Reekes over many years, and by Angus McPhail who has fostered a spirit of intellectual energy in which staff and students can thrive. SR, PRW, TGE, PWG, SRG, ISY, DP, SB and KAM have provided intellectual support in many ways. I remain particularly grateful to TSJ for her constant help, and to my friends and comrades in the Politics Department – Mark Jewell, Timothy Lawson and Matthew Walker (who has been a fantastic addition to the self-labelled 'Dream Team'). David Anderson has built a new Politics Department of which even my good friend Jesse Knight at Charterhouse would be envious. Gareth Hughes and Rachel Batley were kind enough to arrange their wonderful wedding in July 2013 to give Claire and me a weekend away from the children – for which we are grateful (and WOCM ensured that the music worked well).

My parents Rita and Kieran, Theresa and Bart, Rebecca and Rachel, and my brother Richard, have always supported me (and one of them let me drive a JCB at the age of six). Without them I would not have had the confidence to write anything at all. I must also thank Claire's parents, Monica and Colin Castling, who have supported us both these last four-teen years in so many ways.

This book is dedicated to the memory of Dr Gavin Fraser Cameron, friend from Nuffield College days, Fellow of Lady Margaret Hall and Reader in Macroeconomics at Oxford who died from Cystic Fibrosis in 2007 while awaiting a lung transplant. As his obituary in the *RES Newsletter* of January 2008 so beautifully explained, Gavin was a brilliant scholar and a brilliant friend, and among the people who knew him well 'he was not only respected but loved'. We miss him.

If your editor suggests a 'light revision' be afraid, be very afraid ...

New Year's Eve 2013   ROBERT K. MCMAHON

The authors and publishers would like to thank Voteview.com for kindly giving permission for the use of copyright material for Figure 3.1.

Preface to the First Edition and Acknowledgements

Shortly before the publication of his own textbook, my former supervisor directed me in colourful terms never to agree to write one of my own. Textbooks, he insisted, were regarded by colleagues who had written one of their own as unwelcome competition; by those who had not, as intrinsically unscholarly; and by students, degradingly and dispiritingly, as cribs. Many years later, a senior colleague asked me to write a textbook on United States government. Recalling the warning which I had received some years before from my supervisor, I demurred, but the pugnacious reply suggested that it would be unwise to decline. I warmly acknowledge my great debt to Vincent Wright, (then) editor of the series in which this book appears, former supervisor, unembarrassed purveyor of conflicting advice, friend, and colleague. Without his early warning about the pitfalls of writing a textbook, I should have enjoyed his invitation to write it less than I did. Without his steady guidance and patience over the four years that the book has taken to complete, it would not have appeared. Without his unstinting intellectual support, it would be more deeply flawed than it is.

I am also greatly indebted to Katharine Ellis, David Goldey and Desmond King for their intellectual support, friendship, and many kindnesses. All three read the entire text, and the final draft was immeasurably improved by their critical but constructive observations. Desmond generously read several chapters in more than one draft, for which I am particularly grateful. Alan Ware read the full second draft, and made many helpful suggestions; I thank him most warmly, as I do Malcolm Anderson, Roger Crisp, Ruth Deech, and Michael Hart, each of whom read individual chapters. I also thank Herb Alexander for his assistance with campaign finance data. I am also grateful to other colleagues in the Sub-faculty of Politics at Oxford, especially Tim Hames, Gillian Peele, and Byron Shafer, for the intellectual stimulation of their company and conversation. I also thank Mark Habeeb and Richard Hodder-Williams, from whose writings and conversation on American politics over many years I have gained greatly. Warm thanks are also due to Steven Kennedy at (Palgrave) Macmillan for his professionalism and patience.

Undergraduate and postgraduate students with whom I have worked at Edinburgh and Oxford, especially Mark Brough, Gareth Davies, Chris Howard, and Robert Singh, have helped considerably in clarifying for me some of the questions addressed in this book. I am very grateful to them.

Most of the work for the book was undertaken at Oxford in the libraries of Rhodes House, St Anne's College, and the Law Faculty Library; my thanks are due to the staff of all three libraries, especially to Alan Bell and David Smith, for their kindness and professionalism. I am grateful to the Principal and Fellows of St Anne's College, Oxford, for creating a supportive and stimulating environment in which to read, think and write. In particular, I express my warm thanks to my colleagues in the PPE School, Gabriele Taylor and Terry O'Shaughnessy, for their support. Terry drew my attention to Keynes's note of a conversation with President Roosevelt in 1941; I thank him for it.

Thanks are due to many others but there is space to mention just two. Both, sadly, have departed: Tony Allt, who first introduced me to American political history, and Philip Williams, whose knowledge and understanding of this vast subject were profound, and whose enthusiasm for it was inspirational.

Responsibility for errors of fact or interpretation is mine alone.

NIGEL BOWLES

'The other main criticism ... relates to the organs of government. To the outsider it looks almost incredibly inefficient. One wonders how decisions are ever reached at all. There is no clear hierarchy of authority. The different departments of the Government criticise one another in public and produce rival programmes. There is perpetual internecine warfare between prominent personalities. Individuals rise and fall in general esteem with bewildering rapidity. New groupings of administrative power and influence spring up every day. Members of the so-called Cabinet make public speeches containing urgent proposals which are not agreed as Government policy ... Nothing is ever settled in principle. There is just endless debate and endless sitting around ... Suddenly some drastic, clear-cut decision is reached, by what process one cannot understand, and all the talk seems to have gone for nothing, being a fifth wheel to the coach, the ultimate decision appearing to be largely independent of the immense parlez-vous, responsible and irresponsible that had preceded it. Nothing is secret, nothing confidential. The President laughed when I said his method of deceiving the enemy was apparently to publish so much vital information that they would not have the time to read it.'

(John Maynard Keynes, *Collected Writings*, vol. XXIII,
105-k, July 1941)

Map of the United States: State Boundaries and Major Cities

Introduction

Washington DC is a magnificent city. Any visitor must be impressed by the splendour of the buildings that house the three branches of the federal government, and the various departments, agencies and commissions that constitute a large part of central Washington. Those walking its sidewalks appear affluent, many dressed in designer office-wear; almost everyone in central Washington speaks English; many are white and many male. Yet, head south just a few blocks from the grand steps of the US Capitol Building – home of the legislative branch – and you begin to see another Washington: walk along South Capitol Street and across the Frederick Douglass Memorial Bridge (Douglass was a former slave, social reformer, abolitionist and renowned orator), traverse *No Taxation Without Representation Street* (a section of road renamed by Washington DC council in protest against the lack of voting rights in Congress for the city) and into the neighbourhood of Anacostia. Anacostia shows a very different side to the city: poorer, with mainly African-Americans walking the streets – and few grand buildings – federal or otherwise.

The capital city of the United States is a physical symbol of the contradictions of American society; of the gulf between the idealized version of United States society where all can achieve the so-called *American Dream*, where equality is paramount and liberty has delivered a nation in which all are free to pursue their version of this dream. This ideal is in stark contrast to a reality in which wealth is unevenly distributed, where many neighbourhoods are considered too dangerous to walk at night and where minority groups suffer disproportionately from poverty and disenfranchisement.

This gulf between the dream and the reality of a nation characterized by ethnic, religious and geographic diversity, and by widespread inequality, reflects a central feature of the United States: the *political culture* of the nation bolsters a commitment to, and a belief in, a set of shared values which animated the deliberations of the Founding Fathers present at the Philadelphia Convention of 1787 as they struggled to create a set of governing institutional structures that would reflect their commitment to a set of Enlightenment values discussed by some of the most eminent philosophers of the day – values which had, at their core, a commitment both to liberty and to equality, and to the rule of law and not of men.

No introductory textbook could present a comprehensive introduction to the government and politics of the United States without explaining

1

what this political culture *is* and why it *matters*. Indeed, the examination of political culture presented in Chapter 1 is the first of two building blocks on which the rest of this book is built. Rather than launching straight into an examination of the Constitution, we begin with an overview of those values which shaped the crafting of this document and focus on the disagreements between the Founding Fathers with respect to how best to capture these values in a new set of governing structures.

The second building block on which we build the analysis presented in the rest of the book is an examination of the institutional structures created at the founding of the Republic and enshrined in the US Constitution and Bill of Rights (discussed in Chapter 2). We recommend that the student of American government and politics must keep in mind throughout this book how the *values* at the heart of American political culture (examined in Chapter 1) have shaped the structures of American government (examined in Chapter 2), and how these structures reinforce these core values.

American political culture

Americans largely agree about which values are central to American identity. These values shape the ways in which the government and politics of the United States happens. However, although Americans largely agree about which values are fundamental, there is widespread disagreement about what these values mean. For example, Americans agree that the values of liberty and equality are paramount: however, they do not share an agreed understanding of the content of these values.

The political culture of the United States can be understood as the overarching set of dominant beliefs and values about which most Americans agree. These values and beliefs shape and constrain the policy decisions made by government. In short, the values held by the people shape the policy decisions made by governments, but these policy outputs will affect the ways in which these values are understood.

Chapter 1 highlights six principles that underpin the Constitution. These principles are the embodiment of the values on which the Founding Fathers sought to build their new republic. However, as Chapter 2 explains, the widespread agreement about fundamental values within the American polity which were encapsulated by the principles at the heart of the Constitution often mask the *disagreements* within America which arise because the values are agreed but their *meaning* and *application to public policy* are not. One need look no further than a polarized Congress divided over issues which include the federal deficit and the best means to tackle it; the question of whether gun controls should be extended (particularly in light of the Sandy Hook Elementary

School massacre of December 2012); policies to tackle immigration; continued resistance to the Affordable Care Act (ACA – but often called ObamaCare by its opponents), and the attempts by the Obama administration to craft widespread health care reforms.

In short, Americans are committed to a core set of values which include liberty and equality. Yet, what equality means to one American can differ vastly from its meaning for another – and such differences are writ large within the contemporary US Congress. As is clear from even the most cursory glance at American newspapers and news websites, a widespread and commonplace commitment to American political culture does not mean widespread agreement about what core values actually mean when applied to contentious questions of public policy.

The Constitutional framework

The United States Constitution, the Flag, the Declaration of Independence and the Oath of Allegiance are symbols of American values. The Constitution is the touchstone on which debates regarding fundamental values are crafted and then applied to public policy. Without an understanding of how and why the US Constitution was created, it is difficult to appreciate why the Constitution remains the embodiment of American values. Indeed, without an examination of the content of the Constitution and the ways in which it has changed since its creation, it is almost impossible to understand why the Constitution remains at the heart of public policy debate and formation. Politics in America is often couched in terms of fundamental values that are, nevertheless, considered against the guiding principle of *constitutionalism* – that law and its application are consistent with the meaning of the Constitution. And, because disagreements about the ultimate meaning of values and the intentions of the framers of the Constitution are subject to arbitration by the Supreme Court, the Constitution remains a living presence, subject to significant changes in interpretation, rather than a dead document.

The Constitution was written in the summer of 1787 by fifty-five men from the new states of America – the Founding Fathers. The result of the Philadelphia Convention of 1787 was the product of compromise, but a number of central principles were enshrined in the new constitution which are as central to the functioning of American government today as they were when the first Congress sat down to work in 1789. The meaning of those principles is, however, contested and disputed.

The institutional framework created by the Founding Fathers in their constitution is underpinned by the 'Separation of Powers', an idea propounded by Enlightenment philosopher Baron de Montesquieu in his

1748 treatise *The Spirit of the Laws*, in which he argued that the legislature, executive and the judiciary should be distinct and separate branches of government in which no personnel should work in more than one branch. The aim of such separation was to prevent the accretion of excessive power in the hands of any one branch.

Such separation would be bolstered by a system of *checks and balances* in which the powers of the federal government (for example, over taxation; declaring war; making treaties; nominating and confirming executive branch appointments, and legislation) would be shared between branches which ensured that one branch would be able to check the power of the other branches in order to maintain a balance of power between them. As Richard Neustadt explained, 'to share is to limit' (1960: 2). If we share powers, then we have the capacity to place checks on each other and ensure that institutional balance is maintained.

This separation of powers within and across the three branches of the federal government, and the system of checks and balances between the branches, was further bolstered by a division of sovereignty between national (federal) and sub-national (primarily state) governments to create a *federal system*. Finally, the three features outlined above were underpinned by a commitment to *Limited Government* bolstered by constitutionalism and the rule of law, in which the tyranny both of government and of majority rule would, it was hoped, be avoided.

As we walk through Washington DC from the White House (the Executive Branch) to the Capitol Building (home of Congress – the Legislative Branch), and then the further short distance to the Supreme Court building (the Judicial Branch), we see three separate institutions that together constitute the federal government. We see a separation of powers which, the Founding Fathers hoped, would ensure that limited government resulted such that no one branch would ever come to dominate the others. What we may not see on our walk, but which soon becomes apparent as we read the chapters to follow, is that the Founding Fathers created, in the words of Richard Neustadt (1960), 'separate institutions sharing powers'. The Constitution created three separate branches of government in its first three Articles, but this document clearly takes each major federal government power – over money, over appointments to senior posts and over war – and divides it by giving each branch some control over the exercise of power by the other branches. By forcing three separate institutions to share powers, the Constitution created a system of checks and balances in which each branch would balance the power exercised by the others.

The principle of limited government is underpinned by the creation of a federal system in which power is shared between the federal government and the fifty state governments. The fifty-five delegates who met in Philadelphia came from twelve of the thirteen states of the new Republic

(Rhode Island sent no delegates) and all, to a greater or lesser extent, were keen to ensure that the variety and diversity of the states was preserved in any new system of government that they created. And, although the balance between federal and state government has changed dramatically since 1787, the principle that the states must retain a degree of autonomy from the federal government remains a central element in any study of the government and politics of the United States.

The structure of the book

The aim of the book is to guide students through the institutions of government and to consider how Americans influence them. Chapters 1 and 2 examine in greater detail the two building blocks discussed here: the political culture of the United States and its constitutional (governmental) framework. Chapters 3 and 4 examine the principal mechanisms through which citizens can influence government – through the role and influence of parties (Chapter 3), and the electoral system in which they operate (Chapter 4). The three chapters that follow examine the three branches of the federal government: Chapter 5 considers the presidency; Chapter 6 Congress and Chapter 7 the Supreme Court. Chapter 8 considers 'the fourth branch of government', the federal bureaucracy. Chapter 9 examines another means by which citizens seek to influence government – through the influence of interest groups. Chapter 10 examines in detail the relationship between federal and state governments, while Chapter 11 focuses on a number of key issues within the domestic policy sphere. Chapter 12 examines US foreign and defence policy.

Throughout each of these chapters, the two fundamental building blocks of political culture and the constitutional framework remain prominent. The governmental framework seems to present multiple opportunities for influence: the state has many points of access with no single centre of power. Yet, the constitutional framework also represents many points of frustration: checks and balances ensure that quick legislative change is rare. The political culture of the United States created, and is reinforced by, a system of government that offers no more than the possibility of legislative vigour. Such a system makes governing difficult, but its study compelling.

Chapter 1

Beliefs and Values in American Society

This chapter examines the fundamental beliefs and values that form the bedrock of American political culture: the collection of values and beliefs held by ordinary voters and political elites. By creating and sustaining among Americans a commitment to a set of fundamental political values, American political culture acts as the glue that binds together a society characterized by a bewildering diversity. These values are embodied in the structures of American government that citizens regard as sacrosanct. The centrifugal forces created by the diversity of the United States are tempered by the centripetal forces of an American political culture built on a shared set of values. However, conflicts within America persist not least because, as we discussed in the Introduction, the meanings that these values are thought to have are intensely contested. Between and within the two parties, as well as in society at large, disagreements about the way that core values should be applied to policy questions has led to forceful disagreements both among political elites and the mass public. Such divisions are not new but the current level of polarization within the Congress is testament to the continuing disagreements regarding the 'genuine' embodiment of American values and how best to reflect them when crafting government policy. Current public policy debates within both federal and state governments are animated by appeals to fundamental values, and politicians and the public alike claim that those with whom they disagree have failed to understand what these fundamental values mean. Whether it is gun control, immigration or healthcare, debates are couched in terms of values. Yet, opponents and supporters of a given policy proposal will claim that their view represents the 'true' view of liberty, or of equality, or of the 'proper' intentions of the Founding Fathers.

Values and American society

The government and politics of the United States is the product of the distinctive collection of values present from the founding of the new republic in the late 1700s, which contributed to the institutional design settled on by the Founding Fathers in 1787. Indeed, the structure of American government was built on those values that animated the views of the Founding Fathers: liberty, equality, individualism, democracy, the rule of law and constitutionalism.

The political culture of the United States

Over and above the diversity of the nation and the plurality of views within America is a commitment to values thought central to American identity. Despite the diversity of America, its political culture gives meaning to the motto of the United States: *E Pluribus Unum* – out of many, one.

Political culture is that collection of widespread political values shared by citizens and political elites: it shapes not only how and why citizens think about politics and government, but also how and why politicians formulate and oversee public policy. Despite the plurality of views held by a very diverse populace, the political culture of the United States fosters an overarching pattern of widely-held beliefs and values. The core values that constitute this political culture exert a powerful influence on how Americans think about their government, about the role of America as a global power, about the nation as a bulwark of democracy in the face of external threats to liberty and democracy, and about the rights and liberties of citizens. And, despite the disagreements about the content of these values (considered below), it is this particular group of values that underpins the idea of what it is to be an American.

The United States is unique in being the only nation that defines itself – its essence – ideologically. Communist and socialist nations defined themselves ideologically but the citizenry typically paid little more than lip-service to these ideologies. In the United States, by contrast, citizens take the content of American political culture seriously. Other nations define themselves in terms of shared language, history, culture, ethnic background, geography, or a mix of all five. Yet, Americans have created a central and overarching identity built on the political culture born in the earliest days of the Republic.

Being unAmerican

Because American political culture is built on a set of political values, rather than on shared ethnic, religious, racial, historical or cultural traits, failure to adopt and espouse them is considered to be un-American. In almost all modern liberal democracies, there is a consensus about the centrality and desirability of democratic institutions underpinned by the rule of law. Yet, most of these nations do not exhibit a consensus regarding the core political values within their nation. Whether in Canada, Australia, India, Germany or the United Kingdom, there are competing ideologies; in none of these countries is it unusual to find both the public and members of the political elite who espouse dissenting political principles. American identity is different: it equates national identity with a commitment to core political values. Comprehending American political culture is central to an understanding of the way in which America is governed.

It is not easy to imagine being *un-British*, *un-French* or *un-German*; for Americans, such an idea is not merely elementary but elemental. The idea of being un-American is central to our understanding of the government and politics of the United States: to the 'red scares' of the 1920s, the fervent paranoia of the McCarthy era, and the widespread fear of Islam that followed the attacks of 9-11. All are manifestations of the sense that Communism and terrorism comprised attacks not just on the American nation, but also an attack on American values (even as McCarthy portrayed his illiberalism as the protection of those values). And it is the equating of a set of core political values with the idea of being American that helps to explain the sanctity of America's governing institutions, for they are the embodiment of the wisdom of the Founding Fathers and the values which they enshrined in the Constitution.

Insistence on adherence to the values at the heart of American political culture performs an important function in a nation as diverse as the United States. A nation built on successive waves of immigration, with each wave promoting the mantra that the United States was the land of opportunity in which all could achieve, could not easily craft a collective identity based on the identities of Europe from which the first waves of immigrants came. Building an identity on a shared set of political ideas would, in principle at least, allow diversity to co-exist alongside a growing sense of American nationalism but one different to that of the nation-states of Europe due to its being built on political ideals. However, although American political culture projected the values of inclusivity, diversity and tolerance, the reality was somewhat different: African-Americans, Native Americans and Hispanics were specifically excluded from a dominant white (and often anti-Catholic) culture.

Anti-government sentiment

The dominance of the political values at the heart of American political culture has worked against the building of social movements based on collective action. By European standards, trade union membership in the United States has been low. By those standards, too, parties of the left have fared poorly, rarely winning support for policy platforms that advocate the collective rather than the individual. A related consequence of the twinned values of liberty and individualism (discussed in the section on the American Creed) is the rejection of widepsread state intervention and the view of the state as benign. Indeed, central to American political culture is a strong anti-government sentiment which has co-existed with a federal government having significant capacity, even in its early years. Americans often mistrust government and reject the types of welfare state regimes commonplace in Western European liberal democracies. Yet, there are many programmes administered by the federal government that Americans favour (Social Security, Defence, and Medicare are but three clear examples). This seeming paradox reflects a cultural animosity to government combined with the widespread acceptance of specific government programmes.

Underpinning the emphasis on individualism and liberty is an expectation that Americans advocate the tenets of classical liberalism. Yet, this conformity is often accompanied by pervasive distrust of, and sometimes detestation of, forms of government. Many Americans accept the need for individual citizens to protect themselves both from the overweening forces of government and from each other, including from those who are deemed un-American. Central to the heady mix of liberalism and the emphasis on equality is a contradictory emphasis placed on the need to be prepared to use violence to protect against threats from outsiders and from other American citizens. The broader rationale is that of the maintenance of order in the face of chaos. The notion that violence might be necessary even to protect the American people from their government finds ready assent in many American communities.

Adherence to the political values at the heart of American political culture has led many Americans to distrust their government – especially federal government. That distrust is thickened by a commitment to take-up arms to ensure that limited government is maintained. The acquisition and defence of property and wealth has been facilitated in fact, and symbolized in literature and film, by individuals' access to weapons. Violence has not represented a departure from accepted social practices in America but has, rather, often been their expression. Rooted in its revolutionary birth, in the dominance of the classical liberal values, in the Constitution's defence of the right to bear arms, and in the exposed and dangerous extension of the frontier, individual possession of arms and

Exhibit 1.1 Conspiracies and Paranoia: Don't Trust Your Government

Oliver Stone's *JFK* (1991) capitalized on an obsession with government cover-ups that formed the backbone of many successful films and TV series, including ten seasons of Fox's *The X-Files* (1993–2002) with its message that 'the truth is out there'. The success of the internet-based 9/11 conspiracy movie *Loose Change* (2005) – which in later editions has moved to cinema and DVD platforms (having sold more than one million copies on DVD; watched by over four million people in 2006–07 when streamed online, and with a total viewing audience estimated to be in the tens of millions) – is testament to a willingness to believe the obscure and fanciful, rather than the accounts provided by government and serious analysts (Thompson, 2008; Aaronovitch, 2009).

A willingness to embrace conspiracies is neither uniquely American, nor a recent phenomenon (see Robison, 1798; quoted in Hofstadter, 2008: 11). In his Fourth of July discourse of 1798, *The Duty of Americans in the Present Crisis*, Timothy Dwight, President of Yale University, railed against the threat from the Illuminati as 'though the country were swarming with them' (Hofstadter, 2008: 13). Many will know of the Illuminati from the best-selling *Da Vinci Code* by Dan Brown (2003), but the President of Yale feared a Bavarian Protestant sect of the same name. In the 1950s, McCarthyism had gripped America, capitalizing on the increasing Cold War tensions between the USSR and America. And in removing the United States' sole superpower enemy, the Soviet Union's collapse left room for paranoid individuals and radical groups within America to focus on other objects of discontent, of which Muslims, Jews, black Americans and the federal government itself are four examples.

Neither have those who conceive of politics in such ultimate terms been confined to the ranks of opposition: most governments of southern states have, for most of the South's history, conceived of and practised politics around the stimulation of precisely such fears and hatreds. Catholics (save in Louisiana), Jews, the federal government and, above all others, black persons were the objects of southern whites' detestation. In his book *Race and Democracy* (2008), a brilliant historical analysis of racial politics in Louisiana, Adam Fairclough has noted with respect to

➜

their use remains a prominent characteristic of the United States. The United States is, in many inner-city areas, an exceptionally fragile and violent society. Despite significant reductions in rates of gun-related homicides in the 1990s, the United States is ranked fourth in the world in terms of gun-deaths. Yet, despite the revulsion felt by Americans in the face of another gun-toting maniac wreaking murder on a school or

➜

the South that 'the term "racist" has become devalued through overuse: it fails to prepare one for the depths of disgust, contempt, and condescension with which whites, to varying degrees, still regarded their black fellow citizens in the 1950s' (p. 167).

The resurgence of the Republican Right in the 1980s (Peele, 1984) accompanied a significant rise in media celebrities peddling conspiracies – often accompanied by racism and bigotry, and was followed in the 1990s by the rapid growth of militia groups. Most such groups vividly display the characteristics which Hofstadter identified. In his book *Warrior Dreams* (1994), James Gibson has argued that militia groups' growth in the post-Cold War period owed much to a sub-cultural change reflecting an intense distrust of government arising out of America's defeat in Vietnam. The lagged effects of that disastrous engagement are argued to have deepened a sense of abiding grievance among some of the radical right, who charge the federal government with complicity in America's supposed decline. However, part of the contextual development is partisan: the recasting of the Republican Party in the guise of a socially conservative party, a change which began with its electoral success in southern states following the passage of the 1964 Civil Rights Act and the 1965 Voting Rights Act, provided a militant setting for right-wing politics.

Within the subculture depicted by Gibson, legitimacy was, in turn, lent to those such as Sean Hannity, Rush Limbaugh, Bill O'Reilly and Scott Glenn, who use radio and TV talk shows as platforms for the dissemination of political extremism. (Hannity has some 14 million listeners each week, with Limbaugh just behind with 13 million (Parker, 2010).) The success of deregulated talk radio was augmented by the rise to dominance of the cable TV network news, and by Fox News in particular, which became the most watched news channel in America during the 2003 invasion of Iraq.

Extremism and paranoia were not restricted to the right wing within America. When the New Deal coalition broke down amid dissension within the Democratic Party over the Vietnam War and civil rights, some on the left wing of the party 'came to accept the view that America was in the clutches of a remorseless, all-powerful, white male corporate elite – a globalist conspiracy that the included centre-left Democrats such as President Bill Clinton' (Wilentz, 2008: xxv).

university campus (as the shooting at Sandy Hook Elementary School in 2013 showed), the commitment to the core values of liberal individualism and to the need to protect the citizen against the government are not to be given away – even when such horrors bring guns back to the centre of the policy agenda. For many Americans, the core values at the heart of American political culture are absolutes not to be traded-off under *any* circumstances. Those, including President Obama, who sought tighter controls on guns, are denounced by other Americans as thereby abandoning American values. For such critics, values of this kind make one American and are not open to being negotiated away.

Building American political culture on a shared set of core political values has fostered not only a rejection of Western European-style *welfare statism* but, more fundamentally, has also resulted in the widespread mistrust of government in general, and the national (federal) government in particular within *domestic* policy. The intellectual giants of seventeenth- and eighteenth-century classical liberalism advocated little more than the night-watchman state that would ensure that private property was protected and that private markets functioned properly. The Founding Fathers had seen at first hand the dangers of allowing the British to rule over them and so resolved to resist return to the rule of the few over the many. The overthrow of British rule was the result of a bloody revolutionary war in which many of the Founding Fathers had themselves fought. Accordingly, the need to take-up arms to defend liberty was ingrained in the nascent political culture of the United States. Enshrined in the Second Amendment, the right both to 'keep and bear arms' *and* to sustain 'a well-regulated militia' because these rights were 'necessary to the protection of a free state' is for many (but by no means all) Americans as forceful a statement of American political culture today as it was at the founding of the Republic. In light of the considerable distances between many American citizens and their government (London and Los Angeles are about equidistant from Washington DC), the pronounced geographical and cultural diversity of the United States, and the fact that every citizen interacts with their local government and with state government, distrust of government in general and of the federal government in particular ceases to surprise. Distant though they are in time, the disputes of the late-eighteenth century remain central to the framing of debates within the 113th Congress.

Paranoia

When combined with an emphasis on the individual and the need for protection from the state, a consequence of this anti-government strand within American political culture is a form of extremism in which government is perceived as a mendacious and secretive force. Indeed, fifty years after the event, the bizarre conspiracy theories that gained momentum following the assassination of President John Kennedy in 1963 still find support today (Marrs, 1989; Mailer, 1995). Yet, such theories did not travel as far or as fast as the myriad claims of conspiracies surrounding the 9/11 terrorist attacks. The rise of the internet has facilitated the transmission of such fantasies. As Exhibit 1.1 demonstrates, however, such paranoia is as old as the Republic.

The diversity of American society

That Americans share a common identity testifies both to the vigour of American political culture and the civil society it fosters, and to the culture's capacity to transcend the many cleavages within American society. By almost any metric we may choose, America is diverse. In terms of geography, ethnicity, race, religion, and language, the United States is cross-cut by an array of identities. America is a nation of immigrants without the shared common ties of history, culture and language that shaped the emerging nations of eighteenth-century Europe. Neither do Americans fall neatly into one category: an African-American woman working at the senior levels of the federal government in Washington DC may have more in common with a white, male, gay, director of a Foundation in San Francisco than with, for example, a Southern Baptist, male, African-American construction worker. The great diversity of the United States does not mean that we cannot make generalizations about its citizens, but we must recognize the pitfalls inherent in failing to understand that American identities are multi-dimensional. As a result, even if we are correct in asserting that most American subscribe to the values which constitute their political culture, their orientations towards politics and government will be complex. Americans define themselves as what we might term hyphenated-Americans: African-American; Italian-American; Irish-American; Scots-Irish American; Jewish-American.

It is the political culture of the United States that defines what comes after the hyphen, but the diversity of identities is captured in that which precedes it. The diversity and difference present within the United States has the potential to create centrifugal forces that might overcome the stability and consensus within the American polity. Yet, despite this potential for fission, the United States has not in the twentieth or (at the time of writing, at least) the twenty-first centuries experienced the political conflicts and ideological battles present in Western Europe. Despite being a nation of immigrants, the United States has adopted neither the Socialist nor Social Democratic government forms found in Europe. Neither has it experienced the Far Right, nor the Tory, nor the Christian Democratic forms of government also found within Europe. What trumps the centrifugal forces born of this diversity are the aggregative (centripetal) forces within American political culture – those forces that have allowed Americans to overcome both their diversity and the potential for conflicts based on political differences.

Social cleavages within the United States mirror the considerable diversity within the populace. We refer here not just to inherent characteristics (race, ethnicity, gender, birthplace), but also to acquired characteristics such as income, education, and occupation. Indeed, class differences defined in terms of income and occupation are everywhere apparent in America, but their political implications are dulled because of the greater salience of other social cleavages. In particular, they have been sufficiently cross-cut by ties of race and ethnicity (which successive waves of immigration from different regions and countries have reinforced) for their political significance to be further stifled. Embryonic class loyalties have often expressed themselves in impassioned and violent industrial disputes, but have rarely broken out into wider social conflicts. The overlaying of class division by race, and the pervasive belief in the fact and prospect of upward social mobility (a manifestation of political culture) have together drawn the sting of class politics. Save in 1932, 1936 and 1964, it has proved difficult to build presidential majorities on its foundations. Accordingly, democratic socialism has failed to take root. Commitment to the core values of American political culture has left little room for the successful development of socialism, communism or Western-European style welfare-statism.

Marked more than any other society by mass immigration of those seeking economic betterment or relief from political oppression, the United States is also host to a very large population of African-Americans whose ancestors, uniquely in a diverse society, were involuntary immigrants. Where others fled to America from oppression, blacks were forced there in chains. Slavery shattered black social structures, made marketable property of human beings and underpinned the South's feudal agricultural regime in the nineteenth century. At fearful human and financial cost, the Civil War (1861–65) ended slavery but led indirectly to the extended subjugation of black Americans through segregation, sharecropping and the conferment of merely nominal citizenship rights. Only during the period 1954–65 was the lawfulness of southern and border-states' enforcement of segregation ended. Only then were black civil rights confirmed and black voting rights guaranteed. That post-war transformation in black civil and political rights has changed American party politics, altered voting patterns, and assisted in the belated modernizing of the south, much of it still relatively backward economically. Yet, the bitter aftermath of slavery and segregation still distinguishes black Americans from their fellow citizens, not just from whites but also from Hispanics and the several million immigrants from Asia. A substantial black professional middle class has developed since the 1960s, but blacks remain more heavily represented among the victims and perpetrators of violent crime, and are the poorest, least well-educated, unhealthy and worst-housed groups in American society.

The US also has a large and rapidly growing Hispanic population. Already larger than the African-American population, it is projected to double in size by 2050 (by which point the white population will be, narrowly, the minority). Hispanics, like African-Americans, are over-represented in the lowest two deciles of income distribution and also within the criminal justice system. And, as the 2012 election and the policy disagreements between the White House and the Republican House of Representatives in the 113th Congress highlighted, the issue of immigration (both legal and illegal) and the protection of borders (notably the 1,969-mile border with Mexico) suggest that race remains a changing, but central, issue within the US.

Returning to the gulf between rhetoric and reality discussed in the Introduction, persistent black and Hispanic underachievement under-mines the plausibility of the commitment to liberty and equality central to American political culture. Systematic social disadvantage signifi-cantly reduces inner-city black and Hispanic children's prospects of upward social mobility. Despite being an expression of individual free-dom, the more general unequal distribution of income, wealth and prop-erty threatens the coherence of American political values: material inequality diminishes the worth both of formal equality before the law and of individual freedom. The *Occupy* protests in New York and Washington DC, and in many other major cities in the US and other Western nations in 2011 and 2012, drew attention to the inequalities within US society. And the increasing discussion of the '1 per cent versus the 99 per cent' within the mainstream media in 2011 and 2012 focused attention on income inequalities within the US. President Obama made income inequality a recurring theme of his 2012 State of the Union address.

Yet, despite both the considerable inequalities within the contempo-rary United States and the diversity of the nation, a central commitment to the overarching American political culture fosters a persistent sense of being American. Understanding such a powerful cultural force is a prerequisite for understanding the entire system of government and poli-tics.

The core values within American political culture

A democratic ethos underpins public debate in the United States. American politics proceed with the presumption, if not always the fact, of disclosure and openness, of free debate and publication, in pursuit of negotiated agreements about public policy between individuals who are equal before the law. Links between America's political values and its institutions of government were apparent from well before the first stirrings of revolt against Britain in 1773, and have been declared publicly in key documents since. From the Declaration of Independence in 1776, through President Lincoln's Gettysburg Address in 1863 and President Johnson's speech in 1965 before the Joint Session of Congress, to President Obama's first Inauguration Address in 2009, American political rhetoric springs from a tradition in which politicians invoke ideas of progress towards an ideal democratic society within the constitutional framework of republican government. Such rhetoric has been applied not only at home, but also – as the presidencies of Woodrow Wilson, Harry Truman, John Kennedy and George W. Bush show – abroad. As a military superpower since 1945, the United States has wrestled with the tensions arising from turbulent impulses of an evangelistic, democratic creed and the demands of *realpolitik* presented by the need to establish and maintain international order in the interests of American national security. That need was greatly reinforced and palpably strengthened in the aftermath of the atrocity of 9-11 and the wars in Afghanistan and Iraq. And, both abroad and at home, the United States continues to wrestle with the tension between individual liberty and the combined result of great socioeconomic inequality. Underpinning the rhetoric of an ideal democratic society is that set of fundamental values which, taken together, constitute the political culture of the United States.

The constitutional settlement of 1787, and the institutional design which resulted, was animated by a general acceptance by the Founding Fathers of the principles of eighteenth-century classical liberalism with its emphasis on the centrality of liberty, its focus on the individual and the conception of equality as equality of opportunity. While there was considerable debate and often fierce argument regarding the institutional structure of the new republic, there was much greater consensus about the principles on which the government would be based.

The tenets of liberalism were present from the beginning; the political culture of the nascent United States reflected them, and continues to do so. White adult males, from the founding of the Republic, were given rights and liberties under the rule of law that their European counterparts did not wrest from political elites for another century. American women had few rights and were denied the vote until 1920. Black Americans had no rights and remained enslaved until the era of Reconstruction which followed the Civil War of 1861–65, and many suffered *de facto* segregation until the 1970s and beyond.

The political values at the heart of American political culture are often referred to as the American Creed. They are:

• Liberty
• Individualism
• Equality

- Democracy
- The rule of law
- Constitutionalism.

Liberty

The ascendency of classical liberalism in the United States fostered a rather particular approach to the idea of liberty closely allied to the notion of that which President Herbert Hoover dubbed 'rugged individualism'. Those who have adhered to this approach hold that government's proper role is to be limited to the nightwatchman whose task it is to protect private property and civil liberties. In its pure form, the approach leaves no legitimate space for government to mitigate the effects of unfettered market interactions. Adherence to the American Creed has not prevented many Americans from vehemently rejecting the exercise of governmental power and insisting on the need to bear arms to protect against overweening government power, against individuals who threaten the Creed, and those with ideologies alien to the Creed. Yet, even violent disputes within America are often couched in terms of liberty, with opposing camps claiming to be its protector.

The bedrock of the political culture within the US is liberty. Defined not in terms of the Left–Right (liberal–conservative) spectrum with which we are familiar from Western Europe, in a more fundamental sense of the term, its meaning in the United States is underpinned by the traditions of seventeenth- and eighteenth-century Protestantism, in which the individual has primacy. The individual is understood to be prior to society and must retain his or her individual liberty in the face of attempts to limit it. Influenced by the thought of the giants of classical liberalism (including Locke, Montesquieu and Rousseau), liberty meant negative liberty (Berlin: 1958) in which freedom is 'freedom from' state interference (and from other people), not 'freedom to do' something with the help of the state. Negative liberty protects the indvidual against others and against government authority. It creates a zone of non-interference in which the role of the state is to protect and police the boundaries of personal freedom. Positive liberty involves an active state helping us 'to do' those things we cannot achieve without state aid (for example, by providing buses to help black children attend formerly segregated schools in white neighbourhoods).

Individualism

In America, the predominant conception and practice of liberty is negative. The Bill of Rights, the first ten amendments to the United States Constitution ratified in 1791, outlined many liberties as well as rights:

the freedom to carry a gun, to speak openly, to protect one's private property, even to oppose government encroachment on the states and their citizens. The legacy of Protestantism in the thirteeen colonies of the new America, combined with the influence of classical liberalism, created a sense of liberal individualism in which it is effort and ingenuity, ability to overcome adversity and to innovate that lead to success. It is not government or charity which is paramount but individual effort unencumbered by authority or other people. Americans are individuals who can achieve a great deal as long as their sphere of liberty is maintained and protected. Negative liberty underpins the emphasis within American political culture on the individual: the governmental and constitutional framework protects the individual, but it is the responsibility of citizens to make the most of individuals' talents within parameters protected by the state.

Equality

The distinctive political mix in contemporary America is often held to spring from individual freedom, usually regarded as the supreme American political value. Celebrated though this conception of individual freedom is, it collides with equality, another core value, also pronounced in American political thought and practice. Individual freedom has most commonly been understood in the United States as the freedom of individual citizens to become unequal: democracy in America was, as Richard Hofstadter (1948) observed, born in cupidity rather than fraternity. The pursuit of material abundance has blunted the edge of redistributive politics.

The idea of equality can be found in the American Declaration of Independence of 1776, which states that it is self-evident that 'all men are created equal, that they are endowed by their Creator with certain unalienable rights, that among these are Life, Liberty and the pursuit of Happiness'. All men are equal and the Constitution of 1787 (as well as the Bill of Rights of 1789) cemented this conception of equality. Men would be equal in law and none would be treated differently based on accidents of birth or other circumstance. We may call this conception equality of opportunity – both in the political and the economic spheres. Of course, such equality did not extend to women or to the millions of black Americans enslaved in the colonies of the American South. Equality of opportunity did not demand any equality of outcome. Liberty underpinned the equal opportunity of all to strive and, over time, for some to acquire more than others.

The Founding Fathers regarded the values of liberty and equality as complementary (whereas their European contemporaries saw a fixed-sum game in which greater equality would always be at the expense of liberty). The philosopher Michael Walzer puts it thus: 'liberty and equality are the two chief virtues of social institutions, and they stand best when they stand together' (Quoted in Huntington, 1981: 2). Daniel Bell has written that 'the tensions between liberty and equality, which framed the great philosophical debates in Europe, were dissolved by an individualism which encompassed both' (Huntington, 1981: 3). Liberal individualism was compatible with egalitarianism, as long as the content of such equality was thin, so that equality meant only equity under the law and equality of opportunity.

Attempts to increase equality of condition as well as opportunity are not absent in the United States, but such attempts have rested uneasily with the presumption that liberty must always be paramount. In the 1960s, President Lyndon Johnson's Great Society programme, for the first time in the history of America, used the federal government as an instrument to tackle inequality and its consequences. But the hostility of some sections of the nation to this expanded role for the federal government was built on calls to protect the power of the states and individuals against this centralizing leviathan. Policies actively to encourage the participation of minority groups in the political process, as well as attempts to deliver *de facto* equality to black Americans, were met with hostility in many parts of America. Reapportionment of electoral districts, as well as *Affirmative Action* programmes intended to deliver greater equality to black Americans were viewed by some as an affront both to liberty and to individualism. Active government support was an example of positive liberty, which was not the type of liberty enshrined in the Declaration of Independence. Using the state to help some groups in society increase equality (for example, in applying racial or gender considerations to university admissions) was the very antithesis of rugged individualism.

Although an imperfect characterization, a number of members of the Democratic Party favour a conception of positive liberty in which the state is an active participant in the quest to create a more egalitarian society. Most Republican Party activists view such state action as a violation of the liberties enshrined in the Declaration of Independence and in the Bill of Rights. Tensions within the American Creed shaped the formation of the new republic and continue to shape public policy debates in the contemporary United States. Disagreements about the Affordable Care Act (ACA) 2010 saw the legislative vote in the House of Representatives split almost completely along party lines, and the Senate vote was a pure party-line vote – as Democrats portrayed President Obama's healthcare bill as a means to increase healthcare coverage, while some Republicans described the law as a violation of basic liberties and challenged the law in the Supreme Court (and lost). Few public policy debates are not couched in terms of fundamental values.

Democracy

The idea of equality was bolstered by the revolutionary ferment of eighteenth-century Europe – not least the demands for greater involvement in the governing of the nation and the overthrow of absolutist, monarchical rulers. From the creation of the Republic, the idea of consent given by the people to its chosen (elected) rulers was central. So, too, was the related idea that rulers could be removed through the withdrawal of popular consent. In its first Article, the Constitution created a framework for free and fair elections (albeit elections that then excluded most unpropertied men of all ethnicities, all women, African-Americans and Native-Americans) in which the rule of law would replace the rule of kings. Americans approve of the notion of their democratic governing institutions (Almond and Verba, 1965) but evince little support for individual institutions: in 2012, public opinion polling data gave the US Congress an approval rating of less than 20 per cent.

Americans also approve of a majoritarianism in which government is, as President Abraham Lincoln said 'a government of the people, for the people, by the people'. Even when the seeming excesses of majoritarianism leads to episodes and events such as McCarthyism, Guantanamo Bay and 'rendition', illiberal US immigration policies in the 1930s based on the ideas of eugenics made infamous in Nazi Germany and to draconian criminal justice (permanent incarceration for those convicted of three consecutive crimes), Americans retain their support for their governing institutions. Politicians and the government may be fallible, but the institutions that created and nurtured *American democracy* remain sacrosanct.

The rule of law

The Founding Fathers were well aware of the revolutionary ferment in France in the 1780s and the threats to absolute monarchy across Europe. They would have felt first hand the power of a near-supreme Parliament in Great Britain that could tax its colonies without granting them representation within the legislature of the motherland. The new American republic would not be based on the rule of man but on the rule of law.

Despite the love of majoritarianism, the Founding Fathers – influenced by the ideas of Locke, Montesquieu and Rousseau – feared what John Adams called the 'tyranny of the majority'. Replacing absolute monarchy with absolute majoritarianism was to exchange one tyranny for another. Accordingly, limits would be placed on the power of majorities. The presidency would not be chosen directly by the people but, rather, by an electoral college. The Senate would not be elected directly but, rather, its members would be chosen by state legislatures. Not until the Thirteenth

Amendment of 1913 did the Senate become a democratic institution. Also, fundamental rights and liberties protected by law would be enshrined in the Bill of Rights. Individual freedom, the right to private property and the fair exchange of contracts would all be underpinned by the rule of law.

Constitutionalism

Closely allied to the rule of law is the idea of constitutionalism: government would be limited by law, and the law would be enshrined in the Constitution. This sacrosanct document would replace the divine right of kings and would be 'higher' than any authority within the nation. Fundamental constitutional law would not only be a constraint on the behaviour of individuals, but also on government. No man or woman would be above the law.

Constitutionalism is a central tenet of the American Creed because it unifies the two building blocks discussed in the Introduction: the core principles which define American political culture were enshrined in the Constitution of the United States. The Constitution created and sustains the institutional form of government in the United States *but* it is also the embodiment of those principles on which the Founding Fathers built the new republic. And it is the commitment to the structures created by the Constitution and the values it embodies which is what we mean by *constitutionalism*. To question the Constitution is to question what it is to be an American.

Conflict and consensus within American society

There have been periods within America's history when the centrifugal forces within American society looked set to overwhelm the forces that bound the nation together. Most notably, racial divisions have offered repeated examples of deep tensions within American society – with slavery, Civil War, Reconstruction, segregation and race riots threatening to dismember the country. Yet, remarkably, even at the height of the fight against segregation in the 1950s and during the race riots of the 1960s, there were few calls for a wholesale rejection of American values in favour of competing ideologies such as socialism.

There remains considerable political conflict within American society, but conflict takes place within the *arena* defined by American political culture and America's governing institutions. Despite continued public policy disagreements between voters in so-called Red and Blue states, and continued hostility between the Republican House of Representatives and a Democratic president, Americans remain wedded to the political values at the heart of their political culture. They also remain bound to one another in their commitment to their Constitution and the values it is held to embody.

Polarization and American political culture

Americans share a commitment to the values at the heart of their political culture. However, the meaning and content of these values remain contested. While liberty and equality are values that Americans agree are enshrined in the Constitution and are prized, their meanings are, as W.B. Gallie once wrote, 'essentially contested' (1956), always subject to dispute and interpretation.

Disagreements as to the meaning of the values at the heart of American political culture pervade every decade of American history: whether liberty was a concept that applied to slave as well as free-man; whether equality under the 'equal protection' clause of the Fourteenth Amendment of the Constitution did (*Plessy v Ferguson*, 1896) or did not (*Brown v Board of Education*, 1954) allow segregation of white and black Americans; whether the Constitution protects privacy (*Griswold v Connecticut*, 1965) and, if so, whether privacy can form part of the basis on which women were granted the right to choose abortion (*Roe v Wade*, 1973); or even whether the federal government does or does not have the constitutional right to demand that health insurance providers offer people the opportunity to purchase health insurance that does not exclude those with pre-existing medical conditions (*National Federation of Independent Business v Sebelius*, 2012).

Furthermore, politicians and groups in society may seek to lay claim to be the authentic custodians of American political values. During the 2012 Republican presidential primaries, for example, the Republican candidates vied with each other to show that their policies were the genuine embodiment of American political culture – as they discussed plans to reduce immigration, to shrink the deficit and reduce the size of government, and to overturn President Obama's landmark healthcare law. And then, in the general election, a number of Republican politicians attacked the incumbent, President Obama, for his alleged betrayal of American values. Michelle Bachman (R-MN) and Sarah Palin charged him with being un-American. During the 2010 Congressional mid-term elections and the 2012 presidential election, the Tea Party movements sought to equate their fiscal (and often social) conservatism with Americanism, a position which they pressed Republican candidates to accept and declare. In both the 2010 and 2012 electoral cycles (as in the 1968, 1980, 1984 and 2004 presidential elections), the Republican Party attempted to portray their policy platforms as the only ones consistent with a commitment to the political values of *real* Americans.

And while scholars continue to assess whether, and to what extent, the American public have become more polarized in recent years, it remains the case that the two parties in Congress have become highly polarized. The challenge of forging bipartisan relationships in the divided 113th Congress (2013–15) is, accordingly, one of exceptional difficulty.

America seems, at least to some commentators, to be a nation divided between Red states (predominantly Republican) and Blue states (predominantly Democratic). While there is no settled view in the scholarly literature on the question of the adequacy of such a 'red versus blue' characterization of the voting public, the fact of division is an entrenched and enduring feature of American society. Yet, those divisions sit alongside an overarching commitment to the fundamental values at the heart of American political culture. Notwithstanding the mistreatment of Native Americans, the era of slavery and the reconstruction after the Civil War (1861–65) which followed its abolition, McCarthyism in the 1950s and the continuation of *de facto* segregation into the 1970s, home-grown terrorist attacks on American soil in the 1990s (the Oklahoma Bombing in 1995), the historic mistreatment of Jews and Catholics, as well as African and Native Americans, the rhetoric of political division within both federal and state governments in the second decade of the twenty-first century is pronounced but not unprecedented. But what is striking is the capacity of the United States to endure divisions without challenging the fundamental commitment to those values that underpin America's political culture and its governing institutions.

Conclusion

The fundamental values at the core of American political culture, based on the classical liberal ideals that influenced the Founding Fathers, have shaped both the politics of the United States and the shape of the institutional structure at federal, state and local levels. The meaning of values central to the American Creed has altered since the founding of the new republic. These meanings continue to evolve such that debates in contemporary America continue to reflect the central ideals that animated the Founding Fathers. However, and uniquely among liberal democracies, American politicians and the public alike continue to debate vigorously with reference to their over-arching commitment to a core set of values and a core framework of governing institutions. The centrality of the values at the heart of American political culture shape the style, forms and dynamics of government, politics and public policy-making in the United States.

Chapter 2

The Constitution: Creating the Rules of the Game

This chapter examines the constitutional framework of the United States and the way in which the political culture of the new nation helped shape the institutional framework finally settled on in 1787. The chapter examines the precursor to the Constitution, the Articles of Confederation, before moving to the Philadelphia Convention and the crafting of the Constitution which British Prime Minister William Gladstone described as 'as far as I can see, the most wonderful work ever struck off at a given time by the brain and purpose of man'.

Yet, such effusive praise masks deep divisions evident at the Convention where those favouring the creation of a federal constitution (the Federalists) were vehemently opposed by the anti-Federalists who resisted any proposal to create a new tier of government that would be above the states. In reality, Gladstone's 'wonderful work' was the culmination of much hard work and a great deal of compromise. This chapter identifies the core principles that lie at the heart of the Constitution and considers how these principles shaped both the Constitution itself and the idea of Constitutionalism in which the development of the new nation would conform to the principles and design established in 1787.

The Constitution is the institutional embodiment of six overarching constitutional principles: constitutionalism, separation of powers, checks and balances, federalism, judicial review and representative government. These principles, considered alongside the institutional structure of government established in 1787, help to explain how government functions, how disputes are resolved and who triumphs, how the functioning of government has changed since 1787. They also help our understanding of how the Constitution has changed, both through additions to the text and through changing interpretations of the text's meaning. The final task of this chapter is to examine why the Constitution has endured and why it remains the keystone of the American political system.

Why the Constitution matters

In quotidian debates about politics that focus on those matters that concern American citizens and often divide America (such as gun control, abortion rights, immigration, healthcare, the treatment of suspected terrorists, the national debt, jobs and education), frequent reference is made to the foundational document on which the government and politics of the United States is built: the Constitution. The Constitution continues to animate these debates and, in many cases, determines (through Supreme Court judgements) the manner in which public policy questions are answered. The Constitution frames and re-frames what government can do; and debates regarding the way the Constitution is re-framed determine the meaning of constitutional law.

The Constitution is *complex*. More than just the text drafted in 1787, its declarations, provisions and values are subject to interpretations which can, and do, change fundamentally across generations; where interpretations are often politicized; and where heated debates regarding the content of public policy are underpinned by fundamental disagreements about the meaning of the Constitution. The Constitution, sometimes purposefully imprecise and often ambiguous, provides the basis on which judgements are made, but it rarely provides a definitive answer to the complex questions to which the text is applied. Some answers are to be found in the Constitution. For example, that the United States should have a presidential system characterized by the separation of powers, and that the system should be federal rather than unitary are points about which the Constitution is clear. Yet, even these answers generate questions for which the text has no single answer; for example, whether the separation of powers allows the president to find greater constitutional powers during times of emergency, or whether the president can use signing statements to modify the legislature's intent (see Chapter 5).

Today, the Constitution has an almost sacrosanct nature: alongside the Declaration of Independence, the Flag and the Oath of Allegiance, it has become a symbol of American identity and of those values central to the idea of being an American. The framers of the Constitution are also deified in modern America: remembered as men of genius who created a near-perfect document (a view supported by Gladstone, as the quotation at the start of the chapter suggests). Yet, while some of the Founding Fathers were men of genius, all were statesmen and politicians, many of them soldiers, and almost all were motivated primarily with practical concerns created by the failure of the Articles of Confederation and the spectre of British imperial power that threatened the existence of the new republic. The primary pursuit of the Founding Fathers was not the pursuit of truth but the desire to promote their favoured solution to the problems faced by the fifty-five men who met in Philadelphia in the summer of 1787.

It is perhaps because the Constitution has endured for so long that the Constitution is revered, as are the Founding Fathers who crafted it. However, only by examining how and why the Constitution was created in the way that it was will it be possible to identify the *rationale* which underpins *not only* the institutional structures created and the way they were to interact, *but also* the guiding principles that were to determine how these institutions would function, and to what end.

And it is because these principles continue to shape the way that the game of politics is played that it is crucial that the development of the Constitution be considered before its structure and later amendments are examined. The Constitution remains central to the study of the government and politics of the United States precisely because it has endured for so long, has shaped the way the structures of government function, and continues to define the core principles on which the American Creed has been built. And, like the American Creed, the Constitution is 'above' everyday politics: fierce debates about the application of values and the meaning of the Constitution rarely extend so far that they allow challenges to the Constitution and the American Creed to be tolerated. Whether the Constitution *ought* to be considered sacrosanct is the last question examined in this chapter. That the Constitution performs a central role in creating and maintaining national unity is beyond question. So, too, is the role played by the Constitution in creating and maintaining a sense of national identity. It is unlikely the American Creed could survive without the institutional and ideological underpinnings provided by the Constitution. The Constitution is the supreme law of the land; that supremacy shapes every aspect of the government and politics of the United States.

The creation of a new republic

The United States was born in a revolutionary war against colonial Britain, and the country's revolutionary values have never been fully shed. The flight to Canada of 80,000 loyalists during and after the War of Independence (1775–83) accounts partly for the different pattern and culture of politics in Canada and the United States. Unlike Canada, the United States is a republic, has had neither a Tory nor a significant socialist party and, despite its periods of progressive social reform, has lacked both a comprehensive social democratic tradition and discourse. As American socialism has been a marginal political force, so American conservatism has taken neither the welfarist Christian Democratic forms familiar in Italy and Germany, nor the paternalist Tory form adopted in Britain and retained even after the granting of universal suffrage. The two major parties in the United States are united, rather than divided, by their commitment to dynamic, free-market, ideology. As discussed in Chapter 1, this commitment to the free market is compounded by an antipathy to government in general, and to centralized government in particular, that unites most Americans, as does the corollary of a vigorous defence of political and civil rights. The parties are also united in their commitment to the Constitution's centrality, much as they might disagree about its meanings and their application.

The successful struggle of self-reliant and armed individuals against a violent and hostile frontier, racial segregation, ignorance, injustice and poverty has provided the texts, subtexts and contexts of much American film and literature. While supplying fuel for the nation's physical expansion in the nineteenth century, and its rise to industrial supremacy in both the nineteenth and the twentieth centuries, competitive individual freedom in the pursuit of material wealth has had inequality as both its motive and its result. Yet, despite the westward expansion of the nation, its industrialization, the Civil War and the Cold War, the United States remains committed to the fundamental principles identified in the document drafted in the summer of 1787. But the Constitution of 1787 was not the first constitution in the new republic.

Having declared independence from Britain in 1776, the new nation struggled with a core dilemma: how to create an effective government that would avoid the repressive and tyrannical nature of British rule. Even after peace with Britain was agreed in 1783, the new nation continued to struggle with the challenge of uniting thirteen former colonies ranged along the eastern coast of the United States and which differed greatly from one another ethnically, religiously, cultural, linguistically and economically. The logical government form to adopt for thirteen disparate states that had overthrown an overweening central authority was a loose affiliation of states with a weak central authority: the Articles of Confederation, which endured (painfully) from 1781–89.

The social conflicts that Hofstadter (1948) claimed were founded on 'ultimate schemes of values' and which find echoes in the Civil War, Reconstruction and segregation, and the continuing battles between those who view government as a benign force and those who see it as a threat to individual liberty, are rooted in the formation of the new nation. The conflicts that underpinned the formation of the institutional structures in the newly-independent republic determined the birth and development of these governing institutions.

Both the original constitutional design and the formation of the federal constitution which replaced it reflected the ideological division between those who feared the creation of a powerful central government (the anti-Federalists) and those who argued that the new republic could not survive without a central authority to coordinate the actions of the thirteen former colonies (the Federalists). And the war of words between the groupings who rapidly were labelled as the *Federalists* and the *anti-Federalists* was reflected in the final nature and powers of the three branches of the new federal government, as well as in the nature and limits of the relationships between these branches. Beyond their shaping the functioning of the institutional structures in the new republic, the compromises settled on in Philadelphia in 1787 also helped form the party system in the United States.

Before 1787: the Articles of Confederation

Between 1781 and 1789, the United States was governed under the *Articles of Confederation*, a constitution providing for a central government of exceptional weakness and dependent on the goodwill of the individual states for its functioning. In practice, the thirteen states were unwilling to grant to the Congress of the Confederation the powers which they had denied the British Crown. Each state exercised virtually sovereign powers, even asserting its rights to formulate independent foreign policies and to raise armies and navies. Ministers in London and Paris acted simultaneously on behalf of individual states rather than the United States as a whole. Reacting against unaccountable British power, the Articles established neither an executive nor a judicial branch but, rather, a unicameral legislature. Organized along the lines of the Continental Congress, which it replaced, it was comparably weak and had power neither to regulate commerce between the states nor to levy taxes. Under this charter of impotence, each state had one vote. That was a reflection of the sovereignty and nominal equality of each, and an illustration of John Adams's characterization of the Congress as 'not a legislative assembly, nor a representative assembly but only a diplomatic assembly'. Relationships between the states and the centre of government paralleled those between the legislatures of the thirteen states and their governors. Lacking independent political bases, the latter were the agents of the former.

The Confederal Congress did have the power to create Executive Departments, but those it established were hampered by the states' assertions of sovereignty and their denial to the centre of adequate funds for the support of Departments' roles. Imposts (requests for import duty) required the states' unanimous consent (which was not forthcoming). Save when external threats were palpable and immediate, the centre was feebly inadequate: the standing army was once reduced to eighty men. Between sessions of Congress, a *Committee of the States* sat, comprising a single delegate from each state. With power to act only in respect of those matters not requiring the assent of nine of the thirteen states, it was a prescription for a government with neither authority nor power. Although intended, the costs of such weakness were high: in the south and the west, the states faced significant threats from Spain which gave cause for general concern, but questions of separate taxation by states and of growing indebtedness were the particular and proximate causes of the undermining of the Articles of Confederation. Taxes on commerce between the states were freely imposed; causing such resentment that war between the states seemed possible: New York actually imposed a tax on all ships trading through her waters to the neighbouring states of New Jersey and Connecticut. It became plain that the states had individual interests in the collectivity's being strengthened and becoming more than merely the sum of its parts.

The Confederation's collapse

Under the Articles of Confederation, legislative supremacy in the thirteen states had given way to abuses of power, especially unconstitutional incursions into state judiciaries, and interference with property rights and contracts. In many states, pressure grew for the repudiation of debts (both to American and foreign merchants and bankers). External debt rose considerably between the end of the War of Independence in 1783 and the collapse of the Confederation. Gradually, creditors (especially British ones) became the target of state legislative action: in flagrant defiance of the 1783 Paris Peace Treaty, the Virginia legislature passed a law to prevent British creditors suing to collect their pre-war debts. In 1786 alone, seven states issued paper money, thereby alarming all creditors, British and American, loyalist and revolutionary. In Massachusetts, impoverished rural debtors in the west of the state rebelled under Daniel Shays in an attempt to prevent county courts from delivering judgement against them. Violent clashes that followed were suppressed by the state militia (financed by exactions on merchants) and not by United States forces (because the United States had insufficient resources to raise them).

General Washington inferred from the rebellion that the Articles of Confederation were inadequate, and feared that European governments (which already accorded the Confederation's ministers little respect) would draw similar conclusions. Washington's anxieties were sufficiently widely-shared among senior American politicians to intensify pressures for the drafting of new constitutional arrangements in which the centre would be stronger, popular electoral pressure through legislatures reduced and the political problems caused by indebtedness resolved. Following an initial meeting in 1786 at Annapolis, the Maryland state capital, attended by delegates from five states to consider difficulties in the commercial relations between them, it was proposed that a further meeting take place at Philadelphia in May 1787 to discuss the amendment of the Articles of Confederation. Congress supported the call for a meeting of delegates:

> for the sole and express purpose of revising the Articles of Confederation and reporting to Congress and the several legislatures such alterations and provisions.

The Constitutional Convention: the great compromise

At its outset, the Convention's outcome was uncertain, not least because the centre's weakness had attracted some interests as it lost its appeal for others. Smaller states were especially reluctant to cede the sovereignty that they enjoyed under the Articles of Confederation, because the requirement for unanimity on taxation from the centre, and the rule that each state voted as a unit in the Confederal Congress irrespective of resources and size, underpinned their security. To abandon the rule risked domination by the financially powerful and populous states of Virginia and New York.

Fifty-five delegates met in convention at Independence Hall in Philadelphia. Ambassadorial duties in Paris and London, respectively, prevented Thomas Jefferson and John Adams (both of whom were later elected to the presidency) from attending. Otherwise, the Convention was a galaxy of former rebels against British colonial power: George Washington, Alexander Hamilton, Benjamin Franklin, James Wilson, James Madison and Governor Morris were all present. Having participated in the revolution against Britain in 1776, they now found themselves with the task of creating a new political order only six years after the adoption of the existing confederal one. The proceedings were held in secret and, in order that minds might be changed without difficulty or embarrassment, the votes of individual delegates went unrecorded. Instead, states voted as delegations at Philadelphia as they had done in the Confederal Congress. However, Madison took detailed notes of the discussions and, as a result, we know a good deal about who said what.

The Constitution that emerged from the negotiations and debates at Philadelphia was, necessarily, a compromise between politicians with different priorities, interests and objectives. A short document, the Constitution is, in Supreme Court Justice Sandra O'Connor's words, 'animated by an array of intentions'; it not only admits, but also implicitly encourages, competing interpretations. Compromise was essential not only to build a coalition in the Constitution's support, but also to avoid equally unpalatable and unworkable polar options. And the compromises at the heart of the Philadelphia Convention remain at the heart of government today – because compromise remains a central demand placed on elected officials who wish to create public policy within a system characterized by the need for compromise, where ambitions continue to counteract ambition and where the granting of formal power is no guarantee that goals can be realized.

The core principles of the Federal Constitution

The Constitution marked an attempt to avoid the concentration of governing power and also its dilution, the national and confederal alternatives. Its authors had vivid memories of unchecked executive power exercised from London, experience of the vacuum of executive power under the Articles of Confederation, and apprehensions about future usurpation of governing power by a popular legislature. Through the Constitution adopted in 1789, together with the Bill of Rights proposed in December of the same year and ratified in 1791, they addressed all three anxieties. Suspicion of executive power was tempered by the requirements of political order. Crucially, the new Constitution had two features which its predecessor had lacked: an executive, and the power to act directly on individuals. The central (federal) government comprised, in a federal system, an institutionally separated executive, legislature and judiciary. The states delegated specified powers to the central government but retained substantial and inviolable powers over their own affairs. Some states regarded their membership of the new political order as revocable; not until the victory of Union forces in the Civil War was that view refuted.

In seeking to avoid these anxieties, the Founding Fathers created a constitution informed by principles that continue to determine the way that the United States functions today. Each is subsumed by one overarching principle: Constitutionalism (discussed below). The core principles at the heart of the Constitution are: to ensure limited government; to separate the powers of government vertically to create a federal system, and horizontally to create a separation of powers; to create a system of checks and balances in which no branch of government could come to dominate the others; to allow judicial review such that the Supreme Court would determine the meaning of the Constitution; and to encourage popular consent tempered by the protection of minorities against what Madison called 'the tyranny of the majority'. These principles determine the way that the US system of government and politics functions today.

Constitutionalism

The United States' Constitution is where America's political values and political institutions meet. The link which the Constitution supplies enables the United States to cohere, binding a multicultural, polychromatic, multilingual, ethnically complex society into one united whole. The continued centrality of the Constitution rests on the pervasiveness of the principle of constitutionalism. That principle places the Constitution at the heart of US politics and society, serving as a unifying icon within a heterogeneous society characterized by institutional division and competition.

Constitutionalism is the guiding principle within the US system of government that requires all aspects of government and politics to adhere to the principles established in that document and its subsequent amendments – most notably the ten amendments proposed in 1789 that constitute the Bill of Rights, and the Thirteenth and Fourteenth Amendments passed, respectively, just before and just after the end of the Civil War. This principle is essential to the process whereby the US political system has periodically reconstituted itself: creating a party system in the early nineteenth century; establishing the permanence of the Union and abolishing slavery in the Civil War; projecting itself into the international system in the twentieth century; and establishing a large, bureaucratic, federal government to support vast programmes of economic regulation and welfare provision born in the 1930s. The federal Constitution's ambiguities, uncertainties and intrinsically disputatious provisions have lent it a flexibility that has enabled it to survive, by ensuring its legitimacy in a heterogeneous society subject to repeated demographic shocks of migration and immigration. It has, however, also ensured that agreement on the meaning of its provisions for relations between branches of federal government, between federal and state authorities, and for conflicts between competing rights of individuals resists definitive settlement. Although the meaning of the Constitution remains essentially contested, its predominance as the frame of reference in almost every public policy debate has near-universal acceptance. Constitutionalism demands that the Constitution remain at the heart of the US system of government.

Conflicts apparent between those American values discussed in Chapter 1 find structural analogues in competition between and within the separated and federal institutions of government. Had clarity, order and expeditiousness been their priorities, the framers would neither have separated the executive from the legislature, nor established a potentially powerful judiciary, nor divided power between a national government and state governments in a federal, and hence doubly-separated, structure. Both federalism and the separation of powers were necessary features of a Constitution sufficiently flexible to accommodate political strain and change, but sufficiently resilient to endure. America's vastness and heterogeneity made it necessary to limit the federal government as well to establish it.

Limited government

The federal Constitution represents the culmination of a number of compromises during the process of crafting a governmental framework underpinned by core principles based on classical liberal ideals of seventeenth-century Enlightenment thought. The central area of compromise was between those framers who favoured the creation of a new and sovereign authority which would be constitutionally superior to the states and those who opposed the creation of what John Lansing, a New York delegate to the Constitutional Convention, called a 'triple-headed monster'. The clash between Federalists and anti-Federalists led to the compromise which saw the seven articles of the new constitution drafted in 1787. Agreement to create a federal government was balanced by guarantees sought by the anti-Federalists leading to the first action of the new federal Congress being the proposal of ten amendments to safeguard the rights of individuals, of the accused and of the states. Congress approved the Bill of Rights in 1789; ratification was complete by 1791.

The Constitution and the Bill of Rights taken together represent the marriage of Federalist and anti-Federalist sentiment, and the attempt to ensure that the new federal government would remain limited in its reach. The principle of limited government was central to the Founding Fathers who had fought in the revolutionary wars against the British; the principle remains central to political debate today about the proper scope of the federal government in, for example, the provision of healthcare, gun-control legislation and the right of corporations to contribute to political campaigns.

A doubly-separated system: the vertical and horizontal separation of powers

Limited government was bolstered by the creation and protection of rights and liberties and by the superiority of the rule of law in which the actions of government would rest on authority given by the consent of the people, and at all times be bound by law. In order to ensure that government was subject to the rule of law, the Founding Fathers created a system separated along both horizontal and vertical axes with a vertical separation between national and sub-national governments (federalism) and a horizontal separation between the three branches of the federal government (separation of powers) so that, as Madison put it, 'ambition would counteract ambition'. The separation of powers within a federal system generates institutional tensions that necessitate compromise and negotiation at every stage – indeed, these separations continue to define how government functions.

Judicial review

Although the principle of limited government was enshrined in the structure of the Constitution and compounded by the principle of *constitutionalism*, change was possible through the exercise of judicial review, by which is meant the Supreme Court's authority to determine the constitutionality of government's actions at national and sub-national levels. Judicial review is not mentioned in the Constitution. Many commentators argue, nonetheless, that Article III, Section II of the Constitution clearly implies that the Supreme Court should have the power of judicial review. That view finds support in the *Federalist Papers* of which Hamilton, Madison and Jay were the authors. As the body charged with judging the constitutionality, or otherwise, of government actions, the Supreme Court has been able to insist on adherence to the meaning of the Constitution (as a majority of justices define it). Judicial review remains key to public policy's direction and content.

Popular consent, representation and the tyranny of the majority

Having experienced taxation without representation at the hands of the British, the Founding Fathers agreed that the new government would rest ultimately on the consent of the people. However, there was no consensus with respect to the extent of the people's involvement. Agreement was finally reached that the House of Representatives would be directly elected (a position advocated in *The Virginia Plan*), with the more populous states having more members than the smaller ones. In another compromise, the framers agreed that the Senate would not be elected but that individual states would select two senators. No account was to be taken of differences in the population of the states. This position was that advocated in *The New Jersey Plan*. Thus, the compromise agreement between small and large states provided that one chamber favoured the larger and more populous states, while the other chamber favoured the smaller states (the compromise between the two plans was called *The Connecticut Compromise*).

That only one chamber of the legislature was elected ensured that the representation of the people would be limited. Fearing what Madison called 'the tyranny of the majority', the extent of the direct involvement of the people in governing was limited; as well as the unelected Senate, the president would be chosen through the electoral college, where delegates from the states chose the president rather than the people doing so directly. Madison was not alone in fearing that direct participation by the people might allow majorities to subjugate minorities. Limits on representation, alongside the safeguards created in the structures of the Constitution, were calculated to prevent such tyranny. From the passage of the Bill of Rights in 1791 to the Civil War (1861–65) and the Reconstruction that followed, and the through the Civil Rights era of the 1960s, the role and protection of minorities has been underpinned by arguments based on the content and meaning of the Constitution and its interpretation by the Supreme Court. That the Court could judge segregation constitutional (1896) and later judge it not to be (1954) is an illustration that the Constitution is not a fixed text but a text on which has been crafted a body of interpretation and re-interpretation.

The core structural features of the Constitutional settlement: horizontal and vertical separation

Federalism, separation of powers, checks and balances, and judicial review are the distinctive structural features of US government and the Constitution's decisive achievement. The structure provides politicians with the opportunity to make government effective while preventing them from making it oppressive. Rights of states and individuals against government are guaranteed and are enforced by federal courts empowered to determine the constitutionality of Congressional statute and executive action. The federal government itself is constitutionally empowered to act directly, which its predecessor was not. The possibility that any one of the three branches might unbalance the tripartite structure is lessened by granting each a different source of power and legitimacy, vesting each with different prerogatives and characteristics, and inducing the executive and legislature both to compete and to cooperate for influence over policy.

Vertical separation: Federalism

In the vertical separation, the Constitution grants powers over foreign affairs, defence, monetary policy and the regulation of commerce between the states to the federal authorities. The remainder is, in theory (though it has not become in practice), the business of the states themselves, or of lower levels of government such as cities, counties and special governing units such as school districts and commissions, which derive their authority from the states. Since 1937 in particular, the Supreme Court's resistance to incursions by Congress into what had hitherto been regarded as traditional state responsibilities has weakened. The boundaries between federal and state jurisdictions have shifted, and Congress now faces few impediments in constitutional law to extending its regulatory activities, the Supreme Court's contested ruling in 2012 on the constitutionality of President Obama's healthcare law notwithstanding.

Yet states survive, the fact of their separate existence is constitutionally protected and the federal government no longer enjoys the enormous fiscal advantages over the states that it did between the 1930s and the mid- to late 1970s. Although under fiscal pressure themselves, state governments are creative and autonomous actors. They are not independent but, rather, are interdependent and interactive with federal agencies, bound in complex fiscal and administrative patterns of policy-making. That which the Constitution appears completely to separate, policy-making joins.

Horizontal separation: the separation of powers

In the horizontal separation, the Constitution forbids members of one branch to belong at the same time to another. Neither the president nor any of his cabinet secretaries may be members of the Senate or the House of Representatives, or be a federal judge or Supreme Court justice. Congress is entirely separate and politically independent from the presidency, the president's staff and the political leaders (cabinet secretaries and their senior colleagues) of government departments and agencies. As with federalism, however, the completeness of separation is more apparent in the structures prescribed by constitutional text than in the processes of policy-making. For government to be effective, unrestrained competition will not suffice: *cooperation* must constantly be sought and achieved. The most important lesson to be learned from relations between the presidency and Congress since Franklin D. Roosevelt took office for the first time in 1933 is that, without cooperation, the effectiveness of federal government deteriorates. However great the strain of eliciting cooperation through negotiation and bargaining, the Constitution's health cannot long withstand either the president or members of Congress behaving as if the other branch lacked legitimacy. Each has separate sources of legitimacy and strength. Although the American system is often thought to be presidential, the Constitution provides neither formal links between the president and Congress (other than those which the presentation, passage and vetoing of legislation require), nor sanctions by which the president can coerce legislators or federal judges.

The president therefore lacks direct power over legislators. Except in the unimportant and unusual circumstances of disagreement between the two chambers as to the time of adjournment, he cannot dissolve either House of Congress. Since Franklin D. Roosevelt expanded the size and role of American government so dramatically in the 1930s and 1940s, presidents have, however, been expected to present to Congress legislative proposals they favour: the president is, for example, required in law to propose annually a budget for the entire federal government. Nevertheless, the president lacks both the constitutional power and the political means to require or compel them to respond (whether favourably or otherwise) on his proposals. Neither in law nor in practice is Congress the president's creature.

Although, in part, the president's political effectiveness therefore depends on Congressional cooperation, he does not hold office subject to Congress's approval, as does the British prime minister, subject to the approval of the House of Commons. Indeed, he may face a Congress in which his party colleagues are in the *minority*. Until the election of George W. Bush in 2000, every Republican president since 1954 has had to work with a Congress in which at least one of the two chambers was in the control of Democrats. Richard Nixon's and Gerald Ford's presidential terms occurred with large Democratic majorities in both houses; Bill Clinton's second term opened with Republican majorities in both. G.W. Bush spent the last two years of his second term facing a Democratic Congress. President Obama faced a Republican House of Representatives not just following the 2010 mid-term Congressional elections, but even after the elections of 2012, in which his own relatively straightforward victory was not matched by the winning of a Democratic majority in the House.

The glue that joins British government so strongly – its party system – is consequently a weaker constitutional adhesive in America. Party leaderships, whether in the White House, Congress or National Committee, have few sanctions over elected members of the party at any level. Party is usually unable to combine reliably the governing powers the Constitution has so effectively separated. Only under unusual circumstances does it do so, when the normal constitutional constraints weaken, and presidents have greater freedom of political manoeuvre and initiative. Obstacles to presidential leadership then shrink, permitting a

---

Exhibit 2.1 Checks and Balances

There are six arenas in which the branches check and balance each other: each of the three branches checks the others two – thus making six elements to the checks and balances created by the separation of powers.

Checks by the Executive

Over the Legislature

- Can veto acts of Congress
- Administers (carries out through the federal bureaucracy) those laws made by Congress – thus allowing the Executive Branch the discretion to interpret these laws
- The Vice-President casts the deciding vote when Senate is tied
- Can recall Congress into a special session.

Over the Judiciary

- Nominates Supreme Court Justices
- Nominates federal judges
- May not be obliged to enforce Court decisions
- President can pardon those convicted (in federal but not state courts).

Checks by the Legislature

Over the Executive

- Override presidential veto with two-thirds majority in both chambers
- House can impeach and the Senate convict the president

---

resourceful chief executive the opportunity to chart a course, whether of recovery from economic disaster, or of salvation from foreign threat, and to stick to it.

Checks and balances

Although the Constitution formally created three separate institutions of government in order to ensure that no branch would come to dominate the others, such separation works only because the Constitution also ensured that the most significant powers allocated to the federal government would not be placed solely within the grasp of any one institution. As Richard Neustadt (1990 [1960]) observed, the US has not so much a separation of powers as three separate institutions that share powers.

➜

- Senate may reject presidential nominations
- Refuse to pass the president's legislation
- Refuse/curtail funding requested by the president
- Senate may refuse to ratify treaties.

Over the Judiciary

- May alter the number of Supreme Court justices
- Alter the structure of the federal courts
- Reject Supreme Court nominees
- Impeach (House) and convict (Senate) members of the federal Judiciary
- Propose constitutional amendments with two-thirds majority in both chambers.

Checks by the Judiciary

Over the Executive

- Declare actions of the president and the executive branch unconstitutional
- Impeachment proceedings presided over by the Chief Justice of the Supreme Court
- Can issue warrants.

Over the legislature

- Declare laws made by Congress unconstitutional
- Chief Justice presides over Senate impeachment trials.

Indeed, he captures the essence of this system of checks and balances, noting that 'to share is to limit'. And it is this sharing of powers that places limits on each branch, since no branch can adequately exert power without the support of the others.

The system of checks and balances, in which each branch is able to place limits on the actions of the others, is the direct consequence of a constitutional arrangement in which separate institutions share governing. Checks and balances are the result of a system which demands coordinated action across the branches of government. When the system of checks and balances works well, no branch usurps the power of the others; when the separated institutions of the federal government cannot agree as to how they will share power, the system of checks and balances can, and does, produce gridlock.

That the Constitution allocates formal powers to the three branches of government does not mean simply that these powers can be exercised with ease. Only by working with the other branches to overcome the obstacles created by a system of checks and balances can power effectively be wielded. Neustadt summarized this position succinctly in noting that 'powers are no guarantee of power'. Exhibit 2.1 provides a summary of the checks and balances exerted by each branch on the others.

The Constitution and the Bill of Rights

The seven articles drafted in 1787 represent the culmination of arduous debate and much compromise. While the Constitution is reproduced in full in Appendix I, it is important to consider how each of the seven articles created the three branches of government, discussed the relationships between the three branches, considered the relationship between the government and the states, and made provision for amendments to be added. The ambiguities in these seven articles, as well as their clearest provisions, continue to act as the frame of reference when considering how government is to function, where the limits of government lie and what the Constitution will permit.

Article I of the Constitution established a bicameral legislature, Congress, and describe its powers. Members of the House of Representatives (termed Congressmen, Representatives or Members of Congress) were to be popularly elected by white males (subject in most states, until the 1830s, to some property qualifications). Members of the Senate (senators) were to be selected by each state's legislature, but have been popularly elected since the Seventeenth Amendment to the Constitution in 1920. Every state has two senators, irrespective of population, elected for six-year terms. Apportionment of Congressmen between states varies between one and fifty-three, depending on population; House terms are two years. At biennial Congressional elections, therefore, all House seats and approximately one-third of Senate seats are contested. The Constitution in many respects makes Congress a remarkably powerful legislature: its single greatest power derives from its unfettered authority to raise taxes and to spend money (through 'appropriations') and so to share fully and equally in policy-making. Yet, its powers (unlike those of the British House of Commons) are also defined and strictly limited.

Article II established the new executive power in the institution of a single president, separately elected by an electoral college rather than by popular vote, and Article III an unelected Supreme Court. The powers of all three branches were limited and (albeit imprecisely) specified. The remaining Articles IV–VII comprised rules governing processes of policy:

relations between the states, and procedures for the Constitution's amendment and for dealing with state debts incurred before the Constitution's ratification. The supremacy of the US Constitution was affirmed, and the means of ratification of the Constitution described.

Article VII required that, for the Constitution to be ratified, nine of the thirteen states would have to approve it in conventions called for the purpose. It was nonetheless clear that, without the support of New York and Virginia, the new Constitution would probably collapse. New Hampshire was the ninth state to ratify the Constitution but, in Virginia and New York, opponents were powerful and persuasive. Ratification in both states was achieved only with difficulty, after immense political efforts by both proponents and opponents, and no little good fortune. In New York, Hamilton, Madison and Jay energetically wrote and published *The Federalist Papers*, contributing not only to the campaign for the ratification of the Constitution by the New York Legislature, but also to later scholarly and judicial understanding of the nature of the Constitution itself. Their literary efforts apart, the narrow victory for ratification in New York owed much to Hamilton and Jay's manoeuvring in the state legislature where they threatened that, if the Constitution were not ratified, they would promote the secession of New York City from New York State and join the Union separately; relations between the city and the state have rarely been entirely comfortable since. Eleven of the thirteen states ratified by the end of 1788; North Carolina followed in 1789 and Rhode Island in 1790.

The Bill of Rights

One of the first actions of the newly-created Congress in 1789 was the passage of a series of legislative articles introduced to the House by James Madison in August and proposed as a series of constitutional amendments by both chambers of Congress in September 1789. The ten amendments had been ratified by nine of the thirteen states by 1791 (the Constitution requires three-quarters of the states to ratify an amendment and nine was three-quarters of the then-thirteen states) as constitutional amendments. Influenced by the British Bill of Rights of 1689, the ten amendments that constitute the Bill of Rights pacified the anti-Federalists, who had feared the creation of a powerful central government and gained some reassurance from the codification of those fundamental liberties that would place limits on government; enshrine the rule of law within the constitution; protect the autonomy of the states; and promote the protection of individual liberties including rights to property, free speech, assembly and the right to religion (and importantly the absence of religion within the government). Originally, the provisions of the Bill of Rights placed limits only on federal government, but they were extended to cover the states after the passage of the Fourteenth Amendment (through the doctrine of *Incorporation* discussed in Exhibit 2.4).

If the articles of the Constitution remain crucial to the functioning of the institutions of government today, then the Bill of Rights is at least as, if not more, important than these articles. In no other liberal democracy is so much public policy compared with the provisions of the Bill of Rights. In most democracies (including the UK), public policy is made when the executive secures the consent of a majority in the legislature. Yet, in the US, once such consent is achieved there is another hurdle: that policy is found to be congruent with the provisions of the Bill of Rights. The principle of constitutionalism often demands of policy-makers that they secure legislative support and then the consent of the Supreme Court justices – who are frequently asked to judge the constitutionality of public policy. Debates regarding the meaning and application of the Constitution are much more than an historical curiosity. Whether the electric chair can be used in executions; whether the American Flag may be burned; whether erotic dancers require additional licensing to move from almost-nude to nude dancing; whether Franklin D. Roosevelt's Social Security Act or Barack Obama's healthcare reforms are constitutional; whether members of Westboro Baptist Church may protest during the private funerals of soldiers killed in Iraq, have all been questions before the Supreme Court. Each judgement was based, if only purportedly, on the Court's interpretation of the Bill of Rights.

The central provisions of the Bill of Rights

To present a general overview of the Bill of Rights, it is useful to group the ten amendments into four categories:

- Amendment One places *limits on Congress*
- Amendments Two, Three and Four place *limits on the executive*
- Amendments Five, Six, Seven and Eight place *limits on the judiciary*
- Amendments Nine and Ten place *limits on the federal government in relation to the powers of state governments.*

The First Amendment guarantees freedom of speech, religion and assembly; it implies, but does not declare, that Church and State be clearly separated, since, by allowing all religions, the government would be permitted to adopt none. The Second Amendment guaranteed the right to form militia and to bear arms, while the Third prevented the quartering of soldiers in private property (which some interpret as being one element in a right to privacy).

Amendments Four to Eight specify the rights to the accused, which include: no unreasonable search and seizures (Four), the right to silence and the right to be tried only once for one crime (Five), the right to a fair trial (Six) and the right to a trial by jury in civil cases (Seven), as well as a ban on cruel and unusual punishments (Eight).

Amendment Nine states that right not specified (or 'enumerated') in the Bill of Rights should be presumed both to exist and to remain with the people.

Amendment Ten notes that rights not expressly mentioned in the Constitution are assumed to reside with the states and with the people. Although the term 'federalism' appears neither in the Constitution nor in the Bill of Rights, these two amendments – but most notably the Tenth – are known as the 'federalism' or the 'States' Rights' amendments, since they are viewed, correctly, as the basis on which federalism is preserved.

Later amendments

Only seventeen further amendments have been added since the ratification of the Bill of Rights. The number is small, in part because of the difficulty of securing an amendment to the Constitution. Only twelve amendments have been added since the passage of the Sixteenth Amendment in 1913: the average is just one for every eight years in the last century. The relative paucity of constitutional amendments can be explained partly by the less difficult path adopted: that of judicial review to change the meaning, if not the wording, of the Constitution. Constitutional change often results from judicial review, rather than from formal constitutional amendment.

Exhibit 2.2 The Amendment Process

Proposal of amendment	*Ratification*
Two-third majorities required in both chambers of Congress (34 amendments have been proposed in this manner)	Three-quarters of all state legislatures agree to the amendment (26 of the 27 amendments have been ratified in this manner)
A national convention may be called requiring the assent of two-thirds of the states legislatures (this method has never been used)	Constitutional conventions in three-quarters of the states must agree to ratify the proposal (the Twenty-First amendment was ratified in this manner)

Exhibit 2.3 The Bill of Rights and Political Controversies

The First Amendment: The number of Supreme Court rulings based upon the First Amendment is legion, and they have shaped the development of public policy throughout the Republic's history. In the case of *Texas v Johnson* (1989), Gregory Lee Johnson had burned an American flag at a political demonstration in 1984 in violation of the statutes of the State of Texas. In this ruling, the Supreme Court ruled in a 5–4 decision that Mr Johnson was permitted to burn the flag under the First Amendment's right to free speech and that flag-burning was to be understood as a speech act. And, in the 2011 case of *Snyder v Phelps*, the Court ruled in an 8–1 decision that the Westboro Baptist Church could protest at the funerals of servicemen and women killed in the Iraq and Afghanistan wars. Election finances, internet privacy, religion and the right to perform acts that most find reprehensible have led to landmark judgements by the Supreme Court and have, as with many other rights within the Bill of Rights, seen the Court pitted against both popular opinion and the views of many in the elected branches of government.

The Second Amendment: The continuing debate regarding the right to bear arms, and the ability of states and the federal government to regulate gun ownership and gun use has led to continued clashes between the populous and well-financed National Rifle Association and those advocating stricter gun laws. A recent landmark ruling that highlights both the clash over gun laws and the clash over the appropriate role of the Supreme Court in interpreting the Bill of Rights is *DC v Heller* (2008), in which the four liberal justices in the minority faced the four conservative justices who had the support of swing justice Anthony Kennedy. In the ruling, the Court overturned elements of the restrictions in Washington DC on gun ownership and upheld the right to possess a gun within the home. The case was significant both for its re-shaping of public policy in the arena of gun control, and for the split within the Court along the ideological divide between liberal and conservative justices. Chapter 7 considers this divide in greater detail.

The Third Amendment: Provided the constitutional basis for the right to privacy. Justice William O. Douglas used the right to privacy in *Griswold v Connecticut* (1965), which deemed that the home is a private sphere independent of the state, and that led to the overturning of Connecticut's laws on the use of contraception. That the Third Amendment may create a right to privacy was one element in the arguments that led to the

→

➜

momentous *Roe v Wade* ruling of 1973 that granted women the right to an abortion.

The Fifth Amendment: strengthens the principle of due process by protecting against self-incrimination ('You have the right to remain silent ...'); double jeopardy, which protects against a re-trial for a crime of which one has been acquitted; and the right to trial by jury. This amendment, along with the Fourteenth Amendment, explicitly used the term *due process* and has, for example, formed the basis for overturning convictions based upon testimony obtained from a defendant who had not first been informed of the right to legal counsel ('You have the right to have an attorney present ...'). In *Miranda v Arizona* (1966), Ernesto Miranda confessed to the rape of a seventeen-year-old woman. He had not, during two hours of questioning, been advised of his rights (now called 'Miranda rights') including the right to having legal counsel present during questioning.

The Tenth Amendment: often called the *Federalism* amendment and also the *States' Rights* amendment. This amendment states that 'the powers not delegated to the United States by the Constitution, nor prohibited by it to the States, are reserved to the States respectively, or to the people'. The assumption is clearly that if the Constitution has not clearly granted powers to the newly-created federal government, then powers remain with the states or the people. The Tenth Amendment has, since the ratification of the Bill of Rights, been a central element in clashes between national and sub-national governments in relation to the boundary between the two. Indeed, the changing federal–state balance, particularly since the expansion of the federal government in the 1930s, has turned on the Supreme Court's interpretation of the Tenth Amendment. In 1936, Franklin D. Roosevelt, who saw much of his landmark legislation struck down by the Court, proposed the Judiciary Reorganization Bill of 1937 (known as the 'court-packing' plan) which, arguably, pressured Justice Owen Roberts to change position and support New Deal legislation. This 'switch in time that saved nine' in *West Coast Hotel v Parrish* (1937) represented the end of the Lochner Era. However, the boundary between federal and state power was revisited in 2012 when the Supreme Court was asked to rule on elements of President Obama's landmark healthcare legislation, the Patient Protection and Affordable Care Act of 2010. In a much-anticipated and bitterly-contested decision, the Supreme Court upheld the power of Congress to enact the law (in *National Federation of Independent Business v Sebelius* (2012)).

Exhibit 2.4 The Fourteenth Amendment and the Doctrine of Incorporation

The Fourteenth Amendment was ratified in July 1868 in the aftermath of the Civil War; it is one of the three *Reconstruction* (or *Civil War*) *Amendments* alongside the Thirteenth Amendment (which abolished slavery, and was ratified in 1865), and the Fifteenth Amendment (which prohibited the withholding of the franchise on the grounds of race, colour, or previous conditions of servitude and was ratified in 1870). The Fourteenth Amendment contains three clauses which should have transformed US society by consolidating the rights of all citizens in a nation which, after a bloody Civil War, had abolished slavery. The three clauses are:

(i)   *The Citizenship Clause* states that all persons born or naturalized in the US are citizens of the United States, and of the state in which they reside. Government could make no law abridging the rights of these citizens. Previously, the Supreme Court had ruled that blacks could not be citizens of the United States (in the landmark case of *Dred Scott v Sandford* (1857). The Court ruled that people of African descent – whether slave or free – were not eligible for citizenship of the United States)

(ii) *The Due Process Clause* states that 'no person shall be deprived of life, liberty or property without due process of law'. The clause requires that *procedural due process* is ensured so that, for example, the proceedings in criminal cases are properly executed. The clause has also been interpreted to deliver *substantive due process*, which considers due process not just in terms of the process of a case, but also in terms of the outcomes that are sought by the parties to a case, usually arguing that the outcomes are required by the protection of 'liberty' under the Fourteenth Amendment. During the *Lochner Era* (see Exhibit 2.2), substantive due process was used to strike down many of the central legislative elements of the New Deal (the Court cited 'freedom of contract' as the grounds for overturning Franklin D. Roosevelt's legislation), but the Court adopted a different approach

→

Two significant amendments that followed the Tenth are the Thirteenth and Fourteenth, which abolished slavery and guaranteed 'equal protection of the laws' to all. Yet, despite the momentous achievement of President Lincoln in securing passage of the Thirteenth, genuine equality for black Americans was systematically denied for over a century after the ratification of the Fourteenth Amendment in 1868. Amendments Fourteen, Fifteen, Nineteen, and Twenty-Six dealt

→   to the meaning of *substantive due process* after the about-turn in the *West Coast Hotel* case (Exhibit 2.2), after which the Court allowed that freedoms not explicitly mentioned in the Constitution are nonetheless protected by it (see the discussion of Justice Stone's 'preferred freedoms' doctrine in Chapter 10 on Federalism).

(iii) *The Equal Protection Clause* states that no one within the jurisdiction of the United States shall be deprived of 'the equal protection of the laws'. On one reading, this clause would seem to be the constitutional embodiment of the wording in the United States Declaration of Independence (1776) that '*we hold these truths to be self-evident, that all men are created equal*' – a clause which empowered the Supreme Court to demand equality be delivered by the states.

Incorporation

Until the passage of the Fourteenth Amendment, the Bill of Rights had been applied only to the actions of the federal government. Central to the extension of the Bill of Rights to the states was the application of the equal protection clause of the Fourteenth Amendment. Over the course of many years, and on a case-by-case basis, most of the ten amendments to the Bill of Rights were 'incorporated' by being applied to the states instead of, as previously, to the federal government only. Yet, despite this doctrine of incorporation, the equal protection clause has been used by the states, supported by the Supreme Court, as a barrier to social justice. In the *Plessy v Ferguson* case (1896), the Court upheld the doctrine of 'separate but equal' which, in effect, gave a Constitutional sanction to the practice of segregation. The doctrine was overturned in the Brown decision of 1954 (*Brown v Board of Education, Topeka*, which deemed that enforced separation was always unequal.

Despite the passage of the Bill of Rights and its incorporation under the Fourteenth Amendment, the power of judicial review has not resulted in the unimpeded march of social change. The power of the Supreme Court to interpret the Constitution has resulted in landmark decisions which shape public policy, but this power has also been used to maintain a status quo that has neither protected minorities, nor challenged the views of elected politicians at both the state and national levels.

with issues related to voting; the Sixteenth allowed the federal government to levy income tax (the Supreme Court having struck down an income tax in 1895); the Twenty-Second limited a president to two terms of office; and the Twenty-Seventh provided for the direct election of senators.

Changing the Constitution through judicial interpretation

The Constitution and its twenty-seven amendments remain central to every contentious public policy debate. Through its power to interpret the Constitution, the Supreme Court applies a text that has existed for more than two hundred years to contemporary questions from the use of the internet to the incarceration of terrorist suspects in Guantanamo Bay, whether women have the right to an abortion or whether segregation is compatible with the Fourteenth Amendment.

How the Court interprets the Constitution is of central concern to public policy-makers and the public alike. Constitutional uncertainties and ambiguities invite argument: the question of how far the Supreme Court can, and should, *read into* the Constitution resists tidy resolution. A change in the composition of the Court created by the replacement of one justice with another may alter the extent to which the judicial branch is willing to interpret the wording of the Constitution: adhering closely to the text and eschewing decisions that require meaning to be *found* in the document, or using the Constitution as the basis for addressing the challenges of modern society.

At times, the Court has been in the vanguard of social change, striking down segregation in the South in *Brown v Board of Education, Topeka* (1954); limiting the power of the president, even in times of crisis, in *Youngstown Sheet and Tube v Sawyer* (1952) and in *Rasul v Bush* (2004), and granting women the right to an abortion in *Roe v Wade* (1973). At other times, the Court has maintained the *status quo*, leading some to argue that the Constitution is a barrier to social change. For example, segregation, which the Fourteenth Amendment would seem to have prohibited, continued *de jure* until the *Brown* decision in 1954 (and *de facto* well into the 1970s, when bussing was still commonplace in some areas of the United States). The *Plessy* decision upheld the doctrine of 'separate but equal', which declared that segregation was permissible if equality was maintained.

The Court has also determined the size and reach of the federal government through its interpretation of the Constitution: the growth of federal government during the New Deal era was stymied and, after an about-turn by the Court, upheld. The Tenth Amendment can reasonably be interpreted to exclude the growth in federal government and the dominance of national over sub-national governments, witnessed in the twentieth-century. While it has largely been the presidency that has expanded the reach of federal government, it has been the Court that has been asked to decide where the limit of government lies.

Conclusion

Despite the fractured nature of the governing institutions in the US, with a president and Congress that, in recent years, have found it increasingly difficult to find positions of compromise, a near-universal proclaimed adherence to the tenets of the Constitution and its later amendments pervades almost every element of political debate. The Constitution provides the institutional and textual embodiment of the core values discussed in Chapter 1 which constitute the American Creed – the core values of which politicians and public alike remain wedded even as they disagree about the ways in which these values apply to the content of public policy. It is through the power of judicial review that the Supreme Court must compare public policy with the Constitution and its amendments, applying anew its meanings for each generation.

Diffusion and fragmentation, rather than concentration and coherence, characterize American government, and are reflected in the extraordinary vigour of its society. In introducing the subject of the government and politics of the United States, this book attempts to explain the relationships of conflict, competition and cooperation between the different parts of the democratic yet fragmented system that the Constitution encourages and which makes the United States difficult to govern but compelling to study. In each of the chapters that follows, the imprint of the Founding Fathers, and the vigorous debates that characterized the creation of their governmental system, are everywhere apparent. It is the interplay of the political culture of the new republic, superimposed on a new constitutional design, that defined the birth of the new federal government and which continues to define the government and politics of the nation in the twenty-first century. In a system designed to prevent too much overlap between the elected branches, political parties (discussed in Chapter 3) present the best opportunity to create a workable system of government.

Chapter 3

Political Parties: The Politics of Aggregation and Disaggregation

The United States has the purest two-party system of any large liberal democracy in the world. The system has undergone a number of significant changes during the history of the Republic, but the parties have remained the glue binding together a governmental system divided both vertically (as a result of federalism) and horizontally (as a result of the separation of powers). The US party system differs sharply from European party systems. This chapter traces the development of the party system, and examines how and why the US party system is different, and shows the significance of these differences. In examining the parties, the chapter considers whether, in an era of partisan polarization where moderate elite politicians are few, the parties remain the institutional glue they once were. To examine the parties in detail, this chapter considers the parties from three perspectives: as organizations (party machines that seek to elect candidates to office), as parties within the electorate (who votes for which party, why and how often), and as parties in government (how do elected officials and activists behave, particularly within the elected branches of the federal government. Finally, in trying to understand what has happened to the parties within the federal government, this chapter suggests that the parties have become more polarized in the last three decades but that the 'party in government' ('party elites') remain more polarized than voters. The consequence of this 'elite polarization' is a governmental system that works less well than it might. The party system is a significant contributor to this failure.

The nature of American parties

Parties are as important to American government and politics as they are to government and politics in other systems. However, 'party' in America differs radically from that elsewhere: the distinctive structure, rules and culture of American politics produces a party system unlike any other. In Europe, party is everywhere regarded (more or less accurately) as an organizational device binding together members of broadly similar ideological disposition with the purpose of translating that disposition into policy. In the United States, circumstances differ: parties in America have no mass membership, and the combination of the separation of powers and federalism hinders any attempt at the control of party by leaders. When compared with Western European parties, it is clear that US parties and the party system are unusual in eight key respects, each of which is examined below

The two-party system

The American party system is, except for that in Malta, the purest significant two-party system in the world. Although other parties exist, only the Republican and Democratic Parties have any prospect of nominating a candidate with a chance of winning the supreme electoral prize of the presidency. In many states, at different times, and in the South for one hundred years after the Civil War, there has been just one party exercising power, ranging from the hegemonic to the merely dominant. While many states are now two-party competitive, a significant number are dominated by one party.

Electoral bases and political purposes of the parties

Although the names 'Republican' and 'Democratic' have remained unaltered since the Civil War, neither the party system they dominate nor the electoral coalitions that support them has been static. Their electoral bases and political purposes have often altered suddenly: the introduction of a major new issue or crisis has caused new cleavages to emerge in the electorate, thereby precipitating partisan realignments. New issues have often been advanced not by the Democrats or the Republicans, but by third-party or independent candidates. Eventually, one or both of the two major parties has absorbed the issue, causing the demise of the third party. At other times, partisan change has been slower and more complicated (as has been the case since the early 1960s).

The southern states

The southern states have, for most of the Republic's life, had a distinctive party system and, in certain respects, continue to do so. The Jeffersonian tradition of 'States' Rights' was exploited by southern states to preserve slavery until 1865. Thereafter, it was used to buttress sharecropping (payment in kind from crops grown on land rented from whites) and segregation from Reconstruction until the passage of five Civil Rights Acts between 1957 and 1968. The South's political development is of cardinal importance for an understanding of the American party system, both outside Congress and within it (where the chairmanships of major committees between 1910 and 1975 were dominated by autonomous, powerful, southern conservatives). The South stands as the great exception to many general rules about American society and politics, but also as Hamlet's ghost. As will be explained later, in no respect has the South had more powerful significance than in the contribution which its social order has made to the maintenance of the Democratic majority in presidential elections until 1964, and much less importance in presidential elections since (during which time the White House has been occupied by each party for twenty-four years).

Institutional expression at state level

The doctrine and practice of federalism results in parties finding their chief institutional expression at the *state, not at the federal, level*. Until the early 1970s, this focus on state party organizations rendered national party organizations weak. Since then, national party organizations have acquired new powers over state parties, limiting their autonomy, especially with respect to rules controlling the nomination of candidates for the presidency. None the less, federalism fragments American parties and renders national party organizations weaker than their European counterparts.

Quasi-public institutions

Parties in the United States are quasi-public institutions, not private organizations as they are in most of Western Europe: they are subject to, but often determine, state law passed by state legislatures. As Epstein (1986) notes, parties were not treated as private institutions entitled to regulate their own affairs (as is the case with political parties in most other democracies) but resembled public utilities, in that they were privately-owned companies but regulated by the state in order to ensure that they served the public.

Open organizations without mass membership

Parties are open organizations without mass membership. Where local political clubs and caucuses survive, their membership is determined by local and not by national considerations. primaries (see Chapter 4) give to voters a power over the party that is unique in Western political systems. The organization of parties in local government jurisdictions such as the counties is, partly in consequence, invariably weak and often non-existent.

Lack of ideological coherence

American parties are not strongly programmatic and have usually lacked most of the ideological coherence typical of many European parties. Historically, parties in America have depended on their presidential candidates for the articulation of policy objectives. (The reforms to presidential nominating politics prior to the 1972 primary season have, however, sometimes saddled presidential candidates with commitments from factions in the party which later prove politically damaging.) Candidates for all offices now run under their own programme, not one determined (or even heavily shaped by) a central, state, or local party organization. Candidates seek less to control government (not least because the separated and federal structure of American politics makes that very hard to achieve) than to win elections, a characteristic which does not build national or ideologically coherent parties. A centrally-determined ideological programme would have no purpose, could neither be imposed on candidates nor be assured of implementation in a system of fragmented government at both federal and state level. In contrast to the experience of many European states, in the United States since the end of the Civil War there have never been any electorally significant parties dedicated to the overthrow of the political or economic system, or even systematically critical of either. Both major parties support the political and economic orders, save at times of crisis such as that of the Populist challenges in the 1890s. Party competition, though vigorous, occurs within a comparatively narrow ideological range. Agreement on fundamental values is widespread.

Bridge across the political divide between institutions

Weakened though they are in America by the combination of the separation of powers and federalism, political parties are vital for efficient government: the unique structure of government in America requires party for the bridging of the political divide between institutions. While party leaders lack the sanctions available to which party leaders in many Western European states are accustomed, and work in a system where compliance has to be elicited rather than demanded, party ties exert a powerful pull on individual politicians in Congress. In the United States, parties are, indeed, often weaker than their European counterparts, but party also matters – and increasingly so since the mid-1990s. Party remains one of the best indicators of why members of Congress vote and behave as they do.

The development of the American two-party system

Dangers of partisan allegiance

Party has rarely won the approbation of American voters. It enjoyed the favour neither of the founders nor of the first president of the United States, who perceived in partisan allegiance the seeds of social and political strife (see Exhibit 3.1 for a list of US presidents since 1789, to which it might be helpful in this chapter occasionally to make reference). George Washington himself had no need of party: his reputation ensured that he would face no serious competition to become or remain president, as it proved an unshakeable political foundation for his presidency. The Constitution's exclusion of members of Congress from membership of the presidential electoral college was a feeble barrier to party's emergence. Displeased by the factional strife between Jefferson and Hamilton in his own Cabinet, by the fiercely-contested struggle to succeed him in 1796, and fearful of its implications for the future unity of the country, in his Farewell Address of 1796 President Washington issued a forthright warning of the dangers that party, together with sectional interest groups, presented. He and his contemporaries had no experience of party government, but both he and some of them had a lively anxiety about its destructive possibilities, and the rousing of inarticulate and uneducated masses. Nevertheless, as the overwhelming issue of opposition to the colonial power lost its importance after 1776, factional groupings sprang up in several states.

Party before 1800

Most of the delegates to the Philadelphia Convention of 1787, who drafted the Constitution, intended that the role played by the mass of voters should be marginal: a proposal for the president's direct election was rejected because of their aversion to the possible consequences of mass participation. Hamilton, Madison and Jay wrote *The Federalist Papers* to advance not a democracy, but a republic buttressed and sustained by its rules and spirit against an effusion of democracy, parties and mass participation. In *Federalist* No. 10, Madison argued that the separation of power and federalism would prevent the capture by faction of all branches of government. The notion of government coming under frequent attack from members of an opposition nonetheless loyal to the constitutional order (and sensitive to the need to preserve the Union) was entirely anathema to Madison and his colleagues.

As with any complicated document whose drafting is the product of compromise and disagreement, the meanings and silences of the US Constitution became the subject of intense dispute after its ratification. Hamilton and his Federalist colleagues understood the Constitution to be a means to the establishment of a powerful national state; Jefferson and his allies were distrustful of a powerful central government and, instead, saw liberty's best defence in limited government at the centre.

The broad division between commercial (mainly northern and coastal) and rural (mainly southern and western) interests in the early years of the Republic fuelled emerging partisan divisions in the single-term presidency of John Adams (who succeeded Washington), and in the years of Jeffersonian and Madisonian domination that followed. In 1791, Jefferson succeeded in establishing a compact which united anti-Hamiltonian Republican interests in the South and New York. Partisan divisions over Hamilton's financial policies were soon broadened by fervent disagreement over the course of the French Revolution, the question of war with England or France, ratification of the Jay Treaty (which opened the frontier to the west), and the federalist President Adams's Naturalization, Alien and Sedition Acts of 1798 which (among other illiberal measures) criminalized Republican opposition to Federalist politicians.

Many of the sources of division between the earliest parties in the Republic continued to divide voters and politicians in the United States long after the nascent party system of the late eighteenth century had disappeared. Indeed, the tensions between the values dividing the Federalists from the Republicans still appear between and within parties in contemporary America: the ferocity with which the Tea Party Movement opposed both President Obama's Affordable Health Care Bill, passed in March 2010, and the American Recovery and Reinvestment Bill (ARRA), passed in February 2009, indicate that such tensions remain salient.

Washington's Farewell Address, which Hamilton helped to draft, was as much a reaction to developments already apparent as a warning of what might follow. Partisan divisions quickly focused on the office of the presidency, national party alignments preceded state party alignments. That was a clear indication of the special significance of the presidency and the contest for it. Election to the presidency gave rise to national alignments that have passed through five systems:

- The Virginia dynasty (1800–24)
- Jacksonian democracy (1824–56)
- Civil war, sectionalism and reconstruction (1856–96)
- Populist discontent, progressive reform and Republican majorities (1896–1932)
- The New Deal Democratic Coalition (1932–).

The first party system: the Virginia dynasty

The constitutional crisis of 1800 followed divisions within President Washington's cabinet over financial policy, and the struggle to succeed him. Together, they marked the stirrings of party. Reflecting the degree to which party was beginning to determine voting for president in the electoral college, Thomas Jefferson and Aaron Burr, running together on the Republican ticket against the incumbent Federalist President, John Adams, tied for first place with 73 votes each. The election was therefore thrown into the House of Representatives, dominated by Federalists, many of whom had been defeated in the preceding November elections but who retained their seats until the following March. (The Twelfth Amendment, passed in 1804, ended the possibility of another tie between two candidates running on the same ticket; see Appendix II.) After thirty-five ballots, the House, voting by states, elected Jefferson. Jefferson's Republican Party had swept both the House and Senate elections, and the Federalists were firmly in the minority in Washington, the nation's new capital. Jefferson's own transition from opposition, to party, to presiding over the first party system in American history is gently ironic, but telling. In 1789, he had written scathingly of party spirit: 'Such an addiction is the last degradation of a free and moral agent. If I could not go to heaven but with a party, I would not go there at all.'

In fact, Jefferson's heavenly passage was on his own party ticket. Before his death, he enjoyed two terms in the White House. His friend and ally Madison took the next two terms, and his 'disciple' Monroe the following two. The Federalist Party, greatly diminished by Hamilton's death in 1803, disappeared after the Treaty of Ghent in 1814 ended the second war with Great Britain. The Virginia dynasty, which these three presidents represented, ended in 1824; the Congressional Party caucus could not cope with the demands of finding a successor. The election resulted in a stalemate, with none of the four candidates receiving a majority. Accordingly, the election of 1824 was thrown into the House, where John Quincy Adams defeated General Andrew Jackson, the intemperate frontier hero of the Battle of New Orleans.

The second party system: Jacksonian democracy

The 1824 presidential election was a watershed in the early development of the party system: in the succeeding sixteen years, politicians seeking the presidency looked beyond Congressional caucuses to potential supporters in state and local parties. The old cleavage between Federalists and Republicans collapsed under the pressures of the emergence of mass politics, which shifted the selection of the president from Congress to ordinary voters. Between 1830 and 1850, all states removed considerations of property and religion as qualifications for white males to vote. By the time that Martin van Buren (the first president to have been born a citizen of the United States) entered the White House in 1836 in succession to Jackson, parties had become firmly entrenched in American politics. They were the means by which elections were organized, by which a structurally divided Federal government was (occasionally) given some coherence, and by which supporters of elected politicians were rewarded with patronage.

At the centre of this transformation from dynastic to mass politics, structured by parties, lay the procedures by which candidates for the presidency were selected. Either the party had too few elected officials to whom to submit the decision to nominate, or the outcome of a legislative caucus was unacceptable to those early party activists in the states and the counties who would campaign for the nominee (Shafer, 1988: 6–14). The new party system was distinctive not only in its organization and relationship between the elected and the electors, but also (like the Virginia dynasty) in its bridging of the North–South divide over slavery. It was, unusually in the history of American political parties, a genuinely national two-party system.

Under the leadership of Jackson and a succession of Democratic presidents after him, the Democratic Party had both northern and southern bases. So, too, did the disparate coalition comprising the (generally unsuccessful) Whig Party, whose name was supposed to link in the public mind the English Whigs' opposition to George III with the American Whigs' opposition to 'King' Andrew Jackson, whose enemies described his presidency as a 'reign'. Yet, the new Whigs had little more in common than opposition to Jackson's policies and to his methodical fortifying of party through the spoils which he had introduced, and by which he ensured the allegiance of those postmasters and customs officers who owed their posts to him. The systematic rooting of party in federal patronage began with Jackson's presidency. Despite later civil service

Exhibit 3.1   Presidents and Vice-Presidents of the United States

President	Vice-President	Party	Term
George Washington	John Adams	No Party Designation	1789–1797
John Adams	Thomas Jefferson	Federalist	1797–1801
Thomas Jefferson	Aaron Burr George Clinton	Democratic-Republican	1801–1809
James Madison	George Clinton Elbridge Gerry	Democratic-Republican	1809–1817
James Monroe	Daniel D. Tompkins	Democratic-Republican	1817–1825
John Quincy Adams	John C. Calhoun	Democratic-Republican	1825–1829
Andrew Jackson	John C. Calhoun Martin Van Buren	Democratic	1829–1837
Martin Van Buren	Richard M. Johnson	Democratic	1837–1841
William Henry Harrison[1]	John Tyler	Whig	1841
John Tyler	None[2]	Whig	1841–1845
James Polk	George M. Dallas	Democratic	1845–1849
Zachary Taylor[3]	Millard Fillmore	Whig	1849–1850
Millard Fillmore	None	Whig	1850–1853
Franklin Pierce	William R. King	Democratic	1853–1857
James Buchanan	John C. Breckinridge	Democratic	1857–1861
Abraham Lincoln	Hannibal Hamlin Andrew Johnson	Republican	1861–1865
Andrew Johnson	None	Democratic	1865–1869
Ulysses Grant	Schuyler Colfax Henry Wilson	Republican	1869–1877
Rutherford Hayes	William Wheeler	Republican	1877–1881
James Garfield[4]	Chester Arthur	Republican	1881
Chester Arthur	None	Republican	1881–1885
Grover Cleveland	Thomas Hendricks	Democratic	1885–1889
Benjamin Harrison	Levi Morton	Republican	1889–1893
Grover Cleveland	Adlai E. Stevenson (I)	Democratic	1893–1897

→

reform, patronage appointments remain an important feature of American executive politics, both in federal and state governments.

The possibility that interests might divide cumulatively by region and economic interest along new partisan lines between the slave states of the South and the non-slave states of the North had always been a source of

President	Vice-President	Party	Term
William McKinley[5]	Garret Hobart	Republican	1897–1901
	Theodore Roosevelt		
Theodore Roosevelt	Charles Fairbanks	Republican	1901–1909
William Taft	James Sherman	Republican	1909–1913
Woodrow Wilson	Thomas Marshall	Democratic	1913–1921
Warren Harding	Calvin Coolidge	Republican	1921–1923
Calvin Coolidge	Charles Dawes	Republican	1923–1929
Herbert Hoover	Charles Curtis	Republican	1929–1933
Franklin D.	John Nance Garner	Democratic	1933–1945
Roosevelt	Henry Wallace		
	Harry Truman		
Harry Truman	Alben Barkley	Democratic	1945–1953
Dwight Eisenhower	Richard Nixon	Republican	1953–1961
John Kennedy[6]	Lyndon Johnson	Democratic	1961–1963
Lyndon Johnson	Hubert Humphrey	Democratic	1963–1969
Richard Nixon	Spiro Agnew (1969–73)	Republican	1969–1974
	Gerald Ford		
Gerald Ford	Nelson Rockefeller	Republican	1974–1977
James Carter	Walter Mondale	Democratic	1977–1981
Ronald Reagan	George H. W. Bush	Republican	1981–1989
George H. W. Bush	Danforth Quayle	Republican	1989–1993
William Clinton	Albert Gore	Democratic	1993–2001
George W. Bush	Richard Cheney	Republican	2001–2009
Barack Obama	Joseph Biden	Democratic	2009–

Notes:
1. President Harrison died on 4 April 1841.
2. Prior to the ratification of the XXV Amendment to the Constitution in 1967, a vacancy in the vice-presidency would not be filled until the following presidential election (see Chapter 5).
3. President Taylor died on 9 July 1850.
4. President Garfield was shot on 2 July 1881 and died from his wounds on 19 September 1881.
5. President McKinley was assassinated – he was shot on 6 September 1901, subsequently dying on 14 September.
6. President Kennedy was assassinated on 22 November 1963.

anxiety to those who ascribed to the preservation of the Union the highest political priority. The implied threat to the Union was apparent in the Philadelphia Convention, which produced the three-fifths rule compromise in Article I (see Appendix I) to accommodate the South's adherence to slavery. Washington had been conscious of the dangers: his Farewell

Address, cited already for its warning of the 'baneful effects of faction', also contained strictures against the emergence of regional parties. In 1796, the question of the preservation of the Union was prominent in the mind of every senior politician, but the longer-term threat posed by the entrenched retention of the peculiar social order, culture, economics and politics of the South was clearer to Washington than to some of his contemporaries.

The third party system: civil war and sectionalism

Intensified abolitionist opinion in the North, and (most especially) pro-slavery opinion in the South, eventually burst through the bounds of the two established parties in a spectacular increase in support for the Liberty Party in the northern states, especially in New Hampshire. In New York, the Democratic Party (already dividing on other, unrelated, issues) split on the question of whether slavery should be permitted in any territory acquired from Mexico in the Mexican War. In Massachusetts, slavery split not the Democrats but the Whigs; throughout the North, abolitionists nominated Van Buren for the presidency in the 1848 elections under the Free Soil party label. As third-party candidates do at times of incipient or putative realignment, Van Buren ran well but lost: he came second in Massachusetts, New York and Vermont. As third parties usually do after such promising performances, the Free Soil Party then declined. However, the issue threatening to destabilize the party alignment did not recede.

On the contrary, slavery continued to pose problems which the existing party alignment, based on policy differences over banking and the tariff, could not solve. Neither, as support for abolition grew, could the issue be avoided. Northern Whigs faced a stark choice: if they were to survive as a national party, they were bound to seek compromise at the price of anti-slavery opinion finding expression in another party. If they were to survive as a Northern party, they would have to reject compromise with the grievous consequence of casting off from their Southern wing, and so losing the prospect of winning the presidency. Northern Whigs chose the first option, and sought allies of like mind, most of them in the North.

The problem was exacerbated because of manoeuvring over the greatest political problem of the mid-nineteenth century: the extension of slavery into territories as a result of westward expansion, and the conditions under which new states were to be admitted to the Union. California was admitted as a free state in 1850, but at the price of a more stringent law concerning fugitive slaves. The single-most important event that caused the Union to split along new party lines was the passage of the Kansas–Nebraska Act in 1854, which triggered the formation of a new anti-slavery party bringing together many Northern Democrats, Free Soilers and Whigs. The Republican Party, the last major party to be created in American history, was born. Its parents were the former party alignment and the issue of slavery which the old alignment could no longer contain. The new issue cut across existing affiliations, endangering the future of the Union by aligning party with region.

The Court precipitated change. For only the second time in the history of the United States, it declared an Act of Congress (the Missouri Compromise) unconstitutional in the fugitive slave case of *Dred Scott v. Sandford* in 1857 (see Chapter 7). Former Vice-President John Calhoun of South Carolina, brilliant exponent of the States' Rights doctrine and of the claim that slavery was a national condition but freedom sectional, found vindication in a confused and disastrous argument written by Chief Justice Taney, who set out definitively to resolve the legal status of slavery. The Democratic Party – meeting at its singularly ill-chosen convention home of Charleston, South Carolina – split, with many members of Southern delegations leaving the hall. The Convention reassembled at Baltimore, where Stephen A. Douglas was nominated for president by the Northern faction of the Party, and John Breckinridge of Kentucky for president by the secessionists. The Republicans nominated Lincoln on a platform of opposition to the extension of slavery in the territories, but of no interference with slavery in the Southern states.

The election of 1860 confirmed the Republican Party, dedicated to the Union's preservation, as the majority in both Congress and the White House, exposed the North–South rupture of the Democrats, and left Southern Whigs as a dying rump. The South preferred fissure to accommodation, so that its political order might be maintained, and by this preference disposed of the second-party system, with calamitous consequences: America was now thrust into a war more destructive for it than any other in which it has been involved. Throughout the Civil War, two-party politics continued in the North; in the South, there was no opposition to the Confederate government. The cause of good government in the South did not benefit from being denied a vigorous party politics during the War, or after it. Some Democrats in the Northern states supported the Union and fought for it: Lincoln's successor as president, Andrew Johnson, was himself a 'War Democrat'. Other Northern Democrats were, to varying degrees, unsympathetic to the President's war aims. Pressure within the North against the expected emancipation proclamation (issued by Lincoln on 1 January 1863) brought the Democrats substantial gains in the 1862 elections. Lincoln was almost as hard-pressed by radical Republicans as from 'Copperheads', the intense Northern opponents of the war and of emancipation.

The Civil War has been the only social revolution in American history. At stake were not only the hold on political power, but also the unity of the polity, its fundamental character and its social base. After the War, the United States progressed rapidly towards a full capitalist democracy, in which government had an increasingly important hand. In the regulation of banking and, later, of interstate commerce; in the making of land grants in the west under the 1862 Homestead Act; in trade and tariff policy; and in the ending of slavery itself, the Republican Party acted as the engine of social, economic and political change. In this period, the loyalties of many groups of voters to party were established and consolidated; many remained 130 years later.

The fourth party system: the realigning election of 1896

The period between 1874 and 1892 was one of party deadlock. Except for Grover Cleveland's two conservative Democratic administrations, Republican candidates won the presidency (though by small majorities) and the Democratic Party formed the majority in Congress. The forces behind Reconstruction of the South weakened, especially after the 1876 election. Black Americans in the South were excluded from party politics altogether, increasingly ignored by the Republican leadership, and eliminated from electoral politics by the Democratic Party order of enforced segregation in the South. The value of capitalist enterprise came to hold sway over the leaderships of both the Republican and the Democratic parties, although the former was more fully identified with the protection of the interests of industrial and financial capital, as its espousal of the tariff to protect the interests of Northern owners of businesses and of workers in them showed.

This system was broken by the general election of 1896, and left the Republicans, in very different political circumstances from those of thirty-five years earlier, once again in control of the White House and Congress. The fourth party system brought Republican domination of contests for the presidency, Democratic hegemony in the South, and Republican dominance of state-wide and US House elections in the North. The realignment followed a collapse in agricultural prices, and a deep economic depression in 1893, when the two elected branches of the federal government were under Democratic control. This twin catastrophe occasioned deep resentment among small farmers and debtors (most of them in the southern and western states), and the inequality of income and wealth between west and east, and between debtors and creditors, grew.

The Civil War alignment by which the Democratic Party's base in the south was strengthened proved resistant to significant alteration. McKinley defeated Bryan by a majority of 95 regionally concentrated electoral votes. The industrialized north and east turned firmly against the Democrats, aligning ever more staunchly with the Republican Party. The southern states were as solidly Democratic after the convulsions of the 1890s as they had been before, but the Republican Party's significant gains in northern cities sprang from the appeal of the tariff and sound money both to workers and bankers. Bryan's appeal remained rural. His performance in the 1896 election left him and his Democratic successors with little backing in the increasingly important and populous cities of the north and east.

The link between the Republican Party and the interests of finance and business, established so firmly in 1896, has not been broken since. Among workers of the north and east, too, the Republican Party drew on massive support until shortly before the Depression of the 1930s. Except for Woodrow Wilson's victory in 1912 (which Theodore Roosevelt's Progressive candidacy made possible by splitting the Republican vote) and his subsequent re-election, the period from 1896 to 1932 was one of overwhelming Republican dominance. Not until Al Smith's campaign in 1928 attracted the votes of the huge Catholic immigrant populations of the cities did a Democratic candidate for president win a majority of the vote in America's twelve largest cities. Nevertheless, immigrant voters' indifference to the Civil War and incorporation into the Democratic Party through city machines dispensing services (especially patronage) in return for political support caused the Republican plurality to fall in the presidential elections of 1920 and 1924.

However, even in northern states where Democratic presidential candidates always lost and Congressional ones usually did, the Republican Party between 1896 and 1932 was dominant rather than hegemonic. The South was, by contrast, unwavering in its support for Democrats between Reconstruction and the collapse of segregation in the 1960s. No matter how conservative a view southerners might take of the place of gold in guaranteeing price stability, how hostile they were to organized labour, how suspicious of Catholics, their support for the Democrats as the party of white supremacy in the South overrode those and all other considerations. For so long as the Republican Party represented the alien and hostile forces of Union and desegregation, it found scarcely any support in the South.

The fifth party system: the New Deal coalition

The fifth party system which, in modified form, still operates in the United States, formed as a consequence of the shattering blow delivered to American politics and society by the Great Depression. The onset of its collapse was marked by the beginning of the Wall Street Crash on Thursday 24 October 1929. Within a month of that day's record fall in prices, a vast quantity of wealth was destroyed: the value of equities traded on the New York Stock Exchange fell by 40 per cent. Gross national product (GNP) fell by half in the following three years. Coupled

64   *Government and Politics of the United States*

Exhibit 3.2 Critical Elections, Realignments and Issues

Each of the five party systems described here resulted from an election that created a party realignment – what V.O. Key (1955) calls a 'critical election' in which the relationship between the parties and the voters shifts to a new, but durable, alignment. Such critical elections are often the result of political, economic and social upheavals that realign voters with the parties. As noted, 1800, 1828, 1896 and 1932 were critical elections.

A number of elections are certainly of great significance to the development of the party system in the US. For example, 1968 saw the success of Richard Nixon's Southern Strategy which capitalized on the weakening ties of Southern Democrats to the party and enticed conservative voters in the South into the Republican Party. (Many southern Democrats had defected to Barry Goldwater ('Mr Conservative') in the 1964 election; President Lyndon B. Johnson had expected the Civil Rights Act of 1964 and Voting Rights Act of 1965 to hasten the defection of southern conservative Democrats from the party).

Although the South supported southern candidates from the Democrat Party in 1976, 1992 and 1996 (Carter was Governor of Georgia, Clinton was Governor of Arkansas), the South represents a clear change in the New Deal Coalition created by Franklin D. Roosevelt in 1932. Note, however, that no single election led to a realignment in the South. Rather, the South's move to the Grand Old Party (GOP) was a process of drift, and one in which southern states moved from Democratic to Republican and back again. Yet, the election of Reagan in 1980 and the Republican capture of the Senate in the same year do not reflect a new voter alignment. Neither do the 1994 mid-term elections and the *Republican Revolution* reflect any new alignment. The strategy of former President Clinton to campaign as a moderate (influenced by the Democratic Leadership Council), and the victories of Republicans in the House and Senate, and Republican control of both the White House and Congress between 2001 and 2007 represent not a new alignment of voters but, rather, an electorate that seems evenly balanced, as party control of the elected branches of the federal government alternated between 2007 and

➜

---

with the entry of a huge wave of immigrants into the electorate, many of whom were of the Catholic, Orthodox or Jewish faiths from southern and eastern Europe, and who moved predominantly to the large cities of the north-east, the years 1928–36 witnessed a convulsive upheaval of the American party system. Republican domination since 1896 was overturned, control of the Democratic Party by rural interests replaced by a new coalition of the southern and northern underprivileged and

➔

2012. Even the party polarization in Congress at the time of writing is evidence only of a growing ideological coherence both within and between the parties; that the electorate at large is moving apart is a contention less easily supported.

Although no new partisan alignment has emerged, the level of cohesion *within* the parties has led many commentators to suggest that the ideological bonds that united Democrats within the New Deal Coalition have weakened since the early 1980s. Furthermore, as Burnham noted in the 1970s (Burnham, 1971), there were and are a number of *cross-cutting* cleavages that cut straight across the groupings that composed the New Deal coalition. Even in the 1960s, many Democrat voters were left-wing on economic issues (many being members of unions, for example) but right-wing on social issues (such as the Vietnam War) and racial politics. In the 1970s, cross-cutting cleavages continued to generate *intra-party* as well as *inter-party* differences (abortion increased in salience as a divisive issue following the *Roe* decision of 1973). By the 1980s, the Republican Party appeared to be more ideologically coherent as the party moved to the right: the 1990s saw eight years of divided government, with a moderate Democrat in the White House and conservative Republican majorities in the House and Senate. The first decade of the twenty-first century lends itself to an analysis that suggests issues have become increasingly important and division over issues has fostered the ideological polarization between candidates present in contemporary national politics.

It is tempting to suggest that parties have been superseded by 'issue-politics' in which issues matter more than the qualities of a candidate or their party label. Yet, as Shafer and Claggett suggest (1995), caution must be exercised: issues can be grouped together. Some issues favour one party over another, and some issues resonate with particular ethnic, religious or geographic groups. Issues certainly matter, and the parties are more ideologically polarized. Yet, it is incorrect to assert that the centrality of issues means that parties matter less. Neither is it correct to assert that the centrality of core issues in recent elections (for example, abortion, immigration, terrorism and national security) has created the basis for a new realignment. The Fifth party system has metamorphosed, but no sixth party system has emerged.

'outsiders', and old alignments replaced within many states by a system which (temporarily) owed more to class loyalties across state boundaries.

The election of Franklin D. Roosevelt (FDR) in 1932 marked the birth of the New Deal Party System which represented the unlikely marriage of southern, conservative Democratic voters with the newly-mobilized and newly-enfranchised (in very limited form) black American voter and with Progressive liberal voters enticed by the rhetoric of the New Deal.

In the presidential election of 1932, votes split (as they did throughout Roosevelt's four terms) on economic interest and ideology, between those who stood to gain from an enhanced role in economic management and welfare for the federal authorities, and those who feared that they would lose by it. Within the Republican Party Herbert Hoover was a moderate, but the Democratic landslide of 1932 swept him from the White House and Franklin D. Roosevelt into it. Though altered and weakened, parts of the pattern of politics to which the Great Depression gave rise in the United States persist, as Chapter 3 on elections shows. Adherence to lightly-fettered private ownership defended against foreign competition by high tariff walls, characteristic of the Republican Party since Reconstruction, weakened sharply in the course of Roosevelt's four terms. Repeated defeat induced adjustment in all but the most reactionary, the most stubborn and the most electorally secure.

The New Deal did not nationalize voting patterns, but the two-party system nonetheless progressively supplanted sectionalism throughout most non-southern states. The Republican Party was, for the next forty years, merely a minority presidential party: Republican candidates won only twice (Dwight Eisenhower defeated the Democratic Governor of Illinois, Adlai Stevenson, in both 1952 and 1956) between the onset of the Great Depression in 1929 and the combination of Great Society and civil rights legislation in Lyndon Johnson's Administration from 1963 onwards. Johnson's presidency marks the end of the Democratic New Deal majority at presidential elections. It did not mark its end in congressional elections, where the Democratic Party continued in the majority as before. Since the passage of the Voting Rights Act in 1965 and the very rapid rise in the enfranchisement of southern blacks which it caused, only three Democratic candidates have won the presidency: Jimmy Carter (1977–81), William (Bill) Clinton (1993–2001) and Barack Obama (2009–). From 1896 to 1930, the Republican Party was in the majority; from 1932 to 1964, it was supplanted by the Democratic Party. Thereafter, Republican Party candidates dominated the single national race for the White House, while Democratic Party candidates enjoyed natural majorities in the House and the Senate until Republicans formed the majority among southern delegations to the House from 1994 onwards. This majority lasted until 2006, when the Democrats recaptured both chambers of Congress. The brief spell of unified Democratic government lasted from 2006 to 2010, when Republicans regained the House of Representatives. The trends in partisan control of the federal government, if ever clearly discernible, have become increasingly complex. To understand better what underlies these patterns, or their absence, parties can be examined in terms of their organization, their bases of support in the electorate and their command over the elected branches of the federal government.

Parties as organizations

American political parties as quasi-public institutions

American political parties are not (as parties in most other democratic countries are) private organizations but, rather, quasi-public institutions, subject to regulation in public law passed by state legislatures. State governments may, and do, regulate their organization, their rules and the conditions by which individual citizens may register as Democrats or Republicans. They may further require primary elections to be held to determine who the candidates for the two major parties shall be at state and congressional general elections, the dates on which primary elections for different offices take place, the rules governing their administration, and the extent to which parties may lend their support to favoured candidates in primaries. Political parties in America therefore lack what political parties in almost all other democratic countries take for granted: unfettered control over their own rules and structure. The federal government has regulated party only indirectly through campaign finance legislation; regulation of political parties themselves has been left entirely to state governments.

All states in the Union regulate political parties operating within their borders, to different extents, in different ways, and with different consequences for the organizational vigour of state parties, and for parties' influence over politics and policy. Power over the Democratic and Republican Parties in the fifty states is therefore shared between the parties and the state governments, but the balance of influence between state governments and parties varies by state.

The rise of machine politics

Ingrained suspicion of faction, originating in the earliest days of the Republic, provided the cultural foundation for state regulation, but its proximate cause was the rampant corruption in many eastern cities, where party machines developed between the end of the Civil War and the turn of the century, when the power of party over public affairs peaked.

In many port cities in the states of the mid-west and east – especially in Indiana, Missouri, New Jersey, New York, Ohio and Pennsylvania – politics were constructed by highly-organized machines founded on exchange and material interest, rather than policy. The idea of 'machine' suggests a unifying organization which was self-sufficient, inclusive and directed towards its sustenance and the delivery of votes. The relationship between party and voter was contractual: material assistance and helpful intervention of all kinds were afforded in return for energetic political support. Help of whatever kind needed could be supplied: patronage jobs, whether for the straitened or ambitious), financial or housing assistance to the newly-arrived immigrant family from Europe, a hamper for the widowed at Thanksgiving.

For the city machines, the object was to win elections, and then to control the distribution of the fruits of government. Even in cities where the machine did not dominate, the pattern of politics as mercantilism could be found. Machines reached a high level of development and traded on systematic corruption. In Manhattan, Tammany Hall (named after a mythical Native American) was the first classic example of an urban party machine. Its original function was the orthodox one of a bridge between the newly-arrived immigrant and citizenship. For that vital service, it was the monopoly supplier in Manhattan; and on that monopoly its political power was built:

> Whether or not the corner cop would let your youngster play under the water hydrant on a hot day depended on Tammany. It could do anything for a man from granting a bus franchise to a suspension of sentence for a serious crime; whether or not you could build a skyscraper – and how cheaply or expensively. (Gunther, 1947: 565)

Corporate and political power occasionally found expression in party organizations fuelled by corporate and personal finance: state politics in Michigan and Wisconsin were dominated in the 1880s, and to a lesser extent in the 1890s, by businessmen-politicians who later came under attack from Progressives seeking an end to corruption.

Tackling the power of machines

Having arrived at similar diagnoses for the abuse of political as for corporate power, Progressives prescribed similar remedies for them: regulation of economic monopolies was sought at both federal and state levels by the creation of commissions whose remit was to secure the public interest by controlling private interests. The exercise of corrupt political power was similarly controlled: by regulations designed to weaken the influence of party officials in enhancing the power of citizens through the initiative and referendum (by which voters themselves chose by ballot between policy options); by decreasing the autonomy of elected persons by providing for their recall (ejection from office following a popular vote); by prohibiting party labels altogether in elections for many local offices; and, in some cases, by replacing elected mayors with appointed (and supposedly disinterested and expert) city managers; and, most important by removing the power of recruitment from party notables and vesting it in primary electorates. Candidates whose nominations were won through an appeal beyond party bosses were less likely to submit to party discipline thereafter in government.

Primaries

Much the most important aspect of public regulation of parties has been the control by states of entry to the ballot for state and US congressional elections through primaries. Selection of candidates proceeds according to rules set both by the party and by state legislatures. The intended consequence of the introduction of primaries by states for state assembly and US congressional elections was that parties' capacity to determine who stood in their name at general elections was weakened. This power did not disappear completely in all states. Many local and state parties retained influence over the outcome of primary elections by ensuring that the candidate favoured by party elites won; some parties even prevented primaries taking place. In New York, for example, state laws did little to diminish party strength in most counties. Nevertheless, from the time that state governments first regulated them, parties have been unable to determine who participated in primary elections and who did not. Primaries threw open internal party recruitment decisions to a self-selecting electorate. In Europe, rules governing the selection of candidates confine the decision to party members or a subset of the total party membership; in the United States, selection of candidates is opened to those who 'register' themselves as Democrats or Republicans.

States' registration rules vary from severe to lax, but no state confines registration to 'members'. Indeed, there are no members to whom it might be confined, because American political parties are not mass-membership organizations; opportunities for participation are, therefore, greater. Denied control of who ran for office under the party label, parties in America were (southern courthouse party organizations, and some northern city machines excepted) weakened. Easy entry to the party through the primary election lessens the attraction of running on a third-party ticket, as explained below. Since parties have no membership, there is no possibility of dissenters or insurgents being expelled. Where organizational centres exist at all, they have few sanctions to hand. Whatever the nature and extent of primary voters' loyalty to the party, it is unenforceable.

Major city machines (which by the end of Truman's presidency were all Democratic) formed one of the two major organizational pillars (labour unions were the other) on which Franklin D. Roosevelt's Democratic Party was built in government just as it had been constructed against them when seeking the nomination in 1932. Democratic machines did not make for efficient (still less for good) government, but proved bastions of electoral support for Democratic presidential candidates, as reliable as the

'Solid South', where many rural state and local parties had their own tightly-run organizations centred on courthouses. From Franklin D. Roosevelt to Lyndon Johnson, every Democratic president was indebted to the Chicago machine, which was established in the mid-1930s, reached a peak of influence in the early 1960s and lingered until the late 1980s.

Party organization and the demise of machine politics

Machines have largely disappeared, but party organizations of various kinds persist. Parties remain decentralized, but the patterns of organization and the strengths of organizational units vary greatly from state to state, and even from county to county within a state. In organization as in rules, tradition and political culture, it is more accurate to regard the United States as having a hundred parties rather than two. Viewed nationally, the American party system is a loose confederation of parties drawn into a nominal two-party system.

Nowhere in the United States are party organizations any longer hierarchical command structures, as city machines once were, and as some European political parties remain. The organizational form is not that of a branch, but that of a caucus-cadre party, in the sense that Maurice Duverger (1954) used the categories in his classic work *Political Parties*; that is, an elite rather than mass membership party where groups of party notables came together for 'the preparation of elections, conducting campaigns and maintaining contact with the candidates'. The Democratic and Republican Parties are still of this kind, conforming to Duverger's characterization of them as 'decentralized and weakly-knit'. They remain primarily 'electoral machines' at precinct, ward, city, county, state and national levels. The two major American parties recruit activists, not members (although parties have often sponsored the establishment and operation of clubs associated with the parties); they reach peaks of activity in periods leading up to elections. American parties accordingly lack the financial support which most European parties enjoy through membership fees. Party organizations at national level do not dominate those in states, neither do the latter dominate those at county level. Since the Chicago machine's end in the early 1980s, city organizations do not usually control wards, nor wards precincts. Each level possesses substantial autonomy from the others, and party activists in each typically respect the independence of other levels.

State, local and national parties: the 'hundred-party system'

Using a geological metaphor, Samuel Eldersveld (1982) has characterized this form of non-authoritative relationship as a 'stratarchy'. Not all state and local parties correspond strictly with this form, but it captures the essence of most party organizations more accurately than do notions of hierarchy and command. State parties work in collaboration with the city and county party organizations below them, and with the national organizations above. Save in the (usually Democratic) machines of some eastern and mid-western cities and in (Republican) state party organizations in New York, Ohio and Pennsylvania, authority has rarely typified relations between levels of party organization. It certainly does not do so now that party influence over primary election outcomes is typically slight.

American parties at local, and generally at state, level rely on small numbers of staff (though the number of staff employed by the Republican and Democratic National Committees has increased considerably since the mid-1990s). As primary elections open the party nomination to almost anyone willing to run for it, so American parties are open to any who have ambitions to participate; in the great majority of local parties, however, few do. The federal nature of American politics was a powerful inhibition to the emergence of centralized parties with branches throughout the country, and developments after 1824 confirmed this trend: Jackson was the first outsider to be elected to the presidency, having failed to win it as an insider in 1824. The strategy of nomination by Convention that Jackson adopted for his successful campaign in 1828 gave the presidency (for the first time) a base of power independent of Congress.

There are many forms of local organization but almost all local parties are loose, flexible and informal. Factional disputes rarely concern ideological difference, but often have a racial or ethnic dimension; the ordered development of public policy is inhibited by the common condition of rampant factionalism. In the absence of mass involvement, local party organizations are usually run by a stable group of activists virtually autonomously from other local party organizations in the county or city. In the city machines of the eastern and northern past, local party precinct or ward organizations formed part of a much more hierarchical party structure suited to maintaining a full register of party sympathizers, meeting their many needs, and delivering blocks of votes on election day. But this hierarchical form of party based on powerful control of material incentives was never typical of American local or city party organization and, except in attenuated forms, has now disappeared.

If the city machine lay at one pole, so the other was marked by a virtual absence of organization and party activists; it is the latter that has continued. Such leadership as there is in such weak and fluid conditions depends on powers of persuasion, rather than authority deriving from party rules. The leadership's resources are few. The material incentives on which precinct captains in Chicago and Kansas City thrived during the heyday of the Democratic machines in those two cities are now virtually absent. The spread of civil service conditions and the increased density of union membership among state and local government workers have reduced local political patronage. The courts have further eroded the use of patronage for traditional local and state party organizations. As a result, it is now virtually impossible to draw into local and city parties the volunteer labour which engaged in the detailed canvassing essential to the reliable production of blocks of votes at elections. This loss of patronage over local and state governments has dramatically reduced the political power of local and state party organizations. The Supreme Court's reapportionment decisions, by increasing the number of single-member districts for state assembly and US House elections, have made states less amenable to party control. Finally, the key role of mediator between government and voters, which used to be monopolized at elections by parties, has been replaced almost everywhere by electoral organizations based on individual candidates and constructed by political consultants who communicate with voters by television and internet advertisements produced by media consultants, emails, Facebook, tweets and the like. Party labels remain necessary, but local and state party organizations are now often marginal to the tasks of campaigning and winning elections.

Some factors mitigate organizational weakness: most state party organizations now have permanent staff and a head office in which they work to raise money, conduct opinion polls, and supply party candidates running for office at all levels of government within the state with data and analyses of issues. Functions of this kind enhance the capacity of state party officials to defuse factional conflict within the party, and to infuse a spirit of common purpose, but the state party central committee rarely concerns itself with developing policy as a result. Since state party organizations are usually wholly separate from party organizations in the state legislature (as each party's national committee is separate from the two congressional parties) there would be little point in their attempting to do so.

It is commonly observed that American parties find their primary organizational expression at the local, rather than the state or national, level. By contrast, the national organizations have always been weak: Schattschneider (1942) wrote that the national organizations possess 'only the transparent filaments of the ghost of a party'. The national organization of the president's party has, since the 1960s, enjoyed little autonomy from the White House: President Johnson regarded the Chairman of the Democratic National Committee (DNC) as the chairman of his party; and President Nixon took much the same view of the Chairman of the Republican National Committee (RNC). Nixon's campaign for the 1972 presidential election was run wholly independently of the RNC; George McGovern's Democratic campaign in the same year was also largely independent of the DNC. It is therefore especially ironic that Nixon's personal campaign staff, the Committee to Re-elect the President (CREEP), should have revealed their ignorance of the marginal political importance of the DNC by attempting, in 1972, to find campaign intelligence in the Committee's headquarters (where there would have been none of value), as well as their incompetence, by bungling the burglary of the DNC's offices in the Watergate Building.

The continuing importance of national parties

National parties continue to perform important functions that help elect and sustain candidates in office. In particular, they perform three key functions: raising vast amounts of campaign finance; helping to integrate parties at local, state and national levels; and seeking to wrest control of the branches of the federal government from the other party.

In the 1980s, the financial and organizational renaissance of the Republican Party was built by its chairman, Bill Brock, on sophisticated direct mailing techniques to targeted potential supporters. President Reagan had the good political sense not to impose a chairman of his own on the National Committee when he won the Republican nomination in 1980, but to retain Brock, who continued his work until 1981 and was replaced by Frank Fahrenkopf (1981–88) who sought to capitalize on the role to be played by a national party organization within a party to become rapidly more ideologically homogeneous. The greatly enhanced organizational power and financial resources of the RNC contributed to the marked revival in Republican electoral fortunes in the Senate in the early and mid-1980s, and to the success of the Republican Party in altering economic and defence policy during Reagan's presidency.

The Democrats' national party organization also improved in quality and increased in influence, although not to the same extent as the Republicans. The national Democratic Party's new arrangements for delegate selection to the presidential nominating convention following the McGovern–Fraser Commission's reforms after 1968 helped to centralize the distribution of power within it. Karl Rove, President George W. Bush's Senior Adviser, had sold his direct mail company in 1999 but had used his considerable experience in the industry to help candidates identify and target supporters. Rove was key to George W. Bush's successful presidential campaigns in 2000 and in 2004. In 2004, Democratic presidential candidate Howard Dean built an organization around him that was skilfully organized and which made use of the new media – but particularly the internet. In his 2008 campaign, Barack Obama used the internet to raise significant campaign sums from often modest, but numerous, online contributions.

National party organizations are now much more important for fundraising. Not only has the RNC used modern technologies to identify potential supporters and to raise money from them, but its role in disbursing funds to congressional candidates has also grown. The national organizations of both major parties now play major roles in distributing funds to state and local parties in order to maximize the vote in presidential elections (where the candidates are notionally funded entirely from public sources, as Chapter 4 explains).

Changes in campaign finance are discussed in detail in Chapter 4, but it is important to note here that the importance of party organizations rests in part on their centrality to raising funds for candidates. As finance reforms in the 1970s reduced the importance of party organizations as funding vehicles for candidates so, too, did reforms to campaign finance regulations resurrect party organizations as crucial funding mechanisms. The growth of so-called 'soft money' (discussed at greater length in Chapter 4) provided parties with a crucial role in funding campaigns, and the 1996 Supreme Court decision *Colorado Republican Federal Campaign Committee v. FEC* allowed parties to make expenditures that were formally independent of candidates. An example is that of the funding of 'issue-advocacy' adverts that avoid naming any candidate but that clearly highlight a core issue and a specific stance in relation to it which favour one candidate over another (where candidates are clearly divisible in relation to a key issue). National party organizations were free to spend vast sums of money in support, albeit indirectly, of their candidates.

Neither did the 2002 Bipartisan Campaign Finance Reform Act (BCRA) stop soft money. (The BCRA is more commonly known as 'McCain–Feingold' after two of its three key sponsors; Christopher Shays (R-CT) was the sponsor of the legislation that became law.). It did, however, prevent unlimited party-building donations to the parties. Alongside national parties, state and local parties have been important in raising money in the last decade; so, too, have new funding vehicles, including the 527s and 501 (c) groups discussed in Chapter 4.

Parties in the electorate

The bipolar American party system and third parties

State laws regulating political parties discriminate in favour of the two major parties and against third-party and independent candidates which, since the legislators who write the laws are either Republicans or Democrats, is unsurprising. Prime among these laws is the device of making access to the election ballot by third parties contingent on a prior demonstration of support. Before the last decade of the nineteenth century, third parties could not be marginalized in this way, since ballots were then supplied by parties at the polling station. That procedure made voting virtually a public activity, because party workers noted carefully which voters asked for which ballot. Since 1890, so-called 'Australian' ballots have been provided by the state governments on which parties were listed, and between which voters made their choice in secret. Parties were accordingly given the legal status they had previously lacked; equally, it was a standing which states could, and did, deny to minor parties by drafting rules with which (as was intended) they were often unable to comply.

For the presidential election, the task of securing access to the ballot by third party and independent candidates is made more difficult by the variations in rules between the fifty states and the District of Columbia. Demonstrating support sufficient to meet the different demands made by the states is an onerous burden for a candidate's lawyers and campaign managers, especially since the petitions have to be signed and presented within specified periods. Some states require few signatures on a petition for access to the ballot (merely twenty-five in Tennessee) while others require a percentage of the registered electorate (California required more than 100,000 for John Anderson in his independent candidacy for the presidency in 1980). New York law requires that a petitioner obtain a certain number of signatures in every one of the state's counties.

For the presidency, for congressional races and for state contests, the patchwork of state laws inhibits third-party challenges and increases the incentive for candidates to seek access to the ballot by running for a major-party nomination in the primary. Most states hold primaries only for those parties that secured a substantial proportion of the popular vote in the preceding election. Federal courts have, since the mid-1990s, upheld the right of states to prevent the electoral process from slipping into disrepute, but have indicated their unwillingness to uphold the constitutionality of laws designed to protect the two major parties from competition by third parties.

Despite the height of barriers to third parties, elections for offices at all levels attract many more candidates than the nominees of the Democratic and Republican parties alone. Third-party (and fourth- and fifth-party) candidates frequently appear on ballot papers, especially those for the presidency and for governorships in the states. The Libertarian Party, the Communist Party and the Socialist Party invariably nominate candidates for the presidency. In the 1980 presidential election, there were, in addition to the candidates of the Democratic and Republican Parties – President Carter, and Governor Reagan, respectively – eleven minor party candidates. The best known of them, John B. Anderson, ran as an Independent (despite having been the Republican whip in the US House of Representatives) and took 6.1 per cent of the vote. In 1948, Strom Thurmond's segregationist candidacy brought him 2.4 per cent of the vote and thirty-nine electoral college votes. Some third-party candidates have performed more strongly: in the bitter election of 1968, Governor Wallace of Alabama won 13.53 per cent of the popular vote and forty-six electoral college votes, while Ross Perot took 19.0 per cent of the popular vote (but no electoral college votes) in his independent 1992 campaign. Ralph Nader won 2.74 per cent of the popular vote in the 2000 election (with some commentators suggesting his candidacy helped George W. Bush take Florida, and thus the presidency, rather than Al Gore). Most powerful of all was Theodore Roosevelt's candidacy for the Progressive Party in 1912, when he won 27.39 per cent of the popular vote and eighty-eight electoral college votes.

Third parties have displayed political strength in some states at certain times because of new issues or crises of unusual, if parochial, intensity. For example, the Progressive Party was a powerful force in Wisconsin state politics in the 1934 and 1936 elections, having sprung from factional divisions in the Republican Party between the Progressives (dominated by the La Follette family) and the Stalwarts (the party's conservative wing). In New York, Conservative, Liberal and Right to Life parties are still active in the state's politics: James Buckley was elected to the US Senate from New York on the Conservative ticket in 1970. However, New York's party politics are unusually complicated, not least because the state's election law permits nomination by more than one party, and multiple ballot placement. Some candidates secure the backing not only of one or two minor parties, but also of both the Democratic and Republican Parties.

Measured by the number of parties whose names appear on the ballot paper, the party system in the United States is multiple; measured by the distribution of the vote, it is two-party; measured by election result, the system is the purest two-party system in the world. In the 2008 Congressional elections, every member of the US House of Representatives was either Republican or Democrat. Only two members of the US Senate were from neither party – but both chose to caucus with the Democrats. Bernard Sanders from Vermont describes himself as a democratic socialist; Joseph Lieberman (Al Gore's running mate in 2000) stood as an independent candidate having lost the 2006 Democrat primary in Connecticut. His decision to continue to caucus with the Democrats led Senate Majority Leader Harry Reid in 2008 to allow him to maintain his chairmanship of the Homeland Security Committee).

Since 1856, every president has been the nominee of one of the two main parties and so, since 1945, has been every governor of every state. The party labels that apply at the national level have, since the second party system of Whigs and Democrats in the first half of the nineteenth century, also tended to apply at state and local levels.

Another distinguishing feature of American party politics is that no socialist or social democratic party has ever established itself in the United States. All other industrial democracies have (or have had) socialist or social democratic parties of significant size. Class conflict has often broken out in the United States' commercial and industrial development; it has taken intense forms in the coal industry throughout the twentieth century, and has been apparent at various times in vehicle manufacturing, the docks, road and rail transport. Yet, class has played little part in party politics. Only in 1932 and 1936 has the national political alignment been largely founded on class. Several factors account for this distinctive characteristic: universal male suffrage preceded industrialization in America rather than, as in most of Europe, following it, while ethnic and racial cleavages in American society, far from being cumulative with that of class, have cut across it. Socialist and social democratic parties have also been hindered by factors of a more general kind that have militated against the emergence of third parties. Together, discriminatory rules written by state legislatures against third parties, a single-member district voting system, quadrennial elections by a winner-take-all system in the electoral college for a single-person executive discriminate fiercely against all third-party candidates. At state level, too, the executive is single, not multiple. The consequences for states are similar to those for the federal government in the case of the presidency.

The requirement to unite in the campaign of a single national victor exercises a powerful centripetal force on state party organizations. It is in the election to the presidency that powerful regional interests and divisions are overcome. There are no rewards for coming second, and no prospect of displacing the winner before the end of the four-year cycle. Even the questionable luxury of parliamentary opposition as compensation for defeat is denied the loser. The party without the presidency lacks even a leader. The singularity of the presidency and of the competition for it therefore has powerful implications for the nature of the American party system. Like third parties in another polity with single-member districts, the United Kingdom, third and fourth parties with evenly spread minority support fare badly at the polls. Unlike the United Kingdom, however, regional parties enjoying spatially concentrated support and some electoral reward have never emerged in the United States.

President Washington's first concern was the nascent fissure between the South and North on the question of race and which, were it to become aligned with party, would raise the gravest doubts about the capacity of the nation to survive. The Civil War raised such doubts. Since 1865, however, even at times when it seemed to some politicians most propitious to form a regional or ethnic party, the two-party system has not been seriously threatened. With the exceptions of 1948 and 1968, neither the South between Reconstruction and the struggle for civil rights ninety years later, nor blacks at any time in their history, have formed sectional parties. His independent candidacy in 1968 apart, George Wallace remained in the Democratic Party; other southern Democrats changed their registration to Republican. No ambitious southern politician entertained hopes that a third party based on segregationist principles might compete with the Democrats or Republicans over the long-term: a two-party system with primary selection offered sufficient scope for ambition's realization.

The Tea Party Movement

The Tea Party Movement is a movement and not a party, and it is composed of many Tea Parties rather than a single, coherent, whole. It is not, therefore, a third party. Nevertheless, it does seek to influence which candidates are selected and elected. It exerts the pressure that a third party may exert. Fiscally (and often socially) conservative, this movement has supported those candidates who represent the more conservative elements within the Republican Party. Candidates whom Tea Party activists have deemed insufficiently conservative have been targeted for defeat in Republican congressional primaries. The Tea Party Movement has delivered some notable electoral gains in propelling favoured candidates both onto the ballot and, in many fewer cases, into office. Yet, Tea Party candidates found it easier to win primaries for Republican nominations than they did the subsequent congressional elections because the Tea Party's strategy was built around the proposition that an unyielding appeal to fully-committed conservative Republican voters in the primaries was transferable to the congressional elections. Experience showed, as might have been expected, that median voters in the congressional elections were not attracted by candidates who framed their appeal in such a way: Tea Party primary successes were common; Tea Party congressional election successes were less so.

Partisan identification, independents and polarization

Conventional wisdom dictates that political parties are weak, not only in relation to their European counterparts, but also in relation to their earlier selves. Political parties have, it is claimed, declined. As David S. Broder argued in *The Party's Over*, by the 1970s parties were mere shells of their former selves. Yet, while significant changes have occurred in the relationship between the parties and the electorate between the mid-1990s and the present, it is the vigour of parties that strikes most observers. Parties have grown in strength, as their ideological coherence has increased at the expense of a moderate centre. Indeed, as suggested at the end of the chapter, it is the very strength of the parties that has threatened the successful functioning of the governmental system created by the Founding Fathers.

Some commentators claim that the bitter partisanship of the last decade – particularly at the national level – is the manifestation of the so-called 'Culture Wars', discussed below in the section headed 'Party in the government', in which two ideologically opposed parties compete for control of the institutions of government. Culture Wars exaggerates divisions within the electorate, but bitter partisanship within the national government (both within Congress and between Congress and the White House) were prominent features of the 2010 and 2012 electoral cycles, as they have been of the terms of Presidents Bill Clinton, George W. Bush, and Barack Obama. The electorate, however, is much less divided than partisan elites declare themselves to be.

Some scholars claim to observe an increase not only in the number of voters who identify themselves as independents, but also in those who split their tickets by which voters will cast a vote for a candidate from one party in one electoral contest, but for another party in another election. In fact, in neither case is the evidence especially strong. While the phenomenon of 'ticket-splitting' that simultaneous elections for different offices in the same state make possible is important, its incidence does not appear to have increased since, for example, the 1970s.

When Broder published his now classic work in 1971, the parties exhibited evidence of decline measured by a rise in the number of voters identifying themselves as independents. As Table 3.1 shows, by 1976 16 per cent of voters were independents – compared to 11 per cent in 1968 (and just 5 per cent in 1952). However, as Keith *et al.* (1992) argue in *The Myth of the American Voter*, many voters identified as independents *lean* consistently towards one party or the other; that is to say, they behave as weak partisan identifiers. Many of the so-called independents identified in the 1970s were not the 'independent independents' in Table 3.1 but leaners. Voter detachment from parties was less significant than many scholars had reported. Partisan loyalty continues to be a significant determinant of voting patterns (Bartels, 2000; 2010). Examining Table 3.1, we might remind ourselves of Alan Ware's (2010: 55) point that those independents who leaned towards a party 'behaved much more like strong identifiers with parties than they did with weak party identifiers, in voting consistently for the party towards which they leaned' (see also Ware 2011).

If the purported rise in the number of independent voters does not support the party decline thesis, neither do the data on split-ticketing. The high points of 1972 and 1984 have not been repeated. By 2008, the level of split-ticketing had returned to 1950s levels (see the American National Election Studies series on Presidential/Congressional

Table 3.1 *Party Identification 1968–2008*

	'68	'70	'72	'74	'76	'78	'80	'82	'84	'86	'88	'90	'92	'94	'96	'98	'00	'02	'04	'08
Strong Democrat	20	20	15	18	15	15	18	20	17	18	18	20	18	15	18	19	19	17	17	19
Weak Democrat	26	24	25	21	25	24	23	24	20	22	18	19	17	18	19	18	15	17	16	15
Independent Democrat	10	10	11	13	12	14	11	11	11	10	12	12	14	13	14	14	15	16	17	17
Independent	11	13	15	18	16	16	15	13	13	14	12	12	13	11	10	12	13	7	10	11
Independent Republican	9	8	10	9	10	10	10	8	12	11	13	12	12	12	12	11	13	13	12	12
Weak Republican	15	15	13	14	14	13	14	14	15	15	14	15	14	15	15	16	12	16	12	13
Strong Republican	10	9	10	8	9	8	9	10	12	11	14	10	11	15	12	10	12	15	16	13

Source: American National Elections Studies (ANES), Available at www.electionstudies.org (accessed April 2012).

Split-Ticket Voting 1952–2008 at www.anes.org). Data on the number of independent voters and those splitting their tickets do not support the view that the electorate is polarized. Although it is commonplace to discuss Red states and Blue states, the picture is both more complicated and more interesting than that simple dichotomy allows. Indeed, polarization is as hard to identify among voters as it is easy within the political elite.

Parties in government

The ideological divide between the parties has grown considerably since the 1980s. In 1981 party unity votes (those votes that divide the parties with a majority of Republicans who voted pitted against a majority of Democrats who voted) rose to 76 per cent from 70 per cent in 1980. The figure continued to rise: to 78 per cent in 1991, 83 per cent in 1994, and 91 per cent in 1995 at the start of the 104th Congress following Newt Gingrich's leadership of the so-called *Republican Revolution* in which the GOP regained control of both chambers of Congress for the first time since 1953–54. The figure stayed in the high 80s for the rest of the decade. The first decade of this century saw party unity scores remain at these remarkably high levels. In 2008, House Democrats' party unity score was 92 per cent, while in 2009 and 2010, Senate Democrats' score was 91 per cent.

The distance between the parties can also be highlighted by considering how members of each party vote on a collection of issues that, taken together, can give an indication of how likely each party is to adopt a *liberal, moderate* or *conservative* position. For example, by examing how members of Congress vote when considering bills that will lead to greater intervention by government in the economy, one can place members in terms of the three categories outlined above. And, by considering numerous votes, it is possible to create a picture of where members lie on the *liberal–moderate–conservative* spectrum. As members of each party adopt more consistently liberal or conservative positions, we see from Figure 3.1 that the parties began to diverge in 1981 and that this divergence grows in both chambers between 1981 and 2007. By 2011, the parties are very far apart on the 'government's role in the economy' dimension.

The contested 2000 presidential elections did nothing to lessen the parties' polarization. The appearance of unity following the terrorist attacks of 11 September 12001 is not borne out by party unity scores for the first years of this century. Neither the years of Republican unified government between 2001 and 2007 with President George W. Bush bolstered by a Republican Congress, nor Democratic control of the

Figure 3.1   *Distance between the parties in terms of likelihood of adopting liberal, moderate or conservative policy positions*

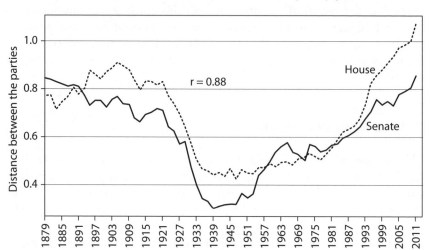

elected branches between 2009 and 2011, led to any lessening of the gap between the parties. President Obama had talked of the need to work across the party divide, but the 2010 mid-term elections were a clear indication that polarization had not diminished. The 2011 budget confrontation and the eleventh-hour agreement that prevented a government shutdown highlight the continued distance between the parties on the role of government in the economy. And, as the 2012 elections showed, social questions continue to divide the parties.

The contemporary Congress: the death of the Moderates

That the parties are more clearly divided than they were does not, as Ware notes, mean that they are ideologically further apart (Ware, 2010: 56). The right flank of the Republican Party shifted to the right. But the Democratic Party did not move leftward in response. As the GOP under Reagan, Gingrich, Bush and Boehner advocated a combination of social and fiscal conservatism, the Democrats under Clinton and Gore (influenced by the Democratic Leadership Council) argued for a distinctive and centrist position in order to recapture the presidency, and consequently moved to the centre. The progressive liberalism which reached its zenith in the Great Society of Lyndon Johnson was not the basis on which Clinton and the *New Democrats* later campaigned. That was a point to which President Clinton was anxious to draw the nation's attention by proclaiming in 1996 that 'the era of big government is over'.

Neither President Obama nor the Democrats in Congress moved significantly leftward. However, part of the story of polarization is that the conservatives within the Democratic Party and the liberals within the Republican Party have largely disappeared, with the result that that the scope for bipartisanship in policy-making remains difficult. The distance between the two parties has left a gulf where the moderates used to be.

The arrival of a responsible party system: be careful what you wish for

Polarization of congressional parties has rectified many of the purported weaknesses of the party system. In 1950, a seminal report produced by the Parties Committee of the American Political Science Association (APSA addressed a 'basic weakness in the American two-party system' (APSA, 1950: v); namely, that the parties were loose associations of state and local parties with little national cohesion and were: 'ill-equipped to organise ... members in the executive and legislative branches into a government held together and guided by the party program'. The solution put forward in this APSA report was to create an effective party system in which parties 'possess sufficient internal cohesion to carry out these programs ... [and where] the opposition party acts as the critic of the party in power, developing, defining and presenting policy alternatives which are necessary for a true choice in reaching public decisions. (pp. 1–2).

The aspirations of the APSA report have been substantially realized. Within the elected branches of the federal government, the parties exhibit a level of cohesion and a clear willingness to act as the 'critic' of the party in power. However, as Quirk (2011: 1) notes:

> An excess of party conflict – or even of cohesion within each party, for that matter – undermines the logic of the American constitutional system. Indeed, an observer of contemporary American politics, reflecting on the Framers' plan, and their hopes to avoid divisive partisanship, might wonder about their vaunted reputation for wisdom and foresight.

The oft-claimed weakness of the American two-party system, not least the lack of partisan ideological coherence, has been greatly attenuated by the polarization of the parties in Congress. Yet, polarization may have created a problem worse than the one it solved: institutional stasis resulting from the creation of an 'effective' two-party system. Some scholars, notably Thomas Mann and Norman Ornstein (2012), lay the blame for partisan deadlock within the federal government squarely on the shoulders of the Republican Party: arguing that the move to the right – what they call the 'new politics of extremism' – has made government practically unworkable.

The resurgence of parties

The constitutional rules establishing and maintaining the separation of powers have not changed fundamentally since 1789. Those concerning federalism have been modified by war, constitutional amendment and Court decisions. Nonetheless, the states retain importance as the basic organizational units around which party is constructed in the United States, and between which quadrennial association takes place through the processes for the nomination and election of the president. The two basic constitutional rules of a separation of powers and presidential system at the national level, with a federal structure, historically have tended towards weakness while ensuring distinctiveness. The presidential system splits parties at the national level by dividing executive from legislative authority, by establishing two elective branches of federal government and two distinct fields of party competition. One is led by the Chief Executive and the other by the majority party (or parties) in the bicameral Congress. And yet, despite the institutional obstacles to party strength, we see from the mid-1990s onwards the resurgence of parties at state, local and national levels characterized by greatly increased voting along party lines, and the polarization that is the result of the disappearance of the moderate centre.

Separating the structures of government does, of course, divide the party system. The full constitutional independence from the Executive enjoyed by Members of Congress invites dissension between them and the president, a phenomenon writ large in the second decade of this century. The prospect of government, so powerful an inducement to political loyalty in many European parliamentary systems, is absent from Congress because the Constitution forbids it. The implication is that, while Members of Congress and the president may share party membership, the separation of powers renders unity of purpose between them weaker than in parliamentary systems. Party is the only bridge across the gulf between president and Congress, but it is alarmingly rickety. The bridge is made more rickety still when president and Congress do not share party identity. It is that condition which is commonly and accurately referred to as 'divided government'.

The creation of two-party systems in the southern states caused by the ending of segregation has resulted in southern Democratic Parties losing almost all politicians having the most conservative views on civil rights: whereas, as recently as 1970, the Democratic Party nationally contained the most conservative and the most liberal voices on civil rights policy, it no longer does so. In most cases, US Senators and House members from southern states are now either conservative Republicans, or Democrats who are fully part of the national Democratic Party alignment. The Republican Party's most moderate voices in Congress are to be found in the Senate, where mobilization by candidates independent of party is easiest. The liberal, progressive wing of the party that was politically significant before the mid-1970s has now virtually disappeared. The Tea Party Movement's active campaigning in favour of those candidates who eschew the liberal, progressive values of the moderate Republicans in the Rockefeller/Eisenhower mould, and against those who, like Richard Lugar (R- IN), were deemed insufficiently conservative, has succeeded in making a largely conservative party organization even more plainly conservative. (Lugar was himself defeated by a Tea Party favourite in the 2012 Republican primaries who was then, in turn, defeated by a Democratic candidate in the Senate election.)

The Democratic Party remains a broader coalition than the Republican Party on issues of defence, fiscal policy, welfare, immigration, education, issues of environmentalism, gay rights, and women's rights – a significant field of battle in the 2012 congressional and presidential elections. Almost all liberal politicians, and most liberal voters, are now Democrats: Presidents Reagan and Bush had little difficulty in marginalizing their Democratic opponents between 1980 and 1988 by stigmatizing them as liberals. The open antipathy of some within the Tea Party Movement towards President Obama highlights the passion generated by opposition to a liberalism categorized by critics as European-style socialism.

The party system from 1932 to the early 1960s, with the Republican Party having large moderate and liberal factions, and the Democratic Party a large conservative wing, has therefore been replaced by one in which ideology no longer cross-cuts party allegiance at wide angles. This development has powerfully affected public policy. Partisan rancour over the passage of the Obama healthcare bill in 2010 and the budget in 2011 echo the partisan bitterness manifest in the 1995/6 government shutdown. Prospects for cross-party collegiality in Congress appear poor.

For Presidents Roosevelt, Truman, Kennedy and Johnson, when neither party was tidily coincident with ideological division, it was necessary to craft legislative majorities from shifting bases of partisan and ideological sources of support. Even President George W. Bush, who presided over six years of unified government until the loss of both the House and the Senate to the Democrats in 2006, was unable to *command* Congress. Despite some notable legislative successes, President Bush's adherence to the theory of the 'unitary executive' (Pfiffner, 2008) highlights the limitations placed on presidential power both by federalism and the separation of powers – and, like Johnson and Nixon, the difficulty faced by a president seeking to govern within seeking the consent of the legislature (see Chapter 4). President Obama's promise to work across the party divide was damaged by the 2010 loss of the House in the mid-term elections.

Since the mid-1990s, parties acted as the bridge between both ends of Pennsylvania Avenue (on which the executive and the legislature are situated), but the bridge has become less secure in the last decade as the parties have grown in strength, ideological coherence and internal discipline. The potential for a bridge with real strength exists, but that quality might well come at the expense of any bipartisan cooperation. Furthermore, where each end of the avenue is controlled by a different party, then the bridge is weakened further. In other words, divided government, where president and Congress are drawn from different parties, combined with strong and disciplined parties, works against any prospect of bipartisan cooperation within Washington. Strong parties and divided government are not conducive to effective policy-making.

Conclusion

Party in America has always been distinctive, and continues to be so. Increased ideological coherence, which has grown dramatically since the early 1990s, has modified the character of American parties but not fundamentally altered their nature. Parties have grown in strength. While machines have vanished, they were never typical of party organization in most of the country where they remain loosely organized. Parties have come to be dominated at all levels by candidates whose campaigns for office are often independent of the party whose label they seek, though often not independent of interest groups from whom many received heavy financial support via political action committees (PACs) and 527s (see Chapter 4). In 2008, Barack Obama was the first candidate of a major party to rely solely on private donations to fund his campaign. He took no federal campaign funding.

Despite periodic claims of party decline and the weakening identification of voters with party, the American two-party system remains substantially intact (Ware, 2010: 64). Buttressed by single-member plurality election rules, the single national electoral prize of the United States's presidency, and the fifty single state prizes of the governorships, the two-party system has, since the early 1970s, extended into the formerly solidly Democratic southern states. It has thereby virtually ended the abnormality of party politics in the South by introducing a party system not dissimilar to that elsewhere in the country. The old one-party system in the South had immense consequences for American politics and government; the transition from a single- to a two-party system has had comparable significance for election processes and results. Neither of the two parties has become a mass membership organization. Both parties continue to find their major organizational expression at state, rather than national, level. National parties have, nevertheless, become important support mechanisms for candidates especially in relation to fundraising; and both remain heavily regulated by state legislatures, which share responsibility with the national Party Conventions and with state and local parties for determining party rules.

The purported increase in the proportion of voters who identify themselves as independents has been exaggerated, as Figure 3.1 shows. Many independents are not significantly independent of party and the number of 'independent independents' has decreased in recent elections. Despite the increased partisanship since the mid-1990s, there has been neither the growth of third parties, nor the significant growth of independent candidacies. The label of one of the parties remains a prerequisite for election to public office (save, of course, for those offices that state legislatures classify as non-partisan). Party remains the major means by which governments are organized, and by which electoral outcomes at all levels of American government are structured. Difficult as government is in America, it would be formidably demanding without party.

Chapter 4

Elections and the Politics of Participation

There are, in the United States, more than 525,000 elective offices. Electoral participation rates are, nevertheless, low. This chapter examines who votes in elections and who does not, and why. It then considers how American elections function, focusing on the oil that wheels the electoral process: money. Campaign finances are central to how Americans run for office and how likely they are to win. Yet, it is essential to focus not only on the role of money, but also on persistent attempts by both federal and state governments to regulate the flows of campaign finances to candidates for public office.

The epic struggles over campaign finance regulation have been the midwife for many new creations: political action committees (PACs); Super-PACs; Leadership-PACs; 527s groups, all of which are examined below. We then consider the processes by which elections happen, and ask which Americans vote for which candidates and why. Related to, but separate from, the question of *who votes for whom* is the question of *which party wins which election and why*. Predicting which party will win which election is difficult. Yet, certain electoral patterns can, in part, be explained by *sociological* factors, an example of which is why Hispanics are more likely to vote for the Democratic Party, or older white men for the Republican Party. We also consider *institutional* factors such as the advantages that accrue to incumbent politicians, and attempts by each party at state level to ensure that the number of safe seats (where incumbents are likely to win) is maximized.

Who votes and who does not

In the most distinguished book ever written on the American electorate, *The American Voter* (1960), Angus Campbell, Philip Converse, Warren Miller and Donald Stokes argued that most Americans in the 1950s knew little about politics, had little interest in the subject, failed to organize their thinking about politics in structured or sophisticated modes, and did not categorize their attitudes to politics in coherent ideological terms Other scholars later argued that much changed in the 1960s as a result of the upsurge of political protest against the involvement of the United States in Vietnam, civil rights marches and urban violence. One theme is that the electorate was said to have become better informed, casting more intelligent votes, and came to think about politics in more sophisticated ways. More recent research has demonstrated convincingly that Campbell *et al.*'s thirty-year-old characterization of the American voter remains broadly accurate (Eric Smith, *The Unchanging American Voter*: 1989; Lewis-Beck *et al.*, *The American Voter Revisited*, 2011; Miller and Shanks: *The New American Voter*, 1996).

Low turnout

Although the elective principle cuts deeper into public life in the United States than in any other democracy, the rate of participation in elections is lower than in every democracy except Switzerland and Poland. The gap has widened even as the legal and institutional barriers to participation have been lowered. This phenomenon has excited much scholarly and journalistic attention, not least because of the implications that low turnout may have for political legitimacy. Part of the explanation for this extraordinary apathy had been thought to lie in cumbersome registration procedures. Registration regulations in some states (such as North Dakota, which required no registration, and Maine, Minnesota and Wisconsin, which permitted voters to register on the day of the election) made entry to the voting roll straightforward. Procedures in many states were much less accommodating, requiring citizens to take positive steps to ensure that their names appear on the electoral roll. An outcome is that, while approximately 80 per cent of those registered to vote turn out on election-day, high non-registration rates in many states keeps participation low. (See Table 4.1.)

Nationally, the highest turnout of voters in a presidential election since Franklin D. Roosevelt's victory in 1932 was just 62.8 per cent, when John Kennedy defeated Richard Nixon in 1960. Although turnout increased dramatically in the southern states following the passage of the Voting Rights Act in 1965, it declined after 1960 in the country as a whole, falling to 50.1 per cent in 1988, and to less than 50 per cent in

Table 4.1 *Turnout in Presidential Elections*

Year	1960	1964	1968	1972	1976	1980	1984
Turnout (%)	62.77	61.92	60.84	55.21	53.55	52.56	53.11

Year	1988	1992	1996	2000	2004	2008	2012
Turnout (%)	50.15	55.23	49.10	54.30	60.70	61.60	58.20

Source: US Bureau of Census, *Current Population Survey.*

1996. Turnout in congressional off-year elections is even lower than in presidential elections. From its highest points of 45.4 per cent, in both 1962 and 1964, it declined to 33.4 per cent in 1986. Many more fail to vote than support either of the two major candidates in presidential elections.

Difficulties of voter registration are greater because of Americans' geographic mobility: one-third of all US adults change their address every two years. Although the federal courts no longer permit states to require more than fifty days' residence before citizens may register to vote, frequency of moving coupled with the disincentive provided by registration requirements reduces registration rates. The blaze of publicity given to the poll leaves few citizens ignorant of the date of the election, but the final date for registration is often little- known.

Two further provisions in many state laws reduce voting participation: first, many states purge voters from the electoral roll if they do not vote in two consecutive elections; second, and for no good reason, most states deny the vote not only to convicts serving sentences, but also to former convicts. Since the United States jails a large proportion of its population, the disenfranchisement effect is marked. Four states – Florida, Iowa, Kentucky and Virginia –withhold the vote from anyone convicted of a criminal offence. In Florida, offenders who have completed their sentences must wait at least five years before they can apply to re-register for the vote. Across the US, more than 5 million Americans are denied the right to vote on grounds that they were convicted of a felony; of those 5 million, 4 million have completed their sentences. Nearly half of the 5 million are black or Hispanic. Thirty-four states have introduced a requirement that voters carry photo ID cards on the day of the election itself. Such measures prompted the National Association for the Advancement of Colored Persons (NAACP) in December 2011 to present evidence of discrimination to the United Nations High Commissioner for Human Rights. And, in the 2009 case *Northwest*

Austin Municipal Utility District v Holder, the Supreme Court upheld a key provision (Section 5) of the Voting Rights Act of 1965 which required those states with a history of 'Jim Crow' laws to seek federal clearance prior to changing any aspect of their elections. In June 2013, the Court agreed to re-examine the constitutionality of Section 5 in the case of *Shelby County, Alabama v Holder*.

Increasing the turnout

There have been many attempts to remedy the problem of low registration, some taking the form of persuasion, others of legislation. Whenever they deem it to be to their advantage, politicians running for office urge voters to register. Jesse Jackson did so in 1984 and 1988, concentrating his efforts among black voters (though this increased the incentive for opponents to persuade other groups, especially poor, white, rural voters to register). The most coherent of reform measures in Congress in the last twenty years, the National Voter Registration Act of 1993 (the so-called 'motor-voter' bill), requires state governments to ensure that when citizens apply for a driver's licence they are enabled to register to vote. All attempts in Congress to make registration easier have met with the opposition of those who fear that their political interests would be threatened by the registration of minority groups, the ill-educated and the poor (smaller proportions of whom are at present registered), and those who claim either that easier registration would encourage voter fraud, or that the federal government ought not to involve itself in matters that are properly the province of the states. Between its passage and early 1996, six states challenged in federal court the constitutionality of the motor-voter law (a federal mandate for which states have had to pay) but without success.

   Following the debacle during the 2000 presidential election in the Miami-Dade district of Florida when a manual recount, followed by a Supreme Court decision, resulted in the victory of Governor George W. Bush (R-TX) over Democratic candidate Vice-President Albert Gore, a great deal of critical publicity was focused on the allegations that the state of Florida had used a private company to perform the first step in 'purging' voters from the electoral roll which led, according to some commentators, to the removal of many potential Democrat voters being unable to vote in the Miami-Dade district. The popular vote in the 2000 presidential election (Bush 50,456,002 to Gore 50,999,897) saw Gore gain more votes; but the electoral college vote (Bush 271 Gore 266) saw the crucial and hotly-contested 25 electoral college votes from Florida go to George W. Bush.

   Voter registration, no doubt as a result of the Florida re-count, was thereafter frequently discussed in Congress. In 2002, the Congress and

President passed the *Help America Vote Act* (HAVA), which replaced punch cards and lever-based voting machines, introduced minimum standards for the administration of elections in every state of the Union, and created a new agency to assist in the administration of elections: the *Election Assistance Commission*. In Miami-Dade, voter registration increased by 65 per cent between 2000 and 2004.

The Republican vote is more easily mobilized than the Democratic: differential rates of turnout therefore have partisan consequences. Some of the statistics are, nonetheless, misleading. In particular, it appears at first sight that the election participation rate of blacks is lower than that of whites, and that of Hispanics even lower than that of blacks. In fact, the racial difference is entirely explained by the higher concentrations of blacks and Hispanics among the working class, the occasionally employed and the unemployed.

How Americans run for election

There have been few amendments to the United States Constitution. Since the Bill of Rights of 1791, only seventeen Amendments have been ratified, of which the Twenty-first (which ended prohibition) cancelled the Eighteenth (which imposed it). An indication of the importance of

Table 4.2 *Amendments to the Constitution Concerned with Electoral Rules*

Amendment	Content
Twelfth	Requires that electors vote separately for president and vice-president (in an attempt to avoid a repeat of the constitutional crisis which developed in the presidential election of 1800)
Fifteenth	Forbids the denial of the right to vote on grounds of race
Seventeenth	Requires that senators be popularly elected, having previously been selected by state legislatures
Nineteenth	Forbids denial of the right to vote on grounds of gender
Twenty-Second	Limits all presidents after Truman to a maximum of two four-year terms of office
Twenty-Fourth	Prohibits the denial of the right to vote by reason of the failure to pay any poll tax or other tax
Twenty-Sixth	Reduces the voting age to eighteen

elections to American politics is that, of the remaining fourteen, seven are concerned with election rules, as Table 4.2 shows (see also Appendix 2).

Central as these Amendments suggest the rules and conduct of elections are to American constitutional law, elections in many states confer limited or contingent power. Elections' legitimating power in American politics is weakened (and the ingrained distrust of politicians exemplified) by the widespread use of the referendum, the initiative and the recall – although these devices are not employed at the federal level.

Election campaigns and finance

Those with ambitions for office must first raise money. Only then can they market themselves. Few candidates do either directly; most hire consultants to do both. Winning elections is costly, and becoming more so, whether the contest be for the presidency, the House of Representatives or the Senate, a state governorship, a state assembly, or the mayoralty of a city. Congressional elections have become particularly expensive. Poorly-financed candidates usually lose (especially if they are challengers). The services of campaign and media consultants, access to prime-time television advertising, opinion polls, advertising hoardings, the creation and staffing of websites, mass mailing, texting and emailing, demand considerable resources, especially for Senate races in large states, where commercials have to be purchased in several media markets. Candidates for the US House running in densely-populated cities such as Chicago, Los Angeles or New York have a problem which, though different in kind, is also expensive: the television time they buy tends to be inefficiently spent because the media market is larger than the Congressional district they are contesting.

Driven by the need to raise large sums of money to deter challengers, or to defend oneself against them, and to raise yet larger ones to make credible challenges against incumbents or build a race for an open seat, the means by which candidates raise money has come under close scrutiny. This has been so both in the states (among which regulation of campaign financing has taken widely differing forms) and in campaigns for federal office, both for the White House and for Capitol Hill.

The mixing of politics with money, and the implied potential the resulting cocktail has for corruption at worst, and the improper exercise of influence at least, is a subject as old as American politics. It gained new currency in the 1996 presidential and congressional elections, in part because of the continuing rapid growth in expenditure and because of the manner in which much of it was raised. President Clinton's victorious re-election was marred by Vice-President Gore's admission that his office had solicited campaign contributions (itself a violation of the federal law, which prohibits solicitation or receipt of campaign funds in federal buildings), by the apparent receipt of funds from foreign sources (a violation of federal law), by the holding of 'coffee mornings' at which Clinton and Gore raised hundreds of thousands of dollars, and by the President's inviting prominent Democratic donors to sleep in the Lincoln Bedroom of the White House. Public concern over fundraising in the 1996 campaign moved the issue of campaign finance closer to centre-stage in the 2000 election. In 2002, Congress passed significant campaign finance regulation.

Financing of federal elections for both the presidency and Congress is regulated, but to differing extents, in differing ways, and with different consequences. Between 1976 and 2008, Barack Obama is alone among candidates for the presidential nomination of a major party to have elected not to receive public financial support in return for adhering to the complicated legal disclosure requirements. Obama set the tone: in 2012, neither President nor challenger accepted public funding.

With the exception of Barack Obama and Mitt Romney, since 1976 (when the public funding of presidential elections was introduced) the two parties' nominees have run their subsequent general election campaigns from public funds, although so-called 'soft' money has increased greatly in amount and importance since 1976. The 2012 campaign may signal the beginning of the end of federal funding in presidential elections. Soft money's impact has undermined the spirit, though not the letter, of the Federal Election Campaign Act (FECA) finance laws of the 1970s and the Bipartisan Campaign Finance Reform Act (McCain–Feingold) of 2002, a law subsequently weakened by the Supreme Court in its 2010 *Citizens United* ruling (see Exhibit 4.1). Members of Congress and senators have not seen fit to apply to their own campaigns even the limitations they set for presidential candidates, and the funding of congressional campaigns is consequently relatively unrestricted: congressional candidates may raise as much as they can, and spend as much as they raise.

Regulating campaign finance

The general statutory framework within which political relations between the presidency and the Congress has developed was deeply affected by the traumatic (and linked) national experiences of the Vietnam War and the abuse of executive power by President Nixon. These changes were important in several respects, including the financing of presidential election campaigns. The Watergate scandal sprang, in part, from the corrupt mixing of money and politics and, in particular, from the illegal activities of Richard Nixon's re-election campaign organization, the Committee to Re-elect the President (CREEP), and the subsequent cover-up of those activities by the President and his most senior staff in the White House.

Among Nixon's numerous violations of the constitutional rights of United States citizens was his use of illegally-acquired secret campaign funds to finance illegal domestic activity by the CIA. The establishment and operation of an investigative unit in the basement of the White House (the so-called 'plumbers' unit on account of its role in plugging leaks from within government) was, in itself, an illegal act but, in addition, was partly financed by an illegal and secret contribution of $2 million which the Milk Producers' Association gave to CREEP in return for President Nixon's backing for increases in milk price supports.

The House Judiciary Committee made reference to the campaign-financing practices of the President in the second Article of Impeachment against the President, which it prepared and approved in 1974.

Exhibit 4.1 Hard Money, Soft Money and Independent Expenditures

Money spent in elections falls into four categories: Personal spending, hard money, soft money and independent expenditures.

Personal spending, since the landmark Supreme Court *Buckley v Valeo* (1976), is limitless. A candidate may spend as much of their own money running for office as they wish. Meg Whitman, former CEO of eBay, spent over $160 million of her own fortune in her (unsuccessful) 2010 bid to become Governor of California.

Hard money is those funds made directly available to candidates seeking office and that are clearly regulated by campaign finance laws with the current funding limits.

Soft money is those donations made by individuals and groups and which go not to individual candidates but, rather, to the parties. In theory, in order to adhere to the letter of the law, such funds were to be used only for so-called 'party-building' activities such as voter registration; get-out-the-vote drives and so on. However, these activities are used by the parties to benefit individual candidates. It was this loophole through which soft money flowed to individual candidates that led to the passage of the Bipartisan Campaign Reform Act (BCRA) in 2002, greatly curtailed by the Citizens United Supreme Court ruling of 2010.

Independent expenditures do not focus directly on either the candidates or the parties. So-called 'issue-ads' are such an example, where an advert may focus on an issue such as gun-control without actually naming a candidate. However, when such adverts run during election time in particular states or districts, the intended focus of the advertising is clear.

Watergate became synonymous with political corruption; Senator Sam Ervin's investigative select committee discovered 'rivers of cash' running through Mr Nixon's campaign in 1972. The total amounted to more than $60 million, including sums ranging from $125,000 to $4.47 million from business corporations, many of which maintained secret funds. Over $1.7 million was raised for the campaign from people who were subsequently given ambassadorships. In the forty-eight hours before the 1971 Federal Election Campaign Act became law, the President's re-election committees spent almost $5 million, much of it in respect of activities directed against Democratic candidates for the presidency.

Watergate's exposure prompted thorough reform of presidential campaign financing, recovering it from the murky reaches of secret contributions in return for presidential favours to the light of public scrutiny through public financing and public disclosure. Amendments to the 1971 Federal Election Campaign Act passed in 1974, 1976 and 1979 led to tighter regulation of campaign contributions; the Bipartisan Campaign Finance Reform Act (BCRA) of 2002 placed further limitations on the legitimate methods by which funds could be channelled to campaigns. However, the rise of 527s groups, PACs and Super-PACs, as well as recent Supreme Court decisions, demonstrate the ongoing battle between the regulations put in place and attempts at their circumvention.

Parties, issue advocacy, and 'soft' money

Parties' direct contributions to candidates' campaigns for election to the US House and Senate are limited by law: $5,000 per candidate in each election cycle for the House and $46,200 per candidate in each cycle for the Senate. In addition to such direct support, each party's national and state committee has a specified amount of so-called 'hard' money which it may spend on behalf of each US House and Senate candidate. A state party committee may either itself spend the same amount as the national committee, or transfer it to the national committee. Candidates' campaigns do not receive such 'coordinated expenditures' direct: party committees may decide in conjunction with the candidates how the money is to be spent, but the law stipulates that responsibility for such contributions lies with the parties. It is the parties that must disclose to the FEC how they are made.

In 1995 and 1996, before the introduction of the limits imposed by the BCRA, the Democratic and Republican national committees spent large sums promoting, respectively, the re-election of President Clinton and the election of Mr Dole. In the 1996 congressional elections, the two major parties spent $11.5 million in independent expenditure. In the 2000 presidential election, the Democratic Party spent $28 million and the

Republicans $37 million. In the 2010 electoral cycle, the total spent by the Democratic Congressional Campaign Committee was $159,490,154 (the Party spend a total of $736,955,120 on all elections in the 2010 electoral cycle). The Republican National Congressional Campaign Committee spent $129,109,330 in 2010 (Center for Responsive Politics at www.opensecrets.org) – their total spend on all elections in 2010 was $638,367,457.

The parties carefully avoided breaching the law: while promoting the two candidates' electoral interests, advertisements did not explicitly urge viewers to 'elect', 'support', 'vote for', or 'defeat' one or the other candidate. Instead, advertisements offered support for, or opposition to, particular views of the two candidates (see the discussion of PACs and '527s' below). In its key 1996 decision, *Colorado Republican Party v Federal Election Commission* (424 U.S. 261), the Supreme Court found such issue advocacy advertising constitutional. The Court judged that political parties have the right to spend unlimited amounts in congressional elections provided that such funds are spent 'independently', thereby raising the question of where the boundaries of that elastic notion might lie. The Court held that the First Amendment prevented the government from imposing any limits on what parties may spend of their own funds when such expenditures are not, in fact, discussed with a candidate or with their agents. The judgement was nearly more radical: four justices made clear in minority opinions that they regarded any expenditure limits on parties as unconstitutional.

Most of the money raised to pay for such issue advocacy advertisements was 'soft', much of it transferred to state parties that were subject to looser Federal Electoral Commission (FEC) rules than national committees. President Johnson's characterization of campaign finance laws in 1967 as 'more loophole than law [which] invite evasion and circumvention' applied with similar force to the corrupting cancer of 'soft' money in modern elections.

The weakness of federal election law on *contributions* was that, while direct contributions to candidates in federal elections from businesses, unions and other interest groups are prohibited, direct donations to political parties are unrestricted. The weakness of current federal election law on *expenditure* is that while certain types of spending might reasonably be regarded in law as 'independent', they are intended to have particular electoral effects in particular campaigns, and often do so. Both parties are skilled at putting 'soft' money to highly creative use while remaining technically independent of individual candidates' campaigns.

From the 1996 campaign onwards, parties became increasingly adept at finding opportunities to fund candidates (McSweeney, 2002: 36). Senator John McCain, who had sought the Republican nomination for the presidency, gained considerable support from advocates of campaign finance reform (as did Democratic Senator Bill Bradley, who made campaign finance reform one of his core issues in the 2000 Democratic presidential primaries), arguing for restrictions to be placed on the role that 'soft money' played in elections.

The Bipartisan Campaign Finance Reform Act (BCRA) 2002

McCain had failed to secure campaign finance reform in 1996, when he and two congressional colleagues saw their legislation fall in the Senate by just six votes. However, in 2002 Senators Russ Feingold (D-WI) and McCain (R-AZ), working with Congressmen Christopher Shays (R-CT) and Patrick Meehan (D-PA), secured passage of the Bipartisan Campaign Finance Reform Act (BCRA) (known as McCain–Feingold despite the final version of the bill bearing a much closer resemblance to the Shays–Meehan House version than the McCain–Feingold Senate version). The BCRA attempted to address two problems. The first was the role played by soft money in the financing of elections; the second was the proliferation of issue advocacy advertisements.

The BCRA broadened the definition of electoral advertisements and attempted to decrease the number of issue advocacy advertisements (many of which took the form of 'attack ads'). The new law required both parties to increase their hard money base (particularly the Democratic Party, which lacked the hard money base of the Republican Party) but this adaptation took time and, perhaps unsurprisingly, the parties increased their reliance on independent expenditures and expenditures by non-profit organizations affiliated to the parties (Marbin, 2004; Cain, 2006: 45). The Supreme Court upheld most of the provisions of the BCRA in *McConnell v FEC* (540 US 93, 2003). Yet, in the run-up to the 2004 presidential election, a number of organizations were created with the intention and effect of circumventing the BCRA restrictions.

Political action committees

PACs exist because the FECA permits them to be used by corporations to make donations to candidates for federal office, something which corporations and labour unions are prohibited from doing direct. Corporations, labour unions and other corporate bodies accordingly establish PACs, for which they solicit financial support. In 1974, 608 PACs were registered with the Federal Election Commission. The number almost doubled by 1976, and reached more than 4,000 by December 1995. In 2011, the total number of PACs was 4,657. Using FEC data, corporate PACs remain the largest category, with 1,652 committees, followed by non-connected (1,601); trade/membership/ health (1,016); and labour (280).

The key provision in FECA was that of permitting large unions and business corporations having contracts with the US government to form political funds. These funds, 'connected' PACs, raise money from people employed by the corporation or from members of the labour union; they rarely solicit donations from the general public, although they are, in law, free to do so. Such 'independent' funding usually takes the form of hostile and negative campaign advertising, of which the most notorious example was the $8.5 million spent by the National Security PAC to produce the 'Willie Horton' television advertisements attacking Michael Dukakis in 1988. Although the Supreme Court has held that independent spending cannot be limited constitutionally, contributions to PACs can: they may not receive contributions of more than $5,000 from any one individual.

Although presidential election campaigns receive public support under the FECA provisions, PACs contribute to the parties' support for the election expenditure of the candidates. Federal law limits to $15,000 the amount that any one PAC may lawfully contribute to a national party, but the amount that PACs may lawfully contribute to state and local parties is subject to restrictions in some states, but not in others. Exploratory, pre-primary campaigns are generally financed from PACs formed by a candidate or by foundations (which have the tax advantage that they may lawfully receive direct and tax-deductible donations). Such candidate and officeholder PACs are used to finance an undeclared candidate's political travel and related expenses.

The consequences of PAC funding are difficult to determine. Some newspapers, of which *The Washington Post* is the leading example, have campaigned for years in favour of a radical reform of the financing of elections, and against what they take to be the corrupting influence of special interest money (Ackerman and Ayres: 2004). It might be thought implausible to claim that the expenditure of large sums of money in support of election campaigns by PAC fund directors does not affect the votes of those financed. Yet, there is no compelling evidence either that PAC money determines the outcomes of election campaigns, or that the receipt of PAC money shapes the voting behaviour of members of Congress. The limitations placed on PAC donations to individual candidates themselves restrict the extent to which candidates may feel themselves under an obligation. Yet, Barney Frank, a US congressman from Massachusetts, once observed that 'Elected officials are the only human beings in the world who are supposed to take large sums of money on a regular basis from absolute strangers without it having any effect on their behavior'. As anthropologists have long understood, no gifts are pure.

The problems presented by the attempts of interest groups to influence election outcomes are not new. Under current law and FEC regulations, PACs' expenditures are at least open to public discussion because they are publicly disclosed. The FEC keeps and scrutinizes full records of the financing of congressional and presidential elections; its records are freely available for public and media inspection. Yet, anxieties remain. The activities of PACs and the rising cost of campaigning prompt troubling questions about the hidden influence that concentrated private interests exercise over legislators. They also expand the already swollen advantages of incumbency. Interest groups' legal circumvention of the limits on individual contributions to PACs by collecting them and distributing them to candidates in so-called 'bundling' operations with the intention of increasing their impact intensifies alarm about PACs' influence, and reduces the worth of limits on PAC donations to individual candidates.

In presidential elections, even after the passage of the BCRA in 2002, 'soft' money has weakened the defences against corruption established by the FECA and its amendments during the 1970s. The 2004 election saw the proliferation of '527' groups – named after the section of the Internal Revenue Service (IRS) tax code that allows such groups (and, indeed, PACs) to fund the advertising of stances on public policy questions. Such 527s are prohibited from funding candidates but, despite the attempts of the BCRA's authors to limit the role of so-called 'soft money', may fund issue advocacy advertisements.

Leadership PACs and Super-PACs

In the post-BCRA landscape, many organizations work alongside the parties in the funding of elections. A good example is the rise of *leadership PACs*, whereby prominent politicians raise money to be used in the campaigns for *other* candidates. Ambitious politicians can use their fundraising ability to shape the electoral success of colleagues and, at the same time, enhance their own career prospects within their party. In 2010, 369 such PACs contributed $33.5 million of which 47 per cent was spent by Democrats and 52 per cent by Republicans (www.opensecrets.org). Provided the funds raised by prominent politicians are not directed to a specific candidate, there is no limit to the money that can be raised.

Following the important 2010 Supreme Court ruling in *Citizens United v FEC* and the DC Circuit Court of Appeals decision in *SpeechNow.Org v FEC* (2010), much of the architecture put in place to limit campaign spending by corporations has been removed.

Citizens United prohibited the government from limiting the expenditures of corporations and labor unions where monies did not flow directly to candidates. *SpeechNow.org*, building on the *Citizens Utd* ruling, allowed a non-profit organization to accept unlimited contributions from individuals for such expenditures (that is, funds would not flow to candidates directly) with the proviso that such an organization register as a PAC. The most significant effect of these rulings was the formation of PACs that (provided that they contributed no funds to candidates, parties, or other PACs) could accept unlimited expenditures from individuals, corporations and unions. The Supreme Court ruled that limitations on such expenditures violated the First Amendment right to freedom of speech.

Such *Independent-Expenditure Only Committees* are more commonly called *Super-PACs* and their influence is considerable: in the 2012 presidential election, super-PACs' spending exceeded that spent by the candidates' election campaigns in the Republican primaries. The Centre for Responsive Politics has shown that the top 100 individual Super-PAC donors in 2011–12 comprised just 3.7 per cent of contributors, but accounted for more than 80 per cent of the total money raised.

Primary election campaigns

Since the early part of the twentieth century, the selection of party candidates for many elective public offices in the United States has lain with voters, and not with party bosses. As Chapter 3 demonstrated, there were exceptions to this rule, especially in many large cities where the bosses of political machines determined who ran under the party label and later distributed the fruits of victory through patronage. It is, nonetheless, now a nearly universal principle that the selection of candidates to run under a party label lies with those voters who identify with a party, rather than with those within a party's organization.

States differ in the severity of the requirements they make of voters intending to participate in primary elections. Approximately 80 per cent of the states demand some form of public statement of affiliation before permitting a voter to participate in a party's primary; in most of these states, the declaration has to be made between two weeks and one year in advance of the election. Primaries can therefore be more or less 'open' to all who wish to participate, or effectively 'closed' to all except those who identify with the party over a substantial period of time.

The primary system provides a means whereby factions within a party struggle for the nomination by appealing to different groups of voters. Primary voters are typically unrepresentative of general election voters, in that their views are further from those of the median voter. Winning a party's nomination through appealing to activists whom a candidate's campaign workers mobilize with energy may constitute a considerable achievement. However, if the factional base on which victory within the party is built is narrow, it might prove difficult to unite the party around a candidacy in the general election, and impossible to expand the coalition to include independent voters and those who normally identify with the opposing party. Under the old order prevailing before the

McGovern–Fraser report (see below), Democratic Party elites could, and did, take these factors into account for presidential elections: the object in selecting a nominee was to select one who maximized the party's prospects of victory in the general election. Primaries at all levels have weakened the capacity of party leaders to exercise this degree of influence. The extension of primaries, which binds delegates to the successful primary candidate in the presidential contest, has increased the clement of randomness in the candidate selection process, as parties exercise less control, and the 'wild-card' candidate can capture the party's presidential nomination.

Both American political parties have as their supreme purpose the quadrennial selection of a candidate who will win the presidency. The increase in randomness through the delegation of the nomination to primary and caucus electorates had graver consequences for the Democrats than for the Republicans, because the greater width of their coalitional base makes it more liable to fragment following the selection of a divisive candidate. Primaries were adopted by most states for the presidential nominating process because it was calculated, correctly, that to do so would enable them to conform safely to the requirements of the national party, which gradually assumed jurisdiction over state party selection rules. These now fall into four types:

- Much the commonest (especially in the Democratic Party) is the *proportional representation preference primary*, in which delegates are distributed between the candidates according to the vote received.
- The *advisory presidential preference primary*, in which votes are recorded for both presidential candidates and delegates to the Convention, who may be denoted as supporting a particular candidate or none.
- The binding *'winner takes all' primary*, in which two types of delegate are elected: those from the state's congressional districts, and those from the state as a whole; delegates are obliged to vote for the winners of the races in each congressional district and that in the state as a whole.
- The *delegate selection primary*, in which only the names of the delegates appear on the ballot, with or without the name of the presidential candidates whom they prefer.

Promoted as an exercise in broadening participation in the selection of the Democratic Party's candidate for the presidency, primaries and caucuses are a minority sport. Rates of participation in Democratic and Republican primaries are much smaller even than in the general election. Indeed, in the 2012 presidential primaries those who did vote constituted only 5.2 per cent of the eligible voting population of the United States as a whole.

The first primary of the presidential election season always takes place in New Hampshire, a small state almost as unrepresentative of the country as it is of the Democratic Party. Low participation exaggerates its unrepresentative character, especially for Democratic candidates: of the 4,419 delegates present at the Democratic Convention in New York City in 2008, 232 were elected from New York and 370 from California, but only 22 from New Hampshire.

Caucuses

Caucuses are even less representative than primaries, and are ideally suited to candidates with unrepresentative but ardent followings, as the etymology of 'caucus' might be thought to indicate: it derives from a Native-American word meaning 'to gather together and make a great noise'. In 1988, Jesse Jackson (the most politically liberal of the Democratic candidates) ran most strongly in those states such as Iowa (which select all of their delegates through caucuses) and those such as Texas (which select some of them in this way). Pat Robertson (much the most culturally conservative of the Republican candidates) also performed markedly better in caucuses than in primaries. By contrast, George H.W. Bush, from the centre of the Republican Party, lost seven of the ten caucuses but only one of the forty-one primaries in which he was a candidate. In the 2012 Republican campaign, the ultra-conservative candidate Rick Santorum won the Iowa caucus while Ron Paul, the least orthodox of the candidates, won the Louisiana caucus.

For candidates in both parties, the object in each primary or caucus is to win as many delegates as possible, so that victory is inevitable at the respective Party Conventions. Unlike the electoral college in the general election, where the winner of a state takes all of that state's electoral college votes, a proportional rule applies in most primaries.

The Democratic Party's nomination rules continue to provide for the representation of senior party officials in addition to the delegates selected by primary and caucus voters. Following the implementation of the McGovern–Fraser Commission reforms in 1972, the number of such delegates fell to just fifty in 1980. In 1984, the number of super-delegates was sharply increased to give senior party officials a louder voice: in 1996, 768 super-delegates (US senators, US congressmen, chairs of state parties and state governors) attended the Chicago Convention, some 20 per cent of the total number of delegates. In 2008, the number of super-delegates was 852.

In 1996, the absence of serious opposition to Clinton's re-nomination had given him walkover victories in primaries and caucuses, and an effective monopoly of delegates at the Convention. In years when the nomination is contested, however, super-delegates may have a role to play. In the 1988 campaign, for example, Governor Michael Dukakis had to secure 50 per cent + 1 of the 4,160 Democratic delegates attending the party's Convention in Atlanta. In the Democratic nomination process, Dukakis won too few delegates in primaries and caucuses to gain the nomination, but had a sufficiently large plurality to ensure that super-delegates switched their support to him. The system was intended to benefit the candidate likely to be closest to the median voter in the general election. So, in this case, it did, by working to the advantage of Dukakis and against that of his main challenger, Jesse Jackson. Unfortunately for Governor Dukakis, he was in the general election only second-closest to the median voter: Vice-President George H.W. Bush defeated him. In the closely-contested 2008 Democratic presidential nomination, Senator Hillary Clinton did not concede until early June (the Party Convention being in August), by which point Barack Obama had secured more of the pledged delegates. The need for super-delegates to decide the nomination was thereby avoided. Unlike Dukakis, Obama was closer to the median-voter in the presidential general election than was his Republican rival, Senator John McCain of Arizona.

Party conventions

Prior to the McGovern–Fraser reforms, accepted by the Democratic National Committee in 1971 and introduced for the 1972 presidential elections, the nominees of the two major parties for the office of president were chosen at the nominating conventions. The highly-divisive Democratic Convention of 1968 saw Hubert Humphrey nominated without his having run in a single primary, a point which factional opponents exploited to secure Humphrey's agreement to the formation of the McGovern–Fraser Commission, whose recommendations have had the effect of virtually nationalizing Democratic Party nominating rules, ceding the task of nomination to primary and caucus electorates, and rendering the convention a political shell. Having lost their central function, the two parties' conventions now ratify decisions taken previously, although, in the unlikely event that no candidate secured the majority required, the nomination would revert to the convention. There is no prospect of the convention regaining its former institutional role.

Enticed by drama, television and press journalists nevertheless continue to cover conventions in depth, often contriving substance from theatrical froth. Convention halls now provide little space for delegates (who have no remaining substantive function save that of being visibly enthusiastic) but much for television, whose demands dominate. While the occasion – funded by federal taxpayers and corporate sponsors – is more memorable for pageantry than political substance, the convention retains three purposes:

- That of *unifying the party* and of *presenting the nominee as a potential president*. Prior to the convention, the focus has been on the struggle within the parties; at the convention, the new theme is on the party as a united force. A divided party convention risks damaging the candidate, as the Democratic Convention damaged Hubert Humphrey in 1968, and the Republican Convention harmed George H.W. Bush in 1992.
- That of *balancing the ticket* by the selection of a *running-mate as vice-president*. The balance generally takes geographical and ideological forms. Thus, in choosing Hubert Humphrey in 1964, Lyndon Johnson selected a northern liberal to balance his own image, rather than his liberal record as a centrist southerner. In choosing Governor Spiro Agnew of Maryland four years later in 1968, Richard Nixon selected a populist conservative from the east coast to counterbalance his own moderate Californian Republicanism. Walter Mondale sought gender balance by his selection of Geraldine Ferraro in 1984. While the choice of Sarah Palin certainly gave a balance to the McCain ticket in terms of gender, age and experience (which he had in abundance and she entirely lacked), Palin neither helped unify the Republican Party nor helped the McCain team appear presidential, since her knowledge of public policy was evidently slight.
- That of presenting the *party's platform*. This purpose is usually carefully constructed in order to placate influential dissidents. Unlike a party manifesto in Britain, where the primary significant constraint on the implementation of its provisions lies in the bureaucracy, and where the executive can usually corral majorities for its policies in the legislature without difficulty, American presidents have no reliable institutional means of converting party aspiration into policy. Party platforms, while given extensive coverage in the major newspapers, are more important for the healing of internal party injuries than they are as statements of policy intent.

General elections

Conventions concluded, running-mates nominated by the candidate, visions of unity extended beyond the party faithful to the undecided electorate, the campaign for the presidency and other federal offices slips into a short summer remission until Labor Day on the first Monday in September. That is traditionally the last day of the lull and heralds the onset of the frenetic two months until election day, which is always held on the first Tuesday after the first Monday in November.

In election years, the presidential election dominates national news, but state and local media markets reflect the importance of state and local electoral politics, too. Even at the level of the presidency, the general election is really fifty-one separate elections, rather than a national election. The object is to win a clear majority in the electoral college; the means to achieving this end is to win a plurality in enough states to secure it, as is explained later in this chapter in the discussion of the electoral college.

In most states, votes are counted by machine. The design of the machine can either facilitate 'party-line' voting, where voters may vote 'down-the-line' for all of a party's candidates for all offices, or make it easier to 'split the ticket' (which, before the introduction of the Australian ballot, meant that party tickets were literally torn by voters) and vote separately for each office. Provision is also made for 'write-in' votes, by which candidates whose names do not appear on the official ballot paper may nonetheless receive support. In 2010, the Senate race for Alaska was decided after a write-in. Having lost the Republican nomination to the Tea Party Movement candidate Joe Miller, incumbent Republican Lisa Murkowski encouraged supporters to place her name on the ballot paper. She was the first senator elected after a write-in campaign since Democratic (as he then was) candidate Strom Thurmond won his 1954 senatorial campaign – having lost the support of his party for endorsing Eisenhower for re-election as president.

The US Constitution did not make the presidency subject to popular election. Article 2, Section I, modified by the Twelfth Amendment, provides for each state to choose (by whatever means each state determines) a number of electors equivalent in number to its total congressional delegation (see Appendixes 1 and 2). It is the electors' task to elect the president. Since each state has two senators irrespective of size or population, and has a number of representatives ranging from one to fifty-three (in California), the variation in voting strength in the electoral college is between three and fifty-five. (Since the ratification of the Twenty-Third Amendment in 1961, the District of Columbia has, purely for the purposes of presidential elections, been treated as if it were a state, and so has as many electors as it would have if it actually were a state.) The electors meet in the month after the popular vote, effectively ratifying it; the person elected takes office on 20 January of the following year, taking the oath of office at the prompting of the Chief Justice and in the presence of the outgoing president, senior members of the old and new administrations, and members of both Houses of Congress.

Each state votes in the electoral college as a unit, and the plurality winner (who, because of the usual absence of third-party candidates is normally also the majority winner) takes all the state's electoral college votes. Unlike in presidential primaries, the presidential election itself does not operate according to proportional or near-proportional voting rules. The winner of the popular vote for the presidency in a state takes all of that state's votes (except in Maine and Nebraska). The state of

Maine awards one electoral vote for each of its two congressional districts, and two by the vote in the state as a whole.

Since all states must have at least three electoral college votes (two from the Senate and at least one from the House of Representatives), states with tiny populations are over-represented in the electoral college; that fact does not, however, induce candidates to spend much time campaigning in them. Most campaigning is undertaken in the eight largest states: California (55), Texas (38), Florida (29), New York (29), Illinois (20), Pennsylvania (20), Ohio (18) and Michigan (16). Together, these account for 207 electoral college votes from predominantly urban and suburban states. This group, in turn, comprises most of the total required to win. Since the total number of votes in the college is 538 (435 votes equivalent to the total number of representatives, plus 100 senators and the three votes for the District of Columbia) a candidate requires 50 per cent + 1 of 538 to win the presidency, which gives 270 electoral college votes. The 2000 and 2004 presidential elections highlight the manner in which the electoral college shapes how the campaigns are conducted. In those many states which lean heavily towards particular party, candidates have little incentive to expend precious campaign resources. For example, New York was known to be a safe state for the Democrats in 2000 and 2004, as was Texas for the Republicans in those two elections. As a result, voters in safe states do not shape the path of presidential election outcomes.

Electors now have autonomy but rarely exercise it; instead, they act not as independent representatives, but merely as agents of the voters' will (there have been nine 'faithless electors' since World War II whereby one of the 535 delegates to the electoral college refuses to vote for the candidate who gained the most votes in their state, thus exercising an autonomy that runs against the convention that votes are cast which represent the outcome of the election). The possibility that a candidate might win the popular vote and lose in the electoral college nonetheless remains. As every student of American politics knows, in the 2000 presidential election Albert Gore won the popular vote: 50,999,897 to George W. Bush's 50,456,002. However, after the Supreme Court decided that the recount in the state of Florida should be terminated, Florida's then 25 (now 29) electoral college votes were allocated to Bush, who won the college 271 to 266 (270 being the winning post). The margin of victory in the Miami-Dade district of Florida (after the first recount) was just 537 votes. In the state as a whole, Bush won 2,912,790 votes to Gore's 2,912,253.

No election has been thrown into the House under the Constitution since the nineteenth century. That is primarily because the stability of the two-party system has come under serious attack only twice: in 1912, with Theodore Roosevelt's defection as a Progressive, and again in 1968.

If it were to happen, the voting strength of the large states would be dramatically reduced and that of the small states enhanced: each state has one vote, which it may cast for any one of the first three candidates in the electoral college's ballot. An absolute majority is required for election. Such a procedure might produce a bizarre result, so undermining the winner's legitimacy and thereby intensifying pressure for modifying the electoral college's rules or even abolishing the college altogether. Widespread though dissatisfaction has been with the potential for difficulty, embarrassment and chaos, no alterations have been made to the rules since the passage of the Twelfth Amendment in 1804.

The media

Even the first president of the United States, General George Washington, was subject to myth-making (consider the account – probably apocryphal – of George chopping down his father's cherry tree and then, when questioned, announcing 'I cannot tell a lie'). The creation of a positive image when running for elected office, and attempts to create a negative image of an opponent, have become defining features of modern political campaigning. First, in the era of radio, such as Franklin D. Roosevelt's fireside chats, and then the era of television, and now the era of modern communications media that include social networking websites and the blogosphere, the roles of the media (both the traditional print media, institutional television and radio networks and the often non-institutional internet sources) have been central to the success or failure of candidates seeking elective office.

Congressional races for the House and the Senate require considerable sums of money to be raised and then spent on campaign advertising (particularly so for senators whose constituencies can be vast) as do races for mayor and gubernatorial campaigns (competition for state governorships). But it is in the competition for the presidency that we see vast sums of money dedicated to the creation or destruction of a presidential candidate and their image. Advertising will focus both on creating a sense of the essence of the candidate (their presidential qualities) and on the core policy choices favoured by a candidate.

Television remains the central medium in presidential election campaigning, but other media now constitute a central plank in electioneering. Howard Dean's campaign for the Democratic presidential nomination in 2004 highlighted how effective the internet could be, both for fundraising and for mobilizing support. The 2008 presidential election saw both candidates make use of modern electronic media alongside the traditional television platform. It was, however, Barack Obama who was most effective in exploiting the potential of the internet, of social

Table 4.3 *Television Revenue from Political Advertising: 1988–2010*

Year	$
1988	227,900,000
1992	299,623,400
1996	400,485,900
2000	665,000,000
2004	1,600,000,000
2006	2,135,104,478
2008	1,709,275,380
2010	4,500,000,000
2012	5,900,000,000

Sources: Television Advertising Bureau, 2013; 2004 value from *USA Today*, 25 November 2004.

networking websites and of blogs. His doing so enabled him to mobilize an activist base, to create support in states which hitherto would have gained little attention from democratic candidates and to raise considerable amounts of money.

How Americans vote

Party and voting

Parties simplify decision-making for the electorate. The party label enables voters to choose without having extensive or detailed comparative information on the candidates whose names appear on the long ballot. Most voters choose how to vote according to their party allegiances, and their voting patterns tend (in the absence of a convulsive realignment of social groups and parties caused by the appearance of a new issue disrupting established alignments and breaking stable coalitions) to be stable over the short-to-medium term. Many of the scholarly debates about electoral behaviour have as their focus the changing relationship between parties and the electorate. The structuring of electoral choice by party remains enormously important in American politics despite the shift towards an entrepreneurial politics in which candidates depend on themselves and their campaign consultants, rather than on the party, for finance and the building of bases of support. The importance of the attachments of voters to parties is plain. These attachments have regional, class, ethnic, educational, gender, age and racial bases, as Table 4.3 shows.

The New Deal coalition

Economic depression fathered the large New Deal coalition. In the early form it took in the 1932 and 1936 presidential elections, the coalition comprised an alliance between voters in the north and the south, workers in industry, and those in agriculture. With the exception of the South, it also comprised the unusual alignment for the United States of party with class: the Democrats represented those without capital or resources, those with only their labour to sell and those millions of unemployed having no one to whom they might sell it. In more detail, the coalition consisted of the industrial working class, the poor, liberal intellectuals, most Catholics, Irish-Americans, Italian-Americans, and later, southern and eastern European immigrants (all of whom Democratic parties in industrial cities accommodated and absorbed), Jews, northern blacks, voters in the (mostly rural) South, the industrial east and mid-west, and the Pacific west. The coalition was united around the common interest that its constituent groups shared in extensive federal macroeconomic intervention in the economy, the creation of social welfare programmes, the regulation of labour markets, capital investment programmes, and the direct creation of work, to counter (as Roosevelt held) the spectacular failures and social injustices of the free enterprise system which President Hoover and the Republican Party represented and defended.

At the presidential level, the New Deal coalition remained intact until 1948. It was weakened as a result of the civil rights challenge that threatened to split its northern and southern wings, fell under the weight of Dwight Eisenhower's wide personal appeal which, in turn, derived from the confidence he inspired in the electorate, and was (with the exception of much of the south and west) reassembled by John Kennedy and spectacularly (though briefly) expanded by Lyndon Johnson in 1964. It collapsed as the Democratic Party was torn asunder by Vietnam, the crisis of the cities, law and order, civil rights, and women's rights in 1968 and 1972. With the qualified exception of 1976, it was not re-assembled in presidential elections until 1992, and then in a form much less dependent on white southern support. Individual candidates have made, and continue to make, a difference to their party's fortunes: Eisenhower would have defeated any candidate whichever party's nomination he decided to seek (or take) in 1952. Ronald Reagan's personal electoral appeal in 1984 would have overwhelmed any Democratic candidate; Lyndon Johnson would have defeated any Republican in 1964, as Richard Nixon knew (which was why he stayed out of the race for the Republican nomination). George McGovern's perceived extremism would have made the task of almost any Republican opponent simple (which makes the decision to burgle the Democratic National Committee Headquarters all the more ill-advised). Nonetheless, it is not accidental

Table 4.4 *Presidential Vote by Social Groups (%)*

	2004		2008		2012	
	Kerry	Bush	Obama	McCain	Obama	Romney
Politics						
Republicans	5	95	7	93	3	97
Democrats	93	7	93	7	95	5
Independents	52	48	51	49	53	47
Conservatives	20	80	23	77	18	82
Moderates	63	37	63	37	67	33
Liberals	88	12	94	6	92	8
Sex						
Male	44	56	50	50	47	53
Female	52	48	57	43	57	43
Age						
Under 30	60	40	61	39	62	38
30 to 49 years	43	57	53	47	53	47
50 to 64 years	48	52	54	46	50	50
65 and older	52	48	46	54	46	54
50 and older	50	50	51	49	49	51
Race						
White (incl. Hispanics)	44	56	45	55	44	56
Non-white	83	17	90	10	89	11
Non-Hispanic white	43	57	44	56	43	57
Non-white (incl. Hispanics)	78	22	86	14	82	18
Black	93	7	95	1	95	5
Religion						
Catholic	52	48	53	47	56	44
Protestant	62	38	47	53	45	55
Education						
College	48	52	55	45	53	47
High School	54	46	47	53	55	45
Grade School	69	31	67	33	48	52
Postgraduate	53	47	65	35	62	38
College graduate only	42	48	51	49	46	54
Some college	44	56	52	48	58	42
High school or less	54	46	51	49	53	47
Grade school	67	33	63	36	63	36
Percentage of vote	48.5	51.5	53.0	46.0	53.0	46.0

that Democratic candidates should have won seven of the nine presidential elections between 1932 and 1964. Yet, in the forty-eight years since the 1964 election the two parties have had equal shares of the White House, although the Democratic Party has enjoyed far less support from southern states than was the case prior to 1964. In short, party allegiances shape outcomes. Beginning in the 1960s, the outcomes began to alter. Party allegiances have altered, too.

Parties still shape the voting behaviour of most individuals, and the attachment of individuals to a party remains strikingly stable over the short term. Most Republican candidates at presidential or congressional elections attract few African-American votes, continuing a pattern begun with Roosevelt's New Deal coalition and confirmed in the early to mid-1960s. John Kennedy, the Democratic president in 1961–63, having associated himself cautiously in the 1960 presidential election with the civil rights cause, later, as president, sponsored executive orders advancing the cause materially. His successor, Lyndon Johnson, succeeded in persuading Congress to pass two major Civil Rights Bills and one Voting Rights Bill. Johnson thereby completed the attachment of blacks to the Democratic Party, at the price of losing the white South (indeed, if one were to look at the electoral map for the 2008 presidential election, we would see that Barack Obama had no more success than the former southern Governor Bill Clinton in capturing the South). Yet, it remains the case that economically successful African-Americans are scarcely more inclined to vote Republican than are poor ones.

Hispanics vote less solidly for the Democratic Party than do African-Americans. Not only do their circumstances and history differ from those of African-Americans, but there are many cleavages among them: many Cubans in Florida and Puerto Ricans in New York are immigrants, but many Hispanics in Texas and California are not. (In the south and southwest, many are illegal immigrants, and hence ineligible to vote.) In 2004, President George W. Bush gained over 40 per cent of the Hispanic vote: the national election poll put the figure as high as 44 per cent. One analyst has attributed Bush's success to his focus in first term on social and moral questions and also national security, which attracted Hispanic Catholics (Schmal: 2004). By 2010, three Hispanic candidates, all Republicans, had gained top state-wide offices: New Mexico gained its first Latino governor in Susana Martinez. Nevada similarly gained its own first Hispanic governor in Brian Sandoval, while Florida's Mario Rubio captured a Senate seat. The Republican Party's considerable efforts to attract Hispanics have met with some success, especially in Florida. However, the 2012 election results showed that the GOP has much more to do if it is to make gains in the 2014 mid-term elections and the 2016 presidential race. Winning the Hispanic vote remains central to the future electoral success of the GOP.

Independents

Only a little over one-third of those who identify themselves as 'independents' lean to neither party and express no preference between them. Accordingly, the concept of 'independent' has therefore to be applied with care. Pure independents (only 7 per cent of the total electorate in 1994; 6 per cent in 1998; and 4 per cent in 2002, 2006 and 2010 (Gallup)) have a lower rate of voting than those with weak or strong partisan attachments. Those who described themselves as independents were less independent than their label implied. Accordingly, presidential elections tend not to be decided by those with a stable and unambiguous party identification, since they change their partisan allegiances only during substantial and sudden realignments, such as 1896 and 1932. They are decided both by those with weaker partisan attachments and by those independents who lean towards one of the two parties who are persuaded either to alter their weaker attachments, or to confirm their leaning according to their view of the policy preferences of the two candidates, or their retrospective judgements of the preceding four years.

How social groups within the electorate vote

Of all groups, only blacks remain firmly wedded to the Democratic Party: 86 per cent of those blacks who voted in 1988 supported Dukakis, and (in a three-way race) 84 per cent supported Clinton in 1996; 95 per cent supported Albert Gore in 2000; 93 per cent John Kerry in 2004; and 95 per cent Barack Obama in 2008. Yet, over 60 per cent of Latino voters are Democrats and 38 per cent are Republicans (Pew Hispanic Center). Since their rates of birth and of immigration are high, Hispanic Americans are increasingly important to the outcomes of elections in California, Texas, Florida and New York; accordingly, both parties pursue them assiduously. According to the Pew Center, Latinos accounted for 15.1 per cent of the population in 2008 – a figure projected to reach 30 per cent by 2050.

As the case of Hispanic voters shows, while Catholics lean to the Democratic cause, they no longer vote as a group. Neither are they decisively swayed by the views of their priests (whose views on social matters are, in any case, by no means uniformly conservative). The new importance in politics and policy, since the 1960s, of social issues such as the role and rights of women with respect to matters such as abortion and contraception, and the changing size and character of family life in contemporary American society, has not met with a unified Catholic response. It has never done so among lay Catholics, and no longer does so among the priesthood, or even the episcopacy. Such expectations as there once were that the conservatism of the Republican Party under the ascendancy of the New Right in general, and Ronald Reagan in particular, would result in Catholics voting *en bloc* for presidential, if not congressional, candidates of the more socially conservative party, have been disappointed. Catholics vote as instrumentally as many other groups have come to do; those who continue to agree with their church's views on social issues do not, for the most part, let it affect their voting decisions.

Jews, women, blue-collar workers, and union members voted heavily for Clinton in 1992 and 1996. Protestants (especially 'born-again' fundamentalists) supported George H. W. Bush heavily, although not as overwhelmingly as they did Reagan, Bush's non-churchgoing, divorced predecessor. In addition to losing some fundamentalist support in 1988, and rather more in 1992, Bush lost many of the Democrats who had defected to Reagan in 1980 and 1984, and other elements of the New Deal coalition who had done the same: those who had come of political age in the 1930s and 1940s, the uneducated and the poor. George H. W. Bush's coalition of support was much closer to the traditional Republican middle- and upper-middle class base of white, Protestant Americans than Reagan's broad base in 1984 had been, and shrank further towards that core in 1992. As Table 4.3 shows, between 2000 and 2012 Jewish voters remained loyal to the Democratic Party in presidential elections: Barack Obama captured 80 per cent of the Jewish vote in 2008. Women still lean more towards Democrats than Republicans in presidential elections, but the Democratic lead is narrow. Union families still lean towards the Democrats, with their level of identification remaining above 60 per cent in the presidential elections of 2004, 2008 and 2012.

Yet, regional loyalties have altered greatly in the post-war era. The disappearance of the solid South is the single-most important such change, but other regions' attachments have also changed. New England, once a Republican stronghold, is now two-party. Even the state of New Hampshire, solidly Republican for most of the twentieth-century, is now a swing state. New Jersey, New York and Pennsylvania in the east, once Yankee Republican strongholds, have, since the early 1970s, had Congressional delegations dominated by Democrats but voted for candidates of both parties for the White House.

Voting patterns in the United States in presidential elections have diverged from those in congressional, gubernatorial, and state legislative elections. 'Ticket-splitting' (voting for one party's candidate for the presidency and for the other party's candidates for most or all other offices) became common for much of the post-war period. The US Congress was controlled almost exclusively by the Democratic Party for most of the period from 1932 until the 1990s. The House went to the Republican for only one Congress between 1932 and 1995 (the 83rd Congress, which lasted from 1953 to 1955). The US Senate was similarly dominated by the Democratic Party until Republicans won a Senate majority in 1980. Since the early 1980s, divided government has been much more commonplace, with both chambers of Congress changing hands much more regularly than the period of Democratic hegemony which began with the election of Franklin D. Roosevelt in 1932. The White House has continued a pattern of alternation between Democratic and Republican control: each party has held the White House for twenty-four years since 1964.

Such persistent divided government suggests why mandates are so difficult for presidents to claim or exploit: they are usually qualified. The key support of common party links to bridge the gap between the White House and the Congress has, since Nixon's presidency, usually been absent. George H. W. Bush rightly inferred from this fact that coopera-tion with his partisan opponents would be essential if he were to have any prospect of achieving his objectives, although George W. Bush coop-erated less willingly with Democratic majorities in his second term. Barack Obama promised cooperation with the Republican-controlled House after the 2010 mid-terms, but successful cooperation has been rare and partisan division commonplace.

The link between Capitol Hill and the White House has weakened in another respect: presidential coat-tails have shortened since Roosevelt's presidency. Whereas Roosevelt brought huge numbers of Democrats into Congress on his coat-tails in 1932 and 1936, and Lyndon Johnson did much the same in 1964, recent presidents have had much less effect on the fortunes of their nominal party colleagues' congressional electoral fortunes. Richard Nixon's victory did not lead to Republican congres-sional successes in 1968: he was the first president in the twentieth century to enter office facing opposition majorities in both Houses. Neither have Nixon's successors done very much better – with the notable exception of George W. Bush in the 2002 mid-term elections, when the Republican Party gained two seats in the Senate and eight in the House, consolidating their success in the 2000 congressional elections.

Why incumbents win

The most striking result of congressional elections in the post-war period is that incumbents win. The outcomes of most elections to the House of Representatives are, therefore, highly predictable; those to the Senate are rather less so. Although incumbent re-election rates have long been high, they have risen in recent years to the point where they now approach 95 per cent. Since 1948, the number of representatives seeking re-election has varied between a low of 368 in 1992 and a high of 411 in 1966. The proportion of those seeking re-election who have won has varied between a low point of 79.3 per cent in 1948 and a high of 98.5 per cent in 1988. The proportion has fallen below 85 per cent only once since 1948, has been above 95 per cent between 1984 and 1990, and above 90 per cent in every election year since 1976, with the two exceptions of the Republican landslide of 1994 (when it fell to 89.9 per cent) and the Republican victories of 2010 (when the rate fell to 87 per cent).

If members of the House are to be politically successful (whether through a long-term career in the House itself, by chairing an important committee or winning a position in the party leadership, or by using their House membership as a springboard for more illustrious office in the Senate, their state's governor's mansion, or even the White House), they must first secure their own re-election. The frequency of elections to the House obliges members of Congress to calculate carefully and constantly the effects on their re-election prospects of their decisions, speeches and voting behaviour. Sam Rayburn, the most capable holder of the Office of Speaker in the twentieth century, on more than one occasion advised Democratic colleagues to 'vote your district'. The Speaker's advice was more guileful than it might appear. As his party's leader in the House, Rayburn's task was to maximize Democratic voting strength by helping Democrats win re-election. As Rayburn thereby implicitly acknowledged, members of Congress cannot rely on party label or organization to shield them from constituents' displeasure if they should be so unwise as to place the interests of another congressional district, or those of their president, above their district's own. The double jeopardy of primary and general elections offers opponents from within and without the representative's own party two opportunities to capitalize. In practice, few members of Congress thus imperil their careers.

Like their colleagues in the Senate, members of the House provide themselves with massive resources drawn from public funds to defend themselves from defeat and advance their interests: personal and committee staff, offices in the home district and state; expert advice from congressional support agencies; free mailings; free trips home; extensive exploitation of the internet and appearances in television studios. Personal staff have a powerful electoral utility for members of Congress. By attending efficiently and creatively to district and constituent politics and problems, they underpin incumbents' electoral security. The permanent allocation of many staff dealing with constituent mail to district or state offices symbolizes and strengthens the link between representative or senator and electors. Postal franking privileges are a significant expense to the taxpayer, but wonderfully useful to incumbents for enabling them to keep voters at home fully apprised of their political qualities. A study by the Congressional Research Service has shown that the volume of House mail through the Capitol Hill Post Office is twice as large in election years as it is in off-years. Television studio facilities are also valuable to members for recording broadcasts to be aired on local television stations.

The systematic exploitation of congressional perquisites, provided at public expense, buttresses incumbents' electoral security. Irrespective of whether the incumbent won in the most recent election with a tiny majority or by a landslide, the tending of electoral roots is a preoccupation: incumbents' first object is to deter plausible opponents from taking up the challenge of running against them; their second, to defend their seats against those who are not so deterred. The acquisition and constant replenishment of campaign treasuries greatly enhances such a deterrent effect: in 2008, the average incumbent in the House spent $1,372,539, but the average loser spent $492,928. In the Senate, the average spend by incumbent senators was $8,531,267, but the average spend by losers was $4,130,078 (www.opensecrets.org). Under circumstances such as these, it is to be expected that the quality of many challengers to incumbent representatives and senators should be poor and their political experience slight: in 1988, only 10 per cent of incumbents seeking re-election faced opponents who had ever been elected to public office, however lowly.

In the 1980s, incumbency was so powerful that it underpinned the Democratic Party's majority in the House, defending it against the growing popularity of conservative Republicanism. In the long run, incumbency offers no defence since the average length of service of members of Congress is less than twelve years. Only when incumbents decline to run again or die in office (thereby precipitating an 'open' race) is a change in the partisan label of the district's representative more than a remote possibility. In 1992, the unpopularity of Congress, fuelled by public discontent with a paralysis of policy-making and with an apparently widespread abuse by congressmen of the perquisites of office, many incumbents retired prematurely in order to stave off anticipated defeat. Others were defeated in primaries, many of them taking place for newly-drawn congressional districts following the decennial reapportionment and redistricting exercises.

Nevertheless, of those who stood for election in November under their party's label, 93.1 per cent were re-elected to office. Even in the 1994 mid-term elections – the so-called 'Republican Revolution', when Republicans made a net gain of fifty-three House seats to recover the majority status they had lost forty years previously – the incumbency re-election rate remained at 90 per cent. Most Republican gains in 1994 were in open seats (in which they won twenty-two of those previously held by Democrats) and in seats defended by Democratic incumbents in their first term (when incumbents are most vulnerable to defeat). Consistent with the discussion in Chapter 2 about the regional patterning of partisan strength, nineteen Republican gains in 1994 came in the South, sixteen in the Pacific west, and fifteen in the central plains.

Exhibit 4.2 The Changing Political Geography of the United States: How the States Voted in Presidential Elections, 1932–2012

Presidential election, 1932

	Popular vote	ECV
Governor Franklin Roosevelt (Democrat)	22,825,016	472
President Herbert Hoover (Republican)	15,758,397	59

Presidential election, 1968

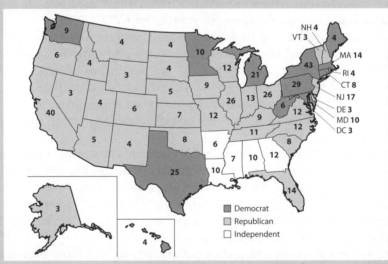

	Popular vote	ECV
Vice-President Hubert Humphrey (Democrat)	31,270,533	191
Richard Nixon (Republican)	31,770,237	301
Governor George Wallace (Independent)	9,906,144	15

Presidential election, 1980

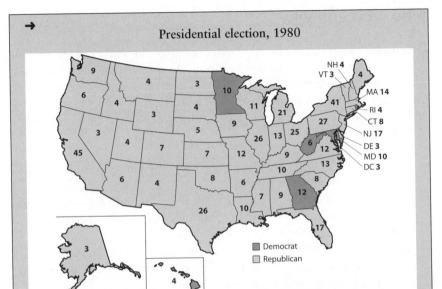

	Popular vote	ECV
President Jimmy Carter (Democrat)	35,480,115	49
Governor Ronald Reagan (Republican)	43,903,230	489

Presidential election, 2012

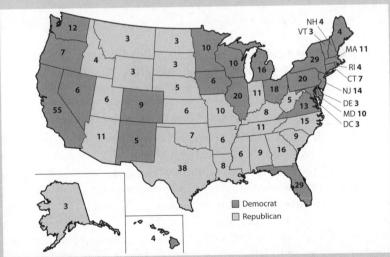

	Popular vote	ECV
President Barack Obama (Democrat)	65,899,660	332
Governor Mitt Romney (Republican)	60,932,152	206

Note: The numbers in this figure represent the total number of electoral college votes (ECVs) for each state.

Who wins and why

Despite the considerable body of evidence that explains how Americans vote when broken down by demographic characteristics, the question of why one party triumphed in a given election is not reducible simply to an explanation based on demographics. As Miller and Shanks (1996: 1–14, 464) show, the outcome of elections can be explained by examining a combination of:

- the *partisan identification of voters* – with which party do voters identify and with what intensity;
- *policy-related predispositions* – in short, whether one describes oneself as liberal or conservative, favours limited government, is pro-union or pro-business;
- *current policy preferences* – whether one favours stronger border protections to limit immigration, favours the Affordable Care Act (ACA), or stricter gun control;
- *predisposition of current conditions* – whether one thinks the economy is improving or worsening, or America's role in the world is weakening/strengthening;
- *retrospective evaluations of personal qualities* – for example, a president seeking re-election has a track-record on which he can be judged;
- *evaluation of personal qualities* – integrity, empathy, leadership and so on;
- *prospective performance evaluations* – how likely the candidate is to improve the huge federal debt, or strengthen American business, or strengthen the role of the nation in terms of foreign policy.

In 1988, Reagan's Vice-President – George H.W. Bush (the father of George W. Bush) – attempted to portray his opponent, Michael Dukakis, Governor of Massachusetts, as another liberal in order to sustain his own appeal among those who had supported Reagan. The 1988 television campaign adverts (www.thelivingroomcandidate.org) show the devastatingly and effective Bush campaign which lambasted Dukakis for his alleged liberalism. The infamous Willie Horton advert that attacked Dukakis's weekend prison furlough programme showed prisoners walking out of a turnstile to freedom as the voiceover explained that Horton had been released on furlough but committed assault, armed robbery and rape while out of prison. The Bush campaign used the same refrain in many adverts: 'Don't let Dukakis do for America what he has done for Massachusetts'.

Yet, in 1992 President Bush faced an opponent who placed the economy at the centre of debate, particularly the deepening recession. As

James Carville, Governor Bill Clinton's campaign strategist explained in typically pithy style 'It's the economy stupid': Governor Clinton remained focused on the Bush administration's economic record. One advert focused on President Bush's claim from the 1988 election when he said 'Read my lips, no new taxes' and super-imposed across the image of the President's mouth a rolling list of twenty-two tax increases introduced in the four years of the Bush presidency. In 1996, the moderate conservative Senator Bob Dole (R-KA) found it difficult to differentiate himself from President Clinton, who had moved to occupy the centre-ground. Dole's inability to exploit ideological divisions, combined with a budget surplus and a healthy economy, helped return Clinton to the White House.

The first four elections of the new century (in 2000, 2004, 2008 and 2012) represent a marked return to battles fought over issues and ideology. During those twelve years, the ideological distance between the parties grew; that gulf was apparent in presidential elections. The two parties were increasingly viewed as a liberal and a conservative party, but the electorate was evenly split with two very close election results in 2000 and 2004. However, in the 2008 race the economy returned to the fore as voters focused on the claims made by Senator Obama (D-IL) that he could rescue America from the Great Recession that, Democrats claimed, was to be attributed to the failures of President George W. Bush. The 2012 election was also characterized by a continued focus on economic policy, but ideology also played an important role as Governor Mitt Romney challenged President Obama on what Romney characterized as a love of 'big government' and a tendency to 'tax and spend'. President Obama's flagship healthcare reform of 2010, the Affordable Care Act, became a key battleground over which the candidates clashed during the election period. The post-2012 period has seen no lessening of the ideological polarization that divides the two parties at both state and national levels.

Conclusion

Party in America is distinctive. Party has, in the several senses identified in the chapter, also experienced resurgence in recent years. Yet, most candidates for office remain dependent on primary electorates, rather than party officials, for nomination. The presidency, which until 1972 was exempt from this rule, is also now subject to it. The politics of entrepreneurship suffuses elections in America; they are, in turn, mediated primarily by television, rather than by party.

Although neither race nor gender is any longer a bar to voting, and the courts act vigorously to ensure the equal value of votes, comparatively few Americans vote. Elections play a conspicuously large part in American politics but do not, in themselves, make citizens active participants. Electoral alignments, and alterations to them, are made by the 50 per cent of America's adult population who participate in presidential elections, and the 35 per cent who take part in congressional elections. The dominant alignment since 1968 has been of divided electoral power within Washington, by which the electorate, certainly until the mid-1990s, tended to send Republicans to the White House and Democrats to Congress. Divided control persisted for all but two years in the 1990s, but in two modes: since 1994, a Democratic president has governed with a Republican Congress; from 2001 to 2007, unified government prevailed until Republicans lost both chambers of Congress in the 2006 mid-term elections. President Obama governed with the Democrats from 2009 until 2011, when the Republicans regained control of the House and the Democrats just managed to retain the Senate. Republican congressional gains in the 'L'-shaped swathe of states in the Rocky Mountains, plains and the South might well be stable in the medium-term. Southern Democrats are in secular decline, but their extinction is not preordained.

There has been no realignment of the classic kind seen in 1896 and 1932, and there is no majority party. Rather, the parties remain polarized, but the electorate is less so. The New Deal party system may have weakened, but no new electoral alignment has replaced it.

Chapter 5

The Presidency and the Politics of Leadership

On first examination, the office of the president of the United States appears to be a powerhouse in which the decisions made are implemented by the other elements within the governing institutions of the United States. However, the Founding Fathers created in the presidency an office with remarkably limited authority in domestic policy. Authority is divided between the two elected branches, and both the authority and the power of each are limited by the decisions made by the Supreme Court. This chapter considers the authority granted to the president in the Constitution before considering the significant changes that have reshaped the presidency since its creation. Consideration is also given to the central elements within the institution of the presidency that aid the president in his attempt to govern within and through a separated system. Under President Franklin D. Roosevelt, the institutional structure of the Executive Branch increased dramatically with the creation of the Executive Office of the President (EOP). As this chapter shows, the creation of the EOP in 1939 marks the birth of the modern or institutional presidency that exists in only slightly modified form today. The final task of the chapter is to consider both how and why presidential power has grown since the crafting of the Constitution, and to examine how and why some occupants of the Oval Office have sought to overcome the limitations created by a separated system through the use of so-called 'direct action'.

Presidential leadership

The Executive Branch of the government of the United States has but two elected members: the president and the vice-president. The former matters for what he is, the latter for what he might become. Election every four years to the presidency shapes the electoral and party systems; the outcome of each presidential election shapes the pattern of government in the succeeding four years. On taking the oath of office, a president becomes Commander in Chief of the armed forces of the most heavily-armed nation-state on Earth, and acquires full command over its strategic and theatre nuclear forces. New roles thrust on the presidency in the twentieth century have enhanced its symbolic and substantive significance. The elected part of the Executive Branch is singular, not collective, and the president is, in consequence, a prominent national figure: his constituency is the nation, and he therefore enjoys a singular electoral legitimacy. Both the United States Congress and the Supreme Court are institutions with multiple memberships. The presidency is a club of one. As George W. Bush once observed, he has no need to negotiate with himself. But he does need to negotiate with almost everyone else.

He needs to do so because those elected to this supreme national office do not govern alone. The presidency of the United States is not the government of the United States. Governing America requires politicians in separated institutions to cooperate because unfettered competition between them obstructs, rather than facilitates, policy-making. While seeking cooperation, a president must also attempt to lead, because the holder of no other office is institutionally equipped to do so. A president must, however, also accept that other politicians in other institutions have their own separate bases of legitimacy, authority and power, their own perspectives on policy and politics, and their own priorities. A president cannot lead unless he appreciates the perspectives of other elected politicians, and recognizes both their legitimacy and its implications.

A president has no party colleagues whose primary task it is to sustain a government in office, or to enable him to prosper against an opposition; such a bulwark of party government in Britain is absent in America. Presidents are obliged to exercise political leadership in a system of government whose structure has survived essentially unaltered through two centuries. Alluring as the potential power of the office appears to presidential candidates, the task of realizing governing power in a federal system of separated institutions has frustrated all post-war presidents – and defeated most. Presidential elections are zero-sum, two-person, single-shot games: governing America is a non-zero-sum, multi-person, multiple-shot game. The structural simplicity of presidential elections is a poor guide to the complexity of American government. Both presidents and scholars of the presidency have sometimes concluded that the institution's power is illusory; the more discriminating have always understood its constitutional grant of authority to be confined in scope and contingent in application. Presidents are obliged to bargain with other politicians, with independent bases of power over whom they have no authority but merely the possibility of influence. President Obama himself recognized the point, reflecting on the autonomous power centres not just of Congress, but also of markets and market-makers:

> there are a lot of different power centers, and so I can't just press a button and suddenly have the bankers do exactly what I want, or turn on a switch and suddenly Congress falls in line. And so what you do is to make your best arguments, listen hard to what other people have to say, and coax folks in the right direction. (President's News Conference, 29 April 2009, *Public Papers of the President*, Barack Obama, Book I)

Presidential leadership consists of two elements:

1. The strategic capacity to set the nation's political agenda by exploiting such prerogatives (formal powers) as the Constitution grants him, and choosing between policy options and priorities.
2. The tactical capacity to negotiate and bargain with other politicians in order that his declared policies might win the approval of Congress and of public opinion, leading to their implementation by the federal bureaucracy and lower-level governments according to his expressed preferences.

The powers of the presidency

Prerogative powers of the presidency

Article II of the Constitution (see Appendix 1) reveals why the office of the presidency should be the supremely attractive elective office in the United States, the office around which the party system is structured and the focus of national political attention.

It is on the constitutional foundations of Article II, on its explicit grants and limitations of authority, and on the statutory delegation of that authority by Congress, that the contemporary presidency is built. Some constitutional authority is exclusive: those of the pardon and the presidential veto, for example, are his alone. In practice, others, such as the formulation and consideration of legislation, are shared between the executive and legislative branches. In any event, the present nature, sweep and grandeur of the presidency cannot be inferred from the explicit grants of authority alone. The modern presidency is the complex product of a Constitution that has itself been amended (though, as far as the presidency is concerned, with respect to the method of election only, and not to its formal executive authority) and reinterpreted by society and the Supreme Court acting in a continuing, if often disputatious, constitutional debate.

Inherent powers of the presidency

The extent and character of presidential power has, in particular, come to be shaped by part of that debate concerning that authority which some occupants of the Oval Office have claimed to be inherent in the office of president, or implied by the Constitutional document itself. Many ends to which government is necessarily and properly devoted (and to which the Constitution's framers plainly expected American government to be) were not specifically provided for in the Constitution of 1789; neither could they have been. This view was Chief Justice Marshall's own. The view had also been Madison's, as he wrote in the forty-fourth of *The Federalist Papers*:

> Had the convention attempted a positive enumeration of the powers necessary and proper for carrying their other powers into effect, the attempt would have involved a complete digest of laws on every subject to which the Constitution relates; accommodated too not only to the existing state of things, but to all the possible changes which futurity may produce ... No axiom is more clearly established in law, or in reason, than that whenever the end is required, the means are authorized; whenever a general power to do a thing is given, every particular power for doing it is included.

The *power* of the president, by which we mean that which a president is capable of achieving through his exploitation of personal and institutional resources, cannot properly be confined to the sources of authority specified in the Constitution. Presidents have claimed for themselves certain powers which they deem to be inherent in the Constitutional grant of authority in Article II, in a statutory delegation of power by Congress to the presidency, or implied by either of these. In the Republic's two hundred years, no such claim was more sweeping than President Lincoln's suspension of *habeas corpus* during the Civil War under a claim of emergency powers. By his action, Lincoln authorized his

---

Exhibit 5.1 The Office of the Presidency: Article II of the Constitution

- The *Executive power* [by which is meant here 'authority'] *of the Federal government* is vested in the President.
- The President has the power to appoint *ambassadors, members of the Cabinet, Justices of the Supreme Court* and *Judges of lower Federal Courts*, with the advice and consent of the Senate.
- The President may recommend to the Congress such *legislative measures* as he deems appropriate and, subject to two-thirds of both Houses of Congress overriding his decision, *veto* bills emerging from Congress.
- The President has the power to make *treaties* with foreign nations, with the advice and consent of two-thirds of the Senate.
- The President is *Commander-in-Chief* of the armed forces of the United States.
- The President may require the *opinion in writing* of the principal officer of each of the Executive Departments.
- The President has the power to grant *reprieves* and *pardons*, save in the cases of impeachment. The President is, like all other officers of the United States, subject to *removal* from office by *articles of impeachment* voted by the House, and to subsequent trial by the Senate, for 'Treason, Bribery, or other High Crimes and Misdemeanours'.

[Emphasis added]

---

military commanders to declare martial law and to try civilian offenders in military courts. The principled objections of Chief Justice Taney to Lincoln's deliberate setting aside of his oath to defend the Constitution did not move the President. Lincoln took the view that the Constitution could not survive if the Union failed.

Unilateral action

The claims of more recent presidents to be acting under inherent powers have met less frequently with assent from Court or public. Acting, like Lincoln, in a time of war, in the spring of 1952 President Truman attempted to resolve a dispute over new wage contracts in the steel industry by ordering that the works be seized. Truman resorted to a defence similar to Lincoln's: it was for the president to determine the national interest and to act accordingly. Having pushed his case dangerously far, he retreated a little, but the Justice Department rashly returned to the fray in the federal district court by claiming that the courts had no power to restrain a president. Only the ballot box, and the ultimate sanction of impeachment, were available to check the chief executive. The Court declared this unattractive doctrine to be unconstitutional. By a majority, of 6–3, the Supreme Court found in *Youngstown Sheet and Tube Co. v Sawyer* (1952) that the president's directive:

> cannot properly be sustained as an exercise of the President's military power as Commander in Chief of the Armed Forces … we cannot with faithfulness to our constitutional system hold that the Commander in Chief of the Armed Forces has the ultimate power as such to take possession of private property in order to keep labour disputes from stopping production. This is a job for the Nation's lawmakers, not for its military authorities.

In its 1952 ruling, the Supreme Court seemed to favour a view of presidential action that allows the president quite considerable scope to act unilaterally *unless* the Congress has clearly stated its opposition to an action. Indeed, Moe and Howell (1999: 173) argue that the Supreme Court was able to resist President Truman's attempt to seize steel mills because Congress had clearly argued against such a power being granted to the president during the debates that resulted in the passage of the Taft–Hartley Act of 1947, which sought to clarify the rights of unions and employers.

Nonetheless, as the presence of three dissenting voices indicates, the problem of the inherent powers of the presidency is contentious and not easily resolved. There is (by definition) no unambiguous constitutional text at hand to resolve the difficulty, since it is to the unwritten constitutional provisions of inherent powers that presidents appeal in such circumstances. Reliance on constitutional commentators is necessary for courts to adjudicate, together with judgements about the gravity of the circumstances in which the inherent power is claimed and the sweep of the inherent power in question. Many incline to the view that claims of inherent powers are empty. Yet, the Constitution's brevity and generality require gaps to be filled if government is to work. It would be make a nonsense of the Constitution, both as a document and as a framework for working and workable government, were powers to be exercised only where they were expressly and explicitly granted. The process of filling constitutional gaps has been untidy, intellectually inconsistent and highly contentious. But it has been necessary. Not confined to the judicial branch, it has involved all three branches, interested groups and mass public opinion.

As Lincoln and Truman had done, President George W. Bush used those powers he claimed were inherent in Article II to wage a *War on*

Terror in the aftermath of the terrorist attacks of 11 September 2001. President Bush exploited those mechanisms that seemed to permit unilateral action (rather than persuasion) in order to secure his objectives (see Exhibit 5.2 for further examples of unilateral action). While President George W. Bush was not the first to choose unilateral action rather than persuasion, the scope and reach of these actions led many commentators to question the constitutional underpinnings of his actions. President Bush used executive orders and national security directives to create military tribunals to try suspected terrorists held at Guantanamo Bay (the US military base in Cuba) and to freeze the assets of those suspected of affiliation with terrorist organizations. Yet, in a 6–3 judgement, the Supreme Court ruled in *Rasul v Bush* (2004) that the executive order that created military tribunals violated the *habeas corpus* rights of detainees. In *Rasul*, the Supreme Court granted detainees the right to access US courts in order to challenge their detention. As Justice Stephen Breyer (who joined the majority) commented:

> It seems rather contrary to an idea of a constitution with three branches that the executive would be free to do whatever they want, whenever they want, without a check.

In his inaugural address, President Obama issued a repudiation of the perceived excesses of the Bush administration, committed himself to close Guantanamo Bay and to end the use of military tribunals. Yet, having frozen the use of tribunals, he resiled from this decision in May 2011. The detention centre in Guantanamo Bay remained open after the Senate voted 90–6 against the closure on 20 May 2009. It remains open in 2013 at the time of writing.

The principle of the presidency's inherent powers is now generally conceded (including those powers that permit the president to act unilaterally), although its extent remains a matter of dispute. The president's special prerogatives in foreign affairs have long been acknowledged by congressional and judicial politicians alike, especially since the Supreme Court's decision in *United States v Curtiss-Wright Export Corporation* (1936). There, the Court held that federal power over external policy was distinct from, and distinctly greater than, federal power over domestic policy, and that the realm of external policy was one in which the president's power was special and pronounced. In foreign affairs, the latitude granted to presidents by courts, Congress, and public alike, is large, but presidents do not have free rein. However, with respect to general claims of inherent power, presidents have fared less well than they have in foreign affairs.

President Nixon spent much of his presidency attempting to expand executive prerogatives across the entire range of government. The judge-

Exhibit 5.2 Presidential Power, Unilateral Action and the Unitary Executive

Every student of American politics will encounter the theory of presidential power put forward by Richard E. Neustadt in his classic work of 1960 *Presidential Power and the Modern Presidents* (Neustadt, 1990). In fact, the book is so well-known that we take it as a maxim that 'presidential power is the power to persuade'. Yet, a number of scholars have sought to explain the use of unilateral action by presidents – that is, those occasions (and they are numerous) when presidents do not seek to persuade but simply *make* a decision. In focusing on unilateral decision-making, such scholars are asking us to move away from a focus on a 'personal presidency' where, like Neustadt, we consider the personal capabilities of presidents and their ability to deliver leadership, towards a focus on the 'institutional presidency' (Nathan, 1983) where scholars examine the tools available to all presidents when they occupy the White House, including the various opportunities to act unilaterally (Krause and Cohen, 1997). The key tools at the disposal of the president which permit unilateral action include:

- *Executive orders*: Although not specified in the Constitution, the ability of the president to make certain policy decisions without the approval of Congress has been viewed by many as a power that is inherent in the Constitution. Both the president and his executive agencies, the powerhouses of the federal bureaucracy, (see Chapter 8) can make orders (rules) which can range from mere housekeeping to the creation of new agencies. That was how the Environmental Protection Agency was created by President Richard Nixon using an executive order on 3 December 1970. Similarly, many affirmative action regulations are the result of executive orders). Executive orders must derive from existing authority. The flurry of executive orders created by Franklin D. Roosevelt in his first two years of the New Deal (1933–35) led Congress to pass the Federal Register Act which requires all such orders to be recorded.
- *Executive agreements*: These allow the president to enter into agreement with foreign leaders to create agreements that, unlike treaties, do not require Senate approval. Such agreements greatly enhance the foreign policy power of a president. The Vietnam Peace Agreement of 1973 was agreed without President Nixon consulting the Congress.
- *Proclamations*: These allow the president to make a statement on an issue of public policy. While they can be contradicted by an explicit ruling in Congress, they have the same force of law as Executive orders. The difference between them is that executive orders are aimed at those inside government – those who work for the president

→

➜

– while proclamations are directed at citizens. Such proclamations are numerous. They include the proclamation of 3 October 1789 when President George Washington created the Thanksgiving National Holiday, and the emancipation proclamation of 1 January 1863 in which President Abraham Lincoln declared that more than 3 million slaves were free. More recent examples include President George W. Bush's *midnight proclamations* when, in his last week in office, on 13 and 15 January 2009 he reasserted his pro-life and religious credentials with the creation of two new public holidays: the National Sanctity of Life Day and the Religious Freedom Day.

- *National Security directives*: Unlike executive orders, which are recorded in the Federal Register, National Security directives do not have to be revealed at all. Such directives allow the president to exploit his control of the intelligence services and the military by issuing directives that may remain hidden from Congress; for example, President Nixon's bombing of Laos and Cambodia. As this example suggests, such directives make Congressional oversight of presidential actions difficult. Recent and controversial examples of such directives include President George W. Bush's creation of military tribunals to try suspected terrorists, the seizure of the financial assets of those suspected of terrorism, and many examples in which the President overruled the regulations created by the Environmental Protection Agency.

- *Signing statements*: These are written comments added to a bill by the president as he signs the bill into law. Such statements can range from the uncontroversial, where the president may state that the bill is a good bill and addresses a pressing public policy challenge, to the more contentious statements that allow the president to state his intention to ensure that certain aspects of the new law will not be implemented by his administration if he deems them to be unconstitutional, or undesirable. Critics suggest that such signing statements amount to the veto being wielded over sections of a law. Signing statements have been issued by many presidents: President Clinton issued more than two hundred. However, the signing statements issued by President George W. Bush generated particular controversy because critics accused the former president of violating the constitutional separation of powers and the rule of law. They did so because the President asserted that he would not act in a way that 'undermined his authority to supervise the unitary executive branch'. (The notion of the 'unitary executive' was used by President Reagan in a signing statement; some scholars regard it as justifying the expansion of presidential authority beyond those grants of authority stated or implied by the Constitution).

ment in the summer of 1974 that triggered his resignation was made in the case of *United States v Nixon* (1974), during which the President declined to release sixty-four tape-recordings of White House conversations. His defence had two elements: first, that the special prosecutor who had secured a subpoena directing Nixon to produce them was a member of the Executive Branch under Nixon's authority as president; and, second, that the tapes could be withheld from the Prosecutor and anyone else who sought them because they were privileged material. (The real reason for his not wishing to release the material was that one of the subpoenaed tapes was of a conversation between Nixon and Haldeman, his Chief of Staff, in which the use of the CIA to obstruct the FBI's investigation of the Watergate break-in was discussed.) Nixon's claim was not founded on the claim that the contents of particular tapes or parts of tapes were privileged but, rather, that all presidential communications were so. The subpoena, by contrast, referred to specified, dated recordings. The Special Prosecutor had not embarked on an unlimited or undefined enquiry. Nixon contended that executive privilege was absolute; the Court judged that it was not.

Claims by presidents that they have certain inherent powers were advanced with greater insistence in the twentieth century because of the growth in the size and importance of both the government and the presidency; such insistence continues in the twenty-first century because of the threat posed by so-called 'rogue states', terrorism and the purported need for the president to identify and confront threats to the national security of the nation pre-emptively. Throughout the twentieth century, but particularly since 1933, the federal government acquired two huge and continuing responsibilities which, as they have fundamentally expanded its capacity and reach, have effected a proportionately greater aggrandizement of the executive. Within an enlarged system of government, Congress has vested the president with responsibility both for the management of national economic policy and for the direction of foreign and defence policies. These two developments have had four related results:

- The *budget* and *programmes* of the federal government have increased in size and number.
- The relation of the federal to the state governments has changed and become infinitely more *complex* fiscally, organizationally, and politically.
- The nature of the presidency has altered, its prominence has increased and its *centrality*, in the political life of the nation, has become established and permanent.
- The relationships of the presidency with Congress and the Executive Branch have become the most significant in American government.

Presidents' *political direction* of their relations with Congress is among their most important tasks and that of relations with the rest of the Executive Branch scarcely less so, because the maintenance of cooperative and productive relations with both is essential if presidents are to make and sustain their priorities at all stages of the policy process.

The expansion of government has caused a greater growth of the presidency. The modern American presidency could not have assumed the large, bureaucratized form it has in the absence of more general political pressures on government to expand. In consequence, the presidency is now far more prominent within the structure of federal government than those who drafted the Constitution envisaged that it either could, or should, be.

The presidency and the mass media

While the presidency's constitutional authority is limited, its prominence is great. That prominence stems, in part, from presidents' adaptation to changing communication technologies: the advent of radio from Roosevelt's presidency onwards; television from Eisenhower's; and the use of the internet in the first decade of the twenty-first century when candidates from both major parties raised their profiles, and considerable sums of money, using internet-based campaign techniques. Electronic media have played a major role in changing the nature of the presidency, in enhancing its significance as the source of strategic leadership in an otherwise fragmented political system, and in establishing it permanently at the centre of the country's government. Theodore Roosevelt and Woodrow Wilson showed that a mass presidential politics could be created without a mass media, but it would probably be impossible to sustain in its absence.

The trappings of presidential office are intimately familiar: Flag, Oval Office, Marine helicopter on the south lawn of the White House, Air Force One touching-down in the major capitals of the world. The rhetoric, actions (whether contrived or important), resignation, successes, failures and deaths of presidents have their place in national and individual memories. Whether of President Kennedy's lonely burden during the Cuban Missile Crisis in October 1962, of his violent death and Lyndon Johnson's taking of the oath of office aboard Air Force One thirteen months later; of Johnson's transformation of both of the legal and political status of black Americans, and the place and politics of the southern states, by his sponsorship of civil and voting rights legislation; of President George W. Bush's reaction during a visit to a kindergarten when his Chief of Staff, Andrew Card, whispered into his ear that a commercial airliner had crashed into the North Tower of the World Trade Center complex on the morning of 11 September 2001; that same president's very different reaction when he visited fire-fighters on 14 September when he brilliantly seized the initiative in response to a worker in the audience who said 'I can't hear you' with his unprepared declaration 'I can hear you. I can hear you. The rest of the world hears you. And the people who knocked these buildings down will hear all of us soon.' The presidency has come to represent, though not always to comprise, the very centre of government. It remains the only possible source of consistent national political leadership.

That the office and its occupants dominate American and non-American public perceptions and understanding of government in the United States is explained in large part by television's focus on them. The technology of television tends to fasten on the graphic images of events and to eschew the complexities of process; the training of television journalists confirms the tendency. If most students studying the American system for the first time bring with them one assumption, it is that the system is fully presidential. This distorting assumption has been reinforced by the need of television itself and those who work with it to simplify rather than to clarify, and to infer presidential government from presidential visual prominence. For presidents themselves, television has a corresponding utility in reaching directly to voters over the heads of congressional politicians and, less easily, over the heads of media producers, editors, journalists (both print and web-based) and bloggers. Appreciation of the subtly contingent nature of presidential power has nonetheless been inhibited, rather than advanced, by television's ubiquity and cultural pervasiveness.

Most voters in the United States acquire most of their information about, and understanding of, politics and government from television. The consequences of the way in which television portrays politics for voters' understanding of politics have prompted much academic disagreement. Television is not a neutral technology: its operation has implications (albeit of imprecise and contingent kinds) for American politics. Television fastens more easily on the actions (whether trivial or important) of an individual chief executive than it does, for example, on the deliberations of a congressional subcommittee taking evidence from expert witnesses on technical but substantively important questions of corporate tax law; the latter are rarely covered by television. Without a single figure, television would be hard-pressed to make sense of American politics. Whereas in the nineteenth century newspaper coverage of Congress exceeded that of the president, the focus is now on the White House, and presidents receive far more television coverage than do Congress or the Supreme Court.

The presidency and the media have a symbiotic but mutually parasitic relationship. Staff in the White House press office strive to control the president's dealings with the electronic and printed media to his (and sometimes their) advantage. This effort is constantly made (and has been made since Theodore Roosevelt first invited journalists into the White House under strict procedural rules), but is most obvious in time of war, where the incentive and opportunities for control are high and coincident. Yet, the press in general, and television in particular, also threaten presidents. Potentially, they may expose corruption and mischief, and enforce accountability. The relationship is rarely smooth, and usually deteriorates as a presidency ages and political problems grow. The development of the relationship between presidents and journalists has not been simple: presidents have not learned to exploit the medium more systematically to their advantage with the passing years, even though the quality of advice from specialist White House staff available to them has become infinitely more sophisticated. Reagan's ease before cameras and his deceptively relaxed exploitation of the medium during his first term in office inclined some observers rashly to conclude that television would henceforth be the ally of presidents and not, as had been the case under Johnson, Ford, Nixon and Carter, their foe. Former president Clinton showed remarkable ease before the camera. Though more formal in style than Clinton, President Obama also displays confidence and calm when surrounded by reporters and cameras.

The vice-presidency

The growth of government in the twentieth century, and the simultaneous focus of the printed and electronic media on the presidency, had left the vice-presidency little changed. Those who hold it still have no constitutional role other than to wait for the president's death, or to seek the succession when the Twenty-Second Amendment prevents an incumbent president from running for office for a third term (see Appendix 2). With four exceptions in the post-war period, Dick Cheney being the most recent and decisive example, all vice-presidents have led institutional lives of political frustration and, usually, of obscurity. Neither the Constitution nor custom grants the vice-president any responsibilities beyond that of presiding over the Senate. With few exceptions, that duty has proven to be trivial: vice-presidents usually prefer to leave the task to the president *pro tempore* and appear in the chamber only to break a tie vote or at the majority leadership's request to assist in procedural manoeuvres.

Few post-war vice-presidents have been able to make much of the office during tenure, whether in the guise of the president's deputy in the

Executive Branch, or as the Senate's president. In an attempt to clothe the institutionally naked, presidents have occasionally given vice-presidents either substantive tasks or party political duties. President Kennedy appointed Vice-President Johnson to the position of Chairman of the Space Council; President Nixon gave Vice-President Agnew the responsibility of maintaining political support for the administration among groups of conservative voters; President G. H. W. Bush named Vice-President Quayle the Chairman of the Competitiveness Council, in which role he strove to weaken the force of regulations issued by executive agencies under the authority of congressional statutes governing environmental protection and civil rights. President Clinton gave Vice-President Albert Gore responsibility for the National Performance Review – which was intended to help the federal government 'work better and cost less', and permit states greater influence on the execution of federal directives. President Barack Obama gave Vice-President Joseph R. Biden responsibility for the implementation of the $787 billion 2009 fiscal stimulus package (The American Recovery and Reinvestment Act). George W. Bush gave Vice-President Richard (Dick) Cheney the freedom to range across any area of policy, a freedom that he used with striking alacrity.

Selection of the vice-president

Although vice-presidents often have little to do, their selection as a presidential candidate's running-mate typically proceeds on the assumption that a ticket must have a 'balance' of geography and ideology, if not of gender and ethnicity. Hence, Adlai Stevenson, the quintessential northern liberal intellectual, balanced his candidacy in 1952 with that of the conservative southerner, Senator John Sparkman of Alabama. John Kennedy balanced the ticket in 1960 by selecting Lyndon Johnson, thereby ensuring that he would win at least both Massachusetts and Texas. By selecting Walter Mondale, Jimmy Carter chose a vice-presidential candidate who was northern, liberal and a distinguished Democratic US senator. Carter had none of these assets, weaknesses which were as apparent in government as on the campaign trail.

To his credit, Carter discerned Mondale's compensating qualities, and used them to the administration's advantage. In contrast to most of his predecessors in the White House, Carter regarded his vice-president as a colleague, rather than as a subordinate. Their staff organizations were effectively integrated, while Mondale had an office adjacent to the president's own in the West Wing of the White House and not in the East Wing, the remote part of the White House to which vice-presidents are usually assigned. Carter worked closely with his vice-president, drawing on his experience and advice in all major policy matters; he ordered that Mondale be party (without exception) to all of the president's national security briefings, and that he be fully conversant with nuclear decision-making procedures. Such openness was wholly unprecedented.

Succession to the presidency

Characteristically, Truman thought the vice-presidency as useful as a 'fifth teat on a cow'. One of his predecessors, John Nance Garner, Franklin D. Roosevelt's vice-president between 1933 and 1941, once declared that the office was 'not worth a bucket of warm spit'. However, while vice-presidents are often nothing, they may become everything. This is so most dramatically following a president's death: a mere fourteen weeks after being told of the existence of America's atomic weapons programme, Truman ordered the use of nuclear weapons against Japan. Less dramatically, it is the case with election to the highest office after having held the second highest. Since 1945, Vice-Presidents Harry Truman, Richard Nixon, Lyndon Johnson, Gerald Ford and George H. W. Bush have succeeded to the presidency: Truman and Johnson by the natural death and assassination, respectively, of Roosevelt and Kennedy; Nixon after a gap of eight years following the end of his vice-presidency under Eisenhower; Ford because of Nixon's enforced resignation; and Bush by election after Reagan's second term.

For much of the post-war period, the vice-presidency became the office most likely to assist presidential ambitions. Yet, the ascendance of the Washington insider weakened in the 1990s: President Clinton had been Governor of Arkansas, President George W. Bush Governor of Texas and President Obama was a one-term senator from Illinois. All three sought, with more or less plausibility, to exploit the age-old (and distinctively Washingtonian) game of presenting themselves as outsiders to the federal government that they so ardently wished to lead.

Prior to the ratification of the Twenty-Fifth Amendment to the constitution in 1967, a vacancy in the vice-presidency would not be filled until the following presidential election. Thus, until January 1965 (when he began the term to which he was elected in November 1964) Lyndon Johnson had no vice-president. Had Johnson himself died in the period between his accession to the presidency on Kennedy's assassination and his taking of the oath of office in January 1965, the presidency would have fallen to the holder of the office next in succession: the Speaker of the House of Representatives, as provided by statute under the authority of Article 2, Section 6 of the Constitution (see Appendix 1). The Twenty-Fifth Amendment stipulates that, in the event of a vacancy occurring in the vice-presidency following the death of the incumbent, or of his succession to the presidency itself, the new president shall nominate a new vice-president who takes office on majority votes of both Houses of Congress. This procedure was followed when Vice-President Agnew resigned his office in 1973. President Nixon nominated Gerald Ford to succeed him. Ford took the oath of office as president following Mr Nixon's resignation in August 1974. Ford's elevation itself caused a vacancy in the vice-presidency which was filled by the nomination and confirmation of Nelson Rockefeller, a former governor of New York. Between the time of Rockefeller's confirmation and the Democratic succession under Carter in January 1977, both the presidency and the vice-presidency were therefore held by people who had been elected to neither office.

Franklin D. Roosevelt, Harry Truman and the modern presidency

A clear break in the nature, possibilities and purposes of the office of the presidency came in March 1933, with Franklin D. Roosevelt's statement of purpose in his inaugural address. Until that point, the presidency usually lay at the heart of American government only in three exceptional circumstances: responses to foreign threats such as those presented by the British incursions in 1812 and by the European war in 1917–18; imperialist policies adopted towards Mexico in the mid-nineteenth century and, later, towards Spanish possessions in the Caribbean and Pacific; and the response to the threat of secession presented to the federal government by the attempted secession of southern states in the Civil War of 1861–65. In each instance, the Constitution's grant of power to the president under the 'Commander in Chief' clause accorded Presidents Madison, Polk, McKinley, Theodore Roosevelt, Wilson and Lincoln a uniquely powerful position within government.

Setting a national agenda

Emergency is still a sufficient condition for presidential domination, but is no longer necessary. Restrictive interpretations of executive power as defined by Article II of the Constitution are redundant. Economic collapse between 1929 and 1933 caused the attention of the nation's new mass electorate to focus on the institution of the presidency in its search for escape from misery. Only from the presidency was there a possibility that a new national agenda might be set, and a plausible hope of the sluggish and disordered responses of a fragmented Congress being overcome by sustained and coherent executive leadership. The constitutional foundation of presidential powers did not alter under the pressure of events. Yet, on an unchanged base, the processes of presidential politics, and especially of presidential–congressional relations, changed radically between the period from 1929–33 and that from 1933–37, between Herbert Hoover's single term and the first term of his successor, Franklin D. Roosevelt.

Herbert Hoover's failure to offer strategic leadership lay not in an intrinsic weakness of the office he held, but in his own lack of political imagination in the face of a collapse of asset markets and demand. Voters responded to the economic disaster over which he presided by electing his Democratic opponent, Franklin D. Roosevelt, to the White House. When Roosevelt took over in March 1933, he chose to attack the financial collapse and huge loss of output through direct federal intervention. In the short term, he proposed a package of emergency measures to Congress to arrest financial and banking collapse and later, during his first two terms, proposed measures that increased the direct role of government in the economy, acknowledged limited federal responsibilities for the welfare of Americans, regulated industry and finance, and provided for a new framework of labour law.

Roosevelt's three complete terms in office marked radical departures not only in the output of policy, but also in the organization of the Executive Branch, in the place of the presidency in the political life of the nation, in the presidency's relation to the other two branches, its relationship to the electorate and the parties, to the federal bureaucracy, and in relations between the federal and state governments. The federal government, which previously spent less than either state or local governments, had by the end of Roosevelt's second term spent almost twice as much.

Roosevelt's economic policies contributed to the salvation of American capitalism, and his foreign policies established the United States as a military and economic superpower. His reformulation of the role of the office he held was, however, imperative for the achievement of both. The change has been sustained and confirmed by all his successors, irrespective of their views on the proper size and role of government. Conservative or liberal, Republican or Democrat, presidents elected since Franklin D. Roosevelt have presided over a heavily-staffed presidency at the nominal head of a substantial federal bureaucracy. Harry Truman, Roosevelt's successor in the White House, willingly embraced an extension of the role of the federal government in the domestic economy and in welfare and education policy. For Truman, too, the role of Commander in Chief was one that carried with it inescapable burdens and responsibilities which most of his predecessors had known either in exceptional circumstances or not at all.

The United States as a world power

The United States's emergence from World War II in the unique condition among Western allies of economic strength, coupled to a novel (albeit short-lived) monopoly of nuclear weapons and overwhelming conventional military advantage, had immense significance for the presidency's conduct of foreign affairs. When America's engagement with the world was occasional, and its maintenance of large standing military forces the exceptional condition of wartime, rather than the constant experience of peace, the importance and prominence of the presidency fluctuated, too. America's spectacular escape from the depression of the 1930s, occasioned by the vast growth in the country's economic and military capacity during the war and the absorption of its production through domestic mass consumption after it, together with the interests attaching to its new status as the pre-eminent world power after 1945, made presidential activism obligatory in the sustenance of the first, and the discharge of the second.

Franklin D. Roosevelt and Harry Truman thus altered permanently the place of the presidency in the American political system. Passivity would never again be an option for holders of the office. Roosevelt's successors could not plausibly claim that the management of the economy was not their responsibility; neither was it in their electoral interests to do so. Despite the still comparatively scant provision of income support and welfare in America, and the widespread antipathy to welfare dependence, they also found it politically impossible to claim that the welfare of American citizens unable to provide for themselves and their dependents in a market economy was none of their concern. Much as Ronald Reagan railed against 'big government' on the hustings, neither a reduction in the size of the presidency nor the complete removal of the welfare safety net was on his agenda.

The obligation to bargain

The fundamental structural distinctiveness of the federal government – separation of powers and federalism – render effective presidential leadership in domestic politics rare. Partisan and ideological divisions, especially when aligned, make it rarer still. Policy change is difficult to effect in America, even for powerful presidents in propitious circumstances. With the loss of American hegemony in the international system since the mid-1960s, the task has become harder still. The United States's mass of treaty obligations, and military, trading, and financial ties with other nations in a global order which it no longer dominates, makes presidents' satisfaction of voters' expectations effectively impossible to realize, not least because such expectations often conflict. Presidents are more often tethered than they are free.

Political skill is indubitably a factor in the success that presidents have in asserting leadership, whether of a kind susceptible to quantification (as in the proportion of bills that have been passed by Congress proposed by presidents), or not (as in the revival of national morale or purpose). Lyndon Johnson's creative political imagination and sense of purpose provides a remarkable instance of the first kind; Dwight Eisenhower's and Ronald Reagan's strategic skills of the second; and Franklin D. Roosevelt's of both. Since presidents can exercise neither strategic nor persuasive leadership by relying on their limited resources of authority, much depends on the skill with which a president is able to bring political influence and persuasion to bear.

The governing problem for presidents is therefore the following: the presidency is an office whose occupants are expected to deliver successful economic, foreign, defence, environmental and educational policy, and to provide the country with a vision and purpose. 'Political leadership' in its strategic sense in the variegated country that is the US can come from no one but the president, since he and he alone has a national constituency, the sole national electoral legitimacy that flows from it, and both the incentive and the opportunity to act. Other politicians exercise great power within their cities, states, rural counties, or congressional committees but, in every case, their jurisdictions are limited. The president's jurisdiction is, by contrast, exclusively national and nationally exclusive.

Yet, the design of federal institutions acts as a forbiddingly high barrier to the president exercising that leadership. The fit between public expectation and constitutional provision is poor. Though potentially harmful to the office and the system of which it is the central part, that condition is, nonetheless, difficult to rectify, short of radical alteration to the structure and rules of government, which are even more difficult to effect. Such changes are improbable, as both constitutional barriers and the evidence of many failed past attempts suggest.

Faced with the problems created by the separation of powers and the appearance – if not the reality – of leadership, presidents are obliged to attempt to make the system work for them. Modern incumbents have employed various institutional devices to make presidential government more than the fleeting outcome of confluential political advantages, the norm rather than the exception. More than seventy years after Roosevelt recognized the need for Congress to create a more extensive, institution-alized presidency in order to address continuing economic and political problems, the dilemma has not been solved: within the framework of the separation of powers and the weak fabric of political parties in America, it cannot be. It has, nonetheless, been mitigated to the extent that able presidents may maximize their influence so as to exploit passing opportunities to their own advantage, and yet do so without infringing constitutional provision.

A president's greatest political asset is that the executive power in the United States is not collective, but singular. All presidents attempt to exploit this compelling singularity in their bargaining with allies and opponents among elected politicians in Congress, unelected politicians in the departments and agencies of the Executive Branch, and in their contact with members of interest groups and the general public. A member of Congress is one of a body of 435, a senator of one hundred, a governor of fifty, a president of one. A national constituency is theirs alone, and the solitariness of the Oval Office an unmatched opportunity. The president has competitors everywhere but no peer. That is his nagging governing problem, and tantalizing political opportunity.

The presidency and the executive branch

The Cabinet

The growth of government to meet burgeoning domestic needs and responsibilities during the 1930s, together with foreign and defence responsibilities during the 1940s, required the development of a federal bureaucracy which, in turn, has presented presidents with political competition from unelected officials on the one hand, and unelected Cabinet secretaries (the heads of the executive departments) on the other.

Presidents' political skills of persuasion and negotiation are as severely tested in their management of relations with the Executive Branch as they are with Congress. All presidents face the predicament of how to prevail against bureaucrats whose priorities may differ from their own and who (rationally) have political loyalties to members of Congress, to congressional staff, to clients and interest groups, and legal obligations in respect of the programmes they administer (see Chapter 8). Bureaucrats have several loyalties, for reasons of law and politics: the Executive Branch is not a Weberian hierarchy led by the president. Such constitutional complexity has not diminished the demands of chief executives for speedier and simpler responses from the departments of government nominally beneath them, but has made the straightforward assuaging of their demands improbable.

Cabinet secretaries, the political heads of executive departments, are nominally the president's subordinates, rather than colleagues. Unlike in Britain, members of the president's Cabinet have no prospect of supplanting the chairman of the Cabinet by political manoeuvre or *coup d'état* between elections; their only means of doing so is through the public quadrennial processes of nomination and election. Nonetheless,

Cabinet secretaries have conflicting priorities. For them, publicly advancing the president's cause might well be politically necessary in the period immediately following confirmation in office, but is usually overcome in the longer term by each secretary's need to attend to the priorities and preferences of the department and its clients. As we show in Chapter 8, Cabinet secretaries serve two masters: the president, who formally is their immediate superior, and congressional committees that create and fund the departments and agencies of the federal bureaucracy and to which Cabinet secretaries must regularly report and to which they are accountable for the implementation of programmes.

The president's Cabinet is not an executive body: it has neither authority nor power to decide government policy. None of its members are independently elected. Of all the politicians who sit around the table in the White House Cabinet Room, only the president has an electoral base. The Constitution in Article II refers to 'the principal Officer in each of the executive Departments', but only in the context of the president's power to 'require the Opinion, in writing' of such officers (see Appendix 1). The Constitution makes no mention of a Cabinet. Cabinet secretaries therefore not only pose no threat to the president's position between presidential elections, but also lack the legitimacy which flows from electoral support. Presidents serve not for so long as they can command the confidence of party colleagues, but (short of death, resignation, or impeachment followed by conviction) for the four years specified by the Constitution.

The Constitution prohibits dual membership of executive and legislature with the (intended) result that American Cabinet secretaries have no roots in Congress. Not only does the Constitution thereby deny them the opportunity to manoeuvre for the presidency, but most lack the motive and will to seek it. To the extent that most withhold from pursuing the chief executive's job, they do not constantly remind the president of his political mortality. Many American Cabinet secretaries come from law firms, corporations, banks, research institutes and universities, to which they return on leaving the department or agency they run temporarily: moving in and out of government is the norm, rather than the exception, in American government. Others join the Cabinet from Congress, from which they must resign before taking office, and to which most do not later attempt to return.

Whether by virtue of their own stature, or because of the importance of the particular offices they hold, individual Cabinet members in the United States are nonetheless frequently significant political figures (see Exhibit 5.3). The Departments of State and the Treasury comprise the core of America's federal bureaucracy; unsurprisingly, most who have led them were already prominent in public life before becoming Secretary of State or the Treasury. Most have confirmed, and some have enhanced, their standing while in the post. Since the war, Secretaries of State George Marshall, John Foster Dulles, Henry Kissinger, George Schultz and James Baker ranked second to the presidents in whose Cabinets they served, not just in protocol, but also in the influence they enjoyed over the administration's foreign policies. All had known Washington's byways, congressional structures and processes, and the national security and foreign policy-making communities well before they took the post, and were consequently advantaged in it. Several secretaries of the Treasury have been no less influential in their own sphere of finance and macroeconomic policy. As Secretary of Defense, Robert McNamara did as much as the two presidents under whom he served to set and sustain United States policy in Vietnam; in the same office, Caspar Weinberger was the architect of American rearmament between 1981 and 1987. Donald Rumsfeld, who had been Secretary of Defense to President Gerald Ford between 1975 and 1977, returned to the Pentagon under George W. Bush from 2001 to 2005 where, frequently in alliance with Vice-President Dick Cheney, he marginalized the State Department and its distinguished Secretary Colin Powell. President George W. Bush's choice of wars and conduct of them was powerfully shaped by Cheney and Rumsfeld.

By apportioning Cabinet posts carefully, presidents can accomplish five ends:

- *Reward important supporters*, as all presidents frequently do, and as George Herbert Walker Bush did with his appointment of James Baker as Secretary of State.
- Build support among the *uncommitted* or *former opponents*, as Nixon tried to do with his offer of the post of Secretary of Defense to the Democratic Senator, Henry Jackson; as former President Bill Clinton succeeded in doing by appointing William Cohen as Secretary of Defense; and as President Obama did by appointing Hillary Rodham Clinton as Secretary of State.
- Build *links with Congress*, as Clinton tried to do by appointing Les Aspin to be Secretary of Defense in 1993, and Daniel Glickman to be Secretary of Agriculture in 1997; as George W. Bush did in choosing Dick Cheney for the position of Vice-President; and as President Barack Obama did by selecting Joe Biden, a Senator with thirty-six years of service, for the vice-presidency.
- Strengthen links with *key racial groups*, and with *women*, as all modern presidents do by appointing at least one African-American and one woman. In his first term, President Clinton appointed an Hispanic (Henry Cisneros, the former Mayor of San Antonio) to be Secretary of Housing and Urban Development, two African-Americans (Jesse Brown and Ron Brown) to be Secretaries of

Veterans Affairs and of the Department of Commerce, respectively, and five women (Hazel O'Leary, Donna Shalala, Madeleine Albright, Carol Browner and Janet Reno) to be Secretaries of Energy, Health and Human Services, Ambassador to the United Nations, EPA Director and Attorney-General, respectively). In his second term, Clinton confirmed his commitment to promoting women by naming Madeleine Albright as Secretary of State; she was the first woman appointed to the post. George W. Bush appointed Condoleeza Rice, an African-American woman, first to the post of National Security Advisor and then to the post of Secretary of State that Colin Powell, an African-American four-star Army General, had previously occupied. Rice was the second woman to serve as Secretary of State and the first to serve as National Security Advisor. President Obama, the first African-American president, has a diverse Cabinet. By asking Robert M. Gates to remain in post as Secretary of Defense, President Obama also created a degree of bipartisanship, since Gates had first been appointed to the post by Republican President George W. Bush.

- Draw into the inner counsels of the Executive Branch those whom a president *trusts*: as Kennedy did with the appointment of his brother, Robert, to the post of Attorney-General in 1961; as Nixon did by his appointment of John Connally to be Secretary of the Treasury in 1971; and as George W. Bush did with the appointments of Rumsfeld and Cheney, whom he trusted as loyal and experienced Washington insiders. The extent to which these four appointments had their intended effects is a matter of continuing debate.

Although the Cabinet has political utility for presidents in its composition, it has much less in governing. Some presidents (such as Kennedy) have virtually ignored it; others (such as Eisenhower) have found it useful; some (such as Johnson) have used it merely as a device to act out a prepared ritual of purported consultation; one (Reagan) had so tenuous a connection with some of the Cabinet's members that he allegedly forgot the name of his Secretary of Housing and Urban Development. In their first years in office, Bill Clinton held six Cabinet meetings, Ronald Reagan thirty-six and George W. Bush nine. Few Cabinet officers have found Cabinet meetings useful to them. Even fewer presidents have done so.

The organization of the Executive Branch, and the political difficulties which its size, complexity and power present for presidents, are among the political consequences of Franklin D. Roosevelt's radical expansion of the role of the federal government. To play the expanded role required of chief executive following the collapse of the United States' economy under President Hoover's administration, Roosevelt required the resources of an expanded Executive Branch. New programmes spawned new departments and new agencies (authorized by Congress) to run

Exhibit 5.3 President Obama's Cabinet, March 2013 (prior occupation in parentheses)

In order of succession to the Presidency		*Prior occupation*
Vice-President of the United States	Joseph R. Biden	US Senator
Secretary of State	John Kerry	US Senator
Secretary of the Treasury	Jack Lew	Head of Office of Management and Budget
Secretary of Defense	Chuck Hagel	US Senator
Department of Justice Attorney General	Eric H. Holder, Jr.	Deputy Attorney General to President Clinton, 1997–01; Lawyer
Secretary of the Interior	Sally Jewell	Company president
Department of Agriculture Secretary	Thomas J. Vilsack	Governor of Iowa
Secretary of Commerce	Penny Pritzker	Business executive
Secretary of Labor	Thomas Perez	Assistant Attorney General, Department of Justice
Secretary of Health and Human Services	Kathleen Sebelius	Governor of Kansas
Secretary of Housing and Urban Development	Shaun L.S. Donovan	Architect/Academic/ Government Official (Housing) New York State

➔

particular programmes (authorized and appropriated by Congress) within them. By his second term, he appreciated the need for the services of an expanded staff organization responsible exclusively to him.

The executive office of the president

Presidents have had the support of staff since 1789. However, until the middle of the nineteenth century, chief executives were expected to pay for them out of their own overall allowance. Congress first specifically appropriated funds for staff (a private secretary, a steward and a messenger) only during Buchanan's presidency in 1857. Throughout the nineteenth century, Congress provided increasing support for staff assistants

→

In order of succession to the Presidency		Prior occupation
Secretary of Transportation	Anthony Foxx	Former Mayor of Charlotte, North Carolina
Secretary of Energy	Ernest Moniz	MIT Physicist
Secretary of Education	Anne Duncan	CEO of Chicago Public Schools
Secretary of Veterans Affairs	Eric K. Shinseki	Four-star Army General
Secretary of Department of Homeland Security	Janet A. Napolitano	Governor of Arizona

The following positions have the status of Cabinet-rank:

White House Chief of Staff	Denis McDonough	Deputy National Security Advisor
Administrator of the Environmental Protection Agency	Gina McCarthy	EPA official
Office of Management and Budget Director	Sylvia Mathews Burwell	President, Walmart Foundation
United States Trade Representative	Michael Froman	Assistant to the President
United States Ambassador to the United Nations	Ambassador Samantha Power	National Security Council Staff member
Chairman of the Council of Economic Advisers	Alan B. Kreuger	Academic

to the president although, as late as 1900, the total number of clerical and administrative staff in the White House was just thirteen. President Hoover benefited from congressional legislation which increased the complement of secretaries to the president from one to three, permitting the president for the first time to allocate particular tasks to his senior staff. The Executive Office of the President (EOP) was formally established by the Reorganization Act passed by Congress in 1939. The Act sprang indirectly from the work of the President's Committee on Administrative Management, established in March 1936, and chaired by Louis Brownlow, a distinguished scholar of public administration. Brownlow and his colleagues argued, in a phrase that has been taken to characterize their approach: 'The president needs help.'

In support of this claim, the Committee recommended the establishment of the EOP as an overarching organization of presidential staff to support the presidency as an institution, and the virtually autonomous creation within the EOP of a White House Office for the president's closest personal staff.

As its recommendation that such a White House Office be staffed by just six executive assistants showed, the intention was not to create a parallel bureaucracy (although that has been the consequence). Each member of the staff should, they argued, in phrases which entertained Roosevelt and the White House press corps to which he revealed them, 'be possessed of high competence, great physical vigor, and a passion for anonymity'. Roosevelt was especially concerned with the place of the new White House Office within the EOP. At the press conference to publicize the Committee's Report, he justified its radical proposals by emphasizing the responsibility carried by the president for the Executive Branch's general management, and the growth of that responsibility since 1933. (It entered a further phase of expansion following Japan's attack on Pearl Harbor on 7 December 1941, and Germany's declaration of war on the United States four days later.) Rejected by Congress in 1937, the president's proposals, modified slightly to take account of opposition from within the Executive Branch and from Congress, were sent again to Capitol Hill in 1939, where they were this time quickly passed into law.

In addition to the Reorganization Act's substantive importance for the presidency in making available to the president resources appropriate for him to make effective his nominal leadership of the Executive Branch, the Act provided for a legislative veto. The legislative veto allows for the delegation (from Congress) of rule or decision-making authority to the presidency or an executive agency by which rules may be issued and decisions made subject to Congress retaining the right to veto them and thereby prevent their being applied. The laws made by Congress are put into effect by the federal bureaucracy – which has a great deal of latitude in the manner in which it makes regulations (administrative law) based on the authorizing legislation created by Congress. If Congress does not concur with the manner in which administrative law is created, then it may use the legislative veto.

The legislative veto was, and remains, a procedure by which the huge task of issuing detailed administrative regulations might be delegated to Executive Branch officials subject to Congress retaining the right to prevent their being issued should it so decide. The Reorganization Act specifically empowered the president to submit reorganization plans to Congress which, unless both houses of Congress vetoed them, would then become law. President Roosevelt submitted such a proposal ('Plan 1') for the establishment of the EOP by incorporating within it the White House Office and the Bureau of the Budget (BOB).

The executive office is now much more complex than at its inception, having had staff agencies added to it under the reorganization authority delegated to the president by Congress, and other units established by separate Acts of Congress. The present size, shape and composition of the EOP are the product of reorganization plans submitted to successive Congresses by successive presidents, and of Acts of Congress establishing staff agencies such as the Council of Economic Advisers (CEA), and the National Security Council (NSC) within it. However, the genesis of the contemporary White House Office, as of the EOP as a whole, lies in the Reorganization Act of 1939.

The presidency expanded, therefore, because of the general growth of the Executive Branch between 1933 and 1955; and it has continued to grow in later years despite the much slower growth in federal civilian personnel. As programmes within the Executive Branch proliferated, so the agencies that ran them developed powerful political links with Congress (which authorized and reauthorized their existence and the programmes they implemented, and regularly appropriated funds for their continuation) and with the congressional committees that oversaw their operation. Shrewd presidents appreciate that their political direction and control of the Executive Branch are necessarily limited. Accordingly, they must rely heavily on the additional, personal governing resources that the EOP affords them in the form of substantial staff assistance within the executive office (see Exhibit 5.4). The provision of specialized staff working on the president's behalf offered the possibility that nominal presidential authority over subordinate but influential bureaucrats might be made more effective by being devolved to his personal senior staff. Executive office staff are, therefore, a means by which a president indirectly extends his persuasive leadership capacity through intervention in policy implementation, particularly by ensuring that his priorities are reflected to the fullest degree possible in decisions, rules and regulations issued by executive agencies.

The White House Office

Although formally a part of it, the White House Office is effectively separate from the rest of the EOP. Unlike the three members of the Council of Economic Advisers, or the Director of the Office of Management and Budget, the responsibilities of White House staff, numbering approximately 400, are defined by the president, rather than specified in law; they are not subject to confirmation by Congress. They are the president's most intimate advisers, to hire and fire as he sees fit, to organize as he wishes, to undertake the tasks he sets, and responsible to the president alone.

Louis Brownlow had hoped that the White House staff would act with restraint, confining themselves to strictly administrative tasks, and

Exhibit 5.4 Expansion of the Executive Office of the President

Between its establishment in 1939 and the end of Eisenhower's presidency in 1960, the Executive Office of the President (EOP) grew rapidly. A rough measurement of the extent of the increase in staff employed in the presidential branch can be made by noting its physical expansion into buildings in and around the White House. The old Navy building into which the Bureau of the Budget (BOB) moved in 1939 was, by Eisenhower's presidency in the 1950s, insufficiently large to house all the staff members of the EOP and, at the time of writing, is one of three buildings within which EOP staff work. During World War I, it had housed the three Executive Departments of State, War and the Navy. In 2011, 1,888 people were officially listed as working in the EOP and the total budget for the year was $739,787,000 (EOP Fiscal Budget Submission to Congress 2011–12).

Roosevelt's object in the late 1930s was, therefore, similar to that of each of his successors: how to make presidential leadership over the Executive Branch effective; how to be Chief Executive in fact, as well as in the theory of constitutional law. Roosevelt required then, as all presidents have required since, direct assistance from people dependent on him personally, rather than on superiors in departments or clients outside them. For Roosevelt, the problem was novel; for his successors, it has been a familiar feature of the difficulties of presidential governance. A president neither can, nor should, personally scrutinize the work of departments on all major matters of government policy. Neither can he alone ensure that Cabinet secretaries resist the temptation, in John Ehrlichman's words, to 'marry the natives' by straying from his policy and advancing their own. An array of senior staff might be able to assist him.

The modern Executive Branch is therefore divided: there is a departmental component (the departments, specialist agencies and regulatory

➜

refraining from interposing themselves between the president and his Cabinet. However, the division between administration and politics does not, in practice, exist. All administrations since the implementation of Executive Order 8248 in 1939 have been coordinated under the president's direction by a clutch of senior staff whose competitive struggles and activities hold a fascination for Washington's political classes, reporters included. Except under President Nixon, their role has not been to assume executive roles by displacing heads of departments and agencies, but to build unity by enforcing the president's perspective over semi-autonomous departments and agencies and a fully autonomous

➡

organizations of the federal bureaucracy) and a presidential component consisting of the EOP which is, in turn, subdivided.

The following ten units form the institutional presidency (the EOP): the White House Office (WHO), which is led by the President's Chief of Staff; the Council of Economic Advisers (CEA); the Council on Environmental Quality (CEQ); the National Security Staff (NSS); the Office of Administration (OA); the Office of Management and Budget (OMB); the Office of National Drug Control Policy (NDCP); the Office of Science and Technology (OSTP); the Office of the United States Trade Representative (USTR); the office of the Vice-President (VP). In addition to these units, the Executive Residence staff is also formally part of the EOP but has no political role.

All EOP staff agencies have their importance for government, although to differing extents and in differing ways. The significance of the Council of Economic Advisers, created by the (Keynesian) 1946 Employment Act, results from the importance of its primary task of providing economic advice to the president. President Clinton established the National Economic Council (NEC) by Executive order in 1993. The NEC resides within the White House Office (nestled within the Office of Policy Development), as does the equally powerful Domestic Policy Council (DPC), which was created when Clinton split the Office of Policy Development into the DPC and the National Economic Council (NEC) in 1993.

The place in foreign policy-making of the National Security Council, created by the National Security Act of 1947, which functions as the highest source of advice to the president on domestic and foreign questions affecting the nation's security, is examined in Chapter 11. Two other key EOP staff agencies are examined here: the White House Office, comprising the personal staff organization immediately around the president himself, and the Office of Management and Budget, the Executive Branch's organization with primary responsibility for the formulation of the president's budget policy.

Congress. White House staff have the task of advising the president when he requests it, but more usually of assessing the advice of others, whether in Congress or in the departments (see Exhibit 5.5). In their covering papers to the president, staff review the recommendations of Cabinet officers. Preferred courses of action by, for example, the Secretary of the Treasury regarding tax policy is assessed by staff (including, but not confined to, those in the CEA) prior to the president reviewing options and deciding between them. This flow of activity is heavy, constant and runs in both directions between the White House and the agencies.

The organization of the White House Office has varied over time, between presidents, and within presidencies, as presidents become discontented with existing arrangements. Some, such as Eisenhower, have employed a broadly hierarchical form with a Chief of Staff in charge to whom all papers routed to the president are directed in the first instance. Others, such as Roosevelt and Kennedy, have preferred a more fluid system, in which several senior staff have direct access to the president by paper and in person. President Reagan operated in his first term with a triumvirate of senior staff but, following the Iran-Contra scandal (also known as *Irangate* and which exploded on the media networks in November of 1986), with just a Chief of Staff of unusual distinction and standing in Howard Baker, Majority Leader of the Senate between 1981 and 1984.

Reagan's successor in the Oval Office, President George H. W. Bush, was criticized by many for what was seen as the excessive power wielded by his surprise choice for the job of Chief of Staff, former Governor of New Hampshire, John Sununu, who served from 1989–1992. Clinton, absorbed and in command of the fine detail of all aspects of policy and neither accustomed to nor at ease in delegating, chose his old school friend Thomas 'Mack' McLarty as his first Chief of Staff. However, McLarty stayed in post for only one year, having failed to establish an effective management structure within the White House. His successor, Leon Panetta, moved from his post as Director of OMB to become Chief of Staff. He, too, struggled to create a staff structure that was both effective and efficient.

George W. Bush's first Chief of Staff, Andrew Card, exercised a more traditional structure, with the intention of ensuring that Cabinet secretaries would gain access to the president only through him. Card's arrangement did not, however, limit Vice-President Cheney's access to President Bush. President Obama's first Chief of Staff, Rahm Emanuel (2009–10) acquired a dual reputation not only as an effective manager, but also as a divisive figure who did not work to foster relationships with Republicans on Capitol Hill.

President Kennedy used the metaphor of 'a wheel and a series of spokes' in characterizing the organization of his White House Office, with himself at the hub. However, the White House is not a smoothly-ordered operation whose processes can be captured in one of several geometric forms; only during Eisenhower's presidency with Sherman Adams's tenure as Chief of Staff did it approach such clarity. Attempts by staff to establish the organization of the White House formally usually fail. Many presidents, especially self-confident ones, find that fluid staff arrangements best suit their needs. Sometimes such fluidity assists a president's effectiveness; sometimes it does not. Lyndon Johnson's use of a mostly very able staff was not always ideally calibrated for his purposes (see Exhibit 5.5).

Exhibit 5.5 The Power of White House Staff

The late Harry McPherson, one of the most distinguished of all senior White House staff in the post-war period, was Special Counsel to Lyndon Johnson (a title that gave him some specific tasks, but a more important, general remit). In his book, much the best and most perceptive of all presidential staff memoirs, he has emphasized the entirely conditional nature of the power of senior White House staff, and contrasted its nature with the place of the vice-president:

> In every case, the special counsel or assistant carried with him the contingent authority of the President. He needed that authority to accomplish anything at all, as the law gave him none of his own. And it was necessarily contingent; the President had to be free to repudiate his assistants' views and apparent commitments. The counsel-assistant's position was almost exactly opposite that of the Vice-President. The Vice-President was powerless, but he was only a moment away from holding enormous power; the special assistant had power, which might be withdrawn just as suddenly. Working for Lyndon Johnson, an assistant did not easily forget that he carried his authority on sufferance.

Source: McPherson (1972: 284–5).

Truman's Counsel, Clark Clifford; Eisenhower's Chief of Staff, Sherman Adams; Kennedy's Counsel, Ted Sorensen; Johnson's two *de facto* Chiefs of Staff, Bill Moyers and Joe Califano; and, most notoriously of all, Richard Nixon's Bob Haldeman and John Ehrlichman, all did as much to shape the content, style and perceptions of the modern presidency as the most senior members of post-war Cabinets have done to shape policy. To have worked in the service of the president of the United States does no harm to one's *curriculum vitae*. On leaving the White House, many have proceeded to lucrative careers in lobbying and the law (often indistinguishable activities in Washington), business, or journalism. Many have written of their experiences in presidential service. Some, especially in the Nixon and Reagan administrations, have, after leaving the White House, spent time in federal courtrooms and jails, and later writing exculpatory memoirs.

Loyalty to the president is a prerequisite for effectiveness in his service; without it, staff members have no value to him. Loyalty is invariably demonstrated by staff having worked for the president in his election campaigns, or in earlier institutional incarnations. Hence, journalists' reference to President Kennedy's staff as 'the Irish Mafia' and to President Carter's as 'the Georgia Mafia'. Most of Kennedy's staff had served him in his campaigns for the House, Senate, or presidency, and many of President Carter's staff had worked for him when he was Governor of Georgia. Of President Reagan's three senior staff in his first term, two (Meese and Deaver) had served him during his tenure as Governor of California. The third was a remarkable exception to the general rule, in that James Baker had run the presidential primary election campaigns of Reagan's Republican Party opponents in both 1976 and 1980: Gerald Ford and George H. W. Bush. The latter followed the usual pattern for similar reasons. His senior White House advisers were those whose political judgement and loyalty to him he had cause to trust by reason of their having demonstrated both qualities during his long career in federal government, and those whose advice and organizational abilities had been apparent during the primary and general election campaigns of 1988. Yet, appointing those whom the president trusts is not always a strategy for success. Clinton's appointment of Mack McLarty shows that loyalty cannot compensate for inexperience (or ineffectiveness), but President Obama's appointment of Rahm Emanuel as Chief of Staff, despite his earlier support for Hillary Rodham Clinton in the 2008 Democratic primary campaign, suggests that effectiveness may be more important than loyalty.

Trust between president and staff is a necessary, but insufficient, condition for the creation of a successful presidency. However, it can hide neither incompetence and inexperience, (as President Carter learned to his cost) nor criminality (as President Nixon learned). Loyalty is a quality most reliably demonstrated in the fire of an election campaign, but experience of the latter is not the ideal apprenticeship for assisting a president in the formidably demanding task of leading America's government. President Carter's staff proved themselves adept at exploiting the new rules of the Democratic primaries and the new technologies of campaigning in 1976. They had less success in assisting their president to circumvent bureaucratic and congressional barriers in Washington. To no individual has this point applied with greater force than to Hamilton Jordan who, at the tender age of thirty-four and with no experience in government before 1977, was appointed as White House Chief of Staff by President Carter following the (predictably disastrous) dismissal of four senior Cabinet secretaries and the centralization of power in the White House in 1979.

As loyalty and trust are the first requirement for staff, physical stamina, astute political judgement and high intellect are the others. Stamina is necessary to survive the punishingly long hours which the difficulty and volume of their work require of senior staff. No senior staff member can expect respite or relaxation during her or his period in the White House. They are never off duty. As McPherson (1972: 123), thinking of Johnson, has observed: 'Every leader bent on great enterprises consumes his staff as fuel'. Staff who lack political judgement are a liability to the president (as Hamilton Jordan was to Carter through his insensitivity to congressional prerogatives). Powerful intellect is essential since, without it, mastering fast streams of politically complicated and connected policy problems is impossible. The finest White House staff combine all four characteristics, serving their presidents with candour and loyalty, over eighteen-hour days for six (and often seven) days a week, clarifying policy and political options for the president in briefing papers where they distil conflicting opinions from numerous agencies across governments within and outside Washington.

EOP – Cabinet rivalries

Although several presidents have begun their administrations as Jimmy Carter did, by declaring their intention to rely on their Cabinets for the making of policy, none have found it a satisfactory instrument for presidential decision-making. All modern presidents, Carter included, have found irresistible the political attractions of using staff in the EOP to centralize policy-making in the White House. Some, such as George H. W. Bush, deliberately created in the EOP new units such as the Office of Drug Control Policy to administer new programmes and so to increase presidential control over them, lessening the chance of their being undermined by established departments. Both Kennedy and Johnson relied heavily on the Council of Economic Advisers, appreciating it as an intellectual and political counterweight to the established (and invariably more conservative) advice of the Treasury, just across the street from the East Wing of the White House.

Others, such as Nixon, have used the National Security Adviser not merely as their primary source of foreign policy advice, but also as an executive and personal ambassador, thereby not just diminishing significantly the influence and standing of the Secretary of State, but also imperilling the dispassionate analytical clarity essential in a national security adviser.

The federal bureaucracy

President Nixon believed, not without justification, that there was intense opposition to his domestic and foreign policies within the federal bureaucracy, as well as from partisan opposition in both Houses of Congress. He accordingly sought to centralize power within the White House, and did so to a greater extent than any of those who preceded or have followed him in the Oval Office. The frustration for presidents in dealing (as they must) with the federal bureaucracy is that their control over federal bureaucrats is limited. Civil servants always have, and the president's political appointees in the agencies quickly acquire, political loyalties to clients in the private sector, to lobbyists, to interest groups and (crucially) to the members and staff of congressional committees and subcommittees that qualify their loyalty to the president of the day. Under these circumstances, presidents are liable to discover that their policies (and even their instructions) are modified, delayed, or simply ignored by bureaucrats who have both the political incentive (protecting their jobs and their clients' interests by defending the programmes they administer) and the means (by allying themselves with powerful coalitions of congressional and private interests) to resist the president.

The danger for presidents in employing a large White House staff to address the problems of bureaucratic resistance and of balkanized administration is that they thereby run the risk of isolating and misleading him. Whereas agency bureaucrats invariably obstruct, White House staff help. Where bureaucrats may delay, White House staff comply. This may delude presidents into supposing that their instructions are being carried out. In fact (since they have no administrative machine below them to implement decisions), staff can merely relay such instructions, and impress on bureaucrats the importance of compliance, and attempt to ensure that the president's wishes have been carried out to the extent that congressional statute and politics grant him such autonomy.

There is a fundamental problem here that often surprises foreign observers, as it also frustrates presidents: the president does not control the Executive Branch. Neither does the degree of presidential control grow with an increase in the number of staff. At the end of Carter's presidency, Zbigniew Brzezinski, the National Security Adviser, had more personal staff than did the Secretary of Defense, while the Special Assistant for international trade negotiations had a larger personal staff than the Secretary of Commerce, and the Special Assistant for wage and price stability a larger staff than the Secretary of the Treasury (Lowi, 1985: 142). Indeed, Carter's presidency was marked as much as any modern administration by tensions between White House staff and departmental heads.

Those whom the president does control – his immediate staff – are not, and cannot be, executives. This rule does not apply with comparable force to the institutionalized part of the Executive Office such as the Special Trade Negotiator. Yet, attempts by the National Security Adviser and his staff to seize executive authority in circumvention of the Departments of State and Defense have often had damaging consequences for the coherence of policy and for the president's political standing. In the most extreme circumstances, members of the president's National Security staff have attempted to execute policy in defiance of explicit congressional prohibitions, as the examples of Admiral Poindexter and Colonel Oliver North between 1986 and 1988 show.

Conversely, as George W. Bush's two terms show, the coordination of foreign policy is damaged when the National Security Adviser, the Secretary of State and the Secretary of Defense (usually with the support of the vice-president) require the president to adjudicate when policy battles are waged.

White House staff are necessary, but insufficient, for making effective presidential leadership. Like the president for whom they work, they are, in practice, obliged to work with an Executive Branch in which power is scattered and divided, where loyalties run to the many agencies in the Executive Departments, to Congress and to private sector clients, as well as to the president (and often before they run to him). It is, moreover, a system in which bureaucrats are party to other political alliances which grant them substantial autonomy from the Executive Branch's one elected member. Citing presidential wishes enhances the staff's prospects of success, but provides no guarantee of it.

The Bureau of the Budget/Office of Management and Budget

No chief executive has any prospect of political leadership without specialist staff to ensure that his fiscal preferences are adhered to throughout the federal government, and that the financial implications of new legislative proposals are thoroughly examined to ensure that they fit his overall spending policies and do not subvert them.

The significance of political relations between the presidency and Cabinet secretaries arises once again here because of their fiscal implications: the practical political independence of Cabinet secretaries made absolutely necessary the establishment and retention by presidents of a degree of fiscal control. Roosevelt's exercise of strategic leadership depended on his being able to impose fiscal policy choices. Had he permitted departments and agencies within the Executive Branch to make their own annual budget requests to Congress, he would have lost all influence over government spending, and hence over policy priorities. All budgets reveal political preferences: accordingly, budget requests by Executive Departments to Congress reveal the preferences and priorities of the government of the United States. Accordingly, it is essential that the president himself should intervene before budget requests are made in order to ensure that they are fiscally coherent, and that they reflect accurately the priorities he wishes to set for the Executive Branch. The president and his staff will have frequently to intervene after submission of the budget to ensure that his priorities and choices are sustained during their consideration by Congress. Such persuasive leadership through negotiation is essential to the achievement of strategic success. But the huge budget request that is sent to Capitol Hill in January of every year must be the president's aggregated and distinctive choice, not the sum of

> ### Exhibit 5.6 Establishment of the Bureau of the Budget (1939)
>
> The President's Executive Order 8248 of 1939 establishing the Bureau of the Budget in the EOP provided the Bureau with authority to perform certain tasks, the four most important of which were:
>
> - To assist the president with the preparation of the budget and the formulation of the government's fiscal policy.
> - To supervize the budget's administration.
> - To promote efficient administration throughout government.
> - To clear and coordinate legislative proposals made by departments and agencies, and to advise the president of their significance for his overall budgetary policies.

departmental aspirations. In this way, the Bureau of the Budget enhanced the president's influence over the Executive Branch, and provided a coherent baseline from which Congress's Appropriations Committees could work in making their judgements of the funds to be spent on programmes within each executive department and agency.

The Bureau's detachment and expertise provided the foundation for its dominance of fiscal and legislative clearance, and the coordination, refinement and improvement of the Executive Branch's administration. If the disparate elements of the Executive Branch were to be drawn together in the causes of professionalism and efficiency, and the asset of institutional memory to be retained, politicization had to be eschewed. Composed mainly of politically intelligent but non-partisan career civil servants with no programmes or clients to defend, the Bureau had been ideally placed to serve the presidency. Until Richard Nixon's administration, it did so. In 1970, Nixon reorganized the Bureau, renamed it the Office of Management and Budget (OMB) and altered its role from that of an institution serving the presidency to an agency of policy advocacy serving a president. Political control was increased by the traditional expedient in Washington of partisan appointments at senior levels. The Bureau was thereby transformed from the agency of 'neutral competence' that Nixon's predecessors had valued to a personal staff unit; and its credibility outside the White House (and especially within Congress) was accordingly diminished. Congress responded by making the OMB director subject to Senate confirmation. Significantly, having itself been content to rely heavily on BOB analysis and estimates, in 1974 Congress created the Congressional Budget Office to ensure dispassionate fiscal analysis because it could no longer trust the OMB's own.

The process having been started, Nixon's successors extended it, apparently indifferent to the damage which such politicization did to the OMB's capacity for disinterested budgetary analysis and, hence, to the public interest. Under Reagan, the Director of the Budget became a national figure by acting as the chief protagonist for the president's budget. In realizing the administration's object of pressing its budgetary reforms through Congress in a matter of months, dissenting interpretations by the OMB's professional economists were excluded in the cause of generating the fanciful economic assumptions supporting Mr Reagan's budget forecasts which, in consequence, were politically expedient aspirations, rather than intellectually robust expectations.

The presidency and Congress

The presidency's single-most important political relationship is that with Congress. Here is the central link in American government. It is not a sufficient condition of presidential achievement that presidents exercise strategic and tactical leadership of Congress by winning votes for their authorizations and appropriations legislation and for confirmation of their nominees to the Executive and Judicial Branches, but it is necessary. Those presidents (such as Jimmy Carter) who do not reliably achieve legislative leadership are generally regarded as having failed. In the postwar period, John Kennedy has been the only exception to this rule: he achieved little legislative movement on Capitol Hill, and saw most of his proposals languish in committees where conservative chairmen suffocated them. Kennedy's historical standing is, nevertheless, high.

Even Kennedy was bound to take the legislative initiative, although he lacked the political opportunity and creativity to sustain it. Since there is no path of retreat either for presidential aspirants from promising much, or for presidents themselves from the expanded presidency, no incumbent can withdraw from political engagement with Congress. For Lyndon Johnson in the mid-1960s, intense lobbying of congressional chairmen and party leaders was necessary to pass Great Society welfare and education reform, and three major Civil Rights bills into law. Even Richard Nixon, who conducted congressional relations with belligerence, was constitutionally bound to seek Senate ratification of the Strategic Arms Limitation (SALT I) and Anti-Ballistic Missile (ABM) Treaties. Fundamentally, his executive agencies' requirement of regular reauthorization and appropriations for their programmes ensured the interaction of Executive and Congress, and compelled Nixon to seek congressional support. Although his behaviour towards the legislature suggested that he wished it were otherwise, Nixon could not govern independently. His need for finance limited him, just as the Founding Fathers

intended, while his own political agenda required authorizing and reau-
thorizing legislation, as Congress helpfully reminded him. Where Nixon
violated explicit Constitutional provision, as in his attempts to wage war
privately in Cambodia and his refusal to spend lawfully-appropriated
funds, Congress belatedly restrained him by the War Powers Resolution of
1973, and the Budget and Impoundment Control Act of 1974. In such a
setting, Arthur Schlesinger's lengthy indictment of what he took to be an
'Imperial' presidency under its incumbents in the 1960s and early 1970s
(he served two of them as a Special Assistant on the White House staff) had
some force. Yet, American presidents act 'imperially' only when
Congresses do not fulfil their constitutional obligations. Though prosecuted by presidents, the Vietnam War was sustained by annual congressional appropriations, and often by supplemental appropriations when the
expansion of the war exhausted funding. Congress has continued to
finance wars in Iraq and Afghanistan, assisted as it has been by being rather
better-informed about the conduct of the two wars than it was when being
systematically misled by Johnson and Nixon about Vietnam. Nevertheless,
decisions taken in regard to the incarceration of terrorist suspects in
Guantanamo Bay and the use of military tribunals highlight the continuing
capacity of presidents to act, if not imperially, then unilaterally.

As with the changing role of the presidency in general, so with its
legislative function, Franklin D. Roosevelt's administration provides the
historical key. Within the constitutional framework, Roosevelt quickly
altered popular and congressional understandings of the presidency's
legislative role. Eisenhower was the last president not to embrace enthusiastically the role of Chief Legislator; his resistance was token, and
lasted for only one year. Between the beginning of Eisenhower's presidency in 1953 and Reagan's in 1981, most major authorizing legislation
that Congress considered originated with presidential proposals.
Appropriations bills come to Congress as part of the annual budget
message. The Constitution, first, grants presidents power with regard to
the vetoing of bills passed by Congress and, second, respecting the
submission of legislative proposals. Hence, the presidency plays key roles
both at the beginning and at the conclusion of the legislative process:

- The first is granted by Article I, Section 7, of the Constitution,
  providing the president with a qualified veto of legislation presented
  to him (as all legislation must be) for signature (see Appendix 1). The
  success of presidents in using the veto has varied between individuals
  and the circumstances of their disagreements with Congress. The
  most successful modern exponent was Gerald Ford, Richard Nixon's
  appointed successor, whose legislative leadership consisted in his
  vetoing all measures of which he disapproved and then in lobbying
  intensively to have the vetoes sustained by Congress. Impossible

though it made the development of strategic presidential leadership, it was the most attractive option for dealing with a hostile Democratic Congress, since it required his opponents to find two-thirds, and not simple, majorities to prevail. President Clinton did not use his veto powers at all during his first two years in office, when Democrats formed the majorities in both Houses of Congress. (That was the first occasion on which a president had not used the veto in an entire Congress since Millard Fillmore withheld his veto-pen between 1851 and 1853). As President Ford had done twenty years before, however, Clinton found the authority to say 'no' to legislation passed by hostile party majorities in Congress useful in his third and fourth years in office: in 1995, he vetoed a $16 billion rescission bill. Later, he vetoed the Republican 1996 fiscal year budget containing provisions for reductions in Medicaid, Medicare, welfare, education and federal environmental programmes. George W. Bush did not use the veto at all until July 2006, when he vetoed a bill to permit the use of embryonic stem-cell research. Unsurprisingly, Bush employed the veto more frequently during the Democratic controlled Congress from 2007 to 2009.

- The second key role is found in Article II, Section 3, of the Constitution, which deals with the powers and duties of the president, and provides that:

> He shall from time to time give to the Congress Information of the State of the Union, and recommend to their Consideration such Measures as he shall judge necessary and expedient.

This power to recommend is the foundation for presidential leadership of Congress in both the strategic and tactical senses; it enables the president to choose between options and to decide on the order of priorities, and the implied power (from which presidential lobbying of Congress derives its constitutional foundation) to advocate publicly and privately the adoption of his recommended measures places no obligation on Congress to respond affirmatively. In resourceful hands, the president's power to recommend Congress's agenda is great. Yet, the legislative branch has complete constitutional freedom to ignore, reject, or re-order the agenda sent to it from the White House (although it is usually politically more constrained than this formal authority might imply). It is nonetheless on the power of recommendation, agenda-setting and lobbying that all modern presidents have organized their relations with Congress. To that end, all presidents since Eisenhower have assigned a number of their White House staff to organize their relations advantageously. Such staff have four main tasks, irrespective of the politics and policies of the president for whom they work:

1. To assume and retain responsibility within the White House for all questions of *legislative strategy* and *tactics*. The timing of legislative initiatives to Congress, the submission to the Senate of treaties for ratification, and of nominations for confirmation, are matters on which the staff is expected to advise the president and senior policy and political staff. Congressional relations staff maintain active and detailed supervision of the progress made by the president's bills, treaties and nominations; identify obstacles and difficulties, and seek to eliminate or circumvent them.

2. To attend to the political needs of congressional *allies*, to cultivate the *uncommitted*, to *marginalize opponents*.

3. To coordinate the *lobbying work* of the entire administration by ensuring that congressional relations staff in every agency advance the president's priorities, rather than those of departments and agencies. The fragmentation of American government makes this task difficult because the Executive Branch is large and its individual components have powerful countervailing incentives to pursue separate interests. But it also makes the task important because the president's causes may easily be harmed by semi-autonomous agencies.

4. To ensure that due regard be paid to the views of *known* and *potential supporters* in both congressional parties on legislation, treaties and nominees, in order that political difficulties are identified before submission, rather than discovered afterwards. The president's congressional relations staff are therefore ambassadors in both directions along Pennsylvania Avenue: representatives of the president's views and purposes to representatives and senators, and of theirs to him.

Presidential leadership in the sense of the president's persuasive capacity to negotiate and bargain is exemplified in his relations with Congress. Persuasion is necessary because the separation of powers grants Congress autonomy, thereby denying presidents authority over them. Neither the president or his staff, nor his Cabinet colleagues or his political appointees within the federal bureaucracy are members of the legislature. There is no requirement that the legislature should respond affirmatively to his requests or, indeed, an obligation on them to make any response at all. Presidents cannot count on congressional acquiescence. Declaration of agenda items and the setting of priorities are but the first strategic steps in making leadership effective. Presidents must exercise to the full their tactical powers of persuasion through political pressure where they can exert it, and bargaining and negotiation where they cannot, in order to win support.

Legislating in America is an imprecise, uncertain and thoroughly political business. The rise of the presidency to permanent prominence in the twentieth century, and the resulting popular expectations of it, have confirmed the role of president as chief legislator, but have not equipped the president to perform it with the reliability that British prime ministers typically enjoy. President Obama's inability to conclude the confrontation with the Republican House of Representatives in order to secure the raising of the US debt ceiling (in October 2013) illustrates the constitutional predicament in which all presidents are placed. Charles O. Jones was surely right to infer from a lifetime of reflection on American government that 'ours is not a presidential system; ours is a separated system' (Jones, 2005).

The president cannot command a legislature from which he is separated because that structural separation weakens the thread of party and so denies him stable support. Even the presence in Congress of majorities for the same party in control of the White House provides no guarantee that a president will secure approval for those legislative proposals, treaties, or nominations he submits to Congress. Nearly unbroken Democratic Party advantage between 1933 and 1994 did not ensure the adoption of a stream of legislation proposed by Democratic presidents; neither did the one-party dominance of both elected branches by the Republican Party between 2001 and 2007. Neither has divided government placed insuperable obstacles in the governing paths of Republican presidents.

Republican presidents had, until the beginning of the twenty-first century, to accustom themselves to the politics of divided party control, and had been obliged to adjust their tactics accordingly. Were parties to command the undiluted support of their congressional members, Presidents Nixon and Ford would have had no success whatever in their relations with Congress, since they faced Democratic opposition in both chambers throughout their terms. If party were all, President Eisenhower would have had little success for the last six years of his two terms, but would have achieved much for the first two when he was buoyed by Republican majorities (albeit small ones) in both the House and Senate. President Reagan's record, too, would have been less impressive in 1981 than it appeared to be, since control of Congress was divided for the first six years of his two terms. Examination of the legislative records of successive presidents and Congresses working under different partisan and external political circumstances shows that Republican presidents are much more successful than they would be if the divisions between congressional parties were pure and the results of party-line votes predictable.

Equally, the history of relations between Democratic presidents and the Democratic Congresses with which they have worked in the post-war period is one of recurrent friction and frustration. John Kennedy's term of office was marked more by legislative frustration, as the then baronial chairmen of the House Judiciary and Rules Committees refused to allow his legislative proposals for new civil rights legislation to come to the floor of the House for debate and a vote. Other committee chairmen emulated their refusal to cooperate. One such was Wilbur Mills of the House Ways and Means Committee, who showed himself to be an effective opponent of Keynesian demand management (not least because its effective implementation would have weakened the political power of his Committee). Jimmy Carter's term of office (1977–81) was conspicuous for politically damaging legislative failure. His proposals for the containment of health care costs expired in Congress. The energy bill which finally emerged from Congress bore little resemblance to the legislation the President had proposed. The SALT II Treaty which he had negotiated with Leonid Brezhnev was withdrawn from further consideration by the Senate when the Soviet Union's invasion of Afghanistan made political defeat certain. President Clinton, too, failed to secure passage of his major health care reform in 1993-94, despite large numerical majorities in both chambers. Ironically, he enjoyed much greater political success in the 104th Congress (1995–96) when he faced Republican majorities in both chambers than he had in the 103rd: the President adapted to mixed government with extraordinary political agility.

President Bush capitalized on the unified government that characterized the first six years of the Bush administrations to secure passage of a major educational reform in 2002, and two tax reduction bills of great significance in 2001 and 2003. President Obama used party advantage to win passage of healthcare reform. Thereafter, after heavy mid-term congressional losses, both presidents enjoyed much less success. After what he characterized as his 'shellacking' in the 2010 mid-term congressional elections, President Obama was forced to work hard to lead in the face of a Republican House of Representatives under Speaker John Boehner.

Yet, the clarity of the presidential imprint on Congress's legislative process depends on much more than the bare numerical indicators of party balance in each chamber. As Chapter 6 (which examines the Congress) shows, ideological divisions in both House and Senate cut across party cleavages because of the peculiar historical pattern of the American party system and, in particular, because of the one-party politics of the South between Reconstruction and the passage into law of the Civil Rights Act of 1964 and the Voting Rights Act of 1965 (see Chapter 4). Since these two Acts helped transform the politics of the South into a two-party competitive system, the nature of the cross-cutting cleavage has altered – and the first decade of the twenty-first century has been marked by higher levels of partisanship in both chambers of Congress and the dwindling of a moderate centre.

However, even major changes in the political agenda have not resulted in the fusing of ideology with party in the classic European mould. While the Democratic Party in Congress claims the loyalties of most congressional liberals, numerous moderates remain. The Republican Party in Congress is an ideological coalition of many conservatives and some moderates willing to seek accommodation with a Democratic president; liberal Republicans, so important a component of the party in the 1950s, 1960s and 1970s, no longer exist. Since 2010, the Republican Party has come to contain within it a number of House members (and a handful of senators) elected on a platform that appealed to, and was supported by, the Tea Party Movement. The dominant questions of public policy have changed so greatly since the period prior to the passage of the Civil Rights legislation of the mid-1960s that the political significance of the conservative coalition, drawn from the bulk of the Republican Party and a minority of the Democratic Party, has effectively disappeared. Successors to the conservative Southern Democrat Boll Weevils, the Blue Dog Democrats, lost half the members of their caucus in the 2010 mid-terms elections (reduced from 54 members to 26). Conservative Democrats are nearly extinct. No Democrat in the 111th Congress had a voting record more conservative than the most liberal Republican. Party unity scores (the percentage of members voting with a majority of their party on roll call votes on which a majority of one party opposes a majority of the other) are, at an average of over 90 per cent, at a post-war high.

The importance of a conservative coalition for the presidency lay with the consequences it had for the legislative role of the chief executive. The coalition dogged four post-war Democratic presidents (Harry Truman, John Kennedy, Lyndon Johnson and Jimmy Carter), often nullifying their nominal party advantage in Congress. By the same token, it aided immeasurably the lots of four Republicans (Dwight Eisenhower, Richard Nixon, Gerald Ford and Ronald Reagan). George W. Bush, his public appeal to compassionate conservatism notwithstanding, was able to mobilize conservative support for his foreign policy initiatives, as well as wide-ranging tax cuts, changes to welfare, and education reform.

Conclusion

Presidential policy-making failure is more common than presidential success. The federal and fragmented American political system is characterized by the scattering of institutional power; the society that sustains it is a mosaic. Such a setting is hostile to presidential government. Yet, limited though the strategic power of the presidents to set the political agenda is, and constrained as they are in their exercise of leadership through persuasion and negotiation, they are bound constantly to attempt both. The reason is plain: if strategic leadership does not come from the president, it is unlikely to come from elsewhere since every other actor faces collective action problems that the president does not. Elective politicians on Capitol Hill, unelected judges in the federal courts, state governors, legislators, and judges in the state courts, city mayors and local politicians, and unelected bureaucrats throughout the 85,000 governments within the United States often have both the capacity and the incentive to delay, weaken, amend, or nullify initiatives and proposals from the president. The president, alone among the very large class of elected officeholders across America, has both the strategic opportunity and obligation to set both an agenda for the United States and the tactical means for its achievement.

Chapter 6

Congress and the Politics of Legislative Competition

The United States Congress has three primary roles: to represent, to legislate, and to scrutinize (or 'oversee') the Executive Branch. This chapter examines how Congress performs the first two of its roles. Its third function, the oversight of the Executive Branch, as well as the many departments and agencies that constitute the federal bureaucracy, is considered in Chapter 9. Congress can be understood as an institution characterized by the interaction of two countervailing forces: one is centripetal and the other is centrifugal. The first comprises those forces that facilitate collective action, while the second force makes collective action hard to secure. In trying to understand how these two conflicting forces interact to shape legislative outcomes, it will be helpful in this chapter to view the legislature in terms of six aspects, or dimensions, which, taken together, help to explain what Congress does, how it does it, and why. These dimensions focus on the structure of Congress with its two distinct chambers, the centrally important relationship between the legislature and the executive and the individualized nature of an institution with 535 men and women, each of whom possesses a form of independence from their parties rare in European legislatures. It also focuses on the incentives and interests of the 535 individuals within the legislature who must work within this set of institutional and procedural structures. The chapter then examines in more detail centripetal and centrifugal forces. The roles of the parties in each chamber are considered before we move to an examination of the ways in which members of each chamber represent their constituents and make laws.

Procedural and structural dimensions

Congress is the first branch of government. A bicameral institution, it is organized by membership of party, committees, subcommittees and bipartisan caucuses. Unlike the UK Parliament, the United States Congress is not constitutionally supreme: it may not invade certain specified (and other implied and inferred) rights of American citizens. These limitations are significant constraints on Congress's capacity to act and, hence, on majoritarianism; the United States remains a polity founded on the defence of individual rights from encroachment by government. Permeated by its members' political calculations, and cross-cut by ideological, regional, racial and ethnic interests, its powers are limited by the principles of separation of powers and federalism in the Constitution, by other constitutional rights (not least the Bill of Rights and the Fourteenth Amendment) and by the Constitution's guardians, the federal courts.

Congress has six dimensions, the first five of which are structural, and the sixth procedural:

- The *bicameral dimension*, as a divided legislature of two contrasting, autonomous and competitive chambers.
- The *institutional dimension*, as the federal legislature separated from the other two branches of government.
- The *individual dimension*, of 535 legislators with their own agendas and the capacities to pursue them.
- The *specialized dimension and the tendency towards fission* (splitting apart) of committees, characterized by a division of labour in respect of the 'marking up' (drafting) of legislation and the oversight of the executive and judicial branches.
- The *collective dimension and the tendency towards fusion* (joining together) of party, whereby the fissiparous tendencies of Congress are partly overcome.
- The *procedural dimension* of legislation, and oversight of the executive, in which the first five dimensions are all, to varying extents, apparent.

Subject to two-yearly primary elections lying beyond parties' organizational control, members of Congress are highly sensitive to their districts' politics. Such sensitivity is apparent in their voting on bills and amendments to them, in their speeches, in their relations with their constituents, in their interventions in committee and subcommittee hearings, and in the choices they make about the committees and subcommittees to which they wish to belong. Nonetheless, this fragmented grounding of congressional behaviour in the politics of 435 districts does not preclude representatives from taking broader views of government's purposes. Still less does it so preclude senators, the demographic and political diversity of whose states affords most of them political latitude denied to members of the House. Both chambers have developed means whereby the fragmentary character of the institution as a whole is contained and productively channelled into legislation which is more than the sum of its many parts.

The bicameral dimension

The federal legislature is not an undifferentiated whole. The bicameral order is reflected in the physical division between the two chambers and the large supporting complexes of offices, committee rooms, restaurants and gymnasia. Bicameral roots support a legislature divided by culture, constituency, prerogatives, rules, size, tenure and organization. In the organization of parties within Congress, in their procedural and organizational rules, the two chambers are separate and self-governing bodies. Neither chamber dominates the other: while the types of power granted to each chamber by the Constitution are not identical, their extent is comparable (see Exhibit 6.1). Each forms a key part in the constitutional order and in the processes of government; each has interests of its own as well as those which it shares with the other. Neither is what Walter Bagehot (1867) called a 'dignified' part of the United States Constitution, as the House of Lords usually is of the UK's constitution (although discussion of the role of the Senate at the Constitutional Convention alluded to the possibility that the Senate might, like the Lords, act to 'cool the passions' of the popularly-elected House of Representatives). Both chambers are much more central to policy processes in the United States than is the House of Commons to them in the UK, primarily because both have autonomy from the executive.

Bicameralism complicates the legislative process. In their constituency bases, members' terms of service, size of chamber, rules, organization and nature of party organization, the Senate and the House differ. Not only

Exhibit 6.1 Exclusive and Concurrent Powers of the House and Senate

Exclusive powers of the House
- To consider all money bills first
- To vote articles of impeachment
- To choose a president if the electoral college is deadlocked

Exclusive powers of the Senate
- To ratify treaties with a two-thirds majority
- To confirm executive appointments
- To try cases of impeachment
- To elect a vice-president if the electoral college is deadlocked

Concurrent powers
- Pass legislation
- Override the president's veto
- Initiate constitutional amendments
- Declare war
- Confirm the vice-president

do individual members of each chamber differ from their colleagues within the same chamber and from those in the other, so the two chambers often have different interests as collectivities. With 435 representatives directed much more towards the production of legislation than are the one hundred senators, the House remains the more formally and hierarchically organized of the two; the division of labour is also more pronounced. Members of the House spend much of their working time in detailed examination of legislation before the standing committee or committees of which they are members.

Bicameralism reflects the framers' determination to weaken the legislature, and so reduce the probability of its dominating the federal executive. It also reflects the compromise between the political interests of populous and less-populated states during the Constitutional Convention in 1787 (when several states already had bicameral legislatures of their own). By the 'Connecticut Compromise', delegates to the Convention eventually agreed that membership of the House should be distributed between states by population, and that of the Senate divided equally among the states irrespective of area or population. The number of representatives is now fixed at 435; the least populous states have just one representative each, and the most populous (California) has fifty-five. The number of senators rises by two with the admission of a new state to the Union: following the admission of Alaska in January 1959, and of Hawaii in August of the same year, the size of the upper chamber therefore increased from ninety-six to ninety-eight, and then to one hundred.

The Constitution makes no distinction in the general extent of powers granted to the two chambers, and competition between them is often sharp. The Constitution does, however, grant the chambers powers of slightly different kinds: the House considers tax legislation first, while the Senate has the responsibility for advising and consenting on nominations to the executive and judiciary, and for the ratification of international treaties. The implication is that the House (and particularly its Ways and Means Committee) has primacy in national fiscal policy, and that the Senate (particularly its Foreign Relations Committee) has primacy in foreign policy (although qualified by the overall leadership of the president in foreign affairs). Responsibility for confirmation and ratification enhances the Senate's role in oversight of the executive and the judiciary.

Formal equality of the two chambers notwithstanding, membership of the Senate carries greater prestige than membership of the House. Members of both chambers subscribe to this view, as is indicated by the many representatives who leave the House to run for the Senate. By contrast, senators never voluntarily leave the Senate to run for a seat in the House. Having a much smaller chamber with longer terms, membership of the Senate is regarded by most politicians as the more desirable for its being rarer and less frequently exposed to electoral contests. Except for the presidency, the speakership of the House of Representatives and one or two senior party colleagues and committee chairs, and the governorships of California, Florida, Illinois, New York and Texas, only senators have the potential to establish themselves as national figures.

Senators are collectively jealous of the powers granted to their chamber by the Constitution, and individually aware that as the House has, for many of them, formed their stepping-stone to the Senate, so the Senate may be a launch-pad for the vice-presidency and presidency. Former Presidents Truman, Kennedy, Nixon and Johnson, as well as President Obama, were all previously senators (three had also been vice-president). At any one time, as many as a dozen senators might be considered (if only by themselves) as plausible candidates for the presidency or vice-presidency, whether at the next or at some future presidential election. Senators' ambitions for the presidency help shape their thinking and voting on the floor and in committee and subcommittee, and in their speechmaking. Many senators now see themselves, not as most of their predecessors in the 1950s and 1960s did, as spokespersons for their states, but for the nation. The Senate, which in the 1950s was generally viewed by most senators as the summit of their political ambitions, is now increasingly viewed as a base for the fulfilment of ambition elsewhere. To this end, senators use the Senate as a forum in which they can offer a lead on matters of national importance with a view to seeking the nation's highest office.

Circumstances, culture and condition differ greatly between the two chambers, but each presents difficulties to a president seeking to lead. It is not merely that Congress is separated from the executive, but that this institutional separation of a divided Congress from the executive presents different incentives for presidents, congressmen and congresswomen, and senators. They have various (but apparently compelling) reasons for having their own perspectives on public policy. The combination of the three electoral bases of the three institutions, the contrasting internal organization of the two chambers, together with the weakness of party (relative to European parties) which, in part, flows from separation, makes the aggregation of interest within Congress politically difficult, since Congress is both a legislative and representative body. The care and attention that members of Congress devote to representing constituents makes legislating in a cause greater than the sum of Congress's individual parts difficult. On many policy questions, members of Congress and senators often have little interest in seeking reasoned solutions to national problems. Their first concern lies with serving their own political needs: those of their party, chamber, president and their country are of less moment. To make this point is not to criticize legislators' behaviour: they do what they do in large part because of the evolution of Congress's and parties' forms.

Bicameralism results in two separately-constituted, separately-elected, legislative bodies, responding in different ways to different constituencies, circumstances and political pressures. Opportunities for delay and obfuscation in such a body are many. Tenacity, invention and bargaining are therefore necessary qualities for successful legislators in the United States Congress, and for presidents who attempt to give legislative leadership by identifying a national agenda and pressing Congress to adopt it as their own.

The institutional dimension

Congress is also a single institution: as the federal legislature, it has collective institutional interests of its own, binding House and Senate together against the executive. This expression can, and does, bridge partisan division: Congress expressed a collective will against the executive with respect to the control both of fiscal and of foreign policy during President Nixon's second term. The Watergate affair's importance lay in the executive's abuse of power and the unconstitutional infringement by the executive of powers held by Congress, rather than in party political struggle. The Constitution's provision for the impeachment of executive officers and members of the federal judiciary illustrates both the separation and the unification of Congress. The articles of impeachment against President Nixon were voted by the House Judiciary Committee; had the President not resigned, he would have been tried by the Senate. Unlike the imminent impeachment and removal from office of Richard Nixon, the impeachment of President Clinton in December 1998 was neither certain, nor bipartisan: the partisan House of Representatives brought two articles of impeachment against him, but the Senate acquitted the President on both in February 1999.

Congress and the executive

Chapter 5 illustrated the importance of staff within the executive in serving the administrative, electoral and governing needs of presidents. The executive's single greatest asset in its relations with Congress until the Nixon presidency was its virtual monopoly of expertise, the experience and understanding possessed by some senior committee chairmen of policy questions notwithstanding. Of all the legacies to the 1950s and 1960s of the expansion of the presidency under Franklin D. Roosevelt and Harry Truman, this was one of the most significant. When members of Congress sought technical information or guidance on a particular topic, they approached executive agencies. The relationship was partly one of reliance borne of an underlying trust, but it also illustrated asymmetries of information and expertise intrinsic to the relationship between Congress and the executive, which became less acceptable to many legislators as both the scope of federal regulation at home and the peacetime interests of the United States abroad grew. It had special political significance in foreign affairs and defence policy, where the executive's monopoly of information was supplemented by Congress's reluctance to probe too deeply for fear of encroaching on presidential prerogatives. Yet, at hearings held by the Joint Committee on the Organization of Congress which drafted the Legislative Reorganization Act of 1946, witnesses testified to the deplorable inadequacy of congressional staff resources, and of Congress's consequent dependence on hastily-gathered information from the Executive Branch, journalists and lobbyists. For Congress, one of three co-equal branches of government to be collectively and individually dependent on external sources of data risks both its independence and its standing. The 1946 Act accordingly provided for increases in the number of staff provided to members and to committees as a counter to the executive's resources, themselves so massively enhanced by adaptation to the demands of the New Deal and World War II.

Vietnam and Watergate, together with the politicization of the Bureau of the Budget, induced Congress to attempt afresh to end its dependence on the executive for policy information and analysis. Congressional trust in the executive was undermined by President Johnson's conduct of the Vietnam War and by pervasive corruption under Nixon. The 'neutral competence' of the Bureau of the Budget, which derived from its being heavily staffed by civil servants, weakened by the late 1960s as the Bureau became more thoroughly politicized. Congress was accordingly less inclined to trust its budgetary proposals. Unable to rely on the expertise of Executive Branch agencies, Congress recruited its own numerous professional staff to work for individual members, committees and for the legislature as a whole.

Increased provision for staff since the Johnson and Nixon presidencies has strengthened Congress as a single institution. The United States Congress is now a competing source of expertise in the formation, legislation and evaluation of public policy. The participation of the United States Congress in legislation and oversight is powerfully shaped by professional staff. They supply data, expertise, analysis, advice, and speeches, draft questions to Executive officials and others giving testimony before Committees, and provide answers to constituents and journalists. Without them, Congress could not have experienced the institutional 'resurgence' that James Sundquist (1981) identified and which sharply altered the politics of presidential–congressional relations (and, hence, the making of public policy) after the mid-1970s. Asymmetries between the two branches remain, nonetheless. Congress delegates powers to the executive to implement particular public policies precisely because of the Executive Branch's huge bureaucratic assets.

Under Speaker Gingrich's leadership, the radical 104th Congress cut staff budgets and numbers, thereby increasing the executive's informational advantages over Congress. Gingrich's reform may appear perverse in its effects, but he intended his policy to increase his own control over his party colleagues. In the short run, it did so; by the end of the 104th Congress, many of his colleagues had asserted their autonomy from him and his agenda. Yet, many within his own party blamed Speaker Gingrich for their losses in the 1996 and 1998 elections. Gingrich's position was difficult: he sought to maintain a balance between moderate Republicans prepared to work with President Clinton and staunch conservatives who were not. John Boehner (R-OH), Speaker in the 113th Congress, faces a recognizably similar challenge in working with a Democratic president while managing conservative Republicans, and those in the Tea Party faction.

Congress as a bureaucracy

Congress is, therefore, not a simple legislature composed of 535 elected members sitting in two chambers. It is also a large bureaucracy sited in more than twenty buildings. In addition to elected representatives and senators, there are more than 25,000 unelected staff. The 2013 budget for the entire legislative branch amounted to some $3.3 billion.

The individual dimension

The points of cohesion within Congress being few, and those of incohesion many, pressures within Congress are more centrifugal than centripetal. The passage of legislation that serves the public interest (rather than the interests of individuals or groups) is, accordingly, difficult. There are in Congress, as in European legislatures, complex relationships between the structures of government and the processes of politics and policy formation: the constitutional order provides incentives to certain types of political behaviour and disincentives to others, as the authors of the Constitution appreciated. *The Federalist Papers* provide a clear statement of the political behaviour expected of representatives, subjected to popular biennial elections, drawing their political strength from constituencies that were in most cases small and reasonably homogeneous. (Although still relatively homogeneous, they are now very large by European standards: the average British constituency has 70,000 voters but the average congressional district has just over 700,000). The authors contended that these circumstances would cause members of the House of Representatives to be highly sensitive to popular opinion. Madison, when arguing in *Federalist* No. 62 for the necessity of a second chamber, the Senate, insisted that the House of Representatives would be liable to:

> yield to the impulse of sudden and violent passions, and to be seduced by factious leaders into intemperate and pernicious resolutions.

This view had force in the early years of the Republic, but did not characterize most of the post-war period. Yet, the febrile atmosphere of the mid-1990s and in the increasingly partisan Congresses of the first thirteen years of the twenty-first century suggest that intemperate behaviour is no longer the exception. Despite the increasing importance of party leaders, their members typically prove difficult to galvanize, their 535 individual interests resistant to aggregation. Innovative departures from incremental additions to policies, whether in economics, welfare, or defence, remain difficult for congressional leaders to secure. Sensitivity to public opinion, however, is palpable; members of Congress spend much time, money, and effort in attending to constituents' complaints about their treatment by federal agencies. Such complaints are usually prosaic, personal and non-political, but members' staff ensure that (where expedient) their successful handling receives favourable publicity in members' districts, as reports on local television stations across the country and postings on members' websites illustrate.

Local pressures weigh heavily with politicians seeking re-election. Whereas, in the early nineteenth century, Congress was characterized by high membership turnover, it has not been since 1945. Unlike in Britain, where members of Parliament are elected or defeated almost entirely because of their party affiliation, congressmen and congresswomen are heavily dependent for their re-election on their advertised capacity to represent their constituents' interests. For the most part, they are (or become) skilled at doing so. The proportion of incumbent members of the House seeking re-election to have been re-elected has long been high. Until the 1992 election, the proportion of incumbents winning by substantial margins was not only high, but was rising to levels of more than 85 per cent; the rate of incumbents winning re-election rose after the aberrant 1992 elections, with rates close to 90 per cent in the House and just below 90 per cent in the Senate. That has been the norm in the last nine congressional elections.

As Madison expected, members of the House of Representatives are highly responsive to their constituents' expressed needs and wishes. However, for presidents seeking to make their role as legislative leaders effective, the House is a body whose structure and rules appear to foster recalcitrant behaviour. Since presidents, unlike House members, attempt to govern under a constitutional prohibition from serving more than eight years in office, the virtual absence of electoral threat to the incumbency of House members is frustrating. Circumstances in the Senate are different, and the incentives to which electoral politics give rise are less clear-cut. Senators run for election every six years, not every two. Many are therefore less sensitive to the electoral consequences of their political behaviour between polls. Senate elections usually attract more able, and better-financed, challengers to incumbents than do elections in the House. Whereas House congressional district boundaries are redrawn (and often gerrymandered) every decade, state boundaries cannot be adjusted. Most elections are, accordingly, rather more competitive than those in the House.

Membership resources

Since World War II, the personal staffs of representatives and senators have grown by between five and six times. Such staff buttress incumbents against challenges; accordingly, congressional politicians fiercely defend the arrangement. Even zealous congressional Republican followers of Speaker Gingrich early in 1995, while agreeing to reductions in committee staff, resisted cuts in their own. In 1995, some 7,500 staff worked for individual representatives and a further 4,200 for individual senators. By 2005, the number of staff had fallen slightly to 7,390 for the House and just below 4,000 for the Senate. Each representative has a staff hiring allowance of $831,252; this amount is supplemented by a consolidated allowance of $194,980 (but the upper limit of the allowance is over $420,000 since the amount varies with the transport, office and other costs encountered in travelling to, and working within, the home district).

Senators' personal staff allowances are larger than those for representatives. Staff hiring budgets vary (but not proportionately) with state population between $3,149,536 and more than $4,967,563 (the average was $3,409,093). There are further substantial allowances for office equipment and furniture expenses, and for the renting of between 4,800 and 8,000 square feet of office space in the home state. Senators from the largest states who also chair a major committee have as many as 70 staff.

There are two organizational points of special importance here:

- Whereas committee staff are concerned with the legislative and oversight work of the committee, personal staff attend solely to the fortunes of the single politician for whom they work.
- Personal staff are not confined to Washington. Particularly in large Senate offices, many staff are employed not in one of the large congressional office buildings on Capitol Hill but at home in offices spread throughout the state or district. It is there, and not in Washington, that much constituency service work is done.

Constituency service work requires several offices across states and districts. Some senators in large and populous states maintain five or more separate offices; and many congressmen keep three or more district offices in addition to their main office in Washington. In state and district offices, most work is concerned with social security, Medicare, veterans' benefits and tax problems. David Price (1989: 437–8) characterizes the work of congressional offices in general as operating an appeals process for bureaucratic decisions functionally similar to that of ombudsmen in Britain, Sweden and Norway. It also resembles that of members of the French National Assembly.

Most staff based in Washington deal with legislative and political matters of concern to their representative or senator. Organization of staff within congressional offices varies with different politicians' differing needs, but all have a senior political adviser, and an administrative assistant charged with the smooth and effective operation of the office. The resulting undertaking is considerable: the concentration of highly-motivated, ambitious, young people (most are under the age of thirty-five) in an entrepreneurial politician's office makes for a competitive and often fraught environment. Struggles for space, status, advancement and influence result. Many staff have political ambitions of their own and quickly discover that there are few political rewards for the self-effacing.

Committee and subcommittee chairs, and ranking members of committees and subcommittees, enjoy the support of specialist committee staff. (Since rule changes instigated by Speaker Newt Gingrich and his Republican leadership colleagues in January 1995, the employment of staff has, however, formally become the exclusive responsibility of full committee chairmen.) Other members of committees are not provided with committee staff and must rely on one or more of their personal staff to support their committee work. Each senator and representative employs legislative assistants in this role, writing speeches, and preparing and giving briefings on committee business. Other personal staff liaise with the media, seeking to feed stories to the press and television, often by means of sending DVDs or other digital files, professionally-produced in studios on Capitol Hill, of their principal's views on the subjects of the week, arranging for media coverage of events organized during the member's visits to the district or state and organizing press conferences. For all but the dozen or so congressional politicians of national standing, this work is primarily with the newspapers and television stations in the home district or state. Most congressional politicians, lacking any prospect of gaining regular national media attention, therefore focus not on Washington, but on viewers and readers back home.

The specialized and fissiparous dimension

Committee/subcommittee structure

Both the House and the Senate organize their legislative and oversight activity around a complicated structure of committees and subcommittees. Committees are of four kinds:

- *Conference committees*, as the procedural aspect of bicameralism, are convened *ad hoc* enabling the senators and representatives selected to serve on them to agree a common version of a bill previously passed by the two chambers in different forms.
- *Standing committees and subcommittees* lie at Congress's heart. Their members consider and examine legislative proposals, whether from the White House or from within Congress. Members of both

House and Senate committees also oversee the work of executive agencies, examining the extent to which departments and agencies (all of which are authorized and funded by Congress, and none of which can exist without congressional approval) execute the law in the manner Congress intended.

- *Select* or *Special committees* are established for special oversight purposes or to examine particular problems. Some are permanent; others have a limited life. Examples include the Senate's select committees on aging, ethics, intelligence, and Indian affairs; and the House's select committee on intelligence. The best-known (and the one having the greatest political impact) was the Senate select committee on the Watergate affair, chaired by Senator Sam Ervin.
- *Joint committees of Congress*, of which there are four. Two, the Joint Economic Committee and the Joint Committee on Taxation, deal with matters of economic policy in general and fiscal policy in particular. The other two, the Joint Committee on the Library and the Joint Committee on Printing, are politically unimportant.

Importance of committees

Committees are central not just to Congress as an institution, but also to the processes of American government. They are organizational centres of legislation, of oversight and of representation. Different committees engage in these three activities in different proportions at different times. Standing committees engage in all three types of work: they are centres of power and expertise, strengthened by the functional division of labour between them. Members of committees and their substantial staffs are therefore specialists, especially in the House, where the principle of the division of labour is more pronounced.

Congress does most of its work in committees and subcommittees. It is here that hearings on authorizing and appropriations bills take place, with testimony given by witnesses from the Executive Branch, members of groups with an interest in the proposed legislation and disinterested experts. It is here, too, that representatives and senators produce a draft of the legislation during the 'mark-up' (drafting) sessions of the committee before reporting the bill to the floor of the chamber.

To an even greater extent than with legislation, standing and select committees and subcommittees are the primary foci for scrutinizing the implementation of policy by executive departments, agencies, bureaux and regulatory commissions. Oversight is necessarily specialized, and one in which subcommittees, with their smaller jurisdictions, are better placed to work than the full chambers. As Chapter 9 shows, cyclic re-authorization and appropriations legislation provide scheduled opportunities for such scrutiny and influence. Even in legislation and oversight, however, members of committees never lose sight of the importance of representing their constituents' interests.

This use of committees shows that Congress does not provide for a simple translation of majority preferences into policy. Building coalitions in Congress for political change is difficult unless its benefits are widely distributed among those voting on the measure: unless, in other words, there is something in it for those whose support is sought. Distributive politics has long been an attractive game to play in Congress: a federal initiative to tighten pollution controls is more likely to win support if it results in the widespread distribution of grants. As the committee structure facilitates distributive politics, so it may inhibit political reform: Congress's multiple institutional points of access may serve as points of veto.

Senate and House committees: similarities

Senate committees now differ from House committees in some respects, but are similar in others. They share the following features:

* Chairs are always in the hands of the *majority party*.
* The most senior member of the *minority party* on each committee has the title 'ranking member'.
* Political power in both chambers is *unevenly distributed* among committees and subcommittees.

The heavy fiscal deficits incurred in the 1980s and between 2001 and 2013, and the associated effective abandonment of the progressive liberal purpose that informed the Roosevelt, Truman and Johnson presidencies, weakened all authorizing committees except Senate Armed Services and elevated the importance of Finance (Ways and Means in the House) and Budget. Committees with an explicitly regulatory purpose, such as the House Commerce Committee, which has jurisdiction over electricity, nuclear power, telecommunications and finance, also became foci of special political attention and governing importance.

Senate and House committees: differences

Senate and House committees differ in the following respects:

* The *remit* of standing committees in the Senate is broader than that in the House. For example, the Senate Committee on Commerce, Science, and Transportation, covers the following policy areas: aviation, consumer affairs, international trade, tourism, manufacturing and competitiveness, telecommunications, merchant shipping, road

and rail transport, commercial fishing, science, technology and space. The House assigns this large cluster of loosely-related fields to four committees.

- There are *fewer subcommittees* in the Senate than in the House.
- Since the Senate is less than one-quarter of the size of the House, senators belong to *more committees* than their House counterparts and so are able to serve *more objectives* by their committee assignments than are representatives.
- Most senators are *generalists*, whereas almost all representatives (apart from the party leaders) are *specialists*.
- Each Senate committee and subcommittee has *fewer members* than do panels in the House. The largest Senate committee, Appropriations, has only thirty members; the largest House committee in the 113th Congress, Armed Services, has sixty members.
- Senate committees are, in most cases, significantly *less important to the careers* of senators than House committees are to the careers of members of Congress.
- Determination of the *ratio of majority* to *minority parties* on committees differs between the Senate and the House. Whereas House majorities are expanded in party ratios on committees in order to increase party control, Senate ratios are set more leniently.

Standing committees in the House and the Senate

There are twenty standing committees (excluding the Select Committee on Intelligence) in the House, and sixteen (excluding the Select Committees on Intelligence, and on Ethics, and the Special Committee on Ageing) in the Senate. Most are further divided into subcommittees. In both chambers, standing committees are one of two kinds: authorizing, or appropriating. The former create new programmes and modify existing ones, while the latter provide finance for them. Committee jurisdictions cover the entire range of public policy, and there is substantial overlap between the jurisdictions of different committees. The correspondence between the committee structures of the House and the Senate is nonetheless incomplete, since each chamber is responsible for the organization of its committees, as it is for its rules. The House of Representatives' rules require that every standing committee with twenty or more members must have at least four subcommittees. This rule was adopted in 1975, partly in order to ensure that the power and influence of committee chairmen was kept under tighter control than in the sixty years following the ending in 1910 of Speaker Cannon's domination of the House. The importance of subcommittees in the House also reflects the growth of federal regulation and programmes, and the consequent need that Congress has to oversee them. Powerful individual incentives also apply: the preoccupation of representatives with re-election and their ambitions for power within the House or for higher office elsewhere mean that subcommittees provide a convenient stage for political entrepreneurship, for demonstrating their political sagacity to existing or potential constituents. The change towards so-called 'subcommittee government' after the 1970s reforms advanced furthest in the House: there, most bills receive at least their first mark-up in subcommittee (in contrast to circumstances in the Senate, where most marking-up of bills and hearings on them occur in full committee).

The distinction between *authorizing* and *appropriating* committees is fundamental. Authorizing committees consider proposals for new agencies or programmes, or for the re-authorization of existing ones. If committees approve them, they attach limits to the public money that may be spent on them. Appropriations committees (one in each chamber, each with functionally-divided subcommittees) finance government programmes by appropriating public money to them. Except for those programmes where entitlements to benefits are included in the bill authorizing the programme, an Act of Congress enjoys no funding and, hence, is null and void, without appropriations being voted by the appropriations subcommittees and committees of both chambers. Appropriations committees derive their considerable power from controlling government finance. With the addition of the budget committees in both chambers under the Budget and Impoundment Control Act of 1974, which have the remit of setting overall budget targets and obliging other committees to meet them, this categorization is inadequate. In addition to considering all standing committees as being either authorizing or appropriating, we may identify a third category of committee (though these are not separately recognized in congressional rules or procedures): control committees. These institutions control money, legislation and the ethical behaviour of members of Congress; all are forms of standing committee.

Within the control category, four committees have particular significance: Senate Finance and House Ways and Means (which write tax legislation); and the budget committees in each chamber. Tax and spending policy is the heart of Congress's work; those committees concerned with the politics of revenue-raising and spending have always exploited their functional importance to their political advantage.

Both appropriations committees (which, because of their financial control function, may also be regarded as control committees) are powerful because they allocate approximately one-third of federal expenditure. Each is similarly organized around groups of semi-autonomous subcommittees responsible for groups of executive departments, agencies, bureaux and regulatory commissions. The full committees, invariably deferring to the subcommittees, may appropriate funds for programmes to the ceilings determined by the authorizing committees and approved by both chambers, but not beyond them. They are not obliged to appropriate funds at the authorized ceilings or at the levels requested by the president in his budget message.

In practice, the spectrum of politically plausible choices is smaller than that which is theoretically possible. Nevertheless, the width of the theoretical choices shows how great are Congress's powers, especially in comparison with the limp financial control exerted by most West European legislatures. The power of the appropriations committees to cut spending has frequently been a source of tension with the committees that authorize defence spending: the Senate Armed Services Committee, and the House National Security Committee. Congress as a whole acts entirely autonomously in determining public spending, subject only to the threat or fact of a presidential veto. Authorizing committees determined to set spending levels for a programme above the president's request face no constitutional obstacle but only the political one of judging whether such determination can be sustained on the floor, in the Conference Committee and in the Oval Office.

Tax-writing committees enjoy jurisdiction over spending programmes for all the major entitlement programmes: Medicare (assistance for the elderly with their hospital costs), unemployment compensation, social security, welfare, and, in finance's case, for Medicaid (a joint federal–state programme to assist the poor with their medical costs). All lie beyond the control of appropriations committees, since payments are made under them as of right according to criteria specified in the authorizing legislation. Both also have the responsibility of considering legislation to raise the debt limit, which must pass if the federal government is to continue to function. These responsibilities are in addition to their primary shared function of writing tax law.

All three categories of committees and their associated subcommittees may hold hearings on subjects within their jurisdictions in order to oversee the implementation of policy by departments and agencies for which they have responsibility. All may also consider legislative proposals referred to them. Hence, the House National Security Committee and Senate Armed Services Committee may hold hearings on whatever defence or security topic they wish: requests by the administration for changes in the force structure of the US Army; for a new class of aircraft carriers for the US Navy; or on topical questions of its members' choosing related to the performance of particular weapons systems; on the wisdom of the president's naval policy; on the quality of advice made by the Joint Chiefs of Staff to the president; or on the lessons to be learned from a military engagement such as the deployment of the US Marines to Lebanon, the invasion of Grenada, the commitment of troops to Kosovo, or the conduct of wars in Afghanistan and Iraq.

House committees

Congressmen and congresswomen are assigned to committees by their parties' steering committees. For representatives – whose policy interests, unlike those of senators, are usually dominated by those which fall within their committees' jurisdictions – these decisions shape their careers. Changes to House rules passed at the beginning of the 104th Congress (1995–1997) provided that members may serve on no more than two full committees and four subcommittees; chairmen and ranking members (the most senior minority party member on a committee) may, however, serve on all subcommittees *ex officio*. A further change for the 104th Congress caused three full committees to be abolished – the first occasion since the Democrats had retaken control of the House forty years earlier that the number of House committees had been cut.

Richard Fenno (1973) has argued that members of Congress have three main political purposes: re-election, the achievement of power and influence within the House, and the making of good public policy. Mayhew (1974) considers members of Congress to be motivated almost exclusively by the desire for re-election; Aldrich and Rohde (1999) in their Conditional Party Government (CPG) model argue, as does Mayhew, that members care greatly about re-election, but also about the formulation of good public policy (like Fenno). Committee membership is a means to these ends: a seat on the House Agriculture Committee will serve excellently both the re-election and policy interests of a representative from a rural congressional district in southern Illinois; conversely, it would not only not assist a representative from Chicago (in the northern part of the same state), but would probably damage her or him politically. Assignments matter also to congressional party leaders and to the congressional parties more generally: committees' ideological balances, the quality of their membership and their importance can be, and are, modified by recruiting certain colleagues to particular committees, and excluding others. Democrats construct the membership of the steering committee to reflect the regional, economic, ideological and ethnic interests within the party. When the Democrats have had the majority, the Democratic speaker has chaired it. Now that they do not, the minority leader (former Speaker of the House (2007–11) Nancy Pelosi does so. Following the election of Newt Gingrich to position of speaker in 1995, the Republicans' Committee on Committees was abolished – replaced by a new Republican steering committee over which Gingrich wielded considerable influence. Gingrich's successor, Dennis Hastert, allowed the committee greater autonomy and the current speaker, John Boehner, is closer to Hastert than to Gingrich in his relationship with the steering committee.

Before 1975, committee chairs were allocated purely by seniority, regardless of capacity, energy, or ideology. This rule encouraged

---

Exhibit 6.2 Conditional Party Government

One of the most influential post-war examinations of Congress is David Mayhew's *Congress: The Electoral Connection* (1974), in which he argued that we can best understand the actions of members of Congress by proceeding from the assumption (which he then tests against evidence) that their motivations are based on the primacy of the desire to seek and win re-election. For Mayhew, political parties were of minimal significance – important only insofar as they help members with re-election.

However, the resurgence of partisanship in Congress – as well as the increased power of the party leadership (notably with the Speakership of Newt Gingrich from 1995 to 1999, but even with the weaker, but still important, Speaker Hastert and the influential Speaker Pelosi in the 110th and 111th Congresses) and the seeming inability of Speaker Boehner to maintain the coherence of the Republican Party in the House during the government shutdown of October 2013 would suggest that partisanship in Congress, or at least within the House of Representatives, has eroded the capacity of the Speaker to control those he purports to lead. John Aldrich and David Rohde (2002) in their study of congressional behaviour propose the Conditional Party Government (CPG) model, in which they accept Mayhew's view that members are motivated by re-election but widen the interests of members to include (as does Fenno, 1973) the desire to formulate good public policy. They allow that members may be motivated by multiple goals, as they explain:

> [Members of Congress] are centrally concerned with winning elections [but this is] not the same thing as assuming that everyone is concerned *only* with winning elections. Some members, because they have policy goals, may be willing to take some electoral risks to achieve them. (1999: 7. Emphasis in original)

For Aldrich and Rohde, members will structure situations so that they can simultaneously achieve policy goals and electoral goals. The CPG model suggests that, as the diversity of preferences within each party lessens, members will be less worried about party leaders choosing positions with which they disagree, and will therefore be more willing to follow the path set by their party leadership. Some commentators view the CPG model as a useful means of explaining the increasing partisanship in Congress.

---

congressmen to serve what amounted to apprenticeships, because they had no prospect of acquiring power without doing so. Sam Rayburn served in every Congress from 1913 to 1961 and waited eighteen years before becoming chairman of the Interstate and Commerce Committee (an especially important committee during the 1930s, when much of

Roosevelt's New Deal legislation was sent to it); later he served as speaker of the House on three separate occasions, from 1940–47, 1949–53 and 1955–61. He had pithy advice for new members of the House with high hopes of gaining power: 'If you want to get along, go along'. Power in committees came to those who obeyed House norms, and survived. Distribution of power within the House was by age; the chamber accordingly became a gerontocracy and, because southern state legislatures avoided redistricting in order to maintain the over-representation of rural bases of political power in their one-party region, a gerontocracy dominated by southern rural conservatives. The seniority rule applied to both Democrats and Republicans; party leaders had to take it into account. John McCormack, speaker of the House during the 1960s, advised freshmen: 'Whenever you pass a committee chairman in the House, you bow from the waist. I do.' Speaker McCormack did no such thing, of course. But his point was well-made.

Those who sought to reform Congress in the 1970s were, in general, antipathetic to the seniority rule, but they had other interests: liberals sought the weakening of the institutional power bases of conservatives, freshmen of all stripes sought power more quickly than the old rules permitted, and Republicans of conservative and moderate persuasions were keen to weaken Democratic power bases irrespective of the ideologies of chairmen. For all three groups, the motives were entirely political, and opportunities were seized in the turbulent circumstances following Richard Nixon's enforced resignation and the last agonizing months of the Vietnam War. The reforms of 1973 (which resulted in the creation of the Subcommittee Bill of Rights – discussed below) and 1975 had four main consequences for committees and their chairpersons:

1. The abolition of the convention that Committee chairs (most of them conservatives) should be assigned automatically on the basis of *seniority*, (a convention that had been but rarely broken before) and its replacement by the rule that it be made subject to the vote of the *caucus* (which conservatives did not dominate).
2. The devolution of a substantial portion of legislative and oversight work to *subcommittees* from committees. In order to diffuse authority and influence, House rules stipulated that every standing committee with twenty or more members must have at least four subcommittees. Later changes to House rules in 1995 restricted all committees except Appropriations, Government Reform and Oversight, and Transportation and Infrastructure, to a maximum of five subcommittees, and concentrated staff recruitment and deployment powers in the hands of full committee chairpersons.
3. The overturning of the rule permitting members to chair more than one subcommittee, thereby weakening the power of chairmen

further and dispersing power through the middle ranks of the House Democratic caucus.

4.   The expansion of the Speaker's power (especially by greatly increasing his formal and practical powers over the Rules Committee), and of the Democratic Party caucus.

Implementation of the 1970s reforms led to the House coming more closely to resemble the Senate in so far as the old hierarchical order with committee chairs at its apex was replaced by a flatter distribution of authority. The concentration of power in the speakership in the early months of 1995 slowed, rather than halted, the broad thrust of House rule changes from 1973 to 1997, which decentralized power from committee chairpersons to committee members. Speaker Dennis Hastert (1999–2007) did grant greater autonomy to committee chairs who, as a result, were able to wield greater power over their committee members. Yet, despite the growth in party leadership in the post-Gingrich House, the weakening of committee chairs (both in the 1970s and in the 104th Congress) has not been undone. Notions of committee chairmen as the twentieth-century's equivalent of mediaeval barons presiding over their fiefdoms have no explanatory power in the twenty-first century.

All institutional rules are politically formed and informed. Though many are unanticipated, all have political consequences, too. By making committee chairpersons subject to confirmation by the party caucus at the beginning of every new Congress, the House majority obliged chairpersons to pay careful attention to their colleagues' views. Furthermore, since the votes of every member of the party caucus count equally, the views of impatient freshmen members of the caucus carry as much weight in the confirmation process as those of the halt, the lame and the venerable. Speaker Gingrich's reforms of January 1995 were not all of a piece: they weakened the autonomy of subcommittees and increased the authority of full committee chairpersons. Yet, the limit of three terms imposed on chairpersons restricted their medium-term leverage over colleagues (and saw some senior party members retire, rather than act as rank-and-file members). However, while Gingrich had selected committee chairs, his successors, from both parties, have usually left the task to their steering committees.

Despite these reforms to committees, the practice whereby the most senior member of a committee *normally* chairs it remains. In the 1950s, 1960s, and the first half of the 1970s, House committees were chaired by old white men, most of whom were southerners. After the reforms, little on the surface might appear to have changed: immediately prior to the 1988 elections, seven House committees were chaired by men over the age of 70. As late as 1992, old white men still predominated – in the 113th Congress white men of marginally less-advanced years predominate. The

Exhibit 6.3 House Committee Chairs and Ranking Members, January 2013

Committee	Chair	Ranking member	Born	Ethnicity	Elected
Agriculture	Frank D. Lucas (R-OK)	Colin Peterson (D-MN)	1960	White	1994
Appropriations	Harold Rogers (R-KY)	Nita M. Lowey (D-NY)	1937	White	1981
Armed Services	Buck McKeon (R-CA)	Adam Smith (D-WA)	1938	White	1992
Budget	Paul Ryan (R-WI)	Chris VanHollen (D-MN)	1970	White	1992
Education and Workforce	John Kline (R-MI)	George Miller (D-CA)	1947	White	2002
Energy and Commerce	Fred Upton (R-MI)	Henry Waxman (D-CA)	1953	White	1987
Ethics	K. Michael Conaway (R-Tx)	Linda Sanchez (D-CA)	1959	White	2003
Financial Services	Jeb Hensarling (R-TX)	Maxine Waters (D-CA)	1947	White	1993
Foreign Affairs	Ed Royce (R-CSA)	Michael McCaul (D-TX)	1952	Hispanic	1989
Homeland Security	Peter King (R-NY)	Bennie Thomson (D-Mis)	1949	White	1992
House Administration	Candice Miller (R-Mi)	Robert Brady (D-PA)	1946	White	2005
Judiciary	Bob Goodlatte (R-VA)	John Conyers (D-MI)	1947	White	1987
Natural Resources	Doc Hastings (R-WA)	Edward Markey (D-MA)	1941	White	1994
Oversight and Government Reform	Darrell Issa (R-GA)	Elijah Cummings (D-MD)	1953	White/Lebanese	2001
Rules	Pete Sessions (R-TX)	Louise McIntosh-Slaughter (D-NY)	1952	White	1980
Science, Space and Technology	Ralph M. Hall (R-TX)	Eddie Bernice-Johnson (D-TX female)	1923	White	1980
Transportation and Infrastructure	John L. Mica (R-FL)	Nick J. Rahall (D-Ill)	1943	White	1993
Veterans' Affairs	Jeff Miller (R-FL)	Bob Filner (D-CA)	1959	White	2001
Ways and Means	Dave Camp (R-MI)	Sander Levin (D-MI)	1953	White	2001
Intelligence	Mike Rogers (R-MI)	Ruppers Berger (D-MD)	1963	White	2001

seniority principle enjoys general support because it provides assurance of promotion in parties that are divided internally. Its application sometimes results in members supporting those with whom they have little in common in order that the established mode of succession may be maintained, and their own prospects of a committee chairmanship enhanced.

Beneath the veil of the seniority principle's continuity, the politics of relations between chairpersons and committees and of recruitment to the chairs of committees have, in any case, changed completely since the reforms. The 'Subcommittee Bill of Rights' in the 1970s enabled astute congressmen to influence particular areas of policy while still in their first few terms. To that extent, chairpersons of full committees prudently took careful account of the views, objectives and capabilities of party leaders and committee colleagues. Where chairpersons failed to take such account and persistently departed from party policy, they imperilled their chairmanships – as the veteran Mississippi conservative Sonny Montgomery discovered when the Democratic caucus came within four votes of depriving him of his chair following the 1992 elections.

Notwithstanding the six-year limits on their chairmanships since the 1995 changes to the House rules, all chairs retain some powers which resourceful politicians exploit to influence their committees' business and policy jurisdictions. All possess the formal authority to summon meetings of their committees; to determine its business; to hasten, retard, or halt the progress of the legislation before it; to recruit and dismiss committee (and, since January 1995, subcommittee) staff, to ensure the orderly management of the committee; and to allocate resources among its members. As power moved from the speaker back to the Republican steering committee in the late 1990s, so the party leadership, empowered once more to select committee chairs, would make it clear that, in considering candidates for chairing committees, they would assess their records in fundraising for their party colleagues.

Senate committees

Although the Senate is the House's full constitutional equal, it labours under the disadvantage of having to organize its work of legislation and oversight (particularly to scrutinize nominations made by the president to the federal judiciary, and the Executive Branch) with a much smaller membership than in the House. Senators' allocation of their time and the choices which they make about the committees to which they wish to belong reflect their political purposes and calculations. As for congressmen in the House, the choices which senators make about committee membership are not free: if they were, most would choose Appropriations, Finance, and Foreign Relations. Nevertheless, with only one hundred senators to authorize, appropriate, and oversee government, each senator sits on more committees than does each representative.

Committees and subcommittees continue to be important as arenas for the Senate at work, and politically significant for senators themselves. However, since the mid-1990s the Senate floor has acquired greater importance as a centre of decision-making. In the 1950s, committee decisions were invariably ratified by the full Senate. Now, committees cannot be certain that their versions of bills will find straightforward confirmation. Senators who are not members of a particular committee have, therefore, the chance of participating in the decision-making on a bill once it reaches the floor where access to the debate is more open. Their counterparts in the House are less fortunate since debate on the House floor is more tightly controlled under the Rule granted by the Rules Committee.

Following the House's review and modification of its committee structure and operation in the 1970s, the Senate made changes of its own, albeit with less sweeping consequences. In practice, most senators retain wide-ranging committee responsibilities. Discharging those responsibilities poses difficulties of judgement and organization, not least because of the risk that a primary or general election opponent might exploit absence or inattention. Yet, compression of the Senate's effective working week to three days causes committee meetings to clash. Senators must therefore choose how to allocate the average of less than two and a half hours in their typical eleven-hour day which one Senate study in 1976 showed they spent in committees. Multiple committee memberships still make it difficult to ensure enough members can be found to attend meetings: the few senators present at most committee meetings usually carry some colleagues' proxy votes, and reliance on staff is heavy. Chairmanship of full committees takes precedence. The unequal importance of Senate subcommittees mitigates the problem: some scarcely ever meet, and are marginal to legislation, representation and oversight.

An underlying problem is that the breadth of committee responsibilities presents attractive political opportunities to individual senators, but problems for the Senate's efficient operation. Coupled with 'sunshine' laws that require Senate committees to hold most hearings in public, resulting in policy-making being more transparent to lobbyists and the press, the tasks of coordinating Senate business, building coalitions and aggregating interests within and between committees is harder.

The Senate is accordingly characterized by a marked dispersion of authority and power, as Republican Majority Leader Trent Lott (R-Miss) discovered in his first, and deeply frustrating, year as majority leader. His experience of that frustration was frequent, and often intense. So it was in 2003, when Senate Democrats sought to block President Bush's judicial nominations. Lott responded by contemplating what he characterized as 'the nuclear option', in which the president of the Senate, Vice-President Dick Cheney, could be called on to prevent Democrats filibustering to block nominations.

An implication of such power dispersal and multiple responsibilities is that senators depend heavily on staff to assist them in every aspect of their work. Clashing committee and other obligations may oblige senators to rely on staff to attend those meetings they themselves cannot. A result is that staff often outnumber senators at committee hearings and mark-ups. Many hearings attract only one or two senators besides the chair; in some, the chair may be alone with the majority committee staff, the minority committee staff and the personal staff representatives of senators busy with duties elsewhere. Under these circumstances, senior staff have the opportunity and the duty to exercise vicarious political judgement.

The aggregative and collective dimension

Party in Congress offers the possibility that interests in each chamber might be aggregated, and individual preferences and district or state concerns overcome in pursuit of collective ends. Committees and subcommittees are Congress in its specialist mode and its fissiparous dimension; party is Congress in its aggregative mode and collective dimension. Party provides the core of coalitions around which legislative majorities are built. Less frequently (although common in the first thirteen years of this century), party provides a means for the expression of opposition to the policies of the president, and the president's party in Congress. The hold of congressional parties over their members is, in most respects, weak; however, the political forces binding them together are more powerful than those that would unfasten them. Their continued existence shows how, even in the American system of government, centripetal forces can overcome centrifugal ones if the calculus of political incentive is appropriately configured.

Such a calculus is the product of an interest that all members of each party share, regardless of their ideology, or regional, economic, ethnic, or constituency interest. They need one another's support to attain their individual objectives. A senator who, after years of service on a committee, finds himself about to succeed the current chairperson following their retirement, has an overriding interest in his party retaining a Senate majority. His political ambitions will be frustrated if he becomes the minority party's most senior member on the committee: opposition is not a happy condition for serious politicians, since it leaves them deciding what to say, rather than deciding what to do. Senators of each party therefore share the objective at each congressional election of ensuring that their party enjoys majority control.

Crucially, however, shared partisanship gives each a common interest in the other securing re-election, insofar as that may be required for either of them to gain the chair of a committee which they have spent their careers seeking. Such mutual interest, realized through the mechanism of party, holds together what would otherwise be a rickety agglomeration of interests. The House is more amenable to party leadership: as events in 1995, and votes on major tax bills in 1981, 2001 and 2003 showed, it can on rare occasions even be characterized by firm party control.

For so long a barrier to conservative Republican hopes, the House briefly became, under Speaker Gingrich's leadership in 1995, a vehicle for them: the 'Contract with America', the electoral vehicle for Gingrich's assault on the Democratic majority in November 1994, took legislative form in ten major floor votes within one hundred days of the 104th Congress convening. The Democratic-controlled 110th Congress, under the leadership of Speaker Nancy Pelosi, embarked on its 100-Day Plan, the name of which echoed Franklin D. Roosevelt's first one hundred days in the White House, and to which Pelosi had committed House Democrats in the event that they captured the House in the 2006 mid-term elections. The Democrats passed all six of their proposed bills with thirteen of their one hundred hours remaining.

If expressed at all, the public or national interest on behalf of which party leaders in Congress build coalitions of support from among their party colleagues is that voiced by the president. Partisan links between a president and colleagues on Capitol Hill are usually weak. Unlike a British prime minister's power over party colleagues in the House of Commons, links between president and nominal party colleagues in Congress are not strengthened by the powerful inducement of patronage. Partisanship is, nonetheless, one of the few instruments of persuasion at his disposal, and one which party leaders in Congress attempt to exploit at his behest. When President Johnson sent numerous legislative proposals on welfare, education and civil rights to Capitol Hill in the mid-1960s, much of the assembly of supporting coalitions for them was undertaken by the congressional leadership. Together, they coordinated supporters and potential supporters on the floor of each chamber, in liaison with the President and the White House staff. President Reagan acted similarly with Republican colleagues in the House and Senate in respect of his fiscal package in 1981. So, too, did President Bush in his 2001 tax cut, the £1.3 trillion Economic Growth and Tax Relief Reconciliation Act, which passed the house by 240 votes to 211. No Republican voted against the bill. President Obama's healthcare package of 2009 saw every Republican in the House vote against, and only a few Democrats joining them to oppose the President's legislation.

Since neither the president nor his Cabinet colleagues may be members of Congress, they must rely on political allies in Congress for assistance with their legislation. For example, in the case of the 1964 Civil Rights Act, President Johnson directed an intensive lobbying operation, with the assistance of his senior staff, who themselves communicated with the Majority Leader of the Senate, Mike Mansfield; the Speaker of the House, John McCormack; and Hubert Humphrey, the Floor Leader for the bill in the Senate. Close collaboration between presidents and their allies in Congress is a necessary, but not a sufficient, condition of legislative success for presidents who give legislative leadership. The further condition to be satisfied is that congressional leaders are themselves able to elicit support from their colleagues: as presidents cannot rely on members of the legislature following their lead, so ccongressional leaders cannot rely on their colleagues following theirs.

Party leaders have, as their first concern, the party's collective interests. Party leaders in Congress must attempt to maintain coherence and order within their own party, so that when the White House is occupied by a president of their own party he may be supported, and when it is not he may be opposed. Congressional party leaders' effectiveness derives from influence, not authority. Leading entails deciding. Most decisions by party leaders on policy matters threaten the interests of at least some colleagues and may provoke open dissent, thereby undermining party harmony. Party leaders therefore have to strike finely-judged balances between defensive caution (which invites frustration) and aggressive entrepreneurship (which risks dissension). Like presidents, prudent party leaders pay their colleagues courteous and close attention, and assess carefully and precisely whose views and intentions they should take into account, to what extent, in respect of what, and when. Since party leaders will always need the assistance of congressional colleagues, they are bound to attend to their political needs and ambitions. Party leaders can assist colleagues during campaigns (both by speaking for them and by financial support through their personal PACs), invite them to social gatherings, and ensure that they receive more than their fair share of the credit at times of political success (such as after the passage of a bill).

Party organization in the House

The speakership

The House party leadership structure has developed from the Constitution's provision for a speaker. The Constitution does not, however, specify the manner of the speaker's election, which is for the House to determine (see Appendix 1). The vote on the speakership takes place with every Congress. It usually does so on pure party lines: every Democratic representative votes for the Democratic candidate, and every

Republican representative for the Republican. Votes were not unanimous in January 1997 or in January 2013 when, respectively, Newt Gingrich and John Boehner drew opposition from a few dissenting party colleagues. But, for the most compelling political reasons, unanimity or something very close to it us the norm.

The speakership developed from the role of presiding officer in the 1st Congress to that of party leader under the formidable Henry Clay in the first decade of the nineteenth century. Clay was elected speaker while a freshman, an unthinkable event in today's House. Until 1910, the speaker sat at the head of the House's power structure. In the speakership were vested powers of recognition of those who wished to speak on the floor, the assignment of members to committees, the choosing of committee chairpersons, and the personal chairing of the Rules Committee, whose power it was to determine which items of legislation from committees should proceed to the floor. The combination of powers resulted in party control of legislative business in the House throughout the nineteenth century, reflecting, in part, the power exercised by party bosses in urban machines over the selection of candidates for Congress. The last three prerogatives were finally stripped from Speaker Joe Cannon between 1909 and 1911 as a reaction against the excesses of party control (which is to say, his control) exemplified during his tenure in office.

The speaker is the *de facto* leader and spokesman of the majority party in the House; a partisan politician, not a neutral chairperson overseeing debate. Because Democrats had majorities in the House from 1955 to 1994 (and for all but four of the twenty-two years prior to 1955), the advantage of electing the speaker irrespective of the party affiliation of the president or of the party balance in the Senate has been theirs for a large part of the twentieth century. But the period from 1995 to 2007 was one in which Republicans controlled one or both chambers of Congress. When, as in President George W. Bush's first six years, both the White House and the House of Representatives have lain in Republican hands, the Democrats' national political fortunes have been considerably weakened.

When a party lacks a president, the speaker is the closest it may come to having a national leader: for six of Ronald Reagan's eight years in the White House, Tip O'Neill served as speaker, which role amounted to that of an unofficial leader of the Democratic opposition. Gingrich played a similar role with great effect for the first year of the 104th Congress. John Boehner played a similar role – working with (and, more often, against) President Obama during the 112th Congress.

Until the revolt of newly-elected representatives in the 94th Congress of 1975–76, legislative power in the House lay with virtually autonomous committee chairmen. As part of the spate of congressional

Table 6.1 *Party Balances in Congress, 1929–2013*

Year	Congress	Senate			House		
		D	R		D	R	
1929–31	71st	39	56	1	167	267	1
1931–33	72nd	47	48	1	220	214	1
1933–35	73rd	60	35	1	310	117	5
1935–37	74th	69	25	2	319	103	10
1937–39	75th	76	16	4	331	89	13
1939–41	76th	69	23	4	261	164	4
1941–43	77th	66	28	2	268	162	4
1943–45	78th	58	37	1	218	208	4
1945–47	79th	56	38	1	240	190	1
1947–49	80th	45	51		188	245	1
1949–51	81st	54	42		263	171	1
1951–53	82nd	49	47		234	199	1
1953–55	83rd	47	48	1	211	221	1
1955–57	84th	48	47	1	232	203	
1957–59	85th	49	47		233	200	
1959–61	86th	64	34		283	153	
1961–63	87th	64	36		262	175	
1963–65	88th	67	33		258	176	1
1965–67	89th	68	32		295	140	
1967–69	90th	64	36		248	187	
1969–71	91st	58	42		243	192	
1971–73	92nd	54	44	2	255	180	
1973–75	93rd	56	42	2	242	192	
1975–77	94th	61	37	2	291	144	
1977–79	95th	61	38	1	292	143	
1979–81	96th	58	41	1	277	158	
1981–83	97th	46	53	1	243	192	
1983–85	98th	46	54		268	167	
1985–87	99th	47	53		253	182	
1987–89	100th	55	45		258	177	
1989–91	101st	55	45		260	175	
1991–93	102nd	56	44		267	167	1
1993–95	103rd	57	43		258	175	1
1995–97	104th	47	53		203	231	1
1997–99	105th	45	55		207	227	1
1999–01	106th	45	55		211	223	
2001–03	107th	50	50		211	221	
2003–05	108th	48	50	2	205	229	
2005–07	109th	49	59	2	201	232	
2007–09	110th	44	55	1	233	202	
2009–11	111th	41	55	2	256	178	
2011–13	112th	51	47	2	193	242	
2013–15	113th	54	45	1	201	234	

Note: Independent/others in third column for each chamber.

Exhibit 6.4 Democratic and Republican House Leadership in the 113th Congress

REPUBLICAN

Speaker	John A. Boehner (Ohio)
Majority Leader	Eric Cantor (Virginia)
Majority Whip	Kevin McCarthy (California)
Conference Chairman	Cathy McMorris Rodgers (Washington)

DEMOCRATIC

Minority Leader	Nancy Pelosi (California)
Minority Whip	Steny Hoyer (Maryland)
Caucus Chairman	Xavier Becerra (California)

reform in the 1970s, the revitalized party caucus returned to the speaker effective control of the Rules Committee. The Speaker does not chair it, but chooses the chair and nominates other members. While that base in authority does not give the speaker a free hand, placing the committee under the speaker's effective control (especially in the short run) does give them the power to determine which legislation moves from committees to the floor. As former Speaker Jim Wright has observed, the Rules Committee is the leadership's agent. The authority to set the agenda is almost as great a political asset as the capacity, imagination and will to dispose of the items on it. Combining the leadership's own abundant scheduling authority with the institutional resource of the Rules Committee is a potent source of political power. As the rapid movement of the legislative components of the 'Contract with America' to floor votes in 1995, and the rapid passage of six bills in the 'First 100 hours' of the Democrat-controlled 110th Congress showed, the change has strengthened the speaker's capacity to manage legislation in the post-reform Congress.

That, in turn, has assisted the majority party, and protected committee versions of bills from amendment in the Committee of the Whole House. The speaker's preferences are rarely opposed by party colleagues, and even less often successfully so.

Making the speakership's formal authority effective is contingent on the abilities and purposes of the individual speaker, the political context and the depth of support from their party caucus. Limited scope for expensive domestic policy initiatives since the financial crisis of 2007–08, coupled with pressure brought to bear by fiscal conservatives (especially the Tea Party Movement) has restricted subcommittees' freedom to modify the Republican congressional party leadership's purposes, but the speaker remains dependent on the support of colleagues for the maintenance of his office's effectiveness. Revolts against the Speaker before

World War I and in 1996–97, and those against Committee barons in the mid-1970s, show that majority sentiment in congressional parties cannot for long be resisted.

The majority leader and majority whip

In support of the speaker, and immediately below them in seniority within the majority party, is the majority leader, whose primary task is that of assisting the speaker in legislative scheduling, bargaining, exhortation and coalition formation. As Tom DeLay showed during his tenure as majority leader from 2003 to 2005 and as majority whip from 1995 to 2003, these positions are intensely and thoroughly political, rather than being merely technical or administrative in nature. Legislation can be scheduled to suit the interests of the House majority, to facilitate liaison with the Senate or to frustrate it, to accommodate or resist a president's wishes, to enhance a bill's prospects of success, or to weaken them. It is also possible for the minority leader and (more unusually) for the majority whip to overshadow the speaker: DeLay overshadowed Speaker Hastert on many occasions by exploiting his power-base within the conservative wing of the House Republican Party.

The complex and diverse coalitions that comprise the two congressional parties in the House require elaborate whip structures for communication within the party. In addition to the majority whip, there is a leadership organization comprising a chief deputy whip (who has their own staff), deputy whips and assistant whips, covering nearly every state. Former Speaker Jim Wright once observed that the two tasks of House whips are:

> gathering intelligence, knowing where the votes are ... Their second function is persuasion, producing the votes.

The first of these tasks is relatively straightforward; the second is not. Since members of Congress are entrepreneurial, individually seeking both re-election and political power, the task of aggregation can be exceptionally difficult, as the crumbling of Republican Party cohesion in 1982–86 and 1996–97 showed. Yet, the first decade of the twenty-first century has shown that increasing partisanship, coupled with party discipline, can be established and maintained to an extent that would have seemed barely conceivable to politicians and political observers of Congress in the mid-twentieth century. Yet, even in an era of increased partisanship, leaders have few usable and durable sanctions with which to enforce their will, and none to compare with those powerful deterrents to dissension which operate in the partly-fused systems of government in Germany and the United Kingdom.

The minority leader and minority whip

There is no minority speaker: the Democratic Party's leader in the House is the minority leader: former Speaker Nancy Pelosi (2007–11). She has no capacity to engage in scheduling but, like the majority leadership, has as her first task the cultivation of party loyalty and effectiveness in an institution whose structures, procedures and culture do not foster authority's concentration. She therefore acts as the party's principal spokesman in the House. The minority leader is assisted by their deputy, the minority whip, and twelve regional whips. Since the House is a more partisan body than the Senate, the minority party there usually counts for less.

Party organization in the Senate

Majority leadership

The Senate has neither a speaker, nor an office with comparable authority or prerogatives. The vice-president of the United States is the president of the Senate, but has no authority other than to make a casting vote in the event of a tie on the floor. He rarely presides over the Senate; in his place, there is the president *pro tempore*, who has no more power over the chamber's proceedings than has the vice-president. Nevertheless, both parties have leaders, and a whip elected by the Senate Conference (the party caucus) when it convenes after each congressional election. For all that it lacks the powers of the House speakership, the office of the leader of the largest party, the majority leadership, has often been important. Since 1955, it has been held by four Republicans (for a total of thirteen years) and nine Democrats (for a total of forty-two years).

There are fewer and weaker mechanisms in the Senate for enforcing majorities than there are in the House. Senate rules have the consequence of elevating individual members of the chamber, rather than creating majorities, and Senate leaders are obliged to exercise their duties primarily through custom, rather than by rules. Emphasizing that party leaders have little authority, that the leadership is informally at least collective, bound in practice to depend on and defer to other senior members, and heavily reliant for day-to-day functions on staff, Davidson (1989: 285) defines Senate party leaders' responsibilities as follows:

1. managing the affairs of their senatorial parties;
2. scheduling Senate floor business in accord with workload needs and individual senators' desires;
3. monitoring floor deliberations, which include seeking unanimous consent agreements governing debates and votes;

4. serving as a conduit between the Senate, the White House, and the House;
5. speaking for the Senate through the media.

No majority leader enjoys the formal powers over the scheduling of legislation and the assignment of members to committees which the rules of the House of Representatives grants the speaker, or that Robert Taft and Lyndon Johnson enjoyed between 1953 and 1958, in which year a large class of liberal Democratic senators determined to forge a new agenda for the national party was elected. Having been elected minority leader in 1953 after only four years' membership of the Senate, Johnson assumed the majority leadership in 1955 when the Democrats regained their majority following the 1954 mid-term elections.

Influential though Robert Taft had been in enhancing the prominence of the office, it was Lyndon Johnson who not only effectively defined the office of Senate Majority Leader, but who also defined it effectively. Positioning himself broadly in the ideological mainstream of his diverse party, he sometimes led from the front; sometimes, too, he allowed colleagues to move ahead of him while nudging them in one direction or another; at other times he led his colleagues by appearing to the less perceptive of them not to be leading at all; occasionally, he exercised leadership by indirection; and he typically led by reconfiguring single-shot games into multiple-shot games. But, all the while, Lyndon Johnson remained in control of himself, of the chamber's dynamics, of the legislative agenda, and of his place in the history of the United States Senate. Exploiting every opportunity to strengthen the majority leadership, he sought (with little success in the 1950s) to promote his own prospects of presidential office, and (with much greater success) the fortunes of fellow Democrats in the Senate. Johnson did these things by attending constantly to long-established

---

Exhibit 6.5 Democratic and Republican Senate Leadership in the 113th Congress

DEMOCRATIC
President *Pro Tempore*	Patrick Leahy (Vermont)
Majority Leader and Caucus Chair	Harry Reid (Nevada)
Policy Committee Chair	Chuck Shumer (New York)

REPUBLICAN
Minority Leader	Mitch McConnell (Kentucky)
Conference Chair	John Thune (South Dakota)
Policy Committee Chair	John Barrasso (Wyoming)

political friendships, establishing the foundations of new ones, and investing political capital in those whom he judged might be induced, whether by fair means or not, to support him on particular policy questions. Where (as was usually the case) he could not achieve complete legislative victory, he sought compromise while supporting President Eisenhower on matters of national importance, and where the President's own position enjoyed such popular support as to make opposition to it unwise.

None of Lyndon Johnson's successors has approached the office as he did. None has had the same objectives or opportunities, or worked under constraints similar in kind or extent. And none has had remotely his breadth of political imagination, willpower, or deep reservoir of resolve. Part of the explanation lies in the changes that Johnson himself wrought. As he paid due regard within the Senate to the norms of collegiality and deferred to the chairmen of committees, his centralization of power weakened the baronial power-bases of these chairmen. Nelson Polsby (1969) rightly attributed the significant weakening of the 'Inner Club' of senior senators partly to Johnson's transformation of the office of majority leader between 1955 and 1960.

Recent majority leaders have worked in an institution that obliges them to cultivate goodwill if collective objectives are to be achieved. Abraham Ribicoff, a member of the Senate in the final phase of its pre-reform period in the 1960s, but who continued to serve in it after the convulsive internal and external changes of the 1960s and 1970s, characterized the difference by pointing to Majority Leader Byrd's anxious willingness to serve his fellow Democratic senators: were he ever to have taken a pencil out of his pocket in the presence of the majority leader, he remarked, it was certain that Senator Byrd would offer to sharpen it for him. Byrd's was a willingness born of necessity. The clashing ambitions of entrepreneurial colleagues have obliged all of Johnson's successors to mediate between the president and senators, persuading, cajoling and cautiously crafting agreement. Robert Dole has himself characterized the post he twice held as 'majority pleader', something which no speaker of the House of recent years could claim about the speakership.

Minority leadership

The post of minority leader in the Senate has acquired an importance which that of minority leader in the House usually lacks, since majorities there have been less durable. Weaker traditions of party control coupled with laxer and fewer rules make the task of leading the majority party in the Senate especially difficult. The majority and minority leaders are bound to work with each other as colleagues in the task of managing Senate business, as well as against each other in their roles as partisan and competitive politicians.

Whip system

By contrast with the House, the whip system in the Senate is undeveloped. There are majority and minority whips, with chief deputy whips and deputy whips below them. Nonetheless, they work in a political setting quite different from that in the House: the Senate is an institution designed to enable its members to gain regional and national attention, not to produce legislation with despatch. Party control is, accordingly, difficult for party leaders to secure.

Party and voting

Where they perceive constituency interests are likely to be affected, members of Congress and senators tread carefully. If, for example, they calculate that to support the president would prompt heavy criticism from constituents, thereby increasing their vulnerability to primary or general election defeat, they will not hesitate to oppose him. Similarly, however assiduous the party whips, they will not persuade colleagues to risk their careers for the sake of supporting the party. Where adherence to the party leadership is not fatal to re-election prospects, members may take some political risks and provide support to their leadership – particularly in an era of increased partisanship and greater ideological coherence within the parties. Where constituency interests are unaffected or marginal, presidential leadership and party membership help to explain why members of Congress vote as they do.

Presidential success in this regard is, nonetheless, mainly a function of the existence, size and ideological composition of the majority held by the president's party in each chamber. President Roosevelt's extraordinary legislative accomplishments between 1933 and 1938 owed much to his capacity to discern and exploit political opportunities amidst the disorder of economic depression, but ideologically favourable large partisan majorities in the House and the Senate were a prerequisite for his success. President George W. Bush's legislative achievements were made possible not only by majorities in both chambers, but by ideological coherence. President Obama benefited from Democrat majorities in both chambers between 2009 and 2011. Without those majorities, his healthcare bill could not have been passed. Likewise, both his fiscal stimulus package and banking reforms drew overwhelming support from his own party, and opposition from the Republican Party that was not merely complete, but intense.

The decline and resurgence of party voting

Rates of party-line voting declined after the high-point of 1995–96 to the levels of the mid-1980s. In the first and second decades of the twenty-first century, high rates of nearly 90 per cent are again the norm. Congress is now sharply and deeply partisan; the South is strongly Republican; and the ideological gap between the two parties is clear and deep. Conservative Democrats are now so few in number as to be politically insignificant; liberal Republicans in Congress have disappeared altogether from Congress. Party polarization is as high now as it was in the late nineteenth-century.

Caucuses

Party membership is the best predictor of how an individual member of Congress or senator will vote but is, on most issues, still an imperfect one. The social, geographic, ethnic, racial and economic heterogeneity of America makes the containing by two parties of social cleavages difficult. In addition to their party membership, most congressional politicians belong to cross-party caucuses or to intra-party caucuses (factions). They may be confined to the House (as most are), to the Senate, or, in some cases, be drawn from both chambers. Within the cross-party (and most numerous) category, different types of caucus cater to distinct kinds of interest: geographic, social, economic and policy. Intra-party caucuses consist of factional groups within each party which seek to enlarge their influence. Most caucuses have a small staff; all elect officers.

The purposes of bipartisan caucuses vary, but the following three features are shared:

- *provision* and *exchange of information* between members;
- offering of *amendments on pending legislation*;
- building of *wider support* for *caucus policy* on particular issues of concern to its members.

For individual members, the costs of joining a caucus are low, but the rewards may be high. While some members will seek the chairmanship of a caucus, most are content to draw on the benefits of membership. Caucuses frequently work closely with interest groups outside Congress to draft legislation, assisting individual legislators in promoting their policies and careers and, at best, mitigating the worst effects of the relative structural and partisan rigidities of Congress.

The procedural dimension

The procedural dimension has two aspects: the first is of the legislative process; the second that of oversight. We consider only the first here, but the second in Chapter 9. Two chambers share the legislative function, and every bill that becomes law has to be passed in identical form by both. Such an outcome rarely occurs at the first time of asking because bills suffer different fates in the two places, being subject to various amendments as they are considered by committees, subcommittees and, finally, by all members of Congress and senators on the floor of each chamber. Conference committees, composed of members from each chamber, have therefore often (in about one-quarter of cases) been constituted for a bill after it has passed all of the stages in each chamber in order to agree a common version of the legislation on which each chamber then votes. As polarization has intensified, however, so the practice of holding conference committees (and especially holding them in public) has declined. In the 110th Congress (2007–08), only nine conference committees were established. Accordingly, these differences between the two chambers' drafts of legislation are resolved by other means. A common approach has been for either the House or Senate to adjourn and oblige the other to accept the bill, or lose it entirely. A second approach, sometimes dubbed 'ping-pong', comprises a limited number of exchanges of amendments between the two chambers until differences are eliminated.

Polarized politics notwithstanding, most legislation is minor, uncontentious and passed quickly. Provided that the two parties' calendar watchers (usually staff members of the policy committees) raise no objection, such legislation before the Senate is listed by the majority leader one day prior to the formal seeking of approval on the floor. Similar procedures apply in the House with respect to uncontroversial legislation.

Most major bills originate in the Executive Branch. The clearest example is that of the annual budget: all departments' and agencies' annual requests for appropriations are supervized by the Office of Management and Budget before being sent to Congress in the president's budget message. Bills re-authorizing agencies and programmes are also prepared in the Executive Branch. Bills are physically despatched from the White House to Congress where they are introduced, under prior arrangement, by sympathetic senators and congressmen whose names appear on the bill as sponsors. In the Senate, bills are introduced either directly from the floor by the sponsoring senator, or by being sent to Senate clerks for publication in the *Congressional Record*. Most bills thus introduced into Congress every session die. In order to become law, a bill must pass all of the many institutional obstacles to passage within the two-year time limit of each Congress.

An example drawn from the 110th Congress (2007–09) makes the point. In those two years, of the nearly 14,000 bills introduced (the largest number since 1980), only 449 bills were passed – a mere 3.3 per cent of the total introduced. Such numbers tell only part of the story of legislative activity: the importance and durability of the law matters more. The 110th Congress resulted in passage of President Obama's healthcare plan, reform of Wall Street, passage of the fiscal stimulus package, proposals to create three million jobs and to invest in green energy. Irrespective of the view that one might take of these bills' purposes and costs, they make for a considerable political achievement by the executive and legislative branches coordinating in their passage.

The procedure for legislation following the introduction of a bill is that the Speaker refers it to a standing committee of the House; in the Senate, a similar referral is made to a standing committee by the Senate's presiding officer. Accordingly, in the House, a bill re-authorizing support for Amtrak, the inter-city passenger railway system, will be referred to the Transportation and Infrastructure Committee and, in the Senate, to the Commerce, Science and Transportation Committee, each of which would, in the first instance, refer it to the Surface Transportation subcommittees. It is in these subcommittees that Congress does most of its work on the legislation, hearing expert testimony from disinterested and interested witnesses alike, from politicians in senior positions within government departments and agencies, and civil servants lower down, and from lobbyists and experts outside government, or operating at the permeable boundaries of government in Washington, where the public world meshes with the private. All witnesses in the hearings are questioned.

The sponsor of a bill in each chamber, together with such of their co-sponsoring colleagues whose names the sponsor finds it advantageous to have associated with the bill, always seek to divert a bill from a committee that may be hostile to it. Presidents and congressional party leaders behave similarly in respect of their own legislation. Where committee jurisdictions overlap, providing no single path for a bill, obstacles presented by particular committees to a bill's passage can be circumvented. Formal powers granted to the speaker by the House make this easier in the larger, rule-bound House, than in the Senate

At the start of the 104th Congress, the Republican majority abolished joint referrals, and amended House rules to enable the Speaker (Newt Gingrich) to 'designate a committee of primary jurisdiction'. With the vigorous support of the seventy-three conservative GOP freshmen, the Speaker and his colleagues drafted the alteration to enhance his discretion in determining the most effective political means for steering the Republican agenda through Congress by granting to him, for example, the power to send different parts of a bill to different committees. Gingrich quickly added to his powers by creating task forces where he thought it advantageous to circumvent established committees. The formal change in rules and practices did not make Gingrich all-powerful:

for he had overreached himself, prompting some of his colleagues to rebel against his presumption.

Committee hurdles cannot, in any case, always be so easily jumped. Many bills are often submitted to more than one committee, either sequentially or simultaneously. Overlapping jurisdictions, deliberately arranged in order to maximize participation and opportunities for the claiming of credit, fuel multiple referrals. Some authorizing committees, of which the House Energy and Commerce Committee is a striking example, have jurisdictions sufficiently broad to enable their chairmen to conduct oversight of an exceptionally wide range of public policy, and to claim major legislative roles. Much as they are resented, attempts by committees to invade the territory of one another reflect the competitive political struggle within Congress and are, accordingly, ineradicable.

When a subcommittee has completed its hearings, and marking-up, it votes on whether to report the bill to the full committee. If the subcommittee chairman wishes to proceed and has judged his colleagues' views soundly, the bill will progress to the full committee. For major legislation, the full committee will hold hearings, consider amendments and eventually produce a (probably somewhat different) draft of its own. Consideration is then given to reporting the bill to the floor. The floors of both chambers are now very much more important to the content of legislation than they were before the reforms of the 1970s.

Legislation in the House

Their varying tenures, constituencies and Constitutional responsibilities, and the exclusive powers that each chamber has over its rules, causes the formal bicameralism of Congress to issue in distinctive legislative cultures. The House is tightly rule-bound: legislation proceeds through dense institutional structures under detailed rules. The Senate gives freer rein to its members' individual characters, needs and ambitions. Davidson and Oleszek (1981) characterize this contrast between the ordered procedures of the House and the relative looseness of the Senate as reflecting the former's pursuit of 'majority rule' within the 435-member chamber, and the Senate's underpinning of its 100 members' 'individual rights'. The difference is incompletely realized. Nevertheless, procedures for considering legislation on the House floor remain formal and detailed; those in the Senate are, by comparison, informal and general.

House rules grant to five committees the right of direct access to the floor for certain bills: Appropriations, Budget; House Oversight, Rules, and Standards of Official Conduct may all bring such measures direct to the floor provided that other business is not pending there. For most purposes, these provisions grant a privileged status to appropriations bills, to budget resolutions and to the leadership's rules for the ordering and scheduling of business on the floor. All three are best understood as instances of the House leadership's power. Accordingly, they may be brought to the floor for debate at any time of the majority leadership's choosing. Otherwise, except in the rare event of its being subject to a discharge petition, no bill may come to the floor without first having its terms of debate set by the Rules Committee, in the form of a 'Rule' being granted to it. Unlike other standing committees, Rules conducts no hearings on legislation. It is the sole gatekeeper to the floor, establishing rules for the consideration of authorizing legislation on the floor of the House.

The Rules Committee may grant four types of rule. All specify the time available for general debate, exclusive of the time necessary to debate amendments:

- An *open rule*, permitting the proposal and debate of amendments germane to the subject of the bill.
- A *closed rule*. If pure, no amendments may be offered to the bill; otherwise, only those amendments from, for example, the primary committee reporting the legislation may be permitted.
- A *modified closed rule*, according to which some parts of a bill may be subject to amendment and some not.
- *Waiver rules* may be granted by the Committee, and are frequently included within one of the above Rules. They may permit the waiving of points of order raised against parts of the bill, or dispense with customary rules of procedure.

The House is not bound to accept a Rule granted by the Rules Committee, and votes on every Rule prior to debating the bill itself. On the rare occasions that Rules are defeated, the consequences may be considerable.

Whoever controls the Rules Committee therefore acts as gatekeeper of legislation to the House floor, and is able to influence legislation by the selective opening, bolting and temporary closing of the gate. When, as in the 1950s and 1960s, the Committee was dominated by southern conservative Democrats, it checked the liberal and moderate majority. The Committee could not act in the absence of the conservative Democratic chairman, Howard Smith, who accordingly used the pretext of attending to urgent business on his Virginia farm when he needed to prevent a bill proceeding to the floor. Alliance with like-minded conservative colleagues on the Committee (most Republicans and southern Democrats) presented a fixed obstacle to liberal legislation, especially on civil rights. Seeking a discharge petition, whereby business before the Committee could be released from it by a vote of the House against the chairman's wishes, was not politically prudent because all members of the House were reluctant to irritate a powerful chairman whose support they might themselves require for other legislation in the future.

A Rule having been granted by the Rules Committee, and approved by the House, general debate proceeds on the floor under the special procedures applying to the Committee of the Whole House, into which form the House then technically resolves itself. The main political activity in the Committee of the Whole occurs not in the general debate, but in the consideration of amendments. This stage, under which amendments can be made and substitute clauses offered, also proceeds under strict rules: each amendment may be the subject of no more than one five-minute speech in support or opposition.

Once all amendments have been voted on, the Committee of the Whole 'rises', and resumes its former existence as the full House under the speaker's chairmanship. The House reviews the Committee's actions by voting on the amendments. The penultimate stage, for a motion to be offered to recommit the bill to the standing committee which reported it, is invariably rejected. A vote is then taken on final passage by each member wishing to vote, who presses a button to indicate whether they wish to vote 'yea', 'nay', or 'present' (abstain). If the bill is passed, and the Senate has not already considered it, it is then sent there.

Legislation in the Senate

The Senate has no functional equivalent of the House Rules Committee: its Rules Committee is not an analogue of the House Rules Committee, but deals with internal procedural matters only. Most legislation reaches the Senate floor by an agreement of unanimous consent (often referred to as a UCA: Unanimous Consent Agreement) which, dispensing with the rules nominally controlling floor procedure, set terms and conditions under which debate is actually to be conducted.

The Senate retains only filaments of the club-like culture for which it was celebrated in the 1950s. Less raucously partisan than the House, it attaches greater importance to floor deliberation and less to detailed legislative work in committees than does its much larger neighbour. Protection of the individual rights and standing of each senator are reinforced by the Senate's procedures, and makes the scheduling of legislation by the Senate leadership a strenuous task. With the aid of his colleagues in the leadership and staff, the Senate majority leader is condemned to initiate legislation, guide its passage through the Senate and speak on its behalf, while lacking any significant control over it. The variable which majority leaders would doubtless most like to control (but which there is least prospect of their controlling) is that of the schedules of their party colleagues. As senators spend more time in their states, aping the behaviour of House colleagues, so the planning of legislative schedules becomes ever harder. In response to senators' pleas to spend more time, and to spend it more predictably, away from Washington attending to their individual political needs, the Senate now works only three weeks in four.

One Senate rule illustrates how the Senate continues to set a higher priority on the protection of the rights of individual members to object to proposed legislation before the Senate: unlike the House, the Senate preserves the practice of permitting unlimited debate through the filibuster, by which individual senators may deliberately prolong debate by continuing to speak. The filibuster's roots are so deep in the Senate's institutional culture that, even when it has been employed (as it often has) since 1945 by conservative southerners against northern liberals to defeat civil rights legislation, proposals to abolish it have been few. Filibustering requires physical stamina and organizational skill: the late Senator Strom Thurmond of South Carolina, then a Democrat, later a Republican, but always a conservative, spoke for more than twenty-four hours continuously in 1957 against the Civil Rights Bill. Such a herculean performance would not be possible in the House of Representatives, where speeches of five to ten minutes are the norm.

Although the Senate had, as early as 1917, weakened the force of the filibuster by providing in Rule XXII that a filibuster might be stopped under certain circumstances, the hurdles to invoking it were high. The 1964 Civil Rights Act passed only after a bitter battle to vote 'cloture' – that is, to close the debate. Thus, it was on the cloture vote that the political struggle concentrated, rather than on the bill itself. To that extent, the battle was especially difficult because a cloture vote requires (under current Senate rules) the approval of three-fifths of the Senate, after which each senator is permitted to speak for a further hour. Until the modification of Rule XXII in 1975 made the granting of cloture easier, few cloture votes had succeeded. Since 1975, many have. However, although more filibusters have been halted by cloture votes in the last quarter of the twentieth century, filibustering itself has become more, not less, common in the same period: only 23 filibusters occurred in the nineteenth century, but 191 occurred between 1970 and 1994 alone (Binder and Smith, 1997: 11). The Senate is an institution in which the majority has increasing difficulty in exercising its will.

The increased threat (if not the use) of the filibuster has increased since the mid-1960s – as has the partisan rancour in the Senate. During President George W. Bush's administration, the filibuster became the focus of controversy when, in 2005, the Democratic minority threatened to filibuster the judicial nominations of the President (on the grounds that the nominees were too conservative on social issues and, therefore, not in keeping with the purported spirit of nominating a candidate amenable to most members of the chamber). Led by senators John Kerry and Edward (Ted) Kennedy, Senate Democrats threatened to filibuster in order to prevent a vote to confirm the nominations. One particularly controversial nominee, Miguel Estrada, asked that his nomination be withdrawn, but the Republicans in the Senate, incensed by what many of them saw as an abuse of Senate procedures, considered one option that Senate Majority Leader Bill Frist (2003–07) threatened – the so-called 'nuclear option' (a term coined by Senator Trent Lott (R-MS)). This option would require the president of the Senate, Vice-President Dick Cheney, to bypass the filibuster by allowing a simple majority vote – rather than the sixty-vote cloture motion – to end the filibuster. Frist argued that judicial nominations should be exempt from the cloture vote rule because it was the duty of the Senate to provide advice and consent on judicial nominations. However, he could not change Senate rules without gaining a two-thirds majority, so the nuclear option was all that was left to him. Senators Kennedy and Kerry withdrew the filibuster threat, but partisan rancour has continued to the point where it harms the Senate's capacity to participate in the business of government.

Conclusion

The United States Congress was not designed so that policy-making might be made simple. Yet, Congress has developed institutional techniques for the control and channelling of problems embedded in the constitutional order. The outcome invariably appears disordered, and often is. Of the two functions of Congress considered in this chapter, as a representative and as a policy-making institution, the former is discharged with conspicuously greater enthusiasm, effectiveness and efficiency than the latter. Here lies the primary interest in analysing Congress: the tensions between five of its dimensions, and their resolution in the sixth: the centrifugal (fissiparous) political and financial forces on the one hand (especially those arising from congressional districts, home states, and constituents within them), and the countervailing centripetal (aggregative) forces of party and president that provide incentives to representatives and senators to participate in the aggregation of interests and the formation, legislation, implementation and evaluation of public policy.

Nonetheless, by comparison with the powers of legislatures elsewhere, Congress's autonomy from the executive grants it powers over public policy and a role in national politics much greater than those of legislatures in all other advanced liberal democracies. In the formation of national budgets, of many aspects of defence policy, in the regulation of industrial pollution, safety at work, banks, financial markets, labour markets, telecommunications and elections, Congress's power to regulate under the provisions of the Constitution's interstate commerce clause is unfettered and intensively employed. The separation of powers ensures that Congress is not subject to the will of the executive; presidents who suppose otherwise are always disabused.

If its autonomy is complete, its capacity to set and sustain the national political agenda is slight. The bicameral Congress is ill-fitted to give coherent leadership or to act speedily. These possibilities it cedes to the presidency. Congress has no prospect of competing durably with the president in national leadership. Insofar as it is an untidy institution with a deficient capacity to aggregate interests, it reflects the diverse and contradictory aspirations and preferences of American voters and interest groups, and of its own membership.

Chapter 7

The Supreme Court and the Politics of Adjudication

This chapter examines the organization of the Court, its power of judicial review and the ways in which the Court interacts with the elected branches examined in Chapters 5 and 6. The Supreme Court is thickly immersed in the formulation, implementation and evaluation of public policy in the United States. Whether or not the authors of the Constitution intended it, many of the Court's judgements have political consequences. The Court's role differs from those of the other branches because its members are politically appointed, not elected. They are, however, bound to maintain the legitimacy of the institution of which they are members. Accordingly, its appointive character does not diminish the extent to which the Court is political, but modulates its expression.

The federal courts in general, and the Supreme Court in particular, are apparent anomalies in a political system characterized more than any in Europe by the principle of electoral accountability. Federal judges are formally neither accountable to electors, nor answerable to a body of elective politicians. Yet, what appears at first to be constitutionally anomalous flows from the characteristically American cultural distrust of the unfettered exercise of power by politicians. Majority and minority groups across the United States and throughout American history have good cause to distrust the rule of politicians unchecked between elections (and sometimes in spite of them). Nevertheless, the Court is not a final arbiter in matters of public policy (although many suppose it to be so). Its lack of enforcement powers has occasionally resulted in its decisions being vigorously (and sometimes successfully) resisted by communities or regions, or overturned by Congressional action or constitutional amendment.

The organization and role of the judiciary

The structure of state courts

Article III, Section 1, of the US Constitution establishes a Supreme Court, and permits Congress to form lower federal courts (see Appendix 1). The Constitution assumes throughout, and at points explicitly discusses, the existence of courts falling under the jurisdiction of the then thirteen states. There is no doubting the superiority of the United States Constitution in the event of a clash between it and the constitutions or laws of the several states. The Constitution of the United States, and the laws and treaties made under it by the federal authorities shall, declares Article VI:

> be the supreme Law of the Land; and the Judges in every State shall be bound thereby, any Thing in the Constitution or Laws of any State to the Contrary notwithstanding.

Equally, the states are sovereign. Legal entities in their own right, they have full authority under the US Constitution to establish their own courts. Accordingly, there are in the United States fifty-two distinct legal systems: one for the United States as a whole, but administered by a three-tier system of federal courts; fifty for the individual states; and one for the District of Columbia. Most law in the United States is state law; some law is entirely a matter for states. Federal law applies to inter-state matters. Most courts are state and municipal courts. Most judges are state and municipal judges: of the 47,000 judges in the United States, only 3,300 are members of the federal bench. While all state law must accord with the provisions of the United States Constitution and federal law, this requirement permits wide latitude in the content of law between the states and in its interpretation by state judges.

Recruitment of judges to state courts varies between states. In seven states, judges are popularly elected on a partisan ticket; and non-partisan elections are used in a further fifteen; in two, the legislature elects; in ten (mainly in the east) the governor appoints (in some states with confirmation by the state Senate, and in others by a council). In sixteen, the 'Missouri Plan' is applied: the governor appoints from a list of three candidates nominated by a special commission generally comprising lawyers selected by judges, and non-lawyers selected by the governor. Judges chosen by this last method are subject to periodic re-election by citizens of the state. The salience of law and order as a political issue notwithstanding, judicial elections rarely arouse much interest among voters. Incumbency offers some advantage in most states, especially since most voters know little of those standing for election. In few judicial elections are policy issues addressed.

The structure of the courts in the states varies in detail; among municipalities, it varies rather more. Some of the differences consist in the idiosyncrasies of local nomenclature and procedural embellishment; others are substantive.

The structure of federal courts

The three layers to the federal court system comprise the US Supreme Court, the US (Circuit) Courts of Appeals, and the US District Courts. Of these three, the Constitution established only the first by name, but enabled Congress to create a supporting federal judicial system by creating 'such inferior courts as the Congress may from time to time ordain and establish'. Circuit courts were created by the Judiciary Act of 1789, one of the first Congress's first Acts, and district courts by the Judiciary Act of 1891.

Federal district courts

There are currently 94 US district courts and 677 US district judges (including seven in Puerto Rico). Twenty-six states consist of just one district; the rest have two or more. New York and Texas have four district courts each, while California has six. Some districts have only one or two judges, while major cities have many (the southern district of New York has twenty-seven). With the minor exception, since 1979, of the appeal of civil cases to the US District Court first heard before a US magistrate, the district courts have no appellate jurisdiction, but an original jurisdiction only: all crimes against the United States, all financially substantial (above $10,000) civil cases under federal law or the federal constitution, the review and enforcement of orders and actions of certain federal agencies, and in other cases determined by the US Congress.

The US (Circuit) Courts of Appeals

The thirteen Appeals Courts and the 179 judges within them are often named 'circuit courts' because, until the Judiciary Act of 1869, each justice of the US Supreme Court, in being assigned to head one of the circuit courts by way of overseeing its work, was required to 'ride circuit' across the states comprising each division, or circuit, of this Appellate division of the federal judicial system. Each judge has three clerks (only one fewer than most associate justices of the Supreme Court).

Eleven of the circuit courts cover defined geographical areas of whole states; the twelfth covers the District of Columbia, the seat of federal government. For example, the second circuit comprises the states of New York, Connecticut and Vermont. In establishing the federal courts by the 1789 Judiciary Act, Congress provided for the number of circuit Courts to be equivalent to the number of Supreme Court Justices. Increased workloads in the late nineteenth century caused Congress, in 1891, belatedly to recognize the need to establish full-time Courts of Appeal between the overburdened district and Supreme Courts. Eighty-five per cent of federal cases reaching the circuit courts proceed no further.

The United States Supreme Court

From 1789 until the Civil War, the relationship between the federal and state governments dominated all other questions before the Court. In McCloskey's words (1960: 29), the survival of the Union 'inhered in almost every constitutional case the Supreme Court faced'. Neither the Constitutional Convention nor the States' ratification of the Constitution had settled the nature of the new polity. Neither did resolution of that question await revelation by close examination of the Constitution's text, of the Constitutional debates, or *The Federalist Papers*. Constitutional arguments proceeded in Courts, in Congress and in state legislatures throughout the period, but not until the end of the Civil War was the question of the polity's indissolubility finally answered. Related questions of the extent of the states' sovereignty and the meaning of the Tenth Amendment still exercise the federal courts, as the discussion in Chapter 10 shows. Neither will the boundaries of federal and state action ever be definitively settled: neither the Constitution nor the judgements of the Court provide for agreement either on underlying principle, or on the application of constitutional principle to new controversies and cases.

Between 1865 and 1941, the Court's prime concern was the constitutional basis of the federal government's intervention in the economy. The period opens in the aftermath of the final establishment of the indissolubility of the Union, of the end to the frontier, in the founding for the first time of a *nation*, in the completion of transcontinental railroad links, through the formation of independent regulatory commissions from 1883 onwards, and the growing regulation of the national economy in the last decade of the nineteenth century and in the period leading up to World War I. Following the quiescence of the decade that followed the war came the assertion by President Roosevelt in the New Deal of the federal government's power to shape macroeconomic policy, and to regulate agriculture, finance and industry. Roosevelt's

Exhibit 7.1 The 'Court-Packing' Plan of 1937

In 1937, President Roosevelt (FDR) proposed the appointment of one additional justice to the Supreme Court for every justice who had reached the age of seventy and yet chose not to retire as they were entitled to do. (Disingenuously, FDR claimed the move was intended simply to aid with a backlog of cases which faced the Court.) What became known as the 'court-packing' plan led to a furore never seen in the history of the Supreme Court. Rumours of the plan reached the press as early as 1934, at which point the Court had yet to overturn FDR's New Deal legislation. During 1935 and 1936, the Supreme Court affirmed a narrow construction of the powers of the Congress and cited the Tenth Amendment as the basis on which to place limits on the reach of federal government into hitherto state activities – notably, welfare and the regulation of commerce. These years saw some landmark New Deal legislation overturned, including the Fair Labor Standards Act, the National Industrial Recovery Act, and the Agricultural Adjustment Act. Many observers anticipated that the Social Security Act and the National Labour Relations Act would be next.

On 5 February 1937, FDR sent his Judicial Procedures Reform Bill to Congress in the face of the Court's conservative and interventionist judgements during the previous two years. Yet, despite the unpopular positions adopted by the Court, the court-packing plan proved hugely unpopular, with Congressional mail running 9–1 against the plan. In April and May, Chief Justice Hughes and Justice Roberts made a tactical retreat. Crucially, Roberts switched position and allowed an expansive reading of the federal government's commerce and general welfare powers. In June, the Senate Judiciary Committee declared that the court-packing plan violated 'every sacred principle of American democracy'.

FDR badly misjudged both his plan's probable reception and the near-sacrosanct status of the Supreme Court within the American framework of government. Yet, the Court was also guilty of poor political judgement in maintaining a position that saw the institution sets its teeth against the will of a monumental president who had embarked on a domestic programme with huge levels of support.

Chapter 10 presents a detailed discussion of the Court decisions that lay at the heart of the period from 1935 to 1937. The role of the Supreme Court rests at the heart of a thorough understanding of federalism – because the federal–state balance is determined in large part by the judgements of the Court.

policies met with short-lived but vigorous resistance from an activist and conservative Court majority (see Exhibit 7.1). Following wholesale changes in the Court's composition, the justices turned their attention gradually to questions of racial equality, privacy and freedom of speech.

Exhibit 7.2 The Supreme Court and Individual Rights

- *Smith v Allwright* (1944) struck down the all-white primary, long-employed as a means of excluding southern blacks from political participation.
- *Baker v Carr* (1962), *Reynolds v Sims* (1964) and *Wesberry v Sanders* (1964) ended the practice of gerrymandering by rural white elites in order to exclude blacks and other disfavoured groups from electoral politics.
- *Gideon v. Wainwright* (1963) guaranteed legal representation to indigent persons charged with serious crimes, and *Miranda v Arizona* (1966) set rigorous procedural standards for the admission of evidence through confession in criminal trials, thereby guaranteeing compliance with the Fifth Amendment's protection against self-incrimination (although the ruling has since been eroded).
- *Griswold v Connecticut* (1965) overturned state laws that forbade the use of contraception. *Roe v Wade* (1973) overturned state laws restricting abortion in the first three months of pregnancy. *Webster v Reproductive Health Services* (1989) limited *Roe*'s scope by upholding the constitutionality of five provisions of a Missouri statute regulating the circumstances under which late abortions should be performed, and banning the use of public employees and facilities to perform abortions not necessary to save the mother's life. By extension, the Court granted greater scope to the state legislatures

→

The importance of racial politics throughout American history has been fully reflected in their appearance before the Supreme Court, culminating in *Plessy v Ferguson* (1896), and *Brown v Board of Education, Topeka* (1954). *Plessy* sanctioned the practice in southern states of maintaining separate but notionally equal schools segregated by race; *Brown* overturned it. In both cases, the Court's decision shaped the way in which race was subsequently addressed by the states, the Congress, and the presidency. While no decision of the Court in the twentieth century has had greater repercussions than *Brown*, individual rights have occupied almost as much of the Court's attention since 1944, as Exhibit 7.2 shows.

The judicial branch has no political role of the kind the executive and legislative branches do. But in establishing a federal judiciary whose members are appointed by the head of the Executive Branch, subject to the confirmation of one part of the Legislative Branch, the framers did not hide their inclusion of the Supreme and inferior federal

→ to determine abortion policy. *Casey v Planned Parenthood of Pennsylvania* (1992) marked a division between those conservatives on the bench who held that *Roe* should be overturned and others who argued that it should be upheld as precedent. In *Stenberg v Carhart* (2000), the Court struck down a Nebraska state law that outlawed partial-birth abortions, holding that the state law violated the Due Process clause of the Fourteenth Amendment. In *Gonzales v Carhart* (2007), the Court upheld the constitutionality of the Partial Birth Abortion Ban Act of 2003, arguing that the ruling did not impose an 'undue burden' on the due process right of a woman to seek an abortion. Some commentators viewed the ruling as a shift in the position of the Court on abortion rights ushered in by the retirement of Justice Sandra Day O'Connor.

- *Citizens United v Federal Election Commission (FEC)* (2010), in which the Supreme Court ruled that the First Amendment prohibited the government from restricting independent political expenditures by corporations and unions. The judgement overturned elements of *McConnell v Federal Election Commission* (2003) in which the Court upheld the constitutionality of the Bipartisan Campaign Finance Reform Act (BCRA) 2002 (also known as 'McCain–Feingold', discussed in Chapter3).

Further cases are discussed in consideration of the last four Supreme Court Chief Justices.

courts within the political realm. Since the legitimacy of American policy-makers rests so heavily on election, an unelected Court armed with the power of judicial review limits majoritarianism, thereby posing problems of legitimacy which justices of the Court cannot escape. The legitimacy of federal judges and justices derives from three sources: first, from the symbolic and substantive importance of their roles as guardians of constitutionally-guaranteed freedoms and rights; second, from the review of their fitness for the task by the president and his staff prior to their nomination, and the Senate's examination of them prior to their confirmation; third, from the Court's application of judicial restraint to avoid finding acts or actions unconstitutional unless they very plainly are.

The Supreme Court's jurisdiction

The Supreme Court is the only judicial body named by the Constitution whose functions are explicitly discussed in it, and on which duties are laid. Article III, Section 2, lists them:

> The judicial Power shall extend to all Cases, in Law and Equity, arising under this Constitution, the Laws of the United States, and Treaties made, or which shall be made, under their Authority – to all Cases affecting Ambassadors, other public Ministers and Consuls – to all Cases of admiralty and maritime Jurisdiction; – to Controversies to which the United States shall be a Party.

Appellate and original jurisdiction

For all practical purposes, the Supreme Court has an 'appellate jurisdiction' only. Its small 'original jurisdiction' (that class of cases for which the Supreme Court is the court of first instance) derives not from an Act of Congress as that of the federal district courts does but from the Constitution itself. Its original jurisdiction is further limited by the Eleventh Amendment. Chief Justice Marshall built his judgement in *Marbury v Madison* (1803), precisely on the ground that the grant of original jurisdiction could not be modified by Act of Congress as (so he claimed) had happened with respect to the Judiciary Act of 1789's grant to the Court of the power to issue a writ of *mandamus* – an instruction.

Though of much greater importance, the Court's appellate jurisdiction may be limited by Congress, as Article III, Section 2, notes:

> In all the other Cases ... the Supreme Court shall have appellate jurisdiction, both as to Law and Fact, with such Exceptions, and under such Regulations, as the Congress shall make.

In *Wiscart v Dauchy* (1796), the Court accepted that in the absence of a statute passed in an Act of Congress, the Court could not assume jurisdiction. In principle, this leaves the way open for Congress to eliminate the Court's appellate functions; that possibility has on occasion appealed to some members of Congress opposed to particular judgements of the Court. In practice, Congress has not legislated exceptions to the Court's 'core' functions, but the Court has always accepted Congress's power to determine what lies within its appellate jurisdiction. Congress's determination to defend the triangular separation of power between itself, the executive, and the Court has increased its reluctance to reduce the Court's appellate jurisdiction. Members of

Congress and others in public life have often displayed (or affected) outrage with judgements of the Court's majority. Yet, most have also been mindful of the defence which the Court may provide to Congress against the executive, and so have been reluctant to consent to the Court being constrained. Others have recalled that, since all Americans are members of at least one minority group, the collective interest is best served by the Court defending Constitutional rights as it judges for itself. Congress has consequently shown little enthusiasm for restricting appellate powers of the Court.

The Constitution's language on this point is, nonetheless, plain. In *Ex parte McCardle* (1869), the Court addressed the petition of a Mississippi newspaper editor that a writ of *habeas corpus* be issued. Mr McCardle, the editor in question, was held in custody for trial by a military commission for his publication of articles in his newspaper that were allegedly 'incendiary and libellous'. Fearing that the Court would move to declare the Reconstruction Acts unconstitutional, Congress, by an Act of March 1868, removed the Court's jurisdiction in respect of appeals from the circuit courts regarding writs of *habeas corpus* arising under the Reconstruction Act of 1867. Quoting the terms in which Article III, Section 2, qualified the grant of appellate jurisdiction to the Court, Chief Justice Chase declared that the Court could not judge the case:

> Without jurisdiction the court cannot proceed at all in any cause. Jurisdiction is power to declare the law, and when it ceases to exist, the only function remaining to the court is that of announcing the fact and dismissing the case ... this court cannot proceed to pronounce judgment in this case, for it has no longer jurisdiction of the appeal; and judicial duty is not less fitly performed by declining ungranted jurisdiction than in exercising firmly that which the constitution and the laws confer.

Congress's reluctance, in practice, to exercise its right under Article III, Section 2, is illustrated by two issues that prompted impassioned debate: anti-Communism in the 1950s, and school prayer in the 1980s. In the 1950s, the force of anti-Communist sentiment was so great and the anxieties it produced so intense that, in 1958, Senate Majority Leader Lyndon Johnson secured by just one vote the tabling of the Jenner–Butler Bill to deprive the Court of jurisdiction in most security cases. In the 1980s, the US Senate defeated an attempt to exclude all school prayer cases from the jurisdiction of the federal courts by a vote of 62–36. Other attempts to restrict the Courts' appellate jurisdiction over elements of the social agenda promoted by President Reagan and some of his supporters also failed in the 1980s.

'Standing' of the parties and judicial restraint

In all cases arising under the Court's appellate jurisdiction, the party or parties bringing suit must have 'standing': they must have a direct and personal interest in the outcome of the case. The rule ensures that great though the wider significance of an individual case may be, it derives from the Court's judgement in a particular case concerning parties who themselves contest the constitutionality of an Act or an action in specific, and not general, terms. In the absence of such a case or controversy, where one of the parties claims that their Constitutional rights (which must be a specific right or rights) have been infringed, the Court may not act. The Court cannot offer advisory opinions on major questions of public concern, or on hypothetical questions, simply because a majority of justices think a constitutional question is involved. This restriction is a key element in 'judicial restraint', a doctrine by no means confined to certain conservatives. Judicial restraint matters. If the Court were to abandon or weaken it, the foundations of its legitimacy and effectiveness would be weakened.

Procedure

Appeal and certiorari

Most cases that come to the Court for review do so either on appeal as a matter of right, or through the granting of *certiorari* where there exists no right but merely the privilege of petitioning the Court for the granting of a writ that the case may be 'made more certain'. Even in cases of appeal by right, the Court may dismiss the appeal (as it does in approximately 90 per cent of appeals brought to it) if the justices determine either that no substantial federal question is involved, or if they discover that the federal question was not raised at an early stage in proceedings in the state Court.

Petitions for *certiorari* are considered at the weekly conference of the nine justices, which meets on most Fridays during the Court's term; under the 1925 Judiciary Act, the Court has unfettered discretion over whether to grant them. Only one justice has to support a petition's inclusion in the 'discuss' list for it to be considered. Records of such cases, the briefs from the plaintiff and the respondent, in addition to any briefs filed by other parties (*amicus curiae*, see below), are then issued to each justice for consideration prior to the conference.

Although only one vote is necessary for the case to be considered at Friday conferences, for *certiorari* to be granted, four votes are required. Occasionally, justices may change their minds after listening to colleagues at the conference, as happened in a case of brutality by prison authorities in Florida: in *Brooks v Florida*, 389 US 413 (1967), Chief Justice Warren dissented, scathingly but alone, from his eight colleagues' refusal to grant *certiorari*. His dissent not only persuaded his colleagues to grant it, but also thereafter to issue a unanimous *per curiam* opinion reversing the lower court's decision.

Such drama is untypical: 85 per cent or more of the petitions discussed at the Friday Conference are not accepted for review. They may be: (i) summarily reversed; (ii) summarily affirmed; (iii) 'vacated and the case remanded' back to the lower court to be decided in the light of a particular decision of the Supreme Court; or (iv) dismissed because the petition is held by six or more of the Justices not to involve a substantial federal question, or because they think that the Supreme Court has no jurisdiction in the case. The Conference is therefore a sifting mechanism, to ensure that the Court's role adheres to Article III of the Constitution, and to control the burden of work.

The conference is the only regular meeting of the nine justices. In his book *The Politics of the US Supreme Court*, Richard Hodder-Williams (1980: 81) cites Justice Lewis Powell's observation that prior to becoming a member of the Court he had supposed that it would act as a collegial body whose dominant procedural characteristics would be 'consultation and deliberation'. In fact, as Powell discovered, the Court is 'a bastion of jealously preserved individualism'. Justices depend very largely on themselves and their law clerks, who usually serve for a year. The associate justices have two secretaries and the chief justice three. Although the federal executive and legislature enjoy large staff resources, the Court does not.

Oral argument

The public phase of the Court's activity takes place in the chamber of the Court itself. Oral argument there takes place during two weeks each month (normally from Monday to Wednesday, but sometimes from Monday to Thursday) in two sessions: from 10 am to 12 noon, and from 1 pm to 3 pm. The public may attend: there are 188 seats in the public gallery and a further 112 for members of the bar, justices' families and the press. Time for oral argument is limited – usually to thirty minutes for each side. Occasionally, this allowance is doubled, and even more rarely increased still further: reflecting the case's importance, argument in *Brown v Board of Education II* (1955) was allotted fourteen hours. Justices' views about the importance of oral argument for the clarification of opinions vary. Justice Douglas thought it often decisive; Chief Justice Warren did not. It is, in any event, the only occasion on which the Court performs its functions publicly. Lawyers admitted to practise before the Court – not itself a difficult hurdle, but a privilege which the

Supreme Court may remove in the event of disbarment by the state bar of which a lawyer is a member (as were former President Richard Nixon and two of his Attorneys-General, John Mitchell and Richard Kleindienst) – must accustom themselves to interruption from the bench. Some justices, of whom Antonin Scalia is a good (though, to some of his colleagues, an irritating) example, make a practice of interrupting frequently. Others interrupt rarely. Some scarcely even speak – Clarence Thomas broke a five-year monastic silence only in late 2012.

Filing of written briefs

By the time that oral argument takes place on one of the six or seven days allotted for it each month, the justices have, with their clerks' assistance, and after much reading and assessment, already considered the case before them. Justices' dependence on written briefs submitted not just by the plaintiffs and respondents in the case, but also by groups with an interest in the case who may file briefs as 'a friend of the Court' (*amicus curiae*), is high. *Amicus curiae* briefs enable interested organizations (especially groups such as the NAACP in the 1950s and 1960s, the American Civil Liberties Union, the American Federation of Labor and Congress of Industrial Organizations (AFL-CIO), or the National Organization for Women, and the United States government) to make known their views and add to the case of the plaintiff or the respondent. The number of such briefs filed has increased in recent years, and some cases attract many of them. Cases having a major commercial significance instantly draw the attention of corporate lawyers. The gender-discrimination case *Liberty Mutual v Wetzel* (1975) attracted the National Association of Manufacturers, the US Chamber of Commerce, AT&T, General Motors, and Westinghouse Electric. Twenty-one major airlines employing more than 100,000 women joined the fray, to the pleasure and profit of their lawyers (Hodder-Williams, 1980: 89–90).

Amicus curiae briefs are often an attractive option for groups denied access or remedy elsewhere, whether in the states, or in the federal executive or legislature. The NAACP employed the tactic in segregation and voting rights' cases in the 1950s and early 1960s. The federal government also employs it: for the Reagan administration, it was one means by which the President (vainly) attempted to implement his policies on school prayer and abortion. *McDonald v Chicago* (2010) attracted thirty-three *amicus* briefs, one of which was signed by 58 senators and 251 representatives – the largest number of congressional signatures in American history.

Oral argument having been concluded, the public phase of the Court's work ends. Justices then meet (without clerical assistance) in conference, privately. This is the same Friday (and, since 1974, on Wednesday afternoons, too) meeting of conference at which petitions for *certiorari* are heard. Cases heard by the justices in oral argument that week, and those recently discussed in conferences without having proceeded to oral argument, are discussed here. The nine justices maintain a tradition during conference that nobody speaks twice until everyone has spoken once.

Both at this stage and later, when the opinion or opinions of the Court on the case in question are written, the chief justice has the opportunity to exercise special influence. He speaks first in conference, chairs the meeting, and votes last. Associate justices vote in ascending order of seniority. The chief justice may, if he thinks it appropriate, decide in the light of his colleagues' votes and arguments to vote differently from the way he had intended. Extensive and frequently vigorous discussion may take place, unlimited by time, following which a preliminary vote is taken. That preliminary vote commits no one. The second, and final, vote takes place later, following drafting of opinions when such general implications as the Court's majority may decide to identify are determined. This initial vote is simply on whether the lower court's judgement should be upheld or rejected (in the language of the Court, 'affirmed' or 'reversed').

If, whether by conviction or calculation, the chief justice finds himself in the majority, he then has the responsibility (which he discharges within a fortnight of the conference ending) of assigning the writing of the 'opinion', or draft judgement. He may either request a colleague to write it, or write it himself. The opportunity to choose is considerable, enabling a resourceful chief justice to frame the opinion in order that it should win the assent of his colleagues, or have wide or narrow implications as he thinks best. This can usually best be done if he writes it himself, but since his colleagues' views will invariably be well-known, to him, he may think it advantageous for political, personal, or collegial reasons to give the job to a colleague. If the Court's heavy workload is to be shared fairly, it is important that assignments be widely distributed. In practice, chief justices assign most opinions to their colleagues, with the result that each justice typically writes between fourteen and eighteen opinions in each term. Both Warren and Burger assigned only about one in ten cases to themselves. If the chief justice finds himself in the minority, then the senior associate justice (at the time of writing, Antonin Scalia: see Exhibit 7.4) assigns the writing of the majority opinion.

The chief justice may think it wise or necessary to write the opinion himself, in order (for example) that the Court's judgement be seen to carry the fullest weight with lower courts, and with congressional and public opinion. *Brown v Board of Education* in 1954 is the paradigmatic example: it was essential that such a momentous case should be written by the chief justice, and that the final draft should command the unanimous backing of the Court. The same was true of the Court's unanimous decision in *United States v Richard M. Nixon*, 418 US 683 (1974), where the president's own appointee to the chief justiceship, Warren Burger, wrote the opinion that precipitated the end of Nixon's career. Chief Justice John Roberts added weight to a controversial decision when he wrote the majority opinion in *National Federation of Independent Businesses v Sebelius* (2012). To the consternation of those both in favour and against the law, Roberts voted to uphold the constitutionality of President Obama's landmark health legislation (the Patient Protection and Affordable Care Act (2010), which is more commonly referred to as the ACA).

While the immediate objective of an opinion's author is to secure the assent of at least four colleagues, the value of the opinion as settled law is diminished if, in the rush to achieve consensus, intellectual coherence, clarity and force are lost. Drafting and redrafting of an opinion often fails to persuade those who were initially unpersuaded at conference. They may then join with other colleagues in the minority and, by means of a single dissenting judgement, oppose the majority judgement. Alternatively, they may write a separate opinion of their own, dissenting from the majority but on different grounds. Past dissents are often cited by members of the Court's majority when overturning judgements made by their predecessors. In writing dissenting opinions, justices occasionally invite future members of the Court to consider their arguments (another indication that the Court's decisions are contributions to constitutional evolution, rather than final and decisive judgements.) The clearest instance of a dissent coming to represent the majority view is the lone argument of John Harlan (a former slave-owner) in *Plessy v Ferguson* (1896):

> Our Constitution is color-blind, and neither knows nor tolerates classes among citizens. In respect of civil rights, all citizens are equal before the law. The humblest is the peer of the most powerful.

The increasing complexity of the issues involved in the cases before the Court has increased the incidence not only of dissents but of plurality decisions, where justices give different reasons for their decision. A majority might therefore contain several separate opinions. *New York Times Company v United States*, 403 US 713 (1971), the so-called *Pentagon Papers* case, drew nine opinions from the bench, as *Dred Scott v Sandford* 19 Howard 393 (1857) had done. Such revealed divisions usually muddy the reasoning undergirding the Court's judgement.

Drafting of the opinion makes heavy jurisprudential and diplomatic demands on the author. In his work on draft opinions printed and circulated within the Supreme Court, Bernard Schwartz (1985: 19) claims that the decision process is 'essentially … political'. Justices are, as he shows, often open to persuasion by the arguments that their colleagues deploy. For example, in the years following *Brown*, the Court granted *certiorari* in cases involving sit-in protests by blacks against restaurants that served food to whites only. Decided shortly before discrimination in public places and public accommodations became illegal, *Bell v Maryland* (1964) concerned the arrest and conviction of blacks for violating state trespass laws for having refused to leave a whites-only restaurant in Baltimore until they were served a meal. Declining to reverse the convictions on narrow, technical grounds (as President Kennedy's Solicitor-General urged in an *amicus curiae* brief), the Court opted to address the central question, and voted five to four in conference to affirm the convictions. The Chief Justice found himself in the minority (adamantly so) and Justice Black, the then senior associate justice, in the majority.

It was therefore Black's task to assign the opinion, and he did so, to himself. He initially drafted an opinion in which he claimed that the state could not itself be held to be acting prejudicially (against the requirements of the Fourteenth Amendment) if it were merely enforcing trespass laws at the request of the owner of the restaurant. The Fourteenth Amendment was designed to prohibit discriminatory action by a state, and not by a private person or company. Such an interpretation had been upheld by the Court as recently as 1948 in *Shelley v Kraemer*.

Circulation of draft opinions occurred at the same time as the Senate filibuster on Title II of the Civil Rights Act, and Justice Brennan was alarmed at the prospect that Black's opinion, as drafted, would unwisely call the constitutionality of Title II into question. He proposed instead that the convictions should be reversed under laws prohibiting discrimination in public facilities in Baltimore, passed since the convictions took place. Three of Brennan's colleagues, including the chief justice, agreed to support his draft. Brennan's opinion became the majority opinion of the Court when Justice Stewart supported it in order to prevent a majority forming behind an alternative opinion circulated by Justice Clark, reversing the convictions on the grounds that they violated the Fourteenth Amendment because of the state's close involvement in enforcing private discrimination. Clark preferred Brennan's politically subtle judgement (that, in the difficult circumstances of 1964, the case would be better decided on narrow grounds) to be supported, and joined him accordingly. The constitutional question involved was therefore avoided by the Court, partly because it was expected that it would be addressed by the Congress and executive shortly afterwards through the 1964 Civil Rights Act.

A justice may (as *Bell v Maryland* showed) alter their mind up to and including Opinion Day, when the final written opinions of the Court are published. A collective view cannot, therefore, be imposed by justices in the drafting of a judgement. It may, by careful crafting and modification, be elicited.

Judicial review

Judicial review occurs frequently in federal systems, where the boundaries between the federal and provincial authorities are often unclear, and in separated systems of government, where boundaries between the branches are imprecisely drawn, contested, or both. For both reasons, judicial review in the United States is especially important because of the Court's capacity to determine the constitutionality of laws passed by a democratically-elected Congress, and the constitutionality of the actions of the single elected executive and of unelected officials. The Court's power of judicial review was implied by the Constitution without being expressly granted. It was certainly regarded by several of the founders as being logically required in order to defend the Constitution they had written. It was not, however, unambiguously affirmed as a power of the Court until Chief Justice Marshall's seminal judgement in *Marbury v Madison* in 1803 (see Exhibit 7.3).

Such apparently sweeping power in a democracy to overrule the actions and decisions of elected people is contentious. The Court was not designed to be a representative institution, but its power, coupled with its appointive character, alarms those who see liberty's best defence in democratic accountability. While judicial review is both anti-majoritarian and undemocratic, the United States Constitution was constructed neither as a simply majoritarian, nor as a wholly democratic, system.

Functions of judicial review

The Supreme Court has two tasks. The first it shares with Supreme Courts in other countries: the interpretation of legislation, and judging the lawfulness of the actions of public officials. Unlike Courts in the United Kingdom, however, the US Supreme Court is a branch of government in a Constitution which divides powers between the branches, between the federal and state governments, and guarantees to citizens of the United States a panoply of rights against government. Unlike the *Conseil Constitutionnel* under the French Fifth Republic, its importance derives from its appellate, rather than its original, jurisdiction. The Court's decisively important task is its second: determining the fit between Constitutional and statute law, pronouncing on the constitutionality of an Act of Congress, of a Title, clause, or clauses within the Act, or the constitutionality of an act of a state legislature, or an action of an elected politician or unelected official.

With respect to the first task, the Court's construction of a statute can be overturned by an Act of Congress, although pressure on Congress's time usually makes achieving that end harder than those members of Congress and senators most opposed to the Court's judgement wish. The greater power of the Court lies in judicial review where Congress may not overturn the Court's construction of the Constitution except by initiating a constitutional amendment (an altogether more difficult task than amending a statute). Congress may also, as explained earlier, forestall judicial review by stipulating exceptions to the Court's appellate powers.

Since government in America at both federal and state level is held accountable not only by the frequency of elections, but also by constitutional guarantees, the arrangement requires an arbiter. Hamilton, in *Federalist* No. 78, reminded his readers of that which the Constitution itself declares: the Constitution is supreme. It is by implication the task of the Supreme Court (and that of those inferior federal courts created by Congress) to determine whether or not individual statutes or actions by public officials accord with it. If they do not, they are unconstitutional, null and void, and must be amended as appropriate or rescinded:

> A constitution is, in fact, and must be regarded by the Judges as, a fundamental law. It therefore belongs to them to ascertain its meaning as well as the meaning of any particular act proceeding from the legislative body. If there should happen to be an irreconcilable variance between the two, that which has the superior obligation and validity ought, of course, to be preferred: or, in other words, the Constitution ought to be preferred to the statute, the intention of the people to the intention of their agents.

This is an instructive commentary on what came to be accepted as the Court's decisive power. Although Hamilton acknowledges that the Constitution does not explicitly grant it, he insists that central to the jurisdiction of the proposed Supreme Court is the power of judicial review. Insofar as any constitution limited a legislature's freedom of action, the doctrine of judicial review was logically entailed. The experience of most of the states themselves showed this clearly enough in different settings: judicial review was a common state practice, both prior to the adoption of the Constitution in 1789, and thereafter. At least eight states, in their conventions held to ratify the new US Constitution, explicitly accepted that the Supreme Court would possess the power to declare Acts of Congress null and void (Abraham, 1986: 322). The lacunae, ambiguities and uncertainties of the Constitution were, from the time of its defence by the authors of *The Federalist*, pregnant with future political dispute. Hamilton was not alone in holding that judgement of cases arising from them was the proper province of the Court. If its members did not defend the new constitutional order's integrity, who might properly, and plausibly, do so? Where else could the Constitution be impar-

Exhibit 7.3 Marbury v Madison (1803)

Although Hamilton's discussion of the Supreme Court's role was predicated on the Court's power to declare 'all acts contrary to the manifest tenor of the Constitution void', and despite a number of State Supreme Courts themselves having practised judicial review, the Court explicitly assumed the power only in 1803, sixteen years after the Republic's founding. It did so in one of the most important cases ever to come before it: *Marbury v Madison* (1803). The case was extraordinary for taking the process by which the Court had, in its first fourteen years, begun to establish its province a decisive stage further: the power of judicial review of federal statutes was here explicitly claimed, and the basis for the further power of judicial review over state statutes and actions laid. It was also shocking by modern standards for the Chief Justice, John Marshall, having, in his previous incarnation as President Adams's Secretary of State, been intimately involved in the political circumstances which gave rise to the case.

After Thomas Jefferson's victory over John Adams, the incumbent president, in the presidential election of 1800, Adams strove desperately to pack the judicial branch with his Federalist supporters before he left office in March 1801. The attempt was largely successful because the Senate, in which the Federalist Party had a majority, was as anxious to confirm the Federalist nominees in their posts before Jefferson took the oath of office as Adams was to nominate them. Among the nominees was Marshall himself. He stayed on in government (long after his mentor had left it) by moving from the State Department to the Chief Justiceship of the Supreme Court. As Adams's Secretary of State, it had been Marshall's official responsibility to deliver letters of commission to the new appointees following their confirmation by the Senate and the signing of their commissions by the President. He did so in all the important cases, but failed in respect of seventeen Justices of the Peace (posts created under the District of Columbia Organic Law Act in early 1801, during the transition between Adams and Jefferson).

On taking office in March 1801, President Jefferson declined to order that the remaining seventeen letters of commission be delivered by James Madison, the new Secretary of State. Four of the disappointed office-seekers challenged the President in the Supreme Court, petitioning it to issue a writ of *mandamus*, commanding Madison to serve the letters of

➜

tially interpreted free from the pressures generated in a popularly-elected legislature? Both the doctrine and practice of judicial review are not merely consistent with the separation of powers and the doctrine of limited government, but implied by them.

→

commission, under the powers granted the Court by Section 13 of the Judiciary Act of 1789. The circumstances were thus highly charged. A Federalist appointee confirmed in office by a Federalist Senate led a Court in judgement of an intensely political case over a question of patronage. Marshall rose to the occasion. In his opinion, he disposed of any doubt either that William Marbury, one of the four, was entitled to his commission, or that the laws of the United States afforded him a remedy. He was; and they did. The third question was the difficult one, the hinge on which Marshall's judgement turned: did the Supreme Court have the power to issue such a writ?

He established by argument that Section 13 of the Judiciary Act of 1789, which granted the Supreme Court the authority to issue writs of *mandamus*, was unconstitutional. Marshall asserted that, by doing so, Congress had expanded the original jurisdiction granted the Court by the Constitution. This was a contentious claim. It could more reasonably have been argued that Congress was merely granting the Court procedural power to issue such a writ when this would be appropriate in respect of cases properly brought before the Court on either its original or its appellate docket. However, Marshall held that Section 13 represented a substantive addition to the powers of the Court; he did so because to have interpreted it as merely a procedural power would have denied him the opportunity he wished to exploit. Article III of the Constitution permitted no such expansion. He reasoned that the writ therefore could not be issued. This judgement circumvented political opposition. Marshall understood well the implications of any miscalculation: Madison would probably refuse to obey a writ of *mandamus* were one to be issued. A constitutional crisis would certainly result.

It was the first and last occasion on which Marshall declared an Act of Congress unconstitutional, an indication neither of his nor of the Court's weakness, but of his circumspection in establishing its legitimacy and power, and of Congress's disinclination to challenge this subtle affirmation of the Court's independence. There was, nonetheless, a further step to the Court's full assertion of judicial review: its capacity to declare acts of state legislatures or actions of state officials unconstitutional. With Marshall's unanimous opinion for the Court in *Fletcher v Peck* (1810), the Court established its right (much as that right was contested) to declare an Act of a state legislature unconstitutional.

The Supreme Court and the elected branches

In the first year of the Republic, Congress established, through the 1789 Judiciary Act, that the Court should comprise a chief justice and five associate justices. The number of judges was increased by an Act of 1869 to nine, at which figure it has since remained (except in the periods between a justice's resignation or death and the confirmation of their successor).

By its powers to create additional district and circuit courts, to alter the number of justices on the Supreme Court, to set judicial salaries, to restrict appellate powers, and through the important role of the Senate in considering the president's nominees to the Courts, Congress involves itself in the politics of the federal courts, in general, and the US Supreme Court, in particular. Recruitment to the federal courts involves both the Senate and the president. Following confirmation, federal judges and justices enjoy substantial autonomy; during the Senate confirmation process, many endure close scrutiny from elected politicians.

The intermeshing of the federal courts, in general, and of the US Supreme Court, in particular, with the elected branches is, however, of greatest significance in the appointments process. The Court comprises five white men, two white women, one Hispanic woman and one black man (see Exhibit 7.4). Like their colleagues in the district and circuit courts, Supreme Court justices are appointed, subject to the confirmation of the Senate. Once confirmed by the Senate, they are formally unaccountable. Their appointments are for life (which usually means that they serve until death, or close to it). In 2010, an intellectually vibrant Justice John Paul Stephens retired after thirty-five years on the Court, having been appointed by President Gerald Ford in 1975. Except when justices move to other posts (as Abraham Goldberg did on his appointment as Ambassador to the United Nations in 1965), they rarely retire when still active and in good health; some continue in post when neither. Article III, Section 1, of the Constitution places just one qualification on life tenure – that justices of the Supreme Court and judges of the inferior federal courts 'shall hold their offices during good Behavior'.

Article III, Section 1, of the Constitution prescribes that members of the Federal bench were to receive at 'stated times … a Compensation which shall not be diminished during their Continuance in Office'. In *Federalist Papers* No. 79, Hamilton held that tenure and a regular salary 'affords a better prospect of their independence than is discoverable in the constitutions of any of the States in regard to their own Judges'. Nonetheless, the Constitution made no allowance for inflation, and hence no provision for judicial salaries to be protected from its effects. Both in 1964 and 1973, when inflation had eroded judicial salaries, in pointed displays of one branch's displeasure with the decisions of another, Congress raised the pay of district and circuit court judges by more than it did the salaries of Supreme Court justices.

Most of those appointed to the Court are well into middle-age; few have been appointed when younger than fifty. Of those nominated to the

Exhibit 7.4 The Composition of the Supreme Court in 2012

Name (Age)	Year appointed	By	Religion	Place of birth
Antonin Scalia (76)	1986	Ronald Reagan	Catholic	New Jersey
Anthony Kennedy (76)	1988	Ronald Reagan	Catholic	California
Clarence Thomas (64)	1991	George H.W. Bush	Catholic	Georgia
Ruth Ginsburg (79)	1993	William Clinton	Jewish	New York City
Stephen Breyer (74)	1994	William Clinton	Jewish	California
John Roberts (57)	2005	George W. Bush	Catholic	New York State
Samuel Alito (62)	2006	George W. Bush	Catholic	New Jersey
Sonia Sotomayor (58)	2009	Barack Obama	Catholic	New York City
Elena Kagan (52)	2010	Barack Obama	Jewish	New York City

Court and confirmed since the beginning of Franklin D. Roosevelt's administration, William O. Douglas was the youngest (aged forty) at the time of his confirmation, and Clarence Thomas almost as young at forty-three in 1991. Most have been in their late fifties or early sixties. The average age of the Court therefore tends to be high; in the 1980s, it became exceptionally so. In late 1987, as President Reagan (the oldest president in American history) struggled to find a successor to Justice Powell, who had resigned earlier in the year at the age of 79: Justice Brennan was 80 years old, his colleagues Marshall and White were 79, and Justice Blackmun 78. Brennan resigned only in 1990, Marshall in 1991, White in 1993 and Blackmun in 1994. Prior to the death of Chief Justice William Rehnquist in 2005, the average age of the nine justices was 71. By April 2009, the average had fallen to just 69. When Stephens retired in 2010 aged 90 and was replaced by Elena Kagan (appointed at the age of 50), the average age of Court members fell to the sprightly age of 64. The intellectual demands made by the job of Supreme Court justice are considerable, and the stamina required to meet those demands by no means insignificant. Justices of advanced years labour under burdens that very few of their peers contemplate, still less endure.

Exhibit 7.5 Justices of the United States Supreme Court from 1916 onwards

Justice	State	Term	Years in office
Louis Brandeis	MA	1916–1939	22
John Clarke	OH	1916–1922	5
William Taft	CT	**1921–1930**	8
George Sutherland	UT	1922–1938	15
Pierce Butler	MN	1923–1939	16
Edward Sanford	TN	1923–1930	7
Harlan Stone	NY	1925–1941	16
Charles Hughes	NY	1930–1941	11
Owen Roberts	PA	1930–1945	15
Benjamin Cardozo	NY	1932–1938	6
Hugo Black	AL	1937–1971	34
Stanley Reed	KY	1938–1957	19
Felix Frankfurter	MA	1939–1962	23
William Douglas	CT	1939–1975	36
Frank Murphy	MI	1940–1949	9
Harlan Stone	**NY**	**1941–1946**	5
Robert Jackson	NY	1941–1954	13
Wiley Rutledge	IO	1943–1949	6
Harold Burton	OH	1945–1958	13
Fred Vinson	**KY**	**1946–1953**	7
Tom Clark	TX	1949–1967	18
Sherman Minton	IN	1949–1956	7
Earl Warren	**CA**	**1953–1969**	16

→

Venting his frustration at his large workload in his old age, Justice Blackmun observed in 1984 that being a justice was 'a rotten way to earn a living'.

Nonetheless, guarding the Court's independence from interference by Congress or the presidency is so important that there have been no serious attempts to require the retirement of justices at a certain age. However, under the compromise eventually passed following the defeat of the core of Roosevelt's 'Court-packing' Bill in 1937 (see p. 215); the financial pain of retirement endured by federal judges and justices has been eased by establishing exceptionally generous pension arrangements. This inducement notwithstanding, Supreme Court justices tend to carry on. Liberal and moderate members of the Court remained on the Court throughout the 1980s partly in order to deny President Reagan (for whose politics they did not care, and whose view of the Court's proper

→

John Harlan	KY	1955–1971	16
William Brennan	NJ	1956–1990	34
Charles Whittaker	MO	1957–1962	5
Potter Stewart	OH	1958–1981	22
Byron White	CO	1962–1993	31
Arthur Goldberg	IL	1962–1965	2
Abe Fortas	TN	1965–1969	3
Thurgood Marshall	NY	1967–1991	24
Warren Burger	**MN**	**1969–1986**	17
Harry Blackmun	MN	1970–1994	24
William Rehnquist	AZ	1972–1986	14
Lewis Powell	VA	1972–1988	16
John Paul Stephens	IL	1975–2010	35
Sandra O'Connor	AZ	1981–2006	25
Antonin Scalia	NJ	1986–	27
William Rehnquist	**AZ**	**1986–2005**	19
Anthony Kennedy	CA	1988–	24
David Souter	NH	1990–2009	29
Clarence Thomas	GA	1991–	22
Ruth Bader Ginsburg	DC	1993–	20
Stephen Breyer	CA	1994–	19
John Roberts	**NY**	**2005–**	8
Samuel Alito	NJ	2006–	7
Sonia Sotomayor	NY	2009–	4
Elena Kagan	NY	2010–	3

Note: Chief Justices in **bold** type.

role they did not accept) the opportunity to nominate their successors. Ironically, the opportunity to replace them fell to another conservative president, George H.W. Bush.

The composition of the Court is the subject of political dispute almost as intense as its judgements. Processes of selection and confirmation of nominees to the Court involve both the Executive and Legislative Branches. The president proposes a name to the Senate which, after hearings and voting by the Judiciary Committee, confirms, denies, or declines to act on the nomination. The Senate is under no obligation to confirm a president's nominees to the Court (although presidents frustrated by the Senate's resistance to their will have often claimed that it is). The Constitution grants to the Senate a full role in considering the worth of nominees to the federal bench at all levels. Its role is not ancillary. By reason of its importance and prominence in American government, nominations to the Supreme Court naturally attract particularly close attention from the Senate Judiciary Committee and the full Senate.

The manner of their appointment made the federal judiciary's role inescapably political from the first. The autonomy which the Constitution guaranteed them after confirmation by the Senate gave them the freedom to judge without fear of retribution. They were obliged only to make judgements on the cases before them, so that limited government within the framework of the Constitution might be ensured. Since the Constitution has been modified more by judgements of the federal courts than it has by the cumbersome process of amendment, this task is at once difficult and essential. It is assuredly political, but equally certainly not just political.

Threats, manipulation and impeachment

Franklin D. Roosevelt's attempt in 1937 to increase the number of justices on the bench, so that the Court's opposition to his New Deal legislation might be overcome, remains the only attempt by a president or Congress to modify the size of the Court for unambiguously ideological ends. Although Roosevelt proposed the expansion of the Court following his own triumphant re-election in 1936, when he benefited additionally from overwhelming partisan advantage in Congress, the plan made no progress. Instead, it weakened the President and divided the Democratic Party. Roosevelt's offence was constitutional, rather than simply political, and widely regarded as such. Buoyed by his enormous victory in the election, he calculated that he could assert his power over the then conservative, activist bench that had assaulted the New Deal. Rashly, he pressed the plan on Congress without prior warning either to the Democratic leadership, or his own Cabinet.

In seeking to make the Supreme Court more pliable in the face of a liberal president's legislative designs, Roosevelt's proposal opened the way for a future conservative president to employ the Court for very different political ends. The Constitution's greatest strength is often held to be its flexibility. Yet, its resilience is as important, tempered by the jealousy with which institutional balances of power are defended. In August 1937, Roosevelt's bill died in Congress, to the relief of his vice-president and other allies, but not before damage had been done to the New Deal coalition in Congress. In the interim, the circumstances that had prompted Roosevelt to strike against the Court had, in any case, changed. Justice Van Devanter (one of the five conservative members of the bench) retired in May (less than four months after the Court-packing bill was sent to Congress), and Justice Owen Roberts, who had voted to strike down much New Deal legislation as unconstitutional, now changed his disposition and, in a series of pending cases, supported the administration's view as represented by the Solicitor-General.

The formal autonomy of Supreme Court justices is virtually complete. The sanction of impeachment, which applies to justices and federal judges as it does to presidents, is so drastic a remedy that, in recent times, it has not been pursued with great seriousness against any justice. Justice Douglas was the subject of a feeble impeachment attempt in 1953 by a minor congressman from Georgia following his vote to grant a stay of execution against Ethel and Julius Rosenberg. In 1970, Justice Douglas was again the subject of an impeachment attempt, but this time in bungled fashion, by the Republican House Minority Leader, Gerald Ford. Ford claimed that Douglas, in his book *Points of Rebellion* (1970), had endorsed revolution; that he had shockingly liberal views on censorship; and, drawing on material supplied from FBI files by Attorney-General Mitchell (later convicted of serious crimes arising from the Watergate Affair), that he had links to organized crime. (The first and third claims were ludicrous, and the second politically expedient for Ford.) The attempt was, as Ford later conceded, unwise. At the prompting of the John Birch Society, following the seminal decision prohibiting school segregation in *Brown v Board of Education, Topeka* (1954), some southern politicians sought to impeach most, if not all, of the Warren Court, but their sally came to nothing. The impeachment of lower federal court judges is rare, but not unknown. In all, eleven federal judges have been impeached by the House; all but one has been convicted by the Senate.

Autonomy, longevity and justices' behaviour

Judges and justices themselves determine the time of their retirement (if death does not come to them first). The arrangement grants federal judges and justices greater autonomy in office than it does power to the presidents who nominate them. What appears to most presidents to be a valuable opportunity to shape the direction of politics and policy after (often long after) they themselves have left the White House amounts to less than it often seems. Thus, Justice William Brennan continued to sit on the Court and exercise influence over its more liberal wing thirty years after his nomination by the Republican President Eisenhower who, under the provisions of the Twenty-Second Amendment, was prevented from offering himself as a candidate for re-election in 1960 to a third term. However indirectly, presidents' influence over policy continues from the graves of both their political and mortal lives.

Such longevity cuts two ways. It can work to the advantage of a president when his nominees to the Supreme Court, and to the federal district and circuit courts, show on the bench the qualities, characteristics and judicial philosophy that originally caused him to nominate them. Where they do not behave according to expectations, disappointment results.

Grants of power to one branch of federal government are normally qualified either by their being shared, or by their setting in train processes that take away with the left hand what the Constitution gives with the right. Both apply here. Presidents, in practice, share the appointment function with the Senate. Following confirmation, presidents lose all control, and most of their influence, over their nominees. Ambitious judges of the district and circuit courts may build a judicial record with half an eye on prospects for future advancement and are, to that extent, constrained. Supreme Court justices, however, can advance no further. Ambition satisfied, their autonomy is complete; their independence, however, is qualified by prudential attention to the political circumstances within which they make their judgements and their anticipated ramifications.

It is therefore unsurprising that justices should sometimes take a different course on the bench from that which the president who nominated them anticipated. Though superficially attractive, classifying justices simply as 'conservative' or 'liberal' often propounds a false polarity. Insofar as presidents think in these terms, they are bound to be disappointed. It is unclear, for example, how a 'conservative' chief justice such as Burger should have judged cases involving enforcement of school desegregation, or variations on the *Miranda* case (*Miranda v Arizona* 1965) involving the exclusion of improperly-obtained evidence. As a conservative, Burger (no doubt with Nixon's support) would feel bound to defend the rule of *stare decisis*, that of letting the precedent stand. Overturning precedent is not the act of a conservative judge, as Justice Souter reminded conservative critics in *Casey v Planned Parenthood* (1992). Yet, to sustain precedent in new cases in the 1970s concerning the exclusion of improperly-obtained evidence was to uphold *Miranda*, a 'liberal' decision. Complexities of judicial decision-making, and the inapplicability of a linear model covering all cases before the Court with 'conservatives' to the right of the scale and 'liberals' to the left, make presidential disappointment still more likely.

There is no logical inconsistency in a justice adopting a conservative interpretation of the Constitutional limits on pornography, and a liberal interpretation of the constitutionality of the federal regulation of the wages and conditions of employees of state and local governments. Many federal judges have done so. In Samuel Alito's confirmation hearings in January 2006, in his discussion of *Casey*, he explained that, if appointed to the Supreme Court, he would proceed from the position of adherence to the doctrine of *stare decisis*, but that he did not like the idea of 'super precedents' or (in poking fun at the term favoured by the then Senate Judiciary Committee Chair, Arlen Specter, R–PA) 'super-duper precedents'. Alito agreed with the underlying thought 'that when a precedent is reaffirmed it strengthens the precedent' but added that he did not want 'to leave the impression that *stare decisis* is an inexorable command because the Supreme Court said that it is not.'

The tangential influence which presidents exert over judicial policy-making has been a cause of great anguish to presidents of all persuasions. Theodore Roosevelt was furious that Oliver Wendell Holmes should have had the temerity to judge an important anti-trust case differently from the way he had expected and wished. Much later, President Truman took the view that his nomination of Judge Tom Clark had perhaps been unwise:

> it isn't so much that he's a bad man. It's just that he's such a dumb son of a bitch. He's about the dumbest man I think I've ever run across ... I never will know what got into me when I made that appointment, and I'm as sorry as I can be for doing it. (Miller, 1974: 226)

Truman's conservative Republican successor in the White House, Dwight Eisenhower, in his first year in office, had the opportunity to nominate a chief justice, and later regretted his choice. Earl Warren, as Republican Governor of California during World War II, had approved of President Roosevelt's executive order confining American citizens of Japanese descent to prison camps. The combination of Warren's leadership of the Court between 1953 and 1969, and William Brennan's liberal jurisprudence, underpinned the Court's reforming opinions in those years. Eisenhower, who died in the year Warren retired, was privately displeased by the Warren Court's decision in *Brown* and angered by its judgements in cases involving the rights of accused people in the 1960s. Eisenhower was unmoved by Warren's defence of the application of the rules of due process to all Americans – including members of the Communist Party. On their way to Winston Churchill's funeral in 1965, Eisenhower angrily told Warren that Communists should be 'killed'.

Expectations of political similarity and support are two crucial reasons why a president appoints a particular individual: payment of political debts is another. Warren's nomination by Eisenhower owed much to the support which the then Governor of California gave to Eisenhower at the 1952 Republican Convention. Cultivation by presidents of political advantage among ethnic, racial and religious groups, and among women's organizations, also informs their choices. Presidents may also hope to cultivate constituents. For example, while Johnson's nomination of Thurgood Marshall in 1967 had much to do with his expectation that Marshall would continue judicially from the bench what Johnson had started politically from the Oval Office in civil rights and the Great Society, it had rather more to do with Johnson's view that it would be politically advantageous to nominate an African-American man to the Court. (Marshall had the added symbolic distinction of having argued the case for the litigants in *Brown v Board of Education* thirteen years earlier.) Equally, by nominating Sandra Day O'Connor in 1981, President Reagan sent to the Senate for confirmation a conservative and distinguished lawyer. She won the support of conservatives and liberals in the Senate. Conservatives voted to confirm her nomination because, on almost every matter except abortion, she was solidly conservative: despite her ideological bent, liberals felt obliged to confirm her because of her intellect and her gender – a testimony to Reagan's shrewdness in nominating her.

Unless there is clear evidence that a nominee is corrupt, has poor financial judgement, low moral standards, or is opposed to the law and established political values on such matters as civil rights, they are likely to be confirmed. Robert Bork's experience notwithstanding (see later), nominees are in little danger of rejection by the Senate Judiciary Committee or the full Senate simply because of their judicial philosophy. While a nominee with a distinct conservative or liberal record provides senators with ideological axes to grind with a public platform for their views, opposition of this kind has not normally been sufficient to persuade a majority of the Senate.

Scrutiny prior to nomination

In addition to the formal procedures by which the Senate examines nominees, thorough security investigations are made by the FBI of all nominees to federal courts, not just those to the Supreme Court. Only rarely are such reports found wanting: the nomination of Alexander Ginsburg to a federal district judgeship in 1986 occasioned an FBI report which failed to disclose that Ginsburg, when a student in the 1960s, and also when an assistant professor of law at Harvard in the 1970s, had smoked marijuana. An independent professional assessment is also made: through its standing committee on the federal judiciary, the American Bar Association (ABA) considers the professional qualifications of people under consideration for nomination and makes them available to the president and the Attorney-General. The committee ranks those it assesses as 'Not Qualified', 'Qualified', 'Well Qualified', or 'Exceptionally Well Qualified'. The ABA's standing committee has no formal veto over nominees, but its imprimatur is effectively a prerequisite for a nomination to be regarded as plausible. For nominees to the Supreme Court, the ABA committee uses just three classifications – 'Not Qualified' and 'Well Qualified', with 'Not Opposed' as the weakest expression of support. Several members of the ABA voiced their anxieties and reservations about Justice Bork's nomination to the Court in 1987. They expressed their 'concerns as to his judicial temperament, e.g., his compassion, open-mindedness, his sensitivity to the rights of women and minority persons or groups and comparatively extreme views respecting constitutional principles or their application, particularly within the ambit of the 14th Amendment'. (Following the rejection of Robert Bork, many conservatives were angered at what they saw as the liberal political leanings of the ABA. In 2001, President George W. Bush announced that the ABA would no longer be given advance notice of judicial nominations.)

Nominations to federal district courts and to the US circuit Courts of Appeals usually arouse little controversy in the Senate. Nominations are frequently made by the president and considered by the Senate Judiciary Committee. While the formal procedure for nomination and confirmation of judges to district and circuit courts is identical to that for justices to the Supreme Court, senators have, in practice, a fuller role in respect of appointments to the lower courts. Under the Constitution, presidents appoint subject to the advice and confirmation of the Senate. In practice, the senator or senators in the state from which the nominee comes have the right at least to be consulted by the White House prior to the nomination being made, and often to suggest a name or names to the president of a person or persons deemed acceptable. This tradition of 'senatorial courtesy' applies in all cases where the president and at least one of the two senators from the nominee's home state are of the same party. If party is shared, the president will at the very least require the acquiescence of the senator or senators concerned for the nomination to proceed unhindered; without it, the risks of the nomination being defeated rise.

Scrutiny following nomination

In the modern era (since Franklin D. Roosevelt was elected to the White House in 1932), only the nominations of Judges Haynsworth, Carswell and Bork have been denied by the Senate. In addition, the nominations of Justice Abraham Fortas to the post of chief justice, and of Judge Homer Thornberry, were filibustered in 1968 and the nominations withdrawn when it became apparent that no vote could be taken on them, and Reagan's nomination of Judge Ginsburg was also withdrawn after it had become clear that it would fail. Between 1789 and 2012, there were 151 nominations to the Supreme Court; 29 failed to win Senate confirmation. Of the 6 failures since 1932, 4 illustrate some of the limits on presidents' capacity to secure confirmation, and on Congress's capacity to deny it.

Of Nixon's six nominations to the Court, two successive ones were rejected (at the time, a unique achievement in the twentieth century, and the first occasion on which it had occurred since 1894, but one that President Reagan emulated). As president, Nixon took the view that the

Senate's role was to be restricted to that of approval after less than searching examination, a convenient view for one who sought to alter the composition of the Court but who anticipated liberal Democratic opposition to his purpose. Nixon nominated the southern conservative Clement Haynsworth (already a federal circuit court judge) for the vacancy created by the resignation of Justice Fortas in 1969. He did so following a search by his appointees in the Justice Department led by Attorney-General John Mitchell for a southerner who would adopt a 'strict constructionist' interpretation of the constitution on the Court. Two 'strict constructionist' Republican senators voted against Haynsworth. The Senate Republican leadership also opposed him because of allegations that he had participated in decisions involving corporations in which he held shares. Haynsworth also proved deeply conservative on civil rights questions, and on labour law. Moderate Democrats might, nonetheless, have supported him had the Court not become so highly politicized since the fierce conservative opposition to Thurgood Marshall's nomination in 1967. The Senate rejected Haynsworth's nomination by 55–45.

Nixon's belligerent response was to nominate G. Harrold Carswell of Florida, also a circuit court judge, whom Mitchell described as 'almost too good to be true', which he was, but not in the sense that Mitchell supposed. Senate investigations revealed that Carswell had, in 1948, defended segregation in the southern states (unsurprising behaviour by a southern public figure) and, at a later date, attempted to secure federal funding for a segregated private golf club in Florida, a new twist on an old southern practice. Carswell suffered from the further, and fatal, defect of stupidity. One of his most ardent supporters confirmed widespread doubts about his own and the nominee's intellectual competence when he argued that the mediocre generality of the population deserved representation on the Court. Senator Roman Hruska, whom Nixon had unwisely charged with the nomination's management on the Senate floor, observed:

> Even if he is mediocre there are a lot of mediocre Judges and people and lawyers. They are all entitled to a little representation, aren't they, and a little chance? We can't have all Brandeises, Cardozos, and Frankfurters and stuff [sic] like that there.

Others, including Louis Pollak, the dean of Yale Law School, found Carswell's intellectual bankruptcy a matter of anxiety rather than celebration. In Pollak's judgement, Carswell had 'more slender credentials than any nominee for the Supreme Court put forth in this century'. The nomination was defeated by 51–45. Among those who voted against it were thirteen members of the President's own party.

Nixon wrongly claimed that his nominees were rejected solely because of their judicial conservatism. Bruised liberal pride at conservative attacks on the Court's decision-making aside, their rejection owed less to judicial philosophy than to well-founded doubts about their competence and integrity. Although Nixon claimed that the defeat of Haynsworth's and Carswell's nominations showed that the Senate would not confirm a strict constructionist southerner, he believed Blackmun to be at least as conservative as either of the rejected southerners on 'law and order', and 'very slightly to the left only in the field of civil rights'. Convinced of this or not, the President was naturally anxious to defend himself against the charge that he had given way to pressure from a liberal majority in the Senate for a more moderate appointment to be made. Nominated within a week of Carswell's defeat, Blackmun was overwhelmingly confirmed by 94–0. Blackmun was thereafter inclined to adopt a self-deprecatory tone when referring to his having been Nixon's third choice: he was, he said, merely 'Old No. 3'. Subsequently, another two Nixon appointees were confirmed by a Democratic Senate: Powell of Virginia, by 89–1, and Rehnquist by 68–26. As with Blackmun's, so Powell's confirmation underlines the disinclination of the Senate to reject nominees *purely* on ideological grounds.

The only other president to have failed to secure confirmation of two nominees, Ronald Reagan, attempted in 1987 to appoint Judge Bork of the DC circuit Court of Appeals. Bork's judicial philosophy was thought by many senators too narrow to be of constructive use in judging cases before the Court. He had opposed the Civil Rights Act of 1964 (although he later changed his mind) and executed President Nixon's instruction to dismiss the Watergate Special Prosecutor after Attorney-General Elliott Richardson had refused to do so. Either would have harmed his chances with liberals and many moderates; the combination was very damaging. However, the single-most important charge against him was that he denied that the Constitution conferred a right of privacy on American citizens. He had taken this view so far as to oppose the Court's decision in *Griswold v Connecticut*, 381 US 479, the 1965 case by which the Court struck down the state of Connecticut's ban on contraception as an unconstitutional invasion of the First Amendment's 'penumbra' right of privacy. (No right of privacy was explicitly conferred by the Bill of Rights, but it has been held to be implied by it.) Bork was the first nominee in the postwar period to be rejected because of his interpretation of the Constitution. Following Bork's rejection by the Senate Judiciary Committee, the full Senate voted against confirmation by 58–42. All but two of the supporting votes came from Republicans (the two Democrats were both southerners), and all but six of the opposing votes from Republicans (three of whom were New Englanders, and one from Oregon – both areas of residual liberal and moderate Republican strength).

For his second attempt, President Reagan nominated Judge Douglas Ginsburg whom, he averred, was 'a man who believes profoundly in the rule of law', and whom he predicted the Senate would dislike as much as they did Bork; the President was wrong in respect of the first, but right on the second. His pose would under any circumstances have been brazen and unwise, but was especially so following the heaviest vote ever against a Supreme Court nominee, when his own influence was palpably waning, and against the considered advice of equally conservative but politically more sensitive Senate colleagues such as Strom Thurmond of South Carolina, who had energetically supported Bork's nomination. In fact, there was no time for Ginsburg's nomination to be considered seriously because he soon disclosed that he had smoked marijuana. The revelation embarrassed conservative supporters, placed Reagan in an impossible position (with his wife Nancy, Reagan had exploited politically his opposition to drug-taking and also set demanding standards of appointees to jobs in the Justice Department). Both the haste with which Ginsburg's nomination was made, and the offence that caused Ginsburg to withdraw his name from consideration, reflected the disarray within the Reagan White House as the President entered his last year in office.

All presidents seek to influence the Court's composition, including those who proclaim the importance of the Court remaining free of political taint. In the short term, however, presidential manipulation of the Court as a whole is virtually impossible. In the long term, ideological manipulation of the entire federal courts poses a more significant threat. Between 1933 and 1969, justices sympathetic to government regulation of the economy but not to government interference in civil and private rights were nominated deliberately by Democratic presidents of similar mind, and mistakenly by a Republican president. Between 1969 and 1992, justices broadly antipathetic to both stances were nominated by Republican presidents overtly hostile to both. Between 1993 and 2001, former President Clinton appointed two justices to the Supreme Court but, by replacing liberals with liberals, the overall composition of the Court altered little. Former President George W. Bush also appointed two justices to the bench (Chief Justice John Roberts in 2005 and Samuel Alito in 2006) but his appointments tipped the balance of the Court towards conservatism. President Obama had, by 2013, appointed two liberals to the Court such that the current composition of the Court is four liberal justices, four conservatives and one swing justice (Anthony M. Kennedy) who has sided with the conservatives in nearly three-quarters of judgements where he has been in a 5–4 majority. The politics of each period show the continued risk of the Court becoming an unbalanced instrument of elected branches, rather than a principled defence against their majoritarian predations.

Chief justices and leadership of the Court

The Warren Court: 1953–69

Earl Warren stands next to John Marshall as the greatest chief justice in the history of the Court, a garland neither easily won nor lightly worn. Chief justices can shape a Court's direction; Marshall and Warren did so. The task is great, for their political circumstances are even less promising than those of presidents. Those around them are close to being their equals and enjoy complete autonomy in law, if incompletely in political practice. The Court is both a collectivity with an institutional consciousness, and nine individual judges with the resources to resist coercion. As former Chief Justice Rehnquist observed in a speech in 1984, the Court is:

> far more dominated by centrifugal forces, pushing toward individuality and independence, than it is by centripetal forces pulling for hierarchical ordering and institutional unity.

Leadership in these circumstances is difficult to achieve: Chief justices have even fewer sanctions than presidents. *Brown v Board of Education* illustrates how a chief justice may lead his colleagues. When the Court granted *certiorari* on the case and it was discussed in conference in December 1952, the chief justice was Warren's predecessor, Vinson. He was disinclined to overrule *Plessy v Ferguson*, by which segregation was held not to violate the Fourteenth Amendment provided that the facilities were equal. No clear view having emerged, the Court set the case for re-argument in the 1953 term, but Vinson died before it could take place. Justice Frankfurter – who, with Alexander Bickel, his law clerk, had applied himself to preparing the ground for overturning *Plessy* in the face of what he expected would be continued opposition from Vinson (of whom he had a poor opinion) – memorably observed on learning of Vinson's death: 'This is the first indication I have ever had that there is a God'. The second conference on *Brown* took place a year after the first, under Warren, the new chief justice, former Republican Governor of California and Thomas Dewey's running-mate in the 1948 presidential election. Warren was thought by most associate justices (but not by Frankfurter, although he changed his view later) to be a safe choice. Eisenhower expected Warren to be reliable, but was to be disabused.

Warren inherited *Brown*. His disposal of it established his reputation, changed the South in particular, and American politics in general. From his first re-examination as Chief Justice of *Plessy*, he took the view that the doctrine of 'separate but equal' rested on 'a concept of the inherent inferiority of the colored race' to which he did not subscribe. While none of Warren's colleagues contemplated sustaining *Plessy* on such grounds, Justice Reed was reluctant to overturn it, and two other justices, Jackson and Clark, had reservations. Warren fully appreciated the case's gravity for black Americans, for the South, and for the notion and practice of equality in the United States.

The case was therefore frequently discussed in conference; Warren regularly postponed votes in order that he might determine precisely where the point of unanimous agreement lay. Warren's first achievement was to recognize the need for unanimity and to persuade his colleagues accordingly; his second was to achieve it. In conference, in informal groups, during lunch, the case was thoroughly discussed. The conference vote resulted in an 8–1 majority to overturn *Plessy*, with Justice Reed voting to uphold it. In conditions of even greater secrecy than those in which the Supreme Court normally operates, Warren circulated his draft opinions personally to justices in their chambers as soon as they were received from the Court's printers. He took a copy to Justice Jackson in hospital and collected an annotated version from him later the same day.

Energy, courtesy, collegiality and good judgement were Warren's decisive advantages as chief justice. He was, and continued to be, a politician, albeit a robed and unelected one, responding to different pressures, demands and circumstances on the Court than those he had known as Governor of California and as a vice-presidential candidate. His political skills served him well in preparing a unanimous decision on *Brown*, and particularly in persuading Justice Reed of the importance of a unanimous judgement. Between Warren's first conference on *Brown* in December 1953 and May of the following year, Warren lunched with his southern colleague Reed on at least twenty occasions. As the Court's opinion gelled, with Frankfurter and Jackson content to subscribe to Warren's opinion and not submit a concurring one of their own (which itself would have impaired the force of the judgement), Warren put his final case to Reed. All the members of the Court had, as Warren impressed on Reed, to judge carefully the impact of the decision and the means by which it was to be enforced.

Warren secured Reed's vote and unanimity for a short judgement (it takes just eleven pages in its original printing, and a mere seven pages in the lawyers' edition of the *Supreme Court Reports*). Lacking much in legal scholarship and elegance, it nevertheless represents an astonishing marriage of Warren's judgement of what his colleagues would accept and what he and his colleagues thought constitutionally required in the country. No decision of the Court in the period since *Brown* has had a greater impact on public policy and politics. The rapid pace of presidential legislative leadership under Lyndon Johnson between 1963 and 1968 in civil rights would have been politically impossible without the Court's momentous decision in *Brown*, which itself could not have occurred under the leadership either of Warren's predecessor or of his successor. Vinson was not disposed to overturn *Plessy*. It is doubtful if, had he found himself in Warren's place in 1953–54, Chief Justice Burger would have done so either. Even if he had, Burger's weak leadership of the Court between 1969 and 1986 suggests that he could not have led his colleagues to secure a unanimous opinion.

The Burger Court: 1969–86

Where Warren, throughout his fifteen years as chief justice, led the Court with diplomatic skill and imagination, Warren Burger's leadership was invariably hesitant and indecisive. His task was, in certain respects, even more difficult than Warren's. In *Brown*, moral leadership was possible; there existed the opportunity to declare ringing principle. The difficulties of implementation, of applying principle to reality in the complicated formation of detailed policy, were not his. Among the consequences of *Brown* were the establishment of private schools subsidized by state governments, and policies providing for 'freedom of choice' in the selection of schools. Both were means of maintaining segregation *de facto* in the light of its withering *de jure*, and were eventually ruled unconstitutional by the Court in *Griffin v County Board of Prince Edward County* (1964) and *Alexander v Holmes County Board of Education* (1969).

In *Swann v Charlotte-Mecklenburg Board of Education* (1971), Chief Justice Burger wrote the unanimous opinion of the Court, affirming the judgement of the federal district court requiring the bussing of students in Mecklenburg County, North Carolina, in order to achieve school desegregation. Bussing aroused considerable controversy throughout the country. Whereas *de jure* segregation was a distinctively southern problem, *de facto* segregation was common in northern cities, a function of racial division in housing. It aroused intense political passions, was exploited in the presidential elections of 1968 and 1972 by Richard Nixon and George Wallace, divided the Democratic Party not just between south and north, but also between liberals and blue-collar, white voters, and made judicial decision-making exceptionally fraught.

From judging whether the doctrine of 'separate but equal' could be maintained, in Burger's period as Chief Justice the Court moved to determining what length of bus ride federal courts might require to achieve the constitutional end of desegregation, whether schools which were predominantly white were less acceptable than predominantly black ones, and where schools should be built in order to promote integration. Ought they to be constructed in the inner cities, in the suburbs, or in areas between them whose racial composition was changing – and changing very often because of the threat of bussing? Details of policy

Exhibit 7.6 Enforcement of Desegregation

Brown fell into two parts: the principle at stake was decided in 1954 and the remedy followed in 1955. Implementation was, however, protracted and complicated. As late as 1963, the US Commission on Civil Rights reported that less than 0.5 per cent of southern blacks were attending integrated schools. Warren's opinion in *Brown I* provoked longer-term conflicts in northern cities intensified by the muddle which followed *Swann*. In the shorter term, the opinion occasioned tenacious and often violent southern resistance. Both reflected the Supreme Court's lack of implementation powers. An opinion having been delivered, it remains for it to be enforced. Remedies for the wrongs the Court rights lay in hands other than its own. The Court is therefore dependent on other Courts, legislatures, executives, and police forces. It is also critically dependent on the willingness of the public to accept its judgements.

It is not the case that decisions of the Court are implemented or not, that they meet with resistance or are accepted. Within this misleading polarity lies a range of responses of affected parties and many possible paths of development. De Tocqueville understood that, even in the early stages of the Republic, America was a highly litigious society; but its enthusiasm for litigation increased greatly from the 1960s onwards. Federal Court decisions are therefore often tested by cases of a slightly different kind by private citizens, corporations, or other affected individuals or bodies.

Apart from for a small police force to guard the justices and the building, the Supreme Court had no greater means of enforcement in the late 1990s than in 1789. Even within the judicial branch, the Supreme Court depends on District and Circuit Courts to apply the opinion to relevant cases. The resistance of District Court Judges to Supreme Court decisions has been rare, but occasionally of great importance. This was especially so following the second of the Court's *Brown* opinions, which set out the remedy that Warren and his colleagues had refrained from providing in *Brown I*. Paying careful attention to the difficulties of implementation (unusually for the Court, but probably necessarily), the opinion in *Brown II* (1955) required the Federal Courts:

→

implementation do not make judicial leadership as straightforward as the pronouncement of simple principle sometimes does; these were unpropitious circumstances for any chief justice. Nevertheless, instead of overcoming the difficulties facing the Court, Burger compounded them, notably by acting after *Swann* to weaken the force of his judgement. Having written the opinion, Burger became alarmed at the prospect of its

→

to take such proceedings and enter such orders and decrees consistent with this opinion as are necessary and proper to admit to public schools on a racially non-discriminatory basis with all deliberate speed the parties to these cases.

Warren's acceptance of Justice Frankfurter's suggestion of the phrase 'with all deliberate speed' was an error, as both men later appreciated. Southern politicians interpreted the phrase as permitting much deliberation and little speed, thereby delaying integration for many years. Most federal judges complied with *Brown*, although with varying enthusiasm depending on their own views and ambitions, local political circumstances and their courage. President Kennedy sought to prevent the appointment of judges opposed to civil rights, although he did not overcome the device of 'senatorial courtesy'. Most resistance came from southern politicians, as an example illustrates.

State courts and state governors vigorously resisted implementation. At Little Rock, Arkansas, in 1957, Governor Faubus used units of the Arkansas National Guard to prevent the Central High School's integration following earlier approval by the Federal District Court for the eastern District of Arkansas of the School Board's desegregation plan. Faubus testified before the Arkansas State Chancery Court that desegregation of the Central High School might lead to violence. The State Court issued a restraining order preventing implementation, whereupon the Federal District Court ordered that there should be no further delay. The Governor responded by ordering the Arkansas National Guard to prevent black students entering the school, and then defied both President Eisenhower's personal request that he desist and the District Court, which issued a further injunction against further interference with its ruling. Mindful of the potential harm which such action might do the Republican cause in the South during the 1960 presidential election, Eisenhower declared that he could not imagine any circumstances in which he would use federal troops to enforce a Federal Court order. Only with great reluctance did he finally resort to federal force: on 24 September 1957, Eisenhower called the Arkansas National Guard into federal service and ordered 1000 paratroopers from Kentucky into Little Rock to oversee the enforcement of the District Court's integration order.

being implemented with what he took to be excessive zeal, and wrote to federal judges drawing attention to the restrictive language which it contained. It was an act of weakness that detracted from the force of the judgement and made it more, rather than less, likely that federal district courts would implement the original opinion differently according to local circumstances and sentiment.

Other aspects of Burger's leadership also contrasted poorly with that of Warren's. His political judgement was myopic, he made little effort to establish cooperative relations with colleagues, and he showed little imagination in assigning opinions. He not only exercised little influence with those justices who were antipathetic to his conservatism, but also exercised little sway with his natural allies. Harry Blackmun, who had been Burger's best man and remained a close friend, thought Burger's leadership of the Court poor, and became disheartened at the lack of humour on the Court. He particularly resented the chief justice's habit of assigning opinions on tedious tax law cases to colleagues with whom he had had a disagreement.

The Rehnquist Court: 1986–2005

William Rehnquist was nominated to the Supreme Court by former President Richard Nixon in 1971 and began service on the Court in 1972. In 1986, on the retirement of Warren Burger, former President Ronald Reagan appointed Rehnquist to the position of chief justice. While Rehnquist was, when viewed through the lens of his previous judgements, more conservative than his predecessor, nonetheless, the Supreme Court did not lurch to the right. Indeed, between 1986 and 1994 the Court did not strike down those landmark cases so disliked by social conservatives: neither the *Roe* (1973) decision, nor the *Miranda* (1966) decision was overturned. However, the scope and reach of the *Roe* decision was narrowed in both the *Webster v Reproductive Services* (1989) and *Casey* (1992) decisions, the Rehnquist Court did not, at least in its first eight years, embark on a period of judicial activism and held instead to the principle of *stare decisis*.

By 1995, the Rehnquist Court had developed a more consistently conservative approach – most clearly in the area of States' Rights. Rehnquist had made clear his commitment to States' Rights in the 1976 *National League of Cities v Usery* case (see Chapter 10), in which he wrote the majority opinion which argued that the sovereignty of the states constituted grounds to overturn the exercise by Congress of the commerce power (last challenged in the 1935–36 Court term and which contributed to the introduction by Franklin D. Roosevelt of his *court-packing* plan). When the Usery decision was overturned in *Garcia v San Antonio* (1985), Rehnquist dissented. Yet, by 1995, in the *US v Lopez*, a narrow majority of the Court was increasingly inclined to challenge congressional statutes based on the commerce clause of the Constitution. The conservative justices on the Rehnquist Court pushed for a construction of the federal–state relationship reminiscent of the pre-New Deal era.

The Rehnquist Court entered the political thicket when it intervened in the Florida election dispute during the presidential election of 2000. In

Gore v Bush (2000), the Court ended the Florida recount process with the result that the state's disputed electoral college votes went to George W. Bush. Critics of the decision were very vocal in their opposition to what they claimed was a partisan decision by a conservative court. Many were surprised by the Court's judgement, not least because of the Rehnquist Court's record of judging in favour of state sovereignty and against any increased reach of the federal government.

The Rehnquist Court increasingly split into two camps with respect to the federal–state balance: the four liberal justices (Stephens, Breyer, Ginsburg and Souter) adhered to the post-1937 position of the Court that allowed the federal government to regulate inter- and intra-state commerce. The conservative majority adopted a position not dissimilar to that established by Rehnquist in his *Usery* (1976) opinion which echoed the pre-1937 'dual federalist' position of the Supreme Court in relation to States' Rights. The Rehnquist Court remained finely balanced between liberals and conservatives, but it was Justice Sandra Day O'Connor, as a swing justice, who determined whether the majority would favour the liberals or the conservatives on the Court. Such was O'Connor's influence that some commentators labelled the court under William Rehnquist the 'O'Connor Court'. While the Rehnquist Court had, by the mid-1990s, developed a consistent approach to the protection of States' Rights, it did not emerge as the consistently conservative court for which conservatives had hoped and that liberals had feared would be the antithesis, or anti-dote, to the Warren Court's liberal activism.

The Roberts Court: 2005–Present

In July 2005, Justice O'Connor announced her retirement from the Court and just two months later the chief justice, who had been diagnosed with cancer the previous year, died. Rehnquist was succeeded by one of his former law clerks, John Roberts, who was nominated by President George W. Bush to the position of chief justice and confirmed in September 2005. In January 2006, the President secured the confirmation of his second nominee to the Court, Samuel Alito, who replaced O'Connor following her retirement. Where Burger had been largely humourless, Roberts's first eight years on the Court suggest him to be an affable yet politically astute chief justice. Although he has sided with the other three conservatives on the Court in most cases, he is less predictably conservative than his supporters might have hoped. His decision to join the liberals on the Court in upholding President Obama's flagship healthcare legislation (*National Federation of Independent Businesses v Sebelius* (2012)) showed imagination and a political acuity which make the attribution of the term 'conservative' an insufficiently subtle categorization of Roberts.

Despite conservatives' hopes that justices Alito and Roberts would give the Court a consistent conservative majority, the Court has remained finely balanced, with Roberts usually constituting the fourth member of the conservative grouping on the Court (alongside Scalia, Thomas and Alito). Four moderate/liberal justices balanced the conservative grouping and Anthony M. Kennedy emerged as the new swing justice. During the 2006–07 session, Kennedy was in the majority of the cases that were decided 5–4 100 per cent of the time; in the 2010–11 session, that figure fell to 88 per cent. Of these 5–4 cases, 6 out of 10 were decided in favour of the conservative majority.

President Obama secured two successful nominees to the Court in his first two years in office, yet the replacement of two liberals with two liberals did not alter the ideological composition of the Court. Sonia Sotomayor, the third woman appointed to the Court and the first Hispanic on the Court, succeeded David Souter in August 2009. Elena Kagan, the fourth woman on the Court, succeeded John Paul Stephens, who had served thirty-five years on the Court. She took office in August 2010.

Kennedy has used his central point in the Court's ideological spectrum creatively. In recent important judgements, Kennedy has joined conservatives in writing the majority opinion in *Citizens United v FEC* (2010), and was joined by the four conservative justices in ruling that elements of the 2002 Bipartisan Campaign Finance Reform Act violated the First Amendment. The second of those two judgements opened the door to unlimited campaign funding by corporations engaged in 'party-building' activities (see Chapter 4). The same conservative majority voted in 2011 to strike down an Arizona state law that provided matching funds to candidates in receipt of public funding. Yet, in *JDB v North Carolina* (2011), Kennedy joined the liberals in supporting Sotomayor's majority opinion, which ruled that age is relevant to the application of the *Miranda* rights that form the bedrock for determining the circumstances in which a suspect is questioned and placed in custody.

Conclusion

In 1936, over the ferocious dissent of Justices Stone, Brandeis and Cardozo, Associate Justice Owen Roberts wrote in the majority opinion in *United States v Butler*, which struck down both the taxation and expenditure provisions of the Agricultural Adjustment Act of 1933 as unconstitutional, that judicial review was much misunderstood:

> It is sometimes said that the court assumes a power to overrule or control the action of the people's representatives. This is a misconcep-

tion. The Constitution is the supreme law of the land ordained and established by the people. All legislation must conform to the principles it lays down. When an act of Congress is appropriately challenged in the courts as not conforming to the constitutional mandate the judicial branch of the Government has only one duty, to lay the article of the Constitution which is invoked beside the statute which is challenged and to decide whether the latter squares with the former.

In his dissent, Stone complained of Roberts's 'tortured construction' of the Constitution. The language of the Constitution provides few straightforward solutions to problems of American government: truths do not lie in the language awaiting discovery by the discerning. Neither is the view that the only construction that judges and justices may properly place on the Constitution is that which its framers intended of much help to Supreme Court justices. Few parts of the Constitution met with universal approbation from delegates to the Constitutional Convention in 1787; even fewer did so in the state ratifying conventions. Even those who voted to ratify the Constitution, and those who later supported the adoption of amendments to it, had different reasons for voting as they did, and different views of its likely operation and meaning. Not only was the language of the Constitution itself the product of disagreement and intense debate from the opening of the convention to Rhode Island's belated ratification, the Constitution itself and the amendments that followed were framed in ways that would allow changing interpretations in a changed future.

What the Constitution has meant, and means; how that meaning might be determined and clarified; how it should be applied by the federal courts to the cases coming before them; and how the general significance of the decision that emerges should be shaped into a remedy are fundamental problems. They lie at the core of debates about America's public policy, American citizens' liberties, the defence of individual rights, and the maintenance of limited but effective government. Insofar as they must concern themselves with these questions, the Court cannot eschew a political role. Politics is ineradicable from the federal courts. It is present in the selection, nomination and confirmation of judges and justices for federal courts as it is in state courts, and it is present both in the formation of judgements that the courts must make about the cases before them and in the consequences that those judgements have. It is not, for example, clear why to adhere to *Miranda* is an instance of politicization while to weaken it is not.

In matters of recruitment, conservative presidents such as Reagan, George H. W. Bush and George W. Bush have assiduously appointed to the federal courts those whom they expect to share their views. Almost all of their nominees (carefully screened by political appointees at the

Justice Department) were judicial conservatives. President Clinton and President Obama were equally committed to the appointment of liberal justices. Politics do not explain all judicial recruitment, still less judicial decision-making: the Constitution is no more warm putty in the hands of a president than it is in the hands of a passing majority of the Supreme Court, or of the lower federal courts. It is not so because *stare decisis* powerfully constrains current action and decision. Another constraint, however paradoxical, is that the Court inhabits a political world. Justices are constrained (though not confined) by public, congressional, and media opinion, and by their need to ensure the broad acceptability of their judgements and to protect their own legitimacy. Accordingly, they do not write on a blank sheet of paper, but contribute to continuing judicial, jurisprudential and constitutional deliberations among politicians, lawyers, judges and the public. It is in these deliberations that constitutional meaning is found and contested.

Chapter 8

Interest Groups

Interest groups play prominent roles in American politics and there are few areas of public policy in which interest groups are not actively involved. As well as influencing policy directly, there is also the perennial question of how much influence interest groups have over policy outcomes and, crucially, whether such influence benefits or hinders the functioning of democracy. In short, the debate regarding the role of interest groups can be broadly categorized into two opposing views: the pluralists, who consider that group activity enhances democracy, and elite theorists, who consider the political system to be dominated by the few at the expense of the many. As former Senator Edward Kennedy said, 'we have the best Congress money can buy'.

Most Americans are members of at least one group, and the porous central state provides multiple points of access for individuals forming groups with the goal of shaping policy outcomes. This chapter examines American interest groups, their roles in American society, and their interactions with the three branches of the United States government examined in Chapters 5, 6 and 7. The chapter begins with an examination of the opportunities open to, and constraints on, interest groups as a whole. The second section considers lobbying of the courts, Congress, the presidency and the executive bureaucracy (examined in Chapter 9), while the third section analyses different types of groups, their purposes, and the means available to them to bring pressure to bear on decision-makers in government. The fourth section of this chapter evaluates the role played by interest groups and asks whether interest groups benefit or hinder the functioning of democracy in America.

Interest groups: opportunities and constraints

The First Amendment to the Constitution affirms the right of the people 'to petition the government for a redress of grievances'. It thereby legitimizes lobbying – of legislatures, executive agencies and courts – by private interests. Business corporations, labour unions, public interest groups, professional associations, single-issue groups, and coalitions of some or all of these, lobby governments in America on behalf of sectional interests, which may or may not coincide with a (or the) public interest.

That private groups pose problems for the polity as a whole has been acknowledged since Hamilton, Madison and Jay defended the proposed Constitution to the electors of New York in *The Federalist Papers*. Penetration of the porous American state by many groups also poses the question of to whom, in practice, elected politicians are accountable, and of how political power is allocated. Not all interests are represented before government; many have no representation at all, while that of others is often poorly-financed, poorly-organized, or both.

The interest industry

Washington owes its existence, employment, and prosperity to government, and the representation of interests. Directly or otherwise, most who work in Washington do so because it is the seat of federal government; interest representation is the third largest source of employment in the city. Metropolitan Washington's rapid spatial and population growth since the late 1960s is primarily the result of the proliferation of groups, a development that has been supplemented by many corporations moving there from New York.

In 2012, there were 12,016 active lobbyists in the capital registered with Congress. Under the *Federal Regulation of Lobbying Act* (PL 601, 1946) any organization which:

> solicits, collects, or receives money ... to be used to aid in the passage or defeat of legislation by the United States Congress [or] whose principal function is to aid in the passage or defeat of legislation by the United States Congress

is obliged to register with the Secretary of the Senate and the Clerk of the House of Representatives, and to submit quarterly reports on their contributions, loans and expenditure. Registration is a gesture toward transparency in policy-making, a necessary condition of democratic plurality. As the total number of groups lobbying the federal government

Exhibit 8.1 Lobbying: Top Ten Spenders in 2012

Organization	Level of spending ($)
US Chamber of Commerce	95,660,000
National Association of Realtors	25,982,290
Blue Cross/Blue Shield	16,238,032
General Electric	15,550,000
Google Inc.	14,390,000
Pharmaceutical Research & Manufacturers of America	14,380,000
AT&T Inc.	14,030,000
American Hospital Association	13,275,200
National Cable & Telecommunications Association	13,010,000
American Medical Association	12,980,000

is large, so also is the range of legislative interests which they represent (see Exhibit 8.1).

However, the number of registered lobbyists understates the number of individuals who are, in effect, involved in the lobbying industry. As the case of Newt Gingrich and others illustrates (see Exhibit 8.2, p. 270), there are numerous so-called *stealth lobbyists* who operate within the law because of a loophole in the Lobbying Disclosure Act of 1995, which allows individuals who spend less than twenty per cent of their time working on lobbying activities for their client to claim that they are not lobbyists and therefore need not register as such. Because these individuals are not registered, we have no record of to whom they talk, when, what they say, or about what. In short, the number of non-lobbying *de facto* lobbyists in Washington is higher than the official total, but the number is indeterminable.

Organization

As the scope of state government activity (both that flowing from the autonomous actions of state legislatures and from regulations imposed by the US Congress) has grown, groups have also organized vigorously in state capitals. As in Washington, groups attempt to influence state executives and party activists during the formation of policy; state legislatures and the public (through the electronic and printed media) during its legitimation; the executive and state judiciary during its implementation; and all branches of government and public opinion during its evaluation. State and local governments regulate the private sector, just as the federal government does; groups in the private sector accordingly have interests to defend and advance before state governments.

In large states such as California and Texas, the number and range of groups approach that in Washington, since there is similar diversity of economic activity, ethnic composition and political purpose. The two state capitals, Sacramento and Austin, attract ranks of lawyer-lobbyists who seek to influence state governments as their counterparts in Washington do the federal government. The particular weakness of political parties in California has itself been partly responsible for the strength of interest groups in the state. Railroad companies dominated California state politics between 1860 and the Progressive revolt in the state of 1910. Progressive reforms deliberately weakened the legislature through the referendum, the initiative and the recall, and so further weakened parties, leaving a gap that interest groups have partly filled. In Texas, circumstances are different: the two-party system is dominated by fiscal conservatives, but weakened by factionalism within the Democratic Party, many of whose members are closer to organized oil, banking and other commercial interests than they are either to their nominal party colleagues, or to their constituents. Penetration of Texas state government by organized interests is, accordingly, pronounced.

Interest groups and access to government

Interest groups and the courts

Federal courts are open to interest group pressure through litigation. Although courts are not lobbied conventionally, groups litigate on their own behalf, and submit *amicus curiae* briefs (see Chapter 7) to supplement arguments presented by the adversaries directly involved. In courts as much as before Congress, the executive, or public opinion, groups work not alone but in concert with others.

The most striking instance of a group pursuing cases through the courts is, perhaps, the National Association for the Advancement of Colored People (NAACP) through its Legal Defense and Education Fund. Founded at the end of World War I, the NAACP sought to enforce civil rights by litigating on behalf of black people denied their constitutional rights under the Fourteenth Amendment. It did so most spectacularly in *Brown v Board of Education* (1954) through its then Chief Counsel, Thurgood Marshall. It has also litigated in order to preserve its avenue of redress through the courts: in *National Association for the Advancement of Colored People v Button*, 371 US 415 (1963), the Court reversed the Supreme Court of Virginia's judgement to uphold the constitutionality of a 1956 Virginia statute extending restrictions on barratry (the vexatious encouragement of litigation) in ways that would have had the consequence (as its authors had the intention) of significantly weakening the NAACP's attempts to enforce the application of *Brown v Board of Education* through state courts. The NAACP continues to pursue civil rights cases before the courts. In 1989, it succeeded with the last desegregation case, securing a favourable court judgement desegregating the public school system in Natchez, Mississippi.

The NAACP's decision to argue the case for desegregation through the courts was *faute de mieux*: neither Congress nor the executive would act. A similar motivation has informed the busy litigation of pro- and anti-abortion groups in recent years. Both the National Right to Life Committee and the National Abortion Rights Action League have (in league with other groups that lobby on one side or the other of the issue) raised income by appeals to sympathetic populations and then pursued cases through both the federal and state courts. Both in civil rights and in abortion cases, it is the structural fragmentation of the federal government that permits groups denied satisfaction in one branch to seek it in another.

Congress: the exploitation of constituency interests

Congress is the most open branch of the United States government, especially to interest groups. Group pressures are often cumulative with the constituency interests of members of Congress: the homogeneity of most congressional districts typically gives rise to ethnic and economic groups with concentrated membership or support in each district. Such cumulation is augmented by private financing of congressional elections through political action committees (PACs), Super-PACs (see Chapter 4) and reinforced by House elections held biennially, so rendering representatives highly sensitive to local opinion. Members of Congress are local political figures running for office by appealing to local people and local groups on local issues: links between local groups and members of Congress are thereby forged when they first run for office. Once elected, the requirement is to maintain the support of those groups which they judge to be politically advantageous, and to resist, deflect, or disarm those thought to be potentially harmful. These pressures are often exerted on representatives during their frequent (publicly-financed) visits to their home district. Local politics form the backcloth against which policy-making in Congress proceeds.

Where a district is dominated by a major economic interest, a member of Congress rarely determines their view on policy matters autonomously. Thus, the representative from the 7th district of Michigan is obliged to defend the interests of General Motors' workers by seeking limits on the importing of Korean Hyundai vehicles. To do otherwise would be to invite the wrath of the United Automotive Workers (UAW) labour union and to invite a primary challenge. The UAW involves itself both in the politics of individual congressional districts, and also in major policy questions, as it did during the negotiation of the US's Free Trade Agreement with Korea. The Agreement having been reached, Ron Gettelfinger, then the president of the UAW, urged the rejection of the deal on the grounds that it would hurt his workers. High-cost tobacco, peanut, rice and sugar producers in southern states have not only sought, but also achieved and maintained, significant protection against imports from more efficient foreign competitors. Prior to former Speaker Newt Gingrich's major reforms of the committee and subcommittee structure in 1995, the success of such producers was facilitated by the power of regionally-concentrated congressional defenders of trade barriers, quotas and tariffs on two of the House Agriculture Committee's key subcommittees: Cotton, Rice and Sugar; and Tobacco and Peanuts. The chairmen of both subcommittees and most of their colleagues repre-sented districts where the relevant farmers and processors and their employees were significant economic and voting forces. American consumers enjoyed no such institutional advantages. American consumers have accordingly long paid higher prices for tobacco, peanuts, rice and sugar than they would have done under free agricul-tural trade. Similar price differentials apply in the case of steel. Speaking in 1999, Congressman Phil English (R-PA) argued for protection of domestic (by which he meant Pennsylvanian) steel through the imposi-tion of tariffs. The evidence suggested no impending tsunami. Indeed, one consequence of higher steel costs (US steel was more expensive than Chinese) was the higher costs of the main component in US automobile manufacture. To ensure that the US automotive sector was not damaged by the high costs of domestic steel it, too, was protected against imports. Here is an excellent example of how interest group activity harms the public interest. Americans suffered a welfare loss when they bought American cars made from American steel that American manufacturers bought at a premium to world prices.

Hearings of congressional committees and subcommittees provide interest groups with formal opportunities to testify on legislative business before the committee. There are also private opportunities to lobby members of Congress and senators. As hearing rooms of committees in session are usually lined with lobbyists, so lobbyists are invariably to be found waiting in anterooms of congressional offices for the opportunity to speak to the politicians whose support they solicit. Interest groups seek and accept opportunities to present their case before committees. If, as Woodrow Wilson once observed, Congress at work is Congress in committee, then Congress in committee is where Congress and interest groups meet, epitomizing society's penetration of the porous state.

Committees are the primary institutional focus for groups on Capitol Hill. Hearings take place at the discretion of the chair of the committee or subcommittee, and the list of those groups testifying is agreed by the chair in consultation with colleagues in both the majority and minority parties. Which groups are heard and when, how they are questioned, by whom, in what order, and on what subjects, can have a critical effect on the influence that the testimony of particular groups may have on the panel's deliberations. Witnesses may or may not represent the range and intensity of opinion on the particular bill but will, to the extent that the chair thinks it expedient, help the Chair to shape the passage of the bill in a manner which suits their intentions. Chairs may encourage particular supporters to attend, in order either to bolster the bill's prospects, or to weaken them. Hearings may be kept short, thereby limiting the time available for groups' formal submissions, to the point where prepared testimony may merely be entered into the committee's records. Alternatively, they may be deliberately protracted, with the consequence either that groups may win sympathy for their cause, or exhaust it. The capacity of chairmen to influence committee decisions by the creative use of discretion during hearings is great.

Committees which were once internally hierarchical, highly suscepti-ble to special producer influences and unsympathetic to consumer inter-ests now have flatter distributions of internal authority and are open to a greater variety of pressures. There are three explanations for this. The first has to do with developments within, and the second and third outside, Congress:

1. In comparison with the decades before the early 1970s, the weak-ened formal power of committee chairs, and the enhanced impor-tance of subcommittees as sites for hearings, increased both the number and the range of interests represented before Congress. Committees that once were dominated by a few special producer interests on major policy questions are now more susceptible to wider influences. Even where a narrow range of interests continues to be protected within committees and subcommittees, the increased importance of the House floor, and the renaissance in the power of party leaders in the 1990s, limits the capacity of specialist commit-tees to protect their legislation from competing pressures in Congress as a whole.

2. The composition of interest groups lobbying Congress has changed greatly since the 1960s. New types of groups representing single issues, fundamentalist Christians, consumer interests, universities and research institutes, associations of state and local governments,

individual foreign governments and their support groups within the
United States, and associations acting on behalf of what they claim
to be the public interest, have established themselves and intervened
in policy-making (especially during the continuous process of policy
evaluation). Pure examples of single-issue groups include pro-and
anti-abortion groups and the National Rifle Association. Common
Cause, founded in 1970, is the clearest example of a public interest
group. The National Governors' Association has, since the late
1970s, become much the most influential representative of sub-
federal governments. Foreign embassies now court Congress on
questions of international trade, government contracts, US foreign
aid and immigration, while the American Israel Public Affairs
Committee works busily on behalf of Israel's interests (and does so
in close coordination with the Israeli Embassy). Exhibit 8.3 provides
a summary of the main types of interest group.

3. Since the early 1970s, the merging of traditional media with the rise
    of modern social media has augmented the capacity of groups to
    produce and disseminate propaganda. These technological develop-
    ments have spawned new industries of public relations and media
    consulting, enabling politicians and lobbyists to promote causes
    with greater speed and sophistication than was possible previously.
    Presentation of material, its targeting towards selected groups, and
    the generation of income from focused email distribution and social
    networking, have greatly assisted lobbying by groups dependent on
    mass memberships. New communications technologies have
    reduced the real cost of group formation and participation in policy-
    making.

These three interrelated developments have not ended the power of niche
producer interests to protect the domestic US industry in league with relevant agencies, departments and congressional subcommittees. They
have, however, been sufficient to weaken them and (for example) the
capacity of American vehicle manufacturers and pharmaceuticals companies to resist consumer demands for safer cars and drugs by modifying
conceptions of newsworthiness and (partly in consequence) the political
agenda with which Congress works. The rise of modern media makes
controlling either the medium or the message difficult for any group or
corporation. Tweets 'going viral' and YouTube clips in the hundreds of
millions underscore the difficulties faced by groups trying to restrict to
Washington insiders an understanding of the directions and effectiveness
of lobbying.

Openness is a necessary but insufficient condition for politics to be
plural in practice as well as in theory. Three other conditions must also be
satisfied:

1. No single group or class dominates politics and public policy processes, and all groups with an interest in the policy under discussion must be represented in its consideration.
2. Leaders of groups accurately and fully represent their members' views, and the intensity with which those views are held (notwithstanding the problems that intensity poses for rules and norms of democratic decision-making).
3. Political assets and resources are widely and evenly distributed.

As the last section of this chapter shows, these conditions are not reliably satisfied in the making of public policy in the United States. While Congress has undoubtedly become a more open institution since the congressional reforms of the early to mid-1970s, both on the two floors and in committees, the executive has always been a less transparent branch. There, many private interests enjoy collusive relations with executive agencies, whether in iron triangles, networks of influence, or through formal mechanisms of their membership of advisory committees in which they seek to deploy their asymmetrical advantages of information and expertise, and thereby exploit their positional advantages over groups without them. Formal equality of access to legislators and executive officials often obscures other paths trodden by groups which enjoy continuous access and influence. Senate Finance and House Ways and Means Committee meetings are open to the public as well as to special interest groups, but the interests of (mostly unorganized) ordinary taxpayers have usually been less well-represented on those two Committees than those of major corporations.

Nonetheless, ample resources avail lobbyists little in the absence of credibility, which is built on the accuracy of the information which a lobbyist provides to policy-makers. Lobbyists and the lobbied trade in the currencies of information, expertise and influence. Lobbyists can, and do, bring to congressional politicians and their staff information, and interpretations of it which, if accurate, can be of significant benefit. As Hall and Wayman (1990: 803) have explained:

> group representatives often serve as 'service bureaus' or adjuncts to congressional staff. They provide technical information and policy analysis; they provide political intelligence; they draft legislation and craft amendments; they even write speeches or talking points that their supporters can employ in efforts on their behalf.

Lobbyists, who are acknowledged masters of their subjects as well as politically resourceful, can often compensate for their group's lack of financial resources. Providing misleading or inaccurate information to politicians, their staff and bureaucrats quickly ruins a lobbyist's standing by undermining the credibility of politicians unfortunate (or foolish) enough to rely on it. Lobbyists who thus damage themselves and others find their access to policy-makers closes and with it any possibility of exercising influence over the marking-up of a ill, the agency's drafting of regulations, or the holding of oversight hearings on government programmes. On the occasions that it has sought to defend the indefensible, as in its support for the sale of armour-piercing bullets, the National Rifle Association has harmed its cause.

Successful lobbying comprises less the application of pressure than the communication of accurate information and analysis: incentives to mislead are weak, since the penalty is the loss of trust and the rupturing of valuable relationships. Some private groups' expertise is such that their advice commands attention. Other groups carry such great political weight that they cannot be ignored. Rather than occasional encounters, relationships develop between interest groups, congressional committees and subcommittees, and executive agencies. Politicians and staff within government learn whom to trust, those on whose judgement and honesty they may safely depend, and whose opposition will cause them more difficulties than they ought prudently to risk. Lobbyists learn the importance of when, with whom, and how it is most advantageous to intervene. Relationships between competent lobbyists, agency bureaucrats and congressional politicians are positive-sum games: all participants gain.

Some groups are advantaged by the nature of their membership. Thirty-seven million citizens over the age of fifty belong to the American Association of Retired Persons (AARP); all have a current or anticipated direct interest in protecting Social Security and Medicare entitlement programmes. All members of Congress have significant cohorts of retired people within their districts, and need no reminding of their high voting propensity or, hence, of their power. No argument is more persuasive than that resting on constituents' votes. In 2005, the AARP played a strong hand with skill in effectively derailing President George W. Bush's plans to privatize Social Security.

The AARP's large membership was acquired, and is maintained, partly for the reasons identified by Mancur Olson in *The Logic of Collective Action* (1965). Olson showed that individuals do not necessarily form or join groups to promote shared interests, even where it would be rational for them all to do so. He noted that the public goods flowing from the activities of groups are provided to all irrespective of whether or not they join the group. In the case of large groups, the temptation is always to 'free ride' on the contributions of others, since the benefits will accrue to those who do not contribute as they will to those who do.

Olson argues that groups must often offer other, material, benefits if they are to persuade people to pay for membership. Furthermore, these benefits must be excludable from non-members. For Olson, group membership can often be explained through the creation and maintenance of selective benefits which accrue only to those who pay for membership. Of course, it remains the case that many members of groups are motivated to join for reasons other than the rational exploitation of selective benefits, yet Olson's analysis remains powerful. For example, the AARP's ability to defend its members' interests is a function of its success in offering a large range of benefits to them. The AARP website presents an extensive array of benefits which, in 2012, could be obtained for an annual subscription of $16.

The successful employment of such techniques by other groups does not necessarily result in their enjoying comparable success. The American Medical Association's (AMA) financial and lobbying resources are abundant: in 2012, it had 216,000 members and an annual budget of almost $200 million. Yet, these advantages have not enabled it to overcome its internal difficulties. Divisions within the Association have grown as the pressures on federal finances have increased. The size and diversity of the medical profession is such that maintaining unity is difficult; accordingly, it becomes easier to defeat.

Establishment of PACs, and the Federal Election Commission's (FEC) regulation of them requiring that sources and destinations of PAC funds be publicly recorded (see Chapter 4), have allowed examination of the relationship between the money that politicians receive and their votes on questions of interest to PACs and their parent organizations. However, voting is only one form of political behaviour. Others may have greater political significance: the content, tone and timing of speeches, and the audience to which (and the setting within which) they are delivered, also matter. So, too, do the meetings (formal and informal, public and private), conversations, arguments, hints, inflections and facial expressions of politicians. The time, energy, intensity and passion that politicians devote to, or withhold from, a cause also hint at their detailed preferences, their views about issues and the importance that they attach to their resolution.

Votes, by comparison, provide only a partial account. They do not disclose intensity. Neither, by definition, do they measure the efforts that politicians make, successfully or otherwise, to prevent votes being taken at all. It might appear that the rational purpose of the expenditure of PAC funds should be to affect crucial swing marginal votes. Yet, research by Richard Hall and Frank Wayman (1990) has shown that this is not how PAC money is spent. Neither is it entirely clear (as it is commonly argued to be) that money enables lobbyists to buy access to politicians. Even if this were so, it should prompt the question of what lobbyists do with such access once they have it. If group influence is mediated by access, the relationship between its exercise and its effect should still be apparent in voting patterns, but (as almost all research has shown) it is not. Hall and Wayman argue that while PACs do not purchase support in measurable form, they do at least partly affect the intensity of politicians' devotion to different causes.

John Wright (1990: 433) also finds no clear relationship between PAC donations and voting, but some between campaign contributions and groups' lobbying patterns. However, studying the Ways and Means Committee, he finds that representatives' voting decisions are best explained by the number of contacts they had with lobbyists on each side of the issue in question. Wright's research demonstrates a further, important relationship. Since lobbying tends to reinforce opinions that legislators already have, information and interpretations of it supplied to legislators by lobbyists are partly shaped by campaign finance. Such a pattern is classically apparent in iron triangle systems of policy-making, where private economic activities are subsidized through distributive policy: subsidies to tobacco, peanuts, rice, and sugar farming are examples. Throughout the post-war period, it has also been true of tax policy, where sectional interests have succeeded in protecting the many special exemptions and deductions in the tax code.

The passage of the Tax Reform Act of 1986 (HR3838) reveals some of the resources available to many financially powerful groups whose interests were threatened by the Act's provisions for reducing and eliminating tax concessions and shelters. It also illustrates an important feature of modern lobbying: groups rarely lobby alone but, instead, pool their resources and expertise in coalition. The Tax Reform Act was opposed by a wide range of groups, including hospitals, charities, bankers and bond underwriters; many groups in this broad coalition without a PAC of their own formed one to channel campaign contributions to Ways and Means members. In the first six months of 1985, PAC contributions to members of the House Ways and Means Committee nearly tripled compared with the same period in 1983. By seeking to delete Investment Tax Credit from the Federal Tax Code, the bill's authors struck at a key provision of tax law for manufacturing companies. In addition to their individual and trade association lobbying, twenty-three large corporations, including Goodyear, Du Pont and AT&T contributed $800,000 to acquire the services of Charles Walker, one of Washington's most senior and most skilful lobbyists, to press their case before Congress and to purchase full-page advertisements in newspapers arguing that the investment tax credit was in the public interest.

The bill nonetheless passed, and investment tax credit was deleted from the US Tax Code. Powerful as the groups lobbying for special exemptions were, the forces arrayed against them were formidable: the President and his White House staff, the Treasury Department, and the chairmen and key members of the Senate Finance and House Ways and

Means Committees collaborated to ensure that winning coalitions of legislators could be assembled to support the President's bill.

Interest groups and the presidency

At all stages of public policy-making processes (initiation, formalization, legitimation, implementation and evaluation), presidents draw both competition and support from groups. In many areas of distributive policy dominated by sub-governments or issue networks where federal programmes proceed incrementally from year to year, presidents may not attempt (whether by deliberate choice or default) to impose their own preferences. In other areas of greater importance to them, presidents are frequently obstructed in their attempts to formulate and implement policies that they declare to be in the national interest over those they identify (or stigmatize) as being merely the sectional interests of groups. All politicians attempt to present their own interests as being coincident with (and often in fact identical to) the public interest, but the president is in a better position than most to do so. As the sole national elective politician of significance, his singular legitimacy affords him a distinctive advantage in making the claim, and then in seeking to enforce it. To that end, presidents and their staff attempt to co-opt groups into their presentation of new policies, their lobbying of legislative proposals through Congress or of presidential appointments through the Senate, and into the detailed implementation of Acts passed by Congress.

The president has the support of specialist White House staff charged with the task of maintaining 'public relations' – the cultivation of productive relations with groups supportive of the president, and with other groups whose support the president needs but does not reliably have. The broad appeal of both political parties results in ties with groups being less clear-cut than they have traditionally been in Europe: since 1933, labour unions have usually been closer to Democratic presidents than to Republican ones, but all Republican presidents have attempted to woo labour unions – or those among them sympathetic to, at least, politically important parts of a president's agenda. President Nixon did so with considerable success, especially in respect of his foreign policy. Democratic presidents have been similarly resourceful in seeking support from corporate sources, not least from the investment banks that supply many Democratic presidents' appointees to key positions in the US Treasury.

President Carter won support from key interest groups such as the National Educational Association (NEA) (the main teachers' union) during his campaign for the presidency in 1976. Once in government, he unwisely paid such groups less attention until the appointment of a specialist staff member, Anne Wexler, in 1978. She achieved some success in integrating consumer, environmental and labour organizations into the President's lobbying of Congress. By contrast, President Reagan's coalition-building was usually as efficient in office as it had been in pursuit of it. Reagan understood that coalitions of support were best assembled in Congress after the laying of their foundations outside among powerful supporting groups. Reagan's approach was evident in passing the Omnibus Reconciliation Act and the Economic Tax Act of 1981, when he secured the support of business and taxpayers' groups. Since Reagan had enjoyed their backing in the 1980 election, his collaborative campaign with them in 1981 offered the virtues of continuity and political rationality. In 2009, President Obama worked very successfully to secure the support of the AARP as he pushed his health-care reforms through both chambers of Congress. Gaining the support of a group as powerful as the AARP reduced the fears of many Democratic members of Congress that their support for Obama risked their losing the support of older voters in their districts. When added to wide and deep public support, the political context within which Congress voted was shaped to the President's temporary congressional advantage and to the fiscal benefit of the groups with which he worked.

As support can be critical to the president's political success, so opposition can cause its failure. Opposition of the United States Catholic Conference to any bill providing for federal aid to public schools but excluding aid to parochial schools, and the equally impassioned opposition of the NEA to any bill that aided parochial schools on the same terms as public schools, long prevented passage of an Act by entwining the issue with the sensitive First Amendment question of the State's separation from the Church. Only the NEA's change of mind enabled President Johnson's Elementary and Secondary Education Act to pass. Although other groups worked with President Johnson to pass the compromise draft bill, the support of the NEA was essential.

More than twenty years later, the opposition of groups including the American Civil Liberties Union (ACLU), the National Association for the Advancement of Colored People (NAACP), and the National Organization of Women (NoW) was instrumental in bringing about the Senate's rejection of President Reagan's nomination of Judge Bork to the Supreme Court (see Chapter 7).

Interest groups and the executive bureaucracy

Congress's general intent has to be implemented by agencies through the drafting and enforcement of detailed regulations. Groups are, accordingly, obliged to scrutinize and act on the rules that agencies issue. Group interests are as dependent on the detailed application of law as on its general construction, and are assisted by sharing two qualities with agencies and congressional oversight subcommittees: first, expertise deriving from their specialization; and, second, a powerful stake in the rules being drafted to maximize the benefits accruing to them and minimize the costs imposed on them. Details of administrative procedure and practice affect present and future profitability and welfare.

Manufacturers consequently attach great importance to rules drafted and implemented by officials in the Occupational Safety and Health Administration (OSHA). Companies that pollute the air, land and water are similarly attentive to technical regulations drafted and enforced by the Environmental Protection Agency (EPA). The same is true of broadcasters regarding the Federal Communications Commission (FCC) and of stockbrokers respecting the Securities and Exchange Commission (SEC). By the same token, regulatory authorities have regard not only for relations with subcommittee parents in Congress, but also with private interest groups. Purposes are not necessarily shared; neither are modes of operation necessarily collusive. Yet, the OSHA, EPA, FCC and the SEC are parts of policy-making, implementing and evaluation networks. These networks may be politically competitive. Enforcement of rules controlling environmental pollution brings competitive group interests to bear: interests of industries and companies may, and do, diverge and conflict, as (more commonly) do those between most business interests and environmentalists.

Groups are often so closely incorporated into decision-making procedures established by agencies that the boundaries between government and groups are unclear. Formal penetration of economic interests into the bureaucracy through advisory committees has been common since the New Deal. Thus, the Department of Commerce formally incorporates business interests through such committees; the Department of Labor, unions; the Department of Defense, weapons contractors; the Department of the Treasury, banks; and the Department of Housing and Urban Development, companies and groups with policy or commercial interests in the Department's programmes. Less formally, departments consult constantly with clients and other interested parties in the private sector. Lobbyists for all organized interest groups appreciate fully that their groups' objectives may depend on how policies affecting them are implemented. Agencies' drafting of rules may confirm political victories embodied in legislation, or negate them. While organized groups must therefore pay heed to bureaucrats' detailed implementation of policy, the activity is so rarefied that none save the informed and organized appreciate it. Fewer still influence those engaged on it. Interest in such activity remains more likely when the interest in outcomes of rule-drafting embraces a public interest and not merely a set of private, sectional interests, whether they be conflictual or coincident.

Participants in the interest industry

Lawyers and lobbyists for hire

Just as many of Washington's political consultants specialize in working for candidates of a particular party or ideological persuasion, so many of the city's lobbyists work primarily for Republicans, Democrats, conservatives, liberals, or another identifiable group, or specialize in certain policy areas. Contract lobbying firms of this kind are often retained by interest groups to conduct a particular campaign or to supplement their own lobbying efforts. Former senators, members of Congress and administration officials figure prominently among Washington's specialized law and lobbying firms. (The lobbying industry is dominated by lawyers, of whom there are over 40,000 in Washington alone.) Washington has, since the late 1960s, increasingly become a city to which many politicians are attracted and which few leave: many remain in Washington in order to exploit their former contacts, to employ their knowledge and understanding of the policy process, and to know how, when and where to intervene to the greatest effect.

Governments

Governments also lobby. Foreign governments represented in Washington lobby, both on their own account through their embassies and by retaining specialist lobbyists to work for them. State, city and county governments lobby individually but also (and increasingly) in associations of state, county, or city governments: the National Governors' Association (NGA) has been especially influential not only in shaping the course of authorizations and appropriations, but also in modifying the agenda of public policy. As Governor of Arkansas, President Clinton used his chairmanship of the NGA creatively to help set the agenda of national debate about both welfare and education policy. Different parts of the federal government also lobby Congress and, through the Solicitor-General and the submission of *amicus curiae* briefs, the federal courts. The White House lobbies Congress constantly, frequently in coordination with the departments and agencies, each of which has its own congressional relations staff.

Classifying interest groups

Classifying the thousands of interest groups that permeate the state is problematic, since few groups fall neatly into a single category (Exhibit 8.3 provides a typology of groups). The National Rifle Association may legitimately be described as a *single-issue* group but its members claim it to be a *public-interest* group. Friends of the Earth similarly claim to be a public-interest group, yet many Americans oppose its policy positions. Many, if not most, groups are underpinned by an ideological substructure – whether it be an opposition to government interference in free markets, or demands for subsidies to protect family farms. We consider here a small selection of interest group types.

Business groups

Much has changed since the early 1960s, when Bauer, Pool and Dexter noted in their book *American Business and Public Policy* (1963) that 129 of the 166 large corporations which they studied had had no contact with Congress in at least two years. The authors concluded that this remarkable instance of the dog that did not bark was indicative less of business's political naivety than of its general satisfaction with government policy, the weakness of unions in most industries and the lightness of regulation. Moreover, the lack of corporate activity reflected politicians' anticipation of business interests: protection by congressmen from Texas, Louisiana and Oklahoma of the oil industry's depletion allowance in tax law is just one example. (The allowance was abolished by a liberal Democratic Congress in 1975, in full cry against conservative congressional privileges and power.)

Lyndon Johnson's administration, and those of the Republican Presidents Nixon and Ford that followed, saw significant growth in federal business regulation. Congresses dominated by Democrats (and often by liberals) between 1964 and 1977 passed a panoply of environmental, health, safety, labour, product standards and civil rights laws and regulations. Regulations written by the Consumer Product Safety Commission (CPSC), OSHA, and EPA, and most decisions of the Departments of Labor, Commerce, and Health, Education, and Welfare reduced the profitability of many American companies, small and large. In the states, too, regulation burgeoned during the same period, with the result that large corporations operating across the United States pressed for federal regulation to avoid working under different regulations in different states. Growth of consumer and public interest groups also stimulated the surge in corporate representation: General Motors, for example, had thought it unnecessary to establish a lobbying office in Washington. In response to Ralph Nader's exposé of the Chevrolet Corvair (a General Motors product) as 'unsafe at any speed', the company changed its view.

There has never, in the United States, been a single overarching organization representing business: partly in consequence, neither the National Association of Manufacturers (NAM) (whose membership is

Exhibit 8.2 The Revolving Doors on K Street

When Congressman Billy Tauzin left the House of Representatives in January 2005 he became the head of PhRMA, a pharmaceutical lobby group. Prior to his departure from the House, he served on the Energy and Commerce Committee which, among other tasks, oversees the drug industry. Tauzin was the subject of two investigations into the ethical implications of his work on the 2003 Medicare Prescription Drugs Bill, which was viewed as favourable to the big drug companies. Tauzin is a classic example of the revolving door syndrome by which Congressmen leave Congress and move into a high-paying job on K Street. The one-year waiting period demanded by the 1978 Ethics in Government Act has done little to limit the hiring by lobbying firms of former legislators.

When former House Speaker Newt Gingrich left office, he worked as a 'strategic consultant' for a number of drug companies. He claimed in a *Fox News* interview of 17 November 2011 that 'I do not lobby and I never have.' Technically this is true, since the Lobbying Disclosure Act of 1995 does not consider individuals who spend less than 20 per cent of their time with a client in lobbying to be lobbyists. Gingrich is on record as having contacted law-makers when seeking to secure votes during the debates surrounding Medicare charges for prescription drugs. So he, like many others in Washington, have left office having served as former legislators, corporate CEOs, or labour union bosses to embark on a career of non-lobbying exploiting the 20 per cent 'Daschle Loophole' (named after former Senate Majority Leader Tom Daschle, who is also a very busy non-lobbyist.

→

drawn mostly from medium-sized firms) nor the United States Chamber of Commerce (USCC) (whose membership comprises mainly small businesses) has enjoyed much political influence, either in the 1950s, when threats to business interests were slight, or in the 1970s, when they became more significant. In both decades, the two organizations were conservative on all political questions, and weakened by their heterogeneous memberships having conflicting interests. Dissatisfaction with both groups among executives of America's largest corporations led to the formation of the Business Roundtable in the early 1970s, which provided higher-quality analysis and lobbying. That, in turn, stimulated the NAM and the USCC to improve their own analytical work; both now provide economic analysis and econometric modelling, meeting the needs of their memberships and of politicians with whom their lobbyists are in regular contact. These successes notwithstanding, employers still face the problems of maintaining unity on divisive issues, of developing

→

We began this book by walking away from Congress and heading into the poorer neighbourhoods of DC. But, if we walk north and west from the Capitol towards Georgetown, we reach K Street. As the number of lobbying firms in Washington has grown so, too, has the number situated in the spiritual home of lobbying, the somewhat unassuming street between J and L Streets. Data from consumer rights interest group *Public Citizen* show that nearly half of all law-makers enter the lobbying industry on departing office. Approximately three-quarters of those former law-makers work on K Street. It is not just the elected officials who become lobbyists. Their senior staff do so, too. In 2010, the average annual salary paid to congressional aides joining K Street was $350,000. Experienced former legislators earn far greater sums.

Following the Republican Revolution in the 1994 mid-term elections, Majority Whip Tom 'the Hammer' DeLay, with the help of Republican political consultant Grover Norquist, sought to influence prominent K Street lobbyists by suggesting that they consider working harder to raise money for the Republican Party, given that it was the GOP which held the levers of power in the 104th Congress. The simple idea was that access to policy-makers would be reduced if lobbying firms worked with Democratic law-makers. Such a quid pro quo was made illegal in the 2007 Honest Leadership and Open Government Act _ the death knell of the K Street Project.

The profusion of well-resourced lobbying firms on K Street may (further) skew the policy process in favour of those with many resources at the expense of those with few. As Exhibit 8.1 shows, the money spent on lobbying each year is substantial. What one buys on K Street for the money is the subject of the final section of this chapter.

services that individual corporations cannot themselves supply, and of the awkward fact that employers speak with several voices.

Large corporations meet most of their lobbying needs in house, or from contract lobbyists and lawyers retained for particular projects. However, like other groups, business lobbies form *ad hoc* coalitions with other groups on matters of shared interest. Business has also been favoured by the 1974 amendments to the 1971 Federal Election Campaign Act, which repealed the prohibition on corporations having business with the federal government from establishing PACs, and by the weakening of the 2002 Bipartisan Campaign Finance Reform Act in the *Citizens United* case of 2010.

Most of the largest 500 companies in the United States have PACs; few that sell their products or services to the federal government, or are affected by federal regulations, do not. Notwithstanding corporate celebration of the virtues of fiscal rectitude and reduced public spending,

Exhibit 8.3 Typology of Interest Groups

Economic groups

Business groups: As Exhibit 8.1 shows, corporations, including General Electric and Google, spend vast sums each year on lobbying. Many corporations are so large that they have little need of peak organizations. Exhibit 8.1 shows that the sum spent by the Chamber of Commerce is less than that spent by the four biggest corporations. Such corporations have a permanent presence on K Street. The central purpose of business groups is to ensure that legislation emanating from Congress, as well as regulations from the federal bureaucracy, and the actions of state legislatures, is congruent with the interests of business. Often, corporations will fund both incumbents and challengers so that the winner might look favourably on the interests of their campaign contributors.

Labour groups: Labour unions are weak in comparison with their European counterparts. Only 11.6 per cent of workers were unionized in 2011, and unions lack the support of one of the two major parties. The American Creed did not facilitate the development of left-wing groups or parties. In particular sectors, however, labour groups have significant leverage. Within the public sector, the percentage of unionized workers was 37 per cent compared with 6.9 per cent for the private sector (www.ilo.org).

Agricultural groups: Despite the US being the largest producer and exporter of food stuffs in the world, its unions lack the power of some of their European counterparts (for example, the Fédération Nationale des Syndicats d'Expoitants d'Agricoles (National Federation of Agricultural Holders' Unions) FNSEA in France) that often occupy a collusive relationship with the state. In large part, agricultural groups suffer from a lack of coordination between key players: the National Farmers Union (NFU) and the American Farm Bureau Federation (AFBF) do not jointly decide strategy, with the result that their policy demands are not always congruent. Nonetheless, agricultural groups wield considerable influence in those states and districts where farming is an important part of the local economy: legislators and executive officials ignore the demands of farmers at their peril.

Professional groups: These groups represent educated, wealthy and well-connected professions. They include the AMA (the American Medical

→

many major corporations are, directly or indirectly, dependent on federal government contracts. Business PACs spend more than twice as much as unions in campaign finance, and very much more than public interest

→

Association) and the ABA (the American Bar Association). The expertise of such groups gives them considerable power. Like most groups, professional groups claim to act in the public interest, but their efforts can be focused more narrowly on the protection of their industry in the face of policies they oppose.

Promotional/cause groups: Promotional groups seek to promote a particular cause or policy position. The National Rifle Association (NRA) is one such example. Its primary purpose is to protect the rights of gun owners against attempts to regulate this constitutional right. The National Association of Women (NOW) is another prominent example. NOW argues for equal rights for women.

Ideological groups: These groups view policy through the lens of an overarching commitment to core values. The Christian Coalition considers all policy from the perspective of a particular reading of the Bible. The American Civil Liberties Union (ACLU) promotes an underlying commitment to individual liberties, which often brings it into conflict with religious groups.

Sectional groups: These groups represent the interest of specific sections of society. They need not be focused on single issues, but focus on all those issues relevant to the group they represent. Prominent examples include: the Association for the Advancement of Retired Persons (AARP); the National Association for the Advancement of Colored People (NAAC); and the American Israeli Public Affairs Committee (AIPAC).

Public interest groups: Given the difficulty of identifying the public interest in America, it is always presumptuous for groups to call themselves 'public interest groups'. Prominent examples of those that do are: Common Cause, which is committed to 'clean and honest government', and Friends of the Earth (FoE), a global environmental lobby group. Workers in the coalmines of West Virginia and the steel mills of Pittsburgh may not agree that FoE represents *their* public interest. However, these groups are most often associated with the new social movements that arose in the late 1960s, such as the second-wave of feminism, or the growth of the modern US environmental movement following the first Earth Day in 1970.

groups. While this fact does not ensure that their views prevail (not least because they often conflict with each other), business remains a vigorous participant in lobbying and facilitates access to policy-makers (though not control over them). Like other PACs, business PACs usually support incumbents more often and more heavily than they do challengers, even where challengers' politics are closer to their own.

Labour groups

The American Federation of Labor–Congress of Industrial Organizations (AFL–CIO), a weak federation which in 1996 represented seventy-eight independent national affiliates and 13 million trade union members, is the product of an amalgamation in 1955 between, respectively, a craft union federation founded in 1886, and a mass industrial union organization (dedicated to the cause of mobilizing those whom the AFL had deliberately ignored) established in labour's politically buoyant days of the New Deal. The AFL-CIO represents a smaller proportion of the workforce than do the Trades Union Congress in Britain, the Swedish Trade Union Confederation in Scandinavia (commonly referred to as LO), or the Federation of German Trade Unions in Germany.

Although the proportion of unionized workers in the public sector is high, that of white-collar workers is low (and markedly lower than in Europe). Including those unions outside the AFL-CIO, just 11.9 per cent of US workers belonged to a union in 2012, the percentage having fallen from more than 25.5 per cent at its peak in 1965. The fall is partly explained by the decline in employment in industries having previously enjoyed high rates of unionization, such as vehicle manufacture and steel. Although American unions have occasionally been courted by Republican presidents, their preferences have rarely been served by them.

Individual unions have, however, known considerable influence. At times of high profitability, steel, docks, road transport and automobile unions have secured favourable wage contracts for their members: steel was the clearest example during the 1950s and 1960s. Even in the more difficult circumstances since the oil-induced recession of 1973–75, car workers were for some years partly cushioned against the worst effects of increased foreign competition and declining domestic profitability by effective union organization.

Public-interest groups

Increased wealth, public awareness of negative externalities, diminished trust in government's probity after the abuse of executive power with respect to Vietnam and Watergate, the growing importance of issues as cleavages in society and the correlative weakening of attachment to party (assisted by the enhanced importance of television, and the growth of social media) have altered group politics. Since the mid-

1960s, public and consumer interest groups have been established to pursue new issues. Broadly within the Progressive tradition, such groups claim to promote not a sectional (often profit-making) interest, but the public (non-profit-making) interest. The establishment and growth of public interest lobbies is implicitly damaging to the classical pluralist account of group formation in the United States that we discuss below. Adherents of such interpretations of American politics thought it axiomatic that there was no identifiable public interest on most issues separate and apart from the sum of group interests: the public interest was the result of private interests freely competing. To the extent that public interest lobbies have won support for their identification of such a separately-defined interest, the plausibility of such a view was weakened.

Sectional groups: the American Israel Public Affairs Committee

American policy towards Israel has been influenced by pressure on successive administrations and Congresses by groups representing over 6.6 million American Jews. Especially influential in New York and the north-east, and disproportionately represented among the nation's academic, professional, financial and political elites, Jewish lobbies have assiduously sought to advance Israel's security and prosperity.

The lobby on behalf of Israeli causes is dominated by the umbrella organization the American Israel Public Affairs Committee (AIPAC). Many AIPAC groups (among them the American Jewish Congress and the Anti-Defamation League of B'nai B'rith) have their own representatives in Washington. AIPAC has close working relations with other Jewish organizations, some of which are represented on its board. It also advises the numerous Jewish PACs across the United States. Its continuing success can be measured by the National Association for Arab Americans, and the main Greek lobby, the American Hellenic Institute Public Affairs Committee (AHIPAC) (which is the second most powerful ethnic lobbying group on foreign policy), having modelled their tactics on AIPAC's own. Despite its acronym, AIPAC is not a PAC: the largest allied PAC is the National Political Action Committee, but nine other PACs, many of them regional, share similar objectives. In law, Israel is not the client of AIPAC, since it is not funded by the Israeli government. Nonetheless, Israel is the *de facto* client of several Jewish lobbies: it is with its interests alone that they are concerned. AIPAC and its allies are able to draw on the support of not only American Jews, but also of most Americans. Most Americans continue to approve of the United States's generous financial assistance to Israel through foreign and military aid.

Promotional/cause groups: the National Organization for Women; the National Rifle Association

Established in June 1966 on the occasion of the Third National Conference of the Commission on the Status of Women, the National Organization for Women (NOW) was, in its first ten years, concerned primarily with the passage and ratification of the Equal Rights Amendment to the US Constitution. Its stated purposes now include the elimination of discrimination and harassment; securing women's reproductive rights; ending violence against women; eradicating racism, sexism, and homophobia; and promoting social equality and justice.

Its efforts were insufficient to persuade three-quarters of state legislatures to ratify the amendment: only thirty-five had done so when the three-year extension granted by Congress to the original 1979 deadline expired. Since the Supreme Court's 1973 judgement in *Roe v Wade*, NOW has also emerged as the foremost proponent of freedom of choice for women in opposition to the large and diverse Right to Life movement, in which cause it has been a tenacious litigant. NOW's membership of more than 500,000 is a source of financial strength, but its diversity one of weakness. NOW mitigates the difficulties that internal divisions present by devolving some policy-making power and 4 per cent of national revenues to state organizations, thereby reinforcing links between the national organization and the membership, so lessening the prospects of the former misrepresenting the latter. The Supreme Court's decision in *Webster* (1989), that state legislatures should have greater latitude to determine abortion policy, illustrates the importance of interest groups organizing themselves in state capitals as well as in Washington.

Pure single-issue lobbying: National Rifle Association

Of all the lobbies in America, none is better-known outside the nation's capital than the National Rifle Association (NRA); few are more influential within it. Like AIPAC, the NRA is a single-issue group with a clearly identifiable group of potential supporters: legal owners of the 200 million guns in American citizens' hands. Its resources are large: in 2012, nearly 3.5 million members paid fees, giving the organization an income of more than $150 million. The group maintains a full-time staff of 700, including twelve professional lobbyists, and retains the services of contract lobbyists in Washington for particular legislative contests. Members are prompted by letter and email to contact legislators when gun controls are being considered, or when the perceived risk of their being considered rises. The organization has a PAC: the NRA Political Victory Fund which, by spending $18,896,442 in 2012, placed it in the top twenty PACs by spending. Of the twenty-eight NRA lobbyists, on K Street, fifteen worked in government prior to joining K Street.

Ownership of guns enjoys constitutional protection under the Second Amendment (see Appendix 2). Some hold that the Amendment precludes any restriction on the type (or quantity) of weapons that may be held, but this is a contentious view. Most who supported the Amendment in 1791 were concerned more with providing for adequate state militia than for individual rights to own a gun; it is accordingly unclear whether the Amendment refers to the collective rights of militia or to the rights of individual citizens. The consequences of an armed citizenry have made the nature of, and limitations on, this right a bitterly-contested question. The Second Amendment is unique within the Bill of Rights in setting the right to which it refers in a particular organizational and political context. With that setting (and, by implication, limitation) in mind, both the US Congress and state legislatures have acted to control the types of weapon sold in interstate commerce and within states. The Firearms Act of 1934 required the registration of automatic weapons and sawn-off shotguns; the Federal Firearms Act of 1938 prohibited licensed gun dealers from selling guns in interstate commerce and (for the first time) made it a federal offence to sell firearms to felons and fugitives: in 1990, Congress prohibited the sale of AK-47-type semi-automatic weapons and, in 1994, introduced a ban on assault weapons. The fact of gun control has been as much a feature of American public policy as its weakness in comparison with all other democracies. As we write, President Obama (in light of the December 2012 school massacre at Sandy Hook School in Connecticut) has been asked by members of his own party in Congress to press for the reinstatement of the ban on assault weapons which lapsed in 2004. If he attempts it, he is unlikely to succeed.

As is invariably the case in American government, where Congress declines to act, governors and state legislatures may do so. Where state legislatures decline to act, local governments may be permitted (by the states under whose authority they fall) to do so. The result is the familiar and turbulent mix of different laws regulating different types of weapon in different jurisdictions: there are more than 20,000 state and local gun laws. Variegated as gun-control laws therefore are, the constitutionality of control is not in doubt. At both federal and state level, the courts have frequently upheld the right of legislatures to restrict the sale, possession and carrying of certain types of weapon. Unable to pursue judicial challenges to action by state legislatures, the NRA has been obliged to supplement private lobbying of legislators with well-financed and energetic public campaigns. The NRA secured a significant victory in the *Heller* case of 2008 when Justice Anthony M. Kennedy supported the four conservative justices in ruling that a ban on handguns introduced by the City Council in Washington DC was unconstitutional. The Roberts

Court has therefore established a generous reading of the Second Amendment in the face of calls for greater gun control.

State and local regulations are weakened where laws of adjoining states or cities vary (as they usually do); the NRA's major task has therefore been to limit federal regulation. Despite increased pressure on Congress to pass more restrictive legislation following attempts on the lives of three post-war presidents – John Kennedy, Gerald Ford and Ronald Reagan – all of them NRA members, federal regulation remains weak. Similar pressure followed the assassinations of Martin Luther King and Robert Kennedy in 1968; the mass killings by a man with an AK-47 semi-automatic rifle of children in a school playground at Stockton, California (1989); as well as the massacres at Columbine High School, Colorado (1999), Virginia Tech University (2007) and Sandy Hook Elementary School, Connecticut (2012). Yet, the profusion of restrictions below the federal level has not been matched in Washington; that marks a significant achievement for the NRA.

The NRA's usual approach to gun control legislation is to oppose all restrictions of any kind, and few members of Congress and senators feel themselves sufficiently immune from defeat to risk incurring the NRA's wrath, and subsequent support for a primary or general election opponent, because it possesses a formidable capacity to bring pressure to bear on legislators from its large membership. The political sensitivity of the question of gun ownership also causes the White House, the Justice Department, and the Treasury Department's Bureau of Alcohol, Tobacco, and Firearms to tread warily for fear of losing the support of gun-owners. Congress and the Executive Branch have little autonomy against the concentrated lobbying and electoral power of the NRA. The NRA's successful resistance to all restrictions has nonetheless left it politically exposed. Its opposition to the proposed ban on the manufacture or sale of plastic but usable guns incapable of detection by airport X-ray security equipment was insufficient to prevent passage of the bill. The Association's opposition to the prohibition of the manufacture and importing of armour-piercing bullets was insufficient to prevent the House passing the bill with the support of all the major police organizations, the National Coalition to Ban Handguns, and Handgun Control Inc. The NRA's view exposed the NRA to ridicule even in Idaho, where hunting is popular, gun-ownership is restricted only with regard to the carrying of concealed weapons, and support for the NRA is widespread and vigorous: former Governor Cecil Andrus (whose hobby is hunting) referred to the Association as 'the gun nuts of the world' for opposing the ban on armour-piercing bullets by observing that he had yet to see an animal in a bullet-proof vest.

In gun-control, therefore, the major lobby dominates, but does not determine, policy. Great as its financial and organizational resources are, its tactical errors, coupled with the publicity afforded violent crime, have enabled its opponents to organize in support of tighter controls – especially on semi-automatic weapons and handguns. The constitutional and ideological foundations of gun-ownership, and the heavy resources which the NRA always brings to bear, makes enactment of controls comparable in their severity to those in Canada and other civilized democracies highly unlikely. It is equally improbable that guns will be decontrolled. The clash of opinions on the issue leaves few congressional politicians exempt from NRA influence. Members from rural areas have even smaller prospects of resisting the Association than those from cities, where pressures from hunters and farmers are slight and those from the families of victims great. Yet, even in the aftermath of the atrocity at Sandy Hook Elementary School in 2012, polling data suggest that the number of Americans committed to the introduction of tighter gun controls is far lower than many (non-American) observers might have expected (see Gallup poll: 23 January 2013 gallup.com/poll/160085/gun violence).

Evaluating interest groups

Implications for representative democracy

By promoting competition between branches of a weak central state, fragmentation of federal government begets weakness of central authority, corresponding penetration of government by groups and relative openness of policy processes. Although an open society, the United States is not an equal one: formal equality before the law sits alongside social and economic inequalities. Congress is most easily lobbied because it is the more open of the two elective branches. However, many corporations have tight and collusive relationships with executive agencies and congressional subcommittees that many other organizations lack. Crucially, too, such corporations have the resources and incentives to pursue their interests by litigating against federal regulatory bodies, decisions and rule-making.

In the twenty-five years immediately after World War II, J. Leiper Freeman (1955), Douglass Cater (1964) and Theodore Lowi (1969) separately considered the implications for representative democracy of such relations between social organizations and government. Moving across the permeable boundary between government and civil society, Cater wrote in *Power in Washington* (1965) that public policy was effectively determined by a nexus linking government agencies with congressional subcommittees and interest groups. Resulting patterns of policy-making exclude the president, non-specialists and the public from most policy areas, and confine the exercise of influence to specialists – in the federal bureaucracy, in functionally-specialized congressional committees and in groups with special interests in particular programmes authorized and appropriated by Congress, and implemented by executive agencies. This model is both an ideal-type and a good starting point for the examination of public policy.

Cater's approach was later modified by Hugh Heclo (1978) who, in a subtle and celebrated paper, argued that the concept of an iron triangle was 'not so much wrong as disastrously incomplete', because it took too little account of the 'loose-jointed play of influence' accompanying the growth of government, and the refined specialization and highly-developed professional expertise that characterizes both senior civil servants and those in think-tanks and research institutes with whom they deal. Although he fails to sustain the charge of 'disastrous' incompleteness, he usefully modifies Cater's account. Cater's metaphor is too rigid, although Heclo acknowledges that he finds it 'difficult' to define an issue network or specify precisely how it differs from Cater's formulation. Heclo, nonetheless, rightly lays emphasis on the extreme complexity and fluidity with which networks of interlaced, overlapping, conflictual groups of individuals in law firms, research institutes, universities, lobby firms, and the mass and specialized media interact to influence the policy process.

Legitimating public policy

Such complexity offers opportunities to presidents and political executives in the bureaucracy in dealing with or struggling against expert and professional members of groups within and outside government. Political executives cannot monitor all that bureaucrats do; however, they may intervene and attempt to lead in those areas that they, or the president, determine to be in their or the president's political interest. Congress is a more complex and formidable participant in the policy process than either the iron triangle or the issue-network metaphors suggest: individual members of Congress and senators, party leaders, chairs of standing committees, participants in Conference committees, other members on the floors of both chambers and members of cross-party caucuses may all shape public policy.

Most public policy in the United States is legitimated and implemented in public, and open to public view and private pressures, thereby exacerbating the weakness of the state and rendering governance more, rather than less, difficult. Steven Krasner has argued in *Defending the National Interest* (1978), that the state in America is weak but society strong. Martin Sklar (1988: 34) takes a similar view, regarding 'the central principle of the American political tradition' as being:

the supremacy of society over the state: Government and law were to adapt to, and serve, the freely developing society. As shaped by strong republican imperatives since the Revolution, this tradition posited the society as one characterized by equal liberty for all full citizens and special privilege or monopoly power for none.

Within this tradition, modern American government is deeply penetrated by private groups, its processes of public policy-making the product of particularistic patterns of interaction between groups and public officials. Nonetheless, there are in the United States no instances of the corporatist policy-making once familiar in Austria, Sweden and Germany. This condition is partly explained by the fragmentation of many major economic interests in the United States: industry, finance and agriculture are all represented by several organizations. Industry is represented by the US Chamber of Commerce, the National Association of Manufacturers and the National Alliance of Business (all of which have usually been louder in their public pronouncements than they have been effective in shaping public policy). Financial interests are represented by several different organizations, and agriculture by the American Farm Bureau Federation, the Grange (another union of farmers), the National Farmers' Union, and the National Farmers' Organization. Although not unknown, peak organizations are uncharacteristic of most policy areas, including those of health, defence, agriculture and the environment.

Evaluating interest group influence

American political culture, underpinned by the American Creed, places great emphasis on individualism and encourages opposition to a powerful, interventionist state. In a civil society as vigorous as America's, the profusion of groups is regarded by many as, at the least, a benign force, and by some as a positive one. In the traditional approach to the influence of interest groups, the state was a neutral force arbitrating between competing group interests. Competition would result in an overall equality between groups, an equality reflected in public policy outcomes that in the aggregate favoured no groups over others (Truman: 1951).

Pluralist theorists accepted the claim that some groups had greater resources than others (General Electric has a greater presence on K Street than does Friends of the Earth), but argued that interest group resources were not cumulative: what environmental groups lacked in resources was compensated for by members' capacity and propensity for direct action. Robert Dahl, in his classic study of politics in New Haven *Who Governs?* (1961), argued that groups provided a second circuit of democracy which empowered citizens outside of electoral cycles by affording access to government institutions. For Dahl, the competition of groups enhanced the functioning of American democracy by increasing the responsiveness of the elected to its electors.

Critics of the pluralist approach argue that groups cooperate in order better to influence policy outcomes. Elite theorists build on the classic analyses of C. Wright Mills (1956) and E. E. Schattschneider (1960) in arguing that policy outcomes are skewed towards the well-resourced (How many dollars can you spend on lobbying?), those with insider connections (Whom do you know in Congress?), and those with funds to direct towards election campaigning (How deep are your pockets?). Elite theorists on both the left and the right point to the inequities within American society and argue that such inequity is reflected in the leverage which certain groups can wield within the policy-making process. For elite theorists, the 'iron triangle' is a useful metaphor because it captures the essence of group activity: a relatively closed nexus of decision-makers who make policy for their own ends, rather than in the *public interest*. The representation of groups within Washington DC and the state capitals is, on this view, a poor representation of the diversity of interests within the American nation.

Decades of scholarship focused on the influence of interest groups has not demonstrated a clear set of winners and losers in the policy-influencing industry that sustain their influence in the long-run. What is demonstrably clear is that interest groups remain a significant force within American policy, that Americans dislike government and, typically, the operations of interest groups. They do, however, approve of *their* groups (Berry, 1989).

Conclusion

Interest groups attempt to influence public policy by persuading public officials of the merits of their causes and cases. They do not compete for electoral office. Having established rules, agreed purposes and memberships, interest groups differ from broader social movements lacking these characteristics. Relations between advanced democratic societies and states are mediated more by groups than by party in the United States, where organizationally enfeebled political parties contrast with a rich civil society.

At different times, groups have been denounced as being threatening to the Republic, celebrated for expressing democratic participation, excoriated for representing partial interests over the unrepresented public interest, and regarded by some as transmitting public preferences but by others as misrepresenting them. There is no simple solution to the problem of assessing in the aggregate the nature and extent of interest groups' influence over public policy, because they vary with the tactics, resources, legitimacy, substantive expertise, political skill and support of different groups, and with issue, field of activity and political circumstances. These groups' influence over government, or parts of it, accordingly ranges from insignificant to determinative; and developing a theoretical account to explain such variation is, accordingly, forbiddingly difficult. Nevertheless, interest groups are rightly regarded as a key characteristic of the American political system, marked more than any other democratic order by the weakness and fragmentation of the central government and by the vitality of its society.

Chapter 9

Bureaucracy: The Fourth Branch of Government

The United States Constitution provides for three branches of government. This chapter examines an unmentioned *de facto* fourth: the Executive Branch's bureaucracy. Nearly one in fifty American workers is employed by the federal bureaucracy, yet it is often the focus for the opprobrium of politicians. The significant growth of an institution unmentioned in the Constitution, combined with the execution of its three core functions, has created a powerful and semi-autonomous fourth branch of government. But the bureaucracy must operate within a system that is separated into three branches in which each checks and balances the others, and is also separated by federalism such that the bureaucracy sits alongside a group of state-level bureaucracies independent of their federal counterparts.

The fourth branch has two masters – President and Congress – and is bound as a matter of practical politics to work closely with interest groups seeking to influence its execution of the law. Added to these structural considerations is the perennial anxiety that the bureaucracy serves no elected master, but only itself. That concern has led both to claims that the bureaucracy is a bloated leviathan and to periodic efforts at root-and-branch reform.

The institutional setting of the Fourth Branch

Separation of powers combined with Federalism renders bureaucracy complicated, dispersed and decentralized (both within Washington and throughout the country), and its accountability to representative politicians problematic. The federal bureaucracy's key organizational units are usually not government departments but the semi-autonomous agencies or bureaux within them. As islands of separately-authorized functional authority, agencies are subject to political pressures from the presidency, from Congress and from interest group clients seeking to influence bureaucrats' decision-making, both during the formation and the implementation of policy. Presidents attempt to enforce leadership over bureaucrats by making political appointments to the upper reaches of departments and agencies of people loyal to them (at the risk of losing experience and expertise), as well as by establishing their own political and bureaucratic resources within the Executive Office of the President. Reliance on civil service neutrality, customary in British government practice, offers no solution to American presidents, who have to compete for influence in a separated and federal system without a powerful central state over which to preside. It is in the space between the general intent of presidency and Congress, and policy's detailed implementation in the forms of administrative decisions and rule-making, that politicians and lobbyists contend with the expertise, experience and longevity of bureaucrats for influence over the implementation of policy.

There is, in the United States federal government, no durably dominant centre of power, and only a qualified sense of a 'state'. The federal government is permanently divided by constitutional separation and by staggered elections to representative posts of different-sized constituencies and often divided further by split-party control of Congress and the executive. Elected and unelected officials therefore often have compelling incentives to compete openly against one another. Federal executive departments are not ideal-types of hierarchical Weberian rationality but shells within which multiple, semi-autonomous agencies are placed, each of them separately created by Congress. Each such agency's programmes are, in turn, authorized and re-authorized, separately funded through appropriations, and overseen by congressional committees and subcommittees. The internal organization of the federal bureaucracy is tightly and continuously integrated politically with that of Congress in committees and subcommittees. Each agency is shadowed by congressional subcommittees which, since they created and sustain them, are sometimes referred to as their congressional 'parents'. Two consequences flow from these arrangements: first, little collective authority inheres in the federal government; and second, public administration is thoroughly politicized.

Variation among bureaucratic forms in the federal government is wide. The major determinants of any and every agency's design are the political choices of those who establish, sustain and modify the agency in question. This pattern was apparent from the first years of the Republic, when Congress granted to the president much greater leeway in determining the policies to be followed by the Departments of State and War, than it did in the case of the Treasury, where congressional prerogatives were greater. As Seidman and Gilmour (1986: 149) have observed:

> Choices are influenced by a complex of tangible and intangible factors reflecting divergent views about the proper sphere of government activity, politics, institutional folklore, program importance and status, visibility, political and administrative autonomy, and, most important, who should exercise control.

The federal civil service

The federal government acquired a civil service later than most advanced European countries. Well before their industrialization, Germany and France had established public bureaucracies. In France, Napoleon's taxation reforms in the early years of the nineteenth century required the services of a large bureaucracy for their enforcement, although the Napoleonic state was little more than a development of the Jacobin structure. By contrast, the United States lacked the apparatus of a state, just as it lacked the popular conception or sense of one. In continental Europe, the modern democratic form was established by the institutions of representation being added to a bureaucratic order. In America, the sequence was reversed.

The first act of presidents from Andrew Jackson onwards was to dismiss all office-holders in the Executive Branch, replacing them with those of proven loyalty, or those whose cases were advanced by supporters to whom they owed political debts. As Senator William March of New York put it, 'To the victors belong the spoils' (from which the phrase 'spoils system' derives). By this system, all posts in the federal bureaucracy were in the gift of presidents.

The Tenure of Office Act, passed in 1867 over President Andrew Johnson's veto, was the first clear indication that congressional sentiment was moving against the spoils system. It attacked the power of presidents by preventing their removing, without the Senate's concurrence, individuals appointed to federal office with the Senate's consent. An amended version of the Act was repealed in 1881, largely because its constitutionality was in doubt. The Pendleton Act was passed in

January 1883 during President Arthur's administration, following (and, in part, because of) President Garfield's assassination by a disappointed office-seeker. It provided for a classified list of merit appointments by 'open, competitive examination'; for an end to the assessment of office-holders for political contributions; and for a Civil Service Commission to administer the rules impartially. The new rules initially affected only about 12 per cent of bureaucrats in federal service, but the proportion grew rapidly under the reforming stimulus of Theodore Roosevelt and Woodrow Wilson, in particular. During the same period, the merit principle was widely applied by state governments to their own administration. Merit posts were reserved for the best-qualified applicant, regardless of party, who would thereafter be immune from removal when a change of administration occurred, not required to contribute to any political fund, and protected from other partisan harassment.

Two presidents (Harrison and Garfield) had lost their lives to the spoils system; another, Theodore Roosevelt, rose to national prominence, in part, because of his indefatigable enforcement of the Pendleton Act as Civil Service Commissioner. As the drive against patronage grew, it became politically advantageous for presidents to expand the list as a proportion of all federal posts, and they duly did so. In the twenty years following the Civil War, the movement for civil service reform took on the character of a crusade, the object being the de-politicization of the bureaucracy on behalf of a public interest. Entire political careers were devoted to the cause. A merit-based civil service was a prerequisite for a modern bureaucracy capable of administering the policies of a government that was taking on regulatory roles. Civil service reform and the attack on the abuse of monopoly power by large corporations were linked in the Progressive movement, and contributed to the growth of the federal government's capacities in the years immediately before World War I. The Pendleton Act did not eliminate the unedifying scramble for federal posts at the beginning of a new administration, but did greatly diminish both its extent and tendency to corrupt.

Introduction of a merit-based civil service did not remove patronage from American politics; chief executives across America, from the president to many city mayors, still have many appointments within their gift. Development of civil service conditions, in federal, state and local governments, has therefore occurred alongside the maintenance of the right of most executives in most governments in the United States to make at least some political appointments. In 1981, there were 3,425 executive-level political appointees in the federal government, the highwater mark of political appointments to the bureaucracy. In January 2009, President Obama appointed 2,900 executive-level appointments (all of whom are subject to Senate confirmation). However, the total number of political appointees exceeds this number, since not all require confirmation: in 2012, that number was over 7,000 (www.opm.gov).

Specialized support and fragmented government

In 2012, 2.8 million civilians worked for the federal government, not many more than when President Eisenhower took office in 1953 (and a reduction from the level during the 1990s); in proportion to the population, the civil service has shrunk considerably over the period. However, the total size of the government workforce is far higher when, as we must, the expansion of contract labour in government activities is taken into account. Paul Light (2006) calculated that the size of the federal government workforce was 14.6 million employees, including civil servants, postal workers, military personnel, contractors and grantees. More than half of that total comprised contractors; that number has declined since the end of the war in Iraq. The fragmentation of the federal bureaucracy's organization is reflected in its personnel structure. Sixty years after Franklin D. Roosevelt initiated the rapid expansion of the federal bureaucracy, there is still little notion of a government-wide career structure for civil servants. In circumstances of functional specialization and agency autonomy, many agencies have effectively independent career structures, and there is little notion of a common civil service as there was in London prior to the creation of the executive agencies, or as there still is in Paris. The United States's government tends, as Robert Wood (1970) explained, to recruit by profession. This practice affords the government specialized support at the cost of persisting fragmentation.

The example of the Forest Service illustrates the relationship between the functional specialization of agencies within departments and the distinct professional groups recruited to run it. The Forest Service is an agency within the Department of Agriculture run, for the most part, by qualified foresters. The high percentage of the Service's employees who work full-time in the field are graduates of forestry schools. They are no more likely to transfer from or to other agencies within the department than they are to other agencies in other departments. Their specialization is of a kind whereby their skills cannot be transferred within government (although they may well be marketable within the private sector). Even where skills are transferable between agencies, as is the case with lawyers and budget analysts, who are to be found in every agency and department, most civil servants remain in the agency to which they were originally recruited.

Concentration of professional expertise underpins agencies' autonomy within departments, creating asymmetries of information and

Exhibit 9.1 Number of Employees in the Federal Bureaucracy, 1990 and 2010

Agency	1990	2010
Total, all agencies	*3,128,267*	*2,841,143*
Legislative Branch	37,495	30,643
Judicial Branch	23,605	33,756
Executive Branch	3,067,167	2,776,744
Executive Office of the President	1,731	1,965
All Executive Departments	*2,065,542*	*1,937,291*
State	25,288	39,016
Treasury	158,655	110,099
Defense	1,034,152	772,601
Justice	83,932	117,916
Interior	77,679	70,231
Agriculture	122,594	106,867
Commerce	69,920	56,856
Labor	17,727	17,592
Health and Human Services	123,959	69,839
Housing and Urban Development	13,596	9,585
Transportation	67,364	57,972
Energy	17,731	16,145
Education	4,771	4,452
Veterans Affairs	2,48,174	304,665
Homeland Security	N/A	183,455
Independent agencies	999,894	837,488
Environmental Protection Agency	17,123	18,740
Equal Employment Opportunity Commission	2,880	2,543
Federal Communications Commission	1,778	1,838
Federal Deposit Insurance Corporation	17,641	6,436
Federal Trade Commission	988	1,131
General Services Administration	20,277	12,820
National Aeronautics and Space Administration	24,872	18,664
National Labor Relations Board	2,263	1,715
National Science Foundation	1,318	1,474
Nuclear Regulatory Commission	3,353	4,240
Office of Personnel Management	6,636	5,892
Peace Corps	1,178	1,082
Securities and Exchange Commission	2,302	3,917
Small Business Administration	5,128	4,037
Smithsonian Institution	5,092	4,984
Social Security Administration	N/A	69,975
Tennessee Valley Authority	28,392	12,457
U.S. Information Agency	8,555	1,953
U.S. Postal Service	816,886	643,420

expertise *within* departments. It therefore affords agencies greater autonomy from the few political appointees with responsibility for the entire department, and yet greater autonomy from the president. Since the Twenty-Second Amendment to the Constitution ensures that the turnover of presidents is high (see Appendix 2), the longevity of professional bureaucrats in specialized agencies makes the task of presidents who seek to give a policy lead exceptionally difficult, particularly since links between specialized agencies, on the one hand, and specialized parental congressional subcommittees, on the other, are intimate.

Civilian federal employees

There are four broad categories of civilian federal employees:

1. Nearly half work for the Post Office, public power systems operated by the Department of Energy or government agencies with special professional requirements and recruitment procedures such as the Secret Service and the Federal Bureau of Investigation (FBI).

2. The 'General Schedule' (GS), a merit-based career system that accounts for slightly more than half of all civilian employees, including, in eighteen grades, the great majority of civil servants working in the main departments and agencies from the most junior grades to the most senior. Recruitment to the GS, until the early 1980s, undertaken by a standard, competitive, aptitude test, the Professional Administrative Career Examination (PACE). However, in 1982 a federal district court judged PACE to be racially discriminatory, and recruitment is now organized by individual agencies to suit their particular requirements. Recruitment procedures have accordingly fragmented and become more complicated, further weakening the civil service as a whole.

3. The Senior Executive Service (SES) was established by the Civil Service Reform Act of 1978, President Carter's single-most significant domestic reform. Carter intended it to revitalize the senior ranks of the civil service, providing greater mobility between agencies and departments for ambitious and creative senior managers, who were enticed into the SES by the prospect of performance-related bonus payments and career advancement. The Civil Service Reform Act established the SES as a hybrid service, including not only civil servants drawn from the four most senior grades in the GS, but also permitting more political appointees in what would previously have been the exclusive preserve of career civil servants. The creation of this hybrid structure can lead to tensions between career civil servants promoted into the SES and political appointees who

join an agency or department at SES level, their goals and motivations may be different (see Exhibit 9.6 and McMahon, 2006).

    Ronald Reagan's politicization of the civil service exploited the freedom which the legislation gave him to remove SES civil servants from their posts and replace them with political appointees. Reagan devoted more resources to politicizing the bureaucracy than any president before him: 100 staff members in the White House's Office of Presidential Personnel examined potential appointees for loyalty to the president, ideological enthusiasm and (less reliably) competence. While, as the history of Mr Reagan's administration revealed, zealotry is an insufficient condition for changing an agency's course, its application between 1981 and 1988 damaged the quality and morale of the civil service considerably. The SES at the time of writing is much more balanced in terms of the division between career officials and political appointees. In 2012, there were 8,328 members of the SES roughly evenly-divided between career civil servants and political appointees. (In an attempt to limit the politicization of the SES, the Office of Personal Management (OPM) issued a regulation in 1980 stipulating that no fewer than 3,571 appointments must be career appointments.)

4.   Schedule 'C' appointments are conventional political appointments which comprise most presidential patronage. The number of such appointments has fallen from its high-point at the start of the first Reagan administration of just under 3,500 in 1981 to just below 3,000 in 2012.

Reforming the civil service

President Reagan's reforms

Reagan's attack on the civil service cut with the grain of public prejudice and was, to that extent, politically helpful to him. Attacking the alleged sloth and inefficiency of the federal bureaucracy is an old and profitable campaigning tactic, but intellectually questionable because government bureaucracies necessarily differ considerably from private-sector bureaucracies: they face distinctive problems and operate under special constraints. In all democracies, governments operate under constraints of equity, accountability, high standards of stewardship, and fairness, which private companies for the most part do not. In no political system are these constraints more elaborate or more closely supervized than in the United States. The view that public administration is inherently less efficient than private industry and commerce, and that government ought to be run like a business is, nevertheless, widespread; it found its clearest expression in President Reagan's attempts to reform the federal civil service along private-sector lines.

As part of his drive to increase the efficiency of the federal bureaucracy, President Reagan launched a programme in 1981 entitled Reform '88 to examine particular aspects of managerial practice in government. It was followed in 1982 by the President's Private Sector Survey on Cost Control (the Grace Commission, after its chairman, J. P. Grace, a businessman) whose approach to the problem, like that of Reform '88, sprang from the assumption that the introduction of what was taken to be the rigour of private-sector management techniques and organization into the civil service would improve its efficiency. Reporting in 1984, Grace concluded that savings of over $400 billion could be made with improved management. The Congressional Budget Office (CBO) and Government Accountability Office (GAO) issued their own joint report on Grace's recommendations, concluding that the true savings would be only $100 billion, of which 60 per cent could be achieved not through management improvements, but only by policy changes. Of the remaining 40 per cent, most of the savings could be made only if additional costs were to be incurred (such as hiring more Internal Revenue Service officials to collect taxes) or by the contracting-out of services to private companies (on contracting-out, see the reforms of President George W. Bush below).

President Reagan took special steps at an early stage of his administration to attack what he and many in his entourage regarded as the generous pay and perquisites of civil servants. Encouraged by many of those whom he had appointed to senior posts in the Office of Personnel Management, he proposed in 1981 that their pay be cut by 5 per cent. He later modified his view, suggesting that the principle of pay comparability with the private sector (which was, in any case, neither universally nor fully applied) should be abandoned in order to allow for government pensions to be uprated in line with the cost of living. Although neither proposal was accepted, Reagan's hostility towards the conception and practice of public service ensured that the conditions of service for federal civil servants worsened during the 1980s, not least because members of Congress lacked the courage to increase their own salaries in line with inflation, and continued to be unwilling to support civil servants' receiving higher salaries than their own.

National Commission on the Public Service

Reagan's undermining of the civil service lowered morale within it, and made for difficulties of recruitment and retention, which became especially severe as private sector salaries grew quickly in the mid-to-late 1980s: the gap between government and private sector salaries increased to an average of 25 per cent by August 1988. Following a symposium on public service sponsored by the Brookings Institution and the American Enterprise Institute in 1986, the National Commission on the Public Service was formed, chaired by Paul Volcker, the distinguished former chairman of the Federal Reserve, to examine the problems plaguing the bureaucracy.

Volcker brought integrity and high public standing to the job, and was able to force onto the political agenda the related anxieties he and his colleagues on the Commission had about the civil service's condition: public perceptions of the service, pay and conditions, recruitment and retention, the relationship between political appointments and civil service career posts, education and training. He met with sympathetic hearings from key congressional committees, and found in President George H. W. Bush one who valued public service and public servants. Yet, nearly two decades after the first Volcker Commission issued its report on the federal public service, the presidential appointment and confirmation process remains long, cumbersome, intensive and embarrassing.

Among the many proposals to emerge in the Commission's report *Leadership for America* were recommendations that there be significant pay increases, in order to stem the flow of experienced civil servants from government to the private sector, and, to restore morale, that the number of political appointments available to the president be set at the reduced figure of 2000; that managerial and personnel authority be devolved; and, as part of a renewed emphasis on the importance of the training of civil servants, that a special programme of scholarships be established to encourage able young people to pursue careers in the civil service. The Commission's signal achievement was to modify the terms of public debate about the value and importance of public service.

President Clinton's civil service reforms

By raising the subject of public sector reform, as he did in 1993, President Clinton responded to intensifying public discontent with the perceived scale and cost of federal regulation. He announced on 7 September 1993 a programme entitled the *National Performance Review* (NPR) comprising an attempt to improve the quality of federal service to the public while cutting costs by $108 billion over five years. The President gave responsibility for the development and implementation of the programme (popularly, if misleadingly, known as 'Reinventing Government') to Vice-President Gore, who approached the subject with an evangelist's zeal, attempting to exploit it to his electoral advantage in preparation for his (unsuccessful) presidential bid in 2000. Among the programme's elements were proposals to introduce commercial practices into federal procurement, to revise the organization of departments, and to make provision for financial inducements to civil servants 'surplus to requirements' to accept redundancy offers. Some of the programme's elements could be implemented by executive order of the president. Crucially, however, others required congressional legislation. After the Republicans won majority control in 1994, the programme's many components became the object of intense partisan dispute as part of a broader attack on a Democratic president and executive agencies led, for the most part, by Democratic appointees. While the Republican majority failed to abolish any major department or agency, it sought (with only partial success) to claim credit for forcing privatization and commercialization onto federal agencies' agenda. As a result of the NPR, and the *Government Performance and Results Act* (GPRA), 1993, (an initiative of the Republican Congress intended to reduce the size of government and to introduce goals that would focus agencies on performance targets), some elements of the bureaucracy were able to transform themselves. Approximately between 12 per cent and 15 per cent of civil service posts were abolished and managers received greater autonomy over policy and budgetary decision-making. However, one of the most notable failures of the reform efforts during the Clinton years was the creation of Performance-Based Organizations (PBOs). The intention was that they would enjoy greater autonomy than traditional agencies and bureaux, and would receive budgets based upon the achievement of performance targets. The creation of PBOs would have strengthened the NPR but, in 1996, Congress defeated the proposal. With the NPR favoured by the White House and the GPRA favoured by the Republican Congress, but with no joined-up effort to reform the bureaucracy, President Clinton enjoyed little success with reform.

The bureaucracy under President George W. Bush and President Obama

When running for office, President George W. Bush discussed the need to reduce government waste and the bureaucracy. Bush was the first president with an MBA (Master's in Business Administration); even better, his MBA came from Harvard. His management style was to delegate so that his closest advisers within the White House might focus on strategic decisions, rather than detailed questions of process. President Bush sought to cut by half the number of personnel in senior- and middle-management roles within the bureaucracy, to win greater involvement of the private sector in government – and fuller competition within it. Yet, President Bush provided no coherent reform agenda beyond familiar requests for reductions in personnel and gains in efficiency. After the terrorist attacks of 2011, President Bush paid the subject little further attention.

In his first two years in office, President Obama gave no indication of a commitment to bureaucratic reform. His first major speech on the subject was his January 2012 State of the Union Address, in which he committed himself to a plan which would *'make government leaner, smarter and more consumer-friendly'*. The President subsequently established the Government Reform for Competitiveness and Innovation Initiative and, in February 2012, and submitted to Congress the *Government Reform and Consolidation Act*. The bill has yet to be translated into law but might succeed, both because congressional Republicans support reductions in personnel and because Democrats know that the projected cost savings are tiny. The bill proposes a reduction in the number of agencies through a process of mergers, with a cost saving of $3 billion over the next decade which, as a proportion of the US budget over that period, is almost incapable of being measured. Estimated total government spending over the next ten years is $70 trillion: accordingly, a saving of $3 billion represents a potential saving of $1 for every $23,000 spent.

The growth of federal regulation

Whatever the bureaucracy's institutional form, delegation of power to bureaucrats is inescapable (see Exhibit 9.2). Legislators cannot provide for every contingency in statute, some discretion must be granted to those who execute laws. Implementation of policy therefore requires bureaucrats also to form policy by making decisions within sets of general parameters about particular events. Implementation of policy by bureaucracies over time is the administrative analogue of the courts' development of case law.

Bureaucratic growth in the United States has three main sources:

1. The establishment of a wide range of federal social security, urban, welfare and education policies.
2. The growth in the regulatory role of federal government.
3. The establishment of the United States as a global military and political power.

The first and second of these are overlapping categories: all federal programmes have regulatory purposes and consequences, irrespective of whether they are administered by notionally independent regulatory commissions, or notionally subordinate departments and agencies of the Executive Branch.

Most of the expansion in federal employment (especially of employment in Washington) to have occurred between 1933 and the high-point in 1990 did so between the beginning of Franklin D. Roosevelt's presidency and the end of Harry Truman's. During the 1933–53 period, the foundations of social security law were laid, the regulatory activity of the federal government expanded greatly, and the United States moved from isolationism to worldwide military and diplomatic involvement. Contrary to popular opinion, agitated by the false claims of politicians seeking election, federal employment growth since the beginning of Eisenhower's presidency has been slow, and much slower than population growth. While the image of Washington as a bloated and expanding federal animal wins easy applause in election campaigns by stirring old populist sentiment, it is misplaced.

Nevertheless, whether measured by the number of programmes, expenditure, extent of administrative regulation, or the number of public employees, the federal government is large and a formidable actor in public policy, politics and society. Metropolitan Washington is overwhelmingly dependent on government for its prosperity; many communities across America also depend on the federal government for the maintenance of prosperity through direct federal employment.

Large though it is, the federal government depends on lower-level governments to deliver most services generated by the expansion of the federal educational, welfare and urban programmes of the New Deal and Great Society programmes of the 1930s and 1960s. During the 1960s, employment in state and local government grew by nearly 40 per cent, fuelled by an increase of more than 230 per cent in federal aid to lower-level governments. Less than 10 per cent of the federal budget is spent on domestic programmes administered directly by federal employees. Most federal programmes are delivered by lower-level governments and other third parties – by officials working for state or city governments, and by private organizations working under contract to federal agencies, or with the assistance of federal grants. Symbolic of the federal government's involvement in all fields of public policy is the profusion of federal buildings and bureaucrats throughout the country: nearly nine of every ten federal employees work outside the Washington metropolitan area.

From the mid-nineteenth century onwards, Congress began to regulate private business on behalf of a wider public interest by devolving powers to executive agencies, usually to independent commissions. Much of the American economy has since fallen under federal or state regulation. The beginning of the first phase of such regulation was marked by the passage of the National Currency Act in 1863, and, the following year, of the National Bank Act, which established a Comptroller of the Currency with the power to charter and supervize national banks. In 1887, the Interstate Commerce Act established the Interstate Commerce Commission (ICC), designed to rationalize disorderly competition between railroad companies.

Exhibit 9.2 The Functions of the Federal Bureaucracy

The bureaucracy performs three main functions which, taken together, represent a considerable grant of power exercised semi-autonomously from the elected branches. The three functions are: executing laws, creating rules and adjudication.

Executing laws

Congress makes the laws but the bureaucracy is charged with their implementation. Laws provide the basis upon which the Internal Revenue Service (IRS) collects and levies taxes. But the IRS has considerable autonomy in how it executes the law.

Creating rules

Laws made in Congress and signed by the President can never be so detailed as to apply to every circumstance to which a law pertains. For example, the Clean Air Act (signed on 31 December 1970 by President Nixon) was intended to improve public health through the effective monitoring of air quality. Implementation of the Act fell to the Environmental Protection Agency (EPA) created just three weeks before the Act became law.

Monitoring of air quality required skills and expertise that were legion within the EPA but not within the elected branches. Acts of Congress are skeletal: it falls to the bureaucracy to provide for detailed implementation. Cascading from primary legislation is a swathe of regulations (or 'regs') drafted and issued by the civil servants to give effect to Congress's legislative intent.

Adjudication

Laws are challenged by affected parties, are often ambiguous; regulations made by agencies based on the law may also be challenged in court. For example, the Supreme Court ruled in 2007 that the Clean Air Act could be used as the basis on which the EPA could regulate carbon emissions – a decision challenged by a number of affected industry groups, as well as states (including oil-rich states like Texas).

The ICC's establishment marked a new willingness by the federal government to control the worst consequences for public health and consumer well-being of hitherto unrestrained market forces. After much vacillation, the Supreme Court upheld the policy-making role of the Interstate Commerce Commission in *Interstate Commerce Commission v Illinois Central Railroad Co.* (1910), and extended it in *Houston, East and West Texas Ry. Co. v United States* (1914) (which has since become known as the *Shreveport* case). In the latter judgement, the Court upheld the right of Congress to regulate not just interstate commerce, but also intra-state commerce insofar as it had 'a close and substantial relation to interstate commerce'. *Shreveport* had powerful implications for the ICC's regulatory authority over intra-state railroad rates, for congressional supremacy over state law in commercial matters and, hence, for Congress's consequent freedom to legislate. Although the Constitution grants Congress no powers to regulate intra-state commerce, by the *Shreveport* case interstate power was deemed effectively unlimited.

The second phase of federal regulation encompassed the period from the beginning of Franklin D. Roosevelt's presidency in 1933 to the midpoint of his second term in 1938, during which time eight separate regulatory agencies were established to address problems arising from financial ruin and economic collapse. Among them were the National Labor Relations Board, formed by the Wagner Act of 1935; the Federal Deposit Insurance Corporation (FDIC) charged by the Glass–Steagall Act of 1933 (which separated commercial from investment banking) with the insurance of bank deposits up to $10,000 against the default of the member bank; and the Securities Exchange Commission (SEC) established by the Securities Exchange Act of 1934. All national banks, and all state banks that were members of the Federal Reserve System, were covered by the Glass–Steagall Act. (Glass–Steagall was repealed, in part, in 1999 but calls for its reinstatement have gained prominence following the banking crisis of 2007–08 and the *London Interbank Overnight Lending Rate* (LIBOR) rate-fixing scandal of 2012/13). Its primary instrument, disclosure of all pertinent information, employed to counter misrepresentation and fraudulent dealing on Wall Street, remains a key weapon in the federal regulatory armoury. In equity markets, the SEC continues to find plenty of work.

Antipathy to federal regulation among many in the Reagan administration found expression in the easing of regulation on home loans and, in particular, on savings and loans associations. The incentives to imprudent, and even criminal, behaviour that the weakening of federal regulation provided had damaging effects on the home loans market. Such imprudent (and often criminal) behaviour contributed to the so-called 'sub-prime' mortgage crash of 2007, which triggered the broader financial and banking crises of 2007–09.

Whereas the first phase of federal regulation sprang from the intention to control the detrimental effects of monopoly capital, and the second from the Great Depression, the third was triggered by the articulation of new concerns, especially social regulation, and control of negative externalities. Among the regulatory agencies created in this latter period were the Equal Employment Opportunities Commission (EEOC); the Occupational Safety and Health Administration (OSHA); and the Consumer Product Safety Commission (CPSC). Reliance on gross

Exhibit 9.3 Agencies and their Congressional Parents

- The *Department of Defense*, as a whole, has as its ostensibly undivided object the defence of the United States. It is, however, subdivided into three major departments (Army, Air Force and Navy, with the Marine Corps being a semi-autonomous agency within the Navy Department) whose interests frequently collide. Prior to 1949, the Army and Navy were run as wholly separate departments. The amalgamation in that year of the Departments of Navy and of War (which had itself combined supervision of the departments of the Army and the Army Air Force) did not end inter-service rivalry. Bureaucratic competition between the services continues, to the detriment of the formulation and execution of American foreign and defence policy.

- The *Department of Justice* also harbours powerful and autonomous fiefdoms. Indeed, the clearest instance of agency autonomy was the Federal Bureau of Investigation (FBI) during its heyday under J. Edgar Hoover, its Director for almost half a century. Even after his death, most Americans regard the FBI as an independent and free-standing organization, not as a division of the Department of Justice, which it nominally is. Hoover did not readily submit to the succession of Attorneys-General (his nominal superiors) or to presidents; as an unelected bureaucrat, he possessed effective independence. Resolute in pursuit of those whom he suspected of Communist sympathies and unenthusiastic in his enforcement of civil rights laws, Hoover was virtually unaccountable.

- The *Department of the Treasury* illustrates the disparate nature of semi-autonomous agencies within a department – a general pattern throughout the federal bureaucracy. Two agencies within the department have, in practice, substantial independence from each other: the US Secret Service and the IRS. Created by Act of Congress in 1860 to suppress the counterfeiting of US coin, bills and securities, the US Secret Service is now known less for this work than for its responsibility for ensuring the safety of the president and his family, former presidents and first ladies, other senior government figures and visiting VIPs. The IRS is one of the largest agencies within the United States government, with offices spread throughout the country, engaged in the business of collecting federal taxes. In addition to its direct relationship with every American tax-payer, it also has close links to the Tax Committees in both Houses of Congress and to the Joint Committee on Internal Revenue Taxation. Within the Treasury, the functional specialization of the IRS and Secret Service renders them special cases, but only in extent, not in kind. The relationship that each has to the Department of the Treasury as a whole and to other agencies within the Department, such as the Bureau of the Mint, is no different, in principle, from those of other agencies in other departments.

national product (GNP) growth as the single-most important indicator of national welfare came increasingly to be questioned in the mid-1960s as the problems of large pockets of rural and urban poverty, of environmental damage, and of the high risks to the health and safety of workers and consumers became important issues on the political agenda. President Johnson had hastened the change by questioning the adequacy of affluence as an indicator of the quality of life.

The burgeoning consumer interest movement was stimulated by the publication of Rachel Carson's *Silent Spring* (1962) which examined the use of the pesticide DDT and which contributed to the birth of the modern environmental movement, and by Ralph Nader's book *Unsafe at Any Speed* (1965), a critical study of the scant attention then paid by car manufacturers to the safety of their products. Nader's book caused the question of car safety in particular, and consumer interests in general, to rise rapidly up the political agenda. It was the first major success for consumer lobbies in America, and prompted government action. The Consumer Product Safety Act, passed by Congress in 1972 with President Nixon's support, established the Consumer Product Safety Commission (CSPC) to protect consumers against unreasonable risk of injury from hazardous products. Two years before, by an executive reorganization plan that consolidated fifteen scattered units into one, Nixon established the Environmental Protection Agency (EPA), charged with writing regulations enforcing new anti-pollution legislation. That work brings the EPA into conflict with powerful industrial interests.

As a result of the 2007–08 financial crisis and the global economic recession it precipitated, the federal government under President Bush and his successor introduced a number of regulations intended to reduce the recurrence of such an economic crisis. The most significant single piece of legislation introduced by Congress in response to the crisis was the introduction of the 2010 *Dodd–Frank Wall Street Reform and Consumer Protection Act*, which sought greater oversight of the financial sector and the re-introduction of a form of the *Glass–Steagall* separation between commercial banks and their investment arms. It remains unclear whether this legislation, complex in itself and certain to produce yet more complex regulation, will reduce systemic risk in financial markets.

Bureaucratic structure and organization

Executive departments

Competition between agencies within departments is endemic and ineradicable. Buttressed by functional specialization, some agencies enjoy almost complete autonomy from other agencies in the same department, and have strongly resisted attempts by the secretaries and inder-secretaries of departments to enforce a wider or a presidential view or policy on them. Agencies are the primary units of importance and interest. Established separately by Congress, they administer distinct programmes authorized and re-authorized by Congress, and for which Congress separately appropriates public money. Their purposes are defined separately in law, and their work is overseen by different subcommittees. Relations between agencies and their congressional parents are often closer politically than relations between agencies within what is nominally a single department. Brief examinations of the Departments of Defense, Judiciary and the Treasury given in Exhibit 9.3 illustrate this characteristic.

Federal corporations

Regulation, not nationalization, has been the federal government's chosen policy instrument to modify the operations of the market, and opportunities for privatization have consequently been fewer. There have been just four major exceptions to this preference:

1. Major failures of commercial or financial undertakings, such as the collapse of passenger railroads leading to the formation of Amtrak; and the failure of the Continental Bank of Illinois; of many savings and loans associations in the late 1980s and early 1990s; and the crisis within the banking system following the collapse of the US housing market in 2007.
2. The operation of public utilities such as the Tennessee Valley Authority and the western power generation plants.
3. The change in the status of the Post Office from a government department to a public corporation in 1970, so that it might have greater autonomy from congressional pressure to keep postage fees artificially low, thereby starving the organization of investment. (The move has scarcely been an unambiguous success.)
4. The US government's takeover of two nominally private mortgage companies, the Federal Home Loan Mortgage Corporation (colloquially known as 'Fannie Mae') and the Federal National Mortgage Association (similarly known as 'Freddie Mac') in 2008, following those organizations' effective collapse, was presented as a 'conservatorship' but amounted to nationalization (or re-nationalization). The US government's investing up to $50 billion and taking 60 per cent ownership of General Motors in June 2009, following the company's bankruptcy, was similarly an act of nationalization, albeit a temporary one. It was also, as events turned out, a successful one both for the government and for General Motors.

Independent regulatory commissions and executive regulatory agencies

Some regulatory bodies, such as the Food and Drug Administration (FDA), are placed within an executive department. Others, such as the Federal Election Commission, are in their operation (though not in the selection of their senior officials) formally independent both of Congress and of the executive. In 1977, the Permanent Subcommittee on Investigations of the Senate Government Operations Committee in 1977 defined a federal regulatory office as one which:

(1) has decision-making authority, (2) establishes standards or guidelines conferring benefits and imposing restrictions on business conduct, (3) operates principally in the sphere of domestic business activity, (4) has its head and/or members appointed by the President and in all but one instance, subject to Senate confirmation (the FDA is the exception), and (5) has its legal procedures generally governed by the Administrative Procedure Act.

Condition (4) underpins the Commissions' independence: federal departments have at their head secretaries appointed by the president subject to Senate advice and consent, who together comprise the president's Cabinet but (like all political appointees in the departments) are subject to dismissal by the president. Independent Regulatory Commissions are led by independent commissioners who, though appointed on the same terms as departmental secretaries, may not be dismissed by the president. Congress has reinforced the relative freedom which this immunity grants them by setting their (staggered) terms of office at between four and fourteen years, according to the provisions of their founding statutes. In most Commissions, the capacity of presidents and Congresses to interfere is further limited by statutory provisions limiting the number of Commissioners on any one Commission who may be drawn from either political party. Long terms of office increase the prospect that Commissioners will become expert in their work, while granting them almost complete immunity from partisan interference. The old faith in expertise, distrust of politicians, and in organizational solutions to policy problems, which together spurred Progressive reformers at the turn of the century, still exercises its sway.

As federal regulations were addressed to interstate commerce, state regulations and regulatory agencies established by state legislatures dealt with intra-state concerns. State regulations are neither necessarily more lax nor more stringent than federal ones. For example, many states operated and enforced civil rights laws long before the federal authorities acted in 1964, while the regulation of the sale of firearms by many state legislatures is stronger than that by Congress.

Until the early 1980s, much of America's commercial life was regulated by regulatory commissions: broadcasting, air travel, and rail and road transport. Exploiting growing public discontent with the harmful consequences for consumer choice and interests within a highly-regulated economy (which invariably operated to the benefit of producers), President Carter initiated the deregulation of airline travel with the abolition of the Civil Aeronautics Board under the Airline Deregulation Act of 1978, and the consequential ending of a federal role in the setting of airline fares. Railroad rates (fares) were similarly deregulated under the Staggers Rail Act of 1980 with the ending of the ICC's original role. Rates are now determined by the market. The activities of savings institutions (whose members' savings were insured by a federal agency) were deregulated (and consequently greatly expanded) by the Garn–St Germain Depository Institution Act of 1982; the setting of rates for cable TV were deregulated in 1984 under the Cable Deregulation Act. Deregulation contributed greatly to the disastrous run of insolvencies and associated criminality that undermined the savings and loan industry from 1989 onwards, with the result that a new federal agency took over the bankrupt institutions at great public expense. Less dramatically, the rapid rise in prices that followed cable TV deregulation resulted in new regulations passed in the autumn of 1992 over President George H. W. Bush's veto.

However, the deregulation of the 1980s was partial, even within the airline and railroad industries. Many aspects of both, from operational safety and the closure of passenger railroad lines to the occupational health of airline and railroad employees, remain firmly regulated by, among others, the Federal Aviation Agency (FAA), and the Occupational Safety and Health Administration (OHSA). Other areas of economic activity were regulated either for the first time (for example, the futures trading of commodities), or more tightly (as with a range of air, water, and ground pollution controls), during the same period in which airline and railroad rates were deregulated. As the fracas over the lax enforcement of anti-pollution laws at the EPA in 1983 showed, congressional and public support for deregulation was greater in some areas than others; where a clear public or consumer interest was at stake, pressure for the maintenance or extension of regulation was greater than where it was not. Independent regulatory commissions remain a major component of the federal bureaucracy, and regulation continues to be a standard instrument for the control of parts of the economy and of other areas of public life where Congress holds that the public interest cannot be served by an unfettered free market.

Business is not universally opposed to regulation. Regulation has as often served the interests of the regulated industries as those of consumers: agencies have frequently fallen under the effective control of the notionally regulated industry. Many leaders of industries have themselves sought the federal regulation of their industry, because of the threat that individual states might set stricter standards than the federal authorities, or because of the extra costs of dealing with different regulations set by different governments, or in the face of pressure from consumers for deregulation. Marver Bernstein (1955) argued that the 'capture' of regulatory commissions by the regulated organization is the final phase of a dynamic relationship between the two. Airline deregulation was, for example, fiercely fought by large American airlines and by the unions within the industry whose different purposes regulation served well, and very much better than it did the purposes of passengers. In setting the prices of airline tickets and licensing airline routes within the United States, the Civil Aeronautics Board protected the interests of high-cost airlines with conservative business practices, rather than the interests of airline passengers. Similarly, broadcasters had long had their interests defended by the Federal Communications Commission (FCC). Indeed, the FCC (like its predecessor, the Federal Radio Commission) was established at the urging of radio and television companies so that local markets might be protected and their use of frequencies defended.

Administrative law

Administrative law comprises regulations, rulings and judgements made by Executive Branch agencies under authority delegated to them by Congress in authorizing legislation. Regulations published by Executive Branch agencies are binding, and identical in their effects to statute or common law. Congress may delegate powers to agencies broadly or narrowly but, in doing so, it retains the absolute right to modify the nature and extent of the delegation. Indeed, most statutory delegations of authority to agencies and regulatory authorities to issue regulations are subject to Congress retaining the right to veto them. Through re-authorization legislation, Congress may extend, diminish, or abolish altogether the right of executive agencies to exercise rule-making authority. The example of deregulation of airline rates and routes in Exhibit 9.4 illustrates aspects of the phenomenon.

The *Federal Register* is a daily federal government publication with a print run of 35,000. The Federal Register Act of 1935 requires all new regulations and administrative orders issued by Executive Branch agencies to be published in it. The Administrative Procedure Act of 1946 similarly requires all presidential executive orders to be published there, and further requires that the details of proposed regulations be published in the Register to give 'interested persons an opportunity to participate in the rule-making', thereby legitimating the place of interest groups in the

Exhibit 9.4 Federal Aviation Administration Regulations

Deregulation of airline rates and routes since 1980 has occurred simultaneously with the tightening of regulations governing aircraft and airport safety by the responsible authority, the Federal Aviation Administration (FAA), an agency of the Department of Transportation. Regular air passengers on a flight to the United States or within it become familiar with federal regulations covering the safety of passengers in flight and the procedures for emergency evacuation of the aircraft. Such regulations have the force of law; passengers who break them risk heavy fines on conviction. FAA regulations address not only those questions of smoking in the gangways, the fastening of seatbelts and the use of the emergency exits, but also thousands of other operational details familiar only to airlines and their employees.

Every detail of civilian aircraft manufacture and operation is subject to FAA regulation and enforced by FAA inspectors. No civilian aircraft may be flown by any airline within the United States unless the type of aircraft and its engines have airworthiness certificates. The individual aircraft is subject to detailed tests specified, approved and implemented by the FAA. Notices of rules to be issued by the FAA are published in the *Federal Register*.

formation of public policy. Executive orders made by the president have the effect of law, and give effect to provisions of statute law under discretionary authority granted to the president in the original authorizing legislation, treaties, or the Constitution itself.

The complexity of published rules and the financial interest that corporations and other groups have in them, result in frequent hearings by agencies to adjudicate on appeals against their decisions. In more serious and substantial cases, groups may seek the rescinding or alteration of a rule or judgement by filing suit in a federal court. By determining the lawfulness of particular administrative rules, Courts are therefore inextricably involved not just in policy adjudication, but also in the implementation and evaluation of public policy itself. Courts must judge whether or not disputed rules accord with the delegation of authority made to agencies by Congress, or whether such rules are, in the language of the 1946 Act, 'arbitrary and capricious'. The court most directly concerned with major questions of administrative law is the US Court of Appeals for the District of Columbia (the seat of federal government). Since the passage of the Administrative Procedures Act in 1946, the District of Columbia Court of Appeals has established criteria by which agencies ought to act in particular cases. In determining whether an agency head acted appropriately in exercising their authority, courts often require bureaucrats to inform them of the basis for their decisions. Prudence therefore requires administrators to ensure that they are acting within the bounds of the authority granted them by Congress, and full records are kept of the reasoning behind each rule. Interest groups scour the *Federal Register* for notices of regulations affecting them or their clients, in light of which they take action. They also take note of agencies' failure to issue detailed regulations which implement congressional statutes.

Congressional control of the bureaucracy

The Senate Governmental Affairs Committee's 1977 report on federal regulation listed six main objectives of congressional oversight:

1. ensuring compliance of executive agencies with congressional intent;
2. determining the effectiveness of regulatory policies;
3. preventing waste and dishonesty;
4. preventing abuse in the administrative process;
5. representing the public interest;
6. preventing usurpation by agencies of legislative authority.

Congress has extensive formal powers to ensure that these objectives are met. There are three main tools at its disposal, which are examined in the following three sections:

(i)   the power of confirmation of presidential nominees to executive posts;
(ii) appropriations and authorization committee hearings;
(iii) the legislative veto.

Congress also has available to it the commissioning of studies by the US Government Accountability Office (formerly General Accounting Office, one of its institutional arms) into the efficiency with which the Executive Branch executes public law.

The US Senate's power of 'advise and consent'

Senate scrutiny of presidential nominees to political positions in executive departments and agencies is, in combination with authorizing and appropriations hearings, a more potent form of oversight than that available to it in respect of appointments to the judiciary. As the Senate

Judiciary Committee has primary responsibility for examining the qualifications of judicial nominees, so other Senate committees are responsible for scrutinizing nominations to departments and agencies within their functional jurisdiction. Hence, political appointments by the president to agencies within the Department of Agriculture are considered by the Senate Agriculture Committee, and those to the Department of Defense by the Senate Armed Services Committee.

Few nominees to executive departments and agencies are rejected, but the greatest value of the advice and consent power lies in deterrence, rather than defence: wise presidents avoid, rather than court, disputes that would be damaging to them, and so nominate those whom the Senate is likely to confirm, not those whom it is likely to reject. Defying the Senate by deliberately nominating those whom a majority are likely to find repugnant invites rebuff and consequent embarrassment.

Presidents Nixon and Reagan held that the power to 'advise and consent' obliged the Senate to accept their choices. Their view neither had, nor has, any basis in constitutional law. In the twentieth century, the Senate has rejected few nominees to Cabinet-level positions: President Coolidge's nomination of Charles Warren to Attorney-General was rejected in 1925; Eisenhower's nomination of Lewis Strauss as Secretary of Commerce was defeated in 1959; Carter's nomination of Theodore Sorensen (formerly President Kennedy's Special Counsel) as Director of Central Intelligence fell in 1977; and President George H. W. Bush's nomination of former Senator John Tower as Secretary of Defense was rejected in 1989. In the last decade, President George W. Bush's nominee for the post of US Ambassador to the United Nations, John Bolton, was rejected by the Senate in 2005. In 2012, Ambassador Susan Rice withdrew her name from the process to replace Hillary Clinton as US Secretary of State on her retirement in 2013. Rice was the subject of considerable criticism within the Senate – in part, because of comments made following the terrorist attacks on the US Embassy in Bengazi, Libya on 11 September 2012. President Obama also saw his 2013 nomination of Senator Chuck Hagel, a Republican, to the post of Defense Secretary subject to the threat of a Republican-led Senate filibuster during the nomination process.

It is more common for careful soundings of opinion to be taken among key opinion-formers in the relevant Senate committee before a nomination is made, so that nominees' acceptability can be tested before the formal process begins. Such a practice enables influential senators to consider the background, politics, character and behaviour of those whom the president appoints to key policy-making positions within his administration. Presidents and their staff who take seriously the Senate's constitutional right to advise on the acceptability of possible nominees are more likely to secure its consent to them.

The time which members of Congress have devoted to oversight in committee and subcommittee hearings has grown in recent years, partly because of the increased complexity of government regulation, but largely because of Congress's decreased trust in the executive since the late 1960s. President Johnson's conduct of the Vietnam War and President Nixon's systematic abuse of presidential prerogatives led to congressional reform and to the revision of formal executive–congressional relations. Congress became, for some years, a livelier competitor of the executive than it had been prior to the late 1960s. By increasing its staff resources, the number and autonomy of subcommittees, the legislature broke the executive's monopoly of expertise, and was able to oversee more effectively the implementation of public laws passed by Congress. Two legislative vehicles have had special importance in Congress's attempts to enforce its prerogatives. In fiscal policy, the reforms of the 1974 Budget and Impoundment Control Act have enhanced Congress's capacity to participate in the formation of federal budget policy. In military matters, the War Powers Resolution of 1973 marked an attempt to constrain the president's capacity to wage war without congressional knowledge or sanction. The Resolution's constitutionality has been contested by every president since its passage over Nixon's veto, has been flouted by them all, but has still not been tested in a federal court. The larger narrative, however, is of Congress having, in the early twentieth-century, effectively resiled from its constitutional obligations under Article I to check the president's use of the war power to use force abroad. Nothing in the US Constitution grants to the president such an unfettered right, but Congress has behaved toward President George W. Bush and to President Obama as if it did.

Both the War Powers Act and the Budget Act were instances and symbols of Congress's reassertion of its right to participate fully in policy implementation and evaluation, as well as legislation. Congress's role in government and policy-making does not end when the president signs legislation into law, the Supreme Court's judgement in declaring the legislative veto unconstitutional in *Chadha* notwithstanding (see p. 313). On the contrary, when it is doing the job given it by the Constitution, Congress participates at all stages of the policy process: initiation, legislation, implementation and evaluation. It does so, moreover, both in domestic and in foreign policy.

Congress cannot itself implement programmes but must ensure that implementation by executive agencies of programmes which it has authorized, and for which it has appropriated public money, accords with its intentions. Presidents and their political appointees to departments and agencies often find such oversight unwelcome, but their dismissal of Congress's right to scrutinize programmes in detail (so-called 'micro-management') has little constitutional weight. The Constitution gives no part of the United States' government a free hand, and Congress has the incentive, the right and, since the congressional reforms of the 1970s, the capacity to examine implementation of programmes and policy as its members please. Executive officials rarely tell congressional committees all that they know – whether from a proper concern to maintain executive privilege, or an improper attempt to deceive. In the long run, however, the powers of Congress are too extensive and fundamental for presidents and their executive subordinates to ignore. Presidents neither may, nor can, govern without Congress; neither may, nor can, Congress govern without the president. By the same token, the powers of Congress are too important for the legislature to do as it has done in the early twenty-first century in foreign and security policy, which is to permit them to wither.

Authorizing and appropriating committee hearings

Congress typically authorizes programmes for a specified period, varying from every year to every few years. If they are to continue beyond the period specified in law, they require re-authorization. Non-entitlement programmes depend for their funding on annual Appropriations Bills. The committee system of Congress is organized to accommodate the periodicity of re-authorization and appropriation; these regular events supply the bulk of authorizing and appropriating committees' work. Authorization bills enable the Executive Branch to suggest, and the Legislative Branch to require, that programmes be added, altered, or deleted. Appropriations Bills permit similar scrutiny of the cost of programmes. Both authorization and appropriations hearings in specialized congressional committees therefore appear to provide excellent opportunities for Congress to oversee Executive Branch activities: executive officials may be examined about the programmes which they administer, while experts from outside government and witnesses from interest groups are also summoned and questioned about policy and programmes. Congress writes its authorizing and appropriating legislation partly on the basis of the views that members and their staff hear at such committee hearings.

Incentives for representatives and senators to use the subcommittees on which they sit as vehicles for overseeing the agencies' execution of programmes which they authorize and finance are, nevertheless, often weak. Relations between agencies and subcommittees are more often cooperative than conflictual: bureaucrats know that whatever the short-term attractions, the medium- and long-term costs of antagonizing congressional 'parents' are high. Where relations between agencies and parent committees are collaborative, there is, however, a risk that a central purpose of oversight (ensuring that Congress's legislative will is executed) will be compromised. Irrespective of whether cooperation between agencies and committees in fact compromises oversight, the incentives to representatives and senators to engage in general scrutiny of agencies' activities are weak. When, by contrast, errors or disasters occur, politicians engage eagerly in retrospective oversight.

It is Congress's task to set the parameters within which Agency officials act; it cannot be Congress's proper task to do bureaucrats' jobs for them by drafting highly-detailed, technical rules. It is neither desirable, nor practicable, for administrative discretion to be eliminated; the point and purpose of the delegation of powers by Congress to the executive is that it should not be. Dispassionate bureaucratic expertise is a valuable resource: airline passengers sensibly prefer regulations governing the detection of metal fatigue in aircraft to be drafted and implemented by aerospace engineers, rather than by politicians. They have that preference not because it eliminates risk, but because it reduces it.

Two difficulties arise: the first is that the volume and complexity of consequential rule-making by agencies are, respectively, so large and so pronounced that Appropriations subcommittees are unable constantly to check that funds are spent by agencies in accordance with the agencies' stated intentions or Congress's will. The second is that Authorizing committees and subcommittees are similarly unable to ensure that all rules and actions of the agency comply with the letter and the spirit of Congress's requirements in the authorizing legislation. Provided that this fact has no damaging consequences, politicians may be unconcerned. There are only weak incentives for members of Congress to cross-examine witnesses from agencies in hearings of their subcommittees simply in order to check whether Congress's intent is being followed. However, in the event (for example) of an airline disaster, the chair of the Aviation subcommittees will certainly call public hearings to interrogate FAA and other witnesses to assess whether the agency has been negligent in the issuing and enforcing of rules under its delegated authority. Attempts by agencies to depart from Congress's appropriating intent are more easily controlled: the Appropriations committees of both the House and the Senate typically restrict the freedom of agencies to move resources from one programme to another (the 'reprogramming' of funds).

Restricting such administrative freedom may be good administrative practice, but it has few political benefits for the members of Congress who write appropriations law. By calling hearings to examine failures by agencies, committee chairs bathe in the light of publicity, projecting themselves as acting in the public interest but to their own political advantage. Examining officials after the fact is both easier and politically more attractive than examining them before it. To that extent, the three-fold objective of congressional politicians – re-election, the achievement of power within Congress, and the making of sound public policy – can be advanced simultaneously. Generalizing from this particular example suggests, however, that Congress's task of overseeing executive implementation may be executed less than satisfactorily. The FAA's failure (and, by extension, the failure of any agency) to make rules for the detailed implementation of Congress's will was, in these cases, corrected only after the event, and not before.

Studies of Congress's oversight function

Most scholars who have written on the subject argue that Congress performs its function of oversight poorly, waiting for intermittent disasters to force issues onto its agenda, rather than seeking to avert policy failures through laborious scrutiny of an agency's activities. However, others have argued that 'police-patrol' oversight (Congress conducting oversight of a sample of agency activities on its own initiative 'with the aim of detecting and remedying any violations of legislative goals and, by its surveillance, discouraging such violations') is not extensively undertaken, but that 'fire-alarm' oversight (by which they refer to the practice of investigating incidents after they occur) is performed extensively and well (McCubbins and Schwartz, 1984). Preferring the latter over the former is, McCubbins and Schwartz write, 'eminently rational'. It is also possible for Congress, in authorizing legislation, to oblige agencies to report to Congress that the law's requirements are being met, thereby reducing the chance of 'fire-alarm' oversight proving inadequate. Yet, that course of action which is rationally in the (short-term) interests of individual members of Congress is not necessarily in the (longer-term) interests of Congress as a whole. Still less is it necessarily in the public interest. Congress is institutionally much better equipped to respond to particular violations of congressional intent than it is to prevent them.

A more comprehensive study by Aberbach (1990), while not disposing of the dilemma of short- versus long-term interests, emphasizes that large and highly-competent professional committee staff have made the general monitoring of agencies' work a less forbidding task than most writers have supposed. Interviews with senior congressional committee staff have demonstrated their many (and intensively used) informal links with senior agency bureaucrats. Such informal links are the firmer for the widespread practice whereby individuals move within the policy-making communities in Washington: between staff positions on Capitol Hill, law firms, interest groups, political appointments in the Executive Branch, research institutes and universities. In this context, oversight is not a series of discrete events, but interconnected processes in a community of policy-makers embracing agencies, subcommittees and interest groups.

In contrast to the circumstances under which Congress worked in the 1950s and 1960s, the quality and quantity of information available to staff about agencies' work is high. Several members of staff working for the Senate Foreign Relations and House Foreign Affairs Committees, or their associated subcommittees, for example, were well-informed about (and alarmed by) the claims made by then Secretary of State Colin Powell in his testimony before this Committee's budget hearings of 2002, in which General Powell explained that Iraqi dictator, Saddam Hussein, had tried to acquire uranium from Niger. In the same testimony, Powell confirmed that President George W. Bush was correct to discuss the threat posed by an 'axis of evil', as President Reagan had in the 1980s. The Foreign Relations Committee had all the evidence that the White House could provide – but much of the evidence that Powell adduced was, in hindsight, at best misleading. Secrets are difficult to keep in Washington; they are nearly impossible to keep over more than the short-term from the extensive staff networks serving congressional commit-tees. Informal patterns of communication of this sort are essential for congressional oversight to be conducted effectively. The expertise, energy and time devoted by congressional committee staff to the maintenance of communications with officials in the Executive Branch acts both as a check on agencies and as a deterrent to their departing from Congress's intent.

The legislative veto

The legislative veto appears nowhere in the Constitution but was devised by Congress in 1932 to enable the president to reorganize executive departments and agencies subject to either House disapproving within sixty days. It has since been incorporated into much public law, typically providing for a period of sixty to ninety days after an executive action during which Congress might approve or reject it. The legislative veto power was lodged in different institutions by different laws: in the House or the Senate (a 'one-house' veto), in both chambers (a 'two-house' veto), in a particular committee, or even in a committee's chair.

A legislative veto on an agency having been effected and the agency's decision either approved or disapproved, the president has no further role: the Constitution's requirement that all legislation be presented to him for signature or veto does not apply to legislative vetoes. Legislative vetoes therefore enable Congress to exercise some control over the exec-utive without resorting to the passage of a new law. The balance is by no means wholly to the disadvantage of the executive: Congress has to act to nullify the executive's action; it may not amend those measures sent to it by the president; the president decides what is sent to it, and when. These are considerable advantages for presidents, especially when compared to the obstacles which their normal legislative proposals must surmount if they are to pass into law.

However, the failure to adhere to the presentment clause of Article I, Section 7, of the Constitution prompted the Supreme Court to declare in *Chadha v. Immigration and Naturalization Service* (1983) that the arrangement was unconstitutional. Arguments supporting it founded on considerations of 'efficiency' were, the Court declared, unsatisfactory, since the founders did not accord that notion high priority. Since it was partly to provide for a more efficient government than the Articles of Confederation that the founders convened at Philadelphia, this was an odd claim for the Court to make. The legislative veto does, indeed, invert the legislative process as specified in the Constitution: under it, the executive proposes rules which Congress has the opportunity to veto. It is not clear that the procedure subverts the Constitution. The legislative veto is better regarded as one of many instances by which procedures are adapted within the framework of the Constitution to cope with new circumstances and demands.

The legislative veto's value for Congress's oversight capacity and for the case with which the executive conducts its business are, in any case, so pronounced that the Court's cry of unconstitutionality has had little effect other than to call its own judgement into question. President Reagan initially approved of the Court's judgement in *Chadha*. However, the President came to recognize that, being denied the opportunity to review executive agency decisions, the Legislative Branch could, if it chose, restrict its delegations of power to the executive by number and scope, thereby hampering the executive. Deprived of the legislative veto or devices with the same practical effect, Congress would simply not delegate authority to the executive on terms which granted agencies any significant discretion.

In practice, however, Congress has both defied and circumvented the Court's decision. Between the judgement in *Chadha* (delivered in the summer of 1983) and the end of 2005, Congress defied the Court by writing more than 400 legislative vetoes into law: the Supreme Court had overreached itself, and Congress had both the incentive and the means with which to respond. With the grudging consent of the White House and agencies, Congress has also circumvented the judgement by arriving at informal understandings with agencies which the Supreme Court is powerless to prevent, but which constitute a substantial and effective means by which Congress can continue to share in the implementation of legislation.

Presidential control and the problems of bureaucracy

The bureaucracy serves two political masters, the Congress and the president, but is an imperfect servant. Those seeking to control the bureaucracy face a number of challenges, some of which are encountered both the Congress and the president, others only by the president. Formally, the president is the head of the civil service: he commands his Cabinet colleagues, as well as agency and bureau heads below Cabinet rank; each head of a department or agency directs both the political appointees and the career civil servants within their organization – so the chain of command is clear. Five challenges compromise this command structure:

(i)   *Hunkering down* (or bureaucratic obstructionism): career civil servants may choose to undermine the efforts of their political masters when the former reject the directions chosen by the latter. Tensions within the hybrid structure of the Senior Executive Service (SES) (as career and political officials work at the same grade, and often in the same offices), and between the SES and the Schedule C presidential appointments, are not uncommon. A high-water mark of bureaucratic resistance was the 1981 clash between career officials and the Reagan appointee asked to head the US Environmental Protection Agency (EPA), Anne Burford. The most senior career staff in the EPA at this time were, in many cases, lifelong advocates of environmentalism and committed to the 'mission' of the agency (Wilson, 1989). Burford, like the President, sought a 30 per cent cut in the EPA budget for 1981–82 (22 per cent cuts were achieved by 1983) and the lifting of regulations on business that she regarded as onerous. Accounts of the lengths to which EPA officials went to resist Burford's 'attack' on the EPA's mission are impressive in their ingenuity (McMahon: 2006).

(ii) *Going native*: Bob Haldeman, senior adviser to President Nixon, commented that the problem with the Cabinet and agency heads was the tendency to 'marry the natives'. Agency heads may become wedded to the mission of their organization. Rather than acting as the instrument of the president in leading the agency, they become the agency's advocate to him. Where agency mission is powerful (in agencies such as the EPA, with its corps of committed environmentalists at senior levels), or where professional norms are dominant (the Department of Justice; the Department of Defense), or where leaders are irresolute, agency heads may 'go native'. Or agency heads may simply disagree with their president and ignore his directives.

(iii) *The principal–agent problem*: this is a significant concern both for the President and for Congress. Effective leadership from the White House and effective oversight of the bureaucracy by Congress is predicated on the possession of good information. The principal (president or Congress) must be able effectively to monitor what its agent (department; agency; bureau) is doing. The problem arises when asymmetries of information exist such that the principal cannot monitor what the agent does. In exploiting such asymmetries the bureaucracy can resist, alter, or compromise the directives issued by the elected branches.

(iv) *What is the maximand?* In public-choice theory, it is a staple to assume that rational agents are maximizers. Accordingly, the challenge is to specify the maximand (that which they maximize). Public-choice scholars in the 1960s and 1970s argued that bureaucrats maximized their agency or department budget, a proxy for power to wield and resources to expend (Downs, 1955; Niskanen, 1971). Scholars within the public-choice field disagree about the maximand (Simon, 1947; Dunleavy, 1991), but agree that the autonomy of bureaucrats creates problems of control and permits waste and inefficiency.

(v) *Clientelism*: the bureaucracy may develop a symbiotic relationship with the groups whom they serve. As long ago as 1960, President Eisenhower warned in his farewell speech of the threat posed by a *military–industrial complex*. He worried that the defence establishment (defence contractors and their largest client – the federal government) had created a machine that would go of itself, with no brake on the growth of the military, because the economy would be increasingly dependent on this *complex* for economic growth. The President reasoned that neither the Department of Defense and its congressional parents, nor the defence contractors, had any incentive to reduce military expenditures.

Controlling and monitoring the bureaucracy represents a formidable challenge, and attempts at reform are often motivated by the related goals of reducing waste (and costs) and improving bureaucratic responsiveness. The achievement of either goal would be welcomed by many Americans, who consider the federal government and the executive bureaucracy to be a necessary evil. However, these same Americans favour limited government and rule by consent. As such, they may benefit from the limits placed by a largely apolitical bureaucracy on both the president and the Congress. In such circumstances, the bureaucracy is, in the Washington lexicon, 'captured' by its clients.

Conclusion

The president's influence over Congress, and hence his control over the legislative process, is limited by the separation of the legislature from the executive. Separation constitutes a major limitation on the president's authority and on his power, because Article II grants to the president no legislative powers beyond those of being permitted 'from time to time' to recommend measures to Congress, to call Congress into special session and the qualified right of veto. The Constitution does, however, explicitly grant him executive powers, as under Article II: 'The Executive Power shall be vested in a President of the United States of America'.

At first sight, nothing could be clearer: the grant of power is his alone, and (except in respect of the Senate's obligation to consider presidential appointments to senior government posts) unqualified. Even where it is explicit, however, the Constitution does not dispose of political problems. In practice, the apparently unfettered power granted to the president over the executive departments by Article II, Section 2, of the Constitution is highly constrained. Large and fragmented federal departments comprising functionally-differentiated agencies are, in many cases, as much the creatures of Congress and interest group clients as of the presidency, and in other cases effectively independent. Clientelism is a prominent characteristic of some federal agencies, and one that presidents have constantly to confront when deciding how they can best implement the programmes which they have succeeded in persuading Congress to pass into law.

The administrative complexities of modern American government do not fit the eighteenth-century Constitution. The framers could not, and did not, anticipate that the federal government could, or would, assume a large role in managing the national economy; in protecting, however imperfectly, its citizens from penury and sickness in old age; or in placing a rudimentary welfare net beneath the poor. Neither could the framers have expected the United States to expand to a nation of 312 million people, to assemble the most powerful military forces in the history of the world, or to become the largest (and for a time, the hegemonic) global economy. All these functions require vast expenditure of public money and the services of many millions of bureaucrats in departments and agencies of federal, state and local governments. Controlling programmes administered by bureaucrats is therefore of central importance to democrats.

The United States federal government is divided, decentralized and fragmented. Executive departments owe their existence to Acts of Congress, and their maintenance to congressional appropriations. The federal governing process in the United States accordingly comprises, in part, a struggle for control over the many functional islands of the federal bureaucracy by the presidency, Congress, the courts, the departments within which individual agencies are placed and the clients whom the agencies serve.

Chapter 10

Federalism and Intergovernmental Policy-Making

Federalism is a core constitutional principle affirmed in the Tenth Amendment to the Constitution. This amendment reflects an American wariness of government in general, and antipathy to a unitary state. Further, it denotes the need to establish criteria for allocating powers to different levels of government without, in fact, determining them. Since ratification of the Tenth Amendment, the authority, capacity and power of the federal government have been augmented beyond recognition but a unitary state has not emerged. Yet, while states retain elements of their sovereignty, their autonomy from the federal government is heavily circumscribed. The states' constitutional standing has weakened since 1937, when the Supreme Court upheld the authority of the US Congress under Article 1, Section 8, of the Constitution to regulate commercial activity effectively without limit. The widespread perceived failure of federal education, welfare and urban initiatives of both the Great Society of the 1960s and the successor programmes of the 1970s weakened Congress's will to act progressively. The 1980s were marked by President Reagan's attempt to shift power from the federal government to the states, and the 1990s by an especially sharp reaction against federal government power following the Republicans' victory in the 1994 mid-term elections. Republican control of both the presidency and Congress between 2001 and 2007 resulted not only in a dominance of States' Rights rhetoric but also of the continued extension and deepening of federal authority, capacity and power. President Obama has not established an overarching vision of the federal–state relationship.

However, in the case of both President George W. Bush and President Obama, the events of 9/11 and the financial and economic crises of 2008 and beyond have elicited responses at the federal level that permitted little scope for placing federalism at the heart of a presidential policy agenda.

Federalism: theory and structure

Although the word 'federalism' does not appear in the Constitution, the document is animated by the concept. Federalism is fundamental to understanding the structure and operation of government in the United States: the Constitution of 1789 replaced the Articles of Confederation, which had provided for a frail centre and powerful states, by a new federal republic. Under the new regime, the federal government was granted autonomy from the states, which the Articles of Confederation had denied to its predecessor. However, the Constitution also afforded the states and localities powerful influence on the new federal government through their representation in Congress.

Social, geographical, ethnic, economic and political diversity, coupled with the great expanse of the thirteen states, required a federal Constitution. Without it, there could not have been a 'United States': the contested meaning of the term enabled proponents and opponents of the proposed republic to find different constructions and implications in its use. Anti-federalists attacked the essence of the proposed new political order that the Philadelphia Convention had asked state conventions to ratify. Their perception was that the Founders (who for the sake of rhetorical advantage mischievously described themselves as 'Federalists') had, in seven short Articles, created not a federation but a national government. For reasons that George III had taught Americans thoroughly, such an arrangement was to be resisted. In order to assuage fears of an excessively powerful central government, the new Constitution's proponents agreed to the adoption of a Bill of Rights, including the flexible Tenth Amendment.

After ratification, dispute persisted over just what had been created. The Constitution's brevity and imprecision did not assist the dispute's resolution. Sovereignty was not unambiguously placed in the people, the states, or the new federal government. Divisions arose. Alexander Hamilton and John Marshall (Secretary of State under Adams, and later Chief Justice) interpreted the Constitution as a broadly nationalist document by which a national government's few enumerated powers were supplemented by implied powers both broad and deep. Hamilton approvingly detected the possibility of a powerful central government in the elasticity of the powers granted to it in Article I. By contrast, Madison and Jefferson (and much later, in starker form, John C. Calhoun) inter-preted it as a compact between states, in each of whom sovereignty resided after 1789 as it had done before. Madison claimed in *Federalist No. 45* that:

> The powers delegated by the proposed Constitution to the federal government are few and defined. Those which are to remain in the State governments are numerous and indefinite.

The Constitution did more than define a ring in which federal and state governments might compete. Some powers were exclusively those of the federal authorities (foreign and defence policy, monetary policy, and the maintenance of a postal service). Others, including the granting of titles of nobility and the passage of *ex post facto* laws, were denied to federal and state governments. Others powers were granted to Congress but not denied to the states; in these cases, Congress retains the power to pre-empt state action by reason of the Constitution's provision for the supremacy of federal over state law in the event of collision. Other powers (including, for example, the maintenance of troops in peacetime) may be exercised by state governments only if Congress permits. Although 'dual federalism' (see Exhibit 10.1) explains more about the division of powers between the federal government and those of the states in the late eighteenth century than in the early twenty-first, some powers were concurrent from the first.

The Federalists provided less for a national government than for the possibility of its being created. In practice, the federal government now has most of the Constitutional powers of a fully national government. Such freedom to act, such sovereignty as the states retain, is theirs only because the United States Congress permits it. Under Article I, Section 8, of the Constitution, Congress has effectively unfettered power over many areas of public policy: the major exceptions are individual rights unambiguously protected by the Bill of Rights and the Thirteenth, Fourteenth and Fifteenth Amendments, together with the states' consti-tutional right to tax and the immutability of their borders. Otherwise, the constitutional guarantee to the states of sovereignty is now, accord-ing to the Supreme Court, in the gift of Congress. That is not an arrangement for which the framers provided, but it is one that the United States has.

Appendix 3 records the Constitution's guarantees to, and limitations on, the states. This definition leaves unaddressed questions of the Fourteenth Amendment, the commerce clause, and the 'necessary and proper' clause. They will be dealt with in the section below on the consti-tutional law of federalism.

Units of government

States and cities evoke loyalties from their citizens which, for example, congressional districts do not. The famous *New Yorker* cartoon cover portraying New York City as both America's and the world's centre speaks to an important truth not just about that pre-eminent city, but about the dominance of local cultures and politics in the perceptions of Americans. The Jeffersonian tenet that 'all authority resides in the people', retains a strong force in American political culture which is, itself, characterized in part by localism's persistence (Wolman, 1996: 160). The federal government was, in 2012, one of no fewer than 89,004 governments in the United States. Those governments fall into eight categories: federal government; state governments; county, borough and parish governments; city governments, township governments, school district governments, special district governments and regional governments.

Federal government: The federal government is the national government of the United States and the prime subject of this book. Divided into three branches, the federal government was established by the ceding of powers by state governments under the Constitution ratified in 1789.

State governments: There are fifty state governments, each of which is guaranteed a Republican form of government, certain rights and (limited) sovereignty by the Constitution of the United States. Each has its own Constitution (the fact of which, according to a survey conducted for the Advisory Commission on Intergovernmental Relations in 1992, 52 per cent of adult Americans were unaware) and government established under it. The District of Columbia, the Commonwealth of Puerto Rico, Guam, the Virgin Islands and American Samoa are not states, but have certain powers of self-government and send non-voting delegates (not representatives) to the US House of Representatives.

In *Atkins v Kansas* (1903), the Chief Justice of the Iowa Supreme Court, Judge John F. Dillon, determined that local governments:

> are the creatures, mere political subdivisions, of the state for the purpose of exercising a part of its powers. They may exert only such powers as are expressly granted to them or such as may be necessarily implied from those granted.

This judgement, 'Dillon's Rule', holds that sub-state-level governments derive their authority from the state and do not possess it in their own right. Though consistently upheld in constitutional law, its practical application is complicated. Dillon's Rule has prevented neither state governments from granting to their local governments measures of home rule, nor federal and state governments from vesting in local governments responsibilities for delivering specified services to local citizens. The former is merely a devolution of authority from state capitals to cities. Relationships of local to state government are therefore different from those between state and federal government: the latter is a federal relationship; the former, unitary. Different states devolve differing amounts of local autonomy (or 'home rule') to local governments. Some devolve substantial home rule powers to cities with regard to the structure of city governments; some devolve such powers to cities with regard to the functions that they may undertake; and some devolve such powers to cities with regard to personnel policies. States also differ in the amount and type of power which they devolve to counties. The practical force of Dillon's Rule is therefore contingent (see Hanson, 1996: 65).

County, borough and parish governments: The *Census of Governments* conducted by the US Bureau of the Census in 2012 recorded 3,031 county, borough and parish governments. All states designate them 'counties' except Alaska and Louisiana, where they are termed 'boroughs' and 'parishes', respectively. They are local governments and judicial districts organized under each state constitution, and generally have a wide range of responsibilities.

City governments: The responsibilities of the 19,522 American cities typically include fire, police, street maintenance and cleaning, water and sewerage services, public works, libraries, inspection and regulation of a wide range of commercial activities, health and welfare. Cities may coincide with county boundaries, or spread across them; larger cities often form part of a 'metropolitan area'.

Township governments: There are more than 16,364 townships in twenty states, but they constitute significant governments in only eleven. Concentrated in the old Progressive states of Minnesota and Wisconsin, in New York and the states of New England, the functions of township governments are concentrated in police, highways, parks and recreation, and refuse collection services.

School district governments: Local control is commonly, if not altogether accurately, regarded as the most distinctive institutional characteristic of education policy in the United States; 12,884 elected school district governments are its institutional expression. In most states, these single-purpose governments provide substantial independence in both administration and revenue-raising. The federal government accounts for between 9 per cent and 10 per cent of total expenditure on elementary and secondary education, the remainder being split (to differing degrees in different states) between state and local sources.

Special district governments: The 37,203 special districts (2012 data) are local governments which have a single (or few) purposes established under state law. They include authorities, boards and commissions; and states have various rules governing their creation. Their functions include the operation of local parks, hospitals and public housing, and the regulation of specialized aspects of local agriculture or commerce.

Regional governments: Regional governments have frequently been established by two or more state or local governments to administer regional policies and public facilities, especially in public transport.

The development of the constitutional law of federalism

As powers were not definitively allocated between the federal government and the states in the debates at the Philadelphia Convention, or the constitutional text itself, or during the discussion of the proposed Constitution in *The Federalist Papers*, it fell to the Supreme Court to play a part in doing so. In *Ware v Hylton* (1796), the Court invalidated a Virginia statute that erased pre-revolutionary debts of British creditors. Ironically, John Marshall argued the case for the debtors, but he failed to persuade the Court, whose judgement rested on Article VI, Section 2, of the Constitution – that treaties should be supreme over state laws. Since *Ware*, many Supreme Court cases have concerned, either directly or indirectly, federal powers over the states, and state powers over US citizens, to whom the Fourteenth Amendment guaranteed due process and equality in law. The incorporation of the Bill of Rights within the Fourteenth Amendment (see Chapter 1) has been one of the most important developments in the constitutional law of federalism in the twentieth century.

Establishment of the federal government's supremacy

In 1810, the Marshall Court acted to prevent states impairing contracts in *Fletcher v. Peck*, and in the case of *Dartmouth College v Woodward* (1819) to prevent states from impairing charters. Their significance lay in the use of federal judicial power to limit the states' freedom of action against private property – in the first case, of individuals; in the second, of corporations. However, much the most important case concerning federal powers arising under Marshall's Chief Justiceship was *McCulloch v Maryland* (1819). *McCulloch* addressed the question of whether the Constitution gave Congress the authority to incorporate a bank (the Bank of the United States) and whether a state government (Maryland) could tax it. The issue had divided politicians from the

Republic's first year, when President Washington first sought his colleagues' opinions. Hamilton claimed that the bank's establishment was constitutional; Jefferson initially disagreed. In finding that Congress had the authority to create such a bank under its implied and resultant powers, Marshall provoked a controversy that went well beyond the confines of the immediate case: the constitutionality of federally-sponsored internal canal and road improvements was disputed and its political appeal waned as nationalist sentiment faded after the war of 1812.

Federal powers to regulate commerce were first addressed by the Court in *Gibbons v Ogden* (1824). The case arose because the Constitution's grant of power to Congress 'to regulate commerce with foreign nations, and among the several States, and with the Indian tribes' defined neither 'interstate commerce', nor the extent of Congress's power. Marshall's opinion in *Gibbons* was plain: Congress did, indeed, have the power of commercial regulation between the states and there was no clearer case of it than the regulation of navigation in the Federal Coasting Act of 1793, designed for the licensing of ships engaged in interstate coastal traffic. In such circumstances, the federal regulatory power overrode that of the states.

Federal power and the interstate commerce clause

Notwithstanding the growth of federal regulation between the Interstate Commerce Commission's establishment in 1887 and World War I, most Supreme Court justices found dual federalism a persuasive doctrine until the 1930s. The doctrine's application struck at the heart of the New Deal, and embroiled President, Congress and Court in constitutional crisis. Three judgements attacked the heart of President Roosevelt's programme. The issue at stake in the first two remained congressional scope under the 'interstate commerce' and 'necessary and proper' clauses; that in the third concerned Congress's power to tax.

1. *Schechter Poultry Corporation v United States* (1935) concerned the code regulating wage rates and working hours of workers in the poultry industry in New York, and the production and sale of poultry. The case itself was trivial, concerning a sale which, under the authority of the National Industrial Recovery Act, was deemed by federal authorities to violate the code's rules. However, the implications of the Court's unanimous finding for the plaintiffs were, potentially, momentous. In judging that 'the authority of the Federal government may not be pushed to such an extreme as to destroy the distinction, which the commerce clause itself establishes, between commerce "among the several States" and the internal concerns of a

Exhibit 10.1 Varieties of Federalism

Confederation: the first form of government in the United States, in which authority resides with sub-national governments and the national government has authority only in those areas where the sub-national government has yielded it.

Federation: the Latin root of the word is *foedus*, meaning 'agreement' or 'partnership'. Power resides ultimately with sub-national government but an agreement is created in the form of a constitution permitting the transfer of some, but not all, power to a national government. Unlike a confederation, sovereignty is now shared between national and sub-national levels. In the United States, the Constitution specified a number of exclusive powers that would be wielded solely by the newly-created national (federal) government. The Tenth Amendment, added two years after the creation of the Constitution, stated that those powers not expressly granted to the national (federal) government would reside with the states and with the people. Since the ratification of the Tenth Amendment in 1791, the balance between the federal and state government has moved in both directions but, since the early twentieth-century, the federal government has grown in authority, capacity and power.

Dual Federalism: the model of federalism which endured from the crafting of the Constitution until the New Deal era in the 1930s in which the national and state governments are partners in a federal system sharing sovereignty. Each partner exercises sovereignty in separate spheres of government with a clear boundary between spheres. Dual federalism most closely approximates to the *States' Rights* view of federalism, in which states are the equal of the federal government. Morton Grodzins (1966) described this type of federalism as *layer-cake* because of the clear delineation between state and federal governments.

Cooperative Federalism: Grodzins used the term '*marble-cake* federalism' to describe the relationship between national and sub-national governments. The clearly-defined boundary between the states and the federal

➔

State', the Court found that 'the Federal Constitution does not provide for it', and thereby found the National Industrial Recovery Act to rest on an unconstitutional extension of the interstate commerce power.

2. *United States v Butler* (1936) concerned the constitutionality of the Agricultural Adjustment Act of 1933 which turned on the federal government's regulatory authority deriving from its general powers

→

government was gone, replaced by an increased intervention by the federal government within states and by a much greater reliance by the states on the funding flowing from federal government coffers. The aftermath of the Wall Street Crash of October 1929 and the growth of federal government during the New Deal era, with the federal government creating government programmes intended to alleviate poverty and to stimulate economic growth, combined with US entry into World War II, and the Cold War that followed, led to a huge expansion in the role of federal government and its reach into the states. As with marble-cake, the boundary between national and sub-national government was no longer easy to discern: federal 'grants-in-aid' flowed from the centre to the states and were 'categorical' grants with funds earmarked for specific purposes. States did not exercise discretion in the disbursement of federal funds. Roosevelt's New Deal and Johnson's Great Society represent the high-water marks of cooperative federalism. (The Great Society has been characterized as creative federalism – a sub-set of cooperative federalism – to make the first occasion in the history of the United States that the federal government was used as a tool explicitly to tackle poverty and inequality.)

New Federalism: in 1969, Republican President Richard Nixon ascended to the presidency and ushered in another chapter in the history of federalism. New Federalism marked the beginnings of an attempt to return authority to the states, or at least to give the appearance of doing so. Nixon sought to persuade Congress to replace the categorical grants of the Franklin D. Roosevelt and Johnson years with *block grants*, whereby federal funds were given to states but with fewer conditions attached to their use. Greater fiscal autonomy was granted to the states but the federal government continued to provide most of the funding. President Reagan's New Federalism resembled Nixon's in spirit, but his policy instrument differed. Reagan sought to shrink the size of federal government through a combination of tax cuts and spending cuts. However, while the states valued the autonomy given to them by the Reagan administration, the cuts in federal funding created fiscal difficulties for states that had become heavily reliant on revenue flows from Washington.

of taxation and expenditure. Basing his judgement on a simple premise of dual federalism (which he thought it 'hardly necessary to reiterate', but did), Justice Roberts wrote a confused opinion, claiming that no power was specifically delegated to Congress to regulate agricultural production, and that the Tenth Amendment therefore forbade any such power. The general power to tax and spend could not justify compliance with a regulatory act that the Constitution did not permit. To argue otherwise would, Roberts claimed, be to acquiesce in the obliteration of the independence of the individual states, with the consequence that the United States would be:

> converted into a central government exercising uncontrolled police power in every state of the Union, superseding all local control or regulation of the affairs or concerns of the states.

3. *Carter v Carter Coal Company* (1936) concerned a challenge to the Bituminous Coal Conservation Act's regulation of prices and wages in the soft coal industry. The regulation was overturned on the grounds that local production of a good or mineral was distinct from its disposal or marketing in interstate commerce. The Court held that where *Schechter* concerned the attempted regulation of a good after it had passed through interstate commerce, *Carter* concerned its production prior to such passage, but that the latter was no more a part of interstate commerce than the former.

Thus, the Court reached the pinnacle of judicial activism in substituting its judgement about policy for that of Congress in the guise of policing the boundaries between Federal and State action. Justice Stone, dissenting with Brandeis and Cardozo, implicitly rejected Roberts's simplistic model of dual federalism that economic depression, the federal government's immense revenue-raising powers and the New Deal's consequential revision of intergovernmental fiscal relations had changed. Stone wrote that the power to tax and spend in promotion of the general welfare belonged to Congress, and that 'the power to tax and spend includes the power to relieve a nationwide economic maladjustment by conditional gifts of money'.

It was the Court's conservative and interventionist judgements in these three cases that prompted Roosevelt to make his 'Court-packing' proposal in 1937 (discussed in Chapter 7) which, while unsuccessful, nonetheless intimidated the Court to the extent that Justices Roberts and Hughes retreated in the face of Roosevelt's confronting the Court. In *West Coast Hotel Company v Parrish* (1937), the constitutionality of state minimum wage laws was upheld over the dissents of Justices Sutherland, Devanter, Butler and McReynolds. Two cases decided on the same day in 1937 upheld the constitutionality of different parts of the Social Security Act of 1935, the foundation of old age insurance (and, from 1965 onwards, of Medicare): in *Charles C. Steward Machine Co. v Davis* and *Helvering v Davis* the Court dealt, respectively, with a payroll tax and unemployment compensation, and with retirement benefits. Relying on a broad interpretation of the general welfare clause of Article I, Section 8, the Court upheld its constitutionality, and also found in the former case that federal funds used to assist states in the administration of unemployment laws constituted not coercion of the states, but merely an inducement to them.

Earlier that year, the Court had upheld the constitutionality of the National Labor Relations Act in *National Labor Relations Board v Jones & Laughlin Steel Corporation*, although only over the dissenting opinions of the four conservative members of the bench. Activist opposition was weaker in *United States v Carolene Products Company* (1938), where the constitutionality of the Filled Milk Act of 1923 prohibiting interstate trade in adulterated milk was upheld. The importance of the case lies less in its facts than it does in Justice Stone's 'preferred freedoms' declaration in the fourth footnote. Following Cardozo's opinion in *Palko v Connecticut* (1937), Stone distinguished between property rights and civil rights. Regulation of commerce would, he wrote, henceforth be presumed constitutional unless it plainly was not. However, legislation which concerned freedoms protected by the Bill of Rights would not be so presumed:

> There may be narrower scope for operation of the presumption of constitutionality when legislation appears on its face to be within a specific prohibition of the constitution, such as those of the first ten amendments, which are deemed equally specific when held to be embraced within the Fourteenth. (*United States v Carolene Products Company* (1938))

Congress's scope for commercial regulation (the interstate commerce clause notwithstanding) was thereby extended, but differentiated from citizenship rights which were accorded special protection. *Carolene* heralded the Court's confirmation of its presumption of the constitutionality of federal laws addressing economic, financial and commercial policy, broadly construed. By 1941, all four conservative justices who had reacted against the New Deal had retired. Following *West Coast Hotel* and *Carolene*, Roosevelt's attempt to legitimate national direction of American politics through presidential leadership of Congress won the Court's unqualified approval.

For the doctrine of dual sovereignty, and the associated retention of certain commercial powers by the states, the implications were plain:

1. In *United States v Darby Lumber Company* (1941), the Court unanimously upheld Congress's right to prohibit the shipment in interstate commerce of goods produced by children, thereby overruling *Hammer v Dagenhart* (1918).
2. In *Wickard v Filburn* (1942), the Court upheld the executive's power to set acreage quotas for wheat even where none was distributed in interstate commerce.

3. The Court's judgement in *American Power and Light v SEC* (1946) completed what *Wickard* had hastened: defining the 'interstate commerce' power was a matter for Congress and not the courts: 'The power', the Court held, 'is as broad as the economic needs of the nation'. The case symbolized the realization of federal supremacy over the states in commercial and economic policy.

The 'interstate commerce' and 'necessary and proper' clauses were used by the Court to sustain the constitutionality of the public accommodation sections in Title II of the Civil Rights Act of 1964 in *Heart of Atlanta Motel Inc. v United States* (1964) and *Katzenbach v McClung* (1964). The Court chose this route because it was thereby enabled to consider the question of racial discrimination in public facilities without confronting the broader question of whether the Fourteenth Amendment could be held to apply not only to state governments, but also to private persons and businesses. In *Heart of Atlanta Motel*, the Court held that:

> the action of the Congress in the adoption of the Act as applied here to a motel which concededly serves interstate travelers is within the power granted it by the Commerce Clause of the Constitution.

In *Katzenbach*, the Court judged that Mr Ollie McClung was engaged in interstate commerce by virtue of his purchasing 46 per cent of the meat used in the kitchen of his barbecue restaurant on the southside of Birmingham from beyond the borders of the state of Alabama. Accordingly, Mr. McClung was accordingly engaged in interstate commerce.

The reasoning in this case was scarcely compelling. Commercial considerations were not a significant motivation in the passage of the Civil Rights Act of 1964. President Johnson and a majority in Congress intended the Act to expunge racial segregation in the South, and thereby asserted the supremacy of Federal over States' Rights. Nevertheless, the import of the Court's judgement in *McClung* was intentionally clear: if the appellant could be compelled to integrate his restaurant in Birmingham on the grounds of interstate commerce, so could all owners of public facilities. A century after the Fourteenth Amendment, federal power over the states in civil rights was at last unambiguously enforced. Mr McClung understood that implication: within hours of the Court handing down the judgement on 14 December 1964, he agreed to serve African-American customers.

Whereas the interstate commerce and 'necessary and proper' clauses were previously constraints on Congress, after 1937 the Court viewed them as licences. In this regard, the constitutional law of interstate commerce's development was effectively complete with the judgement in favour of the federal regulatory authority in *American Power and Light v SEC* in 1946. The Court's reasoning there constrained Warren and his colleagues to decide *McClung* as they did, once the interstate commerce power was selected as the ground for determining the case. Since 1937, there has been only one significant departure from the principle that the 'interstate commerce' and 'necessary and proper' clauses were for Congress to define, and the view that dual sovereignty had no force: in 1976, Rehnquist wrote the opinion for a split Court in *National League of Cities v Usery*, 426 US 833. Rehnquist declared amendments to the Fair Labor Standards Act extending regulation of earnings and hours to employees of state and city governments unconstitutional.

The Court's protection in *Usery* of governmental functions integral to the operations of state and local government survived for just eight years. By a majority of 5–4, the Court in *Garcia v San Antonio Metropolitan Transit Authority* (1985) overturned *Usery*, finding that restraints on Congress's use of its powers under interstate commerce were political, rather than judicial.

It is, nevertheless, *Usery*, rather than *Garcia*, that is the exception in federal constitutional law since *Garcia* (1937) accords with the preferred freedoms doctrine of Justices Cardozo and Stone in *Palko* and *Carolene*, and of the right of Congress to define the nature and limits of interstate commerce. Such institutional abstention might well make for unsatisfactory constitutional law but, nonetheless, has dominated the Court's thinking on federalism for the best part of a century. For that reason, the importance of *Garcia* is frequently exaggerated (though the costs to state and local government of complying with the judgement were estimated at between \$2 billion and \$4 billion). Blackmun's reasoning in the case was implicit in all but one of the Court's judgements on interstate commerce after *West Coast Hotel*. There remains the tension between, on the one hand, the Court's claiming the power to strike down violations of the commerce clause and, on the other, the Court usually declining to strike down any provisions. It is unclear that either of two significant cases that followed *Garcia* represented a reversal of the position taken by the Court in 1937. In *New York v US* (1992), the Court overturned a key provision of the 1985 Radioactive Waste Policy Act (that had required states to dispose of their waste in the manner specified in this law) on the grounds that the law exceeded the powers granted to Congress under the commerce clause. Justice Sandra Day O'Connor, writing for the majority, argued that the law violated a 'core of state sovereignty' protected by the Tenth Amendment. Justice White, joined by Justices Stevens and Blackmun, wrote a dissenting opinion in which he argued that the law was an example of cooperative federalism in action. Neither is it clear that the

Court's 5–4 decision in *United States v Lopez* (1995) – by which it struck down, as an unconstitutional exercise of the commerce power, Congress's prohibition of the carrying of firearms within 1,000 feet of a school – has the broad implications that some contemporary commentators claimed. Although the *Lopez* judgement was the first since *Carter v Carter Coal Co.* in 1936 in which the Court had held Congress to have exceeded the limits of the interstate commerce power, Justice Thomas was the only member of the Court explicitly to urge the adoption of a much more restrictive understanding of the commerce clause's application.

The decision in *Printz v US* (1997), which struck down elements of the 1997 Brady Handgun Violence Prevention Act, was heralded by some commentators as the beginnings of a judicial revolution. In practice, its effects have been less than that term would imply. Despite the confirmation of two of President George W. Bush's nominees – Justice Samuel Alito and Chief Justice John Roberts – there has been no general or durable shift of the Court towards States' Rights in relation to the interpretation of the commerce clause. The successful confirmation of President Obama's nominees to the Court in 2009 and 2010 has reduced further the prospect of a judicial revolution.

Federalism, civil rights and criminal procedure

The long struggles in the federal courts for the establishment of civil rights notionally guaranteed by the Fifteenth Amendment were examined in Chapter 7. All the cases discussed there have importance for the subject of this chapter – the balance between federal and state power: *Smith v Allwright* (1944), *Baker v Carr* (1962), *Reynolds v Sims* (1964), *Wesberry v Sanders* (1964) and *South Carolina v Katzenbach* (1965), together, ended dualist federalism in civil and voting rights, made state governments more representative, disposed of States' Rights arguments in defence of segregation, and federalized them in law and practice.

Similarly, in rights of the accused, the Warren Court presided over a significant extension of federal standards to the states. In *Mapp v Ohio* (1961) and *Ker v California* (1962), the Court established a position towards which it had moved for some time – that the Fourteenth Amendment incorporated procedural rights of accused people. These two cases had the highly significant consequence that procedures under which state police and authorities searched private property and seized evidence as part of a criminal investigation must conform to federal constitutional standards. Evidence presented in state criminal cases which did not was thereafter ruled inadmissible (although later cases under Burger and Rehnquist weakened the rule).

In *Malloy v Hogan, Sheriff* (1964) and *Griffin v California* (1965), the Court reversed its long-standing position that the Fifth Amendment right against self-incrimination applied only to federal, and not state, authorities: the Fifth Amendment was incorporated into the Fourteenth. Similar incorporation occurred regarding the rights of accused people to a defence counsel 'in all criminal prosecutions', as specified in the Sixth Amendment. *Gideon v Wainwright* (1963) overturned *Betts v Brady* (1942) by extending the guarantee of legal representation to indigent people charged with serious crimes under state law. The Fourteenth Amendment's reach was extended still further in 1972 under Chief Justice Burger, when in *Argersinger v Hamlin* the Court held that accused individuals were entitled to a defence counsel in all cases where imprisonment might follow conviction. *Miranda v Arizona* (1966) set rigorous federal procedural standards for the admission of evidence through confession in state criminal trials, thereby guaranteeing compliance with the Fifth Amendment's protection against self-incrimination.

In personal morality and privacy, too, the ability of state governments to prohibit contraceptives and abortion were, respectively, struck down and restricted by the Court in *Griswold v Connecticut* (1965) and *Roe v Wade* (1973). The latter overturned state laws restricting abortion in the first three months of pregnancy, while *Webster v Reproductive Health Services* (1989) limited *Roe*'s scope by upholding five provisions of a Missouri statute regulating the circumstances under which late abortions should be performed, and banning the use of public employees and facilities to perform abortions not necessary to save the mother's life; the Court thereby granted greater scope to the state legislatures to determine abortion policy. In these cases, the Court wrestled with difficult and contentious cases of personal freedom, but the cases also concerned federal–state relations. Whereas the (heavily Catholic) state of Connecticut had prohibited the use of contraceptives, other states had not; in *Griswold*, the Court struck down all state restrictions in favour of a right to privacy which it thought implicit in the Ninth Amendment.

Divisions within the Court over the litmus test – those cases relating to the *Roe* decision – continue to serve as a useful guide to the liberal–conservative split within the Court, and to the attitude of each justice to the balance between federal and state power. Consideration of the cases above, and of later cases including *Casey* (1992), *Stenberg* (2000) and *Gonzalez* (2007) discussed in Chapter 7 (Exhibit 7.3) show the Court once again confronting questions of privacy and individual rights; of whether the federal courts or state legislatures should judge them; and of such judgements' permissible boundaries.

Federalism: structure and process of intergovernmental fiscal and policy relations

Constitutional law supplies only the framework within which relations between the three levels of government in the United States are conducted. The substance comprises their interaction in the formation, legitimation, implementation and evaluation of public policy. Federal, state, and local politics meet in Congress with the legitimation of policy despite the formal exclusion of state and local governments from the federal legislative process. Yet, the House of Representatives comprises politicians elected from single-member districts, whose electoral fortunes depend heavily on their sensitivity to local opinion in order to deter otherwise plausible opponents. Combined with a congressional committee system which divides legislative labour by function corresponding with district, state, or regional interests, local influence on federal legislation is assured, as successful white southern resistance to civil rights initiatives until the 1960s shows. However, three layers of government provide opportunities to reformists as well as to conservatives. Denied redress by state government, the civil rights movement turned to parts of the federal government. Northern congressmen and senators provided one audience, but alone they were insufficiently strong. Black groups and individuals accordingly turned to the Supreme Court (southern state courts and federal courts in the southern states were barriers, not openings), and later to the federal executive.

Mixing of the three levels is as evident in policy implementation as in formation. Most programmes authorized and appropriated by the federal government are not implemented by them directly, but by state and local governments. The latter are also required to meet much of the cost of federal programmes which they administer from state and local taxpayers: Medicaid, the federal programme that pays the hospital costs of some of the poor, is an example. As power in Washington is less separated than shared by separated institutions, so the formulation and implementation of most policy is less separated into discrete federal and state functions than shared by them. Most policy areas involve all three layers of government in their formation and implementation. Even foreign and defence policy, constitutionally the preserve of the federal government, is influenced by regional, state and local considerations.

Intergovernmental fiscal relations

Measured by their revenue bases, their capacities and will in the making of public policy, the three levels' relative importance has changed during the twentieth century. In 1933, the federal government spent the least of all three levels of government. By 1978, it spent nearly twice as much as the two lower levels combined (some 64.4 per cent of all government spending), and more than 500 federal programmes providing grants to state and local governments had been established. By 2012, despite the rhetorical commitments of successive presidents to rebalancing powers, resources and capacity from the federal government to the states, the federal share had increased to 81.0 per cent. As the major changes by the Supreme Court between 1937 and 1946 weakened the standing of the states in constitutional law, so growing fiscal dependency further reduced the extent to which the states could plausibly claim to be sovereign. Financing public services delivered locally from a mixture of federal, state and local taxes nullified the doctrine of dual sovereignty, and established that of interactive federalism, combining shifting elements of cooperation and conflict.

The potential for the expansion of the federal government's revenue base can be dated precisely to 3 February 1913, when ratification of the Sixteenth Amendment to the constitution offered the federal government the prospect of a major new revenue stream from a federal income tax.

The Sixteenth Amendment presaged a shift from local governments' dominance of revenue-raising. Prior to its ratification, local governments accounted for 59 per cent of aggregate government expenditure, and the states for 6 per cent. By 1936, four years into Roosevelt's presidency, these figures had altered, to 36 per cent and 14 per cent, respectively, and by 1970, a year into Richard Nixon's presidency, to 23 per cent and 13 per cent. (In wartime, the balance shifted sharply and temporarily against sub-federal governments, because the federal government has responsibility for all national expenditure on national defence. In World War II, that huge and rapid change resulted in federal agencies accounting for 90 per cent of all government spending by 1944, the year of the Allied invasion of northern Europe.)

The central difficulty in domestic policy is, as Walter Heller, a former Chairman of the Council of Economic Advisors, once expressed it, that 'prosperity gives the national government the affluence and the local government the effluents'. Problems occur locally, be they homeless and drug-dependent youth of northern cities, unemployed former coal-miners of Appalachia, farmers in remote mid-western towns bankrupted by low grain prices, or inadequate public education in in urban and rural areas. Local and state governments have a more rigid fiscal base than the federal government, and different taxes have different buoyancies. Income taxes provide most of the federal government's revenue; sales taxes are the main source for the states; and property taxes are the mainstay of local governments, especially for local school districts. Apart from the direct and indirect effects of the Sixteenth Amendment, taxes on income are buoyant, especially in times of inflation: as taxable income rises, so does total revenue. If the tax system is progressive, a rise in taxable income will produce a disproportionately large rise in government revenue. By contrast, a rise in general income levels does not produce a proportionate increase in sales taxation. Thus, the greater the extent to which a government relies on income taxes, the greater the revenue increase it can obtain without the (politically unwelcome) step of raising tax rates. By contrast, property tax rates have to be increased if revenue from property taxes is to increase faster than the rate of economic growth.

Dillon's Rule has significance for attempts by states to broaden local governments' revenue bases, and so to revitalize relations between them and the states. Thirty-six states authorize local sales taxes; thirteen permit income levies for certain local governments; forty-eight allow local tax increment financing; and twenty-eight facilitate local government access to bond markets. This revitalization has occurred as prospects for growth of federal assistance to states and localities have dimmed. From Roosevelt's presidency to Carter's, state and local government programmes were increasingly financed by federal authorities. In March 1933, federal grants to state and local governments accounted for only 1.5 per cent of state and local expenditure; in Carter's second year, they accounted for 26.2 per cent. Federal grants made direct to local governments (circumventing state governments) accounted for 2.5 per cent of local revenue in 1955 and 17.5 per cent in 1978, by which time direct aid accounted for one-quarter of all federal grants. Since 1979, such fiscal dependence has broadly stabilized (see Table 10.1).

Enhancement of federal fiscal resources notwithstanding, most public services were, at the end of Herbert Hoover's presidency in 1933, delivered and financed by state and local governments; Federal grants-in-aid mattered only at the margins. Hoover left the presidency and Roosevelt entered it in circumstances of deep national economic crisis which had inflicted major fiscal damage on governments at all levels. Revenue fell as GNP halved in three years. State governments, responding in part to the requirements of most state constitutions that their budgets be balanced, coped by reducing capital investment and aid to local governments. While the dependence of cities and other local governments on property taxes afforded them some protection from heavy falls in revenues from taxes on income, rural domination of state legislatures caused states to be less generous in their grants to cities than to rural counties.

Cooperative federalism

Elected to office by a new coalition dominated by working-class voters, Roosevelt had compelling political reasons for confronting, and if possible alleviating, the cities' plight. Federal authorities accordingly began to expand direct financial aid to cities, rather than disbursing it through state capitals. The sums were small, but the principle was established, and grants rose rapidly. They grew again with the Housing Act of 1948 and the Interstate Highways Act of 1956, before accelerating during the Great Society of Lyndon Johnson's presidency. Direct federal aid to cities, besides meeting substantive needs, also enhanced cities' political standing: Dillon's Rule about authority notwithstanding, after 1933 many cities were better able to assert autonomy from their states as their fiscal capacity rose with augmented federal support.

As the New Deal and World War II required expansion of the presidency and federal bureaucracy, so it effected growth of federal regulation. Many responsibilities previously the preserve of the states were now at the instigation of presidents and Congresses assumed by federal agencies. A sample of New Deal legislation (see Exhibit 10.2 overleaf) indicates the extraordinary sweep of the revolution in regulation, which transformed relations between federal and state governments.

These New Deal programmes established new federal activities and new federal regulations; many supplanted or supplemented state regulations. Federal programmes did not, however, eliminate state regulation. As they had long done, many states set stricter standards for commercial activities, welfare policy and civil rights than did the federal government: the governments of California, Michigan, New York and Pennsylvania all adopted 'little New Deals'. Other states set less strict standards, exploiting the scope which much New Deal legislation gave for state discretion within federal parameters. For example, the Social Security Act (1935) gave discretionary powers to states regarding the Aid to Families with Dependent Children (AFDC) programme in setting criteria for eligibility and levels of benefit, but conspicuously omitted to define a single national standard for either eligibility or benefits. (In the final decade before AFDC's abolition under the *Personal Responsibility, and Work Opportunity, Reconciliation Act of 1996*, payments still varied widely: the average monthly payment per family in 1993 varied from $748 per month in Alaska to $120 per month in Mississippi.) Had Roosevelt bowed to liberal pressures for more radical redistribution, conservative opposition in Congress would have been greater (and possibly successful).

Opposition to federal welfare programmes was heavy but especially intense from southern conservatives, since they feared the social and political consequences of black workers achieving some financial independence from white employers. Determined to preserve his electoral coalition of northern industrial states and segregated southern rural ones, Roosevelt's programmes offered little direct help to African-Americans in southern states: the 1935 Social Security Act's exclusion of agricultural workers and domestic workers was designed by southern

---

Exhibit 10.2 A Sample of New Deal Legislation Bearing on Federal–State Relations

- *The National Labor Relations Act (1935)* enhanced labour unions' rights to organize and bargain collectively, established the National Labor Relations Board, and banned certain unfair practices by employers. The measure was initiated by Senator Robert Wagner and was at first opposed by the President, only to win his support after the extent of Congressional backing became apparent. Three years later, the Fair Labor Standards Act set a minimum wage of 25 cents per hour, and a maximum working week for some workers of 44 hours.
- Following a report by his Cabinet Committee on Economic Security, Roosevelt proposed to Congress in 1935 that a system of social insurance be established. The *Social Security Act (1935)* that instituted old age pensions financed by compulsory contributions from employees and employers (except for agricultural and domestic workers) under the Old Age, Survivors, and Disability Insurance system (OASDI). It also established rudimentary systems of welfare for the elderly poor, a similarly-organized and parsimonious welfare system for the care of dependent mothers and children (Aid to Families with Dependent Children), for the disabled and the blind, and a skeletal federal–state system of unemployment insurance.
- Agriculture largely fell under federal control with the *Agricultural Adjustment Act (AAA) (1933)* and the *Soil Conservation and Domestic Allotment Act (1936)* which largely replaced it. Production was regulated, and payments were made to farmers by means of a tax on the processing of food. The *Agricultural Marketing Act (1937)* made provision for product marketing agreements. The *Agricultural Adjustment Act (1938)* established average allotments and production quotas which, with crop loans and parity payments to farmers, effectively set minimum prices for some products.
- The *Glass–Steagall Act (1933)* separated commercial and investment banking, increased Federal Reserve Board powers over national banks,
→

Democrats in Congress to bar black people. White southern businessmen and farmers benefited from Agricultural Adjustment Act (AAA) programmes, but black sharecroppers and tenant farmers did not. Far from undermining segregation, the New Deal largely accommodated it. The price for southern electoral support in presidential elections and (less reliably) political support from southern committee chairmen in legislative battles, was Roosevelt's acquiescence in Jim Crow: the president proposed no civil rights legislation. However, African-Americans not in agricultural or domestic employment benefited from the provisions of

→

and created the Federal Deposit Insurance Corporation to insure bank deposits. The 1935 Banking Act reorganized the Federal Reserve Board, formed the Federal Open Market Committee to fix short-term interest rates and enabled the Board to set reserve requirements.

- The Federal Power Commission, created under Hoover's presidency in 1930 as a conservation agency, acquired new powers over generating companies by the *Federal Power Act (1935)*, and over interstate natural gas by the *Natural Gas Act (1938)*. Also in power generation, but with a much broader remit, the Tennessee Valley Authority (TVA) undertook major public works in the construction of hydro-electric plants, flood control, the promotion of conservation, the control of water-borne diseases and the stimulation of economic activity (which the generation of electricity did so much to promote) in general. Old southern perceptions of the federal government, owing more to folk-memories of Reconstruction than to the possibilities of economic development, began to be modified as the TVA's benefits accrued to the region. The Authority not only fostered economic growth in a poor region, but began to soften racial politics.

- Roosevelt's foundation in May 1935 of the *Rural Electrification Administration (REA)* altered more rural Americans' lives than any of his other acts. The programme begun by the REA (and virtually completed by the 1960s), to supply electricity to the 90 per cent of rural dwellers who lacked it in March 1933, was an extraordinary symbolic and substantive achievement of federal government in the New Deal. By 1940, the proportion of rural Americans having an electricity supply had increased from 10 per cent to 40 per cent. Electricity, often supplied by cooperatives when private companies would not do so, transformed the quality of rural life, improved agricultural productivity and gave New Deal Democrats in Congress a significant platform on which to run for re-election. The REA was especially welcome to Roosevelt's southern supporters, to whom it provided a solid argument against defenders of States' Rights.

the 1935 Social Security Act, and some were appointed to positions in the administration. The latter was a remarkable departure from past Democratic practices, especially those of President Woodrow Wilson, but most federal agencies themselves continued to segregate black from white workers. Washington, in which most of those African-American federal bureaucrats worked, remained thoroughly segregated.

While the leaders of most New Deal agencies conformed to southern segregationist practices, federal bureaucrats' own autonomy in setting the rules for the implementation of policy were occasionally exploited to advantage. The clearest instance was in the National Youth Administration (NYA). By establishing direct links between the federal government and southern black and Hispanic people, by its resistance to racial wage differentials, and by employing black administrators, the NYA did more than other New Deal agencies to alleviate poverty among young black people in the south. Between 1932 and 1938, most African-American voters responded to changed circumstances by shifting their allegiance from the party of Lincoln to that of Franklin D. Roosevelt.

The discretion that Congress deliberately granted to state governments by means of New Deal legislation created wide disparities in the quality of services supplied which the intervening sixty years have not removed. New programmes and changes in constitutional interpretation altered federalism from dual to cooperative, but the simple categories do not capture the complexity: federalism changed rapidly during Roosevelt's administration in commercial policy, less rapidly in welfare policy and not at all in civil rights. If dual sovereignty was past, state autonomy was vigorously defended, and in certain respects remained intact. In welfare policy, state autonomy was, and remained, sufficient (as the Alaska and Mississippi AFDC payments show) to modify federal policy decisively according to states' fiscal capacities and political choices. In civil rights, state autonomy enabled many northern states to enact civil rights laws, and southern states to sustain segregation.

Some New Deal legislation explicitly supported existing state commercial regulations. The Connally Hot Oil Act prohibited interstate trade in oil produced in violation of such controls on production as states imposed, and the Miller–Tydings Act (1937) exempted states having resale price maintenance from federal anti-trust legislation. Other New Deal programmes, by providing employment and public works programmes to ease unemployment, established links not only between three levels of government, but also between society and federal agencies. Penetration of the federal government by groups had always characterized American politics; the systematic peacetime penetration of society by the federal government was a contribution of the New Deal. Federal agencies increasingly presented themselves, and were increasingly regarded, as both legitimate and needed participants in promoting state and local welfare.

All was grist to Roosevelt's electoral mill: throughout, the president's political calculations informed every aspect of his New Deal's alteration of relationships between federal, state and local governments. From his first day in office, he acted to consolidate and, if possible, to expand the New Deal coalition of 1932. To that end, he and his administration formulated and implemented federal programmes. This political operating principle informed Roosevelt's relief programmes. For example, the

Federal Emergency Administration of Public Works – renamed the Public Works Administration (PWA) in 1939, and established at Roosevelt's behest by Congress in 1933 – helped, by 1939, to construct two-thirds of all new courts and school buildings in the United States, more than one-third of its hospitals, and many hundreds of public works projects, large and small. The PWA financed electrification of the railway linking New York and Washington; the building of the Triborough Bridge and Lincoln Tunnel in New York; and the construction of the fine 30th Street Station in Philadelphia. The New Deal's physical legacy symbolizes its transformation of federal–state relations, introducing new federal life to every state, and congressional district.

Creative federalism: the Great Society

The development of intergovernmental fiscal relations proceeded apace after Roosevelt's death (see Table 10.1).

Lyndon Johnson's politics were shaped by Franklin D. Roosevelt's. In his speech at the University of Michigan on 22 May 1964, Johnson committed his administration to a major programme of federal domestic policy initiatives that, in the phrase supplied by his speechwriter, Richard Goodwin, he termed the 'Great Society'. Not least because he understood the political benefits of his doing so, Johnson declared the 'Great Society' to be a natural extension of the New Deal that he had supported enthusiastically when a young congressman in central Texas.

The Great Society marked the second dramatic forward movement of the regulatory and grant-making roles of the federal government, not only in education, welfare, social security, urban housing and transport policy and the alleviation of poverty, but also in civil rights. The federal role lay primarily in initiation, legislation and evaluation (or oversight); implementation lay mainly with state and local governments. Most federal programmes required the involvement of state and local governments for their implementation; the possibility that the federal government might itself implement the programmes it partly funded was never seriously considered by the administration. Under Johnson's leadership, more than 200 new federal programmes of grants to states, cities, counties, school districts, local communities and charities were authorized. Most were categorical grants, authorized by Congress for particular purposes under defined conditions, rather than as block grants for state and local governments to use as they wished. Categorical grants suited Congress and executive agencies because they reinforced links between lower-level governments and federal authorities. The mirrored division of labour in the fragmented federal bureaucracy and legislature increased both the opportunity and the incentive to make grants both categorical and conditional.

Exhibit 10.3 Federal Grants under Presidents Truman, Eisenhower and Kennedy

- Federal grants-in-aid more than trebled during Truman's eight years in the White House, from $844 million to $2,329 million (although the statistics for his presidency are distorted by the fiscal effects of demobilization, the Cold War and the Korean War). The number of federal grant programmes, including the important *Housing Act* (1949), more than doubled, to 71.
- Eisenhower's presidency was lethargic only by comparison with the frenetic pace of the New Deal and Great Society. Eisenhower was, in fact, a conspicuously activist and reforming president. As Table 10.4 shows, real federal intergovernmental aid more than doubled between Eisenhower's election in 1952 and Kennedy's in 1960: 61 grant programmes were added under Eisenhower, including the large inter-state highway programme in 1956, and the environmental grants programmes for sewage treatment and the control of water pollution in the same year.
- Kennedy also used the federal grant-in-aid as a primary instrument of policy implementation, notably in his regional development programme for Appalachia, which informed Johnson's own anti-poverty programme.

Within this new and complex system of federal grants, cities were especially prominent recipients, both directly and indirectly: the extension of federal grants to governments below the states and to non-governmental groups was a distinctive feature of the Great Society. While states themselves also became more important sources of aid to local governments during the Great Society period (as they had during the New Deal), federal aid grew more rapidly still: by 1971, federal aid was the largest single channel of intergovernmental grants. Moreover, approximately one-fifth of state aid to local governments originated from the US Congress, with the states acting as sluices.

The Great Society comprised six major federal programmes, each of which is considered briefly here.

The war on poverty

The War on Poverty, launched by the 1964 Economic Opportunity Act (EOA), was designed to eliminate poverty and free Americans from welfare support. Responsibility for the Act's administration was placed in the Office of Economic Opportunity (OEO), a statutory agency within the EOP in order to bypass established departmental fiefdoms in the

Table 10.1 *Federal Intergovernmental Grant-in-Aid (GIA) to State and Local Governments by Function from before the New Deal to the close of the Great Society, 1930–70, $millions*

Year	Total GIA	Public assistance	Health	Education	Misc. welfare	Highways
1930	100	–	> 0.5	22	1	76
1932	214	–	–	24	2	186
1934	1,803	–	–	22	2	222
1936	1,015	28	4	37	37	224
1938	790	216	15	48	86	247
1940	967	271	22	51	187	165
1942	926	375	29	151	139	158
1944	983	405	60	136	99	144
1946	844	439	71	58	133	75
1948	1,581	718	55	120	335	318
1950	2,212	1,123	123	82	402	429
1952	2,329	1,178	187	156	333	420
1954	2,958	1,438	140	248	519	538
1956	3,441	1,455	133	276	751	740
1958	4,794	1,795	176	308	816	1,519
1960	6,838	2,059	214	441	896	2,942
1962	7,703	2,432	263	491	1,348	2,783
1964	9,774	2,944	322	579	1,507	3,644
1966	12,519	3,528	365	1,595	2,147	3,975
1968	18,173	5,319	823	2,781	3,588	4,197
1970	23,585	7,445	1,043	3,017	5,041	4,392

Source: *United States Historical Statistics*, Series Y 638/51.

federal bureaucracy; implementation avoided state bureaucracies wherever possible, not least because southern ones would probably have used the opportunity to perpetuate racial discrimination in the programme's implementation. Like the Appalachian Regional Commission inaugurated under President Kennedy, and the 1966 Model Cities Programme, EOA was a 'target grant' programme. Whereas most federal programmes are functionally specific, these three had several specified purposes but were directed to defined areas or to specified demographic groups. The Act called for the 'maximum feasible participation of the residents of the areas and the members of groups served': the OEO contracted with non-governmental community groups to develop anti-poverty programmes.

Although Johnson's anti-poverty programme enjoyed considerable success, its deliberate avoidance of established bureaucracies in the states and cities, and its invitation to local communities and individuals to 'participate', angered state and local Democratic politicians whose support the President needed elsewhere.

The Model Cities Program

Created by the *Demonstration Cities and Metropolitan Development Act of 1966*, the Model Cities Program was an ambitious attempt to ameliorate the severe problems faced by cities through federal grants-in-aid to cities. The poverty, violence (including widespread rioting) and often the squalor within some American cities led the Johnson administration to focus its efforts, in the first instance, on a handful of cities: Detroit, Newark, and Oakland were among the first to receive funding through this programme. Johnson anticipated that the programme would allow city-dwellers to gain better access to decent housing, to social services, and to a higher standard of living. The programme was administered by the Department of Housing and Urban Development (HUD) with the intention of bringing together the numerous existing urban development programmes under the umbrella of the Model Cities Program. Members of Congress rejected Johnson's proposal that the policy be targeted on a few cities, and spread the programme more thinly to distribute the benefits among congressional districts (and, hence, among themselves). The programme's effectiveness was thereby reduced.

The Elementary and Secondary Education Act (1965)

Education has figured prominently in federal policy and politics since the Northwest Ordinance of 1787 required every township in the Northwest Territories to provide free public education. The 1917 Smith–Hughes Act's authorization of federal support for state and local governments' vocational education programmes was supplemented by the Lanham Act in 1940. It authorized federal subsidies to 'federally-impacted areas': school districts whose property tax-bases were reduced by the presence of large numbers of tax-exempt federal buildings. In his 1952 platform for the presidency, Eisenhower declared his opposition to further federal aid to education. However, he regarded the Soviet Sputnik programme as sufficiently alarming to propose the National Defense Education Act of 1958 to support modern language and science education. Widespread resistance to federal control of local schools began to be outweighed by fears for national security in the Cold War. President Johnson's 1965 Elementary and Secondary Education Act (ESEA) extended the principle of federal support.

Protestant objections to financing Catholic schools (nominally on the grounds that such support violated the First Amendment's separation of

Church and State), and Catholic resistance to federal support for non-Catholic schools only, were overcome by the Act's support for school children rather than for schools themselves. ESEA was presented as compensation for the poverty of states, schools and individual children; it was not intended to be an undiscriminating programme of federal assistance. Federal grants were calculated according to the formula of 50 per cent of a state's expenditure per school child multiplied by the number of children in the state from families below the Federal poverty line. The formula was made more redistributive in 1967 by permitting states to receive federal grants, either on the basis of 50 per cent of that which it spent per pupil, or 50 per cent of the average amount per pupil across the United States. In practice, state and local governments' implementation of ESEA thwarted the Act's compensatory intent: most school districts benefited, irrespective of their pupils' impoverishment.

Civil rights legislation, and the Twenty-Third Amendment abolishing the poll tax

In conjunction with Supreme Court judgements regarding electoral redistricting, the Civil Rights Act of 1964, the Voting Rights Act of 1965, and ratification of the Twenty-Third Amendment, eliminated southern states' capacity to abridge the civil and voting rights of black Americans. The 1964 Civil Rights Act and the 1965 Voting Rights Act were discussed in Chapter 4. The 1968 Civil Rights Act made racial discrimination in most housing markets unlawful, thereby further restricting the ability of state and local governments to protect or sanction instances of discrimination by private individuals.

Amendments in 1965 to the 1935 Social Security Act

These decisively consequential amendments provided for a payroll tax paid as part of Social Security to an insurance fund (Medicare) to pay for hospital care for the elderly and disabled. The scheme is wholly federal, and its conditions are uniform: benefits are earned and, accordingly, a matter of entitlement, rather than of annual congressional appropriation. The 'Part X' Medicare Trust Fund receives salary deductions and premiums, and pays hospital costs for the elderly and disabled for up to sixty days. The 'Part B' Medicare premium pays an insured person's doctors' fees. A scheme to provide a rudimentary system of medical care for the indigent poor (Medicaid) was established by the same legislation. Medicare was the only significant departure among Great Society programmes from the principle of federal grants-in-aid, being legitimized instead by enriching the politically secure insurance provisions of the 1935 Social Security Act.

Of all the amendments initiated by President Johnson in 1965, Medicaid causes the greatest difficulties for fiscal relations between levels of government. It is means-tested, financed by federal matching funds to state and local governments for welfare recipients and for others who, while not dependent on welfare, cannot pay their medical costs. As a redistributive welfare programme, Medicaid is administered by the states. To qualify for federal matching funds, a state government that establishes a Medicaid programme (every state now has such a programme) must include within its scope all in receipt of welfare, and additional categories specified in the federal law: the blind, the disabled, and the elderly. States enjoy additional discretion in implementation through their power to determine eligibility rules and benefit levels. Since 1993, the federal agency that administers Medicaid, the Health Care Financing Administration, has permitted states to experiment with a variety of managed care systems in attempts to restrain the programme's rampant cost inflation.

The Job Corps Program

The Job Corps Program was authorized by the Economic Opportunity Act of 1964 (EOA, the main legislative vehicle for the Johnson adminis- tration's anti-poverty programme) and designed to provide remedial education and training programmes for adolescents to enable them to enter the labour market. As such, the programme marked a federal foray into a field of policy in which the United States was becoming markedly deficient by comparison with its major international competitors.

Nixon, Reagan and the new federalisms

President Nixon wisely recognized the importance, and shrewdly discerned the political benefits, of (in his words) a 'New Federalism' involving the replacement of categorical federal funding with a mixture of block grants and the disbursement of funds unrestricted by use. Its general purpose was to devolve decision-making about programmes funded in part by federal grants to state governments and to federal bureaucrats employed outside Washington. The political motivation was to weaken Democratic power-bases in congressional committees and federal agencies in Washington. Nixon's chosen primary vehicle for the purpose was General Revenue Sharing (GRS). Implemented in 1972, it comprised a substantial additional source of federal funds that state and local governments could use as they chose, and not as Congress specified.

GRS was abolished during Ronald Reagan's presidency, ironically as part of an attempt to reduce federal power by decreasing federal spending. In his inaugural address, Reagan declared his intention of attacking not only federal grants to lower-level governments but (implicitly) to the federal bureaucracy and the federal courts by restoring the Tenth Amendment to the place it had occupied in *Schechter* (see p. 323):

> It is my intention to curb the size and influence of the Federal establishment and to demand recognition of the distinction between the powers granted to the Federal government and those reserved to the states or to the people.

President Reagan emphasized his determination to reduce the number and value of federal grants to states, and in 1982 dubbed a programme for reducing federal expenditure on redistributive policy 'New Federalism'. It comprised a devolving of responsibility for the funding of AFDC and Food Stamps from the federal government to the states, one of his perennial objects. The President expected local control of welfare to result in lower levels of benefit, thereby increasing the possibility of tax reductions. Seeking to lessen the fiscal burdens on the states resulting from transfer in order to win their support, he offered to assume full federal funding for Medicaid, to establish a trust fund from federal excise taxes to compensate states further and, by 1987, to have reduced federal excise taxes. If achieved, his proposal would have enabled states to compensate by imposing additional excise taxes themselves.

Reagan's New Federalism proposals foundered on the illogical division of responsibility for welfare programmes from medical aid programmes to the poor. Moreover, the enthusiasm of many governors for federal assumption of Medicaid costs was diminished by their assuming responsibility for AFDC and Food Stamps. The Food Stamps programme had reduced disparities in entitlements between welfare recipients among the states; the cost of taking it over would encumber poor states. By the same token, state governments with relatively generous Medicaid benefits and broad entitlements were reluctant to acquiesce in federal standards which cut benefits and narrowed entitlements. For political reasons, such states would probably be constrained to supplement low federal benefits with their own programmes.

There were few attractions in the swap proposals for many states, and none for local governments. Their fiscal support from federal agencies would under Reagan's plan have been redirected via the states. As state budgets moved into deficit in the early 1980s, radical shifts in federal–state financing of major programmes added to the proposals' fiscal risk. Negotiations between the National Governors' Association (NGA) and the White House on a revised package failed, largely because governors sought firmer assurances of a federal floor beneath state income maintenance levels than the administration – beset by ideological pressure from some officials to any federal welfare standards, economic recession, and growing fiscal crisis – felt able to give.

Reductions in federal grants

New federalism's failure should not obscure President Reagan's remarkable political success in transforming intergovernmental relations by reductions in federal grants. What Reagan failed to accomplish quickly by New Federalism, reductions in federal grants and state taxpayer resistance achieved more slowly. Resistant to the reduction of categorical grants though members of Congress and senators were, Reagan persuaded Congress to cut federal grants between 1981 and 1985 extensively and deeply: their value fell by almost one-quarter in real terms during these years. The greatest reduction occurred in 1981, when the Omnibus Reconciliation Act eliminated sixty programmes and consolidated a further seventy-seven into nine new block grants, giving states greater discretion in how they should be spent. The administration also succeeded in persuading Congress to tighten eligibility rules for AFDC and Medicaid – a Hamiltonian twist in a purportedly Madisonian plot. While Reagan's ambitious New Federalism failed to deliver many of its goals, it did succeed in reversing the trend of ever-increasing financial aid flowing from the federal government to state and local governments. Despite pressures in the early 1990s to increase federal grants-in-aid, neither President George H.W. Bush nor President Clinton effected a significant reversal of the funding reversals of the Reagan years; nor did President George W. Bush. The first significant increase in funding occurred in 2009 as part of President Obama's attempts to limit the damage to America of the devastating financial and banking crises.

Sudden changes in patterns of federal grants-in-aid prompted state and local governments in the 1980s and early 1990s to increase their own revenue (Table 10.2). Many state and local governments also reduced services as part of a politically uncomfortable struggle to satisfy not only taxpayers, but also those dependent on public support. States and cities were doubly squeezed by requirements imposed on them by Congress and federal agencies to assume increasing proportions of federal programme costs. (Medicaid poses particularly severe problems of this kind.) As a result, in the 1980s and early 1990s, many state governments experienced severe financial strain: state legislatures and bureaucrats tightened eligibility requirements and reduced benefit levels, both for their own programmes and for those (of which Medicaid is a key example) partly funded from federal sources. Most states raised taxes after the 1981 Omnibus Reconciliation Act which, while not fully compensating for reductions in federal support, in several cases (including Connecticut

Table 10.2 Federal Grants in Aid, 1970–2011

Year	Current dollars				Grants as percentage of			Constant (2000) dollars	
	Total grants ($bn)	Average annual %change	Grants to individuals		State–local govt outlays	Federal outlays	GDP	Total grants ($bn)	Average annual %change
			Total ($bn)	Percentage of total grants					
1970	24	17.8	8.7	36.3	19	12.3	2.4	74	11.3
1975	50	2.8	16.8	33.7	22.6	15.0	3.3	105	0.6
1980	92	1.8	32.7	35.7	25.8	15.5	3.5	128	-0.2
1985	106	1.6	49.4	46.6	20.9	11.2	2.7	113	0.8
1990	135	11.0	77	57.1	25.2	10.8	2.4	198	6.2
1995	225	6.8	144	64.2	31.5	14.8	3.1	284	3.9
1997	234	2.8	148	63.3	30.3	14.6	2.9	284	0.9
1998	246	5.1	160	65.1	31.2	14.9	2.8	294	3.8
1999	268	8.8	172	64.3	27.4	15.7	2.9	315	7.1
2000	286	6.7	183	63.9	28.4	16.6	2.9	327	3.8
2001	319	11.4	204	64.0	29.5	17.1	3.1	355	8.6
2002	353	10.8	227	64.4	30.5	17.5	3.3	387	9.2
2003	389	10.1	247	63.5	30.9	18.0	3.5	416	7.4
2004	408	4.9	262	64.3	30.8	178	3.5	424	1.9
2005	428	5.0	273	64.0	29.7	17.3	3.4	428	0.9
2006	434	1.4	274	62.8	28.4	16.3	3.3	417	-2.5
2007	444	2.2	284	64.1	27.4	16.3	3.2	412	-1.2
2008	461	3.9	300	65.2	33.1	15.5	3.3	411	-0.3
2009	538	16.6	357	66.3	37.5	15.3	3.8	477	16.0
2010	608	13.1	384	63.2	37.6	17.6	4.2	527	10.6
2011	625	2.8	393	62.8	N/A	16.4	4.1	533	1.1

Source: US Office of Management and Budget, *Budget of the United States Government, Historical Tables, Annual Series*, table 43.1.

and New Jersey) prompted fierce resistance by taxpayers and so caused political difficulties for state governments.

Federalism under William J. Clinton (1993–2001)

In intergovernmental relations, as in much else, Mr Clinton's presidency was one of policy and political flux. When campaigning for the presidency in 1992, Clinton appeared to herald a return to the cooperative federalism of the Johnson years by proposing a substantial economic stimulus package to lift the economy out of recession, and legislation to create a federally-mandated universal healthcare system covering all Americans. By 1993, Republicans in Congress had blocked the Clinton stimulus bill; by 1994, the flagship healthcare legislation was defeated. However, with the Republican Revolution in the 1994 mid-term elections, any prospect of a return to cooperative federalism ended.

President Clinton initiated some progressive reforms and, especially after the Republicans victories in the 1994 congressional elections, acquiesced in extremely conservative ones. In welfare reform, he did both: having made the subject a plank in his campaign for the presidency, he finally conceded leadership on the matter to conservative Republicans in the 104th Congress. The Personal Responsibility and Work Opportunity Reconciliation Act, which he signed into law in the summer of 1996, ended the AFDC programme established by Roosevelt's Social Security Act of 1935 with the purpose of relieving poverty among children. At the programme's outset in 1935, all recipients were children. Even after the inclusion of mothers in the programme from 1939, most recipients were children. In 1992, the AFDC caseload was 9.2 million children (of whom half were under the age of six, and one-quarter under the age of three) and 4.4 million adults. Most of the latter were mothers, but only 7.6 per cent were teenagers. Senator Moynihan, a moderate Democratic US senator from New York, observed that the legislation had as its premise the notion that 'the behavior of certain adults can be changed by making the lives of their children as wretched as possible. This is a fearsome assumption.'

The 1996 Act is important not only as a legislative event, but also as a continuation of a process of retreat from earlier practices: welfare support has become increasingly tied to work requirements for recipients, especially since the Family Support Act of 1988 required that all states run 'welfare-to-work' programmes typically comprising short-term training on seeking and retaining employment, and assistance in finding a post (more commonly called *workfare* programmes). States have also availed themselves of waivers from federal programme requirements to experiment with different AFDC provisions or to increase work incentives. The 1996 Act considerably extended these arrangements by further limiting cash support and increasing the incentive to find and keep a job. By deciding to sign the act, Clinton achieved his immediate object of preventing Senator Dole, the Republican presidential nominee, from exploiting the subject of welfare reform to his advantage. Quite apart from the beneficial electoral effects for Mr Clinton of neutralizing the question, the substance of the act (the first example of the transformation of a major individual entitlement programme into a block grant to the states) contained the following chief provisions:

- State entitlements to matching federal funds were ended by the new law: under Temporary Aid to Needy Families (TANF), states receive a fixed (nominal) amount of money equal to the payments received in the early 1990s for AFDC and related welfare-to-work programmes.
- Any parent who has received 24 months of assistance in programmes funded through TANF must be working or in a work programme to be eligible for receipt of further funding.
- By 1997, 25 per cent of all families in the state in receipt of TANF support were required to be working at least 20 hours per week; by 2002, 50 per cent of all such families had to work at least 30 hours per week.
- States face mandatory time limits on support: no family may receive funding from TANF if an adult in that family has already received 5 years of assistance during their lifetime. Some scope exists for states to tighten or loosen these limits.
- The Act limits able-bodied 18–50 year-olds to 3 months of Food Stamp benefits every 3 years unless they work at least 20 hours a week.
- States are permitted to deny Medicaid to adults who are deleted from the welfare lists because of their failure to meet work requirements, and to decide for themselves whether to deny Medicaid coverage to legal immigrants.
- Illegal immigrants may not benefit from low-income child nutrition programmes.

There is little reason to think that the Act has overcome the conflict (first identified by Henry Aaron (1973) in *Why is Welfare so Hard to Reform?*) between the goals of support for those who cannot work, provision of incentives for those able to work, and the need to keep programme costs and caseloads low. As Rebecca Blank (1997) has argued, and as the Great Depression of the early 1930s showed, there is even less reason to think that States that are much less well-fitted to act counter-cyclically than is the federal government will be able to meet the needs of welfare recipients since, irrespective of differences in programme design between states, welfare is a counter-cyclical programme.

Yet, by ending AFDC and creating the cash-limited TANF block grant to the states, Congress effectively delegated complete discretion over welfare programmes' design to state governments with limited fiscal capacity and political will. States may, effectively, determine those groups entitled to apply for welfare support, the amount that they may receive, and the length of time for which they may receive it. Not unusually for conservative measures that ostensibly devolve decision-making powers, however, the 1996 Act also imposes conditions (or 'mandates') on the states, as indicated in the above list of provisions. For a measure designed to liberate individuals from the yoke of welfare dependence through devolutionary principles, the Act is remarkably coercive and centralist.

Clinton also changed the relationship between the federal government and the states when he signed the 1995 Unfunded Mandates Reform Act. This was the second element of the Republican *Contract with America* enacted into law and it sought to end the practice whereby the federal government could impose requirements on states without providing the funds to obey these impositions. By signing both this law and the 1996 welfare reform bill, Clinton ensured that cooperative federalism was not resurrected.

Federalism under President George W. Bush (2001–09) and President Obama (2009–)

When President Bush pledged to be a 'faithful friend to federalism', most expected the continuation of New Federalism in the Reagan mould. Yet, a combination of policy choices and unforeseen events resulted in eight years in which President Bush articulated no clear or coherent vision of federalism.

Expenditure on education increased rapidly, largely as a result of the passage of Bush's flagship education bill, the *No Child Left Behind Act* (NCLB), in June 2001. The act required states to administer annual tests and to take corrective action where students fell below mandated standards. While substantial federal funds flowed to the states, the Act nonetheless marked a significant intervention by federal government into the states. Resenting federal intervention in an arena they considered a state activity, a number of Republican governors opposed the Act.

The terrorist attacks of 11 September 2001 prompted executive and congressional responses: Congress created the Department of Homeland Security, and passed the PATRIOT Act (2001) to increase surveillance of financial transactions and to disrupt terrorist organizations. Both Acts had centralizing implications. So, too, did the conduct and financing of prolonged wars in Afghanistan and Iraq, and the greatly increased budgets and capacities of multiple intelligence and security agencies.

In neither of his elections did President Obama campaign on the issue of federalism, but Table 10.1 clearly demonstrates a substantial increase in the funding flowing from Washington to the states. That increase results, in part, from economic circumstances which President Obama inherited on taking office in January 2009, and his and Congress's responses to them. However, it is also clear that Mr Obama has a different view to his predecessor in relation to the role of government *both* as a lever to pull when the economy is in recession and as a force for engendering social change.

Conclusion

America's vastness has always affected the character and structure of its politics and government. Despite having a political culture that is, in many respects, inchoate and diverse, and (broadly) a decentralized political system, the United States is a stable and modern political order. Amidst the centrifugal forces of federalism, ethnicity, class and religion, there are powerful centripetal forces that enable the system to cohere. The most important of them is the legitimacy conferred on America by the deliberate nature of its creation, and the simultaneous rejection of European political systems. The federal Constitution dispersed and fragmented government; as the Civil War showed, although the Union of States was permanent, it was not centralized. The implication of developments since 1937 is that there are few limitations in constitutional law on the centralization of power in the federal government. But although constitutional law now acts more as licence to the federal government than as a fetter on it, fiscal incapacity constrains the forces in Washington, which, between the New Deal and Richard Nixon's presidency, altered the balance of power between Washington and state capitals. The federal government's extensive regulatory power notwithstanding, more power over policy initiative (and, in the case of welfare, discretion over implementation) now lies beyond the nation's capital than was the case between Franklin D. Roosevelt's first year in office and Jimmy Carter's last.

Chapter 11

Domestic Economic Policy

The economic policy process in the United States is the result of the interplay of multiple institutional actors in government and in markets who, between them, shape fiscal and monetary policy. The former, concerned as it is with decisions about taxing and spending, is largely the preserve of the president and the Congress. Given the obvious appeal of fiscal policy as a political tool, both the president and the Congress may use decisions about taxing and spending as a means to bolster political arguments, rather than technical ones. Monetary policy, which is concerned with using the quantity of money and interest rates as tools to control inflation, is the preserve of a formally independent central bank, the Federal Reserve, which has twin goals of delivering low inflation and high employment.

The first section of this chapter examines the institutional participants in the economic policy process that seek to affect both fiscal and monetary policy. Important though it is to the health of the American economy, trade policy is considered not here, but in Chapter 12, as part of the discussion of foreign policy. The second section of the chapter examines the formation of fiscal policy during recent presidencies. The chapter then evaluates the efforts of President George W. Bush and President Obama to reduce the size of the national debt while ameliorating the effects of the 2007–09 financial and banking crises. This chapter also considers the effectiveness of those regulations created in the aftermath of the 2007–2009 crises and the prospect that such regulations will correct the failures of earlier regulatory regimes.

The economic policy process

President Obama's 2012 re-election marked the first occasion on which a president has been returned to office with an unemployment rate above 8 per cent since Franklin D. Roosevelt was re-elected in 1936. Economic and financial circumstances in the last two years of President Obama's first term were poor: the national debt approached $17 trillion; the annual deficit stood at $900 billion, more than 8 per cent of gross domestic product (GDP); the US suffered its first credit rating reduction of US Treasury securities by S&P, a credit-rating agency, since that company's establishment in 1860; and battles between the president and Congress over fiscal policy were intense, deep, and appeared often to be insoluble.

Yet, gloomy assessments of its condition, prospects and relative decline notwithstanding, the American economy remain the largest in the world. After the oil price shocks of 1973 and 1979, the United States achieved higher rates of output growth than many other industrial countries, but smaller improvements in productivity. Having averaged about 2.4 per cent between 1890 and 1973, the annual rate of growth in productivity (defined as output per hour of all persons working in the non-agricultural business sector) fell to 0.7 per cent between 1973 and 1990. Productivity increased after 1995 and surged between 2001 and 2004, slowing between 2004 and 2007. After rapid and deep falls in economic output during the period of the financial crisis from 2007–09, economic output recovered, but slowly. The average rate of GDP growth between 2008 and 2012 was just 1.7 per cent during those five years. Measuring productivity is more difficult than it was because of the continued relative decline of American manufacturing and the growth in services. At the time of writing, manufacturing now accounts for only 12.2 per cent of US GDP compared with more than 30 per cent in the 1950s; services account for approximately 65 per cent.

The well-being of all other economies continues to depend on the health of the US economy. Indeed, the financial crisis of 2007, which created the conditions which generated the 2008 global economic recession, began in the US. It was in the US that the housing market's collapse revealed large quantities of toxic mortgage debt held by financial institutions, much of which had no market value.

The US economy is, in certain respects, insulated from the pressures of the international economy. For example, the proportion of US GDP exported throughout the twentieth century was lower than that of America's major competitors. Although the proportion has grown since 1945, it still stands at only 14 per cent. The US dollar is the largest internationally-traded currency: huge quantities of the currency are held overseas by foreign governments and companies, most commodities are dollar-denominated, and so is the United States government's own debt. No other country enjoys the immense advantage of borrowing abroad in its own currency to fund its own debt. And, as we write, the US continues to find and exploit huge reserves of oil and gas (in California and in the Dakotas). Nevertheless, the US's high public debt means that it must take into account the policies, preferences and capacities of those nation-states which purchase America's debt.

Decisions that federal, state and local governments make about taxing and spending affect the economy's condition in the aggregate and its regional and local components. Decisions of individuals and corporations also affect the economy, but the federal government's taxing and spending decisions exert the greatest single influence, because its budget is greater than all state and local budgets combined (accounting for more than 15 per cent of GDP) and because, unlike the constitutions of many states, the US Constitution does not prohibit the federal government from running a fiscal deficit.

Economic policy processes in all democracies are conflictual. In America, however, conflict is intensified by the fragmentation of politics, and a cultural antipathy to big government (as discussed in Chapter 1). More especially, the weakness of executive authority renders policy-making exceptionally fraught: the formation, legitimation, implementation and evaluation of American economic policy require agreements between politicians in autonomous and competitive institutions. Since the objectives, perspectives, electoral bases of support, ideological preferences and institutional interests of the politicians and officials who participate in the process diverge more frequently and in more directions than they converge, achieving such cooperation is difficult. Public powers over federal economic policy are shared between the single elected members of the Executive Branch, that Branch's many unelected officials, the 535 elected members of the United States Congress and the independent quasi-public Federal Reserve System. Public officials contribute to economic policy-making in the knowledge that most economic decision-making power remains in private and corporate hands.

Notwithstanding his constitutional restrictions, the president remains the single-most important participant in the economic policy process. No other politician or official in government, and no individual in the private sector, rivals the presidency's institutional capacity for economic policy leadership. The president has the power – and, indeed, the obligation – to identify economic policy objectives, and both the authority and the opportunity to set an agenda for action. Lacking significant authority in fiscal matters, the president must seek to persuade those whose support he needs but is unable to require. He acts, therefore, with or against congressional politicians who themselves have, and use, powers of initiation, formalization, legitimation, implementation and evaluation. The president's prospects of securing assent for his policy preferences are, therefore, institutionally hampered – and designedly so. This unpromising circumstance may be either mitigated or exacerbated by exogenous factors at best only partially within the president's influence. Among these are the partisan and ideological balances within Congress; the identity and policy preferences of appointees to Executive Branch agencies and regulatory authorities (especially the Federal Reserve Board); public opinion; the proximity of elections; and the international political, military, and economic contexts within which policy is formulated and advanced.

In contrast to the president's leadership of the armed forces in peace and war, he has no power of command in economic policy. Authority rests, ultimately and constitutionally at least, with Congress and not with the president. Presidential leadership in economic policy is problematic, not only because of intellectual uncertainties about the effectiveness of different policy instruments and their relationship to each other, but also because of high political risks for the many people and institutions involved in its formulation. Of this difficulty's several dimensions, the reconciliation of fiscal and monetary policy is the most forbidding. Presidents must try to make fiscal and monetary policy economically and politically congruent because of the broad macroeconomic duties assumed by all presidents since March 1933, and imposed on them by the Employment Act of 1946. Nevertheless, the separation of powers, and the Federal Reserve Board's substantial autonomy, usually cause the president to be a negotiator, rather than an executive.

A president's part in economic policy derives from Article II of the Constitution. He exercises further powers and responsibilities through the delegation of powers to him from Congress by the Federal Reserve Act (1913), the Budget and Accounting Act (1921), the Employment Act (1946) and the Budget and Impoundment Control Act (1974), together with their subsequent amendments. Throughout the twentieth century, but particularly since 1932, the political fate of United States presidents has, in large part, been dependent on the achievement of steady output growth, low inflation and high employment, which presidents and scholars alike understand normally to be prerequisites for electoral victory. Inauspicious as their prospects for success are, presidents must attempt to influence macroeconomic outcomes, not least because their re-election prospects often hang on them, as Presidents Carter and Bush discovered in 1980 and 1992, respectively. President Obama's 2012 re-election, against a backdrop of low growth and high unemployment, accordingly appears aberrant. In that election, 69 per cent of voters nevertheless attributed at least some of the improvement in the labour market to

President Obama's policies, indicating that they recognized that his economic and financial inheritance from his predecessor was grave and that matters had improved in the four years since (ABC News/Washington Post Poll, 10–13 October 2012, N = 1,063 registered voters nationwide).

Participants in economy policy-making

The Executive Branch

The executive's interests in economic policy are divided institutionally between presidential and departmental components. To this extent, the federal government's making of economic policy reflects the general difficulty of presidents in attempting to formulate and implement policy across an administration over which they have constitutional and statutory jurisdiction, but incomplete authority. Within the departmental component, agencies and departments have vested interests in the Federal Budget, not least because it affects their activities. Although not simply (or primarily) budget-maximizers, senior bureaucrats have a prudential continuing political commitment to their agencies' fiscal health. Annual appropriations for many federal programmes ensure that senior bureaucrats must have regard to congressional opinion about them.

The federal government is the largest single participant in the American economy: decisions made by executive officials, and laws and regulations written by Congress have consequences for the level and character of economic activity. All governments in the United States affect the economy by implementing public policies and issuing regulations. Tightening federal or state regulations governing, for example, the discharge of carcinogens into the air may be desirable public policy but, like all regulation, it imposes costs on the polluter, its employees and consumers, while benefiting those affected by pollution. Regulation of markets has, nonetheless, always been preferred to nationalization as an instrument of public policy in the United States.

Governments also intervene in the economy by raising revenue, and by expenditure, both on their own and in support of other governments' programmes. Vast public procurement programmes inescapably cause governments (indirectly) to affect economic activity: in the 2012 fiscal year, the federal government spent more than $490 billion on private sector goods and services. Many individuals, companies and localities depend for their survival on federal orders. This pattern is especially marked in the case of defence equipment which, in law and in practice, is subject to detailed federal control: defence procurement programmes powerfully affect patterns of investment, and research and development, in private industry and commerce.

In most years since 1945, the federal government has run a fiscal deficit on a budget larger than that of all state and local governments combined. By 2013, the federal government had accumulated gross debts of $16.7 trillion ($53,000 for every US citizen); it needs regularly to raise more, which requires the negotiation of the president with the Congress. It is a peculiarity of American fiscal governance that Congress's approval is required for the national debt ceiling to rise. We discuss this point further below.

The US Treasury, which exercises authority delegated by Congress for the government's debt management, covers the shortfall between expenditure and revenue by selling US Treasury securities. With a range of maturities of between two and thirty years, demand from dealers in Treasury securities markets sets the price of the debt. Decisions regarding the financing of the federal government's debt have the potential to affect the economy's condition significantly. Unlike bonds issued by many private corporations and some American cities, Treasury bonds are, even in light of the credit downgrade of 2011, almost entirely secure and will remain so, short of a cataclysmic economic collapse. They are so because they are backed, in the official phrase, 'by the full faith and credit' of the United States government.

The Council of Economic Advisors

Reflecting the twin imperatives of economic crisis and international conflict which spawned its birth and growth, the Executive Office of the President (EOP) has the management of economic and national security policy as its two major activities. In addition to several advisers within the White House Office itself, the Employment Act (1946) established the Council of Economic Advisors (CEA) in the EOP in order to promote policies designed to secure full employment, an institutional expression of Keynesianism. The CEA is a staff, not a line, agency and has one client: the president of the United States. Its three members are appointed by the president, subject to the advice and confirmation of the Senate. The 1946 Act established the objectives of seeking 'maximum employment, production, and purchasing power'. It requires the president, at the start of each session of Congress, to present an *Economic Report of the President*, which comprises an analysis of economic trends and conditions, presents a programme for implementing the president's policy objectives, and makes recommendations for necessary legislation. Since the economic crises following the oil price increases of 1973 and 1979, and the rise of monetarist influence, the CEA has set less store by the objective of full employment set by the 1946 Act, but its members continue to advise the president on macroeconomic policy. Members of the CEA since 1946 have, in their different ways, attempted to provide such means for intelligent and informed presidential decision-making.

Walter Heller, Chairman of the CEA under Kennedy and Johnson, identified five functions the Council enjoyed under these presidents, and which have been retained by later presidents:

1. *Provision of information to the president.* Under Kennedy and Johnson, this obligation included (a) keeping the president informed of 'economic events, trends, and prospects' as the 1946 Employment Act required; (b) responding to presidential requests for information, advice, and interpretation of data and events; (c) briefing the president on economic policy for press conferences, or for private meetings with journalists. All three functions continue.
2. *Speech-writing.* This includes preparing drafts of presidential speeches and commenting on drafts prepared by others. CEA chairmen have always had the subsidiary, public task of representing the president's policies to business corporations and associations, to labour unions and to the press. The preparation of the *Economic Report of the President* falls under this heading. The *Report* offers the president the opportunity to win congressional, interest group and public support for his policies.
3. *Briefing of the President.* The CEA briefs the president for his meetings on economic policy with Cabinet members, interest-group representatives, members of Congress and foreign heads of government. The CEA also seeks to persuade the president of the merits of certain policy choices. During Kennedy's administration, the broadly Keynesian Council persuaded the president of the utility of fiscal fine-tuning in promoting faster economic growth. In 1969 and 1970, President Nixon's CEA, influenced more by Milton Friedman's theory of the natural rate of unemployment than by Keynesian theories of demand management, argued that the defeat of inflation should be the administration's first priority, even at the price of accepting a higher 'natural rate of unemployment'. Paul McCracken and his colleagues on Nixon's CEA were less successful in persuading the President of this object's political desirability than Heller and his colleagues had been with regard to fiscal policy in 1963, and failed completely to prevent the President's startlingly pragmatic imposition of wage and price controls in 1971.
4. *Responsibility for the legislative programme.* The CEA had special responsibility for the president's legislative programme under Johnson. Although new and expensive legislative initiatives have been rarer since the mid-1980s, the CEA continues to review, with a

team of senior White House staff, proposals for the following year's legislative programme, and to assign special responsibility to the economic staff of the Council for the analysis of programmes with particular significance for the economy.

5. *Special activities.* In Chairman Heller's formulation, this simply referred to President Kennedy's use of the CEA 'to represent him in interagency discussions on particular policy problems'. Such a role, apparently nebulous, in fact reveals the intimacy of the Council's relations with the president, and the Council's determination to assert itself at the centre of his administration. The influence of the Council in later years has typically been a function of the political skill of its chair.

The Office of Management and Budget

The Executive's budgetary policy is coordinated in the Office of Management and Budget (OMB), whose history was discussed briefly in Chapter 5. Established by the Budget and Accounting Act (1921) in the Treasury, the Bureau of the Budget was moved to the EOP by the 1939 Reorganization Act. The change resulted from Roosevelt's wish to have more immediate staff assistance, the 1937 Brownlow Commission's agreement with his view, and Congress's accession to both. The Bureau provided the presidency with an office to examine the budget proposals from each of the executive departments and form them into a coherent overall package reflecting the president's priorities for submission to Congress in an annual budget message. The Bureau was renamed the Office of Management and Budget in 1970, reflecting President Nixon's desire to centralize management of the Executive Branch in the EOP, and thereby to politicize it. Prior to the 1974 Budget Reform Act, the message related to the budget for the fiscal year beginning on the first day of July following; since 1974, the fiscal year has begun on 1 October and ended on 30 September. The OMB's role in the formation of the federal budget is examined in greater detail below.

The Executive Departments

Chapter 9 showed that the federal bureaucracy has two distinctive features:

1. Unlike government bureaucracies in France or the United Kingdom, the federal bureaucracy's loyalties are divided. Its members attend not just to presidential preferences, but also (and often primarily) to

congressional ones. Only White House staff are exempt from Congress's scrutiny, and even they are dependent on Congress for their salaries. Congress remains the first branch of government.

2.   The US federal bureaucracy is highly fragmented. Executive agencies within departments are semi-autonomous. Having loyalties both to the chief executive and to Congress (which authorizes their existence and activities, and has the power of the purse over them), departments have ample political space. Presidential policies are not easily coordinated across departments. The president depends on the semi-autonomous Department of the Treasury for developing and implementing fiscal policy, and on the OMB within the EOP for formulation of a budget prior to its submission to Congress. The president's political writ runs for a shorter distance than his constitutional position as chief executive implies, and sub-governmental networks are the primary influences on policy.

The Treasury

The Secretary of the Treasury is the main financial officer of the US government and economic adviser to the president, in which role he has overall responsibility for macroeconomic policy. He is also responsible for international financial policy, and for the management of the government's debt, by which he determines the quantities and maturities of debt to be raised through quarterly refinancing.

The Treasury Department is organized in a similar way to other federal departments: the secretary and a few officials have responsibilities covering the entire activities of the department. Immediately below the secretary are two under-secretaries: one has responsibility for international affairs, and the other for finance. However, most of the department's work is led by political appointees at assistant secretary level in specialist agencies and sections including economic policy; fiscal policy; domestic finance; international economic policy; and international monetary affairs. In all cases, the assistant secretaries are supported by political appointees and civil servants engaged in economic analysis and forecasting, and in preparing policy advice to the under-secretaries and thence to the secretary and the president.

The Department of Commerce

The secretary of commerce is the president's main adviser on business and commercial policy. The department traditionally has close links to business groups and often represents business interests to other federal agencies. In addition to the department's semi-autonomous agencies (including the Bureau of the Census, the Patent and Trademark Office, and the National Oceanic and Atmospheric Administration), most of its agencies are concerned with economic development within the United States, with the promotion of exports and with representing American business interests in international trade. The economic affairs division collects data on economic activity, particularly on consumer spending and capital formation, levels of inventories, and prospects for output and employment. Some of the department's work overlaps with that of the Treasury, the Department of Labor, and the Council of Economic Advisors, The Department consequently has to compete with others to exert influence on the president's policy.

Congress

Congress is the first branch, primarily because it creates most of government and finances all of it. Congress, and Congress alone, has the power of the purse, determining what public money the federal government raises and spends. Whatever taxes are raised by the federal government are raised by Congress. Whatever funds are spent on government programmes are appropriated by Congress or, increasingly, through entitlements included in authorizing bills that Congress writes. By authorizing programmes, Congress permits them to exist. By appropriating funds for programmes, Congress provides finance for the authorized programmes up to and including the maximum specified in the authorizing legislation. Except for entitlement programmes, no programme can be financed without appropriations being voted.

Entitlement programmes include Social Security, Medicaid, Medicare and many Veterans' Administration programmes. Expenditure on them occurs not through Appropriations bills, but because the authorizing legislation identifies certain groups of citizens as being entitled to receive money or services. In such cases, the authorizing legislation entails expenditure, and the Appropriations committees lack jurisdiction. Entitlement programmes therefore further enhance the power of tax-writing committees in both chambers. Since Social Security and Medicare are financed through the revenue-raising process, both fall within the jurisdiction of the House Ways and Means Committee and the Senate Finance Committee – thereby affording them control of both taxation for the programmes and the programmes themselves. Entitlement programmes remain immune from the automatic cuts that flow from the so-called sequester imposed in 2012 as a result of the impasse between President Obama and the Republican-controlled House, which resulted from the failed attempt to secure agreement as to how best to tackle the federal deficit.

Congressional Budget Committees

In 1974, Congress altered significantly the means by which it raised and spent public money. The 1974 Budget and Impoundment Control Act (BICA) established budget committees in both chambers so that the budget might be examined in its entirety. Prior to the Act's passage, the spending and taxing parts of the budget were not examined as a whole by a single committee. To set recent budgetary procedures in context, a brief review of the pre-reform system of budget formation is appropriate, particularly because the new budget committees did not supplant the old revenue-raising and Appropriations committees, but supplemented them.

House Ways and Means Committee

The Constitution places the power of taxation with Congress, and grants the House of Representatives primacy in the process. Article I, Section 7, states that: 'All bills for raising revenue shall originate in the House of Representatives; but the Senate may propose or concur with amendments as on other bills'. The Senate has, therefore, to wait until the House has voted on a tax bill before it may act. Once the House has done so, the Senate's freedom of action is complete, thereby enabling the Senate to play a major role if the opportunity exists. Prior to the 1974 Budget reforms, the Ways and Means Committee enjoyed sole jurisdiction over revenue bills within the House (and hence, because of the origination clause, initiating power over such Bills).

The Ways and Means Committee was established in 1802, with responsibility both for taxation and appropriations, but its appropriating powers were reduced in the succeeding sixty-three years and extinguished with the creation of the House Appropriations Committee in 1865. Until the Subcommittee Bill of Rights in 1973, Ways and Means enjoyed special influence within the House because it had no subcommittees. Furthermore, legislation which it reported was sent to the floor by the Rules Committee under a 'closed' rule which permitted of no amendment. The House was therefore obliged to accept or reject the bill as a whole, thereby enhancing the Committee's influence over the bill's fate. Moreover, under the rules of the House, the Committee's business was 'privileged', which meant that the speaker could place it on the calendar ahead of other business.

Although the seniority rule gave considerable autonomy to all chairmen between Speaker Cannon's overthrow in 1910 and the Committee reforms of January 1975, it gave chairmen of the Ways and Means Committee special influence. The confluence of favourable procedural rules gave Wilbur Mills, Chairman of the Committee from 1957 to 1974, as decisive an influence over fiscal policy as any single elected politician has ever enjoyed in the United States. Until the combination of his personal downfall and internal congressional reforms, no tax legislation moved into law without his personal *imprimatur*. He knew the United States Tax Code well, appreciated its provisions' significance for different groups and individuals, and was a clinically accurate judge of colleagues' sentiment in Committee and on the House floor. Mills was, in an era of powerful chairmen, the most powerful chairman of the most powerful Committee in Congress.

Senate Finance Committee

The House Ways and Means Committee's counterpart in the Senate is the Finance Committee. Its right to conduct hearings on taxation policy and legislation only after the House has acted has only slightly diminished its influence over fiscal policy. Congress's bicameral structure invariably causes a bill to be treated differently by the two chambers; like other legislation, a tax bill drafted in two forms is sent to a conference committee. Members drawn from the Senate Finance Committee and the House Ways and Means Committee determine the bill's final text, which must then proceed to the floor of both chambers for a final vote, generally under procedural rules precluding amendment.

Tax-writing Conference Committees

Politics does not stop at the conference committee door. Chairmen of the Senate Finance Committee and House Ways and Means Committee have never been averse to employing conference committees as forums in which to secure objectives they have been unable to attain in earlier congressional deliberations.

Appropriations Committees

Article I, Section 9, of the Constitution decrees that the federal government spend only those monies properly appropriated:

> No Money shall be drawn from the Treasury, but in Consequence of Appropriations made by Law; and a regular Statement and Account of the Receipts and Expenditures of all public Money shall be published from time to time.

Appropriations committees may not appropriate funds until the legislating (authorizing) committees have authorized spending levels for a programme. In the twenty-five years prior to the 1974 Budget and

Impoundment Control Act, most legislating committees authorized programmes annually, thereby reducing the time available to Appropriations committees subsequently to act, and challenging the political primacy of Appropriations committees. A frequent consequence of the resulting pressures on the congressional timetable has been that Appropriations bills were often not enacted into law by the beginning of the new fiscal year. The 1974 reforms have not disposed of the problem: new budget procedures have made punctual completion of appropriating even more difficult. Consequently, when Appropriations bills lie unenacted by a new fiscal year, Congress must pass a 'continuing resolution' for a limited period (sometimes for as short a period as a day or two, occasionally for much longer), by which spending continues at the level for the previous year until a new Appropriations bill establishes new spending levels. Without appropriations, all but the most essential government activities stop: departments and agencies close, federal employees are sent home and fiscal transfers to state and local governments cease. During the rancorous budget negotiations of 1990, Congress passed five continuing resolutions, as successive deadlines for the completion of the appropriations process passed without agreement having been reached.

The full Appropriations committees are large. They are so in order that the thirteen subcommittees in each chamber should have sufficient members to hold hearings on draft legislation, and thereby to oversee the expenditure of funds appropriated earlier. Since Appropriations committees in both chambers regained their power over appropriations in the years following World War I, appropriating has been undertaken less by full committees than by subcommittees. Jurisdictions of the Senate and House Appropriation Committees are identical, and those of their subcommittees are nearly so. Procedures for appropriations legislation derive from dividing Appropriations bills between departments and agencies. Thus, the work of the House Appropriations Committee is divided between its thirteen subcommittees, each of which corresponds to an executive department or group of agencies, the EOP, the judiciary, and the legislature. All are financed by appropriations, providing heavy burdens for the subcommittees.

Prior to congressional reform in the early 1970s, the House Committee comprised mainly senior congressmen, usually from safe seats and virtually immune to defeat in primaries or general elections. Their conservatism was expressed in their marginal reduction of budget requests made by the president. By concentrating the power to appropriate in one Appropriations committee in each chamber, the House and the Senate indicated their determination to control spending which, in the peacetime years between the early 1920s and the mid-1960s, they did with remarkable effectiveness.

Government Accountability Office

In addition to creating the Bureau of the Budget, the Budget and Accounting Act of 1921 also established the General Accounting Office (GAO), led by the Comptroller-General. The Dockery Act of 1894 had established a Comptroller within the Treasury; the 1921 Act altered the Comptroller's status from an executive official removable by the president to one who, though appointed by the president, could be removed from office only by joint resolution of both houses of Congress. As the creation of the Bureau of the Budget (BOB) reflected the president's growing managerial responsibilities, and its move to the EOP in 1939 reflected Congress's recognition of the need for more satisfactory coordination of the federal government's expenditure, so the GAO's establishment confirmed Congress's intention to oversee the executive's expenditure of monies which it had appropriated.

Congress will not cede powers without retaining oversight, either directly through committee hearings, or indirectly through the creation of an agency, owing its primary responsibility and political allegiance to Congress, rather than to the executive. A legislative agency, the GAO is Congress's main investigating arm. Although the bulk of its work is auditing, Congress has also given it the wider remit of examining the federal government's efficiency and effectiveness. Most of its reports are available publicly.

Congressional Budget Office

Created by BICA, the Congressional Budget Office (CBO) is a non-partisan agency of the Legislative Branch, providing objective and impartial analysis of the budget, current and alternative fiscal policies, and the economy generally. Its professional standards are high. Unlike those made by the highly politicized OMB in the EOP, its forecasts of budget deficits are dispassionate; in the past, that has often made them a more reliable guide to the likely size of the fiscal deficit. Between 1993 and 1996, however, CBO projections of the budget deficit were little better than the OMB's, and both were consistently pessimistic. Tiny errors in forecasts matter, not least because the budget deficits which they project determine the size both of expenditure cuts required and tax cuts that can be afforded. Forecasting errors can therefore have disproportionately large consequences for politicians engaged in bargaining over cuts in programmes required to effect budget cuts.

Monetary policy: the Federal Reserve Board and Federal Reserve Banks

Membership, independence and constraints of operation

By the 1913 Federal Reserve Act, and the Banking Acts of 1933 and 1935, Congress chose to vest exclusive responsibility for monetary policy in the Federal Reserve Board, the central bank of the United States. As a regulatory body, the Federal Reserve Board's members are appointed by the president, with the advice and consent of the Senate. Therefore, neither the president, nor the Secretary of the Treasury, nor Congress directly controls monetary policy. The Board guards jealously its managerial and operating independence: its budget is not subject to review by the president or the OMB. Great though its formal powers are, the Board's capacity to use them is constrained by its sensitivity to political pressure and the prospect of such pressure. The mere possibility that it might be applied is usually sufficient to affect its decisions: discounting for the future is the stock-in-trade of unelected officials as it is of politicians, and of financial market-makers. In political practice, therefore, the Board is constrained, although the tightness of the constraints varies with circumstances. Arthur Okun, President Johnson's last chairman of the CEA, rightly concluded that the Board enjoys independence within, but not from, the administration.

Attempts by Congress to constrain Board policy decisions have similarly been unsuccessful. A congressional resolution in 1974 requiring the Board to inform Congress biannually of its money supply targets has been met with the provision of several broad target ranges, leaving the Board considerable freedom. Even when such targets have been missed, congressional oversight has been weak and without effect. The Humphrey–Hawkins Full Employment Act (1978), congressional Keynesianism's last gasp, required the Board to state whether its monetary targets were consistent with the president's macroeconomic policy, but this requirement has similarly been circumvented by the use of wide monetary target ranges in order to preserve its discretion, and by its unwillingness to accept responsibility for economic policy outcomes (which luxury presidents are denied).

The Board itself comprises seven full-time members appointed by the president, subject to Senate confirmation, each for a fourteen-year term. This period is longer than any president may serve, and longer than most members of either the House or Senate. Formal independence from the executive is thereby assured. Furthermore, no American president may remove a board member. Presidents of the twelve district banks in major cities together comprise the Federal Reserve System and serve on the Federal Open Market Committee (FOMC), membership of which is divided into voting and non-voting members. Five district presidents (the president of the Federal Reserve Bank of New York is always one) have voting powers on the FOMC, together with all seven members of the full Board. The Board's domination of the twelve reserve banks is enhanced by two factors:

(i)   it appoints presidents of reserve banks; and
(ii) the United States' capital market is national – a familiar fact, but one with clear political implications for the Board's internal operations.

It is in this setting that the Board has special responsibility for the containment of inflation through regulation of the money supply. No significant means of monetary control are held by any other agency or institution. Three hundred and fifty highly-specialized economic research staff work for the Board. Many do so for a large part of their careers, attracted in part by salaries fixed not on civil service scales, but set by market forces: the most senior staff earn considerably more than the chairman or governors. The staff is as large as it is because of what Herbert Stein (1988: 341) regards as the Board's operating premise 'that it must be continuously informed about everything that goes on in the economy', and be able to supply analyses to the Board which enable it to adjust policy in the light of it. In practice, this means that there are on the staff specialists in every sector of the economy, from machine tools to futures markets in agricultural commodities.

Elected politicians in Congress and the White House retain some influence over monetary policy. The president's power to nominate the chairman and governors enables him to shape the Board's composition, while the Senate's power of confirmation permits it to examine his choices. Even fourteen-year terms do not exempt Board members from political pressures. Under the Federal Reserve Act (1913), the Federal Reserve Board is Congress's creation, but not its creature: Congress may alter its structure, rules and remit. The Board has, indeed, periodically been the subject of pressure from populist members of Congress, anxious to bring the central bank under closer political control. In practice, there is little overt interference, partly because the Board's members understand that their technical judgements about policy are made in the context of intensely competitive democratic politics. As with the Supreme Court, so with the Reserve Board: its formal autonomy increases, rather than diminishes, its sager members' awareness of the contingent character of its legitimacy and power.

There are, however, two good arguments to be made in support of holding the Board more accountable to elected politicians; the first has to do with the principle of accountability in a democratic society, and the second derives from the composition of the Board's personnel. With regard to the first, it is not *prima facie* justifiable that a political system characterized above all else by the use of elections as a legitimating device for the holding of public office should leave the determination of monetary policy in the hands of individuals formally accountable to no one. The argument is the stronger for the Board's being wholly unrepresentative of America: most governors have been male, white, and either academics or bankers. (In March 2013, the Board comprised four men and three women. Three members of the Board have PhDs in Economics. All members are white.) Those feared to be radical, or whose views depart from the acceptable middle ground of monetary thinking, are rarely considered for membership of the Board, regardless of their ability. Not only does the board draw on a narrow range of activities, it tends to select its membership, and especially its regional presidents, from among its own. Necessary though experience is, it is not clear that the narrow backgrounds of most board and district bank members and of the board's staff are entirely advantageous. Populists and liberals have regarded the self-perpetuating character of the Federal Reserve System's narrow personnel selection as evidence of its threat both to democratic accountability and to the interests of individual borrowers.

The Board hovers uncertainly on the fringes of government, exploiting its centrality to macroeconomic policy and its autonomy to arrive at a unique constitutional arrangement. In practice, its equivocal status has worked to its institutional advantage, and (usually) to the benefit of monetary policy itself. Congressional politicians who have shaped the Board's constitution by statute prize the arrangement's utility. By granting the Board autonomy from electoral politics, wise politicians implicitly acknowledge the temptations open to them were the control of monetary policy to be theirs as completely as is that of fiscal policy. Manipulating interest rates for electoral advantage of congressional majorities would be too enticing to resist, but the consequences would be damagingly destabilizing. (On the one occasion in the post-war period when the Board acceded to ferocious presidential pressure, that of President Nixon's harassment of Chairman Burns in 1971–72, the lagged effects on inflation were disastrous.) By delegating responsibility to the FOMC, Congress implicitly accepts that monetary judgements should be made as dispassionately as possible and comparatively free from immediate political pressures, which, since the early 1970s, have warped Congress's own formation of fiscal policy.

Powers and actions of the Federal Reserve Board

As the discussion of the Federal Reserve Board (often referred to simply as 'the Fed') shows, the president lacks even nominal direct control over monetary policy. The power to set the discount rate (the rate at which the

Federal Reserve lends to commercial banks and other institutions which make loans available) is the Federal Reserve Board's alone, giving it special responsibility for the achievement of economic stability (and especially for the containment of inflation) by manipulating short-term interest rates. Institutional control of United States economic policy is, therefore, twin-headed because the Fed controls only monetary policy but the president and the Congress control fiscal policy. Moreover, the contrast between the formation of monetary and of fiscal policy is sharp. Monetary policy is developed in a small, cohesive unit whose members are more respectful of technical analysis than of electoral pressures, and whose institutional circumstances facilitate the making of technical judgements and exempt them from electoral reprisal. By contrast, fiscal policy has, since the early 1970s, been developed and implemented publicly in conditions of extreme electoral sensitivity in open hearings and mark-up sessions of congressional committees and subcommittees.

The quasi-autonomous Federal Reserve provides an appropriate means whereby both president and Congress may influence indirectly the formation of monetary policy while exempting themselves from blame for its consequences. Congress thereby acknowledges its limited capacity to form policy quickly and coherently. Equally, successive presidents have acknowledged that Congresses will withhold from them greater influence over monetary policy than that granted by the Federal Reserve Act of 1913. Congress is a full constitutional participant in economic policy-making. Its bicameral, fragmented condition prevents it from exercising leadership in circumstances where speed of response and tech-nically-informed anticipation are at a premium. The Board may accom-modate fiscal policy, or move against it. In the long term, its ability to counteract the decisions of elected politicians is slight; in the short term, it may act autonomously, as it did in the latter part of Carter's presidency. The Board works through three policy instruments, each exercised (in ways that doubtless cause President Andrew Jackson to turn in his grave) through the Federal Reserve's trading office in New York:

1. It may buy Treasury bonds from private brokers or sell them in 'open-market operations'. Purchases from brokers increase banks' reserves (directly so if bonds are bought from banks themselves; indirectly if through brokers who then deposit the proceeds from the sale). Increased reserves leach through to increased Treasury bond purchases, which raise their price, decrease interest rates on bonds in the Treasury market, increase the money supply, and so stimulate private spending. Selling Treasury bonds reverses this sequence of events. In practice, the Board is constantly engaged in the markets, pushing prices of and interest rates paid on government securities in their perfectly inversely varying directions.

2. It may encourage or discourage bank borrowing by lowering or raising the 'discount rate', which is the rate of interest that it charges on short-term (fifteen days or less) loans to banks or other depository institutions.
3. It may alter the reserve requirement ratio which it imposes on banks.

Of the many difficulties to which regulation of interest rates by these three means gives rise, the consequential problem of reconciling fiscal and monetary policy is perhaps the greatest. Difficult enough intellectually, the structure and culture of United States government render it harder. The Employment Act of 1946 was not directed to the Federal Reserve Board or its role, although, in congressional hearings in 1952, the Board graciously indicated that it was willing to accept the objectives of the Act 'provided it is explicitly within the framework of a stable price level'. In fiscal policy, by contrast, no such arrangement exists. If monetary policy is made by unelected experts in private, then fiscal policy is formed by elected amateurs in public. Significantly, too, professional staff on congressional committees and subcommittees, and those who work for individual members of Congress and senators, are less insulated by professional cultures and norms than are the members of the Federal Reserve.

Objects and processes of economic policy-making

Policy objectives and policy instruments

In common with the governments of most advanced democracies, the United States government has pursued four economic policy objectives in the post-war period. Conveniently, they are codified in the 1946 Employment Act:

1. maintenance of high employment;
2. promotion of economic growth;
3. maintenance of price stability;
4. maintenance of a favourable balance of payments.

In pursuit of these purposes, the federal government nominally has fiscal (taxation and public spending policies), monetary (controlling the money supply and setting the discount rate) and trade policy at its disposal. Its objectives have not differed materially from those of other western States. The two primary differences in policy between the United States, and Japan and most western European States, have lain, first, in the policy instruments employed and, second, in institutional design. The federal government has not adopted an industrial policy of the kind that

Germany, France and Japan have had (although many of the fifty states have implemented industrial policies of their own).

The institutional setting within which policy is made in the United States is exceptional. No other central government functions within a comparably tight constitutional straitjacket, still less one tailored in the late eighteenth century. Fragmenting structures fragments process, particularly so with economic policy, where taxing and spending powers are divided between Congress and the presidency, and between the federal government and the states. Article I of the Constitution gives the House precedence over the Senate in the origination of revenue bills, requires that all money drawn from the Treasury be in the form of appropriations made by law, and requires that national accounts be published. The presentment clause of Article I introduces the executive to the fiscal feast by providing that all bills shall be presented to the president for his signature or veto. On Article I and the Sixteenth Amendment providing for a federal income tax hang all the constitutional laws enabling and constraining the federal government in the making of fiscal policy.

Economic policy choices

In macroeconomic policy, presidential relations with Congress are primarily fiscal in nature, and those with the Federal Reserve System entirely monetary. All economic policy choices are, nonetheless, tightly interrelated. At its simplest, the two consequences of interrelatedness are: first, that a president's decision regarding problem A will have consequences for problems B, C and D, and the range of choice with respect to those problems; second, policy problems have no coherent structural analogues and so fail to fit into tidy organizational channels. The problem of governance for the president is thereby compounded. Macroeconomic policy has, throughout the post-war period, exemplified both consequences, as presidents and their advisors have long appreciated.

With a single client (the president), the CEA's advice is untainted by parochial agency perspectives, and so has eased the problem for presidents' economic leadership of the divisions between the presidential and departmental segments of the executive. Nonetheless, the CEA has not been a panacea for the executive's maladies. Recent presidents have established other coordinating units – such as Ford's Economic Policy Board', Bush's Economic Policy Council (EPC), and Clinton's National Economic Council (NEC) – in an attempt to imprint the president's strategic and tactical priorities more fully on departments. President George W. Bush maintained Clinton's integration within the NEC of domestic and foreign components of economic policy despite calls, primarily from National Security Advisor Condoleezza Rice, to integrate economic and security policy. In January 2011, President Obama appointed former Clinton advisor Gene Sperling to the post of Director of the NEC; Obama intended the appointment to facilitate the NEC's playing the traditional role of assessing the best economic policy options from across the administration, with Sperling acting as an honest broker to the President. Whether the NEC has actually been effective in enhancing coordination of policy-making in a balkanized government remains unclear.

The federal budget process prior to 1974

Roosevelt and his successors used the budget to set their political priorities between programmes by submitting annual fiscal recommendations to Congress. No other single delegation of power from Congress has done more to enable presidents to set the national agenda. Whether that opportunity is seized and fiscal leadership given (as Roosevelt and Eisenhower did throughout their presidencies, and Reagan did briefly in 1981) or squandered (as Carter did in 1980, and Reagan did after 1981) depends on presidential judgement and skill, and not formal statutory authority.

Prior to the implementation of BICA in 1976 (see p. 374), budgeting was a closed and mainly private process in which no examination was made of the national budget as a whole. Decisions about spending and taxing were made by different politicians in different committees, but budgetary fragmentation did not result in fiscal indiscipline: the seniority rule – the recruitment to Revenue and Appropriations committees in both chambers only of those whom congressional leaders trusted to act responsibly and to defer to the established norms of the Committees – made for tight political control of fiscal policy by Congress. Within the Executive Branch, budgets were drafted incrementally. In submitting their requests to the BOB/OMB, agencies typically (and rationally) added a small percentage to their appropriations for the previous fiscal year. The BOB ensured that the many budget requests it examined did not breach the president's overall budget targets.

Congressional Appropriations subcommittees invariably reduced the budget requests for individual agencies. Departments, agencies, the BOB and the president expected them to do so – hence the inflated requests made by departments and agencies to the BOB, and by the president to Congress. Congress, nonetheless, acceded to incremental budgeting: the economy's steady growth made it affordable and politically attractive by dispensing with the need to set priorities between different categories of spending. Although deficits were usually incurred, the federal deficit declined as a percentage of GNP. Total federal debt therefore also grew absolutely, but shrank as a percentage of GNP. Peacetime budget requests of twentieth-century presidents were, until the late 1960s, designed not to result in substantial deficits (a situation which altered dramatically in the first decade of the twenty-first century). Subsequent restraining action of the Appropriations committees reduced any deficit still further. Congressional tax-writing committees confirmed this culture of fiscal conservatism by generally resisting attempts to cut income taxes. Even in 1965, the first year of President Lyndon Johnson's Great Society, when spending on social, welfare and educational policies was rising quickly, the budget deficit was only $1.4 billion – about half the size of the deficit in the peacetime year of 1955 during the fiscally conservative administration of President Eisenhower, and a trivial 0.2 per cent of GNP.

Expenditure on the Vietnam War disrupted stable incremental budgeting. Costing $27 billion per annum by 1967 (one-third of total defence appropriations), the war accounted for almost the entire federal deficit in that year, and burst the institutional levees of financial restraint. Rapidly rising expenditure on the Vietnam War therefore destabilized government finances, led to the unsettling of the dollar, and to the inflation that engulfed the American economy in the 1970s. Struggles over how to finance the war unhinged not only the Revenue committees, but also the Appropriations committees of both chambers, and damaged relations between them.

In theory, Appropriations committees retained complete authority to appropriate funds within the limits set by the authorizing or legislative committee. In practice, controls exercised by Appropriations committees diminished significantly from the 1960s onwards, for three reasons:

1. The very act of *authorizing* a programme vests it in political practice with a claim on *appropriations*. The capacity of the Appropriations committees to resist authorizing legislation – either by declining to appropriate, or by appropriating at levels significantly below those authorized – is limited. Powerful as both committees were, their members were bound to take account of political pressures from elsewhere in Congress. This pressure intensified with the practice of Authorizing committees in the years after 1945 not to make permanent authorizations (thereby effectively ceding the power of life and death over agencies and their programmes to Appropriations committees), but temporary ones for a year or two (thereby keeping Appropriations committees on a shorter political leash).
2. An increasing proportion of congressional spending has bypassed the Appropriations Committees in the post-war years. A large proportion of Johnson's Great Society programmes were funded by long-term contract authority not subject to annual review by Appropriations committees. The decreasing proportion of the budget that is controllable under current law by the Appropriations committees is examined below.

3.   The House Appropriations Committee's closed meetings, its culture of fiscal conservatism, its hierarchical structure and the protection of its legislation on the floor of the House were all weakened by the wave of congressional reforms of the early 1970s. The dispersal of authority within the House had special significance for 'control' committees such as Ways and Means and Appropriations, whose authority and standing had depended heavily on them. The decision of the House Democratic caucus in 1974 to make appointment to chairs of Appropriations subcommittees subject to full party caucus votes in Congress significantly weakened their autonomy. Furthermore, the powers of Appropriations and tax-writing committees were modified by the 1974 budget reforms.

The Budget and Impoundment Control Act (1974)

The Budget and Impoundment Control Act of 1974, the single-most important reform of economic policy-making since the 1946 Employment Act, arose out of the growing fiscal disorder between 1968 and 1973, and the wider institutional conflict between Congress and the Executive during the Nixon presidency. Vast expenditures on the Vietnam War in the late 1960s, along with growing domestic spending, circumvention of established appropriations control procedures and the political divisiveness of raising income taxes and cutting domestic spending in 1968, had placed budget-making under severe strain by the time Nixon became president. Facing opposition majorities both in the House and the Senate, Nixon attempted to govern without Congress, a strategy which the Constitution ensured would eventually fail but which did so only at a damagingly high cost.

Where Congress appropriated funds to programmes of which Nixon disapproved, he impounded them. Prevented from vetoing parts of Appropriations bills (the 'line-item' veto), Presidents Truman, Eisenhower, and Kennedy had all impounded funds that Congress had added to their defence budgets for particular projects. (The line-item veto is held by the governors of forty-three states. In April 1996, Congress granted this to presidents in the weak form of an enhanced rescission power, which was subsequently judged unconstitutional by the Supreme Court in the 1998 case *Clinton v New York*.) Nixon's use of impoundment was on a different scale and of a different kind: appropriations above the amounts he requested were commonly reduced to his preferred levels or abolished altogether. Bellicosity marked all President Nixon's dealings with Congress, but unashamedly so with respect to budgetary politics. He declined to recognize what was plain in Constitutional law and in statute: the White House's budgetary recommendations had no privileged standing, and presidents were obliged to implement public laws, regardless of whether they approved of them. Laws appropriating funds to government programmes were, in this respect, no different from other public laws; Congress's authority to mandate spending was constitutionally incontestable.

Nixon nonetheless resisted, forcing Congress to sue Cabinet secretaries to ensure that appropriations should be spent as required by law. As impoundments of defence appropriations undertaken by Truman, Eisenhower and Kennedy suggest, Congress has, in any case, declined to eliminate all presidential spending discretion for fear of being perceived as abridging the president's role as Commander-in-Chief. Recognizing the desirability of granting presidents some discretion over the spending of appropriated funds, the 1974 Act legitimized two forms of impoundment – rescissions and deferrals – under specified conditions. The Act required that for appropriated funds to be rescinded (cancelled altogether) according to presidential wishes, the House and Senate would have to pass a bill or a joint resolution of Congress within forty-five days of continuous congressional session following the president's action. The Act set a less demanding condition for the sustaining of a presidential decision to defer the spending of lawfully-appropriated funds: in this case, either the House or the Senate had to veto the proposed deferral for it to be halted.

The 1974 Budget Act addressed three problems:

1. Presidential *abuse of impoundment.*
2. The growing difficulty Congress faced in formulating a *coherent fiscal policy* in the wake of the oil price shock of October 1973 (especially with respect to the increasing difficulty Congress had in passing Appropriations bills before the beginning of the fiscal year to which they referred).
3. Widespread dissatisfaction with what appeared an *uncontrolled growth* in *federal expenditure.*

The first problem concerned the balance of power between Congress and the presidency; the second, the inadequacy of Congress's own procedures for formulating policy; and the third, the federal government's capacity to determine priorities and enable members of Congress and senators to make difficult budgetary choices. To these ends, the Act established new House and Senate budget committees, and a congressional Budget Office providing a centre of economic expertise (thereby enabling Congress to subject budget analyses and estimates from the OMB to its own critical analysis). A new budget calendar was set, the beginning of the fiscal year moved from July to October, and a clear timetable for budget decisions was established. The new budget committees did not supplant the existing Appropriations and Tax-writing committees, but supplemented them: the resulting timetable has therefore to accommodate separate but contingent decisions by the Budget, Appropriations, and Tax committees. This muddled and unsatisfactory compromise occurred because of the unwillingness of members of the established (and prestigious) Appropriations, Senate Finance, and House Ways and Means committees to risk losing influence in a comprehensively reformed fiscal policy committee structure.

The Act stipulates that, in March of every fiscal year, House and Senate budget committees examine reports from other committees on the budgets for programmes falling within their jurisdictions. The budget committees then prepare a first resolution, which, since revisions to the procedure in 1981, has set a ceiling on spending and a floor on revenue on the first day of the next fiscal year, unless Congress decides to adopt a second resolution. It was this first budget resolution, coupled with the binding reconciliation procedures originally included in the second resolution set for passage by September, which Reagan exploited in 1981 to secure heavy cuts in previously-authorized spending over a three-year period.

Neither the Appropriations committees nor the Tax-writing committees in the two chambers enjoy the positions of privilege they once did, despite rules being set for the two budget committees which have limited their effectiveness. The Appropriations committees operate under tight fiscal constraints: the Gramm–Rudman–Hollings Acts I and II, coupled with the Omnibus Budget Reconciliation Act (OBRA) of 1990, and the Budget Act of 1997 have jointly greatly reduced the freedom of action appropriators previously enjoyed. While that part of the federal budget that is controllable under current law by Appropriations committees is small, it is on these programmes that most budgetary restraint was focused until Congress belatedly (in the mid-1990s) turned to the problem presented by the growth of entitlements.

Appropriations subcommittee chairs have adjusted to budget committee ceilings by exploiting such freedom of manoeuvre as they continue to retain. Nominally, their freedom is considerable, since the committee exercises control over the salaries of all federal employees (including themselves, but excluding the president and federal judges, whose incomes are constitutionally protected), defence, education, housing and transport, and over federal programmes, scientific research institutes, and grants-in-aid to state and local governments. In practice, new spending may now be undertaken only where cuts are made in other programmes; the room for manoeuvre is consequently small, and their power reduced commensurately. Special additions to appropriations in order to appease or please colleagues must be matched by reductions elsewhere.

It remains one of the striking characteristics of the federal budget process that presidents and Congresses declare their support for a 'balanced budget' (usually without specifying what they mean by it) without proposing one (as any president could) or writing one (as any Congress could). Rhetorical support for fiscal virtue is cheap; practising it risks being politically expensive.

The Republican majority in the 104th Congress

The politics of budget-making were altered by the Republicans' gaining of a majority in the congressional mid-term elections of 1994. One of the main planks in the Republicans' 'Contract with America' was a proposal to amend the Constitution to require a balanced budget. Under the leadership of Newt Gingrich at the height of his powers as Speaker in January 1995, the House passed the proposal by 300 to 132, but the measure just failed to win passage in the Senate. Later attempts to revive the proposal also met with defeat.

As the Republicans had successfully exploited the Democrats' support for Clinton's tax rises in the 1993 budget negotiations, so Clinton successfully attacked the Republicans in 1996 for having twice forced the closure of federal agencies in the winter of 1995/6 (the so-called 'government shutdown') as part of their campaign to secure a budget deal satisfactory to them. Whereas it had previously normally been the case that continuing resolutions were passed to enable the federal government to continue in operation, Gingrich and his allies in the Republican House leadership, their calculations distorted by inflated ambition, decided in 1995 to force the issue. As Senator Dole had rightly warned would prove the case, the Speaker's tactic was a disastrous political error: Gingrich's sway over Republican House colleagues fell sharply as the full extent of public displeasure became apparent. Mr Clinton, accomplished at the politics of adjusting his own political position to that of the median voter, prospered through successfully stigmatizing Gingrich and his allies as extremists while actually embracing fiscal austerity.

The 1997 Balanced Budget Agreement

Clinton's drift to fiscal conservatism moved a stage further in the summer of 1997 with his support for a fiscal 1998 budget resolution heavily promoted by the Republican majority (see Table 11.1). House Concurrent Resolution 84 provided for a balanced budget by 2002 to be achieved by net reductions in the deficit of more than $204 billion. Significant spending reductions were effected in mandatory programmes, sharpening the burden of deficit reduction on the poor, who had already suffered heavy reductions with the cuts in the Food Stamps programme and the abolition of AFDC in 1996: cuts of $115 billion over five years

Table 11.1 *1997 Budget Agreement: Spending Outlays by Functional Category*

Fiscal year	1997	1998	1999	2000	2001	2002
Science, space and technology	17.0	16.9	16.5	16.0	15.9	15.7
Energy	1.9	2.2	2.4	2.3	2.0	1.9
Natural resources	22.4	22.4	22.7	23.0	22.7	22.3
Agriculture	9.9	11.0	11.3	10.7	9.5	9.1
Commerce, housing credit	−9.6	1.8	3.3	8.6	11.6	12.8
Transportation	39.5	40.9	41.3	41.4	41.3	41.2
Community development	12.1	10.4	10.9	11.0	11.4	8.4
Education, social services	50.5	56.1	59.3	60.7	61.9	62.3
Health	127.4	137.8	144.9	153.9	163.1	171.7
Medicare	191.3	201.8	211.5	225.5	238.8	250.8
Income security	237.8	247.8	258.1	268.2	277.3	285.2
Social security	366.4	384.1	402.8	422.8	443.9	466.8
Veterans	39.4	41.3	41.9	42.2	42.5	42.7
Courts, police, prisons	20.7	22.6	24.5	25.2	25.9	24.9
Defence	266.6	266.0	265.8	268.4	270.1	272.6
International affairs	14.5	14.6	14.6	15.0	14.8	14.8
General government	13.9	14.0	14.4	14.7	14.1	13.1
Net interest	247.6	248.6	252	247.7	241.7	236.9
Offsetting receipts	−47.4	−48.8	−44.4	−46.0	−50.0	−64.1
Total spending	**1,622.1**	**1,692.2**	**1,753.9**	**1,811.1**	**1,858.5**	**1,889.1**
Revenues	**1,544.9**	**1,601.8**	**1,644.2**	**1,728.1**	**1,805.1**	**1,890.4**
Deficit (−) or surplus	**−67.2**	**−90.4**	**−89.7**	**−83.0**	**53.3**	**1.3**

Source: House Budget Committee.

were effected in Medicare (serving 37 million elderly and disabled Americans), and of $16 billion in Medicaid (serving some 42 million poor children, women, and impoverished disabled and elderly). Tax changes included reductions in capital gains and estate taxes, and tax credits for children.

Fiscal policy under President George W. Bush

On taking office in January 2001, President George W. Bush inherited favourable projections for continued government budget surpluses well into the first decade of the twenty-first century. By 2002, however, the surplus had turned to deficit as a result of four factors: an economic slowdown which began in 2001; a dramatic rise in expenditure on defence and homeland security following the attacks of 9/11; increased expenditure on Medicare and subsidies to the farming sector; and the introduction by the President of a sizeable tax cut in 2001, followed by a second in 2003. President Bush's tax cuts contained a sunset clause leading to their expiration in 2010, but Congress extended the cuts in its Tax Relief, Unemployment Insurance Reauthorization, and Job Creation Act of 2010.

The defining economic policies of the Bush years were not the tax cuts of his first administration but the response to the 2007–08 financial crisis that dominated the last months of the second Bush administration. The primary challenge for the President was twofold: to restore confidence in the banking sector, and encourage banks to increase their lending. On 3 October 2008, Congress passed two significant pieces of legislation, the *Emergency Economic Stabilization Act* (more commonly called 'the bailout') and the *Troubled Assets Relief Programme* (TARP). The former authorized the Treasury to buy up to $700 billion of troubled assets. Most of those assets were mortgage-backed securities held by banks which were worthless, following the collapse of the US housing market. The Act also authorized the supply of cash to banks in an attempt to increase liquidity within the financial markets in the hope of stimulating new lending. TARP authorized $700 billion of funds made available to the Treasury to purchase assets and equity from financial institutions in an attempt to strengthen the US financial sector. This amount was reduced to $475 billion as a result of the 2010 Dodd–Frank legislation (discussed below).

Fiscal policy under President Barack Obama

President Obama entered office in January 2009 in the midst of the worst economic and financial crisis in the United States since the Great Depression. Its severity was greatly enhanced and complicated by the banking crisis which, for a period of some months in late 2008, threatened the stability of the entire financial system. The crisis was not just of liquidity, but of solvency.

Within a month of taking the oath of office, President Obama had secured passage of the *American Recovery and Reinvestment Act* (ARRA – often called the Stimulus Package). The ARRA looked much like a Keynesian stimulus package that provided $787 billion of investment in infrastructure, green energy initiatives, education and health. Then, in July 2010, the President secured passage of the *Dodd–Frank Wall Street Reform and Consumer Protection Act*, which represented the most significant regulation of the financial sector since the New Deal banking legislation of the 1930s. The act encouraged greater oversight of the financial sector, increased transparency in the nature of complex financial instruments (primarily of derivatives – which would be traded on exchanges), and the introduction of the Volcker Rule (to create a greater separation between high-street banks and their investment banking arms such that depository banks would refrain from proprietary trading). The complexity of the legislation, and of the regulations to which it gave rise, left unanswered, even by as late as 2013, the question of how effective the legislation would prove to be in reducing the probability that excessive risk-taking by individual bankers would threaten the stability of the entire financial sector.

Having supported legislation designed to ameliorate the effects of the 2007–08 financial crisis, President Obama then faced two related challenges in the form of the so-called *fiscal cliff* and the *debt-ceiling crisis*. The 'fiscal cliff' was the projected outcome of a failure on the part of the President and Congress to put in place legislation that would mitigate the effects of the ending of the 2003 George W. Bush tax cuts, which would end in 2010. If no action were taken, taxes would increase and government spending would decrease. The ending of the Bush tax cuts was delayed for two years as a result of the passage of the *Tax Relief, Unemployment Insurance Reauthorization, and Job Creation Act* of 2010. However, the question of how best to deal with the ending of the Bush tax cuts led to a stand-off at the end of 2011, when the Democratic President and the Republican-controlled House of Representatives disagreed about the appropriate level of government spending and the best way to tackle the national debt. Speaker John Boehner and the Republicans opposed any increase in the level of the deficit and called for a reduction in government spending. President Obama wanted the debt ceiling raised. Agreement was reached in July 2011, minutes before the US would have defaulted on some the interest payments on its loans. However, the agreement failed to prevent America's credit rating being downgraded from AAA to AA+. The fiscal cliff debate dominated the first month of Obama's second term but a compromise was signed into law in the form of the *American Taxpayer Relief Act* (ATRA) of 2012 (enacted in January 2013) which made permanent elements of the Bush tax cuts.

Processes of economic policy-making: an assessment

Three explanations can be advanced for the fiscal crisis in which the United States has become enmired since the early 1980s:

1.   the *new processes* were themselves to blame;

2. the deficit results from the *policy choices* made by the Reagan administration and accepted by Congress in 1981;
3. institutional reform made the *formation* and *legitimation* of fiscal policy more difficult.

In support of the first hypothesis, three arguments have been advanced: first, that privacy and closure were prerequisites for overcoming the challenges presented by the need to ensure coordinated action between myriad institutional players, all of whom had some role to play in economic policy formation. Only by ensuring that these players could work together could aggregate budgetary outcomes be internally consistent and, furthermore, would they be consistent with presidential preferences. The second argument is that the openness of policy processes has encouraged greater interest group influence over policy, and increased the difficulty which members of Congress have in resisting them. Finally, it is argued that the Budget process ought to be regarded as part of the wave of congressional reforms in the mid-1970s which have made Congress a more responsive representative institution, but one that is less capable of aggregating interests.

In support of the second hypothesis, it has been contended, first, that the correlation between institutional reform and fiscal chaos is spurious and that, as Hogan (1985) argued, changed political and economic conditions have disrupted old orders. Second, it is argued that the source of the structural deficit lies in the Reagan administration's failure to reduce entitlement spending in 1981, and its increase in defence spending by 42 per cent in real terms between FY 1981 and FY 1988. Third, the revenue base was driven down. Congress's passage of the Economic Recovery Tax Act in 1981 reduced federal revenues by $749 billion between FY 1982 and FY 1986. A correction in 1982 of approximately $100 billion altered the speed, but not the downward direction, of the federal government's revenue base. Fourth, Reagan's budgetary exercises were predicated on optimistic economic assumptions. Some within the Reagan administration knew perfectly well that the result would be large and growing deficits, but anticipated that Congress would respond by cutting domestic spending still further. To a limited extent, it did so: starting in 1982, Congress reduced spending and increased taxes in 1983, 1984, 1985 and 1987, but expenditure was not cut to the level required to hold the deficit steady. The explanation for the failure is that most of the budget was, as it remains, either uncontrollable under existing authorization law (Social Security and Medicare are clear examples); uncontrollable, if the United States were not to breach international obligations (interest payments on the national debt); or ran counter to the president's wishes (defence spending was to increase in real terms by historically large amounts in peacetime). The remainder accounted for only a small proportion of federal expenditure.

In support of item 3 is an integrated institutional approach based on the assumption that institutions matter and that they shape policy outcomes. Institutional structures and rules do not determine such outcomes, but condition them. Thus, the failure of the 1974 Act and subsequent reforms to establish an entirely new committee structure for fiscal policy and the provision in the House for rotation of the chair is explained by the threat to existing bases of power, promotion to which had governed congressional politicians' career planning and calculations. The budget committees were thereby weakened, and their capacity to make enforceable collective choices for Congress as a whole diminished. They are able to overcome this weakness only on exceptional occasions. Reagan's exploitation in 1981 of the reconciliation provisions of the first Budget Resolution under the procedures amended in 1980 is the best example of the interaction of procedure and political opportunity.

For many, the inadequacy of budget processes since 1974 is revealed by the rarity with which the making of fiscal policy overcomes particularistic interests, ironically illustrated by the later incapacity of Congress to make good the fiscal damage done by choices made in 1981. Current institutional structures in Congress offer weak incentives to elected politicians for the overcoming of electoral and interest group pressures. Presidents Reagan and Bush renounced fiscal policy as an instrument of macroeconomic stability, with the consequence that disproportionate emphasis during their administrations was placed on monetary policy (over which they exercise, at best, marginal influence). Congressional direction of fiscal policy has, since 1981, largely been devoted to addressing the aggregate consequences of the sharp upward thrust given to the fiscal deficit by President Reagan's spending and taxing policies in that year. By the end of 1986, Reagan had accumulated a larger aggregate fiscal deficit than all his thirty-nine predecessors combined: the national debt nearly trebled during the eight years in which he occupied the White House.

Institutional reform did not make fiscal deficits of unprecedented size and proportion in peacetime inevitable, but did reduce the obstacles to their creation. Had such proposals come before the four revenue and Appropriations committees of the House and the Senate in the period before the reforms to committee rules and the budget process of the early to mid-1970s (themselves products of the poisonous distrust that had arisen between the White House and Congress), it is unlikely they would have made legislative progress. In 1981, they made a rapid passage into law.

Differences between the institutional circumstances governing the formation of fiscal and monetary policy have had damaging political consequences since 1981 because of the ideological crusade on behalf of income tax rate cuts, huge increases in defence spending financed by borrowing on international capital markets, and deficient policy processes. When ideological fervour informs the formation of public financial policy, as it did in the early 1980s, modified institutional barriers were too weak to resist, while the incentives for elected politicians to remedy the error were, for too long, insufficient. The divided government which resulted from the Republican landslide in the 1994 mid-term elections solidified this ideological crusade and, as discussed in Chapter 10, Democratic President William Clinton affirmed a shift within his party in relation to fiscal policy when, in 1996, he declared (wrongly, as it turned out) that the era of 'big government' was over.

The eight years of the George W. Bush presidency were marked by two heavy cuts in income tax (in 2001 and 2003), accompanied by a commitment to reductions in federal government spending (tax cuts were delivered much more effectively than the promised reductions in federal spending). And, despite the financial crisis of 2007, no bipartisan agreement has been reached concerning the best way to reduce the deficit, as well as the balance to be struck between tax increases and cuts in federal spending. Although less significant than they were in the 2010 mid-term elections, the Tea Party Movements remain a force within the Republican Party that continue in their efforts to ensure that candidates seeking election or re-election have unblemished credentials as *bona fide* fiscal conservatives. The ideological crusade begun with President Reagan's tax cuts and reductions in federal government spending continues to cast its shadow over the fiscal stand-off between the Republican-controlled House and the Democratic-controlled White House.

Conclusion

Despite significant reforms to the financial system in recent years, current institutional processes provide inadequate solutions to major fiscal crises because they provide powerful incentives for elected politicians to support favoured programmes and to reject the deficit that results. Institutions whose rules reward irresponsibility risk failure.

Making fiscal policy has, since the growth of ,ederal budget deficits in the early 1970s and the contemporaneous internal reforms of Congress, rarely been less than disordered – and, on occasion, incapacitated. Fiscal policy in Washington is formed in an institutional setting and through political processes that now exaggerate, rather than mitigate, the weakness of the central state, the disaggregation of the congressional policy-making process, and its permeability to external influence. Important institutional controls, a neutral and expert BOB in the Executive Branch, powerful and semiautonomous Taxation and Appropriations committees in Congress which have shared interests in fiscal order have been undermined by internal reform and the entrepreneurial independence of legislators whose incentives to reach rational aggregate outcomes are insufficient for the public interest to be achieved. In this unpromising setting, the incoherence of successive fiscal changes and the diminishing share of the federal budget that is effectively controllable have together produced historically high fiscal deficits, a reduced revenue base and a quadrupled national debt. During most of the 1980s, it also produced a large external deficit (which is linked to the fiscal deficit because of the low savings ratio in the United States), and a residually chaotic policy in respect of the external value of the dollar. This deficit dominates economic policy-making in the second decade of the twenty-first century.

Government's general purpose is to effect collective action which cannot be undertaken by private individuals, associations, or corporations. This task is necessarily difficult in the United States because of the fragmentation that characterizes its political institutions. Reforms of the budget processes at both ends of Pennsylvania Avenue and changes in Congress's committee structure, culture and rules perversely made the task of effecting collective action in pursuit of collective economic policy purposes even harder. In conjunction with muddled and incoherent policy choices, the results were, for too long, deeply damaging.

The prospects for the generation of coherent policy-choices in the near future are not promising: the ideological polarization between the two parties has resulted in gridlock with regard to fiscal policy – such that fights over the debt ceiling continue, and blame for the credit downgrade of 2011 is attributed to the dysfunctional relationship between the US Congress and the presidency. The effective party system that scholars in the 1950s hoped to see, and that was discussed in Chapter 3, has materialized. However, this has not resulted in a separated system of well-functioning institutions but, rather, in a system in which the institutions separated by the Constitution are no longer brought together by the glue of parties. For so long as the polarization of political elites at both the federal and state levels hinders the opportunity for bipartisan policy-making, fiscal policy is likely to be defined by incoherence, inadequate eleventh-hour compromise and ideological fervour.

Chapter 12

Foreign and Defence Policy

This chapter examines the processes of United States foreign and defence policy by focusing on the key institutional actors which, together, determine the shape and direction of policy. The United States remains the world's sole superpower, despite the rapid growth of a number of nations since the mid-1980s. China might eclipse the United States as the largest economy in the world by 2020. Some commentators question whether the US will remain the global superpower once its status as the largest economy in the world is lost. Yet, its economy remains not only the largest in the world but twice the size of China's; and its armed forces remain much the most potent. No other state has the capacity and will to project force around the globe, or in the air above it. Neither does any other state commit such a panoply of financial, technical and human resources to gathering intelligence about the military, political, diplomatic and commercial capacities and intentions of other states, whether friendly or hostile.

The formation of United States foreign policy, the means of its implementation, and the ends to which policy is directed, are of critical significance to the international political system. They also affect scholarly understanding of American government itself, since competitive struggles within and between institutions of government occur over foreign and defence policy as much as over domestic policy. This chapter examines these processes – examining the key institutions which direct foreign policy, both in military and non-military spheres. Key to understanding the formation of United States foreign policy is appreciation of the relationships between the president and the Congress which the Constitution invites to share not only authority, but also power over the direction of foreign and defence policy.

Foreign policy, defence policy and the national interest

When asked how foreign policy in the United States was made, President Harry S. Truman replied 'I make foreign policy'. His position is supported by the majority opinion of the Supreme Court written by Justice Douglas Sutherland in *United States v Curtiss-Wright Export Corporation* (1936). Oft-cited in textbooks, this case is usually, but erroneously, identified as the definitive word on the broad and implied powers of the president in foreign affairs (in contrast to his limited and specified powers in domestic ones). Presidents certainly face fewer constraints in foreign policy, and even fewer in security and intelligence policy, than they do when seeking to influence domestic policy. But no president has a free hand.

Justice Sutherland's judgement in *Curtiss-Wright* set only distant boundaries to presidential power. Yet, the president's powers are, in practice, more vigorously contested than his breathless account might suggest. Rather, even in the arena of foreign policy, presidential power remains what Edwin Corwin famously described as 'an invitation to struggle'.

While greater than in domestic policy, and while presidents have, from the first, exercised powers which they claim to be implied by Article II of the Constitution (see Exhibit 12.1), their realizable extent is shaped by the exigencies of politics, and the contingencies both of congressional support and of public opinion. Without the latter two, implied powers amount to little over the long term; with them, they can occasionally be as great as Sutherland wrongly suggested they always are.

While defence policy should serve and not drive foreign policy, the relationship is rarely so straightforward. Defence might be expected to be a realm in which the articulation of a 'national interest' by the agencies of the federal government is least subject to amendment by parochial interests. If the state is to express an interest both unambiguous and durable, surely it can, and will, do so in foreign and defence policy. Yet, it does so incompletely, because different bureaucratic, economic and political pressures on and foreign economic policy-making constrain the president, and affect the long-run direction and content of policy. Foreign policy is but one determinant of defence policy. Defence policy is also shaped by the modes and costs of acquiring weapons systems, the political momentum of established defence relationships, bureaucratic power and congressional support for existing deployments.

As Exhibit 12.1 indicates, the framers of the Constitution were as disinclined to grant the president free rein in the formation of foreign and defence policy as in domestic policy. Nonetheless, from granting the power to negotiate treaties, and the bestowal of the power of Commander-in-Chief of the United States's armed forces to the president

Exhibit 12.1 Constitutional Allocation of Authority (or Powers) over Foreign and Defence Policy

Authority Granted to Congress
Under Article I, Section 8:

The Congress shall have power:

To lay and collect taxes, duties, imposts and excises, to pay the debts and provide for the common defense and general welfare of the United States; but all duties, imposts and excises shall be uniform throughout the United States;

To define and punish piracies and felonies committed on the high Seas, and Offenses against the Law of Nations;

To declare War, grant letters of marque and reprisal, and make rules concerning captures on land and water;

To raise and support armies, but no appropriation of money to that use shall be for a longer term than two years;

To provide and maintain a Navy;

To make rules for the government and regulation of the land and naval forces;

To provide for calling forth the militia to execute the laws of the Union, suppress insurrections and repel invasions;

To provide for organizing, arming, and disciplining the militia, and for governing such part of them as may be employed in the service of the United States, reserving to the States respectively, the appointment of the officer, and the authority of training the militia according to the discipline prescribed by Congress;

To exercise exclusive legislation ... over all places purchased by the consent of the legislature of the state in which the same shall be, for the erection of forts, magazines, arsenals, dock-yards, and other needful buildings.

Authority Granted to the President
Under Article II, Section 2:

The President shall be the Commander-in-Chief of the Army and Navy of the United States, and of the militia of the several states, when called into the actual service of the United States.

He shall have power, by and with the advice and consent of the Senate, to make treaties, provided two-thirds of the Senators present concur; and he shall nominate, and by and with the Advice and Consent of the Senate, shall appoint Ambassadors.

He shall receive Ambassadors ... and shall commission all the officers of the United States.

by Article II, Section 2, presidents since George Washington have claimed substantial implied powers over the making of foreign and defence policy.

The presidential prerogative over waging war under Article II, Section 2, has been expansively defined by most presidents since Franklin D. Roosevelt to include the initiation of hostilities. Formal declarations of war by Congress are rare; the deployment of US armed forces and, increasingly, of remotely-controlled advanced weapons in battle is not. The United States engaged in military conflict without a congressional declaration of war in Korea between 1950 and 1953; in Lebanon, in 1958 and 1985; in Vietnam, between 1961 and 1975; in the Dominican Republic, in 1965; in Cambodia, in 1970; in Grenada, in 1985; in Panama, in 1989; and in the first Gulf War following the Iraqi invasion of Kuwait, in 1991. President Clinton committed troops to Kosovo in the former Yugoslavia in 1999 without a congressional resolution, and in the face of opposition from some members of Congress. President George W. Bush secured congressional approval (but not a declaration of war) for military action both in Afghanistan (October 2001) and Iraq (March 2003). President Obama committed US aircraft to the protection of a no-fly zone in Libya in March 2011. As Clinton had been in 1999, so Obama was criticized by some for failing to secure the prior consent of Congress for his action. In addition to such interventions, covert operations occur throughout the world under the auspices of the Central Intelligence Agency (CIA). These have led, either through direct action or sponsorship, to the overthrow of existing governments and the establishment of new ones, usually in the Third World. Perhaps the most striking single recent example of such action was the assassination of Osama Bin Laden in Pakistan on 2 May 2011. Although undertaken by US Navy Seals, the action was prepared and planned by the CIA. US drone attacks on targets in Afghanistan and Pakistan are, for better or worse, now so common as to excite as little comment from within the United States, as they feed resentment within those two countries. War by remote control has become quotidian.

Institutional participants in foreign and defence policy

The president

The distinguished constitutional scholar, Edward Corwin, once famously observed that the Constitution 'is an invitation to struggle for the privilege of directing American foreign policy'. The struggle is conducted almost entirely between the two elected branches: while significant cases have come before the Supreme Court, executive–legislative struggle since the Nixon presidency has not tempted federal courts to pass judgement

Figure 12.1 *The Defence/Foreign Policy Apparatus of the United States Federal Government*

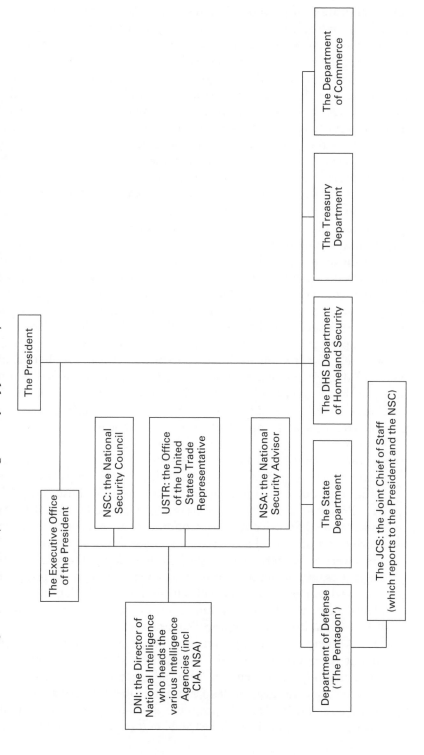

on the allocation of powers. The president is the single-most important participant in foreign and in defence policy, and the Constitution grants him special authority (by which we mean 'powers') in respect of them. The Article II clause conferring the authority of Commander-in-Chief on the president vests him with a singular authority: in war (though not in peace) the president lacks competitors, as well as peers. US soldiers follow presidential commands. Addressing immediate external threats to national security requires organizational clarity and political singularity: they meet in the president. However, conflict about the war power's nature and extent was not disposed of by the constitutional text. Neither has it been settled by subsequent disputes about it.

Whereas, in war, the authority of Commander-in-Chief owes little to persuasion and almost everything to authority, his influence over foreign and defence policy in peace is shared with Congress, and with the civilian and military bureaucracies. Even in peace, however, the president remains the dominant influence in determining what foreign and defence policy actually is. Indeed, although President Obama faced some opposition from within Congress for his so-called 'Pivot to Asia', he did not face the possibility of his decision being vetoed. Congress neither can, nor may, obstruct such a decision by the nation's chief diplomat. The president has both an obligation and an opportunity to lead: US foreign policy is not merely what presidents declare it to be, but is nearly so. In the post-war period, most presidents have accepted the force of the first and the utility of the second, though not to congressional or public acclaim.

Congress's influence on foreign and defence policy is usually exerted in one of two forms, and a president would be unwise to ignore either:

- In the *setting of bounds* to what is *politically acceptable*. Development of United States policy towards Iraq was crafted largely by an inner circle surrounding President George W. Bush comprising Vice-President Dick Cheney, Secretary of Defense Donald Rumsfeld and National Security Adviser Condoleeza Rice. Secretary of State Powell was often excluded from this inner circle. However, discussions were not undertaken independently of Congress, external interest groups, public opinion, or foreign states Although the president's role as Chief Diplomat is formally ensured by Article II, prudent presidents secure the domestic foundations of their negotiating position before committing their political capital abroad.
- In *modifying* particular presidential proposals. Congress has often sought to modify presidential policy, both during its development and after its pronouncement. Informal meetings and conversations between the congressional leadership, members of relevant congressional committees, and the president and his advisers shape policy during formulation. Formal hearings before congressional commit-

tees at which administration witnesses are examined, and after which they give their assessments of congressional sentiment to agency heads and the White House, offer further opportunities for influence. Finally, the ratification of Treaties allows the Senate to judge presidential policy after its establishment. As the Senate's refusal to ratify the Versailles Treaty in 1919 and SALT II in 1979 showed, this power can have momentous consequences: President Carter's withdrawal of the SALT II Treaty in the teeth of Senate opposition to the Treaty's provisions was important both for itself and for reflecting new anxieties within Congress about the erosion of America's military power in the wake of the Soviet invasion of Afghanistan.

Setting the foreign policy agenda

The president's capacity and opportunity to set the foreign policy agenda derive from his legitimacy, a function of his status as the only nationally-elected official. While defining options in policy formation requires the involvement of other parts of the Executive Branch, the pronouncement of foreign policy is primarily the president's responsibility. Yet, Congress's willingness to grant the president virtually unfettered discretion in determining United States foreign policy is a product of Cold War, rather than of peace. The change from the American-led alliance against Nazi Germany to the American-led alliance against Soviet Communism was institutionally nearly seamless: Franklin D. Roosevelt and Harry Truman, as Commanders-in-Chief until August 1945, gave way to Harry Truman as Commander-in-Chief during the Cold War from 1947.

Despite his having laid the legal, organizational, doctrinal and political foundations of America's vast military power in the Cold War, Truman nevertheless depended on Congress. His need for authorizations and appropriations constrained him, as did his need for bipartisan congressional support for his policy of containing the Soviet Union and for rebuilding Western Europe. Truman's achievement of Republican support for his active, internationalist assumption of Western leadership against Soviet expansionism was neither inevitable, nor straightforward. In using the presidency to seek public, congressional and, especially, Republican support, Truman sought approval for a decisive change in American attitudes and policy. The United States had hitherto resisted persisting entanglement in foreign alliances because its leaders perceived high risk in such embroilment, especially with a corrupt European politics fundamentally at odds with American values.

Washington's warning against foreign alliances in his Farewell Address of September 1796 became established as a principle of American foreign policy. The United States, he urged, should eschew 'habitual hatred or an habitual fondness towards any nation', and 'steer clear of permanent alliances with any part of the foreign world'. With the abrogation of the French alliance, isolationism survived even the tuggings at the American heart of the 1848 revolutions. Prior to 1861, the United States took part in no international conference, and few American politicians claimed that American interests were much affected by European events. As late as Franklin D. Roosevelt's first term, when the rationale for isolationism had weakened, isolationist Republicans continued to attribute American entry into World War I to Wilson's determination to protect the arms trade and to save bankers from ruin. Such views were fuelled by persistent distrust of Britain and France, sympathy for Germany and populist antipathy to finance. For some, these sentiments concealed anti-Semitism. Entry into World War II occurred only after the deployment of isolationist arguments similar to those of a century before. The US declaration of war on Japan came on 8 December 1941 after Japanese naval aircraft had sunk the US Pacific Fleet at Pearl Harbor the previous day. Germany and Italy declared war on the United States four days later.

The technological advances that made possible delivery by air of nuclear weapons rendered American boundaries permeable to threats from an ideologically hostile and expansionist enemy in a bipolar international system. Truman adeptly exploited the development, using the presidency to symbolize national purpose in new international involvements designed to protect American interests. Departing from the tradition embraced by all his predecessors of avoiding permanent alliances, Truman sought the advice and won the support of key congressional leaders for the doctrine which bore his name, and by which the United States began its post-war immersion in the defence of western Europe and other allies. He acted similarly in winning the support of Arthur Vandenberg, Republican Chairman of the Senate Foreign Relations Committee, for the Marshall Plan of aid to Western Europe.

Throughout the Eisenhower and Kennedy administrations, and for the first three years of the Johnson administration, an anti-communist ideological purpose united presidents and Congresses. Such agreement failed to settle the question of determining the boundary between the constitutional allocation of the power of Congress to declare war and the power of the president to wage it. This latent problem apart (which, in any event, resists tidy resolution), such disagreement as there was over policy owed more to politicians' attempts to trump others' anti-Communist sentiments with fiercer ones of their own than to a questioning either of the premises of foreign policy, or of the constitutionality of presidential leadership. There was little divergence of strategic view: of the ten treaties submitted to the Senate between 1953 and 1961, none was defeated, and eight were approved with seven or fewer votes against.

Moreover, Eisenhower took careful note of the political harm that President Truman's failure to consult extensively with Congress over the sending of US forces to Korea had caused in 1950. Accordingly, when considering US options in responding to an attack by Communist China on Formosa (now Taiwan) in 1955, Eisenhower sought and secured a joint congressional resolution of approval, underpinning the legitimacy of any actions which he might take later.

In these circumstances, presidential leadership in foreign policy faced little serious constitutional challenge, notwithstanding attempts by the isolationist Republican Senator Bricker to restrict the president's powers to negotiate treaties and executive agreements. Presidents Truman, Eisenhower, Kennedy, and Johnson set US policy in the Cold War with a freedom comparable to that of Presidents Wilson and Roosevelt during the two World Wars. However, Presidents Johnson's and Nixon's frequently deceitful policy in Vietnam eventually disrupted the pattern of congressional deference to presidential leadership, epitomized both in the Gulf of Tonkin Resolution of 1964 and in congressional support for financing the war. Vietnam's human and financial costs were grave for American and Vietnamese combatants, and devastating for the peoples of Vietnam and Cambodia. The war's political consequences for the Democratic Party and the New Deal coalition were bitterly divisive. The trust that Congress was willing to repose in presidents pursuing the bipartisan policy of opposition to what had, since 1948, been regarded as an expansion of territorial control sponsored by the Soviet Union was thereby eroded.

Presidential leadership in foreign policy did not vanish in the years after American withdrawal from Vietnam: the advantages of executive singularity ensured that it could not. Since Ronald Reagan led American rearmament in the early years of his presidency, and both he and George H.W. Bush pursued a policy of negotiating with the Soviet Union in that regime's rapid decline and eventual collapse, the presidency's advantages in foreign and security policy of being the first mover, of operating frequently with diplomatic, intelligence and military secrecy, have again left presidents firmly in strategic control of the agenda setting and execution. Congress is rather less willing now than it was between 1941 and 1967 to acquiesce in the president's agenda, especially in light of the dominant pattern since 1968 of split party control between the White House and Capitol Hill, which has so frequently turned questions of relations between the presidency and Congress into partisan ones. Yet, as Barack Obama's pursuit of covert military and cyber policies against terrorist groups and their state sponsors has shown, even a president who has endured fierce congressional resistance to his domestic agenda has been able to operate only lightly fettered against Iran, Afghanistan and Pakistan.

The National Security Council and National Security staff

The National Security Council (NSC) was established by the National Security Act of 1947, and placed in the Executive Office of the President (EOP) by Truman's Reorganization Plan No. 4 (1949). The president chairs the Council. Three other members attend by statute: the Vice-President, the Secretary of State and the Secretary of Defense. Advisers to the Council also attend. They include the Chairman of the Joint Chiefs of Staff in his capacity as Military Adviser, the Director of National Intelligence (an office created as part of the reorganization of intelligence following the terrorist attacks of September 2001) in his capacity as Intelligence Adviser, the Director of the Central Intelligence Agency and the Director of National Drug Control Policy in the capacity of Drug Policy Adviser. Other officials who attend regularly are the National Security Adviser, the White House Chief of Staff, the Secretary of the Treasury, the Attorney-General and the Secretary of Homeland Security. Others attend by the president's invitation. There is a substantial national security staff, the NSC's secretariat, led by the Assistant to the President for National Security Affairs (National Security Adviser, or NSA), a position created within the White House at President Eisenhower's direction and replicated by each of his successors.

Within the statutory shell provided by the National Security Act and its amendments, operating procedures of national security advice within the White House are determined by presidents themselves. Their practices have varied. In one respect, however, there has been broad similarity between administrations: the post of National Security Adviser has become one of the most important in government. It has been held by (among others) McGeorge Bundy under President Kennedy, Walt Rostow under President Johnson, Henry Kissinger under President Nixon, Zbigniew Brzezinski under President Carter, and Condoleeza Rice under President George W. Bush; all have shaped national security policy. Nixon, distrustful of federal bureaucracies in general, and of the State Department in particular, readily acquiesced in the systematic exclusion of Secretary of State William Rogers from most significant foreign and defence policy decisions by his NSA, Henry Kissinger, with whom he simultaneously formed major new policy initiatives bilaterally and exclusively. President George W. Bush excluded his Secretary of State, General Colin Powell, from key decisions in the days before the invasion of Iraq in 2003. All Secretaries of State and Defense are handicapped by the NSAs' advantage of close proximity to the Oval Office, and of daily scheduled private meetings with the president. Even President Carter, who entered office bent on ending the marginalization of the State Department, eventually fell under the influence of Zbigniew Brzezinski to the disadvantage of both his Secretaries of State.

President Reagan's detachment from foreign policy decision-making left room in the Iran–*Contra* affair of 1986–88 for two of his NSAs, Robert McFarlane and John Poindexter, to conduct an illegal foreign policy operation in defiance of Congress, separately from both the Departments of State and Defense. The breaking of the law besmirched Reagan's presidency, a consequence of which the President seemed incompletely aware. Furthermore, as the *Report of the President's Special Review Board* on the scandal showed, the blurring of the boundary between advising the president (which is the NSA's proper role) and executing policy (which is not) harmed US interests and damaged the integrity of foreign policy-making. The debacle also illustrated anew that, although clear decision-making procedures are important, they are easily subverted by staff and presidents.

The importance of the NSC, as distinct from the NSA and the national security staff, has varied. Eisenhower, whose preference for formal modes of decision-making was clearest in security matters, established a highly-structured system consisting of the NSC itself, a planning board and an operations coordinating board at the centre of foreign policy decision-making. Eisenhower's system worked admirably well. But Kennedy, his Democratic successor, disliked that formal arrangement, and adopted *ad hoc* task forces in an attempt to ensure that policy problems were identified precisely and the options clearly distilled. Working in the guise of an executive committee of the NSC, the group of thirteen that clarified the president's options during the Cuban Missile Crisis of 1962 succeeded in removing Soviet missiles from Cuba without publicly humiliating Nikita Khrushchev, the First Secretary of the Soviet Communist Party. Kennedy made informality work; Johnson, his successor, could not. Confining decision-making to trusted advisers, rather than opening channels to those whose analyses would inform and challenge his own views, Johnson thereby impaired decision-making on Vietnam, his besetting foreign policy predicament, and fatally damaged his presidency.

Eisenhower, more skilled in bureaucratic politics than his critics allowed, understood what Johnson, Nixon, Carter, Reagan and George W. Bush did not: established procedures in which the NSA brokers, communicates, advises the president and coordinates policy development with the Departments of State, Defense, and other agencies benefit not just presidents, but the presidency. The temptations to seek control over policy formation and the esteem of officials within and outside the administration that, together, have fuelled the aspirations and careers of many NSAs may damage the president's own needs. There are recurrent problems of coordination within the Executive Branch: tensions result from the Executive Branch's fragmentation, the gulf between the EOP and the departments, and the struggle for control over both the processes of policy-making and the content of policy itself. Resolution of both requires the full engagement, understanding and resolve of a resourceful president. Few meet this standard.

Office of the United States Trade Representative

The United States Trade Representative (USTR) was created by executive order in 1963, and placed in the EOP by the Trade Act of 1974. The USTR is a member of the president's Cabinet with the rank of ambassador. This representative is assisted by three deputy USTRs, each of whom also holds the rank of ambassador; two are based in Washington and one in Geneva, home of the World Trade Organization (WTO). Following the success enjoyed by President Carter's Trade Representative, Robert Strauss, in leading American negotiators during the Tokyo Round, the President published a Reorganization Plan in 1979 which strengthened the USTR's standing within the administration. Implemented by executive order in January 1980, it conferred the responsibility of setting and administering overall trade policy on the Office, and designated the USTR the chief US representative for the following:

- all matters touching on the World Trade Organization;
- discussions concerning *trade* and *commodity policy* held within the ambit of the Organisation for Economic Co-operation and Development (OECD);
- all other *bilateral* and *multilateral negotiations* concerning trade policy, direct investment incentives and disincentives to trade, incentives and barriers to cross-border investment.

The major trade Act of 1988, the Omnibus Trade and Competitiveness Act, codified the authority granted by the 1980 executive order and added the important duty of implementing enforcement actions under Section 301 of the 1974 Trade Act designed to eliminate barriers to American exports in foreign markets by designating particular practices as 'unfair'.

The nature of trade policy naturally attracts the attention of many government agencies and interest groups. Companies which trade abroad, labour unions dependent on the jobs such trade generates or threatens, cities, congressional districts, states, and regions with economic interests at stake bring pressure to bear on the administration and Congress to protect domestic markets from foreign competition, or to open foreign markets to American competition. During the 1970s and 1980s, for example, many states instituted economic sanctions of their own against the South African regime – and some were slower to remove them than the federal government wished. The involvement of departments such as Agriculture and Commerce ensures that sectional pressures from affected groups are brought to bear. The role of promoting agricultural exports, for example, is reflected in the department's organization, where an under-secretary leads the Foreign Agricultural Service (FAS), an agency that administers export assistance and foreign food assistance programmes, and is represented abroad in more than sixty US embassies by agricultural scientists and economists.

The Department of Commerce

The 1988 Omnibus Trade and Competitiveness Act delegates to the US and Foreign Commercial Service (an agency within the Department of Commerce) responsibility for commercial representation and jurisdiction over trade policy in US embassies and consulates abroad. The Commerce Department is thereby effectively charged with, and the State Department excluded from, the implementation of trade policy determined by the USTR. The Bureau of Export Administration within the Department has responsibility under the 1987 Export Administration Act for promoting American exports of non-agricultural goods, and supervizing countervailing duty and anti-dumping statutes. In implementing the latter, the department is lobbied by domestic industries affected by foreign imports whose prices are artificially low because of subsidies provided to foreign producers, and because of goods being sold in the US market at prices below those in their domestic market, respectively. Three Assistant Secretaries have responsibilities for other aspects of trade policy.

Congress's Commerce Committees have deliberately designed the Department of Commerce to be receptive to complaints by American companies (the department's traditional clients) and politicians about allegedly unfair trading practices. Its structure and programmes encourage such receptivity through triangular political relationships between the private sector, executive agencies and congressional subcommittees. The deliberate placing of the USTR Office within the EOP offers some prospect to American negotiators of their being able to negotiate trade agreements without being subverted by the activities of kaleidoscopic domestic interest groups. Given the intensity with which protectionist pressures are applied in congressional politics, it is striking that presidents have retained such autonomy in making trade policy.

The Treasury Department

The Treasury participates in foreign policy through its responsibility for the management of the world's largest trading currency, the US dollar.

The department's other international responsibilities include the US external balance, tariff policy and managing the public debt. Its international role has become more demanding with the end of United States economic hegemony and the growth of its interdependence with the international economy. The fact of American economic hegemony in 1945 is widely known, but its extent too little appreciated. In 1945, the United States accounted for 50 per cent or more of total world GNP, exported more than twice as much as it imported, and effectively determined (by reason of the dollar's dominance) other countries' monetary policies. To that extent, Bretton Woods was a political fig-leaf, and an earnest symbol of self-restraint. West European dependence on American policy was symbolized by the Marshall Plan in 1947, but was an established fact two years before. American hegemony lasted for barely twenty-five years, but American dominance continues.

The end of the United States's hegemony was expressed in the collapse of the Bretton Woods order in 1971, vividly symbolized by the United States running a trade deficit for the first time in its modern industrial history, and by ending the right of governments to convert surplus dollars into gold. The increasingly multinational character of production, the rapid growth in capital movements across national boundaries, the ending of dollar–gold convertibility, the weakening US balance of payments, and the vigorous economic recoveries from war in Western Europe and Japan undermined American capacity to determine international monetary policy. That development was underlined by the rising proportion of the United States' GNP absorbed by international trade, with its accompanying exposure of the American economy to developments and pressures beyond its control.

A decade later, foreign pressures increased: as the fiscal deficit grew in the early to mid-1980s and the savings ratio remained obstinately low, Treasury debt was bought in larger quantities by foreign customers. The US external deficit also grew rapidly, adding to weaknesses which pushed the Treasury more deeply into foreign policy. The relative decline of the US economy in the 1980s was put into fuller perspective at the end of the decade by the sudden collapse of the Soviet and East European economies, whose consequent vulnerability and dependence on new sources of multilateral finance from the International Monetary Fund (IMF) dominated by the United States lent further weight to the Treasury's voice. As the United States dominates the IMF, it also dominates the World Bank and the Inter-American Development Bank; as important sources of development finance internationally, they were significant sources of Treasury influence on American foreign policy.

The Justice Department

Three bureaux of the Justice Department are involved in foreign policy: the Federal Bureau of Investigation (FBI), the US National Central Bureau (USNCB) and the Drug Enforcement Administration (DEA). (The first of these is not considered below, but in the next section, dealing with the intelligence community.)

- The USNCB represents the United States in INTERPOL and has assumed greater importance in recent years as international police cooperation has grown with intensified efforts to defeat terrorism. The agency coordinates the work of federal intelligence and law enforcement agencies; police services at federal, state, city and local levels of government in the United States; and between the United States and police services abroad.
- The DEA was created in 1973 by President Nixon's Reorganization Plan No. 2, which amalgamated four agencies into one. It is charged with the tasks of investigating drug-trafficking between states within the US and between the US and foreign countries; and with breaking drug manufacturing and distribution networks. In addition to field offices throughout the United States, the DEA is represented in fifty foreign countries.

The intelligence community

The intelligence 'community', in the misleadingly comforting euphemism, is large and extensive. As might be expected in light of the discussion in Chapter 9, it is also riven with inter-agency conflict and competition. The size of the annual appropriations by Congress to the several agencies comprising the community totalled $53.9 billion for 2012.

The Director of National Intelligence (DNI) is required by his office's founding statute (the Intelligence Reform and Terrorism Prevention Act of 2004) to advise the president, the NSC and the Homeland Security Council about intelligence questions bearing on national security. As head of the sixteen-member so-called 'intelligence community', the DNI directs and has responsibility for the National Intelligence Program. The rationale of the 2004 act was to overcome the damaging division between military and civilian intelligence agencies by creating, in one office, authority over both.

The Central Intelligence Agency

The CIA was established by the National Security Act of 1947 as the

NSC's intelligence advisory service and the coordinating agency for the federal government's entire intelligence work. Such an advisory and coordinating role has been hampered by the characteristic dispersion of functions among a number of agencies. As the CIA's coordinating role under the 1947 Act was often foiled by other agencies, the Agency's twin roles of intelligence operative and policy advocate have sometimes impaired its analytical objectivity. Even conservative presidents with a coldly realistic understanding of international politics have privately expressed dissatisfaction with the CIA's work. For example, Richard Nixon regarded the CIA with a contempt similar in kind and intensity to that which he expressed about most federal government agencies: he complained to his senior aide, Bob Haldeman, in the summer of 1971 that 'The CIA tells me nothing I don't read three days earlier in the *New York Times*. The CIA isn't worth a damn' before defining intelligence as 'how to spend $5 billion and learn nothing' (Haldeman, 1994).

Its covert activities have caused the CIA to be regarded with suspicion, especially by liberals and democrats. In 1973, the CIA organized the overthrow of Salvador Allende's elected government in Chile and its replacement by General Pinochet's bloody military dictatorship. The CIA was simultaneously engaged in coordinated, illegal, domestic operations with the FBI against Nixon's political opponents. Abuse of its power angered congressional liberals and prompted President Carter to restrain the Agency by attempting to enforce the 1947 Act. However, under his successor, the DCI's authority over other intelligence agencies was again reduced, and budgets for covert work increased. Establishment by the House and Senate of Select Committees on Intelligence to oversee the CIA has necessarily had only limited success. Intelligence operations require secrecy; democratic procedures require disclosure and accountability.

In 1975, by means of the Hughes–Ryan Amendment to the 1974 Foreign Assistance Act, Congress attempted to hold the CIA accountable by expanding the number of Oversight Committees and requiring reports to be made to them about covert actions. The Senate created a new Select Committee on Intelligence in 1976, and the House followed suit a year later. After the failure of the Iranian hostage rescue, Congress's determination to check the CIA weakened, and Hughes–Ryan was replaced by the less restrictive Intelligence Oversight Act of 1980. It required the CIA to report to the select committees only, and permitted the president to launch covert operations without prior notification if he judged that vital interests were at stake. As the mining of Nicaraguan harbours, the covert war against the Contras, and the Iran–Contra episode revealed, President Reagan showed scant regard either for the spirit of the Act, or for congressional prerogatives. Congress's enthusiasm for restraining the CIA cooled in the 1980s, partly because providing additional information to Select Committees deflected criticism: consulting them was not only required by statute, but often politically advantageous.

Tensions persist. They gained prominence in the public examination of the purported failings of the intelligence community months following the terrorist atrocities of 9/11, and the furore that followed passage of the 2001 PATRIOT Act, which gave the intelligence services a statutory basis for eavesdropping and other means of surveillance even, it was argued, in those cases where little or no evidence warranted such activity.

Other intelligence agencies

Agencies that operate under the Secretary of Defense's authority but remain within the intelligence community include the National Security Agency which, with the world's most extensive and advanced electronic signal gathering system, intercepts and decodes government, commercial and private communications within allied and enemy states; the Central Imagery Office, which has charge of intelligence gathered by satellite; and the Defense Intelligence Agency, which provides the Secretary and the Joint Chiefs of Staff (JCS) with analyses drawn from the intelligence gathering still undertaken (to the detriment of the Defense Department's efficiency) by the four individual services. The Secretary of State depends heavily on the Bureau of Intelligence and Research, headed by an Assistant Secretary of State, for the intelligence input into decisions. The Bureau is, in turn, dependent for raw material on reports from US embassies and stations abroad, and the information that other agencies choose to supply.

Three other departments also have substantial intelligence functions: Justice, Treasury and Energy. Within the Justice Department, the FBI's role is counter-espionage. This broad remit has, in the past, been subject to abuse by some presidents and FBI directors in order to harass domestic opponents: Martin Luther King, for example, was subjected to intensive surveillance throughout his entire political career as part of a campaign by J. Edgar Hoover to label him as having Communist sympathies. During the Nixon administration, the Justice Department illegally wire-tapped many domestic organizations under cover of the President's duty to protect national security, in violation (as the Supreme Court later determined) of the Fourth Amendment. The Bureau of Alcohol, Tobacco, and Firearms (formerly within the Treasury Department) is now located within the Department of Justice. Its task is to monitor smuggling and illegal trading in the three specified goods. The Department of Energy's intelligence work is largely confined to ensuring compliance by foreign states with the Nuclear Non-Proliferation Treaty, and with gathering intelligence on the testing by foreign states of nuclear weapons. The first assumed much greater importance during the search by the International

Atomic Energy Agency for evidence of the alleged continuation of an Iraqi nuclear and chemical weapons programme in the months following 9/11 and before the US-led invasion of Iraq in spring 2002.

The Department of Homeland Security

Eleven days after the attacks of 9/11, President George W. Bush created, by executive order, the new Cabinet post of Assistant to the President for Homeland Security. In November 2002, Congress authorized the creation of the Department of Homeland Security (DHS). As its title suggests, the DHS has lead responsibility for the protection of the security of the mainland United States and it is also charged with the task of working with other federal agencies to respond effectively to disasters, whether natural or man-made. The DHS includes beneath its umbrella the Immigration and Naturalization Service (INS) that had previously been an agency of the Department of Justice. Congress gave to the DHS responsibility for Border Protection and Customs (previously located within the INS). The DHS is the third largest Cabinet department, with 204,000 members and a budget of $59 billion in 2013. In its 2013 budget summary, the DHS declared that its mission had five elements:

- Protecting the United States from terrorism using counter-terrorism techniques.
- Securing and managing the borders of the United States to prevent terrorism or other criminal activity.
- Enforcing and administering immigration laws – focusing, in particular, on illegal aliens who break the law or pose a security threat to the mainland United States.
- Safeguarding and securing cyberspace: the DHS is the federal government lead agency for securing civilian government computer systems, preventing or responding to cyber-attacks and maintaining the security of electronic networks.
- Ensuring resilience to disasters: the DHS provides the coordinated, comprehensive federal response in the event of a terrorist attack, natural disaster, or other large-scale emergency while working with federal, state and local government agencies.

The DHS now also contains the US Secret Service, formerly within the US Treasury. Its task is not only to protect the president and VIPs, but to gather intelligence on threats to them that it seeks to forestall. It also retains responsibility for the federal government's anti-counterfeiting work. Much of the DHS operating budget is spent in grants to state and local government agencies in an attempt to allow them better to execute the five elements of the DHS mission.

The Department of State

Older even than Treasury or Judiciary, the State Department was established by an Act of Congress on 27 July 1789 as the Department of Foreign Affairs, and renamed the Department of State in September of the same year. In 2012, it was staffed by 31,000 employees, 11,500 of whom are foreign nationals working in embassies or consulates abroad (see Exhibit 12.2). The department's congressional appropriation in 2012 was $15.7 billion. Its American employees are divided roughly equally between postings abroad and in Washington: 5,200 are employed as Foreign Service Officers (FSOs), the corps of professional diplomats who represent the United States government abroad in 164 embassies; in twelve missions; one US interests section; sixty-six consulates general; fourteen consulates; three branch offices; and forty-five consular agencies.

The majority of federal civilian employees in foreign postings are drawn from other agencies: approximately 85 per cent work for the Agency for International Development (AID); the Arms Control and Disarmament Agency, (ACDA); the US Information Agency (USIA); the Central Intelligence Agency (CIA); and domestic departments and agencies with international responsibilities such as the Departments of Agriculture, Commerce and Treasury. Such bureaucratic splintering exacerbates the difficulties of coordinating foreign policy and the State Department's prospects of leading it, despite the Foreign Service traditionally regarding other agencies disdainfully as being parasitic on the central purposes of diplomacy.

US ambassadors are drawn both from the ranks of career FSOs and from the pool of political appointees, both those to whom the president has obligations for their contributions to his election campaign, and those with abilities and attributes of potential benefit to the president and the country. Ambassadorships in London and Paris are coveted by, and usually awarded to, close supporters. Most ambassadors to African and Latin-American countries are career diplomats, since the postings have little attraction and much danger. Not unnaturally, the use of ambassadorships as rewards to political friends causes all manner of tensions in the State Department between appointees and career diplomats. Together with the Deputy Assistant Secretaries and Office Directors assigned to cover individual countries within each bureau, State Department officials receive from embassies abroad reports of conversations and meetings, and information from the other intelligence-gathering agencies. In the light of their accumulated understanding, they interpret the material and, with other departments and agencies, develop policy options for the Secretary of State, the NSC and the president towards countries and groups of countries in the region. The involvement of other departments and agencies in

Exhibit 12.2 The Department of State

Seven principal officials based in Washington comprise the top layer of the State Department: the Secretary of State, the Deputy Secretary, and five Under-Secretaries. Below these seven are nineteen Assistant Secretaries in charge of the Department's *bureaux*, its key operating units in Washington (see below). Within each bureau are directors of individual offices, civil servants and Foreign Service officers (FSOs).

As in other departments, the Secretary of State is always a political appointee, as are most of the six colleagues at principal level. (The only exception is that the Under-Secretary for Political Affairs is always a career official, well-placed to bring experience and continuity to the Department.) The four Under-Secretaries (for Global Affairs, for Economic and Agricultural Affairs, for International Security Affairs, and for Management) are invariably political appointees.

In Washington, the State Department is organized into *bureaux*, units similar in origin and function to agencies in other departments. Each is headed by an Assistant Secretary. Conforming to the pattern throughout the federal bureaucracy, every bureau except one has a parent Subcommittee in Congress. The exception is the Department's Congressional Relations office, which coordinates appearances by administration officials in Congressional hearings, especially the Senate Foreign Relations Committee and the House Foreign Affairs Committees. Seven bureaux have functional remits, and five geographic areas: Africa, East Asia and the Pacific, Europe and Canada, Inter-American Affairs, Near East and South Asia. Assistant Secretaries in the latter five areas have charge over the development of US policy towards the countries and regions within each, and chair interdepartmental groups in the National Security Council (NSC) system which prepare papers for the Council and implement Council decisions.

foreign policy denies regional bureaux a monopoly of control over information, analysis and policy formation within the Executive Branch, whose fragmentation obliges each bureau to coordinate constantly with others.

Many State Department officials have relevant academic expertise before joining the State Department (linguistic ability and advanced academic training in a social science are prized advantages) but all, to a greater or lesser degree, acquire it in the course of their careers. But expertise is not always welcomed by new political administrations or political appointees, especially where policy issues are ideologically charged. Neither has analytical detachment always been highly prized: on his appointment as President Nixon's National Security Adviser, Henry Kissinger's distrust of State Department professionals and obsessive concern for his own political influence and status led him to circumvent not only regional bureaux in the Department, but also (in secret preparations for a *rapprochement* with China in 1972) to exclude the State Department from the process altogether. If the president deems a policy question sufficiently important, State Department expertise is (ironically) often nullified, since the important questions are decided by the president in consultation with senior staff and the Secretary of State, rather than at bureau level in the Department. This pattern has applied to all questions touching on US relations, both with major allies and adversaries in the post-war period, thereby reducing the influence of the otherwise prestigious Bureau for European Affairs (which had responsibility for covering both NATO and Warsaw Pact members).

The politicization of the State Department, as of other federal agencies, is necessary and inevitable if the president is to have any prospect of enforcing his policy priorities. Fear of jeopardizing their careers under a president from a different party is usually a sufficient reason for officials to avoid adopting a radical or polar position in a controversial matter. Aggregation of these individual tendencies lends some substance to the claim that the State Department is characterized by a culture of cautious incrementalism which can be overcome only by energetic leadership of appointees loyal to the president and the Secretary of State. Innovative Secretaries of State are, accordingly, inclined to form policy in small groups loyal to them rather than to clients. Having attempted to formulate policy without the aid of the State Department when merely the President's National Security Adviser, Kissinger continued to view the Department with suspicion once he became Secretary of State in his own right. Not all Secretaries have distrusted the department (Cyrus Vance, James Baker, Colin Powell and Hillary Clinton all worked with it, rather than against it), but many have. Political loyalty in Washington is generally more highly-prized by department secretaries than is detached expertise. Such a disposition nonetheless carries the price of uneven attention to potential crises and of discontinuity between administrations, and exacerbates the fragmentation of the policy-making community, rather than overcomes it.

The Department of Defense (the Pentagon)

The Department of Defense was established in 1949 by congressional amendments to the National Security Act of 1947. It comprises the Office of the Secretary of Defense, the military departments and military services within those departments; the Chairman of the Joint Chiefs of Staff and the Joint Staff, the unified and individual commands; the Defense Agencies and the Department's field stations. The Secretary of Defense's authority over this most complex of all departments was increased by the Defense Reorganization Acts of 1958 and 1986 (see p. 407). Unlike the Secretary of State, the Secretary of Defense directs an agency with a huge budget the disposition of which is of vital importance to defence contractors, subcontractors and suppliers, and thus to employees of contractors, and to their representatives in Congress. Acquisition of weapons systems presents one of the purest examples of distributive policy-making by Congress, comprising business worth tens of billions of dollars annually to corporations, thereby generating intense group pressures on the Department and the Congress's Armed Services Committees, who make procurement decisions. All Secretaries of Defense also face political pressures from members of Congress proposing the expansion of defence facilities in their districts or, as is now more often the case, attempting to resist their closure.

Since the Secretary of Defense is designated in law as the 'principal defense policy adviser to the President', and is responsible 'for the formulation of general defense policy and policy related to all matters of direct and primary concern to DOD', he requires a large civilian management team within the Pentagon. Attempting to implement administration policy in so vast a bureaucracy accustomed to incremental budgeting and decision-making, and standard operational procedures is exceptionally difficult. Accountability of civil servants and military officers in the department to the Secretary, the president, and to Congress is often weak. Public alarm at a rash of procurement scandals within the Department helped Senator Goldwater, during the mid-1980s, to build a coalition for improved management structures and procedures in the Pentagon, with the object of reinforcing accountability. Within the 'Office of the Secretary of Defense' (itself a large management structure) there are several senior assistants to the Secretary and the Deputy Secretary. Despite its nominal unification, each armed service maintains its own structure within the Department and, like agencies in other departments, has substantial operating autonomy.

The Joint Chiefs of Staff

The JCS organization comprises the Chairman; the Vice-Chairman; the Chief of Staff, United States Army; the Chief of Naval Operations; the Chief of Staff, United States Air Force (USAF); and the Commandant of the Marine Corps (the Marines are, in principle, a command within the Department of the Navy, but regard themselves as a separate armed service). By their statutory authority, the Joint Chiefs represent military opinion to the president and the Secretary of Defense. The National Defense Authorization Act of 2012 (NDAA) added the Chief of the National Guard Bureau to the Joint Chiefs of Staff.

Although, in law, the armed forces have always been under complete civilian control, their lack of authority in policy matters has not prevented them from exercising influence, often to the advantage of individual branches of the armed forces. None of the four armed services has ever supported a unified Defense Department, because it would threaten its own interests. The combination of cultural and structural differentiation has proved to be an obstacle to presidents, Secretaries of Defense, and chairmen of Congress's Armed Services committees, who have periodically attempted to develop a more rational and efficient organization. The capacity of individual services to advance their own interests at the expense of those of the nation and the taxpayer has often been apparent. Competition is injected into the organization by its representational character: as the JCS represent the four services, so the military members of the Joint Staff (the JCS secretariat) of approximately 400 are drawn equally from the four services. The JCS possesses formidable bureaucratic capacity to resist presidential initiatives, as its successful opposition to President Carter's attempt to end production of the BI Bomber vividly showed.

Many members of the JCS regarded the organization less as a coordinating mechanism than as a forum for pressing their sectional claims and interests. As the JCS was unable to overcome the US Armed Forces' fragmentation, so relations between the Army, Air Force, Navy and Marines within the Pentagon and in theatres of operation have often been less than ideal, leading to inadequate coordination in both peace and war.

Goldwater–Nichols Act (1986)

In an attempt to reduce the damaging competitive rivalry and strife between the four armed services, the Defense Reorganization Act of 1986 (the Goldwater–Nichols Act) enhanced the role of the JCS and weakened individual service departments' influence within the Defense Department. The Act also increased the authority of the chairman of the JCS, in two respects:

1. By designating the chairman as the principal military adviser to the president, NSC and Secretary of Defense. However, it grants him neither membership of the NSC, nor direct command over US forces; the JCS chairman is entitled merely to transmit orders from the president to Commanders-in-Chief (CINCs), but not to give them himself.
2. Colleagues and staff within the JCS organization are now under the chairman's authority and serve at his direction, thereby increasing their incentive to supply disinterested analyses. General Colin Powell (later Secretary of State in the Cabinet of President George W.

Bush), appointed Chairman by President George H.W. Bush, put the powers granted him by the 1986 Act to effective use during the Gulf War of 1991 while leaving field command to a Commander-in-Chief (General Schwarzkopf), as the Act required.

The Goldwater–Nichols Act has given the chairman greater opportunity to influence the president's defence and national security thinking, and it requires him to advise the Secretary of Defense on priorities between different requests of colleagues in the four major commands, but it stripped him of operational command over the armed forces. The chairman is also required to assist the president and the Secretary of Defense by providing for:

- *strategic direction* of the armed forces;
- their *budgeting*;
- *comparison* of US *military capabilities* with those of other states;
- preparation of *contingency plans*, and the *logistic* and *mobility plans* for them to be fulfilled.

The legislative branch

Congress's influence over foreign and defence policy varies with the particular type of policy. In crisis management, it is minimal. In war, it is insignificant in the short-term when there is a premium on supporting forces in the field. Even in the medium-to-long term, it is slight for so long as the president's direction of war meets with success and enjoys public support. When these two conditions are not met, congressional opinion can reflect the (often divided) sentiments of wider public opinion. Presidents Truman and Johnson eventually encountered such medium-to-long-term political difficulties with Congress and public opinion as their conduct of Asian wars faltered. So, too, did President George W. Bush as the Iraq War became increasingly unpopular from 2005 onwards: by June of 2005, 60 per cent of respondents to an ABC Poll thought that the war 'should not have been fought'.

In strategic foreign policy, Congress exercises more influence, and the executive less autonomy. In strategic foreign policy, the executive depends on congressional authorizations and appropriations for foreign and military aid, on Congress's willingness to support presidential trade policy, and on the Senate's willingness to ratify treaties. In structural defence policy-making, the executive enjoys little autonomy and is heavily dependent on the Military Installations and Construction subcommittees of the House and Senate Appropriations committees, and of the (authorizing) House and Senate Armed Services committees. Congress has the opportunity to involve itself in these second and third types of

foreign and defence policy, not only through authorization and appropriations, but also in committee hearings called to examine problems and
controversies. Increases in subcommittees' autonomy from full committees and substantial increases in congressional staff resources in the
1970s complicated the patterns of executive–congressional interaction in
both strategic and structural policy. The lengthy list of congressional
committees and subcommittees with jurisdiction over parts of foreign
and defence policy hints at the complexities of the policy process which
results.

Interest groups

Foreign states with which the United States maintains diplomatic relations have direct representation to the executive in Washington, and the
opportunity to represent their varied interests to congressional, media,
group and public opinion. Foreign countries may be regarded as groups
seeking to influence US policies to their advantage. Allies such as Britain,
Canada, Australia and New Zealand enjoy such close, cooperative ties
with the United States that diplomatic activity between them is constant,
wide-ranging, cooperative and often collusive. Differences of policy are
rarely serious and, since 1945, none (including Suez in 1956) have threatened diplomatic rupture: relations are conducted primarily at official
level between embassy officials and executive departments.
Disagreements remain, but they are mostly confined to trade where, in
any case, EU states are formally represented in trade negotiations by the
European Commission, and not individually. Whatever differences may
appear in public, the submerged bureaucratic cooperation is intense and
institutionalized.

Other foreign states have different relations with the United States.
Even Israel, the single largest recipient of both US Foreign Aid and
Military Aid, does not enjoy an amicable and stable relationship with
every president; President Obama's experience makes the point well. The
Israeli embassy accordingly pursues a broader range of contacts and
employs different techniques in pressing for increased aid, and in opposing US sales of military equipment to Israel's adversaries. Israel bolsters
its political strength with the administration by cultivating friendly relations with the Pentagon, with members of Congress and senators, and
through the maintenance of close contacts with pro-Israel interest
groups, by steering funds to congressional supporters and away from
opponents. Israeli causes are, in any case, strengthened enormously by
the large and influential activities and writings of Jewish academics, journalists and business people. These have been insufficient to prevent the
United States from adopting a Middle East policy at variance with Israel's
own, but they have limited the divergence between the two states and

have been sufficient to preserve the American guarantee of the sanctity of Israel's borders and security.

Most foreign governments have a more difficult task in influencing American policy. Declared enemies during the Cold War, such as the Soviet Union and the Warsaw Treaty Organization clients, had no prospect of modifying American policy while Communist regimes remained in power.

As the processes of trade negotiations and the institutions of the EU show, the United States must increasingly pursue diplomacy with non-state actors. The importance of the United Nations following the end of the bipolar international order and the Soviet Union's collapse was first seen to American advantage in the first Gulf War of 1990, waged under the cover of UN authorization. The lack of United Nations support for UN Resolution 1441 (providing for support for hostilities against Saddam Hussein) resulted in the US-led operation in Iraq in 2003, and reflected the weakness of America's position at the outset and hinted at the risk of the supporting coalition's gradual weakening.

During the 1960s and 1970s, the United States Mission to the United Nations was often engaged in hostile exchanges with other member states. Diplomacy has been calmer (in public) since the end of the Cold War, but the relationship between America's war in Iraq greatly strained relations with the UN. Yet, the UN remains both a forum and an instrument of US policy, as it was during the Korean War. As the utility of inter-state relations diminishes with the increased salience of questions such as global terrorism, environmental pollution, human rights and economic development, susceptible to solution only through the brokerage of international organizations, the importance of their representation in Washington may grow, and that of individual states (or, at least, advanced European ones) decline.

Foreign states and transnational actors exist alongside domestic groups whose agendas either extend to international affairs, or are founded primarily on them. They include ethnic and national pressure groups, economic groups, human rights organizations, intellectual and research organizations on the fringes of government itself, state and legal governments, the electronic and print media, and public opinion.

- Among *ethnic and national groups* are the congressional black caucus, which has taken a close interest in – and, at the margins, exercised influence over – US policy towards South Africa; the National Association for Arab-Americans; and the ten major pro-Israel PACs that help fund supporters' election campaigns.
- *Economic groups* include the defence contractors (whose roles are examined on p. 423) in structural defence policy-making; companies which stand to gain or lose from particular trade agreements to

which the United States is a party; and labour unions with interests in trade, or in the prohibition of imports made by workers employed in oppressive circumstances.

- *Human rights groups* include Asia Watch, an organization specializing in the perpetually demanding tasks of gathering intelligence on the abuse of human rights in Asian countries, and in the difficult task of persuading Congress and the executive to lobby for their remedy; and a host of liberal and church-based organizations with similar purposes.

- *Intellectual and research organizations* are often ideologically driven. These groups include the Council for Foreign Relations, an influential group representing elite business, financial and intellectual interests and perspectives on US foreign policy; the Centre for International Economics, a successful research institute conducting research on international trade; the Brookings Institution, a centrist think-tank; the Centre for Strategic and International Studies, a predominantly conservative research institute of high quality; and the American Enterprise Institute, a conservative, pro-business organization linked to many Republican politicians and to some conservative Democrats. Different administrations are susceptible to varying degrees to the research produced by members of these think-tanks. Presidents also draw on their own personnel when staffing their administrations, and members of Congress and senators when staffing their offices. By the same token, think-tanks draw on those who leave the Executive and Legislative Branches.

- *State and local governments*, most of which seek to attract capital from abroad, to which end, most states and large cities maintain representative offices in foreign countries. Through the National Governors' Association, the National League of Cities, and other representative organizations, lower-level governments attempt to influence policy deliberations within both the executive and Congress on questions affecting state and local commercial and political interests.

- *Electronic and print media groups* The coverage by television network news of foreign affairs is usually slight and superficial, and often banal. Even avid readers of the best American daily newspapers have difficulty in following political developments in major countries such as China, Russia, India, Germany, Japan and Brazil. This parochialism helps to ensure that few know much of foreign affairs, except those who watch public (non-commercial) television, read the foreign press, and view websites carrying news from beyond America's borders. Commercial television, oft-viewed websites and the domestic press nonetheless influence the political agenda, and are subject to influence by government press officers and, occasionally, to control by them. Such control takes different forms: during the invasion of Grenada, journalists were prevented from reporting it, whereas during the Iraq War (2003), journalists were embedded within US military units, with no freedom to move beyond them.

However, the media are (under favourable circumstances) able to shape public thinking and challenge government propaganda. For example, the coverage accorded the Tet offensive in 1968 exposed as hollow the administration's claim that the war was being won, hastened President Johnson's withdrawal from the race for the Democratic nomination, and caused US policy in Vietnam to be reassessed. President George W. Bush's unwise claim in May 2003 that declared the 'mission accomplished' in Iraq was discredited by the war's continuation and unclear outcome. Even after the fall of Saddam Hussein in December of the same year, the Bush administration was unable to control the flow of negative media reports from the region, in part because of news sources (such as the Qatar-based *Al Jazeera*) that offered different perspectives and accounts of the conflict.

Processes of foreign and defence policy-making

Crisis policy

Crisis policy proceeds according to the broad outline of contingency plans. Preparation of multiple contingency plans for the launching of attacks by the Soviet-led World Trade Organization on the Central European front preoccupied Pentagon and NATO planners throughout the Cold War. Nonetheless, however imaginative the planning work or accurate the intelligence assessments, the unexpected usually happens. Worse, the consequences of the unexpected are invariably unforeseen. For example, Japan's attack on Pearl Harbor in December 1941 not only precipitated the entry of the United States into World War II, but also transformed the nature of the domestic debate about continuing isolation from the politics of great power rivalry. Consequences of a different kind flowed from the Gulf of Tonkin crisis in 1964: it galvanized Congress to give the president leave (by margins of 415–0 in the House and 98–2 in the Senate) to respond to aggression as he thought fit. It thereby granted him *carte blanche* to conduct a war which eventually cost the lives of 56,000 Americans, and more than one million Vietnamese, and helped to disable the Democratic Party in presidential elections for a generation.

The attacks of 9/11 led George W. Bush to develop his Manichean foreign policy, crystallized in his West Point speech of 2002, which established the need to launch a *War on Terror* to focus both on Al-Qaeda and on an 'axis of evil' comprising Iran, Iraq and North Korea. And, as early as December 2001, Congress gave its support to the War on Terror in passing the PATRIOT Act which, though not the *carte blanche* of the Gulf of Tonkin Resolution, afforded the president considerable powers to employ the intelligence services in surveillance, to monitor and control immigration, and to scrutinize private financial records and other data.

The President's powers in crises

The Constitution unequivocally grants the power to Congress to declare war (see Appendix 1). Yet, delegates to the Philadelphia Convention acknowledged that the Legislature was too unwieldy and sluggish an institution to respond to sudden attacks. Only six wars (including the first Gulf War of 1990) have ever been declared by Congress. That the president's powers as Commander-in-Chief, the maker of war, include the power to order military responses to attack is universally acknowledged. Even Jefferson, the most assiduous critic of executive power, accepted this understanding and acted on it as president in ordering a response to the British attack on the *USS Chesapeake* in 1807. Had Soviet armoured forces launched the massive thrust through the Fulda Gap in northern Germany after 1949 for which contingency NATO planners prepared, Congress might well have had no time in which to declare war. Yet, the president would certainly have waged it.

Such ideal-type cases are straightforward and prompt no serious constitutional controversy. Presidents not only may, but *must*, defend the country against sudden attack: they may not decline to respond if the price of delay is defeat. The Constitution provides for government in emergency as well as in normality; the rights it defends are vitiated if the Republic it constitutes is destroyed by war. President Lincoln thus acted by suspending *habeas corpus* and imposing a blockade on the rebellious southern states in April 1861, when Congress was in recess. He merely sought (and secured) retrospective congressional approval. Even under Franklin D. Roosevelt and Harry Truman, the Commander-in-Chief clause was abused during time of war: in *Korematsu v United States* (1944), the Supreme Court upheld the internment of 100,000 people of Japanese descent that Roosevelt had ordered. However, President Truman received shorter shrift from the Court in *Youngstown Sheet and Tube Co. v Sawyer* (1952) for his attempt to seize private property under his Commander-in-Chief powers in what he claimed to be the national interest (see Chapter 7).

Where individual and property rights are not involved, the Supreme Court has avoided controversies about the war power, expediently choosing to regard them as political questions for resolution between the executive and the legislature. The Gulf of Tonkin resolution, for example, provoked no intervention by the Court. From its passage in August

1964 until the end of his presidency, Johnson regularly secured congressional appropriations for the expanding war, including the unrelenting bombing campaign from March 1965 and the deployment of ground troops in July of the same year. Johnson regarded securing his political base in Congress for the war as his first priority. In doing so, the President attempted to pursue a middle course between conservative and liberal critics, whose ranks swelled from the middle of 1967 onwards when prospects of winning seemed as remote as those of withdrawal. A president's political need of congressional support for his foreign and defence policy effectively obliges him to consult with Congress, whatever view individual presidents may take of their implied powers under the Commander-in-Chief clause. That which the Constitution does not require of the president the politics of coalition-building may.

Consultation with Congress neither saved Johnson's presidency, nor won the war that split his party, for his policy in Vietnam depended partly on deception, not least of himself. As the prospect (and conception) of victory receded, doubts about the means, purpose, morality and constitutionality of the huge effort grew. Partisan and ideological circumstances changed with Richard Nixon's election in 1968: facing Democratic majorities in Congress, Nixon chose to conduct the war alone, taking account of congressional advice only when it suited his domestic purposes. Disregarding State Department advice and concentrating policy formulation and implementation in the White House restricted Congress's capacity to oversee the conduct of the war. Such reasoning informed the tight control of the invasion of Cambodia in April 1970, which Nixon sought to justify later as an exercise to protect the lives of Americans in Vietnam. Under its Chairman William Fulbright, the Senate Foreign Relations Committee had, as early as 1965, considered whether presidential war powers were being unconstitutionally extended. He exposed as bogus Johnson's claim that the US invasion of the Dominican Republic in April of that year was for the purpose of protecting American lives, rather than that of intervening to prevent a change of government inimical to American interests. That led him to consider whether Congress had also been misled in the information about the supposed North Vietnamese attack on the *USS Maddox* in the Gulf of Tonkin in the summer of 1964, which had enabled Johnson to seek congressional approval for expanded war measures.

From 1965 onwards, therefore, debate about the propriety and conduct of the war in south-east Asia became entangled with the constitutional problem of the scope offered by the Commander-in-Chief clause. Johnson claimed that the Gulf of Tonkin resolution was an affirmation of broad presidential powers; Madisonian critics such as Senators Fulbright and McGovern disagreed. Two factors complicated the problem. The first was that the administration misled Congress about the circumstances under which the *USS Maddox* was alleged to have been attacked on 4 August 1964. Had it been known that, on the 4 of August, the ship was in North Vietnamese and not (as it had been on the occasion of the first attack two days before) in international waters, the justification in international law for the administration's action would have collapsed. The emergency was, as Fulbright himself later rightly argued, contrived. The second was that, as Johnson claimed throughout his term in office, and as Nixon asserted when the Gulf of Tonkin resolution was finally repealed in 1970 amidst bitter congressional dispute about the war's expansion into Cambodia, the President had no need of the resolution. Both claimed that the Commander-in-Chief clause gave him sufficient authority to act virtually as he chose; the Gulf of Tonkin resolution was a political cover that was finally removed.

This was no confined or arcane constitutional question: its origins, course and resolution resonated through American society and politics. It broke two presidents, damaged the presidency, and eventually induced vigorous reassertions of congressional prerogatives. The dispute's importance was plain: if the president could commit American troops to war without congressional authorization in circumstances other than those of response to sudden attack, an important constraint on presidential power was nullified. Moreover, if the executive's purpose in supplying information to Congress was to deceive rather than to inform, the bonds of trust on which bi-partisanship in foreign policy had been built were shattered. The claim that the Constitution afforded presidents powers in foreign and defence policy without let or hindrance offered a Caesarist corruption, rather than a Hamiltonian interpretation, of Articles I and II, with sinister implications for a democratic Republic.

Congress's response began with Fulbright's Senate investigations. Having co-sponsored the Gulf of Tonkin resolution in 1964, he spent his last years in public life resisting Johnson and Nixon's claims that presidential war powers were inherently flexible, a euphemism for their being determined by the president. His own 'Sense of the Senate' resolution, the so-called National Commitments Resolution (1969), declared that grants of power from Congress to the executive in foreign policy would henceforth be limited in extent and duration, unlike the Gulf of Tonkin Resolution which was general and open-ended. The National Commitments Resolution was not law, but marked the beginning of the reassertion of congressional powers. It preceded the invasion of Cambodia and the revelation of the full extent of American military involvement in adjoining countries.

Undeclared presidential war in Cambodia prompted Senators Cooper and Church to attempt to define conditions under which a president could act unilaterally abroad. Although the measure eventually passed the Senate in compromise form, it failed in the House, which was less inclined to challenge the assertion of presidential foreign policy prerogatives. The Chairman of the National Security Policy Subcommittee of the House Foreign Affairs Committee attempted in both the 91st and the 92nd Congresses to pass a resolution, but as Church–Cooper was too restrictive for the House, so his own versions were insufficiently restrictive for the Senate.

Following President Nixon's ordering of the bombing of Hanoi and Haiphong during Christmas 1972, resistance to attempts by congressional liberals to limit presidential war-making powers weakened. The end of the bombing, followed by the withdrawal of US combat forces in March 1973, did not terminate American engagement: President Nixon ordered a secret bombing campaign of Cambodia. When, as was inevitable, the new air war became known, Congress denied appropriations. Although Nixon vetoed the bill, he eventually agreed to end all US combat operations in south-east Asia. Nixon's attacks on Cambodia weakened those who sought an accommodation with the President. The War Powers Resolution (1973), passed under Senator Javits's leadership over the president's veto, required the president to report to the speaker and the president *pro tempore* of the Senate within forty-eight hours of the initiation of hostilities, on their circumstances, nature, extent and likely duration. The resolution required the president to consult with Congress 'in every possible instance' before introducing armed forces into hostilities or circumstances where hostilities were clearly imminent. It further gave Congress the authority to end hostilities within sixty days, and required the president to withdraw US forces within sixty days with another thirty days being allowed for the withdrawal operation if the president declared it necessary. The timetable could be suspended by Congress declaring war or granting specific support for the president's action.

Every president since 1973 has regarded the War Powers Resolution as unconstitutional. Neither in the *Mayaguez* incident of 1975, where President Ford ordered the use of military force without prior consultation with Congress, nor in the rescue of US citizens from Saigon in 1975, did he consult with Congress. Neither did President Carter do so prior to attempting a rescue of American hostages in Teheran in 1980. Although the Supreme Court has declined to adjudicate on it, the Resolution's constitutionality is doubtful, and not merely because it might be regarded as infringing a president's power as Commander-in-Chief. The Resolution, in fact, grants to the president and Congress powers that the Constitution denies: the waging of undeclared war for up to ninety days, and congressional restrictions on the president's command of deployed forces. Nuclear exchanges may occur in the two days between initiating hostilities and reporting to Congress. Less dramatically, such a period may make it politically impossible for Congress to question their deployment for fear of being regarded as treacherous. The War Powers Resolution has not diminished the president's capacity to set the agenda: as Commander-in-Chief, he can initiate and implement policy. It leaves wide scope for presidential discretion regarding the form and timing of consultation, and a choice as to whom he consults. The Resolution's silences permit presidents latitude sufficient for them to act without significant hindrance.

The Resolution has, in practice, thus had less effect than Javits hoped for, whatever its constitutionality. The intense debate in Congress over the wisdom of granting President George H.W. Bush a free hand in the Gulf in 1991, and the fierce debate in Congress in 2007 regarding the powers wielded by President George W. Bush not only in Iraq and Afghanistan but also in relation to detainees at Guantanamo Bay, suggest that, while the bilious distrust marking relations between Johnson, Nixon and Congress had faded, reluctance to cede war powers remained. Given the disastrous initiation and conduct of war in south-east Asia between 1964 and 1973, and because of Congress's own powerful sources of bureaucratic and analytical expertise in its specialist professional staff, it is at first glance surprising, even allowing for the desire to respond to the attacks of 9/11, that Congress granted President George W. Bush such a sweeping grant of authority in passing the 2001 PATRIOT Act. That it did so is a measure of the convulsive effects that the terrorist attacks on New York and Washington in 2001 had on American policy and policy-makers.

Strategic policy

In contrast to crisis policy and the war power, Congress exercises continuous influence on strategic policy. Its decisions about the recipients, amounts and conditions of foreign and military aid; trade policy; ratification of Treaties; confirmation hearings of senior administration officials; its oversight of Executive Branch decision-making; hearings on human rights violations; its controls over arms exports; its authorizing weapons purchases and appropriating funds to pay for them, are all instances of Congress's broad powers over strategic policy.

The Defense Department's 'Quadrennial Defence Review', notionally established to examine the major strategic purposes and modalities of US defence policy, also shows Congress's influence. Indeed, Congress itself required that the department undertake the periodic reviews, retaining for itself (consistent with the argument in the section below on structural policy) the right to determine the mix of modalities (especially base-closures) necessary to enable the United States to meet its self-imposed standard of having the capacity to fight two major regional wars simultaneously.

The Constitution's designation of the president as Chief Diplomat is subject to three qualifications:

- Appointments of Ambassadors and of appointees to non-civil service posts in the Executive Branch (save the president's immediate staff) are subject to *Senate confirmation*.
- The president's treaty-making power is subject to the *advice* and *consent* of two-thirds of the Senate.
- Congress retains full authorizing and appropriating powers over foreign and defence policy.

Treaties and executive agreements

Presidents have generally secured consent more easily when they have sought advice prior to and during the negotiation of treaties: senators respond with warmth to courting, but with heat to neglect. Inadequate consultation risks misjudgement of negotiating positions with foreign states and, so, defeat in the Senate. President Carter's negotiation of SALT II divided the Democratic party in the Senate; President Reagan's proposed sale of AWACS aircraft to Saudi Arabia in 1982 did much the same to his party through his attempt to avoid a legislative veto by the House and the Senate. The law of anticipated consequences obliges presidents to take account of opinion in the Senate Foreign Relations Committee and of the full Senate (in the case of treaties), and the reactions in both chambers (in the case of authorizing and appropriating legislation) before seeking support on Capitol Hill. Drafting of policy proposals only after full consultation reflects political sagacity, not weakness. The need for Senate ratification, coupled with the wisdom of securing bi-partisan support, informed the approach of Presidents Truman and Eisenhower to strategic policy formulation. Such an approach does not ensure foreign policy success, but does offer some prospect of domestic tranquillity.

Presidential failure to secure Senate ratification of treaties can alter the entire course of US foreign policy, as the Senate's rejection of the Treaty of Versailles in 1920 showed. The Senate's action flowed partly from partisanship (symbolized in Wilson's unwise exclusion of senior Republicans from the American delegation to Versailles), his unwillingness to consult fully with the Senate prior to establishing his own negotiating position, and his unyielding opposition to compromise with key senators who sought an amendment of the Treaty's Tenth Article in order to preserve Congress's prerogative to declare war and commit US forces. President Carter's Panama Canal Treaty of 1979 would have been defeated had the Senate leadership not visited Panama to secure amendments necessary for ratification. Carter lacked both the confidence and the foresight to consult influential senators during the Treaty's negotiation, which would have limited the need for remedial action later.

The North Atlantic Treaty (1949) illustrates the utility for presidents of close political collaboration with the Senate. Consultation between the Senate Foreign Relations Committee and the State Department was close throughout the drafting of the Treaty. Moreover, the ground was prepared by a Senate resolution calling for a collective security organization linking the United States and Western Europe. The resolution in question was drafted by State Department officials and senior senators including Arthur Vandenberg and Thomas Connally. Bridging the separation of the executive and legislature in the cause of 'advice and consent' has both force and value, as even Alexander Hamilton acknowledged in *Federalist* No. 75. The constitutional law regarding the termination of treaties is less clear than their ratification, although potentially of comparable moment. The court's majority holding in *Goldwater v Carter* (1979) that the question is political, and thus beyond the court's jurisdiction, does not close the matter; it is likely to return for adjudication when Congress next challenges a president's termination of a treaty.

Recent presidents have sometimes viewed the prospect of securing the ratification of treaties as insufficiently certain or excessively cumbersome, and so have resorted to concluding executive agreements. The destroyer–bases swap arrangement with Britain in 1940 (more than a year before the United States was brought into the war) is the most celebrated example. Roosevelt took the step because he anticipated that the Senate would reject a treaty taking the United States a step further from neutrality. From the president's constitutional authority to recognize foreign governments, he must have an implied power to conclude agreements with foreign states. (He may also be given authority to negotiate agreements by delegated authority, as is the case in trade negotiations.) Executive agreements risk involving the president and Congress in disputes over their respective powers, but conflict has usually occurred when agreements are concluded secretly, or touch the heart of the nation's foreign policy commitments. In the first case, the Senate cannot act if secrecy is maintained; in the second, Congress may protect Senate prerogatives by refusing to appropriate funds for the agreement's implementation, or by so amending authorizing legislation that the agreement is vitiated.

Foreign and military aid

Congress's power of the purse over US foreign and defence policy is clearly evident with regard to foreign and military aid. The president requests aid budgets, but Congress retains complete autonomy in lawmaking: it determines the identity of beneficiaries, the budget's size and

Table 12.1 *Top Recipients of US Foreign Assistance, FY2000 and FY2010 (in millions of current 2010 US$)*

FY2000		FY2010	
Israel	4,069	Afghanistan	4,102
Egypt	2,053	Israel	2,220
Columbia	899	Pakistan	1,807
West Bank/Gaza	485	Egypt	1,296
Jordan	429	Haiti	1,271
Russia	195	Iraq	1,117
Bolivia	194	Jordan	693
Ukraine	183	Kenya	688
Kosovo	165	Nigeria	614
Peru	120	S. Africa	578
Georgia	112	Ethiopia	533
Armenia	104	Columbia	507
Bosnia	101	West Bank/Gaza	496
Indonesia	94	Tanzania	464
Nigeria	68	Uganda	457

the allocation of funds. Foreign aid attracts attention disproportionate to its cost. Unpopular with constituents, many of whom erroneously suppose it to be a large proportion of federal expenditure, and an even larger proportion of whom think it wasteful, the foreign aid budget is the object of intensive lobbying not only by foreign governments to whom the aid is important, but also, for example, from human rights organizations such as Amnesty International and Asia Watch, whose officials regularly testify against US military aid being granted to regimes that flout human rights. Members of the House and the Senate also choose to give committee and subcommittee hearings on foreign aid publicity, because the annual legislative rounds of authorization and appropriation enable them to question officials on US policies towards states and regions.

The cyclical appropriations process not only guarantees Congress influence over administration policy, but also enables distributive politics to be played (see Tables 12.1 and 12.2). As with structural defence policy, military aid gives senators and members of the House opportunities to direct federal spending towards businesses in their state or district. Foreign aid gives them the opportunity to appeal to fiscally conservative voters by attempting to cut the president's foreign aid budget request, or alternatively, for example, to appeal to Jewish voters by supporting increased aid to Israel.

Since the redistribution of power within Congress in the early 1970s, the foreign aid budget has become more politicized and subject to

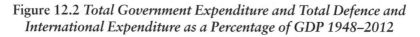

Figure 12.2 *Total Government Expenditure and Total Defence and International Expenditure as a Percentage of GDP 1948–2012*

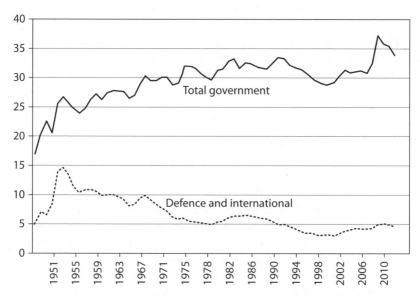

detailed control. This development has been most apparent with human rights and international drug trafficking. Congress requires the State Department to report annually on human rights abuses in foreign countries, which may be taken into account when determining aid. The department's report became embroiled in controversy during Mr Reagan's Administration when, for reasons of *realpolitik*, he sought increased financial support for regimes in Central America which had deplorably bad human rights records. The Anti-Drug Abuse Act (1986) required the executive to certify whether foreign countries were or were not cooperating with American efforts to end international trafficking in drugs: President Reagan reported that General Noriega was cooperating even as it became evident that the Panamanian leader was personally profiting from a huge drug-smuggling operation conducted with American knowledge. Violations of congressional trust during the Vietnam War and Iran–Contra continue to exercise a chilling effect on the conduct of foreign policy. Congress is less likely to grant greater administrative discretion to the executive insofar as its members, or a majority of them, distrust it. The problem worsened in the 1980s as the split partisan control of the two elective branches appeared to have become the dominant pattern. Such a lack of trust was prominent in the aftermath of the 2003 invasion of Iraq when Congress, effusive in its support for the War on Terror in the months just after 9/11, became increasingly troubled by the failure to find any weapons of mass destruction (WMD) in Iraq, the alleged existence of which had been the ostensible *casus belli*. With the Democratic capture of the House of Representatives in the 2006 mid-term elections, tensions within Congress and the executive became increasingly strained when, in early 2007, the Democratic leadership in the House pressed President George W. Bush to announce a timetable for the withdrawal of armed forces from Iraq. The pressure on the President failed.

Trade policy

Trade policy presents fewer but significant opportunities to Congress, which has deliberately chosen to place primary responsibility for negotiating in the World Trade Organization with the USTR, a part of the EOP whose officials are responsible to the President. To delegate responsibility, for example, to an agency of the Department of Commerce would expose trade negotiators to greater and more numerous pressures from Congress and private interests alike. By affording the USTR autonomy from narrow interests, and granting the president 'fast-track' negotiating authority, Congress implicitly recognized the United States' overriding interest in maintaining a liberal trading regime. However, this fast-track presidential authority expired in June 2007 but the Congress decided not to re-authorize this authority for President George W. Bush.

Sectional interests nonetheless abound. In the Doha Round that commenced in 2001, they included agricultural and service industries seeking unfettered access to foreign markets; agricultural interests opposed to lifting barriers against competitive imports; opponents and proponents of the imposition of industrial tariffs and of non-tariff trade barriers. The main divisions within the Doha Round were between the developed states (the EU and the US) and the major developing nations of China, India, Brazil, South Africa and South Korea. One notable area of tension focused on the continued use of agricultural subsidies by the USA and the EU member states that developing nations rightly claimed were, in principle, barriers to trade. The Doha Round of negotiations broke down in July 2008; as we write, the impasse remains unresolved.

Structural policy

Structural policy includes the procurement of weapons and weapons systems; the construction, expansion, reduction and closure of defence bases and facilities; and the hiring, deploying and organizing of military personnel. An excellent example of distributive policy, it comprises the federal government's purchase of goods and services from private businesses with public funds. Except for the lively market in guns sold to American citizens to defend themselves against other American citizens, the federal government is a monopsonist in the domestic market for weapons. The sale by US defence contractors of weapons and weapons systems to foreign governments is tightly regulated in statute, and overseen by Congress.

Structural policy ties the executive, Congress and groups together unusually tightly. Defence contractors depend for their profits, and their employees for their jobs, on decisions made by the president, the Pentagon and, most of all, by Congress. They decide which weapons systems are to be bought, in what quantities, under what conditions, from whom and over what period. Structural defence policy therefore matters for the domestic economy as a whole, for local economies dependent on defence contractors and, so, for American politics in general. Decisions about structural policy are politically informed. To that extent, the location and status of military bases, the number, type and mix of weapons systems do not necessarily address the United States' actual defence needs.

The power of the purse and single-member districts ensure that structural policy is a product of politicians' calculations about the significance of their decisions for their careers. Local politics obstructs policy-making in the national interest: developing a rational policy for the United States's military bases has been bedevilled by Congress's fragmentation. Between the 1930s and early 1970s, southern domination of key committees caused a large proportion of expenditure on weapons and bases to be directed to the South, known by sceptical northerners in the United States Army as that supposedly anti-federal region of the US where federal highways connect federal bases. Only with the slight reduction in real defence spending from 1986 onwards, and the sharper reductions following the Soviet Union's disintegration, did Congress establish a procedure for overcoming this costly collective action problem. Base closures are now proposed to Congress by the Secretary of Defense and voted on in a single package. It is effectively a closed bureaucratic rule which, like the closed rule under which the House Ways and Means Committee once operated in Congress, has the advantage of enforcing hard choices by overcoming particularism.

The new procedure has not diminished politicians' proclivity to judge the country's defence equipment needs by their own political interests. Defence contractors duly exploit this weakness by distributing subcontracts widely, so that as many senators and congressmen as possible have vested interests in defending weapons projects from elimination. Production runs are expensively extended, and research and development programmes continued, to protect congressional politicians from opponents' attacks. Policy is consequently often driven by the weapons acquired, instead of weapons being bought to serve a particular policy.

At $688 billion, Congress's appropriation to the Department of Defense for the 2012 fiscal year was nearly one hundred times greater than that to the State Department. The figures conceal the politics behind their establishment, but every element of Department of Defense expenditures has its constituency of supporters in Congress who find merit in it because part of the system is manufactured in their district.

Each of the armed services has a vested interest in its own overseas bases, often in countries with weak and undemocratic regimes, where the service has its own network of contacts with the armed services of the host government and may pursue its own bureaucratic interest in the guise of its own foreign and defence policy. Without representatives in Congress, these bases may become particularly vulnerable at a time of budgetary constraints and defence cuts.

Conclusion

In foreign and defence policy, the model of a fragmented and separated political system is less straightforwardly applicable to American government. The reasons for the difference are, first, that the constitutional authority of the federal government relative to the fifty states is much greater than in domestic policy; and, second, that with the exceptions of foreign aid and structural defence policy-making, the president's prerogatives are more numerous and substantial than in domestic or economic policy. The executive's autonomy from congressional and interest group pressures is consequently more extensive.

The president lacks competition in forming and executing foreign policy only during the management of crises and wars, and then only in the short term. It is quite different in other areas of foreign and defence policy formation. Congress, intellectuals, journalists, interest groups and public opinion play different, and often important, roles in the construction of defence bases; in the procurement of weapons systems and other supplies; in foreign aid policy; in strategic policy towards regions and countries; in the development of trade policy and the export of sensitive items of high-technology equipment; in immigration policy; and in questions of human rights and their abuse in foreign countries. Even where the autonomy of the Executive Branch is greatest, it is constrained. Even where government appears to be unified, symbolized in the lonely responsibilities of the president as Commander-in-Chief of the world's sole remaining military superpower, the politics of competition and fragmentation remain latent and are readily activated.

Conclusion

Two major crises dominated the first decade of the twenty-first century: the War on Terrorism; and the financial crisis which erupted in 2007 and thereafter developed into consequential crises of credit markets, banks and banking, production and employment. This exceptional series of events had major fiscal and political consequences, and raised fundamental questions both about the legitimate powers of federal government and about that government's capacity to shape public policy outcomes, whether in foreign states or in domestic and international markets. As America's internal fiscal deficit fell sharply in the late 1990s, so did political anxiety about fiscal policy. By the same token, as America's internal fiscal deficit grew with the fall in federal tax revenues after 2001 in response to the combination of a mild recession, major tax cuts and steep increases in national security expenditure, so anxiety about the resultant rise both in annual deficits and total federal debt grew. Among the public and political debates, many of which were notable more for their noise than for their depth, some academics and journalists reflected helpfully and incisively upon the possible institutional sources of the financial and economic crises. Partisan polarization has worsened the difficulty of overcoming the collection action problem which is, under any circumstances, especially severe in a separated system. Such concerns must be viewed against the backdrop of a political culture in which many Americans display considerable ambivalence towards the role of government, and at a time when Republican Party officials, in particular, encouraged by the Tea Party Movement, declare themselves deeply distrustful of government and ideologically opposed to any public policy proposals entailing government intervention and, especially, regulation.

The combination of institutional separation and partisan polarization has re-created a variation upon the common phenomenon of 'gridlock' in which those having incentives to effect collective political action are defeated by those who prefer the status quo. It is under these conditions that charges of a 'do-nothing' Congress and a lame-duck president are generated. Indeed, as we write in the autumn of 2013, members of Congress have failed to pass major agriculture legislation, or respond to the need to raise the debt ceiling, and threaten to rebuff the President's limited political ambition to punish President Assad's regime in Syria for his use of chemical weapons against his own people. One of the few initiatives with bipartisan support is President Obama's attempt to bring Israelis and Palestinians back to the negotiating table. Yet, in the first year of the 113th Congress the GOP has proposed 42 bills intended to eradicate, or at the least to emasculate, the President's flagship healthcare bill, the Affordable Care Act (ACA).

Constitutional divisions between institutions, as well as partisan polarization, are underpinned by the influence of powerful interest groups and the private financing of Congressional campaigns. Most Congressional districts are wholly or substantially uncompetitive, and most politicians are aided by campaign consultants and by the increasingly sophisticated use of the internet and social media to target potential voters. The influence of groups and money was bolstered by the Supreme Court's relaxation in 2010 of campaign finance regulations that were, in any case, strikingly weak. Politicians appear better adapted to satisfying group and individual demands than to identifying a public interest, and expressing it through legislation and action.

Popular distrust of politicians and cynicism about their ethical standards and motives has measurably increased. Public opinion poll data lend some support to the claim that popular distrust of government (especially of federal government) has become both deeper and more extensive since the poison of Vietnam and Watergate entered politics: in 2012, American voters regarded the United States Congress scarcely more favourably than it did Fidel Castro. American government remains infected with, and deeply affected by, the enduring poison of Watergate; since 1980, polarization has increasingly characterized public and Congressional debate, and often overwhelmed Congress's capacity to reason, educate, examine and legislate. As the discussion of American political culture in Chapter 1 showed, anti-government sentiments are older than the Republic itself, underpinned by an antipathy to government bolstered by the ambiguities of the confederal and US Constitutions. Revolutionary values coexist with principles of stable government, leaving open spaces for Jacksonian sentiments to express themselves - sometimes with violence, but more frequently with violent rhetoric.

Distrust of government notwithstanding, institutional separations have ensured that parties remain central to the functioning of democracy in America. The much vaunted decline of parties is a less plausible account of American politics than it once appeared. In the early twenty-first century, members of Congress are much more likely to vote along party lines, leaving little scope for politicians to form cross-party coalitions. This extreme weakness of bipartisanship has made the prospect of reaching consensus, and therefore of making policy in an era of divided government, problematic. The rise of strong, disciplined parties akin to those in parliamentary systems has led to gridlock in a system that encourages divided government.

The fundamental problem presented by politics in the United States, especially in the federal government, is that collective decisions are difficult to achieve in a multiply-fragmented system that inhibits articulation of the public interest, penetrated by a vigorous, diverse, and dynamic civil society. The high premiums placed upon democratic accountability and individual rights accordingly make the governing of the United States uncommonly demanding.

The composition, content, and ordering of the agenda of public policy in the United States are competitively determined and subject to change. While some matters high on the federal agenda in Mr Obama's second term appear forbiddingly complex and resistant to collective public remedy, there is no good reason for thinking that current problems of public policy are harder to solve than the combination of deep economic depression and world war which Franklin D. Roosevelt faced, or the threatened sundering of the United States that Abraham Lincoln successfully overcame, or the creation and establishment of the Republic to which Washington, Adams, Jefferson, Madison and Jackson in their several ways devoted themselves.

As the citing of these examples suggests, the presidency is not only the centrepiece of the United States Constitution and of its politics, but provides the starting point for understanding the Republic's capacity to endure. It does so because the presidency is a symbol of the country's ability to reconstitute itself, the means whereby old problems may be examined afresh, new objectives identified and old values invoked anew. The Constitution grants little authority to presidents but, as this book has shown, numerous opportunities to his competitors and nominal allies to deflect, disrupt and delay. Yet, the Constitution offers the possibility of renewal by giving a new president not only heavy responsibilities, but also the fresh opportunity to lead this most diverse of nations and complex of governments. The cyclical prospects of change and possibilities of progress are not the least of the Constitution's complex legacies.

The Constitution of the United States, Bill of Rights and Later Amendments

We the People of the United States, in order to form a more perfect union, establish Justice, insure domestic tranquillity, provide for the common defence, promote the general Welfare, and secure the Blessings of Liberty to ourselves and our Posterity, do ordain and establish this Constitution for the United States of America.

Article I

Section 1. All legislative Powers herein granted shall be vested in a Congress of the United States, which shall consist of a Senate and a House of Representatives.

Section 2. The House of Representatives shall be composed of Members chosen every second Year by the People of the several States, and the Electors in each State shall have the Qualifications requisite for the Electors of the most numerous Branch of the State Legislature.

No Person shall be a Representative who shall not have attained to the Age of twenty-five years, and been seven Years a Citizen of the United States, and who shall not, when elected, be an Inhabitant of that State in which he shall be chosen.

Representatives and direct Taxes shall be apportioned among the several States which may be included within this Union, according to their respective Numbers, which shall be determined by adding to the whole Number of free Persons, including those bound to Service for a Term of Years, and excluding Indians not taxed, three fifths of all other Persons. The actual Enumeration shall be made within three Years after the first Meeting of the Congress of the United States, and within every subsequent Term of ten Years, in such Manner as they shall by Law direct. The Number of Representatives shall not exceed one for every thirty Thousand, but each State shall have at Least one Representative; and until such enumeration shall be made, the State of New Hampshire shall be entitled to chuse three, Massachusetts eight, Rhode-Island and Providence Plantations one, Connecticut five, New-York six, New Jersey four, Pennsylvania eight, Delaware one, Maryland six, Virginia ten, North Carolina five, South Carolina five, and Georgia three.

When vacancies happen in the Representation from any State, the Executive authority thereof shall issue Writs of Election to fill such Vacancies.

House of Representatives shall chuse their Speaker and other Officers; and shall have the sole Power of Impeachment.

Section 3. The Senate of the United States shall be composed of two Senators from each State, chosen by the Legislature thereof, for six Years; and each Senator shall have one Vote.

Immediately after they shall be assembled in consequence of the first Election, they shall be divided as equally as may be into three Classes. The Seats of the Senators of the first Class shall be vacated at the Expiration of the second Year, of the second Class at the Expiration of the fourth Year, and of the third Class at the Expiration of the sixth Year, so that one third may be chosen every second Year; and if Vacancies happen by Resignation, or otherwise, during the Recess of the Legislature of any State, the Executive thereof may make temporary Appointments until the next Meeting of the Legislature, which shall then fill such Vacancies.

No Person shall be a Senator who shall not have attained to the Age of thirty Years, and been nine Years a Citizen of the United States, and who shall not, when elected, be an Inhabitant of that State for which he shall be chosen.

The Vice President of the United States shall be President of the Senate, but shall have no Vote, unless they be equally divided.

The Senate shall chuse their other Officers, and also a President pro tempore, in the Absence of the Vice President, or when he shall exercise the Office of President of the United States.

The Senate shall have the sole Power to try all Impeachments. When sitting for that Purpose, they shall be on Oath or Affirmation. When the President of the United States is tried, the Chief Justice shall preside: And no Person shall be convicted without the Concurrence of two thirds of the Members present.

Judgement in Cases of Impeachment shall not extend further than to removal from Office, and disqualification to hold and enjoy any Office of honor, Trust or Profit under the United States: but the Party convicted shall never the less be liable and subject to Indictment, Trial, Judgement and Punishment, according to Law.

Section 4. The Times, Places and Manner of holding Elections for Senators and Representatives, shall be prescribed in each State by the Legislature thereof, but the Congress may at any time by Law make or alter such Regulations, except as to the Places of chusing Senators.

The Congress shall assemble at least once in every Year, and such Meeting shall be on the first Monday in December, unless they shall by Law appoint a different Day.

Section 5. Each House shall be the Judge of the Elections, Returns and Qualifications of its own Members, and a Majority of each shall constitute a Quorum to do Business; but a small Number may adjourn from day to day, and may be authorized to compel the Attendance of absent Members, in such Manner, and under such Penalties, as each House may provide.

Each House may determine the Rules of its Proceedings, punish its Members for disorderly Behavior, and, with the Concurrence of two thirds, expel a Member.

Each House shall keep a Journal of its Proceedings, and from time to time publish the same, excepting such Parts as may in their judgement require Secrecy; and the Yeas and Nays of the Members of either House on any question shall, at the Desire of either House of one fifth of those present, be entered on the Journal. Neither House, during the Session of Congress, shall, without the Consent of the other, adjourn for more than three days, nor to any other Place than that in which the two Houses shall be sitting.

Section 6. The Senators and Representatives shall receive a Compensation for their Services, to be ascertained by Law, and paid out of the Treasury of the United States. They shall in all Cases, except Treason, Felony and Breach of the Peace, be privileged from Arrest during their Attendance at the Session of their respective Houses, and in going to and returning from the same; and for any Speech or Debate in either House, they shall not be questioned in any other Place.

No Senator or Representative shall, during the Time for which he was elected, be appointed to any Civil Office under the Authority of the United States, which shall have been created, or the Emoluments whereof shall have been increased during such time;

and no Person holding any Office under the United States, shall be a Member of either House during his Continuance in Office.

Section 7. All Bills for raising Revenue shall originate in the House of Representatives; but the Senate may propose or concur with Amendments as on other Bills.

Every Bill which shall have passed the House of Representatives and the Senate, shall, before it becomes a Law, be presented to the President of the United States; If he approve he shall sign it, but if not he shall return it, with his Objections to that House in which it shall have originated, who shall enter the Objections at large on their Journal, and proceed to reconsider it. If after such Reconsideration two thirds of that House shall agree to pass the Bill, it shall be sent, together with the Objections, to the other House, by which it shall likewise be reconsidered, and if approved by two thirds of that House, it shall become a Law. But in all such Cases the Votes of both Houses shall be determined by Yeas and Nays, and the Names of The Persons voting for and against the Bill shall be entered on the Journal of each House respectively. If any Bill shall not be returned by the President within ten Days (Sundays excepted) after it shall have been presented to him, the Same shall be a Law, in like Manner as if he had signed it, unless the Congress by their Adjournment prevent its Return, in which Case it shall not be a Law.

Every Order, Resolution, or Vote to which the Concurrence of the Senate and House of Representatives may be necessary (except on a question of Adjournment) shall be presented to the President of the United States; and before the Same shall take effect, shall be approved by him or being disapproved by him, shall be repassed by two thirds of the Senate and House of Representatives, according to the Rules and Limitations prescribed in the Case of a Bill.

Section 8. The Congress shall have Power To lay and collect Taxes, Duties, Imposts and Excises, to pay the debts and provide for the common Defence and general Welfare of the United States; but all Duties, Imposts and Excises shall be uniform throughout the United States;

To borrow Money on the credit of the United States;

To regulate Commerce with foreign Nations, and among the several States, and with the Indian Tribes;

To establish an uniform Rule of Naturalization, and uniform Laws on the subject of Bankruptcies throughout the United States;

To coin Money, regulate the Value thereof, and of foreign Coin, and fix the Standard of Weights and Measures;

To provide for the Punishment of counterfeiting the Securities and current Coin of the United States;

To establish Post Offices and post Roads;

To promote the Progress of Science and useful Arts, by securing for limited Times to Authors and Inventors the exclusive Right to their respective Writings and Discoveries;

To constitute Tribunals inferior to the supreme Court;

To define and punish Piracies and Felonies committed on the high Seas, and Offences against the Law of Nations;

To declare War, grant letters of Marque and Reprisal, and make Rules concerning Captures on Land and Water;

To raise and support Armies, but no Appropriation of Money to that Use shall be for a longer Term than two Years;

To provide and maintain a Navy;

To make Rules for the Government and Regulation of the land and naval Forces; To provide for calling forth the Militia to execute the Laws of the Union, suppress Insurrections and repel Invasions;

To provide for organizing, arming, and disciplining the Militia, and for governing such Part of them as may be employed in the Service of the United States, reserving to the States respectively, the Appointment of the Officers, and the Authority of training the Militia according to the discipline prescribed by Congress;

To exercise exclusive Legislation in all Cases whatsoever, over such District (not exceeding ten Miles square) as may, by Cession of particular States, and the Acceptance of Congress, become the Seat of the Government of the United States, and to exercise like Authority over all Places purchased by the Consent of the Legislature of The State in which the Same shall be, for the Erection of Forts, Magazines, Arsenals, dock-Yards, and other needful Buildings; – And

To make all Laws which shall be necessary and proper for carrying into Execution the foregoing Powers, and all other Powers vested by this Constitution in the Government of the United States, or in any Department or Officer thereof.

Section 9. The Migration or Importation of such Persons as any of the States now existing shall think proper to admit, shall not be prohibited by the Congress prior to the Year one thousand eight hundred and eight, but a Tax or duty may be imposed on such Importation, not exceeding ten dollars for each Person.

The Privilege of the Writ of Habeas Corpus shall not be suspended, unless when in Cases of Rebellion or Invasion the public Safety may require it.

No Bill of Attainder or ex post facto Law shall be passed.

No Capitation, or other direct, tax shall be laid, unless in Proportion to the Census or Enumeration herein before directed to be taken.

No Tax or Duty shall be laid on Articles exported from any State.

No Preference shall be given by any Regulation of Commerce or Revenue to the Ports of one State over those of another; nor shall Vessels bound to, or from, one State, be obliged to enter, clear, or pay Duties in another.

No Money shall be drawn from the Treasury, but in Consequence of Appropriations made by Law; and a regular Statement and Account of the Receipts and Expenditures of all public Money shall be published from time to time.

No Title of Nobility shall be granted by the United States: And no Person holding any Office of Profit or Trust under them, shall, without the Consent of the Congress, accept of any present, Emolument, Office, or Title, of any kind whatever, from any King, Prince, or foreign State.

Section 10. No State shall enter into any Treaty, Alliance, or Confederation; grant Letters of Marque and Reprisal; coin Money; emit Bills of Credit; make any Thing but gold and silver Coin a Tender in Payment of Debts; pass any Bill of Attainder, ex post facto Law, or Law impairing the Obligation of Contracts, or grant any Title of Nobility.

No State shall, without the Consent of the Congress, lay any Imposts or Duties on Imports or Exports, except what may be absolutely necessary for executing its inspection Laws: and the net Produce of all Duties and Imposts, laid by any State on Imports or Exports, shall be for the Use of the Treasury of the United States; and all such laws shall be subject to the Revision and Control of the Congress.

No State shall, without the Consent of Congress, lay any Duty of Tonnage, keep Troops, or Ships of War in time of Peace, enter into any Agreement or Compact with another State, or with a foreign Power, or engage in War, unless actually invaded, or in such imminent Danger as will not admit of delay.

Article II

Section 1. The Executive Power shall be vested in a President of the United States of America. He shall hold his Office during the Term of four Years, and, together with the Vice President, chosen for the same Term, be elected, as follows.

Each State shall appoint, in such Manner as the legislature thereof may direct, a Number of Electors, equal to the whole Number of Senators and Representatives to which the State may be entitled in the Congress: but no Senator or Representative, or Person holding an Office of Trust or Profit under the United States, shall be appointed an Elector.

The electors shall meet in their respective States, and vote by ballot for two Persons, of whom one at least shall not be an Inhabitant of the same State with themselves. And they shall make a List of all the Persons voted for, and of the Number of Votes for each; which List they shall sign and certify, and transmit scaled to the Seat of the Government of the United States, directed to the President of the Senate. The President of the Senate shall, in the Presence of the Senate and House of Representatives, open all the Certificates, and the Votes shall then be counted. The Person having the greatest Number of Votes shall be the President, if such Number be a Majority of the whole Number of Electors appointed; and if there be more than one who have such Majority, and have an equal number of votes, then the House of Representatives shall immediately chuse by Ballot one of them for President; and if no Person have a Majority, then from the five highest on the List the said House shall in like Manner chuse the President. But in chusing the President, the Votes shall be taken by States, the Representation from each State having one Vote; A quorum for this Purpose shall consist of a Member or Members from two thirds of the States, and a Majority of all the States shall be necessary to a Choice. In every Case, after the Choice of the President, the Person having the greatest Number of Votes of the Electors shall be the Vice President. But if there should remain two or more who have equal Votes, the Senate shall chuse from them by Ballot the Vice President.

The Congress may determine the Time of chusing the electors, and the Day on which they shall give their Votes; which Day shall be the same throughout the United States.

No Person except a natural born Citizen, or a Citizen of the United States, at the time of the Adoption of this Constitution, shall be eligible to the Office of President; neither shall any Person be eligible to that Office who shall not have attained to the Age of thirty five Years, and been fourteen Years a Resident within the United States.

In Case of the Removal of the President from Office, or of his Death, Resignation or Inability to discharge the Powers and duties of the said Office, the same shall devolve on the Vice President, and the Congress may by Law provide for the Case of Removal, Death, Resignation or Inability, both of the President and Vice President, declaring what Officer shall then act as President, and such Officer shall act accordingly, until the Disability be removed, or a President shall be elected. The President shall, at stated Times, receive for his Services, a Compensation, which shall neither be encreased nor diminished during the Period for which he shall have been elected, and he shall not receive within that Period any other Emolument from the United States, or any of them.

Before he enter on the Execution of his Office, he shall take the following Oath or Affirmation: –"I do solemnly swear (or affirm) that I will faithfully execute the Office of President of the United States, and will to the best of my Ability, preserve, protect and defend the Constitution of the United States".

Section 2. The President shall be Commander in Chief of the Army and Navy of the United States, and of the Militia of the several States, when called into the actual Service of the United States; he may require the Opinion, in writing, of the principal Officer in each of the executive Departments, upon any Subject relating to the Duties of their respective Offices, and he shall have Power to grant Reprieves and Pardons for Offences against the United States, except in Cases of Impeachment.

He shall have Power, by and with the Advice and Consent of the Senate, to make Treaties, provided two thirds of the Senators present concur and he shall nominate, and by and with the Advice and Consent of the Senate, shall appoint Ambassadors, other public Ministers and Consuls, Judges of the Supreme Court, and all other Officers of the United States, whose Appointments are not herein otherwise provided for, and which shall be established by Law; but the Congress may by Law vest the Appointment of such inferior Officers, as they think proper, in the President alone, in the Courts of Law, or in the Heads of Departments.

The President shall have Power to fill up all Vacancies that may happen during the Recess of the Senate, by granting Commissions which shall expire at the End of their next Session.

Section 3. He shall from time to time give to the Congress Information of the State of the Union, and recommend to their Consideration such Measures as he shall judge necessary and expedient; he may, on extraordinary Occasions, convene both Houses, or either of them, and, in case of Disagreement between them, with Respect to the Time of Adjournment, he may adjourn them to such Times as he shall think proper; he shall receive Ambassadors and other Public Ministers; he shall take Care that the Laws be faithfully executed, and shall Commission all the Officers of the United States.

Section 4. The President, Vice President and all civil Officers of the United States, shall be removed from Office on Impeachment for, and Conviction of, Treason, Bribery, or other high Crimes and Misdemeanors.

Article III

Section 1. The judicial Power of the United States, shall be vested in one Supreme Court, and in such inferior Courts as the Congress may from time to time ordain and establish. The Judges, both of the supreme and inferior Courts, shall hold their Offices during good Behaviour, and shall, at stated Times, receive for their Services, a Compensation, which shall not be diminished during their Continuance in Office.

Section 2. The judicial Power shall extend to all Cases, in Law and Equity, arising under this Constitution, the Laws of the United States, and Treaties made, or which shall be made, under their Authority; – to all Cases affecting Ambassadors, other public Ministers and Consuls; – to all Cases of admiralty and maritime Jurisdiction; to Controversies to which the United States shall be a Party; – to Controversies between two or more States; between a State and Citizens of another State; – between Citizens of different States, – between Citizens of the same State claiming Lands under Grants of different States, and between a state, or the citizens thereof, and foreign States, Citizens or Subjects.

In all Cases affecting Ambassadors, other public Ministers and Consuls, and those in which a State shall be party, the supreme Court shall have original jurisdiction. In all other Cases before mentioned, the supreme Court shall have appellate Jurisdiction, both as to Law and Fact, with such Exceptions, and under such Regulations, as the Congress shall make.

The Trial of all Crimes, except in Cases of Impeachment, shall be by Jury; and such Trial shall be held in the State where the said Crimes shall have been committed; but when not committed within any State, the Trial shall be at such Place or Places as the Congress may by Law have directed.

Section 3. Treason against the United States, shall consist only in levying War against them, or in adhering to their Enemies, giving them Aid and comfort. No Person shall be convicted of Treason unless on the Testimony of two Witnesses to the same overt Act, or on Confession in open Court.

The Congress shall have Power to declare the Punishment of Treason, but no Attainder of Treason shall work Corruption of blood, or Forfeiture except during the Life of the Person attainted.

Article IV

Section 1. Full Faith and Credit shall be given in each State to the public Acts, Records, and judicial Proceedings of every other State. And the Congress may by general Laws prescribe the Manner in which such Acts, Records and Proceedings shall be proved, and the Effect thereof.

Section 2. The Citizens of each State shall be entitled to all Privileges and Immunities of each Citizens in the several States.

A person charged in any State with Treason, Felony, or other Crime, who shall flee from Justice, and be found in another State, shall on Demand of the executive Authority of the State from which he fled, be delivered up, to be removed to the State having Jurisdiction of the Crime.

No Person held to Service or Labour in one State, under the Laws thereof, escaping into another, shall, in Consequence of any Law or regulation therein, be discharged from such Service or Labour but shall be delivered up on Claim of the Party to whom such Service or Labour may be due.

Section 3. New States may be admitted by the Congress into this Union; but no new State shall be formed or erected within the Jurisdiction of any other State; nor any State be formed by the Junction of two or more States, or Parts of States, without the consent of the Legislatures of the States concerned as well as of the Congress.

The Congress shall have Power to dispose of and make all needful Rules and Regulations respecting the Territory or other Property belonging to the United States; and nothing in this Constitution shall be so construed as to Prejudice any Claims of the United States, or of any particular State.

Section 4. The United States shall guarantee to every State in this Union a Republican Form of Government, and shall protect each of them against Invasion; and on Application of the Legislature, or of the Executive (when the Legislature cannot be convened) against domestic Violence.

Article V

The Congress, whenever two thirds of both houses shall deem it necessary, shall propose Amendments to this Constitution, or, on the Application of the Legislatures of two thirds of the several States, shall call a Convention for proposing Amendments, which, in either Case, shall be valid to all Intents and Purposes, as Part of this Constitution, when ratified by the Legislatures of three fourths of the several States, or by Conventions in three fourths thereof, as the one or the other Mode of Ratification may be proposed by the Congress; Provided that no Amendment which may be made prior to the Year One thousand eight hundred and eight shall in any Manner affect the first and fourth Clauses in the Ninth Section of the first Article; and that no State, without its Consent, shall be deprived of its equal Suffrage in the Senate.

Article VI

All Debts contracted and Engagements entered into, before the Adoption of this Constitution, shall be as valid against the United States under this Constitution, as under the Confederation.

This Constitution, and the Laws of the United States which shall be made in Pursuance thereof, and all Treaties made, or which shall be made, under the Authority of the United States, shall be the supreme Law of the Land; and the Judges in every State shall be bound thereby, any Thing in the Constitution or Laws of any State to the Contrary notwithstanding.

The Senators and Representatives before mentioned, and the Members of the several State Legislatures, and all executive and Judicial Officers, both of the United States and of the several States, shall be bound by Oath or Affirmation, to support this Constitution; but no religious Test shall ever be required as a Qualification to any office or public Trust under the United States.

Article VII

The Ratification of the Conventions of the nine States, shall be sufficient for the Establishment of this Constitution between the States so ratifying the Same.

DONE in Convention by the Unanimous Consent of the States present the Seventeenth Day of September in the Year of our Lord one thousand seven hundred and Eighty seven and of the Independence of the United States of America the Twelfth. IN WITNESS whereof We have hereunto subscribed our Names.

George Washington
Presid^t and Deputy from Virginia

Amendments to the Constitution of the United States

[The first ten amendments were proposed on 25 September 1789 and declared ratified on 15 December 1791.]

First

Congress shall make no law respecting an establishment of religion, or prohibiting the free exercise thereof, or abridging the freedom of speech, or of the press; or the right of the people peaceably to assemble, and to petition the government for a redress of grievances.

Second

A well regulated Militia, being necessary to the security of a free State, the right of the people to keep and bear Arms, shall not be infringed.

Third

No Soldier shall, in time of peace, be quartered in any house, without the consent of the Owner, or in time of war, but in a manner to be prescribed by law.

Fourth

The right of the people to be secure in their persons, houses, papers and effects, against unreasonable searches and seizure, shall not be violated, and no Warrants shall issue, but upon probable cause, supported by Oath or affirmation, and particularly describing the place to be searched, and the persons or things to be seized.

Fifth

No person shall be held to answer for a capital, or otherwise infamous crime, unless on a presentment or indictment of a Grand Jury, except in cases arising in the land or naval forces, or in the Militia, when in actual service in time of War or public danger; nor shall any person be subject for the same offence to be twice put in jeopardy of life or limb; nor shall be compelled in any Criminal Case to be a witness against himself, nor be deprived of life, liberty, or property, without due process of law; nor shall private property be taken for public use, without just compensation.

Sixth

In all criminal prosecutions, the accused shall enjoy the right to a speedy and public trial, by an impartial jury of the State and district wherein the crime shall have been committed, which district shall have been previously ascertained by law, and to be informed of the nature and cause of the accusation; to be confronted with the witnesses against him; to have compulsory process for obtaining Witnesses in his favor, and to have the Assistance of Counsel for his defence.

Seventh

In suits at common law, where the value in controversy shall exceed twenty dollars, the right of trial by jury shall be preserved, and no fact tried by a Jury shall be otherwise re-examined in any Court of the United States, than according to the rules of common law.

Eighth

Excessive bail shall not be required, nor excessive fines imposed, nor cruel and unusual punishments inflicted.

Ninth

The enumeration in the Constitution, of certain rights, shall not be construed to deny or disparage others retained by the people.

Tenth

The powers not delegated to the United States by the Constitution, nor prohibited by it to the States, are reserved to the States respectively, or to the people.

Eleventh

[Proposed 4 March 1794; declared ratified 8 January 1798]
The Judicial power of the United States shall not be construed to extend to any suit in law or equity, commenced or prosecuted against one of the United States by Citizens of another State, or by Citizens or Subjects of any Foreign State.

Twelfth

[Proposed 9 December 1803; declared ratified 25 September 1804]
The electors shall meet in their respective states, and vote by ballot for President and Vice-President, one of whom, at least, shall not be an inhabitant of the same state with themselves; they shall name in their ballots the person voted for as President, and in distinct ballots the person voted for as Vice-President, and they shall make distinct lists of all persons voted for as President, and of all persons voted for as Vice-President, and of the number of votes for each, which lists they shall sign and certify, and transmit scaled to the seat of the Government of the United States, directed to the President of the Senate; – The President of the Senate shall, in the presence of the Senate and the House of Representatives, open all the certificates and the votes shall then be counted; – The person having the greatest number of votes for President shall be the President, if such number be a majority of the whole number of Electors appointed; and if no person have such majority, then from the persons having the highest numbers not exceeding three on the list of those voted as President, the House of Representatives shall choose immediately, by ballot, the President. But in choosing the President, the votes shall be taken by states, the representation from each state having one vote; a quorum for this purpose shall consist of a member or members from two-thirds of the states, and a majority of all the states shall be necessary to a choice. And if the House of Representatives shall not choose a President whenever the right of choice shall devolve upon them, before the fourth day of March next following, then the Vice-President shall act as President, as in the case of the death or other constitutional disability of the President. The person having the greatest number of votes as Vice-President, shall be the Vice-President, if such number be a majority of the whole number of Electors appointed, and if no person have a majority, then from the two highest numbers on the list, the Senate shall choose the Vice-President; a quorum for the

purpose shall consist of two-thirds of the whole number of Senators, and a majority of the whole number shall be necessary to a choice. But no person constitutionally ineligible to the office of President shall be eligible to that of Vice-President of the United States.

Thirteenth

[Proposed 31 January 1865; declared ratified 18 December 1865]

Section 1. Neither slavery nor involuntary servitude, except as a punishment for crime whereof the party shall have been duly convicted, shall exist within the United States, or any place subject to their jurisdiction.

Section 2. Congress shall have power to enforce this article by appropriate legislation.

Fourteenth

[Proposed 13 June 1866; declared ratified 28 July 1868]

Section 1. All persons born or naturalized in the United States, and subject to the jurisdiction thereof, are citizens of the United States and of the State wherein they reside. No State shall make or enforce any law which shall abridge the privileges or immunities of citizens of the United States; nor shall any State deprive any person of life, liberty, or property, without due process of law; nor deny to any person within its jurisdiction the equal protection of the laws.

Section 2. Representatives shall be apportioned among the several States according to their respective numbers, counting the whole number of persons in each State, excluding Indians not taxed. But when the right to vote at any election for the choice of electors for President and Vice-President of the United States, Representatives in Congress, the Executive and Judicial officers of a State, or the members of the Legislature thereof, is denied to any of the male inhabitants of such State, being twenty-one years of age, and citizens of the United States, or in any way abridged, except for participation in rebellion, or other crime, the basis of representation therein shall be reduced in the proportion which the number of such male citizens shall bear the whole number of twenty-one years of age in such State.

Section 3. No person shall be a Senator or Representative in Congress, or elector of President and Vice President, or hold any office, civil, or military, under the United States, or under any State, who, having previously taken an oath, as a member of Congress, or as an officer of the United States, or as a member of any State legislature, or as an executive or Judicial officer of any State, to support the Constitution of the United States, shall have engaged in insurrection or rebellion against the same, or given aid or comfort to the enemies thereof. But Congress may by a vote of two-thirds of each House, remove such disability.

Section 4. The validity of the public debt of the United States, authorized by law, including debts incurred for payment of pensions and bounties for services in suppressing insurrection or rebellion, shall not be questioned. But neither the United States nor any State shall assume or pay any debt or obligation incurred in aid of insurrection or rebellion against the United States, or any claim for the loss or emancipation of any slave; but all such debts, obligations and claims shall be held illegal and void.

Section 5. The Congress shall have power to enforce, by appropriate legislation, the provisions of this article.

Fifteenth

[Proposed 26 February 1869; declared ratified 30 March 1870]

Section 1. The right of citizens of the United States to vote shall not be denied or abridged by the United States or by any State on account of race, color, or previous condition of servitude.

Section 2. The Congress shall have power to enforce this article by appropriate legislation.

Sixteenth

[Proposed 12 July 1909; declared ratified 25 February 1913]

The Congress shall have power to lay and collect taxes on incomes, from whatever source derived, without apportionment among the several States, and without regard to any census or enumeration.

Seventeenth

[Proposed 13 May 1912; declared ratified 31 May 1911]

The Senate of the United States shall be composed of two Senators from each State, elected by the people thereof, for six years; and each Senator shall have one vote. The electors in each State shall have the qualifications requisite for electors of the most numerous branch of the State legislature.

When vacancies happen in the representation of any State in the Senate, the executive authority of such State shall issue writs of election to fill such vacancies: PROVIDED, That the legislature of any State may empower the executive thereof to make temporary appointments until the people fill the vacancies by election as the legislature may direct.

This amendment shall not be so construed as to affect the election or term of any Senator chosen before it becomes valid as part of the Constitution.

Eighteenth

[Proposed 18 December 1917; declared ratified 29 January 1919]

After one year from the ratification of this article, the manufacture, sale, or transportation of intoxicating liquors within, the importation thereof into, or the exportation thereof from the United States and all territory subject to the jurisdiction thereof for beverage purposes is hereby prohibited.

The Congress and the several States shall have concurrent power to enforce this article by appropriate legislation.

This article shall be inoperative unless it shall have been ratified as an amendment to the Constitution by the legislatures of the several States, as provided in the Constitution, within seven years from the date of the submission hereof to the States by the Congress.

Nineteenth

[Proposed 4 June 1919; declared ratified 26 August 1920]

The right of citizens of the United States to vote shall not be denied or abridged by the United States or by any States on account of sex.

The Congress shall have power, by appropriate legislation, to enforce the provisions of this article.

Twentieth

[Proposed 2 March 1932; declared ratified 6 February 1933]

Section 1. The terms of the President and Vice-President shall end at noon on the twentieth day of January, and the terms of Senators and Representatives at noon on the third day of January, of the years in which such terms would have ended if this article had not been ratified; and the terms of their successors shall then begin.

Section 2. The Congress shall assemble at least once in every year, and such meeting shall begin at noon of the third day of January, unless they shall by law appoint a different day.

Section 3. If, at any time fixed for the beginning of the term of the President, the President-elect shall have died, the Vice-President-elect shall act as President until a President shall have qualified; and the Congress may by law provide for the case wherein neither a President-elect nor a Vice-President-elect shall have qualified, declaring who shall then act as President, or the manner in which one who is to act shall be selected, and such person shall act accordingly until a President or Vice-President shall have qualified.

Section 4. The Congress may by law provide for the case of the death of any of the persons from whom the House of Representatives may choose a President whenever the right of choice shall have devolved upon them, and for the case of the death of any of the persons from whom the Senate may choose a Vice-President whenever the right of choice shall have devolved upon them.

Section 5. Sections 1 and 2 shall take effect on the 15th day of October following the ratification of this article.

Section 6. This article shall be inoperative unless it shall have been ratified as an amendment to the Constitution by the legislatures of three-fourths of the several States within seven years from the date of its submission.

Twenty-First

[Proposed 20 February 1933; declared ratified 5 December 1933]

Section 1. The eighteenth article of amendment to the Constitution of the United States is hereby repealed.

Section 2. The transportation or importation into any State, Territory, or possession of the United States for delivery or use therein of intoxicating liquors, in violation of the laws thereof, is hereby prohibited.

Section 3. This article shall be inoperative unless it shall have been ratified as an amendment to the Constitution by convention in the several States, as provided in the Constitution, within seven years from the date of the submission hereof to the States by the Congress.

Twenty-Second

[Proposed 21 March 1947; declared ratified 3 March 1951]

Section 1. No person shall be elected to the office of the President more than twice, and no person who has held the office of President, or acted as President, for more than two years of a term to which some other person was elected President shall be elected to the office of the President more than once. But this Article shall not apply to any person holding the office of President when this Article was proposed by the Congress, and shall not prevent any person who may be holding the office of President, or acting as President, during the term within which this Article become operative from holding the office of President or acting as President during the remainder of such term.

Twenty-Third

[Proposed 17 June 1960; declared ratified 3 April 1961]

Section 1. The District constituting the seat of Government of the United States shall appoint in such manner as the Congress may direct:

A number of electors of President and Vice President equal to the whole number of Senators and Representatives in Congress to which the District would be entitled if it were a State, but in no event more than the least populous State; they shall be in addition to those appointed by the States, but they shall be considered, for the purposes of election of President and Vice President, to be electors appointed by a State; and they shall meet in the District and perform such duties as provided by the twelfth article of amendment.

Section 2. The Congress shall have power to enforce this article by appropriate legislation.

Twenty-Fourth

[Proposed 27 August 1962; declared ratified 4 February 1964]
Section 1. The right of citizens of the United States to vote in any primary or other election for President or Vice President, for electors for President or Vice President, or for Senator or Representative in Congress, shall not be denied or abridged by the United States or any state by reason of failure to pay any poll tax or other tax.

Section 2. The Congress shall have power to enforce this article by appropriate legislation.

Twenty-Fifth

[Proposed 6 July 1965; declared ratified 23 February 1967]
Section 1. In the case of the removal of the President from office or of his death or resignation, the Vice President shall become President.

Section 2. Whenever there is a vacancy in the office of the Vice President, the President shall nominate a Vice President who shall take office upon confirmation by a majority vote of both Houses of Congress.

Section 3. Whenever the President transmits to the President pro tempore of the Senate and the Speaker of the House of Representatives his written declaration that he is unable to discharge the powers and duties of his office, and until he transmits to them a written declaration to the contrary, such powers and duties shall be discharged by the Vice President as Acting President.

Section 4. Whenever the Vice President and a majority of either the principal officers of the executive department of such other body as Congress may by law provide, transmit to the President pro tempore of the Senate and the Speaker of the House of Representatives their written declaration that the President is unable to discharge the powers and duties of his office; the Vice President shall immediately assume the powers and duties of the office as Acting President.

Thereafter, when the President transmits to the President pro tempore of the Senate and the Speaker of the House of Representatives his written declaration that no inability exists, he shall resume the powers and duties of his office unless the Vice President and a majority of either the principal officers of the executive department or of such other body as Congress may by law provide, transmit within four days to the President pro tempore of the Senate and the Speaker of the House of Representatives their written declaration that the President is unable to discharge the powers and duties of his office. Thereupon Congress shall decide the issue, assembling within forty-eight hours for that purpose if not in session. If the Congress, within twenty-one days after Congress is required to assemble, determines by two-thirds vote of both Houses that the President is unable to discharge the powers and duties of his office, the Vice President shall continue to discharge the same as Acting President; otherwise, the President shall resume the powers and duties of his office.

Twenty-Sixth

[Proposed 23 March 1971; declared ratified 30 June 1971]
Section 1. The right of citizens of the United States, who are 18 years of age or older, to vote shall not be denied or abridged by the United States or any state on account of age.

Section 2. The Congress shall have the power to enforce this article by appropriate legislation.

Twenty-Seventh

[Proposed 1789; declared ratified 7 May 1992]
No law varying the compensation for the services of the Senators and Representatives shall take effect, until an election of Representatives shall have intervened.

Constitutional Allocation of Powers over Foreign and Defence Policy

Powers Granted to Congress

Under Article I, Section 8:

The Congress shall have power:

To lay and collect taxes, duties, imposts and excises, to pay the debts and provide for the common defense and general welfare of the United States; but all duties, imposts and excises shall be uniform throughout the United States;

To define and punish piracies and felonies committed on the high Seas, and Offenses against the Law of Nations;

To declare War, grant letters of marque and reprisal, and make rules concerning captures on land and water;

To raise and support armies, but no appropriation of money to that use shall be for a longer term than two years;

To provide and maintain a Navy;

To make rules for the government and regulation of the land and naval forces;

To provide for calling forth the militia to execute the laws of the Union, suppress insurrections and repel invasions;

To provide for organizing, arming, and disciplining the militia, and for governing such part of them as may be employed in the service of the United States, reserving to the States respectively, the appointment of the officer, and the authority of training the militia according to the discipline prescribed by Congress;

To exercise exclusive legislation ... over all places purchased by the consent of the legislature of the state in which the same shall be, for the erection of forts, magazines, arsenals, dock-yards, and other needful buildings.

Powers Granted to the President

Under Article II, Section 2:

The President shall be the Commander-in-Chief of the Army and Navy of the United States, and of the militia of the several states, when called into the actual service of the United States.

He shall have power, by and with the advice and consent of the Senate, to make treaties, provided two-thirds of the Senators present concur; and he shall nominate, and by and with the Advice and Consent of the Senate, shall appoint Ambassadors.

He shall receive Ambassadors ... and shall commission all the officers of the United States.

Further Reading

Journals and Newspapers

The *New York Review of Books* is a good and pleasurable source of political debate. The *New York Times*, and the *Washington Post* remain America's two best newspapers; both provide excellent news websites. Each of those newspapers' Apps are useful and user-friendly. An examination of the App Store yields an embarrassment of riches which include *Slate Magazine*, and the *Huffington Post*. Some apps, as with some online versions of these newspapers, charge a small monthly subscription, but many are free. Although the availability of such Apps is large, you might wish to consider viewing either the Apps or the websites for the following:

RealClearPolitics.com
HuffingtonPost.com
WashingtonPost.com
NYTimes.com
OpenSecrets.org
Slate.com
C-Span.org
nbc.com
foxnews.com
msnbc.com
usatoday.com
time.com

The quality of European analysis of American politics varies: all of the British so-called 'quality' newspapers report daily on American politics, but often unimaginatively. The *Financial Times* is the clearest exception to this rule: its coverage of the United States is usually excellent. The *Economist*'s coverage is often useful, particularly the eight or so pages dedicated to the examination of North America.

The Palgrave series *Developments in American Politics*, now in its eighth edition (2014), is an invaluable source of up-to-date information and analyses from eminent scholars.

Almost all of the sources below can be found both in hard copy and as electronic downloads.

Chapter 1 Beliefs and Values in American Society

De Tocqueville's 1835 analysis of American political culture, *Democracy in America* (1969), provides a readable account – and one of the earlier works of political science. A classic statement of the view that American political culture is built on a liberal tradition can be found in Louis Hartz's *The Liberal Tradition in America* (1955). An excellent critical assessment of the Hartzian legacy is provided in Mark Hulliung's edited volume *The American Liberal Tradition Reconsidered: The Contested Legacy of Louis Hartz* (2010). Rogers M. Smith's *American Political Science Review* article *Beyond Tocqueville, Myrdal, and Hartz: The multiple traditions of America* (1993) provides a thoughtful re-assessment of the dominant approaches to the assessment of American political culture. Samuel Huntington's discussion of 'the American Creed' in his 1983 book *The Promise of Disharmony* is a stimulating and oft-quoted account.

Chapter 2 The Constitution: Creating the Rules of the Game

French constitutions were once regarded merely as 'periodical literature'; the *Constitution of the United States of America*, endless subject of disputatious interpretation, could never be so stigmatized. It is central to United States government and politics; reading it and thinking about it in the context of American history is essential if United States government and politics are to be understood (a searchable version of the United States Constitution, with annotations and commentary, can be found as a free App and is most useful). For the same reason, *The Federalist Papers*, early and sophisticated propaganda in defence of the proposed Constitution, remain essential reading; Isaac Kramnick's 'Introduction' to the Pelican edition is splendid (Hamilton *et al.*, 1987). Louis Hartz's classic liberal exposition of American political values, *The Liberal Tradition in America*, together with Charles Beard's *An Economic Interpretation of the Constitution*, which advances a radical, if unpersuasive, interpretation of the motives and interests of the Constitution's founders, are important and stimulating arguments. Among the plethora of scholarly work on the Constitution's operation, Maurice Vile's *Constitutionalism and the Separation of Powers* has lasted well and fully repays reading. Louis Fisher's more recent *Constitutional Dialogues* is a subtle and perceptive interpretation of the most important and complex constitutional relationships in United States government: those between Congress and the executive. Seymour Martin Lipset's *The First New Nation* and his *Continental Divide* offer informed, comparative and historically rich interpretations of the Republic's founding, development and distinctiveness. Byron Shafer addresses himself to some of the many facets of the problem of American exceptionalism in his excellent edited collection of essays *Is America Different?* Robert Singh's *The Farrakhan Phenomenon* is a splendid critical analysis with much of importance to say about the immediate subject and the wider questions of extremism in America. James Gibson's *Warrior Dreams* sets right-wing militia groups in historical and cultural contexts, whilst Richard Hofstadter's *The Paranoid Style in American Politics* is a magisterial treatment. (The 2008 edition has an excellent introduction by Sean Wilentz.)

Chapter 3 Political Parties

An excellent textbook examination of parties is Hetherington and Larson's *Parties, Politics and Public Policy in America* (2010). Sandy Maisel's *American Political Parties and Elections: A Very Short Introduction* (2007) is part of OUP's VSI series and is a good place to start. Alan Ware's 2011 *Political Conflict in America* provides a fascinating and insightful overview of the current state of the political parties. Leon Epstein's *Political Parties in the American Mold* is a fine interpretation of the distinctiveness of political parties in the United States. Nelson Polsby's *Consequences of Party Reform* examines what its title declares; Byron Shafer's *Quiet Revolution* is a detailed, scholarly account of party reform. On party organization, A. J. Reichley's *The Life of the Parties* is an authoritative plea for party revival, while Alan Ware's *The Breakdown of Democratic Party Organization* is a sophisticated argument about the decomposition of the organizational base of parties. Sundquist's *Dynamics of the Party System* is a fine study of alignment and realignment of political parties, while Key's superb *Southern Politics*, and Bass and De Vries's *The Transformation of Southern Politics* explore the tortured history of the great regional exception to most rules about party politics in the United States. Katznelson's *City Trenches* advances a compelling argument about the weakness of class as a basis for party politics in the United States. Stanley Greenberg's revised edition of *Middle Class Dreams* is a stimulating account of a supposed middle-class rebellion against the federal government and the two major political parties.

Chapter 4 Elections and the Politics of Participation

Three problems of major interest receive extensive attention in the literature: (i) for whom Americans vote; (ii) why voting participation is comparatively low; and (iii) why presidential elections have recently so often had different partisan outcomes to Congressional ones.

With regard to those for whom Americans vote, Polsby and Wildavsky's *Presidential Elections* is the best introductory text. Burnham's *Critical Elections and the Mainsprings of American Politics* remains a classic study. Nie *et al.*'s *The Changing American Voter*, and Smith's *The Unchanging American Voter* address the same problem with different data. Philip M. Williams's 'Party Realignment in Britain and the US' (1985) sets the American debate about realignment in a comparative context. *Primary Colors* is an entertaining novel about the entirely fictional campaign of an unprincipled southern governor running for president in the early 1990s. Shafer and Claggett's *The two Majorities* is an important and illuminating account of, in the authors' words, 'the grand substantive framework for political conflict'.

With regard to why voting participation is comparatively low, Piven and Cloward's *Why Americans Don't Vote* has provoked much controversy and debate, as shown by Bennett's article 'The Uses and Abuses of Registration per cent Turnout Data' in *PS* (June 1990), and the ensuing exchanges in the same journal. E. C. Ladd's *Where Have all the Voters Gone?* is a useful study, as is W. D. Burnham's essay 'The Turnout Problem' in A. J. Reichley's edited collection *Elections American Style*.

With regard to the varying partisan outcomes between presidential and Congressional elections, Beck *et al.*'s article 'Patterns and Sources of Ticket-Splitting on Subpresidential Voting' (1992), together with Jacobson's excellent study *The Electoral Origins of Divided Government* and Shafer's stimulating article 'The Election of 1988 and the Structure of American Politics' (1989) provide a good interpretation of the nature and dimensions of one of the most fascinating problems in American politics.

Dan Balz's *Collision 2012: Obama vs. Romney and the Future of Elections in America* is probably the most readable book on the 2012 presidential elections by one of America's most distinguished reporters.

In terms of explaining elections outcomes, perhaps the most extensive and yet readable text is Miller and Shanks' *The New American Political Voter* which was published in 1996. Maisel and Brewer's *Parties and Elections in America* (2011) is another excellent source of information and analysis of who wins, what and why.

Chapter 5 The Presidency and the Politics of Leadership

A very good introductory textbook is James Pfiffner's and Roger M. Davidson's *Understanding the Presidency* (6th edn: 2010). Still the defining study more than forty years after it was first written, Neustadt's *Presidential Power* is a subtle and brilliant scholarly proof of the proposition that the Presidency and Congress are locked in complex relationships of mutual political dependence. Unfortunately, Neustadt's work is more often cited than it is read. Bob Haldeman's *The Haldeman Diaries* comprise the finest single source of published evidence on the Nixon presidency, rich with insights into the institution of the presidency itself. Another excellent source is Joseph Califano's *The Triumph and Tragedy of Lyndon Johnson*.

Louis Fisher also sets the presidency in the appropriate context of relations with the other two branches in *The Law of the Executive Branch: Presidential Power* (2013). James Sterling Young's *The Washington Community 1800–1828* (1966), a study of the dilemmas of leadership in Jeffersonian America but with much to tell us about modern American politics, has (with Neustadt's *Presidential Power*) a good claim to be one of the dozen finest books ever written on United States politics. Rockman's *The Leadership Question* (1984) is a stimulating study, exceptionally well-grounded in the comparative literature on political leadership, as is Macgregor Burns's *Leadership* (1978). Relations between presidency and Congress are scrutinized in Peterson's *Legislating Together*, and in Jones's study of President Carter, *The Trusteeship Presidency*. Leuchtenburg's *In the Shadow of FDR* explains well the consequences of Franklin D. Roosevelt's restructuring of government, policy and politics in the United States. Studies of individual modern presidents and presidencies abound. Among the best are Leuchtenburg's *Franklin D. Roosevelt and the New Deal*, Greenstein's ambitious (though not entirely persuasive) interpretation of Eisenhower's leadership, *The Hidden-Hand Presidency* and Lou Cannon's excellent book *President Reagan*.

Chapter 6 Congress and the Politics of the Legislative Competition

Attracted by the prospect of quantification through the statistical analysis of congressional voting patterns, American political scientists have written more widely on Congress than on either the presidency or the Supreme Court. Jones's large textbook, *The United States Congress*, is a splendid introduction. Another distinguished student of Congress, Richard Fenno, has written extensively on the subject; his *Congressmen in Committees* (1973) and *Home Style* (1979) have been the most influential. The first analyses members of Congress at work on Capitol Hill, while the second examines them at work in their districts. The influence of electoral considerations on congressional behaviour is the subject of

Mayhew's classic study *Congress: The Electoral Connection*, and of Fiorina's scarcely less well-known *Congress: Keystone of the Washington Establishment*. Fowler and McClure's enjoyable and informative *Political Ambition* examines the problem of the factors that determine who runs for Congress. Sinclair's *The Transformation of the US Senate* is one of the best recent studies of the smaller chamber. Fenno has written a series of studies of individual senators: his excellent *The Making of a Senator* is a case study of the Senate career of Danforth Quayle; *Learning to Legislate*, is a study of Arlen Specter; *The Emergence of a Senate Leader*, examines Senator Pete Domenici's role in budgetary politics; while *The Presidential Odyssey of John Glenn* considers that senator's failed presidential bid. Questions of political process are considered by Dodd and Schott in their highly intelligent, if dated, *Congress and the Administrative State* and by Smith in his *Call to Order: Floor Politics in the House and Senate*. Hall's article 'Participation and Purpose in Committee Decision Making' (1987)) is seminal; his book *Participation in Congress* is an impressively fine (and useful) piece of social science research.

Lou Fisher's *On Appreciating Congress: The People's Branch* (2009) sets out a sophisticated argument inviting fuller understanding of the first branch of US Government, whilst M.N. Green's *The Speaker of the House* (2010) is a most helpful guide to that critical institution of legislative leadership.

Hibbing and Theiss-Morse's *Congress as Public Enemy* offers a careful account and analysis of the American public's opinion of the federal legislature. Two very useful edited collections of essays are Cox and Kernell's *The Politics of Divided Government* (1991), and Davidson's *The Postreform Congress* (1992). Thomas Mann and Norman Ornstein's *The Broken Branch* (2008) provides a stimulating and critical appraisal of the contemporary Congress.

Chapter 7 The Supreme Court and the Politics of Adjudication

Congressional Quarterly Weekly Report is a great help in keeping up to date with judgements when they are handed down in a rush during the summer, and the November issue of the *Harvard Law Review* contains a useful account of the preceding term's judgements. The many American law school journals also contain articles in which the Court's judgements are examined. All of these cases can, of course, be searched with ease online.

However, there is no substitute for reading the full decisions in the original: all good law library websites contain the full text of Supreme

Court judgments. Hall's *The Oxford Companion to the Supreme Court of the United States* is a magnificent and enjoyable compendium with concise explanatory entries on Court rules, procedures, cases, controversies, points of law and justices.

With respect to the large secondary literature, Richard Hodder-Williams's *The Politics of the US Supreme Court* and David O'Brien's *Storm Center* are excellent introductions to the subject. Hodder-Williams's article, 'Six Notions of "Political" and the United States Supreme Court' (1992) provides a helpful analysis of a problematic concept. Schwartz's *Super Chief: Earl Warren and his Supreme Court* is an admirable study of one of the greatest chief justices in the Court's history, while Blasi, in his edited collection entitled *The Burger Court*, and Schwartz in *The Ascent of Pragmatism* advance our understanding of the Court under Earl Warren's less remarkable successor. Michael Perry's *The Constitution in the Courts* is a skilful and subtle interpretation of the problems of original intent. Witt's *A Different Justice: Reagan and the Supreme Court* is a useful examination of that frequently conflictual relationship, while in *The Judicial Process*, Abraham gives an indispensable comparative treatment of courts in Britain, France and the United States.

Chapter 8 Interest Groups

Truman's *The Governmental Process* (1951) and Latham's *The Group Basis of Politics* (1952) are classic pluralist statements; Dahl's *Who Governs?* (1961) is social scientific research of the highest quality, and still essential reading. Schattschneider's *The Semi-Sovereign People* (1960) is a less sanguine account of the distribution of political power. Dahl and Lindblom's *Politics, Economics, and Welfare* (1953) still has the capacity to surprise. Cater's *Power in Washington* is an early but excellent interpretation of the power of sub-governments in Washington; Heclo's later article, 'Issue Networks and the Executive Establishment', in King (ed.), *The New American Political System* (1978) is a clever interpretation of a more fluid system than that which Cater analysed. Building on the theoretical foundations established in his seminal book *The Logic of Collective Action* (1965), Olson considered the relationship between interest group activity and economic decline in *The Decline of Nations* (1982). Walker's article, 'The Origins and Maintenance of Interest Groups in America' (1983) addresses himself to the same theoretical problem with which Olson was concerned in 1965. Lindblom's *Politics and Markets* (1977) marked a change of view by one of the most distinguished scholars of interest groups, confirmed in his later presidential address to the American Political Science Association, reprinted as

'Another State of Mind' (1982). Gaventa's *Power and Powerlessness* is an excellent application of Lukes's theory developed in *Power* (1974) to a coal-mining community in Appalachia. Wilson's *Unions in American Politics* is a good introduction to labour unions in the United States. Among recent articles, Peterson's 'The Presidency and Organized Interests' (1992), and Quinn and Shapiro's 'Business Political Power: the Case of Taxation', *American Political Science Review* (1991) are excellent.

Chapter 9 Bureaucracy: The Fourth Branch of Government

Crenson and Rourke's essay 'By Way of Conclusion: American Bureaucracy since World War II', in Galambos's edited collection *The New American State*, provides a brief introduction to the subject. Fuller accounts may be found in Rourke's own *Bureaucracy Politics, and Public Policy* and 'Bureaucracy in the American Constitutional Order' (1987), in Johnson and Libecap's *The Federal Civil Service System and the Problem of Bureaucracy* and in Woll's *American Bureaucracy*. Seidman and Gilmour's *Politics, Position, and Power* (4th edn) is a politically sensitive interpretation of the fourth branch. Dodd and Schott's *Congress and the Administrative State* is admirable, though now rather dated. The delegation of congressional powers to agencies is further examined in McCubbins and Page's essay 'A Theory of Congressional Delegation', in McCubbins and Sullivan's edited collection *Congress: Structure and Policy*; the other half of that problem, congressional oversight of agencies' operation through the appropriations and authorization processes, is well treated in Aberbach's *Keeping a Watchful Eye* (1990). Distributive politics has received considerable attention: Arnold's *Congress and the Bureaucracy: A Theory of Influence* is excellent, while Rich's 'Distributive Politics and the Allocation of Federal Grants' (1989), and Hird's 'The Political Economy of Pork: Project Selection at the US Army Corp of Engineers' (1991) are excellent pieces of research. Moe considers the persistent problem for presidents of how they might exercise influence over bureaucrats only nominally subordinate to them in his essay 'The Politicized Presidency', in Chubb and Peterson's *New Directions in American Politics*; Wood and Waterman's article on the same subject 'The Dynamics of Political Control of the Bureaucracy' (1991) repays reading. James Q. Wilson's *Bureaucracy: What Government Agencies Do and Why They Do It* (1991) provides a thoughtful and detailed analysis of the motivations of bureaucrats within a selection of departments and agencies.

Chapter 10 Federalism and Intergovernmental Policy-Making

Good introductions are to be found in Dye's *American Federalism*; Elazar's *American Federalism: A View from the States*; Reagan and Sanzone's *The New Federalism*; Riker's *Federalism: Origin, Operation, and Significance*; Walker's *Toward a Functioning Federalism*; and Wright's *Understanding Intergovernmental Relations*. O'Toole's edited collection entitled *American Intergovernmental Relations* is a useful introductory reader. Sam Beer's splendid book, *To Make a Nation*, is fine scholarship founded on his long immersion in the subject. Chubb explores the difficulty of altering the balance of power between the federal and state governments in his essay 'Federalism and the Bias for Centralization', in Chubb and Peterson's *New Directions in American Politics*. McKay considers the development of policy embracing the federal and state governments in his *Domestic Policy and Ideology*, and Kettl asks hard questions about difficult problems of regulatory growth in *The Regulation of American Federalism*, using a detailed case study of a programme administered by the Department of Housing and Urban Development. The general subject of politics below the federal level is nowhere better introduced than by Burns *et al.* in their excellent *State and Local Politics*. Governorships provide the subject of Larry Sabato's valuable *Goodbye to Good-time Charlie*, and governors' relations with state assemblies the subject of Alan Rosenthal's *Governors and Legislatures: Contending Powers*. The processes of election to, and the structures and processes of politics within state assemblies themselves, are considered in Rosenthal's *Legislative Life*.

Chapter 11 Domestic Economic Policy

The websites run by the Office of Management and Budget and the Congressional Budget Office contain a wealth of statistical detail in presidential budget proposals and congressional budget legislation. Many of the tables reproduced in this book are from these websites.

The *Congressional Quarterly Weekly Report* and *National Journal* provide detailed accounts of the authorization and budgetary processes. Collender produces an annual *Guide to the Federal Budget* which is an essential reference. The best account of the reform of budgetary law in the 1970s is in Sundquist's *The Decline and Resurgence of Congress*. Hogan provides an assessment of the effectiveness of those reforms in his article 'Ten Years After: the US Congressional Budget and Impoundment Control Act of 1974' (1985). Other sources on the politics and procedures of the budget are Savage's *Balanced Budgets and American Politics* and Stein's *Presidential Economics*. Mr Reagan's bout of tax-cutting and aggregate budget increases are addressed by Stockman in his badly-written but revealing account, *The Triumph of Politics*, by Penner in his edited collection, *The Great Fiscal Experiment*; and by Friedman in *Day of Reckoning*. The history of the budgetary process is the subject of Stewart's *Budget Reform Politics*, Fisher's *Presidential Spending Power*, and of Schick's *Congress and Money*. Monetary policy is examined in Mayer's edited book, *The Political Economy of American Monetary Policy*, and by Woolley in *Monetary Politics*. Greider's *Secrets of the Temple* is a sensational but entertaining account of Federal Reserve perfidy during the 1980s. Berman's *The Office of Management and Budget and the Presidency, 1921–1979* provides a good account of the development of that key institution within the Executive Office of the President. Brownlee's edited collection *Funding the Modern American State, 1941–1995* contains much important scholarship on the history of taxation and public finance. For an accessible but intellectually rigorous overview of economic policy under George W. Bush, see Paul Krugman's *Fuzzy Math: An Essential Guide to the Bush Tax Plan* (2001). His overview of the 2008 economic crisis is analysed in his 2009 edition of *The Return of Depression Economics*.

Chapter 12 Foreign and Defence Policy

The literature in this field is vast, but as with economic policy, so Sundquist's *The Decline and Resurgence of Congress* provides the single-best account of the struggle between the two elective branches over policy in the 1960s and 1970s. *Congressional Quarterly Weekly Report* and *National Journal*'s detailed reports provide a useful running account of the bargaining between presidency, Congress and interest groups over the formation of foreign and defence policy. Kegley and Wittkopf's *American Foreign Policy* is a good introductory textbook, and John Gaddis's *Strategies of Containment* a superb account of relationship between the United States and the Soviet Union during the Cold War. Rubin's *Secrets of State* is a study of the State Department's role in the formation of United States' foreign policy, and Christopher Shoemaker's *The NSC Staff* is an examination of the National Security Council's secretariat. The intelligence community provides the subject for Johnson in *America's Secret Power: The CIA in a Democratic Society*, and Bamford's *The Puzzle Palace*. The Vietnam War has spawned a minor publishing industry of its own, but Halberstam's *The Best and the Brightest* retains its capacity to shock, while Gelb and Betts's *The Irony of Vietnam*, the three volumes of Gibbons' *The US Government and the Vietnam War*, and Berman's *Planning a Tragedy* repay careful reading.

The list of memoirs by former participants is very large. Among the best are Kennan's *Memoirs*, Nitze's *From Hiroshima to Glasnost*, and Monteagle Stearns's *Talking to Strangers*. Kissinger's two volumes, *White House Years* and *Years of Upheaval*, should be read in conjunction with Shawcross's *Sideshow* and Seymour Hersh's *The Price of Power*. Strobe Talbott's *Endgame* and *Deadly Gambits* are splendidly revealing accounts of nuclear arms negotiations between the United States and the Soviet Union. More general arguments about the processes of foreign and defence policy-making processes are Destler *et al.*'s *Our Own Worst Enemy* and George's *Presidential Decisionmaking in Foreign Policy*. International economic policy is the subject of Bergsten's 'The World Economy after the Cold War' (1990), Spero's *The Politics of International Economic Relations*, and Macchiarola's edited collection of essays *International Trade: The Changing Role of the United States*.

Bibliography

Aaronovitch, D. (2009) *Voodoo Histories: How Conspiracy Theory Has Shaped Modern History* (London: Random House).

Aaron, H. J. (1973) *Why is Welfare so Hard to Reform?* (Washington, DC: Brookings Institution).

Aberbach, J. (1990) *Keeping a Watchful Eye* (Washington, DC: Brookings Institution).

Abraham, H. J. (1982) *Freedom and the Court*, 4th edn (New York: Oxford University Press).

Abraham, H. J. (1986) *The Judicial Process*, 5th edn (New York: Oxford University Press).

Abrams, C. (1955) *Forbidden Neighbors* (New York: Associated Faculty Press Inc.).

Abramson, P. R. and Aldrich, J. H. (1982) 'The Decline of Electoral Participation in America', *American Political Science Review*, vol. 76, no 3.

Abramson, P. A., Aldrich, J. H. and Rohde, D. W. (1999) *Change and Continuity in the 1996 and 1998 Elections* (Washington, DC: Congressional Quarterly Press).

Ackerman, B. and Ayres, I. (2004) *Voting With Dollars: A New Paradigm for Campaign Finance* (New Haven: Yale University Press).

Aldrich, J. and Rohde, D. (2002) 'Conditional Party Government in the States', *American Journal of Political Science*, vol. 46, no. 1, January: 164–72.

Almond, G. and Verba, S. (1965) *The Civic Culture: Political Attitudes and Democracy in Five Nations* (New Jersey: Princeton University Press).

Anonymous (Joe Klein) (1996) *Primary Colors* (London: Vintage Books).

Ambrose, S. E. (1985) *Rise to Globalism*, 4th edn (Harmondsworth: Penguin).

Arnold, R. D. (1979) *Congress and the Bureaucracy: A Theory of Influence* (New Haven, CT: Yale University Press).

Bachrach, P. and Baratz, M. S. (1962), 'Two Faces of Power', *American Political Science Review*, vol. LVI, no. 4.

Bachrach, P. and Baratz, M. S. (1963), 'Decisions and Nondecisions: An Analytical Framework', *American Political Science Review*, vol. LVII, no. 3.

Balz, D. (2013) *Collision 2012: Obama vs. Romney and the Future of Elections in America* (New York: Viking Books).

Bamford, J. (1983) *The Puzzle Palace* (New York: Penguin).

Banfield, E. C. (1974) *The Unheavenly City Revisited* (Boston: Little, Brown).

Bartels, L. (2000) 'Partisanship and Voting Behaviour, 1952–1966', *American Journal of Political Science*, vol. 44: 35–50.

Bartels, L. (2010) *Unequal Democracy: The Political Economy of the New Gilded Age* (New Jersey: Princeton University Press).

Bass, J. and De Vries, W. (1976) *The Transformation of Southern Politics* (New York: Basic Books).

455

Bauer, R., Pool, I. and Dexter, L. A. (1963) *American Business and Public Policy* (New York: Atherton).

Beard, C. (1913) *An Economic Interpretation of the Constitution* (New York: Macmillan).

Beck, P. A., Baum, L., Clausen, A. and Smith, C. E. (1992) 'Patterns and Sources of Ticket-Splitting on Subpresidential Voting', *American Political Science Review*, vol. 86, no. 3.

Beer, S. (1993) *To Make a Nation* (Cambridge, MA: Belknap Press).

Bellesiles, M. A. (1996) 'The Origins of Gun Culture in the United States, 1760–1865', *Journal of American History* (September), p. 425.

Bennett, S. E. (1990) 'The Uses and Abuses of Registration and Turnout Data', *PS* (June).

Bergsten, C. F. (1990) 'The World Economy after the Cold War', *Foreign Affairs*, vol. 69, p. 2.

Berlin, I. (1958) 'Two Concepts of Liberty', in Isaiah Berlin (1969) *Four Essays on Liberty*. (Oxford: Oxford University Press).

Berman, L. (1979) *The Office of Management and Budget and the Presidency, 1921–1979* (Princeton, NJ: Princeton University Press).

Berman, L. (1982) *Planning a Tragedy* (New York: W.W. Norton).

Bernstein, M. H. (1955) *Regulating Business by Independent Commission* (Princeton, NJ: Princeton University Press).

Berry, J. M. (1989) *The Interest Group Society* (Ann Arbor, MI: Little, Brown).

Bickel, A. (1955) 'The Original Understanding and the Segregation Decision', *Harvard Law Review*, vol. 69, no. 1.

Binder, S. A. and Smith, S. S. (1997) *Politics or Principles? Filibustering in the United States Senate* (Washington, DC: Brookings Institution).

Blank, R. M. (1997) 'The 1996 Welfare Reform', *Journal of Economic Perspectives*, vol. 11, no. 1.

Blasi, V. (ed.) (1977) *The Burger Court* (New Haven, CT: Yale University Press).

Brass, C. (2011) Shutdown of the Federal Government: Causes, Effects and Consequences (Congressional Research Service – Research Paper), 18 February.

Brownlee, W. E. (2003) *Funding the Modern American State, 1941–1995* (Cambridge University Press).

Bureau of the Census (2000) *Historical Statistics of the United States* http://hsus.cambridge.org/HSUSWeb/HSUSEntryServlet.

Bureau of the Census (2012) *State and Metropolitan Area Data Book, 2012* (Washington, DC: US Government Printing Office).

Bureau of the Census (2012) *Statistical Abstract of the United States, 2012* (Washington, DC: US Government Printing Office).

Burnham, W. D. (1970) *Critical Elections and the Mainsprings of American Politics* (New York: W.W. Norton).

Burnham, W. D. (1971) *Critical Elections: And the Mainsprings of American Politics* (London: W.W. Norton).

Burnham, W. D. (1987) 'The Turnout Problem', in A. J. Reichley (ed.), *Elections American Style* (Washington, DC: Brookings Institute).

Burns, J. M. (1978) *Leadership* (New York, Harper & Row).

Burns, J. M., Peltason, J. and Cronin, T. (1984) *State and Local Politics*, 4th edn (Englewood Cliffs, NJ: Prentice-Hall).

Cain, B. and Goux, D. (2006) 'Parties in an Era of Renewed Partisanship', in *Developments in American Politics 5* (Basingstoke: Palgrave): 37–53.

Califano, J. (1991) *The Triumph and Tragedy of Lyndon Johnson* (New York: Simon & Schuster)

Campbell, A., Converse, P. Miller, W. and Stokes, D. (1960) *The American Voter* (New York: John Wiley).

Cannon, L. (1991) *President Reagan* (New York: Touchstone).

Carson, R. (1962) *Silent Spring* (New York: Houghton Mifflin).

Cater, D. (1964) *Power in Washington* (New York: Random House).

Cater, D. (1965) *Power in Washington* (London: Collins).

Chubb, J. E. (1985) 'Federalism and the Bias for Centralization', in J. E. Chubb and P. E. Peterson, *New Directions in American Politics* (Washington, DC: Brookings Institution).

Chubb, J. E. and Peterson, P. E. (1985) *New Directions in American Politics* (Washington, DC: Brookings Institution).

Collender, S. (1990) *Guide to the Federal Budget* (Washington, DC: Urban Institute Press).

Conlan, T. (1988) *New Federalism* (Washington, DC: Brookings Institution).

Constitution of the United States of America, The.

Corrado, A. (1997) 'Financing in the 1996 Elections', in W. D. Burnham, *The Election of 1996* (Chatham: Chatham House).

Corwin, E. (1957) *The President: Office and Powers* (New York: New York University Press).

Cox, G. W. and Kernell, S. (1991) *The Politics of Divided Government* (Boulder, CO: Westview Press).

Crenson, M. (1971) *The Unpolitics of Air Pollution* (Baltimore, MD: Johns Hopkins University Press).

Crenson, M. and Rourke, F. E. (1987) 'By Way of Conclusion: American Bureaucracy since World War I', in L. Galambos (ed.), *The New American State* (Baltimore, MD: Johns Hopkins University Press).

Dahl, R. (1961) *Who Governs?* (New Haven, CT: Yale University Press).

Dahl, R. and Lindblom, C. (1953) *Politics, Economics, and Welfare* (University of Chicago Press).

Dash, L. (1996) *Rosa Lee* (New York: Basic Books).

Davidson, R. H. (1992) 'The Senate: If Everyone Leads, Who Follows?', in L. C. Dodd and B. I. Oppenheimer (eds), *Congress Reconsidered*, 4th edn (Washington, DC: CQ Press).

Davidson, R. (ed.) (1992) *The Postreform Congress* (New York: St Martin's Press).

Davidson, R. H. and Oleszek, W. J. (1981) *Congress and its Members* (Washington, DC: CQ Press), ch. 9.

Davidson, R., Oleszek, W. and Lee F. (1989) *Congress and Its Members* (Washington, DC: Congressional Quarterly Press).

Davis, M. (1993) 'Who killed LA?', *New Left Review,* vol. 197.

de Tocqueville, A. (1969) *Democracy in America* (Anchor Books), p. 287.

Destler, I. M., Gelb, L. H. and Lake, A. (1984) *Our Own Worst Enemy* (New York, Simon & Schuster).

Dodd, C. and Oppenheimer, B. I. (1997) *Congress Reconsidered*, 6th edn (Washington, DC: CQ Press).

Dodd, L. C. and Schott, R. L. (1979) *Congress and the Administrative State* (New York: John Wiley).

Douglas, W. O. (1970) *Points of Rebellion* (New York, Random House).

Downs, A. (1957) *An Economic Theory of Democracy* (London: Harper & Row).

Dunleavy, P. (1991) *Democracy, Bureaucracy and Public Choice* (London: Harvester Wheatsheaf).

Duverger, M. (1954) *Political Parties* (London, Methuen).

Dye, T. R. (1990) *American Federalism* (Lexington, MA: Lexington Books).

Elazar, D. (1972) *American Federalism: A View from the States* (New York: Crowell).

Eldersveld, S. J. (1982) *Political Parties in American Society* (New York: Basic Books).

Epstein, L. (1986) *Political Parties in the American Mold* (Madison, WI: University of Wisconsin Press).

Fairclough, A. (1995) *Race and Democracy* (Athens, GA: University of Georgia Press).

Feigert, F. B. (1984) 'On the "Decline" in Congressional Party Voting', Paper presented at the annual meeting of the Southern Political Science Association, Savannah, Georgia.

Fenno, R. (1973) *Congressmen in Committees* (Boston, MA: Little, Brown).

Fenno, R. (1979) *Home Style* (Boston, MA: Little, Brown).

Fenno, R. (1989) *The Making of a Senator* (Washington, DC; CQ Press).

Fenno, R. (1990) *The Presidential Odyssey of John Glenn* (Washington, DC: CQ Press).

Fenno, R. (1991a) *Learning to Legislate* (Washington, DC: CQ Press).

Fenno, R. (1991b) *The Emergence of a Senate Leader* (Washington, DC: CQ Press).

Fiorina, M. (1974) *Congress: Keystone of the Washington Establishment* (New Haven, CT: Yale University Press).

Fisher, L. (1975) *Presidential Spending Power* (Princeton, NJ: Princeton University Press).

Fisher, L. (1987) *The Politics of Shared Power,* 2nd edn (Washington, DC: CQ Press).

Fisher, L. (1988) *Constitutional Dialogues* (Princeton, NJ Princeton University Press).

Fisher, L. (1991) *Constitutional Conflicts between Congress and the President,* 3rd edn (Lawrence, KS: University Press of Kansas).

Fisher, L. (2009) *On Appreciating Congress: The People's Branch* (New York: Oxford University Press)

Fisher, L. (2013) *The Law of the Executive Branch: Presidential Power* (New York: Oxford University Press).

Fowler, L. L. and McClure, R. D. (1990) *Political Ambition* (New Haven, CT: Yale University Press).

Freeman, B. I. (1965) *The Political Process* (New York: Random House).

Freeman, J. Leiper (1955) *Political Process: Executive Bureau–Legislative Committee Relations* (New York: Random House).

Friedman, B. (1988) *Day of Reckoning* (New York: Random House).

Gaddis, J. (1982) *Strategies of Containment* (New York: Oxford University Press).

Gaventa, J. (1980) *Power and Powerlessness* (Oxford: Clarendon Press).

Gelb, L. and Betts, R. K. (1979) *The Irony of Vietnam* (Washington, DC: Brookings Institution).

George, A. (1980) *Presidential Decisionmaking in Foreign Policy* (Boulder, CO: Westview Press).

Gibbons, W. C. (1986) *The US Government and the Vietnam War: Part II, 1961–1964* Princeton, NJ: Princeton University Press).

Gibson, J. (1994) *Warrior Dreams* (New York: Hill & Wang).

Glazer, N. (1997) *We are all Multiculturalists Now* (Cambridge, MA: Harrard).

Glazer, N. (2010) 'Notes on the State of Black America', *The American Interest*, magazine, July/August issue, Hollywood, California)

Gray, V. and Jacob, H. (1996) *Politics in the American States*, 6th edn (Washington, DC: CQ Press).

Green, M. N. (2010) *The Speaker of the House: A Study of Leadership* (New Haven, CT: Yale University Press).

Greenberg, S. (1996) *Middle Class Dreams* (New Haven, CT: Yale University Press).

Greenstein, F. (1982) *The Hidden-Hand Presidency* (New York: Basic Books).

Greenstein, F. (1990) *Leadership in the Modern Presidency* (Cambridge, MA: Harvard University Press).

Greider, W. (1987) *Secrets of the Temple* (New York: Simon & Schuster).

Grodzins M. (1966) *The American System: A New View of Government in the United States* (Chicago: Rand McNally).

Gunther, J. (1947) *Inside US* (London: Hamish Hamilton).

Gurr, T. R. and King, D. S. (1987) *The State and the City* (Chicago University Press).

Halberstam, D. (1992) *The Best and the Brightest* (New York: Random House).

Haldeman, R. (1994) *The Haldeman Diaries* (Santa Monica, CA: Sony Corp).

Hall, K. (1992) *The Oxford Companion to the Supreme Court of the United States* (New York: Oxford University Press).

Hall, R. (1987) 'Participation and Purpose in Committee Decision Making', *American Political Science Review*, vol. 81, no. 1.

Hall, R. (1996) *Participation in Congress* (New Haven, CT: Yale University Press).

Hall, R. and Wayman, F. (1990) 'Buying Time: Moneyed Interests and the Mobilization of Bias in Congressional Committees', *American Political Science Review*, vol. 84, no. 3.

Hamilton, A., Madison, J. and Jay, J. (1987) *The Federalist Papers*, intr. Isaac Kramnick (Harmondsworth, Penguin).

Hanson, R. C. (1996) 'Intergovernmental Relations', in V. Gray and H. Jacob (eds), *Politics in the American States*, 6th edn (Washington, DC: CQ Press).

Hartz, L. (1955) *The Liberal Tradition in America* (New York: Harcourt, Brace, Jovanovich).

Heclo, H. (1978) 'Issue Networks and the Executive Establishment', in A. King (ed.), *The New American Political System* (Washington, DC: American Enterprise Institute).

Hersh, S. (1983) *The Price of Power* (New York: Summit Books).

Hetherington, M. and Larson, B. (2010) *Party, Politics and Public Policy in America* (Washington DC: CQ Press)

Hibbing, J. R. and Theiss-Morse, E. (1995) *Congress as Public Enemy* (Cambridge University Press).

Hird, J. A. (1991) 'The Political Economy of Pork: Project Selection at the US Army Corp of Engineers', *American Political Science Review*, vol. 85, no. 2.

Hodder-Williams, R. (1980) *The Politics of the US Supreme Court* (London: Allen & Unwin).

Hodder-Williams, R. (1992) 'Six Notions of "Political" and the United States Supreme Court', *British Journal of Political Science*, vol. 22, no. 1.

Hofstadter, R. (1948) *The American Political Tradition* (New York: Knopf).

Hofstadter, R. (1966) *The Paranoid Style in American Politics* (London: Jonathan Cape).

Hofstadter, R. (2008) *The Paranoid Style in American Politics and Other Essays* (New York, Random House).

Hogan, J. (1985) 'Ten Years After: the US Congressional Budget and Impoundment Control Act of 1974', *Public Administration*, vol. 63, no. 2.

Hughes, M. A. and Sternberg, J. E. (1993) *The New Metropolitan Reality* (Washington, DC: Urban Institute).

Hulliung, M. (ed.) (2010) *The American Liberal Tradition Reconsidered: The Contested Legacy of Louis Hartz* (Kansas: University of Kansas Press)

Hunter, F. (1953) *Community Power Structure* (Chapel Hill: University of North Carolina Press).

Huntington, S. (1981) *American Politics: The Politics of Disharmony* (Harvard: Harvard University Press).

Huntington, S. (1983) *The Promise of Disharmony* (New York: Bellknap Press)

Jackson, K. T. (1985) *Crabgrass Frontier* (New York: Oxford University Press).

Jacobson, G. C. (1990) *The Electoral Origins of Divided Government* (Boulder, CO: Westview Press).

Johnson, L. (1989) *America's Secret Power: The CIA in a Democratic Society* (New York: Oxford University Press).

Johnson, R. N. and Libecap, G. D. (1994) *The Federal Civil Service System and the Problem of Bureaucracy* (University of Chicago Press).

Jones, C. O. (1982) *The United States Congress* (Belmont, CA: The Dorsey Press).

Jones, C. O. (1988) *The Trusteeship Presidency* (Baton Rouge, LA: Louisiana State University Press).

Jones, C. O. (2005) *The Presidency in a Separated System* (2nd edn) (Washington DC: Brookings Institution).

Kain, J. (1992) 'The Spatial Mismatch Hypothesis: Three Decades Later', *Housing Policy Debate*, vol. 3, no. 2.

Katznelson, I. (1981) *City Trenches* (Chicago University Press).

Kegley, C. W. and Wittkopf, E. R. (1991) *American Foreign Policy*, 4th edn (New York: St Martin's Press).

Keith, B., Magleby, D. B., Nelson, C. J., Orr, E., Westlye, M. C. and Wolfinger, R. E. (1992) *The Myth of the Independent Voter* (Berkeley: University of California Press).

Kennan, G. (1967) *Memoirs* (Boston, MA: Little, Brown).

Kerner Commission (1967) *The Challenge of Crime in a Free Society* (Washington, DC: US Government Printing Office).

Kettl, D. F. (1987) *The Regulation of American Federalism* (Baltimore, MD: Johns Hopkins University Press).

Key, V. O. (1949) *Southern Politics* (New York: Knopf).

Key, V. O. (1955) 'A Theory of Critical Elections', *Journal of Politics*, vol. 17, no. 1.

Kincaid, J. (1994) 'Governing the American States', in G. Peele, G. Peele, C. J. Bailey, B. Cain and B. G. Peters (eds), *Developments in American Politics 2* (Basingstoke: Macmillan), p. 209.

King, D. S. (1992) 'The Changing Federal Balance', in G. Peele, C. J. Bailey and B. Cain (eds), *Developments in American Politics* (London: Macmillan).

King, D. S. (1995a) *Actively Seeking Work?* (Chicago: Chicago University Press).

King, D. S. (1995b) *Separate and Unequal* (Oxford: Clarendon Press).

Kissinger, H. (1979) *White House Years* (London: Weidenfeld & Nicolson/Michael Joseph).

Kissinger, H. (1982) *Years of Upheaval* (London: Weidenfeld & Nicolson/Michael Joseph).

Kluger, R. (1975) *Simple Justice*, vols I and II (New York: Knopf).

Krasner, S. (1978) *Defending the National Interest* (Princeton, NJ: University Press).

Krause, G. A. and Cohen, D. N. (1997) 'Presidential Use of Executive Orders, 1953–1994', *American Politics Quarterly*, 25(October): 458–81.

Krugman, P. (2001) *Fuzzy Math: the Essential Guide to the Bush Tax Plan* (New York: Norton).

Krugman, P. (2008) *The Return of Depression Economics* (London: Penguin)

Ladd, E. C. (1977) *Where Have all the Voters Gone?* (New York: W.W Norton).

Lamis, A. P. (1984) *The Two-Party South* (New York: Oxford University Press).

Latham, E. (1952) *The Group Basis of Politics* (Ithaca, NY: Cornell University Press).

Leman, N. (1991) *The Promised Land* (New York: Knopf).

Leuchtenburg, W. (1963) *Franklin D. Roosevelt and the New Deal* (New York: Harper & Row).

Leuchtenburg, W. (1989) *In the Shadow of FDR*, rev. edn (Ithaca, NY: Cornell University Press).

Lewis-Beck, M. S., Norpoth, H., Jacoby, W. G. and Weisberg, H. F. (2011) *The American Voter Revisited* (University of Michigan Press).

Light, P.C. (2006) 'The Tides of Reform Revisited: Making Government Work, 1945–2002', Public Administration Review 2006, vol. 66, no. 1: 6–19.

Lindblom, C. (1977) *Politics and Markets* (New York: Basic Books).

Lindblom, C. (1982) 'Another State of Mind', *American Political Science Review*, vol. 76, no. 1.

Lipset, S. M. (1963) *The First New Nation* (London: Heinemann).

Lipset, S. M. (1990) *Continental Divide* (London: Routledge).

Lowi, T. (1969) *The End of Liberalism: The Second Republic of the United States* (New York: Norton).

Lowi, T. (1979) *The End of Liberalism*, 2nd edn (New York: Norton).

Lowi, T. (1985) *The Personal President* (Ithaca, NY: Cornell University Press).

Lukes, S. (1974) *Power* (London: Macmillan).

Macchiarola, F. J. (ed.) (1990) *International Trade: The Changing Role of the United States* (New York: Academy of Political Science).

Mailer, N. (1995) *Oswald's Tale: An American Mystery* (New York: Random House).

Maisel, S. (2007) *American Political Parties and Elections: A Very Short Introduction* (New York: Oxford University Press).

Maisel, S. and Brewer, M. D. (2011) *Parties and Elections in America: The Electoral Process* (Lanham, MD: Rowman & Littlefield).

Malbin, M. (2004) 'Political Parties under the Post-McConnell Bipartisan Campaign Finance Reform Act', *Election Law Journal*, vol. 3, no. 2: 177–91.

Mann, T. and Ornstein, N. (2008) *Congress: The Broken Branch* (New York: Oxford University Press).

Mann, T. and Ornstein, N. (2012) *It's Even Worse Than It Looks: How the American Constitutional System Collided with the New Politics of Extremism* (New York: Basic Books).

Marrs, J. (1989) *Crossfire: The Plot That Killed Kennedy* (New York: Carroll and Graf).

Mayer, T. (ed.) (1990) *The Political Economy of American Monetary Policy* (Cambridge University Press).

Mayhew, D. (1974) *Congress: The Electoral Connection* (New Haven, CT: Yale University Press).

McCloskey, R. G. (1960) *The American Supreme Court* (Chicago: University of Chicago Press).

McCubbins, M. D. and Page, T. (1987) 'A Theory of Congressional Delegation', in M. D. McCubbins and T. Sullivan, *Congress: Structure and Policy* (Cambridge University Press).

McCubbins, M. and Schwartz, M. (1984) 'Congressional Oversight Overlooked', *American Journal of Political Science*, vol. 2, no. 1 February.

McKay, D. (1989) *Domestic Policy and Ideology* (Cambridge: Cambridge University Press).

McMahon, R. (2006) *The Environmental Protection Agency* (Brighton: Sussex Academic Press)

McPherson, H. C. (1972) *A Political Education* (Boston, MA: Little, Brown).

McPherson, J. M. (1988) *Battle Cry of Freedom* (New York: Oxford University Press).

McSweeney, D. (2002) 'Political Parties', *Developments in American Politics 4* (Basingstoke: Palgrave Macmillan): 35–51.

Miller, M. (1974) *Plain Speaking* (London: Coronet).

Miller, W. E. and Shanks, J. M. (1996) *The New American Voter* (Cambridge, MA: Harvard University Press).

Mills, C. Wright (1956) *The Power Elite* (New York: Oxford University Press).

Milton, S. (Eisenhower Foundation) (1993) *Investing in Children and Youth, Reconstructing Our Cities* (Washington, DC: Eisenhower Foundation).

Moe, T. (1987) 'The Politicized Presidency', in J. E. Chubb and P. E. Peterson, *New Directions in American Politics* (Washington, DC: Brookings Institution).

Moe, T. M. and Howell, W. G. (1999) 'Unilateral Action and Presidential Power: A Theory', *Presidential Studies Quarterly*, vol. 29, no. 4, December: 850–73.

Mollenkopf, J. H. (1993) *The Contested City* (Princeton, NJ: Princeton University Press).

Mollenkopf, J. H. (1994) *Phoenix in the Ashes*, new edn (Princeton, NJ: Princeton University Press).

Morris, C. R. (1996) *The AARP* (New York: Times Books)

Nader, R. (1965) *Unsafe at Any Speed* (New York: Grossman).

Nathan, R. P. (1983) *The Administrative Presidency* (New York: John Wiley).

Nathan, R. P. and Doolittle, F. C. (1987) *Reagan and the States* (Princeton, NJ: Princeton University Press).

Neustadt, R. E. (1990 [1960]) *Presidential Power and the Modern Presidents* (New York: Free Press).

Nie, N. H., Verba, S. and Petrocik, J. R. (1979) *The Changing American Voter* (Cambridge, MA: Harvard University Press).

Niskanen, W. (1971) *Bureacracy and Representative Government* (Chicago: Aldine Atherton).

Nitze, P. (1989) *From Hiroshima to Glasnost* (London: Weidenfeld).

O'Brien, R. (1990) *Storm Center*, 2nd edn (New York: W.W. Norton).

Obama, B. (No date) President's News Conference, 29 April 2009, *Public Papers of the President, Book I*.

Oleszek, W. J. (1996) *Congressional Procedures and the Policy Process*, 4th edn (Washington, DC: CQ Press).

Olson, M. (1965) *The Logic of Collective Action* (Cambridge, MA: Harvard University Press).

Olson, M. (1982) *The Decline of Nations* (New Haven, CT: Yale University Press).

Organisation for Economic Co-operation and Development (1997) *Economic Outlook* (Paris: OECD).

O'Toole, L. J. (ed.) (1985) *American Intergovernmental Relations* (Washington, DC: CQ Press).

Peele, G. (1984) *Revival and Reaction: The Right in Contemporary America* (Oxford: Clarendon Press).

Peirce, N. and Hagstrom, J. (1983) *The Book of America* (New York: W.W. Norton).

Penner, R. (ed.) (1991) *The Great Fiscal Experiment* (Washington, DC: Urban Institute Press).

Perry, M. (1994) *The Constitution in the Courts* (New York: Oxford University Press).

Peterson, M. (1990) *Legislating Together* (Cambridge, MA: Harvard University Press).

Peterson, P. (1981) *City Limits* (Chicago University Press).

Peterson, P. (1991) *New Directions in American Politics* (Cambridge, MA: Harvard University Press).

Peterson, P. E. (1992) 'The Presidency and Organized Interests', *American Political Science Review*, vol. 86, no. 4.

Pfiffner, J. and Davidson, R. (2010) *Understanding the Presidency* (London: Pearson)

Piven, F. F. and Cloward, L. R. A. (1989) *Why Americans Don't Vote* (New York: Pantheon).

Polsby, N. (1969) 'Goodbye to the Inner Club', *Washington Monthly*, August.

Polsby, N. (1983) *Consequences of Party Reform* (New York: Oxford University Press).

Polsby, N. and Wildavsky, A. (1988) *Presidential Elections* (New York: Free Press).

Pomper, G., Burnham, W. W., Mayer, W. G., Just, M. R., Corrado, A., Keeter, S., Hershey, M. R. and McWilliams, W. C. (eds) (1996) *The Election of 1996* (Chatham: Chatham House).

Pool, I. and Dexter, L. A. (1963) *American Business and Public Policy* (New York: Atherton).

Price, D. (1989) 'The House of Representatives: A Report from the Field', in L. C. Dodd and B. I. Oppenheimer (eds), *Congress Reconsidered*, 4th edn (Washington, DC: CQ Press).

Quinn, D. P. and Shapiro, R. Y. (1991) 'Business Political Power: The Case of Taxation', *American Political Science Review*, vol. 85, no. 3.

Quirk, P. J. 'A House Dividing: Understanding Polarization', *The Forum*, vol. 9, no. 2, article 12.

Reagan, M. D. and Sanzone, J. G. (1981) *The New Federalism*, 2nd edn (New York: Oxford University Press).

Reichley, A. J. (ed.) (1987) *Elections American Style* (Washington, DC: Brookings).

Reichley, A. J. (1992) *The Life of the Parties* (New York: Free Press).

Rich, M. J. (1989) 'Distributive Politics and the Allocation of Federal Grants', *American Political Science Review*, vol. 83 no. 1.

Riker, W. (1964) *Federalism: Origin, Operation, and Significance* (Boston, MA: Little, Brown).

Rivlin, A. (1992) *Reviving the American Dream* (Washington, DC: Brookings Institute).

Rockman, B. (1984) *The Leadership Question* (New York: Praeger).

Rosenstone, S. J., Behr, R. L. and Lazarus, E. H. (1984) *Third Parties in America* (Princeton, NJ: Princeton University Press).

Rosenthal, A. (1981) *Legislative Life* (New York: Harper & Row).

Rosenthal, A. (1990) *Governors and Legislatures: Contending Powers* (Washington, DC: CQ Press).

Rourke, F. E. (1987) 'Bureaucracy in the American Constitutional Order', *Political Science Quarterly*, vol. 102, no. 2.

Rourke, F. E. (1984) *Bureaucracy, Politics, and Public Policy*, 3rd edn (Boston, MA: Little, Brown).

Rubin, B. (1985) *Secrets of State* (New York: Oxford University Press).

Sabato, L. (1983) *Goodbye to Good-time Charlie* (Washington, DC: CQ Press).

Savage, J. D. (1988) *Balanced Budgets and American Politics* (Ithaca, NY: Cornell University Press).

Schattschneider, E. E. (1942) *Party Government* (London: Holt, Rinehart & Winston).

Schattschneider, E. E. (1960) *The Semi-Sovereign People* (New York: Holt, Rinehart & Winston).

Schick, A. (1980) *Congress and Money* (Washington, DC: Urban Institute Press).

Schmal, J. P. (2004) 'Electing the President: The Latino Electorate (1960–2000)', *La Prensa*, San Diego, http=www.laprensa-sandiego.org/archieve/april30-04/elect.htm.

Schwartz, B. (1983) *Super Chief: Earl Warren and his Supreme Court* (New York: New York University Press).

Schwartz, B. (1985) *The Unpublished Opinions of the Warren Court* (New York: Oxford University Press).

Schwartz, B. (1990) *The Ascent of Pragmatism* (Reading, MA: Addison-Wesley).

Seidman, H. and Gilmour, R. (1986) *Politics, Position, and Power*, 4th edn (New York: Oxford University Press).

Shafer, B. (1983) *Quiet Revolution* (New York: Russell Sage).

Shafer, B. E. (1988) *Bifurcated Politics* (Cambridge, MA: Harvard University Press).

Shafer, B. E. (1989) 'The Election of 1988 and the Structure of American Politics: Thoughts on Interpreting an Electoral Order', *Electoral Studies*, vol. 8, no. 1.

Shafer, B. E. (ed.) (1991) *Is America Different?* (Oxford: Clarendon Press).

Shafer, B. E and Claggett, W. J. M. (1995) *The Two Majorities* (Baltimore, MD: Johns Hopkins University Press).

Shawcross, W. (1986) *Sideshow*, 2nd edn (London: Hogarth Press).

Shefter, M. (1992) *Political Crisis, Fiscal Crisis* (New York, NY: Columbia University Press).

Shoemaker, C. (1991) *The NSC Staff* (Boulder, CO: Westview Press).

Simon, H. (1947) *Administrative Behaviour: A Study of Decision-Making Processes in Administrative Organisation* (New York: Macmillan).

Sinclair, B. (1989) *The Transformation of the US Senate* (Baltimore, MD: Johns Hopkins Press).

Singh, R. (1997) *The Farrakhan Phenomenon* (Washington, DC: Georgetown University Press).

Singh, R. (1998) *The Congressional Black Caucus* (Thousand Oaks, CA: Sage).

Sklar, M. J. (1988) *The Corporate Reconstruction of American Capitalism, 1890–1916* (Cambridge: Cambridge University Press).

Skowronek, S. (1982) *Building a New American State* (Cambridge: Cambridge University Press).

Smith, E. (1989) *The Unchanging American Voter* (Berkeley, CA: University of California Press).

Smith, S. S. (1989) *Call to Order: Floor Politics in the House and Senate* (Washington, DC: Brookings Institution).

Sorauf, F. (1976) *Party Politics in America*, 3rd edn (Boston, MA: Little, Brown).

Spero, J. E. (1990) *The Politics of International Economic Relations*, 5th edn (New York: St Martin's Press).

Stearns, M. (1999) *Talking to Strangers* (Princeton, NJ: Princeton University Press).

Stein, H. (1988) *Presidential Economics* (Washington, DC: American Enterprise Institute).

Stein, H. (1989) *The Fiscal Revolution in America* (Chicago: Chicago University Press).

Stewart, C. (1989) *Budget Reform Politics* (Cambridge: Cambridge University Press).

Stockman, D. (1986) *The Triumph of Politics* (London: Bodley Head).

Stone, C. (1989) *Regime Politics* (Lawrence, KA: University of Kansas Press).

Stubbing, R. A. with Mendel, R. A. (1986) *The Defense Game* (New York: Harper & Row).

Sundquist, J. (1973) *Dynamics of the Party System* (Washington, DC: Brookings Institute).

Sundquist, J. L. (1981) *The Decline and Resurgence of Congress* (Washington, DC: Brookings Institute).

Talbott, S. (1979) *Endgame* (New York: Harper & Row).

Talbott, S. (1985) *Deadly Gambits* (London: Picador).

Thompson, D. (2008) *Counterknowledge* (London: Atlantic Books).

Thurber, J. (1996) *Rivals for Power* (Washington, DC: CQ Press).

Truman, D. (1951) *The Governmental Process* (New York: Knopf).

United States Office of Management and Budget (1997) *Budget of the United States Government, Fiscal Year 1998, Historical Tables* (Washington, DC: United States Government Printing Office).

Vile, M. (1967) *Constitutionalism and the Separation of Powers* (Oxford University Press).

Walker, D. B. (1981) *Toward a Functioning Federalism* (Cambridge: Winthrop Publishers).

Walker, J. (1983) 'The Origins and Maintenance of Interest Groups in America', *American Political Science Review*, vol. 77, no. 2.

Ware, A. (1985) *The Breakdown of Democratic Party Organization, 1940–1980* (Oxford: Clarendon Press).

Ware, A. (2010) 'Political Parties and the New Partisanship', *Developments in American Politics 6* (Basingstoke: Palgrave Macmillan): 50–64.

Ware, A. (2011) *Political Conflict in America* (New York: Macmillan).

Warner, S. B. (1968) *The Private City* (Philadelphia, PA: University of Pennsylvania Press).

Warren, E. (1977) *The Memoirs of Chief Justice Earl Warren* (New York: Doubleday).

Wayne, S. (1978) *The Legislative Presidency* (New York: Harper & Row).

Wildavsky, A. (1974) *The Politics of the Budgetary Process* (Boston, MA: Little, Brown).

Wilentz, S. (2008) 'Introduction', in R. Hofstadter, *The Paranoid Style in American Politics and Other Essays* (New York: Random House).

Williams, P. M. (1979) 'Party Realignment in Britain and the US', *British Journal of Political Science*, vol. 15, no. 1.

Wilson, G. (1979) *Unions in American Politics* (London: Macmillan).

Wilson, J. (1991) *Bureaucracy: What Government Agencies Do and Why They Do It* (New York: Basic Books).

Witt, E. (1986) *A Different Justice: Reagan and the Supreme Court* (Washington, DC: CQ Press).

Woll, P. (1977) *American Bureaucracy*, 2nd edn (New York: W.W Norton).

Wolman, H. (1996) 'Theories of Local Democracy in the United States', in D. King and G. Stoker (eds), *Rethinking Local Democracy* (London: Macmillan).

Wolpe, B. C. and Levine, B. J. (1996) *Lobbying Congress*, 2nd edn (Washington, DC: Congressional Quarterly).

Wood, R. (1970) 'When Government Works', *Public Interest*, vol. 18, Winter.

Wood, R. and Waterman, L. (1991) 'The Dynamics of Political Control of the Bureaucracy', *American Political Science Review*, vol. 85, no. 3.

Woolley, J. (1984) *Monetary Politics* (Cambridge: Cambridge University Press).

Wright, D. (1983) *Understanding Intergovernmental Relations* (Pacific Grove, CA: Brookes/Cole).

Wright, J. R. (1990) 'Contributions, Lobbying, and Committee Voting in the U.S. House of Representatives', *American Political Science Review*, vol. 84, no. 2.

Young, J. S. (1966) *The Washington Community 1800–1828* (New York: Columbia University Press).

Index